Guide to Basic Reference Materials for Canadian Libraries

SEVENTH EDITION, REVISED & ENLARGED

Edited by Claire England

With contributions by Patricia Fleming, Diane Henderson and Kirsti Nilsen

Published for the Faculty of Library and Information Science
by University of Toronto Press
1984

© Faculty of Library and Information Science
University of Toronto
1984
Printed in Canada
ISBN 0-8020-6581-3

No part of this book may be reproduced
without written permission of the
Faculty of Library and Information Science
University of Toronto

Canadian Cataloguing in Publication Data

Main entry under title:

Guide to basic reference materials for
Canadian libraries

First 4 eds. edited by: Edith T. Jarvi; 5th and
6th eds. edited by: Diane Henderson.
Includes indexes.
ISBN 0-8020-6581-3

1. Reference books - Bibliography. 2. Bibliography -
Bibliography. I. England, Claire, 1935-
II. Fleming, Patricia. III. Henderson, Diane, 1935-
IV. Nilsen, Kirsti. V. University of Toronto.
Faculty of Library and Information Science.

Z1035.1.G84 1984   011'.02   C84-099480-X

TABLE OF CONTENTS

ACKNOWLEDGEMENTS		iii
INTRODUCTION		v
Key to Locations, Reference Citations and Abbreviations		vi
TITLE INDEX		289

SECTION A -- GENERAL REFERENCE

AA	Library and Information Science	1
AB	Book Trade and Information Industries	10
AC	Aids to the Selection of Books and Materials	15
AD	National Bibliography	24
AE	Periodicals and Newspapers	46
AF	Indexes to Periodicals and Other Materials	51
AG	Audio-Visual Materials	58
AH	Annuals, Directories and Handbooks	63
AI	General Encyclopedias	72
AJ	Language Dictionaries	78
AK	Atlases, Maps and Related Materials	90
AL	Biography	95
AM	Government Information	106
AN	Publications from International Organizations	119

SECTION B -- HUMANITIES

BA	General Reference in the Humanities	125
BB	Philosophy	126
BC	Religion	129
BD	Literature	137
BE	Fine and Applied Arts	151
BF	Music	165
BG	Performing Arts	173

SECTION C -- SOCIAL SCIENCES

CA	General Reference in the Social Sciences	181
CB	Economics	189
CC	Business	192
CD	Political Science	199
CE	Law and Legal Materials	204
CF	Anthropology and Ethnology	208
CG	Sociology and Related Topics	212
CH	Psychology	220
CI	Education	223
CJ	History	227

SECTION D -- SCIENCE AND TECHNOLOGY

DA	General Reference in Science and Technology	237
DB	Mathematics	245
DC	Computer Science	247
DD	Astronomy	249
DE	Physics	253
DF	Chemistry	256
DG	Earth Sciences	260
DH	Biological Sciences	265
DI	Health Sciences	270
DJ	Agricultural Sciences	275
DK	Environmental Sciences and Energy Resources	279
DL	Engineering and Technology	283

ACKNOWLEDGEMENTS

This edition, as earlier editions, reflects the advice and help of librarians and students who suggested and verified entries and who contributed to the content in this GUIDE TO BASIC REFERENCE MATERIALS FOR CANADIAN LIBRARIES. My thanks to my colleagues at the Faculty of Library and Information Science who contributed major sections; to Professor Patricia Fleming for Section B: HUMANITIES; to Chief Librarian Diane Henderson for her continuing support as a former editor of this work and for Section C: SOCIAL SCIENCES; to associated instructor Kirsti Nilsen for the subject fields in Section D: SCIENCE AND TECHNOLOGY. Additional thanks to Gale Moore, Book Selector at John P. Robarts Library, University of Toronto for revision of HEALTH SCIENCES. My gratitude is also extended to three colleagues who revised and enlarged a section on official documents. Edith Jarvi, retired Professor, FLIS, and long associated both with this GUIDE and with government publications revised the material on CANADIAN GOVERNMENT INFORMATION. Kirsti Nilsen, a former government documents librarian, revised the section on U.S. GOVERNMENT DOCUMENTS. Peter Hajnal, Head, Government Publications Section, University of Toronto libraries, revised and enlarged a new separate section for PUBLICATIONS FROM INTERNATIONAL ORGANIZATIONS. The efforts of all who contributed to this 7th edition are much appreciated.

                                                          Claire England
                                                          Editor
                                                          FLIS

INTRODUCTION

This selection of reference works is designed primarily as a guide to materials for students in the Faculty of Library and Information Science. Intended for use with courses in the reference, collections and literature streams at the Faculty, the GUIDE is an introduction to basic and representative reference works in all major fields. Because general reference works, taught in fundamental reference and collection courses are studied more intensively than works in the subject fields, the section (A) GENERAL REFERENCE MATERIALS is more extensive than sections in (B) HUMANITIES, (C) SOCIAL SCIENCES and (D) SCIENCE AND TECHNOLOGY.

Characteristic of each successive edition of the GUIDE, the size gradually increases, and that is true of this revised and expanded edition. A section on library and information science, the book trade and information industries, has been expanded beyond the size representative of most collections in libraries but not beyond the needs for students in the field to be aware of the publications within their chosen discipline. Various enlargements have also occurred within the sections so that topical interests and newly developed fields are represented.

Sections are organized in a way that the compilers hope is useful to a student in understanding and learning the organization of a literature. The ordering of entries is not alphabetical except when groups of entries are reasonably few in number. Items similar in function or format are grouped together. In the A section, many groupings are initially organized by area (international, Great Britain, United States, Canada) and then by type of reference work (abstracts and indexes, encyclopedias etc.). Chronology is a factor in the sequence of some entries. In other sections (B,C,D) or sub-sections (AA), entries are initially grouped by type of reference, with either an alphabetical or geographical sub-order.

This edition increases the use of title entries for the works cited. THE CHICAGO MANUAL OF STYLE (13th ed., Univ. of Chicago Press, 1982), with some variation, is the basis for the bibliographical style. Style follows the humanities for sections A, B and C; style follows the sciences for section D. Capital letters highlight titles; subtitles are always given but overlong subtitles following the colon have only the initial letter of important words capitalized. A series statement, also with mixed capitals and small letters, may follow the title. Call numbers follow the bibliographical citation, and refer to the FLIS library, the Univ. of Toronto libraries and/or the Metropolitan Toronto Central Library. If the item is the most recent edition and is available at FLIS, only the FLIS number may be given. Notes are given for many entries except for those entries where the title itself is a sufficient description. The titles are annotated to describe their scope, arrangement and other features. The length of the annotation does not necessarily reflect the importance of the work. In section A, a reference is given to Sheehy's GUIDE TO REFERENCE BOOKS or, if Canadian, to Ryder's CANADIAN REFERENCE SOURCES in order that other notes on the entries may also be examined. In other sections, a reference to Ryder normally accompanies Canadian entries, and a reference to Sheehy is made only when the additional information might be useful.

The GUIDE is not intended as a buying guide for any library; obviously it is representative rather than comprehensive in many instances and should be used as a stepping stone to understanding and using literatures. The principle in compiling this work has been utility for students in library and information science courses. The compilers hope that the work is useful, and are grateful for any suggestions that would improve any future editions.

KEY TO LOCATION SYMBOLS

R025.5 A12   DDC no. is a location in the FLIS library. An 'R' preceding the no. indicates the Reference Collection. (The Metropolitan Toronto Central Library also uses DDC, and these call nos, when given, are identified as MCL).

Z1035 T4   LCC no. is a location in the Univ. of Toronto libraries, frequently the Reference Dept, John P. Robarts Library. In the (D) SCIENCE section call nos (e.g. QA5 J4) are a location in the Science and Medicine Library. Additional symbols indicate specific areas, e.g. GOVT (Government Documents Section); PASR (Physical and Applied Science Reference Dept) or libraries, e.g. BOTA (Botany). Location symbols at Univ. of Toronto catalogues should be consulted.

FLIS   Faculty of Library and Information Science library
  (IND)   Index Tables
  (PER)   Periodical Collection
  (SC)   Special Collection
MCL   Metropolitan Toronto Central Library, 789 Yonge St
  BU   Business
  FA   Fine Art
  MUS   Music
  TH   Theatre
OISE   Ontario Institute for Studies in Education, 252 Bloor St W.

KEY TO REFERENCE CITATIONS

Sheehy AB1   Sheehy, E.P., GUIDE TO REFERENCE BOOKS. 9th ed. 1976.
Sheehy 1AB1   _____. _____. SUPPLEMENT. 1980
Sheehy 2AB1   _____. _____. SUPPLEMENT. 1982.
Ryder GR1-1   Ryder, D.E. CANADIAN REFERENCE SOURCES. 2d ed. 1981.

KEY TO ABBREVIATIONS

ALA   American Library Association
Aslib   Association of Special Libraries and Information Bureaux
BL   British Library
CGPC   Canadian Government Publishing Centre
CIP   Cataloguing in Publication information
CISTI   Canada Institute for Scientific and Technical Information
CLA   Canadian Library Association
Cum. ind.   cumulation; cumulative or cumulated index
Dist.   Distributor
DDC   Dewey Decimal Classification
GPO   see USGPO
HMSO   Her Majesty's Stationery Office
i.p.   in print
LC   Library of Congress
LCC   Library of Congress Classification
NLC   National Library of Canada/ Bibliothèque nationale du Can.
OCLC   OCLC Inc. (formerly Ohio Colleges Library Consortium)
o.p.   out of print
o.s.   out of stock
UDC   Universal Decimal Classification
USGPO   United States Government Publishing Office

Section A
General Reference

LIBRARY AND INFORMATION SCIENCE

GUIDES

AA1   Lilley, D.B., and R.M. Badough, eds. LIBRARY AND INFORMATION SCIENCE: A GUIDE TO INFORMATION SOURCES. Detroit: Gale Research, 1982. 151 p.
020.202 L729L
"A practical guide for practicing librarians."

AA2   Purcell, Gary R., and Gail A. Schlacter. REFERENCE SOURCES IN LIBRARY AND INFORMATION SERVICES: A GUIDE TO THE LITERATURE. Santa Barbara, CA: ABC-Clio Information Services, 1984. 359 p.
R020 AP985R
An annotated guide in two parts. Part 1, arranged by type of publication, covers nearly 700 works. Part 2, arranged by subject, lists more than 450 works on library-related issues, developments, institutions or techniques. Title, author and geographic indexes.

BIBLIOGRAPHIES

AA3   ABHB: ANNUAL BIBLIOGRAPHY OF THE HISTORY OF THE PRINTED BOOK AND LIBRARIES, 1970-   The Hague: Martinus Nijhoff, 1973-   irregular. (Dist.: Kluwer Boston).
R070.5 A615A
(Vol. 11, 1980 {1984}). International and "aims at recording all books and articles of scholarly value which relate to the history of the printed book, to history of arts, crafts, techniques, equipment and of the economic, social and cultural environment" of the book. Topical arrangement with author, anonym, geographical and personal name indexes; a list of periodicals (title, place) reference only.

AA4   Cannons, Harry G.T. BIBLIOGRAPHY OF LIBRARY ECONOMY. Chicago: American Library Association, 1927. 680 p. Reprint/ New York: Burt Franklin, 1970.
R020 AC22
Classified index to library literature, 1876-1920. Author access provided by AN AUTHOR INDEX WITH CITATIONS (Scarecrow Press, 1976). (R020.AC22A)

AA5   Columbia University Library Service Library. DICTIONARY CATALOG. 7 vols. Boston: G.K. Hall, 1962. SUPPLEMENT 4 vols (1976).
R020 AC726
This collection, begun by Melvil Dewey, dates back to 1876.

AA6   INFORMATION REPORTS AND BIBLIOGRAPHIES, 1972-   New York: Science Associates International. 6 issues a year.
(PER)
Title varies. Each issue on a topic useful to librarians in their work. Issues also normally cite items from ERIC Information Resources clearinghouse (see AA12n), and cite articles from library and information science periodicals.

AA7   Schlachter, Gail A., and Dennis Thomison. LIBRARY SCIENCE DISSERTATIONS 1925-1972: AN ANNOTATED BIBLIOGRAPHY. Research Studies in Library

Science, no. 12. Littleton, CO: Libraries Unlimited, 1974. 293 p. SUPPLEMENT 1973-1981 (1983, 414 p.).
R020.7 AS338L
    Set covers more than 1600 doctoral dissertations in library science and related fields accepted by academic institutions in the U.S. and Canada. Entries are chronological by date of acceptance.

AA8   "Serials Currently Received." Toronto: University of Toronto, Faculty of Library and Information Science, March, 1969- twice yearly.
(at desk; 5th floor)

ABSTRACTS AND INDEXES

AA9   Danton, J. Periam. INDEX TO FESTSCHRIFTEN IN LIBRARIANSHIP 1967-1975. New York: R.R. Bowker, 1970. 461 p.
R020.8 AD194

AA10   --------, and Jane F. Pulis. INDEX TO FESTSCHRIFTEN IN LIBRARIANSHIP 1967-1975. Munich: K.G. Saur, 1979. 354 p.
R020.8 AD194A
    From both indexes, some 4800 articles written to honour an individual, from international sources. Author/ subject listing.

AA11   CURRENT RESEARCH IN LIBRARY AND INFORMATION SCIENCE, 1983- London: Library Association, 1974- quarterly.
(PER)
    Continues RADIALS BULLETIN (Research and Development Information and Library Science), 1974-83, which was published twice yearly as a cumulative listing of research projects in the U.K. or done by U.K. nationals abroad. The title change marks expanded international coverage and increase in frequency of issue. The scope includes archives, documentation, library and information. Research citations, with abstract, are in a classed order; name, subject indexes.

AA12   ERIC. CURRENT INDEX TO JOURNALS IN EDUCATION, 1969- Phoenix, AZ: Oryx Press [for ERIC], 1979- monthly, semi-annual cumulation. (CIJE MAIN ENTRY CUMULATION 1969-1980, annual updates, microfiche.)
(IND)   Sheehy CB81
    Part of the ERIC family of publications, AA12-AA16, see note below. Indexes about 780 journals in the education and related fields like library science. INDEX TO EDUCATION JOURNALS (Macmillan Information, 1979-) duplicates CIJE.
    The Educational Resources Information Center (ERIC), established in 1964, is composed of 16 clearinghouses, e.g. IR: Information Resources, and covers all significant facets of education and cognate fields. ERIC is sponsored by the National Institute of Education, U.S. Dept of Health and Welfare. In addition to print format (publisher varies), ERIC is widely available through online services, (DIALOG, ORBIT, BRS; CAN/SDI).

AA13   _____. RIE/RESOURCES IN EDUCATION, 1975- Washington: GPO [for ERIC, National Institute of Education, U.S. Dept of Education]. monthly; semi-annual cum. index.
(IND)   Sheehy CB85
    Supersedes RESEARCH IN EDUCATION, 1966-1974. Abstracts of report literature (research findings, technical reports, speeches). Resumes

cite author, source, 200 word description with conclusions. Subject, name, publication type, institution indexes. From 1981, a 'highlights' page features citations for 15 to 20 publications selected from the 16 clearhouses. RIE MAIN ENTRY CUMULATION 1966-1980 (Oryx Press); RIE/CIJE COMBINED SUBJECT INDEX (Oryx Press), annual updates, microfiche.

AA14 _____. EDUCATIONAL DOCUMENTS ABSTRACTS, 1968- 2 vols. Phoenix, AZ: Oryx Press [for ERIC]. annual. (Vols 1979- available on microfiche)

AA15 _____. EDUCATIONAL DOCUMENTS INDEX, 1968- Phoenix, AZ: Oryx Press [for ERIC]. annual. (Vols 1979- available on microfiche).
Provides titles, subject, author, identification/accession (ERIC Document, ED) numbers to documents and report literature abstracted in AA14.

AA16 _____. THESAURUS OF ERIC DESCRIPTORS. 10th ed. Phoenix, AZ: Oryx Press, 1984. 544 p.
(IND)
Controlled vocabulary useful for searching ERIC. Each 'descriptor' explained in scope notes; with posting (no. of items in database) and terms defined as broader, narrower, related or invalid.

AA17 INFORMATICS ABSTRACTS, 1977- Moscow: VINITI. monthly.
(IND)
The English language version of REFERATIVNYJ ZHURNAL, Section 59 "Informatika"; supersedes ABSTRACT JOURNAL: INFORMATICS 1963-76. Covers much material, particularly non-English, not included elsewhere in English language sources.

AA18 INFORMATION SCIENCE ABSTRACTS, 1966- New York: Plenum Pub. Co., 1981- bimonthly; cum. index.
(IND)
Supersedes DOCUMENTATION ABSTRACTS. Founded by American Society for Information Science, a division of the American Chemical Society and the Special Libraries Association, the service is still edited by Documentation Abstracts. Covers 450 journals plus books, conference proceedings, reports, patents; has foreign-language coverage. Intended for information scientists, (special) librarians, educators, equipment developers, systems analysts and for persons in related fields of publishing, translation, technical writing. Abstracts are classified by subject, then listed alphabetically by author; author, subject index. Annual indexes in last issue to Dec. 1981; cum. ind. from 1982.

AA19 LIBRARY AND INFORMATION SCIENCE ABSTRACTS, 1969- London: Library Association. monthly. CUMULATIVE INDEX 1969-73 (1975).
(IND)   Sheehy AB11, AB12
LISA bimonthly until 1982; it continues LIBRARY SCIENCE ABSTRACTS 1950-68. A classified listing of abstracts of journal articles, books and reports in library, information science and related fields, e.g. printing, electronic publishing and databases, media. Name and subject indexes. Available online.

AA20 LIBRARY LITERATURE, 1921- New York: H.W. Wilson, 1934- bimonthly; annual, biennial cumulations to 1977; annual cum. 1978-
(IND)   Sheehy AB10
An author and subject index to books, periodicals, proceedings,

pamphlets, theses, films, filmstrips and microforms dealing with library and information science. Non-library science periodicals indexed selectively. Book review section.

AA21   R & D PROJECTS IN DOCUMENTATION AND LIBRARIANSHIP, 1971-   The Hague, International Federation for Documentation. bimonthly.
(PER)
"Information System on Research in Documentation" (ISORID) lists national and individual activities; lists names of projects and people. The Library Documentation Centre, NLC, reports to ISORID.

REVIEWS AND ANNUALS

AA22   ADVANCES IN LIBRARIANSHIP, 1970-   New York: Academic Press. annual.
R020 A244
Articles and bibliographic essays critically reviewing published literature of library and information science in broad areas.

AA23   THE ALA YEARBOOK, 1976-   Chicago: American Library Association.
R020.62273 A512Y   Sheehy 1AB14
A review of library events. American emphasis, but international coverage. Short and feature articles, obituaries. The (U.K.) Library Association issues the LIBRARY ASSOCIATION YEAR BOOK (PER) annually; this yearbook is limited to the LA's charter, bylaws, membership list.

AA24   ANNUAL REVIEW OF INFORMATION SCIENCE AND TECHNOLOGY, 1966-   Washington: American Society for Information Science. CUMULATIVE INDEX 1966-75 (1976).
R010.78 A615
Bibliographic essays reviewing the literature, recent developments in information science and related areas. KWOC index to vols 1-14, in vol. 14, 1979.

AA25   THE BOWKER ANNUAL OF LIBRARY & BOOK TRADE INFORMATION, 1956-   New York: R.R. Bowker.
R027.07 B786   Sheehy AB118
Title varies. Almanac of statistics, legislation, grants, literary commendations, directory information, bibliographies and short articles on topics of current interest to library and publishing fields.

AA26   SCHOOL LIBRARY MEDIA ANNUAL, 1983-   Ed. by Shirley Aaron, and Pat Scales. Littleton, CO: Libraries Unlimited.

ENCYCLOPEDIAS AND HANDBOOKS

AA27   ALA WORLD ENCYCLOPEDIA OF LIBRARY AND INFORMATION SERVICES. Ed. by R. Wedgeworth. Chicago: American Library Association, 1980. 616 p.
R020.3 A111A   Sheehy 2AB3
Short articles, statistics, biographies, North American emphasis.

AA28   CANADIAN LIBRARY HANDBOOK/GUIDE DES BIBLIOTHEQUES CANADIENNES, 1979/80-   Toronto: Micromedia. irregular.
R027.071 C212CB   Ryder SS8-8
(3d ed. 1983) Concise directory and brief information on

libraries, library education, events, statistics.

AA29 ENCYCLOPEDIA OF LIBRARY AND INFORMATION SCIENCE. 35 vols. New York: M. Dekker, 1968-83. SUPPLEMENT 3 vols. Vol. 36- (1983- In progress).
R020.3 E56   Sheehy AB23, 1AB8, 2AB4
   Vols 34 and 35 are the author and subject indexes to this set; articles of varying length in a topical arrangement. Vol. 36, has the updated article, "Libraries in Canada 1970-1979" (pp. 94-155) to supplement information in the main set. Planned completion for supplement is 1984, with periodic future supplements intended.

AA30 LIBRARY TECHNOLOGY REPORTS, 1965- Chicago: American Library Association. bimonthly; cum. index.
R025.078 A512
   Evaluations, descriptions of systems, equipment, supplies etc. for libraries. The SOURCEBOOK OF LIBRARY TECHNOLOGY cumulates reports from 1965-79 in microfiche with hardcopy table of contents and index.

AA31 Taylor, L.J. A LIBRARIAN'S HANDBOOK. 2 vols. London: Library Association, 1977-80.
R020.941 T243L; R020.941 T243LA
   A guide to British librarianship. Vol. 1 (1977, 882 p.) covers documents, statistics; vol. 12 (1980, 1182 p.) has full texts of key extracts of policy statements, standards, regulations from govt and professional bodies. Single index to both volumes.

DICTIONARIES AND GLOSSARIES

AA32 LIBRARY AND INFORMATION SCIENCE DICTIONARIES AND GLOSSARIES: A SELECTIVE LIST BASED ON NATIONAL LIBRARY OF CANADA HOLDINGS. Prepared by Claire Renaud Frigon. Ottawa: Library Documentation Centre, National Library of Canada, 1979. 17 p.
R020.3 F912LA

AA33 THE ALA GLOSSARY OF LIBRARY AND INFORMATION SCIENCE. Ed. by Heartsill Young. Chicago: American Library Association, 1983. 245 p.
R020.3 A512AA

AA34 ELSEVIER'S DICTIONARY OF LIBRARY SCIENCE, INFORMATION AND DOCUMENTATION IN SIX LANGUAGES. Comp. by W.E. Clason. New York: Elsevier Scientific Publishing, 1976. 708 p.
R020.3 E49E
   Includes English/American, French, Spanish, Italian, Dutch, German arranged in English alphabet, with Arabic supplement.

AA35 Longley, Dennis, and Michael Shain. DICTIONARY OF INFORMATION TECHNOLOGY. New York: John Wiley, 1982. 390 p.
R020.3 L856D

AA36 Harrod, Leonard Montague. THE LIBRARIANS' GLOSSARY OF TERMS USED IN LIBRARIANSHIP, DOCUMENTATION AND THE BOOK CRAFTS, AND REFERENCE BOOK. 4th ed. rev. Boulder, CO: Westview Press, 1977. 903 p.
R010.3 H32L4   Sheehy AB29, 2AB5

AA37 Montgomery, A.C. ACRONYMS AND ABBREVIATIONS IN LIBRARY AND INFORMATION

WORK: A REFERENCE HANDBOOK OF BRITISH USAGE. 2d ed. London: Library Association, 1982. 102 p.
R020.148 M787A2

AA38 Pipics, Z. THE LIBRARIAN'S PRACTICAL DICTIONARY IN 22 LANGUAGES. 7th ed. Munich: Verlag Dokumentation, 1977. 385 p.
R020.3 P665D7

AA39 Tayyeb, Rashid, and K. Chandra. A DICTIONARY OF ACRONYMS AND ABBREVIATIONS IN LIBRARY AND INFORMATION SCIENCE. Ottawa: Canadian Library Association, 1979. 146 p.
R020.148 T247DA   Ryder SS8-61

AA40 Vaillancourt, P.M. INTERNATIONAL DIRECTORY OF ACRONYMS IN LIBRARY, INFORMATION, COMPUTER SCIENCES. New York: R.R. Bowker, 1980. 500 p.
R020.148 V131I

DIRECTORIES

Directories of Libraries

Canadian libraries are identified in general library directories or in publications from associations or from provincial jurisdictions responsible for libraries. Directories usually group libraries by type, collection or geographic region. For example, DIRECTORY OF ONTARIO PUBLIC LIBRARIES (1979), DIRECTORY OF SPECIAL LIBRARIES IN THE TORONTO AREA (1979), DIRECTORY OF INDUSTRIAL RELATIONS LIBRARIES (1979), HEALTH SCIENCES INFORMATION IN CANADA (1979), DIRECTORY OF LIBRARIES IN COMMUNITY AND TECHNICAL COLLEGES (1980), DIRECTORY OF LIBRARIES AND ARCHIVAL INSTITUTIONS IN PRINCE EDWARD ISLAND (1980), DIRECTORY OF OCCUPATIONAL HEALTH AND SAFETY LIBRARIES AND COLLECTIONS IN CANADA (1981), DIRECTORY OF SASKATCHEWAN LIBRARIES (1981) and so on.

AA41 DIRECTORIES OF CANADIAN LIBRARIES/ REPERTOIRES DES BIBLIOTHEQUES CANADIENNES. Prepared by Jacqueline Tomlinson. Ottawa: Library Documentation Centre, National Library of Canada, 1984. 17 p.
R021.002571 AD598D
  Library Documentation Centre, NLC, prepares several bibliographies in English and French language reversed, as a service to the profession and normally free on request. Other examples: GUIDE TO LEGISLATIVE LIBRARIES AND PUBLIC AND SCHOOL LIBRARY AGENCIES IN CANADA (4th ed., 1980, 16 p.) (R027.071 C212G4); GUIDE TO PROVINCIAL LIBRARY AGENCIES IN CANADA (1984, 16 p.) (R354.7100852 R649G).

AA42 AMERICAN LIBRARY DIRECTORY, 1908- 2 vols. 1983- New York: R.R. Bowker. irregular.
R027.07 A51   Sheehy AB43
  Frequency varies; biennial to the 1979 ed., and in one vol. before 1983. With an updating service, ALD covers all types of libraries in the U.S. and Canada, listed geographically, including networks, consortia, public and school library agencies, library schools.

AA43 ASLIB DIRECTORY. 2 vols. 4th ed. Ed. by Ellen M. Codlin. London: Aslib, 1977-80.
R026 A835D4
  Prepared by the Association of Special Libraries and Information Bureaux in Britain as access to over 6400 British and Irish libraries

etc. Vol. 1 (1977) INFORMATION SOURCES IN SCIENCE, TECHNOLOGY AND COMMERCE. Vol. 2 (1980) INFORMATION SOURCES IN THE SOCIAL SCIENCES, MEDICINE AND THE HUMANITIES.

AA44 CANADIAN LIBRARY DIRECTORY. 2 vols. Ottawa: National Library of Canada, 1974-76.
R027.071 C212D   Ryder SS8-9,SS8-10
   Vol. 1, FEDERAL GOVERNMENT LIBRARIES (partially updated in 1977, R027.071 C212DA). Vol. 2, UNIVERSITY, COLLEGE AND SPECIAL LIBRARIES. Alphabetical by name of library, with geographical, personal name and subject indexes. French edition.

AA45 DIRECTORY OF SPECIAL LIBRARIES AND INFORMATION CENTERS. 3 vols. 8th ed. Ed. by Brigitte T. Darnay. Detroit: Gale Research, 1983.
R026 D598D8
   Describes holdings, personnel, services; covers U.S. and Canada. Vol. 1, in 2 pts, arranged alphabetically by name of library with subject index. Vol. 2, geographic and personnel indexes. Vol. 3, is a semi-annual supplement, NEW SPECIAL LIBRARIES. Also issued as a five vol. set, SUBJECT DIRECTORY OF SPECIAL LIBRARIES, 8th ed., (1, Business and Law Including Military and Transportation Libraries; 2, Education and Information Science Including Picture, Audiovisual, Publishing, Rare Book and Recreational; 3, Heath Sciences; 4, Social Sciences and Humanities; 5, Science & Technology Including Agricultural, Energy, Environment and Food Science Libraries.).

AA46 DIRECTORY OF LIBRARY STAFF ORGANIZATIONS. Ed. by Frances M. Jones, and Patrick L. Jarvis. Phoenix, AZ: Oryx Press, 1984. 208 p.

AA47 WORLD GUIDE TO LIBRARIES: INTERNATIONALES BIBLIOTHEKS-HANDBUCH. 6th ed. Ed. by Helga Lengenfelder. Munich: K.G. Saur, 1983. 1186 p. (Dist.: Gale Research).
R027 I61I5 (1980 ed.)
   Directory and brief collection information on some 43 000 libraries (govt, school, special). Entries are by type of library within country, name index.

AA48 WORLD GUIDE TO LIBRARY SCHOOLS AND TRAINING COURSES IN DOCUMENTATION/ GUIDE MONDIAL DES ECOLES DE BIBLIOTHECAIRES ET DOCUMENTALISTES. 2d ed. Paris: UNESCO/ London: Clive Bingley, 1981. 550 p.
R020.711 W927W (1972)
   Additional information appears in NEWSLETTER ON EDUCATION AND TRAINING PROGRAMMES FOR INFORMATION PERSONNEL, 1977- (UNESCO/FID). AA48 provides information on regular training programs at various levels; supplemented by the REGISTER OF EDUCATION AND TRAINING ACTIVITIES IN LIBRARIANSHIP, INFORMATION SCIENCE AND ARCHIVES, edited and compiled by Eric de Grolier (UNESCO, 1982) (020.7 R337R).

Directories and Guides to Library Collections

AA49 Ash, Lee. SUBJECT COLLECTIONS: A GUIDE TO SPECIAL BOOK COLLECTIONS AND EMPHASES AS REPORTED BY UNIVERSITY, COLLEGE, PUBLIC AND SPECIAL LIBRARIES AND MUSEUMS IN THE UNITED STATES AND CANADA. 5th ed. rev. and enl. New York: R.R. Bowker, 1978. 1184 p.
R026 A819S5   Sheehy 2AB11

AA50   DIRECTORY OF CANADIAN RECORDS AND MANUSCRIPT REPOSITORIES. Ottawa: Association of Canadian Archivists, 1977. 115 p.
R025.171 A849D   Ryder HA4-3
   Under province or territory, the archives (federal, provincial, city, church, university) and museums (federal, provincial, municipal, private, military, marine etc.) are listed alphabetically.

AA51   Downs, Robert. AMERICAN LIBRARY RESOURCES: A BIBLIOGRAPHICAL GUIDE. Chicago: American Library Association, 1951. 428 p. SUPPLEMENT 1950-61 (1962); 1961-70 (1972); 1971-80 (1982).
R011 D751A   Sheehy AB100
   Each vol. has a subject index. ALR CUMULATIVE INDEX 1870-1970 compiled by C.D. Keller (ALA, 1981, 89 p.) (R011 D751AD).

AA52   _____, assisted by Elizabeth C. Downs. BRITISH AND IRISH LIBRARY RESOURCES: A BIBLIOGRAPHICAL GUIDE. 2d ed. New York: Mansell/H.W. Wilson, 1982. 448 p.
R020 AD751B (1973 ed.)   Sheehy AB100
   More than 6700 entries for catalogues, guides, articles describing collections for all subjects and in all types of libraries. A similar title, also by R.B. Downs, covers AUSTRALIAN AND NEW ZEALAND LIBRARY RESOURCES (Mansell/H.W. Wilson, 1979, 164 p.) (R026.00099 D751A).

AA53   Lewanski, Richard C. SUBJECT COLLECTIONS IN EUROPEAN LIBRARIES: A DIRECTORY AND BIBLIOGRAPHICAL GUIDE. 2d ed. New York: R.R. Bowker, 1978. 495 p.
R017 L669S5   Sheehy AB97
   Expands approach of AA49 to Europe, arranging libraries by country within broad classes based on DDC.

AA54   RESEARCH COLLECTIONS IN CANADIAN LIBRARIES. Ottawa: National Library of Canada, 1972-   occasional.
R026 R432   Ryder SS8-44
   In two parts with several volumes/ nos in each part. Part 1, UNIVERSITIES. Vol. 1, PRAIRIE PROVINCES; vol. 2, ATLANTIC PROVINCES; vol. 3, BRITISH COLUMBIA; vol. 4, ONTARIO; vol. 5, QUEBEC. Part 2, SPECIAL STUDIES. No. 1, THEATRE RESOURCES IN CANADIAN COLLECTIONS; no. 2, FEDERAL GOVERNMENT LIBRARIES; no. 3, LAW LIBRARY RESOURCES; no. 4, SLAVIC AND EAST EUROPEAN RESOURCES; no. 5, COLLECTIONS OF OFFICIAL PUBLICATIONS; no. 6, I,II, FINE ARTS LIBRARY RESOURCES IN CANADA; no. 7, MUSIC RESOURCES IN CANADIAN COLLECTIONS; no. 8, DANCE RESOURCES IN CANADIAN LIBRARIES; no. 9, RESOURCES FOR NATIVE PEOPLES STUDIES.

AA55   Roberts, S., and others. RESEARCH LIBRARIES AND COLLECTIONS IN THE U.K.: A SELECTIVE INVENTORY AND GUIDE. London: Clive Bingley, 1978. 285p.
R026.0002541 R642R
   Entries are grouped as (1) national, special, public libraries; (2) university libraries; (3) polytechnic libraries; (4) Scottish central institutions. (See also AA43).

Directories of Librarians and Library Associations

Directories frequently carry personnel listings, and as with directories of libraries, some "who's who" exist for regions or types of libraries. For example WHO KNOWS WHAT (AA62) or WHO'S WHO IN SPECIAL LIBRARIES 1983/84 (Special Libraries Association, 1983).

AA56   ALA HANDBOOK OF ORGANIZATION AND MEMBERSHIP DIRECTORY, 1980/81- Chicago: American Library Association, 1980- annual.
R020.62273 A512H
   Title varies. An ALA MEMBERSHIP DIRECTORY (R202.622 A51) has appeared since 1948, and a handbook has also separately appeared at various times. The present HANDBOOK combines an outline of the structure of ALA, its officials, committees, and key publications together with a membership roster. (See related title, AB23).

AA57   CLA DIRECTORY & MEMBERS' HANDBOOK, 1983/84- Ottawa: Canadian Library Association. irregular.
R020.67 C21
   Supersedes CLA DIRECTORY 1978/79, with SUPPLEMENT 1979/80. AA66 lists CLA personal and institutional members, their addresses and divisional affiliation plus a guide to the organization and governance of CLA.

AA58   DICTIONARY OF AMERICAN LIBRARY BIOGRAPHY. Ed. by B.J. Wynar. Littleton, CO: Libraries Unlimited, 1978. 595 p.
R020.922 D554D   Sheehy 1AB13
   Sketches of 302 prominent persons, including Canadians. Supplementary sketches in the JOURNAL OF LIBRARY HISTORY.

AA59   DIRECTORY OF LIBRARY ASSOCIATIONS IN CANADA/ REPERTOIRE DES ASSOCIATIONS DE BIBLIOTHEQUES AU CANADA. 5th ed. Ottawa: Library Documentation Centre, National Library of Canada, 1979. 1 vol. unpaged.
R020.6 C212   Ryder GR10-5, SS8-1

AA60   DIRECTORY OF LIBRARY CONSULTANTS '85. New York: R.R. Bowker, 1984.
   Lists more than 250 people in areas of management, acquisitions, appraisals, systems analysis, publicity, libraries by type, work flow and cost studies, standards, legislation. Arranged alphabetically, geographically and by specialty.

AA61   Fang, Josephine R., and Alice H. Songe. INTERNATIONAL GUIDE TO LIBRARY, ARCHIVAL AND INFORMATION SCIENCE ASSOCIATIONS. 2d ed. New York: R.R. Bowker, 1980. 400 p.
R020.6 F211I (1976 ed.)

AA62   WHO KNOWS WHAT: CANADIAN LIBRARY RELATED EXPERTISE. Ed. and comp. by Susan Klement. Ottawa: Canadian Library Association, 1984. 174 p.

AA63   WHO'S WHO IN LIBRARY AND INFORMATION SERVICES. Chicago: American Library Association, 1982.
R020.922 W628W
   Replaces A BIOGRAPHICAL DIRECTORY OF LIBRARIANS IN THE UNITED STATES AND CANADA, 5th ed. last published 1970.

BOOK TRADE AND INFORMATION INDUSTRIES

REVIEWS AND ANNUALS OF THE BOOK TRADE

AB1   THE BOOK TRADE IN CANADA/ L'INDUSTRIE DU LIVRE AU CANADA, 1975-   Ed. by E. Thorne and E. Matheson. Caledon, Ont.: Ampersand. annual.
R070.50971 B724B   Ryder GR9-5
    Supersedes BOOK PUBLISHERS IN CANADA. A directory of publishers, distributors, booksellers; notice of awards, short articles on copyright, book trade etc.

AB2   THE BOOK PUBLISHING ANNUAL, 1984-   New York: R.R. Bowker. annual.
    Replaces PUBLISHERS WEEKLY YEARBOOK (1st ed., 1983) (R070.50973 P976PA). AB2 has "Highlights, Analyses, & Trends" by industry expects in collaboration with the editors of PW (AB5). News on the "business of books", e.g. mergers, statistics, imports, exports plus articles reviewing the year in books through articles on types (text, trade, scholarly etc.) and on pertinent topics (law, milestones, etc.).

AB3   THE BOWKER ANNUAL OF LIBRARIES AND THE BOOK TRADE. (See AA25).
    From 1982, a bibliography of "Basic Publications for the Publishing and Book Trade" has been included.

AB4   U.S. BOOK PUBLISHING YEARBOOK AND DIRECTORY, 1979/80-   White Plains, NY: Knowledge Industry Publications Inc., 1979-   annual.
R070.50973 U5891U
    The first edition published by Facts on File as a Knowledge Industry Publication series. Knowledge Industry has conducted major surveys for the publishing trade; that research is reflected in this review of domestic publishing with comparative information on Canada, Great Britain, West Germany, Japan. Records trends, trade information, statistics. Directory section is smaller than LMP (AB12); other information is comparable to, and sometimes extends, overviews in the BOWKER ANNUAL (AB3) or THE BOOK PUBLISHING ANNUAL (AB2).

NEWSPAPERS

AB5   PUBLISHERS WEEKLY: THE BOOK INDUSTRY JOURNAL, 1872-   New York: R.R. Bowker.
(PER)
    Brief announcements, interviews, articles on every aspect of the trade, e.g. electronic publishing, copyright, legislation, economics, trends. Annual summary statistics and regular seasonal features.

AB6   QUILL AND QUIRE, 1935-   Toronto: Greey de Pencier Publications. monthly
(PER)   Ryder GR9-17
    Paper of the Canadian book trade with library, publishing news, reviews, recent trade and educational books. A "forthcoming" insert with CIP entries in each issue. A regular special issue on education. Subscription includes the CANADIAN PUBLISHING DIRECTORY listing publishers and agents plus other seasonal flyers, "Books for Everybody" (promotional) and "New & Forthcoming Books." On microfilm with index, 1935-75 (McLaren Micropublishing).

DICTIONARIES AND GLOSSARIES

AB7 BOOKMAN'S GLOSSARY. 5th ed. Ed. by J. Peters. New York: R.R. Bowker, 1975. 169 p.
R655.03 H72B5

AB8 THE LANGUAGE OF THE FOREIGN BOOK TRADE: ABBREVIATIONS, TERMS AND PHRASES. 3d ed. Ed. by Jerrold Orne. Chicago: American Library Association, 1976. 333 p.
R010.3 O74L3   Sheehy 1AA58

AB9 THE PUBLISHER'S PRACTICAL DICTIONARY IN 20 LANGUAGES. Ed. by E. Mora. Munich: Verlag Dokumentation, 1979. 587 p.
R070.5 M827W

DIRECTORIES

Directories of the Book Trade

AB10 AMERICAN BOOK TRADE DIRECTORY, 1915-   Comp. by Jaques Cattell Press. New York: R.R. Bowker. biennial.
R655.473 A512
   With a subscription updating service. Canada included since 1979; lists retail, antiquarian stores, wholesalers, publishers with area of speciality. Arranged alphabetically by state/ province, city. Similar coverage in INTERNATIONAL BOOK TRADE DIRECTORY (R.R. Bowker, 1979-) for firms outside North America; INTERNATIONAL LITERARY MARKET PLACE (R.R. Bowker, 1965-) (R070.52 I616I) has directory and related trade information, literary agents, sales and rights on a nation by nation basis with section on literary prizes.

AB11 CANADIAN ANTIQUARIAN BOOK SELLERS DIRECTORY. 5th ed. Comp. by Maria Szivos. Brandon, Man.: Brandon University Library, 1983. 46 p.
R658.8090705 S998C5

AB12 LITERARY MARKET PLACE, 1972/73-   New York: R.R. Bowker, 1972- annual.
R070.52L776L
   LMP is published in the Fall; its "yellow pages" section is the telephone book for American publishing, including print and micro-publishers, agents, photographers, columnists, wholesalers, packagers, translators, public relations people. Directory information, ISBN prefix, product or service descriptions of firms, individuals in some 2000 U.S., Canadian firms. MAGAZINE INDUSTRY MARKETPLACE, 1980- (R.R. Bowker, 1979-) is a related annual title, also published in the Fall and geared to periodical publishing. MMP has a bibliography of over 2500 consumer, trade, professional, literary and scholarly periodicals plus extensive list of periodicals in fields like printing, graphics.

AB13 MICROFORM MARKET PLACE: AN INTERNATIONAL DIRECTORY OF MICROPUBLISHING, 1974/75-   Westport, CT: Meckler Pub., 1974-   annual.
R070.57 M626D
   Excludes micrographics and supply manufacturers but includes the publishers and their fields of activity in subject list. Directory, names and numbers, geographic index with information on mergers, organizations in micrographics education etc.

AB14   PUBLISHERS' DIRECTORY. 5th ed. Ed. by Linda S. Hubbard. Detroit: Gale Research, 1984. 1630 p. (inter-edition PD SUPPLEMENT)
Supersedes BOOK PUBLISHERS' DIRECTORY. Described by publisher as including "over 7000 U.S. and Canadian publishers not in LMP (AB12); records new, established, private, special interest, avant garde, government and institution presses. Information on discounts, returns, stock. Subject, publisher, geographic indexes.

AB15   PUBLISHERS, DISTRIBUTORS & WHOLESALERS OF THE UNITED STATES. 5th ed. New York: R.R. Bowker, 1983. 772 p.
R070.502573 P976P
Paperbound list taken from the database for BOOKS IN PRINT series; "A directory of 45 600 publishers, distributors, associations and wholesalers, listing editorial, ordering addresses and ISBN prefix."

AB16   PUBLISHERS' INTERNATIONAL DIRECTORY/ INTERNATIONALS VERLAGS ADRESSBUCH. 11th ed. Munich: K.G. Saur, 1984. Inter-edition supplement. (Dist.: Gale Research).
R070.5 P976P (8th ed., 1979)
Access to some 7000 trade and non-trade, active publishers, their specialities and ISBN prefix. Geographically arranged, addresses are in Europe, the Americas, Africa, Asia and Oceana.

Directories of the Information Industries and Services

AB17   ENCYCLOPEDIA OF INFORMATION SYSTEMS AND SERVICES. 5th ed. Ed. by John Schmittroth. Detroit: Gale, 1983. 1242 p. Inter-edition supplement.
R029.7 E56E5
Details on over 2500 organizations in the U.S., 60 other countries that produce, process bibliographic databases, text or micrographic information. Multiple access through subject, name, geographic, analytic indexes to computerized information or data management services, vendors. Suppl: NEW INFORMATION SYSTEMS AND SERVICES.

AB18   INFORMATION INDUSTRY MARKET PLACE 1980- An International Directory of Products and Services. New York: R.R. Bowker, 1979- annual.
R025.04025 AI43IA
Provides a quick-reference to organizations in the U.S., Europe and elsewhere in sections for production, distribution, retail support services and suppliers, associations, government agencies, conferences and courses, sources of information (reference books, periodicals). Geographic index; a "yellow pages" name and number index (see related title, AB12); IIMP is similar to EISS (AB17) in content.

Directories: Computerized Information

AB19   COMPUTER READABLE DATA BASES: DIRECTORY AND DATA SOURCEBOOK, 1969- Washington: American Society for Information Science. biennial. (Dist.: Knowledge Industries Publications).
R025.04025 C738CA
Alphabetical list of publicly available bibliographic and numeric databases. Details include producer, processor, name, subject index.

AB20   COIN: A DIRECTORY OF COMPUTERIZED INFORMATION IN CANADA. Edmonton: Alberta Information Retrieval Association, 1980. 771 p.
R025.0402571
Covers bibliographic and numeric databases. In three parts: directory, keyword and contact index.

AB21   DIRECTORY OF CANADIAN SCIENTIFIC AND TECHNICAL DATABASES. Ottawa: Canada Institute for Scientific and Technical Information, 1984.
Lists over 100 machine-readable collections of bibliographic or scientific numeric data, produced by Canadian organizations. Also includes international databases with significant Canadian content.

AB22   DIRECTORY OF ONLINE DATABASES, 1979- Santa Monica, CA: Cuadra Associates. 4 issues a year, including 2 directory issues and 2 supplements.
R025.04025 D598D
Covers both bibliographic and text data bases, with descriptions, addresses of producers and services, indexes by subject, producer, online service, names. Directory issues are cumulative.

AB23   ONLINE BIBLIOGRAPHIC DATABASES. 3d ed. Ed. by James L. Hall and Marjorie J. Brown. London: Aslib, 1983. 383 p. (Dist.: Gale).
R025 04025 H177HA
Over 170 bases covering medicine, education, music, business, engineering, languages etc., offered by 44 international suppliers.

AB24   ONLINE DATABASE SEARCH SERVICES DIRECTORY. Ed. by John Schmittroth and Doris M. Maxfield. 2 vols. Detroit: Gale Research, 1983-84.
A guide to libraries, commerical firms that provide online searches for the public or specific clientele. Has six indexes to cover organizations, systems (e.g.: DIALOG, BRS) and bases (e.g.: ERIC, INSPEC) used, subjects, search personnel, and geographic area.

SEARCH MANUALS FOR ONLINE DATABASES

AB25   BRS MANUAL, 1979- 3 vols. Scotia, N.Y.: Bibliographic Retrieval Services. looseleaf; bulletin updates
R025.524 B111B
(Last ed. 1981) Vols are SYSTEM REFERENCE; USER and DATABASE DESCRIPTIONS manuals.

AB26   CAN/OLE MANUAL, 1974- 2 vols. Ottawa: Canada Institute for Scientific and Technical Information. looseleaf; bulletin updates.
R025.524 C111CC3
(3d ed., 1982) French ed.: MANUAL DE L'UTILISATEUR CAN/OLE. Vols are a user and a database description for databases available on CANadian/OnLine Enquiry.

AB27   CAN/SDI PROFILE DESIGN MANUAL, 1969- Ottawa: Canada Institute for Scientific and Technical Information. looseleaf.
R025.525 C111C
(6th ed., 1982) French ed.: MANUEL DE REDACTION DES PROFILES. Instructions on formulating a subject interest for running against databases described in the manual as available at CISTI.

AB28   CANSIM USER'S MANUAL FOR DATA RETRIEVAL AND MANIPULATION. Ottawa: Information Canada [for Statistics Canada], 1972. various paging.
R650 C212CA 1972
   Describes the (batch mode) use and programs of the Canadian Socio-Economic Information Management System database. Other occasional titles are THE INTERACTIVE SYSTEM USER'S MANUAL (1977)(R650 C212D) and information on the contents in the system. (For further note on CANSIM, see CA36).

AB29   GUIDE TO DIALOG SEARCHING, 1979- Palo Alto, CA: Lockheed DIALOG Information Retrieval Service. looseleaf; updates.
R025.524 G946G

AB30   ORBIT USER MANUAL, 1979- Santa Monica, CA: SDC Search Service, System Development Corp. looseleaf; updates. QUICK REFERENCE GUIDE. looseleaf
R025.524 O111U

AB31   QL SYSTEMS MANUAL, 1980- 2 vols. Ottawa: QL Systems Ltd. looseleaf
R025.524 Q1Q
   Vols are a users' manual and a database descriptions manual.

AB32   UTLAS SYSTEMS MANUAL/ MANUEL DES SYSTEMES, 1983- Toronto: UTLAS. looseleaf.
R025 308504 U11US
   (First ed. 1983 in manual format). Has 2 parts; the SYSTEMS MANUAL: GUIDE TO USE OF THE CATALOGUE SUPPORT SYSTEM (CATSS) AND REFCATSS and the GUIDE TO USING ACCORD (R025 30854); also with UTLAS MARC CODING MANUAL FOR MONOGRAPHS (1982; updated to March 1983, looseleaf) (R025 302854 U11UM).

AIDS TO THE SELECTION OF BOOKS AND MATERIALS FOR LIBRARY COLLECTIONS

GUIDES TO REFERENCE WORKS

AC1   AMERICAN REFERENCE BOOKS ANNUAL, 1970- Littleton, CO.: Libraries Unlimited. CUMULATIVE INDEX, 1970-74 (1974); 1975-79 (1979).
R025.5 AA512
     Short descriptive, evaluative reviews. Arranged by broad subject with author, title and subject index. BEST REFERENCE BOOKS SELECTED FROM ARBA 1970-76 (1976) (R025.5 AB561B) and RECOMMENDED BEST BOOKS FOR SMALL AND MEDIUM-SIZED LIBRARIES AND MEDIA CENTERS (1981-   ) (071.02 R331R) provides an annual selection from ARBA.

AC2   Bibliothèque nationale du Québec. LES OUVRAGES DE REFERENCE DU QUEBEC. Compilée sous la direction de Réal Bosa. Quebec: Ministère des Affaires culturelles du Québec, 1969. 189 p. SUPPLEMENT 1967-74 (1975).
R025.5 AB582   Ryder GR1-89, -90

AC3   Malclès, Louise-Noelle et André d'Héritier. MANUEL DE BIBLIOGRAPHIE. 3d ed. Paris: Presses universitaires de France, 1975. 398 p.
R011 AM242M3   Sheehy AA5, 1AA1

AC4   Ryder, Dorothy E., ed. CANADIAN REFERENCE SOURCES: A SELECTIVE GUIDE. 2d ed. Ottawa: Canadian Library Association, 1981.
R025.5 AR992C
     An annotated guide grouping works, published to the end of 1980, under general reference, history and allied subjects, humanities, science, social sciences. This ed. notes an emergence of works on women's studies, labour movement, archives, ethnic groups and children's literature.

AC5   Sheehy, Eugene P., ed., and others. GUIDE TO REFERENCE BOOKS. 9th ed. Chicago: American Library Association, 1976. 1015 p. SUPPLEMENT 1981; 1982.
R025.5 AM94G9
     An annotated, comprehensive guide; international with emphasis on American sources and materials distributed in America. Brief notes sometimes cite reviews. The second supplement lists nearly 2100 items, bringing publication up to 1980 in coverage. Older materials appear as they come to the attention of compilers.

AC6   Walford, A.J., ed. GUIDE TO REFERENCE MATERIAL. 4th ed. 3 vols. London: Library Association. Vol. 1, SCIENCE AND TECHNOLOGY (1980). Vol. 2, SOCIAL AND HISTORICAL SCIENCES, PHILOSOPHY AND RELIGION (1982). Vol. 3, GENERALITIES, LANGUAGES, THE ARTS AND LITERATURE (1977).
R025.5 AW174G3   Sheehy AA404
     Complements AC5, with emphasis on British, European and non-western reference titles. The 3d vol. contains a subject index. WALFORD'S CONCISE GUIDE TO REFERENCE MATERIALS, (Library Association, 1981; 434 p.) contains 2560 entries selected and updated from the larger volumes.

AC7   Wynar, Christine G. GUIDE TO REFERENCE BOOKS FOR SCHOOL MEDIA CENTERS. 2d ed. Littleton, CO: Libraries Unlimited, 1981. 377 p.
          A selection of titles based on the appropriateness of title for K to 12 curriculum, broadly interpreted.

RETROSPECTIVE SELECTION

General Retrospective Selection (Guide; and then Aids. See also AC1-AC7)

AC8   BOOKS IN OTHER LANGUAGES, 1979: A GUIDE TO SELECTION AIDS AND SUPPLIERS. 4th ed. Ed. by L. Wertheimer. Ottawa: Canadian Library Assoc., 144 p
          018.1 M594B4   Ryder SS8-78
          Dated, but still useful source. Items grouped by language.

AC9   BOOKS FOR PUBLIC LIBRARIES. 3d ed. Chicago: American Library Association, 1982. 374 p.
          011 AP976B3
          "A starter list" of more than 4000 titles, half of which are new, useful for smaller libraries. Arranged by DDC, titles are non-fiction and chosen as sound, readable reflecting contemporary interest.

AC10   CANADIAN BOOK REVIEW ANNUAL, 1975-   Ed. by Dean Tudor, and Ann Tudor. Toronto: Simon & Pierre. annual.
          R819.08 C212B
          Evaluative short reviews of English language trade and educational books by broad classes (e.g.: reference, humanities, applied arts, science and technology, social sciences). With author/ title/ subject index; incidental information includes an "annual awards" list. (Related publication for French language materials, AC16).

AC11   CANADIAN SELECTION: BOOKS AND PERIODICALS FOR LIBRARIES. Compiled by Edith Jarvi, Isabel McLean and Catherine MacKenzie. Toronto: University of Toronto Press, 1978. 1060 p. SUPPLEMENT 1977-79, (1981).
          R015.71 C212C   Ryder SS8-75
          A buying guide for small, medium-sized libraries. Classified list with author, title, subject index. New rev. edition, by M.O. Cariou, A.M. Bregman and S. Cox, is planned for publication in late 1985; it continues the same arrangement, has a cut-off date of Dec. 1983 and includes selected significant English language Canadian items.

AC12   CATALOG OF MUSEUM PUBLICATIONS AND MEDIA. 2d ed. Ed. by P. Wasserman, and E. Herman. Detroit: Gale Research, 1980. 1044 p.
          Z5052 C32
          Clues for publications, av and other media not always found in more standard sources. Covers some 1000 institutions, galleries, museums etc. in the U.S., Canada. Title, subject, geographic indexes.

AC13   CURRENT BOOK REVIEW CITATIONS, 1976-1982. New York: H.W. Wilson. monthly; annual cumulation until publication ceased.
          (PER)   Sheehy 1AA84
          Author or main entry/ title index to all reviews in over 1000 periodicals covered by the Wilson indexes, plus references to reviews in BOOKLIST, LIBRARY JOURNAL, CHOICE, SCHOOL LIBRARY JOURNAL.

AC14   FICTION CATALOG. 10th ed. Ed. by Estelle A. Fidell. Standard Catalog
        Series. New York: H.W. Wilson, 1980. 800 p. Four annual supplements
        between editions.
        R823 AF448C10   Sheehy BD200
            The 'Wilson Standard Catalogs' (see AC17, AC23, AC27, AC28) are in
        three parts, a classified main section with bibliographic cataloguing,
        classification information and annotation; an index section and a
        publisher or distributor directory.
            The FICTION CATALOG cites over 5000 works of fiction, arranged
        alphabetically by main entry, with full citation, plot summaries (for
        anthologies, a list of contents), excerpts from reviews or criticism.
        Title, subject indexes. AC14 is a companion to AC17 and to the more
        specialized fiction in AC28.

AC15   Katz, William A., and Linda Sternberg Katz. MAGAZINES FOR LIBRARIES: FOR
        THE GENERAL READER AND SCHOOL, JUNIOR COLLEGE, COLLEGE, UNIVERSITY AND
        PUBLIC LIBRARIES. 4th ed. New York: R.R. Bowker, 1982. 958 p.
        R050AM189   Sheehy AA419a
            Appr. 6500 magazines selected for libraries noted in title. Basic
        bibliographic information, availability of samples, microform
        editions, audience level in brief description of magazine.

AC16   LIVRES ET AUTEURS QUEBECOISES. Critical Review of the Year/ Revue
        critique de l'année, 1961-   Quebec: Les Presses de l'Université
        Laval, 1973-   annual.
        (PER)
            Supersedes LIVRES ET AUTEURS CANADIENS, 1961-1968 (Editions
        Jumonville, 1962-1968). Overview of the year's literary production in
        extracts taken from reviewing media. Incidental information includes
        list of prizes, doctoral theses and bibliogs. (Related publication for
        English materials, AC10).

AC17   PUBLIC LIBRARY CATALOG. 8th ed. Ed. by G.L. Bogart and E.A. Fidell.
        Standard Catalog Series. New York: H.W. Wilson, 1984. 1353 p. Four
        annual supplements between editions.
        R011 AP976C7   Sheehy AA342
            Designed for use in public, college, university libraries. DDC
        classified list of non-fiction titles with author/ title/ subject/
        analytic indexes; directory of publishers. Complements AC14.

AC18   THE READER'S ADVISER: A LAYMAN'S GUIDE TO LITERATURE. 12th ed. 3 vols.
        New York: R.R. Bowker, 1974-77.
        R011 R286   Sheehy AA339,1AA68
            A standard reference covering the 'best' or 'best-known' works in
        subjects. Vols 1-2, British, American and world literature in English.
        Vol. 3, reference literature.

AC19   REFERENCE AND SUBSCRIPTION BOOKS REVIEWS, 1975/76-   Chicago: American
        Library Association, 1977-   annual.
        R016 S941A
            An annual reprinting of reviews of reference materials as the
        reviews appeared in BOOKLIST (AC30). Reference reviews appeared
        separately as SUBSCRIPTION BOOKS BULLETIN, 1930-56; then cumulated
        from THE BULLETIN AS SUBSCRIPTION BOOKS BULLETIN REVIEWS, 1956-68; as
        a biennial, REFERENCE AND SUBSCRIPTION BOOKS REVIEWS, 1968/70-74.

AC20   REFERENCE BOOKS FOR SMALL AND MEDIUM-SIZED LIBRARIES. 4th ed. Ed. by Jovian Lang and Deborah Masters. Chicago: American Library Association, 1984.
011.02 AA512R4
An annotated buying guide.

Academic Retrospective Selection (See also previous titles in this section)

AC21   BOOKS FOR COLLEGE LIBRARIES: A CORE COLLECTION OF 40,000 TITLES. 2d ed. 6 vols. Chicago: American Library Association, 1975.
R011 AB724B2   Sheehy AA348-AA352
Five vols cover major subject areas, emphasizing social sciences and humanities; vol. 6 is the index. A 3d ed., 6 vols, is planned; work beginning in 1984. The new edition will list 50 000 titles for a core undergraduate collection; it excludes serials but includes non-print materials. Vol. 5, covering psychology, science, technology and bibliography is to be published first.

Children and Young Adults

AC22   CANADIAN BOOKS FOR YOUNG PEOPLE/ LIVRES CANADIENS POUR LA JEUNESSE. Rev. ed. Ed. by Irma McDonough. Toronto: University of Toronto Press, 1980.
R028.52 C512LA   Ryder HU6-66
Expansion of CANADIAN BOOKS FOR CHILDREN/ LIVRES CANADIENS POUR ENFANTS (1976). Annotated titles, some adult titles, series, fiction and non-fiction, for pre-school to age 14, grade nine.

AC23   CHILDREN'S CATALOG. 14th ed. Ed. by E. Dill. Standard Catalog Series. New York: H.W. Wilson, 1981. 1296 p. Four annual supplements between editions.
R028.5 AW74C14   Sheehy AA375
Features "quality" books suitable for preschool, grades K to 6. The classified section organizes the titles into nonfiction (including biography), fiction, story collections and easy books. Author/ title/ subject/ analytic index; directory of publishers.

AC24   IN SEARCH OF CANADIAN MATERIALS. Winnipeg: Manitoba Dept of Education, 1978.
015.71 AP558I
School library associations, education depts or ministries have typically issued guides featuring Canadian content. For example, ATLANTIC BOOK CHOICE: RECOMMENDED CANADIAN AND REGIONAL TITLES FOR ELEMENTARY SCHOOL COLLECTIONS (Vol.1; Canadian Learning Materials Centre, Dalhousie and the N.S. School Library Association, 1983) with two more vols planned for junior, senior high school collections.
CIRCULAR 15 (French ed.: REPERTOIRE 15) (Ontario Min. of Education, 1974), no longer published, listed English language materials for elementary and secondary school curricula. CIRCULAR 14: TEXTBOOKS and CIRCULAIRE 14: MANUEL SCOLAIRES published annually in January and followed by two supplements, 14A (Spring) and 14B (Fall), lists texts, not necessarily but emphasizing Canadian, approved by the Minister of Education for use in Ontario schools.

AC25   IN REVIEW: CANADIAN BOOKS FOR YOUNG PEOPLE, 1967-1982. Toronto: Libraries and Community Information Branch, Ministry of Culture and Recreation. quarterly to 1979; bimonthly to 1982. CUMULATIVE INDEX 1967-76 (1977).
(PER)
Ryder GR9-9, HU6-64
   An Ontario bicentennial ed. (1984) is in preparation as a final edition. Books reviewed in IN REVIEW, and collected by the publication, are now retained as a collection in the FLIS library.

AC26   NOTABLE CANADIAN CHILDREN'S BOOKS/ UN CHOIX DE LIVRES CANADIENS POUR LA JEUNESSE. Rev. [by Irene Aubrey] to include notable books published in 1973 and 1974. Ottawa: Children's Literature Service, National Library of Canada, 1976. 94 p. (typescript). SUPPLEMENT 1975 (1977); 1976 and 1977 (1979); 1978 (1980); 1980 (1982); 1981 (1984).
028.52 N899N2
   The original edition is an annotated catalogue, prepared by Sheila Egoff and Alvine Bélisle, for a 1973 exhibition at NLC. The Children's Literature Service of NLC then revised, and continues to prepare an annual supplement, compiled by Irene E. Aubrey [and others].
   NLC provides various lists, usually free upon request, related to Canadian children's literature, Lists normally accompany NLC exhibits or displays, e.g., PICTURES TO SHARE: ILLUSTRATION IN CANADIAN CHILDREN'S BOOKS, exhibition 1979, (1980); SPORTS AND GAMES IN CANADIAN CHILDREN'S BOOKS (1982); MYSTERY AND ADVENTURE IN CANADIAN BOOKS FOR CHILDREN AND YOUNG PEOPLE (1983) or may simply be compiled as an aid, e.g. ANIMAL WORLD IN CANADIAN BOOKS FOR CHILDREN AND YOUNG PEOPLE (rev. list, 1983). (See related title, AC29).

AC27   JUNIOR HIGH SCHOOL LIBRARY CATALOG. 4th ed. Ed. by Gary L. Bogart, and Richard H. Isaacson. Standard Catalog Series. New York: H.W. Wilson, 1980. 939 p. Four annual supplements between editions.
R027.8 AW95H4
Sheehy AA376
   Continues from CHILDREN'S CATALOG (AC23), grades 7 to 9.

AC28   SENIOR HIGH SCHOOL LIBRARY CATALOG. 12th ed. Ed. by G.L. Bogart and K.R. Carlson. Standard Catalog Series. New York: H.W. Wilson, 1982. 1300 p. Four annual supplements between editions.
R027.8 AW74S12
Sheehy AA377
   Covers grades 10-12, some adult titles suitable to high school curricula are included.

AC29   SOURCES OF FRENCH CANADIAN CHILDREN'S AND YOUNG PEOPLE'S BOOKS/ SOURCES D'INFORMATION SUR LES LIVRES DE JEUNESSE CANADIENS FRANÇAISES. Rev. and enl. Compiled by Irene E. Aubrey. Ottawa: National Library of Canada, 1984. 18 p. (free pamphlet)
028.5 AA895SA
   A comprehensive list, important for English libraries because it collates information that otherwise requires searching through sources not readily accessible in most libraries. Bilingual pamphlet refers to general Canadian bibliographies (AD73, AD77 and so on) which contain references and/or list the children's titles; refers to retrospective bibliographies, e.g. PLEINS FEUX SUR LA LITTERATURE DE JEUNESSE AU CANADA FRANÇAISE (Lémeac, 1972) and to current aids, e.g. LURELU, 1978-   (3 issues a year, Communication Jeunesse). (See related title, AC26).

CURRENT SELECTION

General Current Selection

AC30   THE BOOKLIST, 1905-   Chicago: American Library Association. semi-monthly.
       (PER)   Sheehy AA343
       Title varies. A reviewing journal. Reference reviews also published separately (see AC19).

AC31   BRITISH BOOK NEWS: A GUIDE TO BOOK SELECTION, 1940-   London: British Council. monthly.
       (PER)   Sheehy AA344

AC32   CANADIAN LITERATURE/ LITTERATURE CANADIENNE: A Quarterly of Criticism and Review, 1959-   Vancouver: Univ. of British Columbia.

AC33   CHOICE, 1964-   Chicago: Association of College and Research Libraries. 11 issues a year, annual index 1980-
       (PER)   Sheehy AA353
       CHOICE reviews print (and non-print) materials of potential value for undergraduate libraries. Reviews non-print as well as print. A "Reviews on Cards" reprint service available to subscribers. CHOICE 1964-74 (1976-77) is a classified cumulation in 9 vols, vol. IX is the author/title index. THE OPENING DAY COLLECTION, 3d ed. (1974) (R027.7 AC545) lists selected titles for newly created academic libraries. Selected reviews published from March of one year to Feb. of the next year appear in a Spring brochure, OUTSTANDING ACADEMIC BOOKS AND NONPRINT MATERIALS. Titles are arranged as in the original magazine; citations with no annotations but with reference to original review, which "should be consulted ... especially if the list is to be used as an acquisition guide."

AC34   FREE: The Newsletter of Free Materials and Services, 1979-   Vancouver: Dyad Services. 5 issues a year. pamphlet.
       Materials recommended as useful for teachers and school, public libraries, vertical files. Short description of item.

AC35   KIRKUS REVIEWS, 1933-   New York: Kirkus Service. semi-monthly.
       R011 K59K
       Owned since 1971 by New York Review of Books, this looseleaf service is oriented to public libraries, general readers. Reviews pre-publication for adult, juvenile books. Author indexes cumulate quarterly and semi-annually.

AC36   LETTERS IN CANADA, 1936-   Toronto: Univ. of Toronto Press. Summer issue of the UNIVERSITY OF TORONTO QUARTERLY, 1931-
       Z1375 C34   Ryder HU6-19a
       An annual feature since vol. 5; a critical survey of both French and English publications in the humanities and social sciences. Issue is enlarged; since 1980-   the issue is completely devoted to reviews.

AC37   LIBRARY JOURNAL, 1876-   New York: R.R. Bowker. semi-monthly. Section: Book Reviews.
       (PER)   Sheehy AA415
       Journals features articles and reviews. Over 5000 reviews annually for books of interest to wide variety of institutions from small

public to large academic library. Special lists in various subject areas. The annual May list of the year's outstanding reference sources appears, from May 1984, in AMERICAN LIBRARIES. Reviews from LJ are cumulated annually in THE LIBRARY JOURNAL BOOK REVIEW, 1967- (R028.1 AL697).

AC38   NOS LIVRES, 1977-   Montreal: L'Office des communications sociales 10 issues a year.
    Formerly LE LIVRE CANADIEN, 1972-77. Reviews books published in Canada, in original French or translation; articles on authors.

AC39   QUILL & QUIRE. (See AB6)

AC40   READERS ADVISORY SERVICE; SELECTED TOPICAL BOOKLISTS, 1974-   New York: Science Associates International. quarterly, cum. index.
    Reading lists, sometimes briefly annotated, for broad range of popular and academic interests in humanities, social sciences, sciences and technology. Title, name indexes.

Reference Collections

AC41   COLLEGE & RESEARCH LIBRARIES, 1939-   Chicago: Association of College and Research Libraries. bimonthly. Section: Selected Reference Books.
(PER)

AC42   MICROFORM REVIEW, 1972-   Westport, CT: Microform Review. quarterly, CUMULATIVE INDEX 1972-76.
(PER)

AC43   RQ: (REFERENCE QUARTERLY), 1960-   Chicago: American Library Association. quarterly. Section: Sources: Databases, Reference Books, Professional Materials.
(PER)
    Specializes in reviews of reference works; has annual update on U.S. national bibliography and abstracting services.

AC44   REFERENCE SERVICES REVIEW, 1973-   Ann Arbor, MN: Pierian Press. quarterly.
(PER)
    Contains only reviews, review articles and bibliographic essays. Surveys the reference literature for variety of subjects. Pierian also published REFERENCE BOOK REVIEW INDEX (R028.1 AS659R)

AC45   REPRINT BULLETIN BOOK REVIEWS, 1955-   Dobbs Ferry, NY: Glanville Publishers. quarterly. (Title varies).
(PER)

AC46   WILSON LIBRARY BULLETIN, 1914-   New York: H.W. Wilson. monthly. Section: Current Reference Books.

Children and Young Adults

AC47   APPRAISAL: SCIENCE BOOKS FOR YOUNG PEOPLE, 1967-   Boston: Boston University School of Education and the New England Round Table of Children's Librarians. 3 issues a year.
(PER)

AC48   BULLETIN OF THE CENTER FOR CHILDREN'S BOOKS, 1947-   Univ. of Chicago, Graduate Library School. monthly (except August).
(PER)

AC49   CANADIAN CHILDREN'S LITERATURE, 1975-   Guelph, Ont.: Canadian Children's Press. quarterly
(PER)
Annually features a bibliog. of imprints. Long review articles.

AC50   CM: CANADIAN MATERIALS FOR SCHOOLS AND LIBRARIES, 1971-   Ottawa: Canadian Library Association. 6 issues a year.
(PER)
Continues CANADIAN MATERIALS: AN ANNOTATED CRITICAL BIBLIOGRAPHY FOR SCHOOLS AND LIBRARIES. Evaluates 800 or more items annually, all media including games and kits produced in Canada or about Canada for young people from pre-kindergarten to post-secondary levels. Citation includes price, audience level. Subject arrangement.

AC51   THE HORN BOOK MAGAZINE, 1924-   Boston: Horn Book. bimonthly.
(PER)

AC52   THE REVIEWING LIBRARIAN, 1974-   Toronto: Ontario School Library Association. quarterly, annual cum. index.
(PER)
Reviews all media. Emphasizes Ontario curriculum, noting Ont. govt publications useful to school librarians. Other provincial school library associations also provide reviews either in their journals or separately, e.g. BCSLA REVIEWS.

AC53   SCHOOL LIBRARY JOURNAL, 1954-   New York: R.R. Bowker. monthly (September to May).
(PER)
Reviews are cumulated annually in THE SCHOOL LIBRARY JOURNAL BOOKS REVIEW, 1968-   (R028.5 S372).

BOOK REVIEWING PERIODICALS

AC54   BOOKS IN CANADA, 1971-   Toronto: Canadian Review of Books. 10 issues a year.
R011 B724B
Emphasizes trade books with articles on the trade, authors etc. Also on microfiche, 1971-78 (McLaren Micropublishing); BOOKS IN CANADA: AUTHOR, TITLE, REVIEWER INDEX, 1971-76, (McLaren, 1977).

AC55   THE NEW YORK REVIEW OF BOOKS, 1963-   New York: New York Review Inc. 22 issues a year.
(PER)

AC56   THE NEW YORK TIMES BOOK REVIEW, 1896-   New York: New York Times. weekly. CUMULATED INDEX 1896-1968. 5 vols. (1972).
(PER)   AP2 N658; AP2 N658 (Index)

AC57   THE TIMES LITERARY SUPPLEMENT, 1902-   London: Times Newspapers. weekly, (Friday edition). TLS INDEX: 1902-39. 2 vols. (1978); 1940-80. 3 vols. (1982).
AP4 T55; AP4 T553 (Index)

INDEXES TO BOOK REVIEWS OF GENERAL LITERATURE

AC58   BOOK REVIEW DIGEST, 1905-   New York: H.W. Wilson. monthly (except Feb., July); quarterly, annual cumulations.
R016 B72   Sheehy AA411
   BRD AUTHOR/TITLE INDEX 1905-1974 (4 vols, 1976) provides access to almost 300 000 titles covered in the digest. BRD surveys 81 periodicals, in U.S., U.K. and Canada, for excerpted reviews of books receiving a minimum number of reviews to qualify for the digest. Covers about 6000 books a year. Previous restriction to books pub. or dist. in the U.S. extended to include Canada from 1983.

AC59   BOOK REVIEW INDEX, 1965-   Detroit: Gale Research. bimonthly; quarterly, annual cumulations.
R028.1 AB724B   Sheehy AA412
   BOOK REVIEW INDEX: A MASTER CUMULATION 1969-79 (7 vols, 1980) ed. by G.C. Tarbert, places reviews in single alphabetical sequence by author with title index. Files from 1969 available online with 3 updates a year. CHILDREN'S BOOK REVIEW INDEX, 1976-   (PER) is an annual excerpt of juvenalia reviews from BRI.

AC60   CANADIAN PERIODICAL INDEX (See AF12)
        (IND)
   Reviews listed by book's author under form heading: Book Reviews.

AC61   COMBINED RETROSPECTIVE INDEX TO BOOK REVIEWS IN SCHOLARLY JOURNALS, 1886-1974. Comp. by E.I.Farber, and others. 15 vols. Arlington, VA: Carrollton Press, 1979-82.
Z1035 A1C64
   Scope is more narrow than title implies. Offers author, title access to reviews in 458 journals in history, political science, sociology and is a companion to a COMBINED RETROSPECTIVE INDEX TO JOURNALS IN HISTORY, 1838-1974 (11 vols, 1977); ... IN SOCIOLOGY, 1893-1974 (6 vols, 1977); ... IN POLITICAL SCIENCE (8 vols, 1977) and ... IN SCHOLARLY HUMANITIES JOURNALS, 1802-1974 (10 vols, 1982-83).

AC62   TECHNICAL BOOK REVIEW INDEX, 1935-   New York: Special Libraries Association. monthly (Sept. to June)
Z7913 T36 ENGR
   Book reviews of scientific, technical books in ca 2500 journals are indexed, with extracts from the published reviews.

NATIONAL BIBLIOGRAPHY

LIBRARY CATALOGUES

France

AD1   Bibliothèque nationale. CATALOGUE GENERAL DES LIVRES IMPRIMES DE LA BIBLIOTHEQUE NATIONALE: AUTEURS. 231 vols. Paris: Imprimerie nationale, 1897-1981. Reprint/ 1974.
R018.1 B582   Z927 P2   Sheehy AA105
    Vols. 1 to 186 contain all works of an author held at the BN to the date of volume's publication. From vol. 187, only works published before 1960 entered. Detailed, accurate entries; more than 5 million works in the set. Separate purchase is available for ACTES ROYAUX (6 vols); INCUNABLES (1 vol.) and an extracted set, AUTEURS: D'ARISTOTE A ZOLA 1895-1981 (57 vols).

AD2   _____. CATALOGUE GENERAL DES LIVRES IMPRIMES: AUTEURS, COLLECTIVITES -- AUTEURS, ANONYMES, 1960-69. 27 vols. Paris: Imprimerie nationale, 1965-67.
R018.1 B582   Z927 P22   Sheehy AA106
    In two sets, Série 1: Caractère latins, 23 vols; Série 2: Caractère non latins, 4 vols.

Great Britain

AD3   British Library. THE BRITISH LIBRARY GENERAL CATALOGUE OF PRINTED BOOKS TO 1975. 360 vols. London: Clive Bingley/ Munich: K.G. Saur, 1979- In progress.
Z921 B86G4 1975   Sheehy 2AA12
    Anticipated completion 1985. Cumulates in one alphabetical sequence the BM CATALOGUE (AD4) and supplements (1st, 2d, 3d) plus additions and corrections. Includes holdings of printed books, except those in Oriental languages. The sequence for England (8 vols, 1982) is available for separate purchase with independent title and subheading indexes (2 vols, 1982).

AD4   British Library [Museum]. Dept of Printed Books. BRITISH MUSEUM GENERAL CATALOGUE OF PRINTED BOOKS TO 1955. Photolithographic edition. 263 vols. London: Trustees of the British Museum, 1959-66. SUPPLEMENT 1956-65, 50 vols; 1966-70, 26 vols; 1971-75, 13 vols [British Library]; microfiche ed. 402 fiche, 1976-82.
R017 B86   Z921 B86G4   Sheehy AA100
    The original edition and supplements to 1970 are o.p. Several separately published catalogues for specific collections or subjects or languages are available, e.g, BLC OF PRINTED MAPS, CHARTS AND PLANS; CATALOGUE OF BOOKS PRINTED IN THE 15TH CENTURY; CATALOGUE OF PRINTED MUSIC and catalogues for oriental languages, mss collections.

AD5   _____. _____. BRITISH LIBRARY GENERAL CATALOGUE OF PRINTED BOOKS, 1976-1982. 50 vols. Edited by the British Library. Munich: K.G. Saur, 1983.
Z921 B86G4 1983
    This is the fourth supplement to AD3 or AD4; it records British and overseas acquisitions.

AD6   _____. _____. SUBJECT INDEX OF MODERN BOOKS. 1881-   London: Trustees of the British Museum, 1920- quinquennial to 1960; 1961-70, 12 vols (1982); 1971-75 (in preparation).
R017 B86   Z921 B87/toB8722   Sheehy AA101
   These indexes provide a subject guide to British and foreign works. Indexes before 1946, 1956-60 are o.p.; 1946-50, 4 vols (1961; reprint/ 1968); 1951-55, 6 vols (1974); 1956-60, 6 vols (1966); then becomes a set covering a decade.

United States

AD7   Library of Congress. A CATALOG OF BOOKS REPRESENTED BY LIBRARY OF CONGRESS PRINTED CARDS ISSUED TO JULY 31, 1942. 167 vols. Ann Arbor, MI: J.W. Edwards, 1942-46.
R018.1 N275   Z881 A1C3   Sheehy AA99
   The main catalogue of the Library of Congress closed in January 1981; it contains over 24 million cards. No complete reproduction (author, title, subject) of this catalog exists although information in the catalogue is available through various published catalogues and services. From 1984, K.G. Saur is reproducing the complete main catalogue, 1898-1980, on COM fiche with a projected completion date of 1987. On appr. 10 000 fiche, this dictionary catalogue (author, title, subject, series, related entries) gives access to some 7½ million items including the appr. 5½ million items for which machine readable access is not available. (LC cataloguing data is available weekly on magnetic tape through its MARC distribution service, online as LIBCON, and in microfiche.)

AD8   _____. SUPPLEMENT: 1942-47. 42 vols. Ann Arbor, MI: J.W. Edwards, 1948. (Cards issued Aug. 1, 1942 to Dec. 31, 1947).
R018.1 N275 Suppl   Z881 A1C312

AD9   _____. AUTHOR CATALOG: A CUMULATIVE LIST OF WORKS REPRESENTED BY LIBRARY OF CONGRESS PRINTED CARDS, 1948-1952. 24 vols. Ann Arbor, MI: J.W. Edwards, 1953.
R018.1 N275A   Z881 A1U352

AD10   _____. THE NATIONAL UNION CATALOG: 1952-1955 IMPRINTS: An Author List Representing Library of Congress Printed Cards and Titles Reported by Other American Libraries. 30 vols. Ann Arbor, MI: J.W. Edwards, 1961.
R018.1 N277 1952/55   Z881 A1U352   Sheehy AA92-95

         _____. THE NATIONAL UNION CATALOG: A CUMULATIVE AUTHOR LIST, 1953-1957: Representing Library of Congress Printed Cards and Titles Reported by Other American Libraries. 28 vols. Ann Arbor, MI: J.W. Edwards, 1958.
R018.1 N277

         _____. _____, 1958-1962. 54 vols. New York: Rowman and Littlefield, 1963.
R018.1 N277 1958/62

         _____. _____, 1963-1967. 67 vols. Ann Arbor, MI: J.W. Edwards, 1969.
R018.1 N277 1963/67

_____. _____, 1968-1972. 128 vols. Ann Arbor, MI: J.W. Edwards, 1973.
R018.1 N277 1968/72

_____. _____, 1973-1977. 135 vols. Totowa, NJ: Rowman and Littlefield, 1978.
R018.1 N277 1973/77

_____. _____, 1978-1982. Washington: Library of Congress. monthly; quarterly, annual cumulation. 16 vols, 1978: 16 vols, 1979; 18 vols, 1980; 18 vols, 1981; 18 vols, 1982.
R018.1 N277

Annual cumulations of NUC in print format ceased with the 1982 set. From January 1983, LC, using computer software developed by NLC, began publication of NUC in microfiche only, (see AD11).

The **arrangement** of NUC (AD10) is alphabetical by author or title with cross references. The **scope** covers currently issued cataloguing for monographs, pamphlets, maps, atlases and serials regardless of publication date. Roman and non-Roman alphabet materials catalogued by LC and monographic publications reported by 1100 North American libraries.

The NUC REGISTER OF ADDITIONAL LOCATIONS (NUC/RAL) 1968- (microfiche only, 1978-) is a supplement to NUC listing added locations for monographs which appear in the catalogues.

AD11 _____. _____. BOOKS, 1983- Washington: Library of Congress. monthly; cum. index. microfiche publication.
R018.1 N277B (MR)

Cumulations in the twelve monthly issues are complete within one year, and do not carry forward into the next year. NUC BOOKS consolidates information formerly included in the printed paper editions, NATIONAL UNION CATALOG: A CUMULATIVE AUTHOR LIST, SUBJECT CATALOG, MONOGRAPHIC SERIES and CHINESE COOPERATIVE CATALOG.

The **form** of NUC BOOKS is microfiche, 1:48 reduction; the **arrangement** is in two registers (see also CANADIANA, AD77). One register with the full record and one register with four cumulative indexes (name, title, LC subject, LC series). The **scope** is somewhat altered from NUC (AD10); NUC BOOKS contains records for monographs, pamphlets, printed sheets and some microforms in Roman alphabets and with Romanized records for various scripts catalogued by LC or by the 1500 contributing institutions.

AD12 _____. _____. U.S. BOOKS, 1983- Washington: Library of Congress. monthly; cum. index. microfiche publication.

Cumulations in the twelve monthly issues are complete within one year, and do not carry forward into the next year. NUC U.S. BOOKS is the first U.S. national bibliography to be published by LC. It is similar to NUC BOOKS (AD11). But, its scope is restricted to items bearing U.S. imprints in all languages; including monographs, pamphlets, printed sheets as well as some microforms and atlases in book form. LC provides this catalog as being "of particular interest to small and medium-sized libraries."

Other LC/NUC Cumulations or Catalogues

AD13   _____. LIBRARY OF CONGRESS AND NATIONAL UNION CATALOG AUTHOR LISTS, 1942-1962: A Master Cumulation ... Compiled by the editorial staff of the Gale Research Company. 152 vols. Detroit: Gale Research, 1969-71. Also available on microfiche.
R018.1 N276

AD14   _____. THE NATIONAL UNION CATALOG PRE-1956 IMPRINTS: A Cumulative Author List Representing Library of Congress Printed Cards and Titles Reported by Other American Libraries. 754 vols. London: Mansell, 1968-82. SUPPLEMENT 70 vols.
                        Z881 A1U372   Sheehy 2AA9
    Known as 'Mansell', this catalogue has a reputation as the last of the monumental printed catalogues. Some 12 million items (books, pamphlets, periodicals, maps, atlases, music and ephemera) in many languages and for all disciplines. Retrospective strength complements computer-based bibliographic utilities; duplication of published catalogs and major bibliographic networks (RLIN, OCLC, WLN) is estimated at less than 20%. PRE-1956 is the largest, most comprehensive, single record of the world's historic literature.

AD15   _____. THE NATIONAL UNION CATALOG: 1956 THROUGH 1967. 125 vols. New York: Rowman and Littlefield, 1970-72.
                        Z881 A1U352   Sheehy AA97

AD16   _____. LIBRARY OF CONGRESS/ NATIONAL UNION CATALOG, 1953-1980. Andover, MA: Advanced Library Systems. annual sets 1978- ; quinquennial sets 1953-77. microfiche publication.
R018.1 N276

AD17   _____. LIBRARY OF CONGRESS CATALOG - MONOGRAPHIC SERIES, 1974-1982. Washington: Library of Congress. Annual cum. 5 vols, 1974; 4 vols each year, 1975 through 1981; 3 vols, 1982.
R018.1 N277L   Z1033 S5U55
    A quarterly with annual cum. until absorption by NUC BOOKS (AD11), 1983- . All monographs catalogued by LC as parts of a series; popular or scholarly series; non-print (e.g. filmstrips) series excluded.

AD18   _____. LIBRARY OF CONGRESS CATALOG - BOOKS: SUBJECTS: 1950-1954: A Cumulative List of Works Represented by Library of Congress Printed Cards. 20 vols. Ann Arbor, MI: J.W. Edwards, 1955.
R017.U58   Z881 A1U376   Sheehy AA99
    Includes entries for books, pamphlets, serials, maps and atlases arranged by subject. Entries are primarily current publications. (Note continues below.)

      _____. _____: 1955-1959: A Cumulative List of Works Represented by Library of Congress Printed Cards. 20 vols. Ann Arbor, MI: J.W. Edwards, 1955.
R017 U58 1955/59

      _____. _____: 1960-1964. 25 vols. Ann Arbor, MI: J.W. Edwards, 1965.
R017 U58 1960/64

_____. _____: 1965-1969. 42 vols. Ann Arbor, MI: J.W. Edwards, 1970.
R017 U58 1965/69

_____. _____: 1970-1974. 100 vols. Totowa, NJ: Rowman and Littlefield, 1975.
R017 U58 1970/74

_____. SUBJECT CATALOG, 1975-1982. Washington: Library of Congress. monthly; quarterly, annual, quinquennial cum. 1950 through 1974; [1975-1980, to be announced]. Annual cum. 18 vols, 1975; 17 vols, 1976; 15 vols, 1977; 19 vols, 1978; 21 vols, 1979; [1980, no cumulation]; 15 vols, 1981; 17 vols, 1982.
R017 U58   Sheehy 2AA11
   (Note cont.) Incorporated in NUC BOOKS (AD11), 1983- . Catalogues from 1950-82 available on microfiche from Advanced Library Systems, MA.

AD19   _____. CUMULATIVE TITLE INDEX TO THE CLASSIFIED COLLECTIONS OF THE LIBRARY OF CONGRESS. 150 vols. Arlington, VA: Carrollton Press, 1979- In progress.

Canada

See entries for Canada, AD64 to AD66, under "National and Trade Bibliographies."

BIBLIOGRAPHIES

Bibliographies of Bibliographies

AD20   Besterman, Theodore. A WORLD BIBLIOGRAPHY OF BIBLIOGRAPHIES AND OF BIBLIOGRAPHICAL CATALOGUES, CALENDARS, ABSTRACTS, DIGESTS, INDEXES AND THE LIKE. 4th ed. 5 vols. Lausanne: Societas Bibliographica, 1965-66.
R011 AB56W4   Sheehy AA14,1AA5
   Of interest for retrospective searching. Includes only separately published bibliographies (stating number of items in bibliog.) arranged under broad subjects, personal and place names, with author index. Also published as subject volumes, e.g. A WORLD BIBLIOGRAPHY OF ORIENTAL BIBLIOGRAPHIES (1975). A WORLD BIBLIOGRAPHY OF BIBLIOGRAPHIES 1964-74, comp. by A.F. Toomey (2 vols, Rowman and Littlefield, 1977) is a decennial supplement based on Library of Congress holdings.

AD21   BIBLIOGRAPHIC INDEX: A CUMULATIVE BIBLIOGRAPHY OF BIBLIOGRAPHIES, 1937- New York: H.W. Wilson, 1938- 3 a year; annual cumulation.
(IND)
   A subject index to bibliographies of fifty or more citations, published separately or included in books, pamphlets or periodicals; includes Romance or Germanic languages.

AD22   BIBLIOGRAPHICAL SERVICES THROUGHOUT THE WORLD, 1951/52- Paris: UNESCO, 1953- annual; decennial, then quinquennial cumulations. 1950-59 (1961); 1960-64 (1969); 1965-69 (1972); 1970-74 (1977); 1970-74 (1983, French ed.; English ed. in preparation).
R010 B582BA   Z1008 A9523
   Annual reviews are conducted for/by UNESCO. Such surveys, and subsequent cumulations, are prepared by different authors. The last

issue LES SERVICES BIBLIOGRAPHIQUES DANS LE MONDE 1975-1979 with added 1980 supplement, compiled by Marcelle Beaudiquez of the Bibliothèque Nationale in Paris. This edition recounts the bibliographical activity in 121 member states, using data supplied by the National Commissions of UNESCO and other information. The annual survey for 1980, included with this 1983 publication, also appeared in GIP UNISIST NEWSLETTER which reports such activity on an ongoing and annual supplement basis.

AD23   Lochhead, Douglas. BIBLIOGRAPHY OF CANADIAN BIBLIOGRAPHIES/ BIBLIOGRAPHIE DES BIBLIOGRAPHIES CANADIENNES. 2d ed. rev. and enl. Toronto: Published in assocation with the Bibliographical Society of Canada by the Univ. of Toronto Press, 1972. 312 p.
R015.71 AL812B2   Ryder GR1-1

First ed. by Tanghe may still be of some interest; its main approach is by broad subject. AD23 has bibliographies with "some Canadian connection either by subject, compiler, geographical location." Most bibliographies listed were separately issued, but a few formed parts of books or periodical articles. Arranged alphabetically by main entry, with subject, compiler and editor indexes. The Publications Committee of the Bibliographical Society of Canada is assuming responsibility for a 3d edition.

NATIONAL AND TRADE BIBLIOGRAPHIES

Great Britain

AD24   Pollard, A.W., and G.R. Redgrave. A SHORT-TITLE CATALOGUE OF BOOKS PRINTED IN ENGLAND, SCOTLAND & IRELAND AND OF ENGLISH BOOKS PRINTED ABROAD, 1475-1640. London: Bibliographical Society, 1926. 609 p.
R015.42 P77   Sheehy AA647, 1AA123

Catalogue of extant titles, in brief form, arranged by author according to the British Museum rules; no indexing. Gives a limited number of locations, mostly British. Related material includes A CHECKLIST OF AMERICAN COPIES ... of STC locations in North American libraries by W.W. Bishop (2d ed., Greenwood Press, 1968) (015.42 B62); AN INDEX OF PRINTERS, PUBLISHERS AND BOOKSELLERS ... by P.G. Morrison (Univ. of Virginia Library, 1950).

AD25   _____. _____. 2d ed. revised and enlarged. Compiled by W.A. Jackson, F.S. Ferguson, and K.F. Pantzer. London: Bibliographical Society. In progress. (Vol. 2, I-Z, 1976)
R015.42 P77S2

AD26   Wing, Donald. SHORT-TITLE CATALOGUE OF BOOKS PRINTED IN ENGLAND, SCOTLAND, IRELAND, WALES AND BRITISH AMERICA AND OF ENGLISH BOOKS PRINTED IN OTHER COUNTRIES, 1641-1700. 3 vols. New York: Columbia Univ. Press, 1945-51.
R015.42 W769S   Sheehy AA660

Continues Pollard and Redgrave's STC, listing publications of the period following, with locations. An index of printers, publishers and booksellers compiled by Paul G. Morrison. Wing compiled A GALLERY OF GHOSTS (Modern Language Association, 1967) (R015.42 W769A) adding about 5000 entries.

AD27 _____. _____. 2d ed. revised and enlarged. Edited by Timothy J. Crist. 3 vols. New York: Modern Language Association, 1972-82.
R015.42 W769S2   Sheehy AA660
   The revised edition includes new titles, locations and has corrections to the first edition.

AD28 THE EIGHTEENTH CENTURY SHORT TITLE CATALOGUE. Ed. in chief, Robin C. Alston. London: British Library, 1977-1983. microfiche publication; ca 175 microfiche.
                              ZB7576 Ref. Desk (ESTC:BLC)
   FACTOTUM (PER), the ESTC newsletter, outlines the history and progress of the project. Available online from 1982, in Europe on BLAISE, in North America on RLIN, with a base file of microfiche available from 1983. ESTC includes every notable item, appr. 200 000 in no., except some ephemera, newspapers, serials, maps or music, printed in any language in Great Britain and its colonies or printed in English anywhere in the world from 1701-1800. It is an author/title file (with added entries) and with indexes by date and place of publication and by selected genres. THE ESTC: THE BRITISH LIBRARY COLLECTIONS (BL, Reference Division Publications, 1983), ed. by R.C. Alston, assisted by Michael J. Crump, 113 microfiche with printed introd. (22 p.) is separately available and represents the fiche publication to date.
   Based on the ESTC, Research Publications, 1983- is producing a microfilm collection of the titles. Arranged in units of 35 microfilm reels, by broad subject (religion, philosophy, fine arts, science and technology, etc.) within unit, and randomly within subject.

AD29 THE NINETEENTH CENTURY SHORT TITLE CATALOGUE: SERIES 1, PHASE 1, 1801-1815. 5 vols. Newcastle upon Tyne: Avero Publications, 1984- In progress.
   Publication schedule for Phase 1 is Feb. 1984 to June, 1985. The NSTC series is planned to cover 1801 through 1918 in three phases (1801-15; 1816-70; 1871-1918) with multiple volumes in each phrase. Compiled from the in-house and published catalogues of libraries covered; the NSTC lists works published in the U.K., its colonies, the U.S., books published in English or translations from English published anywhere in the world. Each phase will be initiated by a printed union catalogue of relevant books in the BL, the National Library of Scotland, the Bodleian, Cambridge, Trinity College (Dublin) and the university library of Newcastle. Author entry in each vol.; a final vol. has general sections on directories, periodicals, ephemera, with headings for England, Ireland, Scotland, London plus a subject/ imprint index and fiche addenda for titles in alphabetical order.

AD30 Lowndes, William Thomas. THE BIBLIOGRAPHER'S MANUAL OF ENGLISH LITERATURE: Containing an Account of Rare, Curious, and Useful Books, Published in or Relating to Great Britain and Ireland, from the Invention of Printing ... London: H.G. Bohn, 1858-64. Reprint/ 8 vols. Detroit: Gale Research, 1967.
R015.42 L919   Sheehy AA639

AD31 Watt, Robert. BIBLIOTHECA BRITANNICA: OR, A GENERAL INDEX TO BRITISH AND FOREIGN LITERATURE. 4 vols. Edinburgh: Constable, 1824. Reprint/ New York: Burt Franklin, 196?.
R011 W346   Sheehy AA640

AD32   WHITAKER'S CLASSIFIED MONTHLY BOOK LIST, 1983-   London: J. Whitaker & Sons.
Books published in the U.K. during the month plus books forthcoming within ensuing two months. Books are entered under 53 subject headings (derived from Dewey and UNESCO) including divisions within fiction (e.g. historical, war, short stories). Main entry, with full order information, is alphabetical by author, editor, (or first significant word in title) within each classification. Whitaker's, the major U.K. book trade publisher, also prepares trade directories, e.g. WHITAKER'S PUBLISHERS IN THE UNITED KINGDOM AND THEIR ADDRESSES (R070.5042541).

AD33   WHITAKER'S CUMULATIVE BOOK LIST, 1924-   London: J. Whitaker & Sons. annual.
R015.42W57   Sheehy AA668
Until 1984, issued quarterly with annual cumulation. Published in April, CBL is an alphabetical author/ title list with some subject access supplied by an abbreviation or by subject as part of a title. Whitaker series is based on the author-title lists in the weekly trade periodical, THE BOOKSELLER (PER), which lists new publications of the past week, and on the monthly periodical, WHITAKER'S BOOKS OF THE MONTH & BOOKS TO COME (PER) which lists new titles of the past month plus forthcoming titles for two months ahead (see also entry AD32).

AD34   BRITISH BOOKS IN PRINT, 1965-   2 vols. London: J. Whitaker & Sons. annual. microfiche ed. available, 1983-   monthly.
R015.42B862P   Sheehy AA673
Supersedes REFERENCE CATALOGUE OF CURRENT LITERATURE, and earlier titles, 1874-1965. Author/ title/ catchword subject in one alphabetical sequence listing more than 350 000 titles from over 9000 publishers with directory information and ISBN prefixes. Appears in the Fall recording books available at the end of March of the same year. A monthly cumulative edition, 1978-   available in microfiche.
THE ENGLISH CATALOGUE OF BOOKS, 1801-1968, is also useful for retrospective searching (015.42 E58).

AD35   BRITISH PAPERBACKS IN PRINT: A REFERENCE CATALOGUE OF ... PAPERBACKS IN PRINT AND ON SALE IN GREAT BRITAIN, 1960-   London: J. Whitaker & Sons. annual.
R015.41 B862B   Sheehy AA674
Supersedes PAPERBACKS IN PRINT. Author/ title/ subject list.

AD36   BOOKS 1976-82 NOW OP -- ON MICROFICHE. London: J. Whitaker & Sons, 1983.
Lists over 63 000 titles for books recorded in BBIP (AD34) published between 1976 and 1982 and reported o.p. as of December 1982. Entries are alphabetical under author, title, catchword subject with complete bibliographical (order) information.

AD37   THE BRITISH NATIONAL BIBLIOGRAPHY, 1950-   London: British Library, Bibliographic Services Division. weekly; interim, annual cumulation, 1964-   (in 2 vols; microfiche ed. available, 1981-   ).
R015.42B862R   Sheehy AA667
A list of new British books received by the Copyright Receipt Office, BL. From 1977 has CIP entries for forthcoming titles. (UK/BNB MARC tapes and BLAISECOM service available.) Entries in BNB are in full cataloguing form, arranged by modified DDC, with author/ title/ series index in each weekly issue. Last issue for each month contains

cumulated author, title and PRECIS subject index. Final cumulation: Vol. 1, SUBJECT CATALOGUE; vol. 2, INDEXES.
Cum. subject catalogues (1951-54; 1955-59; 1960-64; 1965-67; 1968-70) and cum index catalogues (1950-54; 1955-57; 1960-64; 1965-67; 1968-70; 1971-73) are available.

AD38   BOOKS IN ENGLISH, 1971- London: British Library, Bibliographic Services Division. bimonthly; annual cumulation. microfiche.
Began as a negative ultra-microfiche listing compiled from UK & LC MARC tapes; changed in 1981 to 1:42 reduction compatible with other BL COM products. BOOKS IN ENGLISH 1971-1980 (forthcoming Fall 1984, 600 fiche) combines previous annual ultrafiche listings in a total of 3 million entries for over a million records.

United States

AD39   Sabin, Joseph. A DICTIONARY OF BOOKS RELATING TO AMERICA, FROM ITS DISCOVERY TO THE PRESENT TIME. New York: Sabin, 1868-92; 29 vols. Bibliographical Society of America, 1928-36. Reprint/ 15 vols. Amsterdam: N. Israel, 1961-62.
R015.73 S116   Sheehy AA451
Sometimes known as BIBLIOTHECA AMERICANA. It includes books, pamphlets, periodicals, some government publications printed in North America, works about North America printed elsewhere from 1493-1892.

AD40   Thompson, Lawrence S. THE NEW SABIN: Books Described by Joseph Sabin and his Successors, Now Described Again on the Basis of Examination of Originals, and Fully Indexed by Title, Subject, Joint Authors, and Institutions and Agencies. Troy, NY: Whitston Pub. Co., 1974- In progress. (Vol. 8, 1981; each vol. with separate index). CUMULATIVE INDEX, vols 1-5, 1979.
R917.303 A7473N

AD41   Molnar, John E. AUTHOR TITLE INDEX TO JOSEPH SABIN'S DICTIONARY OF BOOKS RELATING TO AMERICA. 3 vols. Metuchen, NJ: Scarecrow Press, 1974.
R015.73 S116A

AD42   Evans, Charles. AMERICAN BIBLIOGRAPHY: A Chronological Dictionary of all Books, Pamphlets and Periodicals Printed in the United States of America from the Genesis of Printing in 1639 Down to and Including the Year 1820, with Bibliographical and Biographical Notes. Chicago: Privately Printed for the Author, 1903-34. Vols 1-12. Worcester, MA: American Antiquarian Society, 1955-59. Vols 13-14. Reprint/ Gloucester MA: P. Smith, 1967. SUPPLEMENT (Univ. Press of Virginia, 1970).
R015.73 E92   Sheehy AA445, AA446
Evans' intention was to take entries to 1820, but he only reached 1799. In 1955 the bibliography was completed through 1800. Entries are arranged by year, subarranged by author or other main entry; author/ title indexes in each volume. Vol. 14 is a cumulated index to authors and titles. The supplement, by Roger P. Bristol adds 11 000 items.
EARLY AMERICAN IMPRINTS 1639-1800 (Readex Film Products, 1981-82) (AC E274 MICR) is the result of a project, begun in 1955, to film the items in Evans, arranged according to Evans nos. Initially produced in microprint versions, the 1981-82 series, is in microfiche. It corrects Evans which "while still embodying a work of considerable achievement ... lost considerable eminence", and adds 12 000 overlooked works.

AD43   Shipton, Clifford K., and James E. Mooney. NATIONAL INDEX OF AMERICAN
          IMPRINTS THROUGH 1800: THE SHORT-TITLE EVANS. 2 vols. Worcester, MA:
          American Antiquarian Society, 1969.
          R015.73 E92A   Sheehy AA453
               Items from Evans, additions and corrections in one alphabetical
          order with locations.

AD44   Shaw, Ralph R., and Richard H. Shoemaker, comps. AMERICAN BIBLIOGRAPHY:
          A PRELIMINARY CHECKLIST FOR 1801-1819. 19 vols. New York: Scarecrow
          Press, 1958-63.
          R015.73 S535   Sheehy AA453
               This basic impetus for early 19th century materials has associated
          aids in a TITLE INDEX (1965); CORRECTIONS AND AUTHOR INDEX (1966) and
          AMERICAN BIBLIOGRAPHY ... PRINTERS, PUBLISHERS AND BOOKSELLERS INDEX,
          GEOGRAPHICAL INDEX, (1983, 443 p.) compiled by Frances P. Newton.

AD45   Shoemaker, Richard H. A CHECKLIST OF AMERICAN IMPRINTS, 1820- Metuchen,
          NJ: Scarecrow Press, 1964- In progress. TITLE INDEX, 1820-29 (1972).
          AUTHOR INDEX, CORRECTIONS & SOURCES, 1820-1829 (1973).
          R015.73 S559   Sheehy AA454
               Continues AMERICAN BIBLIOGRAPHY (AD44) and will replace various
          individual bibliographies, e.g. Roorbach's BIBLIOTHECA AMERICANA,
          1852-61 (R015.73 R779) and Kelly's THE AMERICAN CATALOGUE OF BOOKS ...
          PUBLISHED IN THE UNITED STATES FROM JAN. 1861 TO JAN. 1871 (R015.73
          K29) in an attempt to bring the sequence into the 1870's. Compilers
          vary; last title available A CHECKLIST OF AMERICAN IMPRINTS, 1834
          (1982), compiled by Carol Rinderknecht and Scott Bruntjen.

AD46   AMERICAN CATALOGUE OF BOOKS, 1876-1910. New York: Publishers Weekly,
          1876-1910. Reprint/ New York: P. Smith, 1941.
          Z1215.A5   Sheehy AA457

AD47   THE UNITED STATES CATALOG: BOOKS IN PRINT. New York: H.W. Wilson, 1899.
          (2d ed., 1902; 3d ed., 1912; 4th ed., 1928).
          R011 C971   Sheehy AA460

AD48   CUMULATIVE BOOK INDEX: A WORLD LIST OF BOOKS IN THE ENGLISH LANGUAGE,
          1898- New York: H.W. Wilson. monthly; cumulates.
          R011 C971A   Sheehy AA461 AA468
               CBI records current publishing (excluding government publications,
          periodicals, maps, music, pamphlets) in one list by author, title,
          subject, series, editor and translator. English language books from
          countries other than the U.S., U.K. and Canada are listed by country
          at the beginning of each monthly issue. Directory of publishers and
          distributors in the back of annual volumes.

AD49   THE PUBLISHERS' TRADE LIST ANNUAL, 1873- 5 vols. New York: R.R.
          Bowker.
          R015.73 P97   Z1215.P972   Sheehy AA472
               PTLA is a compilation of over 200 U.S. and Canadian publishers'
          catalogues in alphabetical order by publisher. Includes overseas
          publishers with U.S. agents plus a special large section of small or
          specialty press firms. THE PUBLISHERS' TRADE LIST ANNUAL 1903-1980
          (R.R. Bowker/ Meckler Pub., 1983) is a microfiche publication giving
          year-by-year coverage; cloth and fiche indexes.

AD50   PUBLISHERS' CATALOGS ANNUAL, 1983/84   Westport, CT: Meckler Pub., 1983-   microform publication. (1983/84 ed. 301 microfiche).
          Published in October; reproduces more than 2000 catalogs, appr. four times the no. in PTLA (AD49). Major U.S., Can. publishers plus specialty, society, museum publishers; their catalogues filed in one alphabetical sequence with printed subject, publisher indexesd to microfiche. PUBLISHERS' TRADE LISTS, 1903-1963 (1979) is a retrospective fiche compilation with print index.
          Related microform publications: SOFTWARE PUBLISHERS' CATALOGS ANNUAL, 1983- with subject, publisher printed index to catalogues on microfiche; MICROPUBLISHERS' T.L.A.; EUROPEAN P.T.L. 1980/81- biennial; BRITISH P.T.L. 1980/81- biennial.

AD51   BOOKS IN PRINT, 1948-   6 vols. New York, R.R. Bowker. annual.
          R015.73 P97A   Sheehy AA474
          "The record of U.S. publishing activity." Well over 600 000 books from appr. 15 000 publishers. Separate author and title volumes contain information for verification and acquisition. Coverage is primarily current and trade books; includes forthcoming titles and any binding (e.g. paperback, spiral) with publishers' directory. Published in the Fall for books available to July; the SUPPLEMENT (AD52) published in the Spring lists books published after July. Available online, 1981- with monthly updates; also microfiche ed. (see AD53). Separate vols available for children's books; elementary/ high school books; bilingual education; business; medical; religious; scientific and technical books; large type books; books published by associations (see AD55) with separate publications for serials in print (AE3, AE4).

AD52   BOOKS IN PRINT SUPPLEMENT, 1973/74-   2 vols. New York: R.R. Bowker. annual (in Spring).
          R015.73 P97A Suppl   Z1215 P974

AD53   BOOKS IN PRINT ON MICROFICHE, 1984-   New York: R.R. Bowker. quarterly.
          (See AD51 for print version). Each quarterly set of fiche, ca 140, is a new, updated ed. with forthcoming titles for six months; changes for in-print titles, entries for o.p., o.s.i. titles; separate author and title indexes contain full information.

AD54   SUBJECT GUIDE TO BOOKS IN PRINT, 1957-   3 vols. New York: R.R. Bowker. annual.
          R015.73 P97AB   Sheehy AA474
          Published simultaneously with AD51, listing non-fiction under LC subject headings with cross-references.

AD55   ASSOCIATIONS' PUBLICATIONS IN PRINT, 1981-   2 vols. New York: R.R. Bowker. annual.
          R015.73 A849A   Z1220 A8
          Pamphlets, journals, bulletins, newsletters, books, and audio-visual materials from some 3500 associations arranged under LC subject headings in vol. 1. Index of titles, associations, acronyms, publishers, distributors in vol. 2.

AD56   BOOKS OUT OF PRINT, 1980/1983-   New York: R.R. Bowker, 1983- annual.
          Lists o.p. and o.s.i. titles.

AD57   FORTHCOMING BOOKS: NOW INCLUDING NEW BOOKS IN PRINT, 1966-   New York: R.R. Bowker. bimonthly.
R015.73 F739B   Sheehy AA475
   Each issue has author and title listings of books to be published for the next five months, as well as books published since the previous summer.

AD58   SUBJECT GUIDE TO FORTHCOMING BOOKS, 1967-   A Bi-monthly Subject Forecast of Books to Come. New York: R.R. Bowker.
R015.73 F739S   Sheehy AA463

AD59   BOOKS IN SERIES, 1876-1949: Original, Reprinted, Inprint, and Out-of-print Books, Published or Distributed in the U.S. in Popular, Scholarly and Professional Series. 3 vols. New York: R.R. Bowker, 1982.
Z1215 B63
(See related title, AD60)

AD60   BOOKS IN SERIES. Original, Reprinted, Inprint, and Out-of-print Books, Published or Distributed in the U.S. in Popular, Scholarly and Professional Series. 3 vols. 3d ed. New York: R.R. Bowker, 1980.
Z472 B652   Sheehy 1AA97
   Title changed from BOOKS IN SERIES IN THE UNITED STATES. New subtitle reflects the inclusion policy of this title which has information on more than 21 000 series (some 200 000 titles) from 1950 to 1980. Foreign titles appear if available from a U.S. distributor.

AD61   WEEKLY RECORD, 1974-   New York: R.R. Bowker.
R015.73 A51B   Sheehy AA477
   Current American book listings. Excludes government publications, subscription books, dissertations, pamphlets, periodicals, most school texts, specialized works. Mass market paperbacks, reprints, annual and yearbooks listed only if item sent to R.R. Bowker for inclusion. Arranged by main entry with LC/CIP cataloguing. (See also AD62).

AD62   AMERICAN BOOK PUBLISHING RECORD, 1960-   New York: R.R. Bowker. monthly; annual, quinquennial cumulations. ABPR CUMULATIVE 1876-1949, 14 vols. (1980); 1950-1977, 15 vols (1979); 1975-1979, 5 vols (1981, microfiche available).
R015.73 A51   Sheehy AA463
   ABPR cumulates WEEKLY RECORD (AD61). A classified listing by DDC with separate sections for adult and juvenile fiction. Author/ title/ subject indexes. There is a microform ABPR CUMULATIVE 1876-1981 (Advanced Library Systems, 1982, 650 fiche).

AD63   PAPERBOUND BOOKS IN PRINT, 1955-   2 vols. New York: R.R. Bowker. annual
R015.73 P214   Sheehy AA471
   Title, author and subject listings.

<u>Canada</u> (See also the bibliographies, AM65-AM99, in Government Information.)

Library Catalogues

AD64   Gagnon, Philéas, ESSAI DE BIBLIOGRAPHIE CANADIENNE: Inventaire d'une bibliothèque comprenant imprimés, manuscrits, estampes, etc., relatifs à l'histoire du Canada et des pays adjacents avec des notes

bibliographiques. Québec; L'Auteur, 1895. AJOUTES A LA COLLECTION (La Patrie, 1913).
FLIS(SC) 015.71 G13　　　　　　　　　　　　　　　　Ryder GR1-27

AD65 Lande, Lawrence. THE LAWRENCE LANDE COLLECTION OF CANADIANA IN THE REDPATH LIBRARY OF McGILL UNIVERSITY. Montreal: Lawrence Lande Foundation for Canadian Historical Research, 1965. 301 p. RARE AND UNUSUAL CANADIANA: FIRST SUPPLEMENT TO THE LANDE BIBLIOGRAPHY. (1971, 779 p.).
FLIS (SC) R015.71 M145　　　　　　　　　　　　　　Ryder GR1-29
   The collection, "a valuable, unique and historically significant accumulation" of mss, maps, pictures, prints, published or unpublished items relating to Canadian political, cultural, economic development, is now in the Public Archives of Canada. From 1981- key documents are being microfilmed and made available, in biennial installments, for purchase (Micromedia). "Time Frames" is a multi-media kit of this material suitable for senior students of Canadian history.

AD66　　LAURENTIANA PARUS AVANT 1821. M. Vlach avec la collaboration de Y. Buono. Montreal: Bibliothèque nationale du Québec, 1976. 120 p.
　　　R015.714 B582C　　　　　　　　　　　　　　　　Ryder GR1-94
   Descriptive bibliography of 770 Quebec imprints and titles about Quebec to 1820, held in BNQ. Title, name, subject, illustrator, maps and plans, place of publication, printer and imprint date indexes. LES IMPRIMES DANS LE BAS-CANADA, vol. 1, 1801-1810, by J. Hare and J-P Wallot, (Presses de l'Univ. Montréal, 1967, 381 p.) covers books, pamphlets, broadsides and nine newspapers for the first decade of the 19th century.

Bibliographies

AD67　　Toronto Public Library. A BIBLIOGRAPHY OF CANADIANA: Being Items in the Public Library ... Relating to the Early History and Development of Canada. Edited by Frances M. Staton and Marie Tremaine. Toronto: Toronto Public Library, 1934. 828 p. SUPPLEMENT by G.M. Boyle and M. Colbeck, 1959. SECOND SUPPLEMENT (forthcoming 1984-86).
　　　R015.71 T68Bi　　　　　　　　　　　　　　　　Ryder GR1-17
   Items are arranged by date of subject matter to form a chronological record of the history and development of Canada to 1867. Included are all Canadian imprints (books, pamphlets, broadsides, government publications) to 1841 held in the library and material on Canadian subjects from 1534 to 1867 wherever printed. The entry describes Toronto Public Library's copy. Author index, with some title and subject entries.
   SECOND SUPPLEMENT, edited by Sandra Alston and assisted by Karen Evans, will describe some 3500 titles, arranged by imprint date, and not appearing in the first two bibliographies. This supplement is planned for 3 vols; 1300 titles covering the period 1801-1849 are included in vol. 2, planned for publication, by the Metropolitan Toronto Library Board, in late 1984. Vol. 1, 1511-1800 and Vol. 3, 1850-67 are proposed for publication in 1985-86. Eight computer generated indexes for names (including illustrators), titles, subjects, illustrations, maps and plans, place of publication, printers and publishers are being created for this supplement to pre-Confederation Canadiana.

AD68   Amtmann, Bernard. CONTRIBUTIONS TO A SHORT-TITLE CATALOGUE OF CANADIANA. Montreal: 4 vols. Bernard Amtmann Inc., 1971-73.
R015.71 AB522   Ryder GR1-6
  About 45 000 entries compiled from listings in the Amtmann catalogues since 1950.

AD69   _____. EARLY CANADIAN CHILDREN'S BOOKS, 1763-1840/ LIVRES DE L'ENFANCE ET LIVRES DE LA JEUNESSE AU CANADA. Montreal: B. Amtmann Inc., 1976. 151 p.
R809.89282 AA528E   Ryder HU6-61A

AD70   _____. A BIBLIOGRAPHY OF CANADIAN CHILDREN'S BOOKS AND BOOKS FOR YOUNG PEOPLE, 1841-1867/ LIVRES DE L'ENFANCE ET LIVRES DE LA JEUNESSE AU CANADA. Montreal: B. Amtmann Inc., 1977. 124 p.
R809.89282 AA528EA   Ryder HU6-61B

AD71   Morgan, Henry J. BIBLIOTHECA CANADENSIS: Or, A Manual of Canadian Literature. Ottawa: G.E. Desbarats, 1867. 411 p. Reprint/ Gale Research, 1968.
015.71 M84   Ryder GR1-13
  Materials published from 1760 to 1867 in Canada, about Canada or written by Canadians in English or French. Includes books, periodical articles, pamphlets with short description and note on the authors.

AD72   Haight, Willet Ricketson. CANADIAN CATALOGUE OF BOOKS, 1791-1895. Toronto: Author, 1896. 130 p. SUPPLEMENT 1896 (1898); 1897 (1904). Reprint/ London: H. Pordes, 1958.
R015.71 H14   Ryder GR1-12
  The main volume is a retrospective list with the annual supplements planned as a tool for the publishing trade. Arranged by author with title and chronological indexes.

AD73   CANADIANA 1867-1900: MONOGRAPHS. Ottawa: National Library of Canada, 1980- irregular; cumulates, cum. indexes. Four SUPPLEMENT(s) 1984- microfiche.
R015.71 C21BA (MR)   Z1365 C35   Ryder GR1-5
  Prepared in the Canadiana Editorial Division, under the direction of Michel Thériault, with a proposed completion date sometime in 1985. (Revisions or additions likely to continue on irregular basis.) The first part of this retrospective bibliography lists some 36 000 publications. Includes books, pamphlets, leaflets, offprints, broadsides, official publications, serials (with some exceptions). Excludes newspapers and maps. A cumulation to Dec. 1983 was issued in early 1984, bringing the number of records to 41 002. A total of four supplements (two each year 1984, 1985 appearing appr. in May and Nov.) to conclude project. A final cumulation and corrected editions thereafter are possible. New cumulations, suppl. revise earlier entries and add new material. Format is a register for full bibliographic record with five indexes (see CANADIANA AD77).

AD74   THE PRINTED RECORD: A BIBLIOGRAPHIC REGISTER WITH INDEXES/ CATALOGUE D'IMPRIMES CANADIENS: REPERTOIRE BIBLIOGRAPHIQUE AVEC INDEX. [Ottawa]: Canadian Institute for Historical Microreproductions, 1982. microfiche publication.
                                Z1365 C36 VUPR
  CANADA'S PRINTED HERITAGE (CIHM, 1983) explains the project behind this bibliography. Briefly, CIHM, est. 1978 by the Canada Council, and

working with NLC, is developing a collection of pre-1900 Canadiana in microform. Titles microfilmed are distributed annually to subscribers; U.S. distribution by University Microfilms International. Includes monographs, pamphlets, playbills, pictures, advertisments, municipal and county publications. Largely excludes manuscripts, journals, news papers, engravings, provincial and territorial govt publications and engravings. Some 5600 records are in this first CIHM fiche catalogue modelled on the CANADIANA (AD77) format of register and indexes. CIHM records available online through UTLAS.

AD75   Tod, Dorothea D., and Audrey Cordingley, comps. A CHECK LIST OF CANADIAN IMPRINTS, 1900-1925. Ottawa: Canadian Bibliographic Centre, 1950. 370 l.
R015.71T63   Ryder GR1-16
   Intended as a preliminary checklist, with entries arranged alphabetically by author. Excludes pamphlets, government publications, serials, and has no index or annotations.

AD76   THE CANADIAN CATALOGUE OF BOOKS: Published in Canada, About Canada, as well as Those Written by Canadians, with Imprint 1921-1949. 2 vols. Toronto: Toronto Public Libraries, 1959. Reissued/ Consolidated English language reprint with cumulated author index. 1 vol., 1967.
R015.71 T68CCr   Ryder GR1-9
   Vol. 1, 1929-1939. Vol. 2, 1940-1949. Prepared annually, it includes books, pamphlets and selected government publications. the cumulation retains the arangement by year and broad class, but does not include French language books with appeared irregularly in the original edition. NOTICES EN LANGUE FRANCAISE DU CANADIAN CATALOGUE OF BOOKS 1921-1949 (Reprint/ Bibliothèque nationale du Québec, 1975) (R015.71 T68CD) consolidates the French listings in one volume.

AD77   CANADIANA: CANADA'S NATIONAL BIBLIOGRAPHY/ :LA BIBLIOGRAPHIE NATIONALE DU CANADA, 1950-   Ottawa: Supply and Services [for NLC], 1953- monthly; annual cumulations. CANADIANA 1973-1980 (1981, on microfiche).
R015.71 C21   Ryder GR1-4; (history in Appendix A)
   To 1979, subtitled Publications of Canadian Interest Received by the National Library. Created at NLC, CANADIANA includes material received under book deposit regulations as well as that material published in other countries but written by Canadians or about Canada. Format varies. Before 1981, arranged by DDC and divided into eight parts with one part separately published (see AG18) and with indexes for author, title, series and English or French subject headings.
   From 1981, the print version adopts the format of the microfiche edition, i.e. is in two parts with five indexes. The first part is a **register** showing in one numerical sequence complete bibliographic entries, including all notes and tracings and locations. The second part is the **indexes.**

   Index A: author/ title
   Index B: chronological
   Index C: publishers/ printers
   Index D: place of publication/ printing
   Index E: subject (proper names only)

   CANADIANA 1973-1980 is the first multi-year cumulation of both text and indexes of the bibliography since 1951. The format is as noted above, and the items include 72 000 monographs, 32 000 theses,

15 000 serial titles, 44 000 govt publications, pamphlets and sound recordings.

AD78   CANADIAN BOOKS IN PRINT: AUTHOR AND TITLE INDEX, 1983/84-   Toronto: Univ. of Toronto Press, 1968-   annual. quarterly supplement, 1980- (microfiche publication).
R015.71 C212A   Z1365.C22   Ryder GR1-2, GR9-1
   CBIP 1983/84 represents a slight title change reflecting a change in recording date. Previous title bore the year during which the information was gathered, i.e. the first edition CBIP, 1967 (pub. 1968). Editions now bear the date of publication, i.e. CBIP 1983/84 (pub. 1984). From 1967-1973, the title was bilingual to demonstrate inclusions, i.e. CBIP/ CATALOGUE DES LIVRES CANADIENS EN LIBRAIRIE.
   CBIP includes imprints, available as of August, from Canadian publishers or subsidiaries; has directory information. CBIP also has the microfiche supplement (issued Apr., July, Oct. and available only to hard-copy subscribers). Coverage is primarily English language; French (see also AD88), or other, language material is included if published by an English language Canadian publisher. General interest items published by the government and available through (trade) book stores are included; maps, sheet music, newspapers, periodicals, catalogues, annuals or materials not of general interest are excluded.

AD79   CANADIAN BOOKS IN PRINT: SUBJECT INDEX, 1983/84-   Toronto: Univ. of Toronto Press, 1974-   annual.
R015.71 C212A   Ryder GR1-2, GR9-2
   The first edition covered the year 1973; for explanation of method of citing date in the title, see AD78. CBIP:SI is in three sections, (1) list of subject headings with cross references and preceded by listing of broad areas (e.g., art, literature, history, technology etc.) of coverage; (2) the subject index, with headings based on LC and Canadian supplementary terms, and (3) the publisher index (a directory). The work includes biographies, placing them under a subject (e.g., Biog. - Science); also includes literary works (and children's literature) entered such materials under form headings (drama, poetry, fiction).

AD80   LA LISTE DES LIVRES DISPONIBLES DE LANGUE FRANÇAISE DES AUTEURS AT DES EDITEURS CANADIENS/ CANADIAN AUTHORS AND PUBLISHERS FRENCH BOOKS IN PRINT, (Sept/Oct.) 1981-   Montreal: Biblio-Informatica. quarterly. (microfiche ed. also available; 10 issues a year)
   Published in two parts: Ptie 1: Classement alphabétique par titres; Ptie 2: Classement alphabétique par auteurs. Published in cooperation with la Société de développement de livre et du périodique (S.D.L.P.) and Edi-Québec. Includes imprints (books or periodicals) from Quebec province and from any French language publishing from other provinces.
   CATALOGUE DE L'EDITION AU CANADA FRANÇAISE, published from 1965 to 1970 (Z1377.F8R4), was superseded by an irregular annual REPERTOIRE DE L'EDITION AU QUEBEC (Edi-Québec) published to cover the years 1972 to 1976.

Regional Bibliographies (From East to West and North)

AD81   ATLANTIC PROVINCES CHECKLIST: A Guide to Current Information in Books, Pamphlets, Government Publications and Magazine Articles Relating to

the Four Atlantic Provinces ... 1957-65. 1972. Halifax: Atlantic Provinces Library Association in cooperation with the Atlantic Provinces Economic Council, 1958-74.
R015.715 AA881   Ryder GR1-47
   Arrangement is by province, then by general subjects with an author index. Publication suspended with the 1965 issue, revived with 1972 issue (1974) and then ceased.

AD82   O'Dea, Agnes C. A BIBLIOGRAPHY OF NEWFOUNDLAND, 1611-1975. Toronto: Univ. of Toronto Press. In preparation.

AD83   "The Prince Edward Island Bibliography." Directed by Andrew Robb. N.p.: N.p. In preparation.
   Work in progress at the Univ. of P.E.I., Charlottetown, anticipated completion date 1985. More than 8000 monographs and serials published to cut-off date of December 1980 and relating to the Island in the areas of humanities and social sciences are expected to appear in this bibliography.

AD84   LA BIBLIOGRAPHIE DE BIBLIOGRAPHIES QUEBECOISES. Compilé sous la direction d'Henri-Bernard Boivin. 2 vols. Montreal: Bibliothèque nationale du Québec, 1979. SUPPLEMENT(s) vol. 1, 1980; vol. 2, 1981.
R015.714   Ryder GR1-91
   Set records nearly 4000 items (books, pamphlets, theses, government publications) arranged by subject with author, title, subject index. Items are Quebec imprints or works about Quebec or by Quebec authors.

AD85   Hamelin, Jean; André Beaulieu, and Gilles Gallichan. BROCHURES QUEBECOISES, 1764-1972. Quebec: Ministère des communications, Direction générale des publications gouvernementales, 1981. 598 p.
R015.714 H213B
   A checklist of some 10 000 brochures alphabetically ordered in a chronology; author, subject indexes. Entries are in their language (English, French) of publication. Items were compiled using libraries "particulièrement riches en brochures" and locations are given for these Quebec libraries, the Library of Parliament and the Public Archives of Canada. Compilers used LC definition of a pamphlet (less than 49 pages; excluding periodicals, offprints, circulars, government publications, calendars and manuals) as a basis for inclusion but exercised their discretion to enlarge the definition and include certain monographs and documents.

AD86   Dionne, Narcisse-Eutrope. INVENTAIRE CHRONOLOGIQUE. 5 parts. Québec: Royal Society of Canada, 1905-12. Reprint/ New York: B. Franklin, 1969; New York: AMS Press, 1974 (5 parts in 1).
R015.71 D59A   Z1392.Q3D52   Ryder GR1-97
   Records French-Canadian publishing from 1764 and books about the Quebec published elsewhere to the publication date. Arranged chronologically by imprint.

AD87   BIBLIOGRAPHIE DU QUEBEC 1821-1967: Notices Etablies par le Bureau de la bibliographie rétrospective, BNQ, 1980- Quebec: Editeur officiel du Québec. In progress.
R015.714 B582B   Ryder GR1-93
   Vols 1 to 6 available, (Tome VI, 1983). Covers all books published in Quebec by non-government sources. Each vol. in two parts; pt 1,

about 1000 notices; pt 2, an index with six approaches (author, editor, printer, name, place, chronology). LES IMPRIMES DANS LE BAS-CANADA, vol. 1, 1801-1810, by J. Hare and J-P Wallot, (Presses de l'Univ. Montréal, 1967, 381 p.) covers books, pamphlets, broadsides and nine newspapers for the first decade of the 19th century.

AD88   BIBLIOGRAPHIE DU QUEBEC: Liste mensuelle des publications québécoises ou relatives au Québec, 1968-   Montreal: Bibliothèque nationale du Québec, 1970-   monthly; annual cum. INDEX 1968-73; 1974-76; annual index, 1976- .
R015.714 AB582B   Ryder GR1-92
   One vol. pub. for 1968; then 3 issues a year, 1969- April, 1972; then monthly. In two parts, books or pamphlets arranged by broad LC class and Quebec government publications. Author/ title and subject index to both parts.

AD89   LA LISTE DES LIVRES DISPONIBLES DE LANGUE FRANÇAISE DES AUTEURS AT DES EDITEURS CANADIENS. (See AD80).

AD90   Bishop, Olga; Barbara Irwin, and Clara G. Miller. BIBLIOGRAPHY OF ONTARIO HISTORY, 1867-1976: CULTURAL, ECONOMIC, POLITICAL, SOCIAL. 2 vols. Toronto: Univ. of Toronto Press, 1980.
R971.3 AB622B   Ryder HA4-109
   A revision and expansion of ONTARIO SINCE 1867: A BIBLIOGRAPHY (Min. of Colleges and Univ., 1973). A comprehensive list of printed items; some 15 000 bibliographies, monographs, pamphlets, articles and theses. Library location; author/ title/ subject index.

AD91   Fleming, Patricia. A BIBLIOGRAPHY OF UPPER CANADIAN IMPRINTS, 1801-1841. Toronto: Univ. of Toronto Press. In preparation, forthcoming.
   Descriptive listing of imprints; includes books, pamphlets, broadsides, serials. Arrangement is chronological, with indexes. Locations for all copies examined. Directory of newspapers; biographical directory of the printing trade.

AD92   Artibise, Alan F. WESTERN CANADA SINCE 1870: A SELECT BIBLIOGRAPHY AND GUIDE. Vancouver: Univ. of British Columbia, 1978. 312 p.
                Z1365 A7   Ryder GR1-56
   Arranged by subject, then by province with author/ name/ series indexes. Includes books, articles, and theses to 1977 in the social sciences and humanities.

AD93   Peel, Bruce B. A BIBLIOGRAPHY OF THE PRAIRIE PROVINCES TO 1953: With Biographical Index. 2d ed. Toronto: Univ. of Toronto Press, 1973. 780 p.
R015.712 P374B2   Ryder GR1-78
   Books and pamphlets relating to the Prairie Provinces arranged chronologically by date of publication with some exceptions, such as accounts of early travels published later but listed by date of event. Subject/ title/ author indexes.

AD94   Arora, Ved P. THE SASKATCHEWAN BIBLIOGRAPHY. Regina: Saskatchewan Provincial Library, 1980. 500 p. SUPPLEMENT (forthcoming, Dec. 1984).
R015.7124 A769S   Ryder GR1-86
   Nearly 6400 entries for all forms of material, including government publications, fiction, theses, published in or about Saskatchewan from 1905 to cut-off date of 1979. Author/ title/ subject

indexes. Suppl., using same arrangement, adds 3000 items new to 1983 or missed in the original edition.

AD95 Strathern, Gloria M. comp. ALBERTA BIBLIOGRAPHY 1954-1979: A PROVINCIAL BIBLIOGRAPHY. Edmonton: Univ. of Alberta, 1982. 745 p.
Z1392 A4A45
Published in honour of Alberta's 75th anniversary. Lists popular, scholarly works (books, theses, pamphlets etc.) excluding serials, scientific, technical materials (some exception for agriculture) and govt publications. (Complements AD93; related to AD94).

AD96 A BIBLIOGRAPHY OF BRITISH COLUMBIA. 3 vols. Victoria: Univ. of Victoria, 1968-75.
R015.711 B582   Ryder GR1-60,62,63
The three vols are separately titled. NAVIGATIONS, TRAFFIQUES & DISCOVERIES, 1774-1848 by Gloria M. Strathern; LAYING THE FOUNDATIONS, 1849-1899 by Barbara Lowther; A BIBLIOGRAPHY OF BRITISH COLUMBIA: YEARS OF GROWTH, 1900-1950 by Margaret H. Edwards and John C. Lort.

AD97 Arctic Institute of North America. ARCTIC BIBLIOGRAPHY. 21 vols. Washington: GPO (vols 1-12)/ Montreal: McGill/ Queen's Univ. Press (vols 13-21), 1947-75.
R919.8 AA675 Z6005 P7A7 ENGR GEOL Ryder GR1-111
Prepared, with support of U.S. and Can. government agencies, at McGill Univ. The first three vols covered all pertinent items in many languages located to time of publication. Subsequent annual vols list then current material and older works not previously listed. Entries, with abstracts, are arranged alphabetically by author with subject/ geographic index. (See related title DG9).

AD98 YUKON BIBLIOGRAPHY: 1897-1963. Ottawa: Dept of Northern Affairs and National Resources, 1964. 151 p. UPDATE 1963-1970; 1971-1973; 1974- Boreal Institute Publications no. 8: 1- Edmonton: Boreal Institute for Northern Studies, Univ. of Alberta. irreg. annual.
Z1392.Y8L6 Ryder GR1-120,-121
(No. 8-11, UPDATE TO 1982 {1983}). YUKON BIBLIOGRAPHY: CUMULATED SUBJECT INDEX TO 1980 (1984) and YUKON BIBLIOGRAPHY: CUMULATED AUTHOR INDEX TO 1980 (1984), both prepared by J. MacDonald and G. Cooke. Brief, indicative abstracts compiled from items received at the Boreal Institute or selected from the Yukon Archives. Includes books, government and consultant reports, theses, periodical articles, and any unpublished items to which the owner provides access. Maps and non-print not included.

WESTERN EUROPE

For additional information or information on other national or trade bibliographies, see listing of various bibliographies in Sheehy AA677-AA945, 1AA92-1AA159, 2AA2-2AA16.

AD99 INTERNATIONAL BOOKS IN PRINT: English Language Titles Published Outside the United States and the United Kingdom, 1980- 4 vols. Munich: K.G. Saur, 1979- biennial. SUBJECT GUIDE 1984- (2 vols). (Dist.: R.R. Bowker).
Z1011 15
Expanded in size from one vol. first edition, to 2 vol. AUTHOR

TITLE LIST plus a SUBJECT GUIDE in 2 vols to create, for the 1984 edition (1983) a 4 vol. complete set. One alphabetical sequence for authors or main entries and titles; Dewey classes plus country arrangement for subject vols. The 1984 ed. covers about 140 000 titles from some 4600 publishers in 95 countries. The majority of entries are from Canada, Australia, New Zealand, India, the Netherlands, Japan, Israel, Federal Republic of Germany and the Scandinavian countries. Includes in-print fiction, non-fiction, books or microforms, pamphlets, trade and non-trade items.

A number of 'in-print' sources (many dist. by R.R. Bowker or Gale) are available for various countries, e.g. LIBROS EN VENTA for Latin American and Spanish books, ITALIAN BOOKS IN PRINT, AUSTRALIAN BOOKS IN PRINT etc.

AD100   BIBLIOGRAPHIE DE LA FRANCE-BIBLIO: JOURNAL OFFICIEL DU LIVRE FRANÇAISE, 1972-   Paris: Cercle de la librarie. weekly; quarterly, annual. (Dist.: Bibliorama, Montreal)
R015.44 AB582B   Z2165 B58   Sheehy 1AA117
Includes publications, maps, music received at the Bibliothèque nationale (France). Weekly classed lists become LES LIVRES DU MOIS, cumulated in TABLES TRIMESTRIELLES DES NOUVEALITIES and annually in LES LIVRES DE L'ANNEE - BIBLIO, 1971- (Z2165 L5). For publication mergers and name changes, see Sheehy AA611 to AA617, 1AA117.

AD101   LES LIVRES DISPONIBLES/ FRENCH BOOKS IN PRINT, 1977-   3 vols. Paris: Cercle de la Librairie. annual. microfiche edition available. (Dist.: in Montreal, Bibliorama for print; Periodica for fiche.)
Z2161.L82
Supersedes CEF-CATALOGUE DE L'EDITION FRANÇAISE (1970-76) and REPERTOIRE DES LIVRES DISPONIBLES (1972-77). Author, title, subject volumes provide worldwide coverage of French language publishing; inclusion is to July 1st of the year previous to publication. Microfiche edition available.

AD102   GESAMTVERZEICHNIS DES DEUTSCHSPRACHIGEN SCHRIFTTUMS, 1700-1910. 160 vols. Munich: K.G. Saur, 1979-83.

AD103   GESAMTVERZEICHNIS DES DEUTSCHSPRACHIGEN SCHRIFTTUMS, 1911-1965. 150 vols. Munich: K.G. Saur, 1976-79. also microfiche ed. 1983, ca 390 fiche.
Z2231 G4
These (GV) bibliographies of German language publications cumulate three national and several quasi-national bibliographies and university library retrospective catalogues including Austria and Switzerland. Does not replace current national bibliographies since subject indexes are not integrated and some sources are only partly represented. GV 1911-1965 however does combine in one alphabet some 3 million main title and subsidiary entries; it includes books, maps, journals and non-trade publications (e.g. theses).

AD104   DEUTSCHE BIBLIOGRAPHIE: WÖCHENTLICHES VERZEICHNIS. Frankfurt a.M.: Buchändler-Vereinigung GmbH, 1947-   weekly; semi-annual, quinquennial cumulations.
Z2221 D4632   Sheehy AA632-AA635.
Includes publications for East and West Germany, as well as German language publications issued elsewhere. In three parts, issued at

different frequencies: trade (weekly), non-trade (monthly) and maps (bimonthly).

AD105   DEUTSCHE NATIONALBIBLIOGRAPHIE UND BIBLIOGRAPHIE DES IM AUSLAND ERSCHIENENEN DEUTSCHSPRACHIGEN SCHRIFTUMS. Leipzig: Verlag für Buch und Bibliothekswesen, 1931-   weekly; quarterly, annual, quinquennial cumulations. (Quinquennial title: DEUTSCHES BUCHER-VERZEICHNIS.)
        Z2221 D453   Sheehy AA627-AA631
Similar in coverage to DB (see AD104). In three parts, issued at different frequencies: trade (weekly), non-trade (semi-monthly), dissertations (monthly).

AD106   VERZEICHNIS LIEFERBARER BUCHER/ GERMAN BOOKS IN PRINT, 1971/72-   4 vols. Frankfurt a.M.: Verlag der Buchändler-Vereinigung, GmbH. annual, semi-annual (Spring) supplements. (Dist.: Gale Research).
R015.43 V574   Z2221 V4   Sheehy AA636
Items in VLB are from publishers in West Germany, Austria, Switzerland with author, title, catchword approaches. To complete the VLB set, there are four additional publications, ISBN INDEX, 1978- ; SUBJECT GUIDE, 1978-   (3 vols, 7th ed. 1984); SPRING SUPPLEMENT and ISBN INDEX TO SPRING SUPPLEMENT.

BUYING GUIDES

Rare, Out-of-Print Materials, Reprints, Remainders

AD107   AMERICAN BOOK-PRICES CURRENT: A Record of Literary Properties Sold at Auction in the United States and in London, England, 1894/95-   New York: American Book-Prices Current. annual; quinquennial cum index.
R018.3 A512   Z1000 A5

AD108   BEST BUYS IN PRINT, 1978-1983. Ann Arbor, MI: Pierian Press. annual.
R015.73 B561B
Was a guide to "quality books" at reduced prices, pre-publication offers, special reprinting, remainders, from original publishers and secondary vendors.

AD109   BOOKS ON DEMAND 1980. 3 vols. Ann Arbor, MI: University Microfilms International, 1979. SUPPLEMENT 1980 (1981).
        Z1033 E3B65
Author, title, subject guide to some 93 000 o.p. books available from UMI as xerographic reprints.

AD110   GUIDE TO REPRINTS, 1967-   Kent, CT: Guide to Reprints. annual.
R011 G946   Z1033 E3G7
The 1981 ed. in 2 vols; some other ed. with supplements.

Microforms (See also "Newspapers" AE22-AE24)

AD111   GUIDE TO MICROFORMS IN PRINT, 1961-   2 vols. Westport, CT: Meckler Pub., 1983-   annual.
R001.5523 AG946   Z1033 M5G8
From 1977, has subtitle: Incorporating International Microforms in Print. Books, journals and other materials excluding theses, in microform offered for sale by publishers worldwide. Author/ title

GUIDE and SUBJECT GUIDE TO MICROFORMS IN PRINT (Meckler Pubs, 1983-) available separately.

AD112 Library of Congress. NATIONAL REGISTER OF MICROFORM MASTERS, 1965- Washington: Library of Congress. annual, 1976-   CUMULATION 1965-75. 6 vols (1976).
R018.1 N277AA   Z1033 M5N3   Sheehy AA123
   A listing of microfilmed library materials and locations at which the master negatives are held. Annual cumulations in 1 or 2 vols. Includes U.S. and non-U.S. books, pamphlets, serials, technical reports, mss and foreign dissertations. Copies of microforms are entered in the NATIONAL UNION CATALOG(s).

ARCHIVES, MANUSCRIPT COLLECTIONS, CATALOGUES

AD113 British Library. Dept of Manuscripts. INDEX OF MANUSCRIPTS IN THE BRITISH LIBRARY. 12 vols. Cambridge: Chadwyck-Healey, 1984-   In progress.
   Expected completion, 1985. Represents all major collections with items, in one alphabetical sequence, indexed by personal or place name giving name of collection for item and its number with the collection. Consolidates, with corrections, the indexes to over 30 separate (unpublished, printed or o.p.) catalogues describing the collections.

AD114 Library of Congress. Manuscripts Section. NATIONAL UNION CATALOG OF MANUSCRIPT COLLECTIONS, 1959-   annual.
            Z6620 U5N3
   Few vols. biennial; some vols with index. Collections reporting are in American repositories. Mss include letters, transcripts of oral recordings and other items of research value.

AD115 DIRECTORY OF CANADIAN RECORDS AND MANUSCRIPT REPOSITORIES. (See AA50)

AD116 Public Archives of Canada. CATALOGUE OF THE PUBLIC ARCHIVES LIBRARY/ CATALOGUE DE LA BIBLIOTHEQUE DES ARCHIVES PUBLIQUES: Public Archives of Canada, Ottawa: A Collection of Published Material with a Chronological List of Pamphlets. 12 vols. Boston: G.K. Hall, 1979.
            Z1365 A35   Ryder GR1-26
   PAC, responsible for govt records of historical value and other historical material, contains primary, secondary material received as mss, federal records (particularly early government material). PAC collects in the traditional areas of Canadiana, e.g. cartography, exploration, travellers' narratives, etc. The catalogue is in three parts (1) an author/ title (2) bilingual subject and (3) chronological catalogue of pamphlets extending from 1495- . The author/ title and pamphlet chronology are reproduced to date of publication in this set.

AD117 _____. GENERAL INVENTORY: MANUSCRIPTS/ INVENTAIRE GENERAL: MANUSCRITS. 8 vols. Ottawa: CGPC, Supply and Services, 1971-1977.
R971 6212G   Ryder GR5-1A
   Supersedes a PRELIMINARY INVENTORY (1952-59). Covers documents in the public "Records Group" (RG) and "Manuscript Group" (MG) in the Manuscript Division of the PAC. A related title, prepared by the PAC, is A UNION LIST OF MANUSCRIPTS IN CANADIAN REPOSITORIES, 2d ed. (2 vols, 1975) (R091 AC212A) with SUPPLEMENT 1976 (1977); 1977-78 (1980); 1979-1980 (1982) (Z6620 C3A4).

PERIODICALS AND NEWSPAPERS

BIBLIOGRAPHIES AND PERIODICAL DIRECTORIES

AE1 PERIODICAL TITLE ABBREVIATIONS: Covering Periodical Title Abbreviations in Science, the Social Sciences, the Humanities, Law, Medicine, Religion, Library Science, Engineering, Education, Business, Art and Many Other Fields. 2 vols. 4th ed. Ed. by Leland G Alkire. Detroit: Gale Research, 1983. Suppl.: NEW PERIODICAL TITLE ABBREVIATIONS.
050 W187 (1969)
   Began as a guide to language, literature, linguistics periodicals and expanded to include other fields. Vol. 1 lists over 50 000 abbreviations commonly used for periodicals together with full title; vol. 2 is the reverse dictionary. Cumulative suppl., in 2 issues, 1984, adds 10 000 titles. Vols contain no publishing histories nor bibliographic information to distinguish similar titles, but are helpful for reading abstracts, indexes, union lists, etc.

AE2 SERIALS FOR LIBRARIES: An Annotated Guide to Continuations, Annuals, Yearbooks, Almanacs, Transactions, Proceedings, Directories, Services. Comp. by J.K. Marshall. New York: Neal-Schuman/ ABC-Clio, 1979. 494 p.
R050 M368S
   Over 2000 titles arranged in broad discipline or subject categories. Descriptive annotations indicate audience level.

AE3 ULRICH'S INTERNATIONAL PERIODICALS DIRECTORY: A Classified Guide to Current Periodicals, Foreign and Domestic, 1932- 2 vols. New York: R.R. Bowker. annual.
R050 AU45   Sheehy AE10
   (23d ed., 1984) An extensive list of current periodicals, arranged by broad subjects with subdivisions. Title, subject indexes. Separate lists for new and ceased periodicals and publications available from international organizations or congresses. Supplemented by ULRICH'S QUARTERLY, 1977- , formerly BOWKER SERIALS BIBLIOGRAPHY SUPPLEMENT, 1972-76. Online, Fall 1981. SOURCES FOR SERIALS: International Serials and Their Titles with Copyright and Copy Availability Information (1977- irreg.) (R050 AU45C) has directory and other infromation derived from the database for ULRICH'S.

AE4 IRREGULAR SERIALS & ANNUALS: AN INTERNATIONAL DIRECTORY, 1968- New York: R.R. Bowker, 1967- biennial
R050 AU45A   Sheehy AE8
   Companion to AE3. Information on serials issued annually, or less frequently, or at irregular intervals. Updated by ULRICH'S QUARTERLY.

AE5 AYER DIRECTORY OF PUBLICATIONS: The Professional's Directory of Print Media Published in the United States; Puerto Rico; Virgin Islands; Canada; Bahamas; Bermuda; the Republics of Panama and the Philippines, 1869- Philadelphia: Ayer Press. annual.
R070AA97   Z6941.17   Sheehy AE24
   A comprehensive list, arranged geographically, with title and classified indexes. Economic description, maps, gazetteer information for places of publication.

AE6   CANADIAN ADVERTISING: RATES AND DATA, THE MEDIA AUTHORITY, 1928-
         Toronto: Maclean Hunter. monthly.
         R659.1 S785C   HF801.C272
            Canadian periodicals and other media that accept advertising are
         listed by type, e.g. business, foreign language publications, radio
         stations, supermarkets.

AE7   CANADIAN SERIALS DIRECTORY/ REPERTOIRE DES PUBLICATIONS SERIEES
         CANADIENNES. Toronto: Univ. of Toronto Press, 1972-77. annual.
         R050 AC212CA   Ryder GR7-5
            Of retrospective interest only.

AE8   NATIONAL DIRECTORY OF NEWSLETTERS AND REPORTING SERVICES: A Reference
         Guide to National and International Information Services, Financial
         Services, Association Bulletins and Training and Educational Services.
         2d ed. 8 parts; 2 series. Detroit: Gale Research, 1978-   In progress.
                        Z6944 N4G3
            Parts 1-4, Series 1 (1978-81) lists more than 3000 publications,
         with subject, publisher, title index. Parts 5-8, Series 2 (1983-)
         adds another 3000 publications; cum. indexes.

AE9   THE STANDARD PERIODICAL DIRECTORY, 1964/65-   New York: Oxbridge
         Communications. biennial.
         R050 AS785   Z6951.S78   Sheehy AE29
            (8th ed. 1983/84, 1613 p.) Comprehensive coverage of American and
         Canadian periodicals from dailies to biennials, excluding general
         newspapers. Includes special newspapers, newsletters, directories,
         consumer or trade or house magazines, government publications.
         Alphabetical by subject with a title index. Oxbridge also publishes
         separate directories for religious, ethnic periodicals, newsletters.

AE10   WILLING'S PRESS GUIDE: A Guide to the Press of the United Kingdom and to
         the Principal Publications of Europe and the U.S.A., 1871-   London:
         T. Skinner Directories. annual.
         R070 AW733   Z6956.E5W5   Sheehy AE68
            Geographical then title alphabetic title listing of periodicals
         and newspapers, with a subject index for U.K. publications only.

AE11   Uhlan, Miriam. GUIDE TO SPECIAL ISSUES AND INDEXES OF PERIODICALS. 3d
         ed. New York: Special Libraries Association, 1983. 289 p.

AE12   CONSER. (CONversion of SERials database published by the National
         Library of Canada) Ottawa: Supply & Services. microfiche. 1975-78 base
         register with 1979, 1980, 1983 (1984) supplements; cumulative index.
            The base register, with supplements contains over 197 000 records.
         Includes all serial records authenicated either by the Library of
         Congress, which distributes CONSER in the U.S., or by NLC. Records are
         in English only, with exception of those for which English and French
         name, subject headings are assigned by NLC. Five indexes (author/
         title/ series; ISSN; LC card no.; CANADIANA serial no.; OCLC control
         no.) refer to base register of bibliographic information arranged
         sequentially. Locations and holdings are not included. Unauthenicated
         records are also available through MARC service. CONSER TABLES (LC,
         1982 ed.) is a looseleaf publication designed as a reference tool for
         use by participants in the CONSER project.

Union Lists

AE13   BRITISH UNION CATALOGUE OF PERIODICALS: A Record of the Periodicals of the World from the Seventeenth Century to the Present Day, in British Libraries. 4 vols. London: Butterworths, 1955-58. SUPPLEMENT TO 1960 (1962). CUMULATION OF NEW PERIODICAL TITLES, 1960-1968.
R050 AB86D2   Z6945.B87   Sheehy AE146
    BUCOP lists holdings in 440 libraries of 140 000 titles in many languages.

AE14   BRITISH UNION CATALOGUE OF PERIODICALS, INCORPORATING WORLD LIST OF SCIENTIFIC PERIODICALS: NEW PERIODICAL TITLES, 1964- London: Butterworths. quarterly; annual cumulation.
R050 AB862A   Sheehy AE147
    Continuing supplement to AE13, recording titles which began or changed since 1960. Scientific serials also published separately.

AE15   UNION LIST OF SERIALS IN THE LIBRARIES OF THE UNITED STATES AND CANADA. 5 vols. 3d ed. New York: H.W. Wilson, 1965.
R050 AU58G3   Sheehy AE133
    Holdings of 956 libraries for 156 000 serials which began publication before 1950.

AE16   NEW SERIAL TITLES: A Union List of Serials Commencing Publication after December 31, 1949, 1950- Washington: Library of Congress. 8 monthly issues; quarterly, annual (except quinquennial years). Cumulation: (quinquennial year cumulation replaces annual) : 1950-60; 1961-65; 1966-69; 1950-70 (sold by R.R. Bowker, microfilm or xerographic copy); 1971-75; 1976-78; 1976-79; 1980 and annually thereafter.
R050 AN532   Sheehy AE134-AA136
    Continues AE15, entries in an alphabetical arrangement by title with locations, are holdings reported by more than 800 libraries in the U.S. and Canada. Serials not in the Roman alphabet are included in romanized form. Until the end of 1980, newspapers, looseleaf publications, books in parts, municipal government serial documents, publishers' series, and audio-visual formats were excluded. NEW SERIAL TITLES, 1950-1970: SUBJECT GUIDE (R.R. Bowker, 1975) arranges entries by DDC, subdivided geographically; no holdings. Beginning with the 1981 cumulation, NST created by an automated system using MARC records through CONSER (AE12) without restricting type of serial entered.

AE17   HOLDINGS OF CANADIAN SERIALS IN THE NATIONAL LIBRARY/ INVENTAIRE DES PUBLICATIONS CANADIENNES EN SERIE DANS LA BIBLIOTHEQUE NATIONALE. Ottawa: National Library of Canada, 1974. 278 p.
R052 C212H   Ryder GR7-4
    Comp. in the Collections Development Branch, NLC. Lists holdings as of March 1974; both current and ceased titles. Also available is a bilingual CHECKLIST OF CANADIAN ETHNIC SERIALS (1981, 381 p.) (050 AB675C), comp. by the Newspaper Division, NLC, and containing some 3000 newspapers, periodicals, almanacs, directories, church bulletins, proceedings etc.

AE 18   UNION LIST OF SCIENTIFIC SERIALS IN CANADIAN LIBRARIES. 3 vols. 10th ed. Ottawa: CISTI, 1984.
    Lists holdings of over 69 000 titles in 294 libraries. The French 10th ed., CATALOGUE COLLECTIF DES PUBLICATIONS SCIENTIFIQUES DANS LES BIBLIOTHEQUES CANADIENNES, 3 vols, was published in 1983.

AE 19   UNION LIST OF SERIALS IN THE SOCIAL SCIENCES AND HUMANITIES HELD BY CANADIAN LIBRARIES. 2d ed. Ottawa: Supply & Services, 1981. microfiche. semi-annual updates.
R050 AU58G
    Compiled at NLC, and available online (NLC/DOBIS). This list created from previously published NLC lists, e.g. PERIODICALS IN THE SOCIAL SCIENCES AND HUMANITIES CURRENTLY RECEIVED BY CANADIAN LIBRARIES (2 vols, 1968); ULS INDEXED BY SOCIAL SCIENCES CITATIONS INDEX; ULS IN EDUCATION AND SOCIOLOGY; ULS INDEXED BY P.A.I.S. BULLETIN; ULS IN FINE ARTS IN CANADIAN LIBRARIES.

AE 20   CUSS LIST. (Cooperative Union Serials System List). 10th ed. Toronto: Ontario Council of University Libraries, 1983. 67 microfiche.
    An unedited COM list created from the merged serial files of 15 Ontario university libraries. Over 124 000 main entries with cross references arranged alphabetically.

AE 21   GUIDE TO PERIODICALS AND NEWSPAPERS IN THE PUBLIC LIBRARIES OF METROPOLITAN TORONTO. 2 vols. 9th ed. Toronto; Metropolitan Toronto Library Board, 1979.
R050 AM59A
    Lists ca 4650 retrospective, 7000 current titles; by main entry.

Newspapers

AE 22   Library of Congress. NEWSPAPERS IN MICROFORM, 1948-1983. 3 vols. Washington: Library of Congress, Catalog Publication Division, 1983.
R071.3 AU584M, 84N (2 vols, 1973)   Z6945   Sheehy AF26
    Continues NEWSPAPERS ON MICROFILM. Several cumulated editions published; format and no. of vols offers a purchase choice between cumulated U.S. and Foreign (full ed., 3 vols); U.S. only (2 vols); foreign only (1 vol.). (See AE23).

AE 23   _____. NEWSPAPERS IN MICROFORM, 1978- Washington: Library of Congress, 1979- annual.
    Supersedes NEWSPAPERS ON MICROFILM. Compiled by the Catalog Publication Division of LC, these catalogues cover newspapers in microform, both masters and service copies, housed in U.S., Canadian and other foreign libraries as well as held by domestic and foreign commercial micro-publishers. Entries are arranged geographically by state and city, with alphabetical title list providing the geographical key. (See also AE22).

AE 24   CANADIAN NEWSPAPERS ON MICROFILM/ CATALOGUE DE JOURNAUX CANADIENS SUR MICROFILM. Ottawa: Canadian Library Association, 1959-1973. looseleaf; irregular supplements.
R070 AC212   Z6954.C2C25   Ryder GR6-4
    Part I lists newspapers microfilmed by CLA. The newspapers, with note on their history, are entered by province with a title index.

Part II, revised in 1969, includes both CLA and non-CLA microfilms -- over 1500 Canadian newspapers entered with briefer notes. This part also arranged by province, then place of publication, with title index. Both parts list holdings.

AE25 UNION LIST OF CANADIAN NEWSPAPERS HELD BY CANADIAN LIBRARIES. Ottawa: Newspaper Section, National Library of Canada, 1977. 483 p.
R071.1 AC212U   Ryder GR6-15
    A location source for original and microform copies of Canadian newspapers held in over 125 libraries. Includes titles publilshed at any time and in any language. Arranged by province, city then title, with title index. Also, A UNION LIST OF NON-CANADIAN NEWSPAPERS HELD BY CANADIAN LIBRARIES. (NLC, 1978) (R071 AR953).

INDEXES TO PERIODICALS AND OTHER MATERIALS

DIRECTORY AND BIBLIOGRAPHY

AF1　　ABSTRACTING AND INDEXING SERVICES DIRECTORY. Ed. by John Schmittroth. 3 nos. Detroit: Gale Research, 1982-　In progress.
　　　　"A descriptive guide to abstracting journals, indexes, serial bibliographies, catalogs, title announcement bulletins and similar information access or alerting publications in science, technology, medicine, business, law, social sciences, education and humanities" Each of the 3 issues covers ca 500 services with cum. title index.

AF2　　INDEXES, ABSTRACTS, DIGESTS. Ed. by Annie M. Brewer. Detroit: Gale Research, 1982. 801 p.
　　　　Reproduced LC cards, in a classified arrangement, providing a bibliography of some 5000 publications that index, abstract or otherwise identify contents of books, periodicals, other documents.

GENERAL INDEXES TO PERIODICALS

AF3　　POOLE'S INDEX TO PERIODICAL LITERATURE, 1802-1906. Vol.1. Boston: Osgood, 1882; Vols 2-6. Boston: Houghton, 1888-1908.
　　　　R050 AP822　　　　　　　　　　Sheehy AE164-AE166
　　　　A catchword subject index to 479 British and American journals. Entries lack inclusive paging and year of cited volume. DATE AND VOLUME KEY (1957) (R050 AP822A) and CUMULATIVE AUTHOR INDEX FOR POOLE'S INDEX (Pierian, 1971) (R050 AP822C) improve access.

AF4　　NINETEENTH CENTURY READERS' GUIDE TO PERIODICAL LITERATURE, 1890-1899, WITH SUPPLEMENTARY INDEXING 1900-1922. 2 vols. New York: H.W. Wilson, 1944.
　　　　R050 AN71　　　　　　　　　　Sheehy AE168
　　　　Author, subject index to 51 periodicals, 7 not in POOLE'S. Supplementary indexing adds missing years in other Wilson indexes.

AF5　　CUMULATED MAGAZINE SUBJECT INDEX, 1907-1949: A Cumulation of the F.W. Faxon Company's Annual Magazine Subject Index. 2 vols. Boston: G.K. Hall, 1964.
　　　　R050 AC971　　　　　　　　　　Sheehy AE180, AE181
　　　　The annual volumes are here consolidated in one alphabetical sequence indexing 175 American, Canadian, British journals not included in the Wilson indexes; subjects emphasize state and local history, art, architecture, geography, education and political science.

AF6　　READERS' GUIDE TO PERIODICAL LITERATURE, 1900-　New York, H.W. Wilson, 1905-　semi-monthly (Sept. to June), monthly (July, Aug.); quarterly and annual cumulation.
　　　　(PER)　　　　　　AI3.R48　　　　　　Sheehy AE169
　　　　Author, subject index to about 160 general U.S. periodicals in all fields. Subheadings divide subjects; there are some form headings, e.g. book reviews, and stories in the magazines indexed are entered under title. AN ABRIDGED READERS' GUIDE indexes about 60 periodicals for smaller public, school libraries. RGPL is the most general of several similiar 'Wilson indexes' covering various disciplines or forms. Sixteen of the indexes will be available online on 'Wilsonline'

late in 1984. The online service, updated twice weekly, will cover a total of 3000 journals and an average of 60 000 monographs yearly. Until the appearance of Wilson indexes online, THE MAGAZINE INDEX, 1976- (Information Access) indexing about 400 popular magazines, had provided the only online and similar print competition for RGPL.

AF7 GENERAL SCIENCE INDEX, 1978- New York: H.W. Wilson. 10 issues a year, cumulates.
  Subject index to 89 English language layman's periodicals in the pure and applied sciences, health, biology, medicine, psychology, environment and related topics.

AF8 HUMANITIES INDEX, 1974- New York: H.W. Wilson. quarterly; annual cumulations.
 (IND)   Sheehy AE172
  Author, subject index to periodicals in archaeology and classical studies, area studies, folklore, history, language and literature, literary and political criticism, performing arts, philosophy, religion, theology and related topics. Separate listing of citations to book reviews.
  AF8 and AF9 supersede the SOCIAL SCIENCES & HUMANITIES INDEX.

AF9 SOCIAL SCIENCES INDEX, 1974- New York: H.W. Wilson. quarterly; annual cumulations.
 (IND)   Sheehy AE172
  Author, subject index to 263 periodicals in anthropology, area studies, economics, environmental science, geography, law and criminology, medical sciences, political sciences, psychology, public administration, sociology and related topics. Separate listing of citations to book reviews.

AF10 PUBLIC AFFAIRS INFORMATION SERVICE BULLETIN, 1915- New York: PAIS. weekly; annual cumulation
 (PER)   Z7163.P9   Sheehy CA34, CA35
  Subject index to over 1000 periodicals, books, government publications, pamphlets and reports, selected for material in public administration, international affairs, social and economic conditions. CUMULATIVE SUBJECT INDEX 1915-74 (Carrollton Press, 1976). AUTHOR INDEX 1965-69 (Pierian Press, 1973). Available online. PAIS FOREIGN LANGUAGE INDEX, 1968/71- is a quarterly subject index to French, German, Spanish periodicals on the same topics.

AF11 BRITISH HUMANITIES INDEX, 1962- London: Library Association. quarterly; annual cumulation.
 (PER)   AI13.B7   Sheehy AE175
  Subject index to about 400 British and Commonwealth journals. Author index in the annual volume.

AF12 CANADIAN PERIODICAL INDEX/ INDEX DE PERIODIQUES CANADIENS 1928-32; 1938- Ottawa: Canadian Library Association. monthly, annual; CUMULATION 1938-47 (microfiche); 1948-59; 1960- annually.
 (PER)   Ryder GR7-13
  Title varies. Indexes by author and subject 137 periodicals in all subject areas (business, economics, fine arts, librarianship, literature, popular culture and social sciences). Indexes by form for book reviews, poems, short stories. Has French-language, bilingual journals in the primarily English-language coverage.

AF13 PERIODEX: Index analytique de périodiques de langue française, 1972-
Montreal: Centrale des bibliothèques. 10 issues a year; annual cumulation.
(PER)   AI7.P4   Ryder
Supersedes INDEX ANALYTIQUE 1966-72. Indexes French Canadian and other French language periodicals.

AF14 RADAR: Répertoire analytique d'articles de revues du Québec, 1972-
Montreal: Bibliothèque nationale du Québec. 6 issues a year; annual cumulation.
(PER)   Ryder

AF15 FRENCH PERIODICAL INDEX (REPERTORIEX), 1973/74-   Westport, CT: F.W. Faxon. annual.
                          AI7.F7   Sheehy 1AE54
Covers ten major French language journals (L'Actualité, Le nouvel Observateur, Paris-Match, Realités).

AF16 INTERNATIONALE BIBLIOGRAPHIE DER ZEITSCHRIFTENLITERATUR AUS ALLEN GEBIETEN DES WISSENS, 1963/64-   Osnabruck: Dietrich, 1965- semi-annual, (in 2 parts).
                          AI9.I6   Sheehy AE163
English title: INTERNATIONAL BIBLIOGRAPHY OF PERIODICAL LITERATURE COVERING ALL FIELDS OF KNOWLEDGE. Known as IBZ or DIETRICH. Subject index to about 8000 periodicals of many countries. Cross references in English and French to German subject headings. Author index.

CITATION INDEXES

AF17 SCIENCE CITATION INDEX, 1961-   Philadelphia: Institute for Scientific Information. monthly; annual cumulation.
                  Z7401.S365 PASR   Sheehy EA87,1FE14
SCI is the oldest of the three best known and most extensive citation indexes. These indexes offer a multi-disciplinary approach, listing every substantive item in each indexed journal plus indexing many selected monographs. Citation volumes offer author/ corporate name reference to full bibliographical data in source (main) volumes. Permuterm subject volumes offer keyword access. Available online.

AF18 SOCIAL SCIENCE CITATION INDEX, 1973-
                  Z7161.S65   Sheehy CA37,1FC14

AF19 ARTS & HUMANITIES CITATION INDEX, 1977-
                  AI3.A6   Sheehy 1AE41

INDEXES TO NEWSPAPERS

AF20 CANADIAN NEWS INDEX, 1979-   Toronto: Micromedia. monthly
(IND)   AI3.C26   Ryder
Supersedes CANADIAN NEWSPAPER INDEX, 1977-78. Subject or corporate name, biographical index to events in 7 major dailies and several national or regional news and public affairs magazines. Major cities,

with the exception of Ottawa, have newspapers represented. OTTAWA JOURNAL publishes its own index. CNI available online.

AF21 CANADIAN PRESS NEWSFILES, 1984-   Toronto: Micromedia. monthly.
   A clipping file service on microfiche.

AF22 THE NATIONAL NEWSPAPER INDEX, 1979-   New York: Magazine Index,
   Subject index to major American newspapers (WALL STREET JOURNAL, CHRISTIAN SCIENCE MONITOR, WASHINGTON POST). Available online.

AF23 INDEX DE L'ACTUALITE: Vue à travers la presse écrite, 1972- Montreal: Microfor. monthly; annual cumulation.
                    AI21.D42
   Continues INDEX DU JOURNAL 'LE DEVOIR' and adds selective indexing to LA PRESSE (Montreal) and LE SOLEIL. Microfor also issues FRANCE ACTUALITE, 1978- , for major French newspapers.

AF24 NEW YORK TIMES INDEX, 1851-   New York: New York Times, 1913- semi-monthly; quarterly and annual cumulations.
                    AI21.N44   Sheehy AF76,1AF23
   Summarizes in chronological order, under subject headings and names, important items from the late city edition. N.Y. TIMES also available through AF22.

AF25 THE TIMES INDEX, 1973-   Reading, Eng.: Newspaper Archive Developments. monthly; annual cumulation 1977-
                    AI21.T462   Sheehy AF76,1AF23
   Indexes issued by various publishers from 1790 to the present.

RESEARCH OR DISSERTATIONS ABSTRACTS AND INDEXES

AF26 AMERICAN DOCTORAL DISSERTATIONS, 1955/56-   Compiled for the Association of Research Libraries. Ann Arbor, MI: University Microfilms, 1957- annual.
   378.73 AD637A   Z5053.D52   Sheehy AH12,AH13
   Continues DOCTORAL DISSERTATIONS ACCEPTED BY AMERICAN UNIVERSITIES, 1934-55.

AF27 Aslib. INDEX TO THESES ACCEPTED FOR HIGHER DEGREES IN THE UNIVERSITIES OF GREAT BRITAIN AND IRELAND, 1950/51-   London: ASLIB, 1953- annual.
   R378.42 I38   Z5055.G69A8   Sheehy AH44
   Arranged by subject with author index. RETROSPECTIVE INDEX TO TO THESES OF GREAT BRITAIN AND IRELAND, 1716-1950 (ABC-Clio, 1975-76).

AF28 British Library. RESEARCH IN BRITISH UNIVERSITIES, POLYTECHNICS AND COLLEGES, 1983-   3 vols. Boston Spa, West Yorkshire: British Library Lending Division. annual.
   Supersedes SCIENTIFIC RESEARCH IN BRITISH UNIVERSITIES AND COLLEGES. RBUPC is a national register of current research, vol. 1 "Physical Sciences"; vol. 2 "Biological Sciences": vol. 3 "Social Sciences" including research from govt depts and other institutions. Name, department or institution, keyword subject indexes.

AF 29　　DISSERTATIONS ABSTRACTS INTERNATIONAL: Abstracts of Dissertations Available on Microfilm or on Xerographic Reproductions, 1938-　Ann Arbor, MI: University Microfilms. monthly.
Z5053.D5; Z5055.U49C6

The major North American source for access to doctoral theses from about 400 institutions around the world. Format varies. From July 1967- Section A: "Humanities and Social Sciences" (IND); Section B: "Physical Sciences and Engineering"; (with from May, 1977) Section C: "European Abstracts." Keyword and author indexes to all parts. Available online. COMPREHENSIVE DISSERTIONS INDEX 1861-72, 32 vols; 1973-77, 19 vols; then annual supplement. Also available are MASTERS ABSTRACTS, 1962- and RESEARCH ABSTRACTS, 1976- for published research other than that done for the academic degree. Separate paperbound volumes are available for grouped by subject or regional areas, e.g. NORTH AMERICAN INDIANS, ENERGY.

AF 30　　National Library of Canada. CANADIAN THESES/ THESES CANADIENNES, 1952- Ottawa: Ministry of Supply and Services, 1983-　irregular annual; triennial cumulation in 2 vols. (microfiche ed. available from NLC).
R378.71 AC21Ta　　　　Z5055.G69　　　　　Ryder

First appeared in 1953 with some theses dating to 1947. Currently, nearly 70% of all Canadian theses are processed at NLC. Doctoral and master's theses done at some 30 Canadian universities are produced. All theses filmed by NLC appear in CANADIANA (AD77; NLC adds microform copies of each thesis filmed to its collection for reference or lending purposes and sells microform editions of theses. CANADIAN THESES records, under broad subject headings then by university, all theses accepted by participating Canadian universities in a given academic year with author index. CANADIAN THESES 1976/77-1979/80, 2 vols (1983) is last cumulation with combined author index to all four years in Vol. 2. CANADIAN THESES ON MICROFICHE: CATALOGUE (NLC) is free and lists theses catalogued since 1981 numerically by order no. in one volume with supplements at irregular intervals.

GENERAL INDEXES TO ANTHOLOGIES, BOOKS, OTHER MATERIALS

AF 31　　CANADIAN ESSAY AND LITERATURE INDEX, 1973-75. 3 vols. Toronto: University of Toronto Press, 1975-77.
R819 C212E

Of retrospective interest. An author, title, subject index to form groupings of literature (essays, book reviews, poems, plays and short stories) in English language Canadian magazines and anthologies, not indexed elsewhere. Poetry is also indexed by first line. Fifty collections of essays, short stories and plays published in 1971-72 are indexed by subject, author in CANADIAN ESSAY AND COLLECTIONS INDEX, 1971/72 (CLA, 1976) (R819 C212D)

AF 32　　ESSAY AND GENERAL LITERATURE INDEX, 1900-　New York: H.W. Wilson, 1934-　semi-annual; annual, quinquennial cumulation.
(PER)　　　　　　　　AI3.E752; AI3.E753　　　Sheehy BD189

EGLI:WORKS INDEXED 1900-1969 (1972, 437 p.) is a cum. index to this index. AF32 analyzes recently published collections of essays and other composite works with reference value. Author/ subject/ distinctive title index in one alphabet.

AF 33   VERTICAL FILE INDEX: A Subject and Title Index to Selected Pamphlet Materials, 1932- New York: H.W. Wilson, 1935- monthly except August.
(PER)   Z1231.P2V48   Sheehy AA479

INDEXES TO SPEECHES, QUOTATIONS

AF 34   Bartlett, John. FAMILIAR QUOTATIONS. A Collection of Passages, Phrases and Proverbs Traced to their Sources in Ancient and Modern Literature. 14th ed. rev. and enl. Edited by Emily Morison Beck. Boston: Little, Brown, 1968. 1750 p.
R808.8 B28F14   Sheehy BD98

    A standard collection of quotations familiar to Americans, arranged chronologically by author, with separate sequences for Bible and anonymous quotations. Extensive index of key words has an average of four to five entries for each quotation.

AF 35   THE OXFORD DICTIONARY OF QUOTATIONS. 3d ed. London: Oxford University Press, 1979. 928 p.
R808.8 O98   Sheehy BD105

    Quotations familiar fo British users, arranged by author, with a detailed keyword index, at least two references for each quotation. THE CONCISE OXFORD DICTIONARY OF QUOTATIONS (1964) is a selection from the second edition.

AF 36   Partnow, Elaine. THE QUOTABLE WOMAN, 1800-1975. Los Angeles: Corwin, 1977. 539 p.
PN6081.5 Q6   Sheehy BD22

    Arranged by contributor's birthdate, 8000 quotes, mostly British or American. Author, subject indexes.

AF 37   Roberts, Kate Louise. HOYT'S NEW CYCLOPEDIA OF PRACTICAL QUOTATIONS. 2d ed. New York: Funk & Wagnalls, 1966. 1343 p.
R808.8 H86H2   Sheehy BD102

    Arranged by subject with an extensive keyword index.

AF 38   Stevenson, Burton. THE MACMILLAN BOOK OF PROVERBS, MAXIMS AND FAMOUS PHRASES. New York: Macmillan, 1968. 2957 p.
R808.8 S847M   Sheehy BD154

    Formerly STEVENSON'S HOME BOOK OF PROVERBS, MAXIMS AND FAMILIAR PHRASES (1948). Traces sayings from their original source to current English and American use. Foreign entries are given in English translation followed by original language. Subject arrangement with keyword index.

AF 39   Sutton, Roberta Briggs. SPEECH INDEX: An Index to 259 Collections of World Famous Orations and Speeches for Various Occasions. 4th ed. New York: Scarecrow Press, 1966. 947 p. SUPPLEMENT 1966-70 (1972); 1971-75 (1977).
R808.85 S96S4   Sheehy BD250

AF40   Columbo, John Robert. COLUMBO'S CANADIAN QUOTATIONS. Edmonton: Hurtig, 1974. 735 p.
R808.8 C718C   Ryder HU6-97
   Includes 6000 "familiar quotations and ... memorable passages that should be better known" with keyword and subject index. Published also in an abridged edition, COLOMBO'S CONCISE CANADIAN QUOTATIONS (1976).

AF41   _____. COLOMBO'S CANADIAN REFERENCES. Toronto: Oxford Univ. Press, 1976. 576 p.
R971.003 C718C   Ryder GR2-2
   Introductory, not comprehensive, source on Canadian subjects.

AF42   Hamilton, R. M., and D. Shields. THE DICTIONARY OF CANADIAN QUOTATIONS AND PHRASES. Rev. enl. Toronto: McClelland and Stewart, 1979. 1063 p.
R808.8 H21   Ryder HU6-99
   More than 10 000 quotes or phrases about Canada or Canadians, from predominantly but not exclusively Canadian sources. Subject aranged.

INDEX TO TRANSLATIONS

AF43   INDEX TRANSLATIONUM: Répertoire international des traductions/ International Bibliography of Translations, 1948- Paris: UNESCO. irregular annual.
R011 AI38   Z6514 T7I   Sheehy AA129, AA130
   (Vol. 38, 1978 {1983}). Worldwide; vol. 38 typically has representation from 64 countries; several thousand items. The CUMULATIVE INDEX TO ENGLISH TRANSLATIONS 1948-68 (1973) lists works from 61 countries; arranged by country then by UDC. JOURNALS IN TRANSLATION: A GUIDE (Delft, Netherlands: International Translation Centre, 1978) lists journals which are fully or selectively translated or have translations from multiple sources (Z694 T7B74 BMER).

AUDIO-VISUAL MATERIALS

GUIDES

AG1   AUDIOVISUAL MARKET PLACE: A MULTIMEDIA GUIDE, 1969-   New York: R.R. Bowker. biennial.
R371.33 A912A
     Lists "media producers & distributors, equipment manufacturers, services and organizations, conventions, film festivals, reference sources & review media."

AG2   EDUCATIONAL MEDIA YEARBOOK, 1973-   Ed. by James W. Brown. Littleton, CO: Libraries Unlimited, 1980-   annual
371.33 E24E
     First five editions (1973-79) published by Bowker. Reviews important developments, lists on new publications, has directory.

AG3   Rosenberg, Kenyon C., and Paul T. Feinstein. DICTIONARY OF LIBRARY AND EDUCATIONAL TECHNOLOGY. 2d ed. rev. and expanded. Littleton, CO: Libraries Unlimited, 1983. 197 p.
R371.33 R813M2
     First ed. titled MEDIA EQUIPMENT: A GUIDE AND DICTIONARY (1976). New ed. adds computer hardware and software to consideration of all types of audiovisual hardware including reprographics, micrographics. Text in 3 sections: criteria for equipment selection with evaluation checklists; dictionary of terms, orgs and suppliers; bibliography.

AG4   Sive, Mary Robinson. MEDIA SELECTION HANDBOOK. Littleton, CO: Libraries Unlimited, 1983. 171 p.
R371.33 AS624EA (1978)
     Earlier issues titled SELECTING INSTRUCTIONAL MEDIA (1978); EDUCATOR'S GUIDE TO MEDIA LIST (1975); retains emphasis on building collections responsive to curriculum and school library needs.

BIBLIOGRAPHIES AND INDEXES (See also Music, BF, and Performing Arts, BG)

General

AG5   British Library. BRITISH CATALOGUE OF AUDIOVISUAL MATERIALS. London: Bibliographic Services Division, British Library, 1979. 487 p. SUPPLEMENT 1980; 1983.
LB1043 Z9B75 AVL
     Material processed by the BL and Inner London Education authority. Initial classified catalogue lists over 5000 multimedia items for purchase or rent in the U.K. Subject and title/ series/ name indexes.

AG6   Library of Congress. NUC AUDIOVISUAL MATERIALS, 1983-   Washington: Library of Congress. quarterly; annual cumulation. microfiche pub.
R018.1 N277FA (to 1982); R018.1 N277FB (MRR)
     Microfiche replaces print version. Title varies for the print version; AG6 supersedes the LC catalogue, AUDIOVISUAL MATERIALS, 1979-82, formerly FILMS AND OTHER MATERIALS FOR PROJECTION. The scope includes all motion pictures, video recordings, filmstrips, slide sets, transparencies, slide sets, transparencies released in the U.S.

or Canada. Restricted to films which have instructional or educational value and catalogued by LC.

AG7 NICEM. INDEX TO EDUCATIONAL AUDIO TAPES, 1971- Los Angeles: National Information Center for Educational Media, Univ. of Southern California. irregular. (5th ed., 1980)
R371.33 AN278D   Sheehy AA427

    NICEM approximates an 'in print' control for non-print materials, although publication schedules lag well behind the original intention of biennial frequency for most of the indexes. Five of the 15 NICEM indexes are a multi-media coverage for specific subjects, e.g. ENVIRONMENTAL STUDIES, PSYCHOLOGY, VOCATIONAL AND TECHNICAL EDUCATION, HEALTH AND SAFETY EDUCATION, and SPECIAL EDUCATION in 2 vols. Other indexes (AG7-AG15) are by form of material. Editions from 1983 are available in microfiche and print formats; OISE has a number of these indexes. Each index has a subject guide, lists titles with full bibliographic citation with a directory of producers and distributors. NICEM UPDATE OF NONBOOK MEDIA, 1973- (3 a year; at OISE) supplements the basic indexes.

    NICSEM (National Information Center for Special Education) is a parallel organization with an online database (NIMIS: National Instructional Materials Information System) and publishing in print and microfiche format. NICSEM publications include a SPECIAL EDUCATION INDEX TO LEARNER MATERIALS (1979); ... TO PARENT MATERIALS (1979); ... TO ASSESSMENT MATERIALS (1980).

AG8 _____. INDEX TO EDUCATIONAL OVERHEAD TRANSPARENCIES, 1969-
R371.33 AN278T   (6th ed., 1980)

AG9 _____. INDEX TO EDUCATIONAL RECORDS, 1971-
R371.33 AN278E   (5th ed., 1980)

AG10 _____. INDEX TO EDUCATIONAL SLIDES, 1973-
R371.33 AN278S   (4th ed., 1980)

AG11 _____. INDEX TO EDUCATIONAL VIDEO TAPES, 1971-
R371.33 AN278V   (6th ed., 1983)

AG12 _____. INDEX TO 8MM MOTION CARTRIDGES, 1969-
R371.33 AN278M   (6th ed., 1980)

AG13 _____. INDEX TO 16 MM EDUCATIONAL FILMS, 1964-
R371.33 AN278A   (8th ed., 1983)

AG14 _____. INDEX TO 35MM EDUCATIONAL FILMSTRIPS, 1967- 2 vols.
R371.33 AN278B   (8th ed., 1983)

AG15 _____. INDEX TO PRODUCERS AND DISTRIBUTORS, 1971-
R371.33 AN278C   (6th ed., 1983)

FILMS, FILMSTRIPS, VIDEO

AG16   THE BRITISH NATIONAL FILM CATALOGUE, 1963-   London: British Film Institute. bimonthly; annual cum.
R791.438 B862   Z5784.M9B75
    A record of British and foreign films released in the U.K. Classified by subject, with subject and title indexes, listing of distributors, production companies, sponsors, technicians.

AG16   CANADIAN FEATURE FILMS, 1913-1969. (See BG37)

AG17   FILM CANADIANA, 1980/82-   Montreal: National Film Board of Canada, 1984- biennial.
R791.438 F487F   Ryder HU3-9B
    Publisher, frequency varies. From 1948-64, films produced in Canada were listed in CANADIAN INDEX TO PERIODICALS AND DOCUMENTARY FILMS (AF12). From 1964-76 as Part 6 "Films and Filmstrips" in CANADIANA (AD77). From 1976, Part 6 not published with CANADIANA; published with FILM CANADIANA (Canadian Film Institute, 1969- quarterly, then annual). Previously covering Canadian and some foreign films, this publication became solely dedicated to Canadian films in 1972/73 ed. NLC, from 1973, provided data sheets to CFI on all Canadian feature, short, or made for TV films. CANADIANA and FILM CANADIANA duplicated coverage until 1976- when FILM CANADIANA became "the national bibliography" of film. This yearbook of Canadian cinema, in five sections (filmography, bibliography, organizations, festivals and awards, statistics) carried the bibliographic record from 1976 to discontinuance, in 1979, of CFI's FILM CANADIANA.
    A machine readable data base, cooperatively sponsored by NLC, PAC National Film Television and Sound Archives and CFI, has been created and has filled the gap in publication with a new issue of FILM CANADIANA. Now publihsed by NFB, the films are listed, by title, in bilingual format, with indexes. Available online and in print formats.

AG18   NFB FILM CATALOGUE, 1971/72-   Montreal: National Film Board, 1971- annual. supplements
R791.438 C212   Ryder HU3-12
    NFB, est. 1969, is Canada's official film-maker and distributor. The catalogue, once restricted to NFB films, now lists some commercial films and CBC videotapes.

AG19   16MM FILMS AVAILABLE FROM THE PUBLIC LIBRARIES OF METROPOLITAN TORONTO, 1969-   3 vols. Toronto: Metropolitan Toronto Library Board. annual. (Title varies).
R791.438 T686
    A typical local guide, produced for patrons' use, as a guide to public library holdings. Subject index; main entry by title.

PHONORECORDS AND TAPES

AG20   CANADIANA, 1950-   (see AD77)
R015.71 C21
    In Part V "Sound Recordings" until change of format in 1983.

AG21   HARRISON TAPE GUIDE, 1969-   New York: M. & N. Harrison. bimonthly.
ML157.3 H3 MUSI
   Covers all types of tapes, with other Harrison catalogues, e.g. ... OF STEREO 4-TRACK TAPES; ... OF STEREO 8 TAPE CARTRIDGES.

AG22   Library of Congress. MUSIC, BOOKS ON MUSIC AND SOUND RECORDINGS, 1953-   Washington: Library of Congress. semiannual; annual cumulation. quinquennial cumulations 1953-1977.
R018.1 N277M
   Formerly LC CATALOG - MUSIC AND PHONORECORDS, 1953-1972. Sound recordings entered are of all kinds, e.g. educational, musical, literary or political. Music is broadly defined to include scores, sheet music, libretti, books about music and musicians catalogued by LC and other libraries selected by the Music Library Association as representative of spectrum of music collections.

AG23   SCHWANN-1 RECORD & TAPE GUIDE, 1949-   Boston: Schwann. monthly. semiannual (title: SCHWANN-2).
ML156.2 S3862 MUSI
   Title varies; has CHILDREN'S GUIDE; ; ARTIST ISSUE, 1963-   irreg.

PICTURES AND REPRODUCTIONS

AG24   PHOTOS CANADA, 1963-   Ottawa: Information Canada. occasional.
R779 C212   TR199.C35   Ryder HU4-85
   Supersedes CANADIAN PICTURE INDEX issued by the NFB. Mostly b&w white photographs, arranged by subject; includes order instructions.

AG25   Public Archives of Canada. GUIDE TO CANADIAN PHOTOGRAPHIC ARCHIVES/ GUIDE DES ARCHIVES PHOTOGRAPHIQUES CANADIENNES. Ottawa: Public Archives, 1979. 222 p.
R779 G946G   Ryder HU4-86

AG26   UNESCO CATALOGUE OF REPRODUCTIONS OF PAINTINGS, 1860-1969. (See BE51)

AG27   UNESCO CATALOGUE OF REPRODUCTIONS OF PAINTINGS PRIOR TO 1860. (See BE52)

SELECTION AIDS (See also section AC)

AG28   EFLA EVALUATIONS, 1948-   New York: Educational Film Library Association. looseleaf.
OISE
   Critical evaluations summarize content, technical quality and give suggestions for audience use. FILM EVALUATION GUIDE, 1946-64 (EFLA, 1965) (R371.335 AF487) with SUPPLEMENT 1964-67 (1968); 1967-71 (1972) is a compilation of EFLA evaluations with subject guide.

AG29   Rothwell, Helene. CANADIAN SELECTION: FILMSTRIPS. Toronto: Univ. of Toronto Press, 1980. 537 p.
R371.335 AR848C   Ryder HU3-15
   Buying guide for school, public libraries. Lists about 1900 filmstrips, produced in Canada, for K-13. Arranged by DDC with subject, title, series indexes and directory of distributors.

AG30   LE TESSIER. Montreal: La Centrale des Bibliothèques, 1983. 1100 p.
   Named for Quebec motion picture pioneer, Albert Tessier, this French language catalogue lists nearly 7000 Canadian 16mm films, video recordings, filmstrips and other AV in the French language. Entries arranged by DDC with title, subject, author, series indexes and directory of Canadian producers, distributors.

REVIEWS AND INDEXES TO REVIEWS

AG31   MEDIA REVIEW DIGEST, 1970-   Ann Arbor, MI: Pierian Press, 1971- annual, with supplement.
R371.33 AM961
   Continues MULTI-MEDIA REVIEWS INDEX. An annual index to and digest of reviews, evaluations, descriptions of all forms of non-book media appearing in over 145 periodicals and reviewing services. Has films, (feature and short, some non-U.S.), filmstrips, videocassettes, records, tapes, slides, globes, charts, kits and games etc. Several indexes, a "Film Awards and Prizes" section and a mediagraphy.

AG32   INTERNATIONAL INDEX TO MULTI-MEDIA INFORMATION, 1970-   Pasadena, CA: Audio-Visual Associates, 1971- quarterly. looseleaf.
R791.43 F487
Supersedes FILM REVIEW INDEX. Index to reviews, often with brief quotations from the review. Wide range of media covered.

AG33   THE NEW YORK TIMES FILM REVIEWS, 1913-   (See BG49)

ANNUALS, DIRECTORIES AND HANDBOOKS

ANNUALS, ALMANACS

AH1   THE ANNUAL REGISTER: A RECORD OF WORLD EVENTS, 1758-   London: Longman, 1761-   irregular.
        R905.8 A615   D2.47   Sheehy DA50
        Title, publisher vary. A brief summary of the year's events. Arranged by political unit such as the U.N., Commonwealth, or regions, Middle East; then by subject such as law, religion, science and technology, arts, economics. Obituaries, statistics, text of documents, abstracts of important speeches in last chapter.

AH2   THE EUROPA YEAR BOOK: A WORLD SURVEY, 1926-   2 vols. London: Europa.
        R320.5 E89   D2.E8, JN.E8503   Sheehy CJ62
        Vol. 1 covers international organizations and Europe, and begins the alphabetical sequence of countries which is continued in vol. 2. Information includes an overview, economic and demographic statistics, government and directory addresses in religion, tourism, publishing, universities. Europa also issues regional yearbooks, FAR EAST AND AUSTRALASIA, MIDDLE EAST AND NORTH AFRICA and AFRICA SOUTH OF THE SAHARA, and a yearbook on education THE WORLD OF LEARNING (CI28).

AH3   THE STATESMAN'S YEAR-BOOK: STATISTICAL AND HISTORICAL ANNUAL OF THE STATES OF THE WORLD, 1864-   London: Macmillan.
        R320.5 S797   JA51.57   Sheehy CG45
        Similiar, but more concise, information to that found in AH2. From the 115th ed. (1978/79) countries, formerly grouped under political units, are listed alphabetically. For each country, information on history, government, geography, defense, economy, resources, communications, law, education with bibliography. Companion volume: THE STATESMAN'S YEAR-BOOK WORLD GAZETTEER (2d ed., 1979) (G103 5S8).

AH4   INFORMATION PLEASE ALMANAC, ATLAS AND YEARBOOK, 1947-   New York: Information Please. annual.
        R317 I43   AY64.I55   Sheehy CG66
        Some overlap with AH6. One or two topical articles; mainly concise facts, statistics of general interest.

AH5   Whitaker, Joseph. AN ALMANACK: The Yearbook: An Invaluable Guide to British and World Affairs of the Past Year and Essential Dates and Data for the Year Ahead. 1869-   London: Whitaker. annual.
        R310 W577   AY754 W5
        Subtitle varies: "Containing an Account of the Astronomical and Other Phenomena and a Vast Amount of Information Respecting the Government, Finances, Population, Commerce and General Statistics of the Various Nations of the World." WHITAKER'S is available in three editions; the "Shorter" containing an miscellany of information emphasizing Britain; the "Library" (with maps) and the "Complete" both of which cover the Commonwealth, foreign countries and add more information on Britain, etc.

AH6   THE WORLD ALMANAC AND BOOK OF FACTS, 1868- New York: Newspaper Enterprise Association. annual. Canadian edition/ Toronto: Toronto Star Syndicate.
R317 W927   AY67.N5W7   Sheehy CG75
   The oldest of the American handbooks of miscellaneous information. Some overlap with AH4. Detailed index to the records, lists, dates and statistics for countries, personalities, sports, churches, historical events and disasters etc. GEODATA: THE WORLD ALMANAC GAZETTEER (1983) (G103 15K87) in four sections (the U.S.; the world; major landmarks; miscellaneous ranked data).

Great Britain

AH7   BRITAIN: AN OFFICIAL HANDBOOK 1950- London: Central Office of Information. annual.
R914.2 G786   DA630.A17   Sheehy CJ177
   Like CANADA YEAR BOOK (AH12), it is primarily concerned with the work of government, but extends to non-government features such as sports, list of newspapers, British books. Presentation reflects a policy of combining promotion with general information. THE ANNUAL ABSTRACT OF STATISTICS (CA33) provides more detailed information.

AH8   WHITAKER'S ALMANACK. (AH5)

United States

AH9   INFORMATION PLEASE ALMANAC, ATLAS AND YEARBOOK. (AH4)

AH10   THE WORLD ALMANAC AND BOOK OF FACTS. (AH6)

AH11   STATISTICAL ABSTRACT OF THE UNITED STATES. (See CA34)

Canada

AH12   CANADA YEAR BOOK: AN ANNUAL REVIEW OF ECONOMIC, SOCIAL AND POLITICAL DEVELOPMENTS IN CANADA, 1905- Ottawa: CGPC, Supply and Services [for Statistics Canada], 1972- biennial, 1978/79-
R317.1 C212   Ryder GR3-10;SS10-5
   Frequency varies. French ed., ANNUAIRE DU CANADA. Records in statistics and brief descriptions the work of the federal government. Discusses constitution, physical geography, population and other aspects. Appendices feature special articles, books about Canada, synopses of legislation, a chronology, honours, etc.

AH13   CANADA HANDBOOK: THE ANNUAL HANDBOOK OF PRESENT CONDITIONS AND RECENT PROGRESS, 1930- Ottawa: CGPC, Supply and Services [for Statistics Canada], 1972- biennial, 1979- .
R371.1 C212C   Ryder GR12-1
   (The 1982/83 ed. subtitled THE 50TH ANNUAL. 1984 ed., 344 p.) French ed.: LE CANADA: LE REVUE ANNUELLE. Based on CANADA YEAR BOOK (AH12), but produced in a more popular format and style, with colour photographs for widespread appeal, very general information on country, environment, culture, government.

AH14　　CANADIAN ANNUAL REVIEW OF PUBLIC AFFAIRS, 1901-38. 35 vols. Toronto: Canadian Review Co., 1903-40.
　　　　971 C212A　　　　　　　F5003 C325　　　　　　Ryder GR12-5
　　　　Reviews the year in a series of essays. Lists Canadian books published for the year, and is still helpful as a publishing record for the early years of this century.

AH15　　CANADIAN ANNUAL REVIEW OF POLITICS AND PUBLIC AFFAIRS, 1960-　Toronto: Univ. of Toronto Press, 1961-　irregular.
　　　　R971 C212AB　　　　　F5003.C326　　　　　　Ryder GR12-4
　　　　(1981 ed. {1984}) Former title: CANADIAN ANNUAL REVIEW, 1960-71. Reviews the year in a series of essays by specialists.

AH16　　CANADIAN ALMANAC & DIRECTORY, 1847-　Toronto: Copp Clark Pitman.
　　　　R317.1 C212A　　　　AY414 C2　　　　　　　Ryder GR12-3
　　　　Canada's oldest almanac (1848 ed.) A variety of useful information, arranged in four sections: directory; almanac; information and statistics; law firms and lawyers. Almost 90% directory information.

AH17　　THE CORPUS ALMANAC OF CANADA, 1966-　Toronto: Corpus Publishers Services. annual.
　　　　R317.1 C822　　　　　F5003 M3　　　　　　　Ryder GR12-6
　　　　Title varies: McGRAW-HILL DIRECTORY AND ALMANAC OF CANADA, 1966-71; CORPUS DIRECTORY AND ALMANAC OF CANADA, 1971-72. Some overlap with CANADIAN ALMANAC & DIRECTORY (AH16). Information for over 5000 associations, societies, labour unions; emphasizes business, government. Facts on real estate, taxation, native peoples, sports.

AH18　　QUICK CANADIAN FACTS: THE CANADIAN POCKET ENCYCLOPEDIA, 1945-　Toronto: Quick Canada Facts. annual.
　　　　R317.1 Q6　　　　　　F5003 M3　　　　　　　Ryder GR2-7
　　　　Published in January, contains concise information and a chronology of Canada's history to the present.

AH19　　ANNUAIRE DU QUEBEC, 1914-　Quebec: Bureau de la statistique du Québec. irregular annual.
　　　　R317.14 A615　　　　HA747 Q2A32 GENR; GOVT　Ryder GR12-17
　　　　Separate French, English editions 1914-34; bilingual; unilingual French from 53d ed. (1973).

CURRENT EVENTS (See also Indexes to Newspapers, AF20-AF25)

AH20　　DEADLINE DATA ON WORLD AFFAIRS, 1956-　Greenwich, CT: DMS. weekly. card service.
　　　　　　　　　　　　　　D843 D4
　　　　Current information on all countries and major international organizations. Arranged by country; subject index.

AH21　　FACTS ON FILE: A Weekly World News Digest, 1940-　New York: Facts on File. weekly; cum. index; quinquennial index. looseleaf.
　　　　　　　　　　　　　　D410 F32
　　　　Last quinquennial index is 1976-1980 (1981). Reports from more than fifty foreign, U.S. newspapers, magazines. Editors write concise news summaries highlighting factual content. Forthcoming in 1984, an online availability with file beginning from first issue 1982. Related publication, OBITUARIES ON FILE 1940-78.

AH22   KEESING'S CONTEMPORARY ARCHIVES: Record of World Events, 1931-   London: Keesing's Publications. monthly; annual cum. index. looseleaf.
R905 K26   D410 K4
   Subtitle varies; formerly "Record of International Current Affairs with Continally Updated Indexes." Available in five languages. Weekly until 1983; when frequency changes to monthly and arrangement is focussed under geographic areas. Covers developments in economics, sciences, other fields with verbatim accounts, excerpts of international treaties, charters, conferences. Indexes are an analytic subject (twice yearly) with names in final cumulation. Some separately published reports covering countries, e.g. AFRICA DIARY, or topics, e.g. TREATIES AND ALLIANCES.

AH23   CANADIAN NEWS FACTS: The Indexed Digest of Canadian Current Events, 1967-   Toronto: Marpep Publishing Co. semi-monthly. looseleaf.
R905 C212   F5000 C283   Ryder GR6-11
   A topical summary of news in Canada, from the major newspapers, with detailed cum. indexes (quarterly; annual).

AH24   NEWSCOM: Canada's Complete News Summary, 1982-   Winnipeg: Wordswest Publications. semi-monthly; cum index each issue. looseleaf.
   A competitor for AH23. Summaries, derived from some 200 newspapers, financial publications, magazines representative of the Canadian media, have citation to source.

DIRECTORIES OF ORGANIZATIONS

Bibliographies of Directories

AH25   DIRECTORY OF DIRECTORIES, 1980-   Ed. by James M. Ethridge. Detroit: Gale Research. irregular. Inter-edition supplement. 2 issues.
R011 D598D
   (2d ed. 1983). This edition revises nearly 7000 directories originally from issues of DIRECTORY INFORMATION SERVICE, 1977-78; the title for the inter-ed. update. Second ed. has more foreign entries in the general listings of industrial, business, professional and scientific directories. Subject, title indexes.

AH26   Ryder, Dorothy E. CHECKLIST OF CANADIAN DIRECTORIES, 1790-1950/ REPERTOIRE DES ANNUAIRES CANADIENS, 1790-1950. Ottawa: National Library of Canada, 1979. 288 p.
R971.0025 AR992C   Ryder HA4-15
   Over 900 titles listed chronologically within geographic areas. Locations given unless information is from dealers' lists.

Directories

AH27   ENCYCLOPEDIA OF ASSOCIATIONS, 1956-   5 vols. Ed. by Denise Akey. Detroit: Gale Research. irregular. Inter-edition supplement.
R061 G151E12   HS17 G32   Sheehy CA67
   ('84 18th ed., {1983}). The base of this set is vol. 1, in 2 parts, covering appr. 17 700 American national organizations; vol. 2 is the geographic and executive index; vol. 3 is the supplement, NEW ASSOCIATIONS AND PROJECTS. Expanded in size from the national coverage of earlier editions (in 3 vols); this latest edition adds vol. 4 (a 3

issue subscription, 1983- in progress) for non-profit organizations outside the U.S. having international aims and membership. Also new, vol. 5, in 2 parts, edited by A.T. Kruzas and K. Gill, provides details (facilities, grants, programs) about 1000 associations with research as a primary activity.

AH28 THE INTERNATIONAL FOUNDATION DIRECTORY. 3d ed. Ed. by H.V. Hodson. London: Europa, 1983. 450 p.
HU7 157 ROBA; 060.25 I612 OISE
Guide to activities, executives of non-profit foundations, etc. in 45 countries. Reviews science, medicine, conservation, education, aid and social welfare etc. Arranged by country; indexes for foundations, activities.

AH29 RESEARCH CENTERS DIRECTORY, 1960- Detroit: Gale Research. irregular. Inter-edition supplement: NEW RESEARCH CENTERS.
R007 R432R4   AS25 R47   Sheehy CA68
(8th ed., 1983, 1081 p.). Nearly 6600 university and non-profit organizations in the U.S. and Canada listed under broad subjects (mathematics, education etc.) with detailed subject, sponsoring institution, research unit indexes. Related publications from Gale Research are (primarily U.S.) GOVERNMENT RESEARCH CENTERS DIRECTORY (2d ed., 1982); RESEARCH SERVICES DIRECTORY (2d ed., 1982) which is a guide to U.S. commercial firms, individuals providing services for business, industry; and INTERNATIONAL RESEARCH CENTERS DIRECTORY, 1981-82, in 3 issues, covering independent, university-related and government centres.

AH30 YEARBOOK OF INTERNATIONAL ORGANIZATIONS: The Encyclopedic Dictionary of International Organizations, their Officers, their Abbreviations, 1948- Ed. by the Union of International Associations [Brussels]. Munich: K.G. Saur, 1983- irregular. (Dist.: Gale Research)
R060 Y39   JX1904 Y4   Sheehy CK214
(20th ed., 1983). Nearly 20 000 orgs that are international in their aims, membership with a geographic and subject index.

AH31 DIRECTORY OF ASSOCIATIONS IN CANADA/ REPERTOIRE DES ASSOCIATIONS DU CANADA, 1973- Ed. by Brian Land. Toronto: Micromedia Ltd. biennial
R061.1 D598C   AS40 A7D57   Ryder GR10-8
(5th ed., 1984) Former publisher: Univ. of Toronto Press. Lists voluntary, non-government associations alphabetically. Includes local, regional, provincial and national associations; international, foreign associations with branches in Canada. Subject index.

HANDBOOKS

Awards and Prizes

AH32 AWARDS, HONORS AND PRIZES: An International Directory of Awards and their Donors. 2 vols. 5th ed. Ed. by Paul Wasserman: G. Siegman, and K. Wassermann. Detroit: Gale Research, 1982.
R001.44 W322   AS8 A83
All fields covered. Comprehensive set for information on the awards themselves; recipients are not listed.

AH33   LITERARY AND LIBRARY PRIZES. 10th ed. New York: R.R. Bowker, 1980. 651 p
         807.9 L776   PN171 P75L5
            In four sections: international, American, Canadian, British. Lists terms, recipients since inception, of prize.

AH34   WORLD DICTIONARY OF AWARDS AND PRIZES. London: Europa, 1979. 580 p.
                               AS911 A2W58
            Alphabetical, geographic, subject indexes to details of eligibility and recipients of prestigious lectureships, medals, etc. in arts and sciences.

Consumer Information

AH35   CANADIAN CONSUMER, 1971-   Ottawa: Consumers' Association. 6 a year.
                               TX335 A1C34
            French ed.: LE CONSOMMATEUR CANADIEN.

AH36   CONSUMER REPORTS, 1936-   Orangeburg, NY: Consumers Union. monthly
                       TX335 A1C602   Sheehy CH215
            Results of product tests, investigations of consumer services. December issue is an annual buying guide.

AH37   CONSUMER SOURCEBOOK. 2 vols. 4th ed. Ed. by P. Wasserman and G. Siegman. Detroit: Gale Research, 1983.
                               HC110 C63W37   Sheehy 1CH106
            Comprehensive listing of American agencies for consumer protection and guidance with their publications.

AH38   CONSUMERS INDEX TO PRODUCT EVALUATIONS AND INFORMATION SOURCES, 1973- Ann Arbor, MI: Pierian Press. quarterly, annual.
            "Aimed at general consumer, business office and educational or library community." Indexes articles from a variety of non-technical journals, including CONSUMER REPORTS, CONSUMER'S RESEARCH and focussing on finance, health and well-being of buyer.

Holidays and Events (See also History, Chronologies and Tables, CJ18-CJ21)

AH39   Allen, G.P. DAYS TO REMEMBER: Observances of Significance in Our Multicultural Society. Toronto: [Ontario] Ministry of Culture and Recreation, 1980. 159 p.
         R394.269713 A425D   Ryder SS2-4
            Covers the public holidays and observances in Ont., whether general or particular cultures (84 cultural groups noted).

AH40   Foster, Annie H., and Anne Grierson. HIGH DAYS AND HOLIDAYS IN CANADA: A Collection of Holiday Facts for Canadian Schools. Rev. ed. Toronto: Ryerson Press, 1956. Reprint/ 1970. 96 p.
         R394 F754   GT4813 F6   Ryder SS2-5

AH41   Gregory, Ruth W. ANNIVERSARIES AND HOLIDAYS. 4th ed. Chicago: American Library Association, 1983. 262 p.
         R394 AH42   GT3930 H38   Sheehy CF49

AH42   NEWNES DICTIONARY OF DATES. Comp. by Robert Collison. London: Newnes, 1966. 428 p.
R902 C713N2
   An older standard in two sections. The first section gives dates and a few brief words about persons, places, events in an alphabetical sequence. The other section lists people and events in a calendar.

AH43   THE PEOPLE'S CHRONOLOGY: A Year by Year Record of Human Events from Prehistory to the Present. Ed. by J. Trayer. New York: Holt, Rinehart and Winston, 1979. 1206 p.
D11 T83
   Organized by the year; brief entries are flagged in groups using easily understood graphics ($ for economics). Any trivia entries appear strongly to favour U.S. Name/subject index.

AH44   THE WORLD ALMANAC DICTIONARY OF DATES. Ed. by Lawrence Urdang. New York: Longman in coop. with World Almanac, 1982. 318 p.
D9 WT3
   More than 10 000 events from B.C. to the present in a subject/proper name arrangement. Events chosen reflect popular interest.

Emblems, Heraldry

AH45   THE ARMS, FLAGS AND EMBLEMS OF CANADA. 3d ed. Ottawa: Deneau, in coop. with Secretary of State, 1984. 113 p.
CR212 A85; CA1 SS67 A62 GOVT
   French ed.: LES ARMOIRIES DRAPEAUX ET EMBLEMES FLORAUX DU CANADA. An illustrated (in col.) description, display of the heraldic symbols and emblems for each province and territory. With glossary; flag etiquette. Useful brief information for any age, from elementary school on.

AH46   Swan, Conrad. CANADA: SYMBOLS OF SOVEREIGNTY: An Investigation of the Arms and Seals Borne and Used from the Earliest Times to the Present in Connection with Public Authority in and over Canada, along with Consideration of Some Connected Flags. Toronto: Univ. of Toronto Press, 1977. 272 p.
R929.60971 S972C   CR212 S9   Ryder HA3-7

Etiquette

AH47   DEBRETT'S ETIQUETTE AND MODERN MANNERS. Ed. by Elsie B. Donald. London: Debrett's Peerage, 1981. 400 p.
BJ1873 D34
   A British view on everyday conventions and manners.

AH48   THE AMY VANDERBILT COMPLETE BOOK OF ETIQUETTE. Rev. by L. Baldridge. New York: Doubleday, 1978. 879 p.
R395 V228   BJ1853 V27   Sheehy CF63
   A paper edition, with subtitle, "A Guide to Contemporary Living" (Bantam, 1981. 272 p.). A North American view on deportment.

AH49   THE NEW EMILY POST'S ETIQUETTE. Rev. by Elizabeth L. Post. New York: Funk and Wagnalls, 1975. 880 p.
R395 P85E2   BJ1853 P6   Sheehy CF60

Parliamentary Procedure

AH50   Bourinot, John G. BOURINOT'S RULES OF ORDER. 3d ed. rev. by Geoffrey H. Stanford. Toronto: McClelland and Stewart, 1977. 112 p.
      R328 B77R2 (1963)   JL164 B68   Ryder SS6-36
      The standard source for Canadian parliamentary procedure and procedures at public assemblies.

AH51   THE SCOTT FORESMAN ROBERT'S RULES OF ORDER. Newly rev. by Sarah C. Robert, and others. Glenview, IL: Scott Foresman, 1981. 594 p.
      R328 R641 (pocket ed.)   JF515 R692
      "Robert's Rules" are a North American standard for the conduct of deliberative assemblies. A copyright notice states that this 1981 version is the official replacement for earlier editions.

Records

AH52   GUINNESS BOOK OF RECORDS, 1955-   Ed. by Norris McWhirter. London: Guinness Superlatives. annual, 1973-   (Dist.: Sterling; Bantam)
      R031 G964   AG243 G85
      American ed.: GUINNESS BOOK OF WORLD RECORDS. Records are achievements that are "measureable and comparable to other performances in the same category." Unique occurences, interesting peculiarities are not necessarily a category for record. In similar tradition to this widely recognized reference source, Guinness produces a "Facts & Feats" series (e.g. THE GUINNESS BOOK OF WEATHER FACTS AND FEATS (1977); ... OF MOTORCYCLING FACTS AND FEATS (1979); ... OF RAIL FACTS AND FEATS (1979). A feat is "a notable achievement, an unusual accomplishment or a difficult act displaying courage or skill." Other related titles include GUINNESS BOOK OF ESSENTIAL FACTS (1979) a miscellany of curious facts or useful lists (e.g. ranking of populous nations, prize winners) and sports records books (see AH57).

AH53   PRUDENTIAL'S BOOK OF CANADIAN WINNERS AND HEROES. Ed. by J. Brown; B. Brown, and F. Matthews. Scarborough, Ont.: Prentice Hall, 1983. 365 p.
      F5009 B87
      Intended for popular appeal, browsing. Lists most recent winners and miscellaneous information about persons, awards in broad areas (arts, commerce, communications, sciences, humanities and Canadian life, athletics and recreation).

AH54   THE WOMEN'S BOOK OF WORLD RECORDS AND ACHIEVEMENTS. Ed. by Lois D. O'Neill. New York: Doubleday Anchor, 1979. 800 p.
      CT3234 W65

Sports and Games

AH55   SPORT BIBLIOGRAPHY/ BIBLIOGRAPHIE DU SPORT. 8 vols. Ottawa: Sport Information Resource Centre, 1981-82.
                  Z7511 S64   Ryder SS2-15
      Basically, SIRC's bibliography is a subject index to the online database (see AH56). Vols 1-4 cover sports in groups (aquatic, boating, ice, outdoor, winter, bowling and golf, team, combat, gymnastics and dance, martial arts, racquet, track and field,

weightlifting, aeronautical, animal, bicycling, pentathlon, target etc.). Vols 5-8 add items on sport generally (medicine, history, coaching, competing, psychology.

AH56　SPORTS AND RECREATION INDEX/ INDEX DE LA LITTERATURE DES SPORTS ET DES LOISIRS, 1977- Ottawa: Sport Information Resource Centre, 1974- 8 issues a year.
　　Supersedes SPORTS ARTICLES 1974-77. SIRC indexes the worldwide literature of individual and team sports, recreation planning, physical education, sports medicine, facilities and history. Monitors newspapers, appr. 800 journals (from 1975), monographs (back to 1949), theses and conference proceedings. From Feb. 1984, the full file (1975 to date) available online (CAN/OLE at CISTI). (See also AH55).

AH57　GUINNESS BOOK OF SPORTS RECORDS WINNERS AND CHAMPIONS. Ed. by Norris McWhirter and others. New York: Sterling, 1980. 352 p.
　　Compiled from the GUINNESS BOOK OF WINNERS AND CHAMPIONS (1979) (GV11C65) and the ...BOOK OF RECORDS (1962 to 1979 eds), AH57 lists 84 sports in alphabetical order. Some sports are grouped (under Martial Arts, Track and Field etc.) with large section devoted to Olympic Games. Each entry gives brief history of sport, followed by records, winners, record holders. Charts, tables, some photographs; subject, but no name, index. Related titles are GUINNESS BOOK OF WOMEN'S SPORTS RECORDS (1979) covering 46 sports with miscellaneous facts about women in sport, and GUINNESS BOOK OF OLYMPIC RECORDS (1984) covering the winter and summer winners, 1896-1980, for the 28 sports.

AH58　THE INTERNATIONAL DICTIONARY OF SPORTS AND GAMES. By J.A. Cudden. New York: Schocken, 1980. 870 p.
　　　　　　　　　　　　GV567 C8
　　Brief definition, history, etymology, rules and other pertinent information for major sports. Has a chronology of events from 5200 B.C. to A.D. 1979.

AH59　Menke, Frank G. THE ENCYCLOPEDIA OF SPORTS. 6th ed. Rev. by F. Palmer. South Brunswick, NJ: A.S. Barnes, 1978. 1132 p.
　　R796. 03 M545　　　　　GV11 M4
　　Histories, descriptions, rules. Information on records only to 1976.

AH60　THE BIG BOOK OF HALLS OF FAME IN THE UNITED STATES AND CANADA: SPORTS. New York: R.R. Bowker, 1977. 1042 p.
　　R920.3 B592B　　　　　　　　　　　　　　　　Ryder SS2-7
　　Groups fields with applicable halls arranged alphabetically; a historical sketch for hall plus members with biographical notes. CANADA'S SPORTING HEROES: THEIR LIVES AND TIMES, by S.F. Wise and D. Fisher, (General Pub., 1974) (R796.0971 W813C) has biographies, written in a popular style with pictures, to appeal to any age and to promote information on Canadian sport performance.

AH61　RULES OF THE GAME. New York: Diagram Visual Information, 1974. 320 p.
　　　　　　　　　　　　GV731 D52
　　A visual layout, for major sports, of official international rules, playing areas, equipment, objectives. Companion vol.: THE WAY TO PLAY (1975).

GENERAL ENCYCLOPEDIAS

GUIDE

AI1   Kister, Kenneth F. ENCYCLOPEDIA BUYING GUIDE: A CONSUMER GUIDE TO GENERAL ENCYCLOPEDIAS IN PRINT. 3d ed. New York: R.R. Bowker. 530 p.
R031 AE56B
(1st ed., 1976) Contains general information on evaluating encyclopedias, followed by long reviews, and appendixes including information on discontinued titles, directory of publishers.

COMPREHENSIVE GENERAL ENCYCLOPEDIAS

For Adults

AI2   COLLIER'S ENCYCLOPEDIA. 24 vols. New York: Crowell, Collier and Macmillan. illus. maps. issued annually.
R031 C69   AE5.C682
A standard, general encyclopedia with space allocated according to studies on the information needs of the general reading public. Style, vocabulary at the junior college level. Bibliographies are grouped under broad subjects in the index volume. Supplement: COLLIER'S ENCYCLOPEDIA YEAR BOOK, 1939-

AI3   THE ENCYCLOPEDIA AMERICANA. 30 vols. New York: Americana Corp. illus. maps. issued annually.
R031 E56   AE5 E333
The 1983 ed. marks a 150ieth anniversary of this well balanced authoritative encyclopedia with good illustrations and separate index (Vol. 30). Most articles are short and on specific topics, with some extensive articles on broader topics. Particularly useful for coverage of American material , places, topics in business, industry, science and technology. Supplement: THE AMERICANA ANNUAL, 1923- has events, survey articles and a necrology.

AI4   ENCYCLOPEDIA BRITANNICA. 15th ed. 30 vols. Chicago: Enycylopedia Britannica Educational Corp. illus. maps. issued annually.
R032 E56BN   AE5.E363
Designated BRITANNICA 3 (1974), the 15th ed. marked a major revision of content and a new format in three parts. The "Propaedia" (1 vol.) is a detailed outline of the structure of human knowledge; the "Macropaedia" (19 vols) contains in-depth articles on over 4000 topics; the "Micropaedia" (10 vols) has concise, 'ready reference' material and the index. The format provides information at varying levels of interest and readability. Supplements: BRITANNICA BOOK OF THE YEAR, 1938- with feature articles, short entries on the year's events; YEARBOOK OF SCIENCE AND THE FUTURE and MEDICAL AND HEALTH ANNUAL.
The 1983 issue, throughout the set, underwent the most extensive updating and revision since 1974. Complementary vol.: the BRITANNICA ATLAS (1 vol, rev. printing 1983), prepared by EBC and Rand McNally, is a polylingual atlas. EB available online, 1981-

AI5   FUNK & WAGNALLS NEW ENCYCLOPEDIA. 29 vols. New York: Funk & Wagnalls, illus. maps.
R031 F982E

A compact, average encyclopedia intended for home and high school readers with little background in the material. Many articles written by authorities. Most articles are short; any long articles present the general and simple information first. The set underwent a major revision in 1983 to increase the no. of illustrations, update the Hammond maps, revise the bibliogs (in Vol. 28) and content.

AI6   THE RANDOM HOUSE ENCYCLOPEDIA. New rev. ed. New York: Random House, 1983. illus. maps.
AG5 R25

A family encyclopedia. In two sections, the "Colorpedia" has articles arranged under broad topics (Earth; History and Culture); the "Alphapedia" has concise, factual entries on specific topics taken from the longer articles.

For Young Adults

AI7   ACADEMIC AMERICAN ENCYCLOPEDIA. 21 vols. New York: Grolier. illus. maps. issued annually.
R031 A168A

The first ed. (1980) created and published by Arete; purchased by Grolier in 1982. A good standard "ready reference" encyclopedia suitable for the high school and undergraduate user. Advertised as between WORLD BOOK and BRITANNICA in audience appeal. Emphasizes North American curriculum for secondary to college students doing initial research. Has factual short articles; many col. illustrations all with captions; with index vol. Designed from inception with an online edition, 1980- ; it is now online as THE ELECTRONIC ENCYCLOPEDIA with bibliographies, 30 000 brief articles (300 words) or "factboxes" on contemporary, curriculum topics.

AI8   COMPTON'S ENCYCLOPEDIA AND FACT-INDEX. 26 vols. Chicago: F.E. Compton/ Enyclopedia Britannica Educ. Corp. illus. maps. issued annually.
R031 C738

Keyed to curriculum needs, interests of students from upper elementary through secondary school, it also provides practical information for adults. Articles written for age level at which subjects are first encountered; simple concepts given first. Bibliogs have materials for various age levels. Fact-index in each vol. defines many terms not in the main text and refers to main text. Supplements: THE COMPTON'S YEARBOOK and YEARBOOK OF SCIENCE AND THE FUTURE.

AI9   ENCYCLOPEDIA INTERNATIONAL. 20 vols. New York: Grolier. illus. maps. issued annually.
R031 E57   AE5 E497

A family encyclopedia but accomodating students at various levels. Most articles are short; some topics given longer treatment.

AI10   MERIT STUDENTS ENCYCLOPEDIA. 20 vols. New York: Macmillan Educational.
         illus. maps. issued annually.
         R031 M562
            Intended for students from 5th grade through secondary school.
         Clearly written, extensively illus. in b&w., col. with overlays for
         some illustrations. Longer articles have bibliogs.

AI11   THE WORLD BOOK ENCYCLOPEDIA. 22 vols. Chicago: Field Enterprises. illus.
         maps. issued annually.
         R031 W92   AE5 W55
            A well-designed and balanced family encyclopedia, but intended
         especially for the reference needs of elementary to secondary school
         students. Tied closely to U.S. and Canadian curriculum, but with
         definite American emphasis. Most articles are short and factual, with
         long articles on broad subjects. Articles, vocabulary designed to be
         understood at the level at which the subject is likely to be studied.
         A research guide and index added with the 1972 ed. Extensively illus.
         in b&w. and col. Supplements: WORLD BOOK YEAR BOOK; SCIENCE YEAR and
         WORLD BOOK DICTIONARY (see AJ15).

Children's to Young Adult

AI12   THE NEW BOOK OF KNOWLEDGE. 21 vols. Danbury, CT: Grolier. illus. maps.
         issued annually.
         R031 N532
            Primarily for elementary school children and based on analysis of
         school curricula. Articles area tested against the Dale Chall
         readability formula. Dictionary index, on blue pages, in each vol.
         Reading lists in a separate HOME AND SCHOOL READING GUIDE.

AI13   BRITANNICA JUNIOR. 15 vols. Chicago: Encyclopedia Britannica Educ. Corp.
         illus. maps. issued annually.
            Set is geared to the curriculum needs and interests of students in
         upper elementary grades. Much illus., col., b&w., photos, with
         simplified vocabulary, definitions in context, fact index in first
         vol., bibliogs and reading guide. Supplement: BRITANNICA JUNIOR: THE
         ILLUSTRATED ENCYCLOPEDIA YEARBOOK.
            BRITANNICA DISCOVERY, 12 vols, available in an English or Spanish
         ed., is a set for pre-school children.

AI14   COMPTON'S PRECYCLOPEDIA. 16 vols. Chicago: Encyclopedia Britannica Educ.
         Corp. illus. issued annually.
            With aids for separate purchase, e.g. TEACHER'S GUIDE AND INDEX,
         EARLY CHILDHOOD ACTIVITIES, this set has material for children in the
         pre-school to early school years.

COMPREHENSIVE FOREIGN ENCYCLOPEDIAS

AI15   ENCYCLOPAEDIA UNIVERSALIS. 20 vols. 2d ed. Paris: E.U. France, 1968-75.
         SUPPLEMENT. 2 vols. 1980. illus.
                            AE25 E46
            Designed for advanced secondary school (college) level interests
         and audience. Has separately published index pamphlets. Supplement: a
         yearbook, UNIVERSALIA, 1974-

AI 16 LA GRANDE ENCYCLOPEDIE. 21 vols. Paris: Larousse, 1974-78. illus. maps.
  AE25 G69
   Signed articles grouped under broad topics; emphasis on the 20th century. Vol. 21, index.

AI 17 GRAND DICTIONNAIRE ENCYCLOPEDIQUE LAROUSSE. 10 vols. Paris: Librairie Larousse. 1982-   In progress (to 1985). illus.
  R034 G751   AE25 G64
   Last ed. of "Larousse" (GRANDE LAROUSSE ENCYCLOPEDIQUE, 1972-81) discarded the dictionary emphasis to concentrate on encyclopedic entries. This new ed. returns to the original format of dictionary combined with encyclopedia. Encyclopedia entries are basically short with some few longer articles. Bibliogs at end of each vol.; no index.

AI 18 DER GROSSE BROCKHAUS. 15 vols. Wiesbaden: F.A. Brockhaus, 1977-82. illus
  R033.1 B864   AE27G67
   A previous edition of this standard German multi-volume set was titled BROCKHAUS ENZYKLOPADIE (20 vols, 1966-75; five supplements) (AE27 G672). Articles are usually short; authoritative but unsigned following Brockhaus tradition. DGB is a comprehensive family edition with an atlas (vol. 13) and a dictionary (vol.14).

AI 19 ENCICLOPEDIA UNIVERSAL ILUSTRADA EUROPEO - AMERICANA. 72 vols. Madrid: Espasa Calpe, 1905-1933. With supplements, 1934-   irreg.; annual.
  AE61 E6
   (Most recent annual supplement, 1979-80 {1983}). "Espasa" is the standard, multi-volume important historical encyclopedia for Spanish speaking peoples. With illustrations, long bibliographies, maps.
   A middle range standard is "GER"; GRAN ENCICLOPEDIA RIALP, 20 vols. (Madrid: Ediciones Rialp, 1971-76). An encyclopedia written for more popular appeal and for the student is ENCICLOPEDIA BARSA (16 vols, Enc. Brit., 1981). "Barsa" is Latin American in orientation and North American in its format, general revision program.

AI 20 ENCICLOPEDIA ITALIANA DE SCIENZE, LETTERE ED ARTI. 36 vols. Rome: Istituto della Enciclopedia Italiana, 1929-38. APPENDICE I-IV (in 8 vols). 1939-1978.
  AE35E5
   (Most recent supplement: IV: 1961-1978, 3 vols, {1978-81}).

AI 21 THE GREAT SOVIET ENCYCLOPEDIA. 32 vols. New York: Macmillan, 1973-83.
  AE55 B6
   An approved English translation of the official encyclopedia, BOL'SHAIA SOVETSKAIA ENTSIKLOPEDIIA (30 vols, 3d ed., Moscow: S.E., 1970-78). Translated vols are not in correspondence, and recent volumes are supplementary updating. There are interim indexes (vols 1-15; vols 1-25; with vol. 32 as final index). Vol. 31 (1982) is devoted to the USSR.

NATIONAL AND REGIONAL ENCYCLOPEDIAS

Canada

AI22   ENCYCLOPEDIA CANADIANA. 10 vols. Toronto: Grolier of Canada. illus. maps. (issued annually; o.p.)
R971 E561   Ryder GR2-3
    (1st ed. 1957; last printing 1977; o.s.i. 1983) Based on the earlier ENCYCLOPEDIA OF CANADA (6 vols, Univ. Associates of Canada, 1st ed. 1935-37). AI31 is in popular style, covers Canada's political, economic development, geography, flora and fauna; many articles about people and places. Atlas in vol. 10; no index.

AI23   THE CANADIAN ENCYCLOPEDIA. 3 vols. Edmonton: Hurtig Publishers. forthcoming, Fall 1985. illus. maps.
    In preparation since 1980; this encyclopedia contains some 8000 articles on a broad range of topics, including biography, with 300 maps; cross references and index. Written for a family audience. Subsidized by the Alberta govt as part of the province's 75th anniversary celebrations. First ed. will not be reprinted; Hurtig proposes a rev. ed. (about 20% of the text rewritten or updated) every three years. A French ed. proposed for 1987.

AI24   ENCYCLOPEDIA OF NEWFOUNDLAND AND LABRADOR. 3 or 4 vols. projected. Ed. in chief, Joseph P. Smallwood; Man. ed., Robert Du Pitt. St John's: Newfoundland Book Publishers, 1981-   In progress. b&w illus. maps.
F5403 E52
    (Vol. 1 A-E {1981}). Replaces THE BOOK OF NEWFOUNDLAND (6 vols, Newfoundland Book Pub., 1937-75). Written primarily by a group of major contributors with recourse to consultants, numerous archival and other resources. Population figures current to 1976. The topics are alphabetically arranged; cross references, no index planned.

AI25   ENCYCLOPEDIA OF ONTARIO. 7 vols. Ed. and comp. by Nick Mika, and Helma Mika. Belleville, Ont.: Mika Publishing, 1974-   In progress. illus.
F5512 M55 (vol. 1); F5501 P4   Ryder GR2-9
    Vol. I (1974) HISTORIC SITES OF ONTARIO. Vol. II (3 pts, 1977-83) PLACES IN ONTARIO covering their name origins and history. Proposed vols are: III: the people; IV: cultural life; V: transportation; VI: sports, and VII: a chronology.

AI26   ENCYCLOPEDIE DU QUEBEC: Un Panorama de la vie québécoise. 2 vols. Louis Landry, comp. Montreal: Les Editions de l'Homme. 1973.
F5453 L34   Ryder GR2-11
    Topics arranged in broad DDC; index in each vol.

Other Countries

AI27   THE CAMBRIDGE ENCYCLOPEDIA OF CHINA. Ed. by B. Hook. Cambridge: Cambridge Univ. Press, 1982. 492 p. illus. maps.
DS705 C35
    Emphasizes contemporary China in its economic, social, political structure. Good example of an authoritative, single vol. source. One of three titles in a recently instituted series, 'Cambridge Regional

Encyclopedias.' Other titles: THE CAMBRIDGE ENCYCLOPEDIA OF AFRICA (1981) (DT3 C35); THE CAMBRIDGE ENCYCLOPEDIA OF RUSSIA AND THE SOVIET UNION (1982) (DKC14C35).

AI28 KODANSHA ENCYCLOPEDIA OF JAPAN. 9 vols. Tokyo: Kodansha, 1983. illus. (Dist.: New York: Kodansha) SUPPLEMENT (forthcoming, 1985).
DS805K598

(1st ed., 1983) Entirely in English, with romanized and some ideographic Japanese. Presents Japan to the English-speaking world. Audience is the general, scholarly reader. Some 10 000 articles, varying in length, many signed, with bibliog. Vol. 9, the index, and text references lead from general to detailed explanation of topic. A suppl. planned to update articles, statistics.

AI29 ENCYCLOPEDIA OF UKRAINE. 5 vols. Ed. by Volodymyr Kubijovyc. Toronto: Univ. of Toronto Press, 1984- In progress. illus. maps.

Replaces UKRAINE: A CONCISE ENCYCLOPEDIA (Univ. of Toronto Press, 1963-71). Articles are short with essential information about the people, history, geography, economy and cultural heritage. Estimated at some 20 000 entries; arranged alphabetically and intended as a principal reference for students of Slavs and Eastern Europe.

AI30 ENCYCLOPEDIA OF THE THIRD WORLD. 3 vols. Rev. ed. Ed. by George T. Kurian. New York: Facts on File, 1982. illus. maps.
HC59.7 K87

(1st ed., 1978) Information is current to 1981 on 122 developing countries of Africa, Australasia, island nations, excluding China and Taiwan. Information on politics, economics, society and a miscellany of topics (students, tourism, poverty, treaties with the U.S.) with a "fact box" for ready reference. (Cf. FACTS ON FILE, AH21; EUROPA, AH2; STATEMAN'S, AH3).

LANGUAGE DICTIONARIES

GUIDES AND BIBLIOGRAPHIES

AJ1   WORLD DICTIONARIES IN PRINT 1983: A Guide to General and Subject Dictionaries in World Languages. New York: R.R. Bowker, 1983. 450 p.

    Identifies some 20 000 dictionaries in English and all major languages. Includes special purpose lexicons, wordbooks, thesauri, uaage manuals, etymological and translations dictionaries plus the subject dictionaries (science, engineering, law, medicine etc.). Access by subject, language, title, indexes.

AJ2   DICTIONARIES, ENCYCLOPEDIAS AND OTHER WORD-RELATED BOOKS. 3d ed. Ed. by Annie M. Brewer. Detroit: Gale Research, 1981-82.
R030 AB47D

    Provides reproductions of LC shelflist cards; this ed. contains all entries in the 2d ed (1979) with some 3000 additional titles. Vol. 1 covers English language; vol. 2 is polyglot including English, and vol. 3 is foreign language works.

AJ3   Kister, Kenneth F. DICTIONARY BUYING GUIDE: A Consumer Guide to General English Language Wordbooks in Print. New York: R.R. Bowker, 1977. 358 p.
R423 AK61D

    Evaluates 58 adult, 50 school or children's dictionaries and 225 special wordbooks on etymology, use, slang, abbreviations etc.

ENGLISH DICTIONARIES

AJ4   THE OXFORD ENGLISH DICTIONARY. 13 vols. Oxford: Clarendon Press, 1933. SUPPLEMENT, 4 vols. In progress, 1972-
R423 O98E   Sheehy AD25

    The subtitle states that OED is a corrected re-issue of A NEW ENGLISH DICTIONARY ON HISTORICAL PRINCIPLES (10 vols, 1888-1928) (423 M98N) with SUPPLEMENT (1933). NED was "founded mainly on the materials collected by the Philological Society" edited by Sir James A.H. Murray and others. OED is the great scholarly dictionary of the English language, tracing its development from 1150 to publication date. Definitions are supported with dates and almost 2 million quotations from 5000 authors. The present supplement, about 60 000 words, is a major addition in 4 vols. (3 vols pub. to 1982; vol. 4 forthcoming.) THE COMPACT EDITION (2 vols, 1971) is a mini-print edition.

AJ5   THE SHORTER OXFORD DICTIONARY ON HISTORICAL PRINCIPLES. 3d ed. completely reset with etymologies rev. and rev. addenda. 2 vols. Oxford: Clarendon Press, 1973.
R423 M98S3   Sheehy AD28

    The authorized abridgement of the OED; it has two thirds of the vocabulary with shortened definitions and many fewer quotations. Includes in the new addenda material also used for the new supplement.

AJ6   THE CONCISE OXFORD DICTIONARY OF CURRENT ENGLISH. 7th ed. Ed. by J.B. Skyes. Oxford: Clarendon Press, 1982. 1264 p.

    This ed. updates the extensive revision, based on OED and its supplements, done for the 6th CONCISE (1976). A descriptive dictionary, but with two new marks in the 7th ed., a "D" for disputed words and an "R" for words which might offend some ethnic or religious group. THE OXFORD ILLUSTRATED DICTIONARY (2d ed., 1975) (R423 O98) is an encyclopedic dictionary based on the CONCISE.

AJ7 THE LONGMAN DICTIONARY OF CONTEMPORARY ENGLISH. London: Longman, 1978. 1303 p.
PE1628 L64
Describes spoken English, using phonetic alphabet, controlled vocabulary and examples for over 55 000 entries. For people who use English as a second, or foreign, language. Complemented by THE LONGMAN DICTIONARY OF ENGLISH IDIOMS (1979) (PE1460 L65) which explains some 1000 idioms (or clichés) in use in Great Britain.

AMERICAN DICTIONARIES

AJ8 THE NEW CENTURY DICTIONARY AND CYCLOPEDIA. Rev. and enl. 12 vols. New York: Century, 1911.
423 C39   Sheehy AD5
Of interest as probably the most complete dictionary, after the OED, of the English language to the time of publication. Vol. 11 is an atlas, containing the entries for proper names.

AJ9 WEBSTER'S THIRD NEW INTERNATIONAL DICTIONARY, UNABRIDGED: THE GREAT LIBRARY OF THE ENGLISH LANGUAGE. Springfield, MS: Merriam Webster, 1981. 2728 p.
R423 W38N3 (1961)   PE1625.W3   Sheehy AD9
Noah Webster's AN AMERICAN DICTIONARY OF THE ENGLISH LANGUAGE (1828) was the early significant progenitor of AJ9, called WEBSTER'S NEW INTERNATIONAL in the 1909 edition. The second ed. (1934) (R423 W38N2) was reprinted many times. It includes words in use from 1500, with obsolete and seldom used words at the bottom of the page. It has several appendices, was more encylopedic and more helpful for usage and pronunciation than WEBSTER'S THIRD NEW INTERNATIONAL DICTIONARY OF THE ENGLISH LANGUAGE (1961). This 1961 ed., called simply Webster's III or Third, featured new words but with fewer entries than the 2d ed., partly because it excludes words obsolete before 1775; it also has long with many shades of meaning and variant pronunciation. Labels are used less frequently to indicate usage. Some new words, and older words not in III, appear in 6000 WORDS: A SUPPLEMENT TO WEBSTER'S THIRD NEW INTERNATIONAL (1976) (R423 W38N3). Latest illustrated ed. has some 460 000 entries, usage examples, simplified pronunciation key and etymologies.
Most major, unabridged dictionaries have one or more "College" editions in print. WEBSTER'S NEW COLLEGIATE DICTIONARY (1981) is the 8th in the Webster's series. It has over 150 000 entries, including 20 000 new words, with usage examples. The 7th ed. (1976) had fewer words; with sections for biographical names, geographical locations.

AJ10 AMERICAN HERITAGE DICTIONARY OF THE ENGLISH LANGUAGE. Ed. by William Morris. Boston: American Heritage Pub. Co., 1969. 1550 p.
R423 A512H   PE1625 A54   Sheehy AD12
A standard with later printings, from which the college editions and THE CONCISE AMERICAN HERITAGE DICTIONARY (Houghton Mifflin, 1981) derive. Indicates informal, non-standard or slang forms. THE AMERICAN HERITAGE DICTIONARY: SECOND COLLEGE EDITION (Houghton Mifflin, 1982) (PE1625 A54) is an encyclopedic, illustrated dictionary with place and

proper names, a style manual, articles on language, biographical list and list of American colleges.

AJ11 FUNK & WAGNALLS NEW COMPREHENSIVE INTERNATIONAL DICTIONARY OF THE ENGLISH LANGUAGE. 2 vols. Newark, NJ: Publishers International, 1982.
PE1625 F77
Copious encyclopedic material is added to this revision of FUNK & WAGNALLS NEW (INTERNATIONAL) STANDARD ... (1964) (R453 F98N192). An unabridged, illustrated dictionary arranged according to current principles, i.e. contemporary, common definition given first. Explanations for each word are brief; pronunciation given. Appended material includes atlas, quotations list, articles on U.S. political history; world's population and religions, business letter writing.

AJ12 OXFORD AMERICAN DICTIONARY. Comp. by E. Ehrlich and others. New York: Oxford Univ. Press, 1980. 816 p.
PE2835 O9
Not intended as comprehensive; short definitions, simplified pronunciation with some help for determining correct American usage. Includes slang, informal, technical words, phrases, geographical place names for U.S. and Canada.

AJ13 THE RANDOM HOUSE DICTIONARY OF THE ENGLISH LANGUAGE. New York: Random House, 1966. 2059 p.
R423 R192   PE1625 R3   Sheehy AD8
An encyclopedic dictionary with over 250 000 entries and a miscellany of geographical facts, an atlas, a manual of style and concise bilingual dictionaries for English with German, Italian, French and Spanish. A concise ed. issued in 1980. THE RANDOM HOUSE COLLEGE DICTIONARY (rev. ed, 1975) (R423 R1920) is a large desk dictionary, thumb indexed, with about 150 000 entries and featuring a "Bad Speller's" list.

AJ14 THE SECOND BARNHART DICTIONARY OF THE NEW ENGLISH. Ed. by C.L. Barnhart; S. Steinmetz, and R.K. Barnhart. Bronxville, NY: Barnhart/ Harper & Row, 1980. 520 p.
R423 B262D   PE1630 B3   Sheehy AD68, 2AD8
Completes, and continues practices of THE BARNHART DICTIONARY OF NEW ENGLISH SINCE 1963 (1973) (R423 B262D) which culled British, American, Canadian periodicals, books printed from 1963-1972 to select over 5000 new entries without adequate explanation or entrance in standard dictionaries. SECOND adds 5000 entries with etymologies for foreign terms and references to quotations. Excludes specialized technical or scientific terms, dialect, slang of limited use.

AJ15 THE WORLD BOOK DICTIONARY. 2 vols. Ed. by C.L. Barnhart and R.K. Barnhart. Chicago: Field Enterprises, 1983.
R423 W927   PE1625 W65   Sheehy AD24
Formerly THE WORLD BOOK ENCYCLOPEDIA DICTIONARY and compatible with WORLD BOOK ENCYCLOPEDIA (AI11) which carries supplementary words annually in WORLD BOOK YEAR BOOK. This frequently updated dictionary underwent major revision in 1976 to a basis in Thorndike Barnhart principles of graded dictionaries. It is comprehensive, and suitable for grades 4-12. Defines words for the age level at which they are encountered. No personal or geographical names.

Canadian Dictionaries

AJ16   THE GAGE CANADIAN DICTIONARY. Ed. by W. S. Avis, and others. Toronto: Gage Pub., 1983. 1313 p.
R423 D554CA   PE3235 B45   Ryder HU5-7, -8, -11
    Gage produces a set of graded dictionaries based on the U.S. Thorndike Barnhart series with the inclusion of Canadian words. There is a BEGINNING (1962): JUNIOR (1977); INTERMEDIATE (1979) and SENIOR (1973) (called College Rev. ed. in the U.S.). AJ16 revises the SENIOR under changed title. Earlier editions were titled, DICTIONARY OF CANADIAN ENGLISH; this is now the series title.

AJ17   FUNK & WAGNALLS STANDARD COLLEGE DICTIONARY. Rev. Canadian ed. Ed. by W.S. Avis. Toronto: Fitzhenry and Whiteside, 1983. 1590 p.
R423 F98S (1978)   PE1628.S586
    A encyclopedic desk dictionary, appr. 150 000 entries, based on AJ11, with Canadian words added.

AJ18   THE WINSTON DICTIONARY OF CANADIAN ENGLISH. Intermediate ed. Toronto: Holt, Rinehart and Winston, 1969. 844 p.
R423 W783   Ryder HU5-13, -12
    Designed for secondary grades; includes slang, idioms. In paper as THE COMPACT DICTIONARY OF CANADIAN ENGLISH (1970/ reprint, 1976). An elementary ed (1975) was designed for children in grades 4 to 6.

Children's Dictionaries

See entries for GAGE (AJ16) and WINSTON (AJ18) elementary, junior dictionaries.

AJ19   CANADIAN DICTIONARY FOR CHILDREN. Toronto: Collier Macmillan,1979.724 p.
                                                          Ryder HU5-6
    Coloured, illustrated, large type dictionary for children 8 to 12; closely based on the American ed., the MACMILLAN DICTIONARY FOR CHILDREN (1977).

Canadian French Dictionaries

AJ20   Bélisle, Louis-Alexandre. DICTIONNAIRE NORD-AMERICAN DE LA LANGUE FRANCAISE AU CANADA. Montreal: Beauchemin, 1979. 1196 p.
R447.971 B431   PC3637 B4   Ryder HU5-17
    Earlier editions titled DICTIONNAIRE GENERALE DE LA LANGUE FRANÇAISE AU CANADA. An illustrated, general French dictionary with some 8000 Canadianisms.

AJ21   Bergeron, Lèandre. DICTIONNAIRE DE LA LANGUE QUEBECOISE. Montreal: VLB Editeur, 1980. 574 p. SUPPLEMENT (1981).
                          PC3635 B47
    Large type and well-spaced entries extend the size of this general dictionary featuring words commonly found in a LAROUSSE or ROBERT but adding, with supplement, over 18 000 entries (including slang, phrases) that are distinctively French Canadian. THE QUEBECOIS DICTIONARY (Lorimer, 1982) (PC3635 B4713) is an abridged translation.

AJ22   DICTIONNAIRE CANADIEN: FRANCAISE ANGLAIS, ANGLAIS FRANÇAISE/ THE CANADIAN DICTIONARY: FRENCH ENGLISH, ENGLISH FRENCH. Concise ed. Ed. by J-P. Vinay. Toronto: McClelland and Stewart, 1962. 862 p.
          R443.2 D554   PC2640 D53   Ryder HU5-26
     About 40 000 words, intended as a general dictionary of Eng/ French with added Canadianisms. Lacks history; few scientific or technical terms. An expanded version with more emphasis on Canadian words and terms in preparation, no publication date announced.

European and Slavic Languages (Monolingual; Bilingual/ English)

AJ23   Dupré, Paul. ENCYCLOPEDIE DU BON FRANÇAIS DANS L'USAGE CONTEMPORAIN. Difficultés, subtilités, complexités, singularités. 3 vols. Paris: Editions de Trévise, 1972.
                              PC2640 D88   Sheehy AD295
     Some 10 000 words which pose problems of genre, use, spelling documented by opinions as found in major dictionaries, quotations.

AJ24   GRANDE DICTIONNAIRE ENCYCLOPEDIQUE LAROUSSE. 10 vols. Under the direction of C. Dubois, and others. Paris: Librarie Larousse, 1982- In progress.
                              PC2625.G7
     Last ed., GRANDE LAROUSSE DE LA LANGUE FRANÇAISE (7 vols, 1971-78).

AJ25   Robert, Paul. DICTIONNAIRE ALPHABETIQUE ET ANALOGIQUE DE LA LANGUE FRANÇAISE. 6 vols. Paris: Société du Nouveau Littré le Robert, 1966. SUPPLEMENT 1970.
                              PC2625 R55   Sheehy AD271
     Sponsored by the Academie Française; organized on historical principles with etymology and quotations. PETIT ROBERT (1977).

AJ26   TRESOR DE LA LANGUE FRANÇAISE XIXe-XXe SIECLE (1789-1960). Vols 1-7 under the direction of P. Imbs; Vol. 8- under the direction of B. Quemada. Paris: Centre nationale de la recherche scientifique, 1971- In progress.
                              PC2625 T74   Sheehy 1AD48, 2AD27

AJ27   HARRAP'S NEW STANDARD FRENCH AND ENGLISH DICTIONARY. 3 vols. Ed. by J.E. Mansion, and others. London: Harrap, 1972.
                              PC2640 H3   Sheehy AD277
     With a HARRAP'S NEW SHORTER ... (1 vol., 1974). Complemented by HARRAP'S ENGLISH FRENCH DICTIONARY OF SLANG AND COLLOQUISMS (1975).

AJ28   Grimm, Jacob, and Wilhelm Grimm. DEUTSCHES WÖRTERBUCH. 16 vols. Leipzig: Hirzel, 1854-1962.
                              PF3625.G7   Sheehy AD318, 2AD33
     The German equivalent of the OED. Revised, enlarged edition, 1965- In progress.

AJ29   DUDEN DAS GROSSE WÖRTERBUCH DER DEUTSCHEN SPRACHE. 6 vols. Under the direction of G. Drosdowski and others. Mannheim: Bibliographisches Institut, 1966-1981.
                              PF3625 G75

AJ30   HARRAP'S STANDARD GERMAN AND ENGLISH DICTIONARY: Part One: German English. 3 vols. Ed. by T. Jones. London: Harrap, 1963-74.
PF3640 H37   Sheehy AD330
Comprehensive for general use; has scientific terms. Part Two English German not published.

AJ31   LANGENSCHEIDT'S ENCYCLOPEDIC DICTIONARY OF THE ENGLISH AND GERMAN LANGUAGES. 2 pts in 4 vols. Berlin: Langenscheidt, 1962-75.
PF3640 L3   Sheehy AD332
In Roman type; emphasizes definitions over equivalent meanings. A LANGENSCHEIDT'S CONDENSED MURET SANDERS GERMAN DICTIONARY (1982) covers everyday current language, specialized terminology from all major fields translating from German to American/ British Englisn.

AJ32   OXFORD DUDEN PICTORIAL GERMAN ENGLISH DICTIONARY. Ed. by J.A. Pheby. New York: Oxford Univ. Press, 1980. 960 p.
Sheehy 2AD35
A general technical dictionary based on the DUDEN BILDWÖTERBUCH; complements standard dictionaries. Explains, by illustration, daily and technical activities. (English lang. ed.: OXFORD DUDEN PICTORIAL ENGLISH DICTIONARY 1981)

AJ33   Academia Española. DICCIONARIO DE LA LENGUA ESPANOLA. 19th ed. Madrid: Espasa Calpe, 1970. 1970.
PC4625 A35   Sheehy AD636
A standard for use, etymology.

AJ34   AMERICANISMOS DICCIONARIO ILUSTRADO SOPENA. Barcelona: Editorial Ramon Sopena, 1983. 670 p.
PC4822 A59
Encyclopedic approach to words from politics, culture, history, geography of Hispanic America; organized by country with sections for native peoples.

AJ35   THE CAMBRIDGE ITALIAN DICTIONARY. 2 vols. Under the direction of B. Reynolds. Cambridge: Univ. Press, 1962-81.
R453.2 C178   PC1640 R4   Sheehy AD450
Vol. 1, Italian English (1962); vol. 2, English Italian (1981). Extensive dictionary of words, terms, phrases to help Eng. speakers in Italian expression. Follows principle of translational equivalence, but lacks pronunciation, labelling of irregular verbs and other common aids.

AJ36   ENGLISH ITALIAN, ITALIAN ENGLISH DICTIONARY. Under the direction of Malcolm Skey. New York: Oxford Univ. Press, 1981. 1890 p.
An adaptation of DIZIONARIO INGLESE ITALIANO, ITALIANO INGLESE (4th ed., 1981); with English based on the ADVANCED LEARNERS DICT. OF CURRENT ENGLISH (Oxford, 1963). Emphasis is on current language, idioms and phrases; has technical and scientific terms.

Russian Language

AJ37   Galperin, I.R. BOLSHOI ANGLO RUSSKII SLOVAR/ NEW ENGLISH RUSSIAN DICTIONARY. 2 vols. Moscow: Sovetskaia entsiklopediia, 1972.
        PG2640 G3   Sheehy AD591
    Intended for Russians reading English, but useful to English students of Russian. Emphasizes modern idiom; marks stress.

AJ38   Katzner, Kenneth. ENGLISH RUSSIAN, RUSSIAN ENGLISH DICTIONARY. New York: John Wiley, 1984. 904 p.
        PG2640 K34
    Based on American English, with all explanations in English. Information on verbs, declensions; glossary of proper names.

Chinese Language

AJ39   THE PINYIN CHINESE ENGLISH DICTIONARY. Under the direction of Wu Jingrong. New York: Wiley, 1982. 976 p.
PL1455H34 (1979)   Sheehy 2AD21
    Prepared by the Beijing Foreign Languages Institute, and first published in Hong Kong (Commercial Press, 1979), this dictionary gives all lexical units in characters and official romanization.

Semitic Languages

AJ40   Alcalay, Reuben. THE COMPLETE HEBREW ENGLISH DICTIONARY. 4 vols. Tel Aviv: Massadah Publishing, 1959-61.
        PJ4833 A45   Sheehy AD382

AJ41   Wehr, Hans. A DICTIONARY OF MODERN WRITTEN ARABIC. Ed. by J. Milton Cowan. Trans. from the German. 4th ed. Wiesbaden: Otto Harrassowitz, 1979. 1110 p.

Classical Languages

AJ42   A GREEK ENGLISH LEXICON. Comp. by H.G. Liddell and R. Scott. New ed. rev. by H. Jones. 2 vols. Oxford: Clarendon Press, 1940. SUPPLEMENT 1968.
        PA2365 E5088

AJ43   OXFORD LATIN DICTIONARY. Ed. by P.G.W. Glare. New York: Oxford Univ. Press, 1982. 2126 p.
    A one vol. ed. of OXFORD LATIN DICTIONARY, in 8 fascicles, 1968-1982 which replaces the older standard LATIN DICTIONARY (1879/ reprints: variant title) (R473.2 L673) of C.T. Lewis and C. Short; follows the format of the OED examining classical Latin from its beginnings to second century A.D., excluding Christian latin.

SPECIAL DICTIONARIES

Etymology (See also Eponyms and Names, AJ63-AJ64)

AJ44   Klein, Ernest. A COMPREHENSIVE ETYMOLOGICAL DICTIONARY OF THE ENGLISH LANGUAGE. Dealing with the Origin of Words and Their Sense Development Thus Illustrating the History of Civilization and Culture. 2 vols. Amsterdam: Elsevier, 1966-67. (Re-issue/ 1 vol. ed., 1971).
R422 K64
    Has scientific, technical terms and proper names.

AJ45   THE OXFORD DICTIONARY OF ENGLISH ETYMOLOGY. Oxford: Clarendon Press, 1966. 1024 p.
R422 O98
    A standard reference; some emphasis on humanities.

Pronunication

AJ46   BBC PRONOUNCING DICTIONARY OF BRITISH NAMES. 2d ed. Ed. by G.E. Pointon. London: Oxford Univ. Press, 1983. 274 p.
PE1660 B3

AJ47   Lass, Abraham H. DICTIONARY OF PRONUNCIATION. New York: Quadrangle, 1976. 334 p.
PE1137 L38

Usage

AJ48   Fowler, H.W. A DICTIONARY OF MODERN ENGLISH USAGE. 2d ed. Rev. by E. Powers. Oxford: Clarendon Press, 1965. 725 p.
R428 F78D3
    Opinion on the use, spelling, pronunciation, meaning of common words; many comparisons of Eng. and American use.

AJ49   Follett, Wilson. MODERN AMERICAN USAGE: A GUIDE. New York: Hill & Wang, 1966. 436 p.
R425 F667
    American counterpart of AJ48.

AJ50   THE OXFORD GUIDE TO ENGLISH USAGE. Comp. by E.S.C. Weiner. London: Oxford Univ. Press, 1984. 577 p.
PE1628 O87
    Combines THE OXFORD MINIDICTIONARY (1984) with short essays on language ("inflated" diction; English overseas) and guide including word formation, pronunciation, grammar, vocabulary, punctuation.

Synonyms

AJ51   Roget, Peter M. THESAURUS OF ENGLISH WORDS AND PHRASES. New rev. ed. London: Longmans, 1982. 1247 p.
R424 R73T4 (1962 ed.)   PE1591 M37   Sheehy AD100
    In a 'Roget' thesaurus words are without definition, usually arranged in classified in classified list of ideas under broad headings, such as time and space, with subdivisions. Alphabetic word

index. Many editions and versions available, e.g. ROGET'S II: THE NEW THESAURUS (American Heritage, 1980). Some editions, like WEBSTER'S COLLEGIATE THESAURUS (Merriam, 1976) or THE NEW ROGET'S THESAURUS OF THE ENGLISH LANGUAGE ... (1978) re-arrange the entries alphabetically, and as in WEBSTER'S, add antonyms and a brief definition of the word.

AJ52   WEBSTER'S NEW DICTIONARY OF SYNONYMS. A Dictionary of Discriminated Synonyms with Antonyms, Analogous and Contrasted Words. Springfield, MS: Merriam, 1968. 909 p.
R424 W38D1
Differentiates synonyms with illustrations from literature.

Regional and Dialect

AJ53   A DICTIONARY OF AMERICAN ENGLISH ON HISTORICAL PRINCIPLES. Comp. by Sir William A. Craigie, and James R. Hulbert. 4 vols. Chicago: Univ. of Chicago Press, 1938-44.
R427.973 C886   Sheehy AD105
A companion set to the OED; its purpose is to distinguish American English from English elsewhere. Included are words and phrases clearly of American origin; connected with the history of the U.S. or having greater currency in the U.S. Quotations, in chronological order, trace the history of a word from its earliest use in the colonies to 1900. (See related title AJ54)

AJ54   A DICTIONARY OF AMERICANISMS ON HISTORICAL PRINCIPLES. Ed. by Mitford M. Matthews. Chicago: Univ. of Chicago Press, 1951. 1946 p.
R427.973 D554   Sheehy AD106
Supplements AJ53. From early printed U.S. sources to 1950, AJ54 gathers words and expressions added to English in the U.S.; also lists words for which new meanings have evolved. An abridged ed. (1966).

AJ55   A DICTIONARY OF CANADIANISMS ON HISTORICAL PRINCIPLES. Dictionary of Canadian English. Toronto: Gage, 1967. 926 p.
R427 971 D554   Ryder HU5-10
Produced at the Univ. of Victoria "to provide a historical record of words and expressions characteristic of the various spheres of Canadian life," with illustrations, explanation, meaning, etymology. A CONCISE DICTIONARY OF CANADIANISMS (1973) omits bibliographies and adds no new words.

AJ56   DICTIONARY OF NEWFOUNDLAND ENGLISH. Ed. by G.M. Story; W.J. Kirwin, and J.D.A. Widdowson. Toronto: Univ. of Toronto Press, 1982. 625 p.
PE3245.N4D5
Based on OED principles; words, phrases are documented with a discussion of sources; introd. on English in Newfoundland.

AJ57   Bergeron, Lèandre. DICTIONNAIRE DE LA LANGUE QUEBECOISE. (AJ21)

Idioms and Slang

AJ58   Berrey, L.V., and M. Van den Bark. THE AMERICAN THESAURUS OF SLANG. 2d ed. New York: Crowell, 1953. 1272 p.
R427.09 B533   Sheehy AD87
Expressions categorized by topic, type of slang, e.g. underworld, military. Alphabetic word index.

AJ59   Wentworth, Harold, and Stuart B. DICTIONARY OF AMERICAN SLANG. 2d ed. New York: Crowell, 1975. 766 p.
R427 0973 W478   Sheehy AD93
Comprehensive, alphabetical list with classified lists appended. In two parts; a basic (earlier) vol. with supplements for added terms.

AJ60   Partridge, Eric H. A DICTIONARY OF SLANG AND UNCONVENTIONAL ENGLISH: Colloquialisms and Catch-Phrases, Solecisms and Catachreses, Nicknames, Vulgarisms and Such Americanisms as Have Been Naturalized. 2 vols. 7th ed. London: Routledge, 1970.
R427.09 P275   Sheehy AD91
Originally designed as companion to OED. Partridge has compiled several specialized dictionaries, e.g. A DICTIONARY OF THE UNDERWORLD, BRITISH AND AMERICAN (1963), A DICTIONARY OF CATCH PHRASES (1977), A DICTIONARY OF CLICHES (5th ed., 1978).

AJ61   PICTURESQUE EXPRESSIONS: A THEMATIC DICTIONARY. Ed. by Nancy Laroche. Detroit: Gale Research, 1983. 500 p.
Some 3000 expressions grouped under themes (bravery, escape etc.) with explanation of origin, with quotations, usage notes.

Suffixes

AJ62   -OLOGIES AND -ISMS: A THEMATIC DICTIONARY. 3 ed. Ed. by Laurence Urdang, and others. Detroit: Gale Research, 1983. 400 p.
PE1680 04 (1981)
Using common suffixes, AJ21 has over 5000 words, omitted or not easily accessible in standard dictionaries, arranged under themes covering ideas, actions, attributes. Alphabetic word index. A similar title, also edited by L. Urdang and others is SUFFIXES AND OTHER WORD FINAL ELEMENTS OF ENGLISH (Gale, 1982) which, for each word ending, gives examples, origin, meaning, use and variant.

Eponyms and Names

AJ63   EPONYMS DICTIONARIES INDEX: A Reference Guide to Persons both Real and Imaginary and to Terms Derived from Their Names. Ed. by James Ruffner, and others. Detroit: Gale Research, 1977. 730 0.
PE1596 E6
Lists about 20 000 words and the 13 000 persons upon which the word is based with citations to biographies and dictionaries.

AJ64 PSEUDONYMS AND NICKNAMES. 2d ed. Ed. by J. Mossman. Detroit: Gale Research, 1982. 995 p. NEW PSEUDONYMS AND NICKNAMES SUPPLEMENT, 1982- In progress (2 issues).
CT120 P8
Includes figures from all walks of life. Entries furnish original and assumed names, birth and/or death dates, nationality and occupation with reference to some sources of additional information. Second of two supplements with cumulate the 1st supp. now in print.

Abbreviations (Guide; then Abbreviations)

AJ65 ABBREVIATIONS, ACRONYMS, CIPHERS AND SIGNS. Ed. by A.M. Brewer. Detroit: Gale Research, 1981. 323 p.
Reproduction of LC cards for some 900 titles in the area.

AJ66 ACRONYMS, INITIALISMS AND ABBREVIATIONS DICTIONARY, 1960- 3 vols, in 6 pts. Ed. by E.T. Crowley. Detroit: Gale Research. irregular. Vol. 2; inter-edition supplement.
R421.8 R452R   PE1693 G3; PE1680 O4
(8th ed., 1982). Vol. 1, 2 pts, is the base vol. emphasizing American material with terms from Britain, France, Germany, Russia and other countries. Contains some 250 000 short forms etc in alphabetical sequence. Vol. 2, 2 pts, NEW ACRONYMS ... is the suppl. Vol. 3, 2 pts, REVERSE ACRONYMS ... arranges entry alphabetically by complete word or term with abbreviation following. (See related title AJ68)

AJ67 De Sola, R. NEW INTERNATIONAL ABBREVIATIONS DICTIONARY. 6th ed. New York: Elsevier/ North Holland, 1981. 966 p.
R421.8 D46A4   PE1693 D4
Long subtitle varies to show coverage, e.g. "Abbreviations, Acronyms, Anonyms, Appellations, Computer Terminology, Contractions, Criminalistic and Data Processing Terms; Eponyms, Geog. Equivalents, Historical, Musical, Mythological Characters, Initials, Nicknames, Short Forms, Shortcuts, Signs and Symbols, Slang, Superlatives, Winds of the World, Zip Codes, Zodiacal Signs."

AJ68 INTERNATIONAL ACRONYMS, INITIALISMS AND ABBREVIATIONS DICTIONARY: A Guide to Foreign and International Acronyms, Initialisms, Abbreviations, Contractions, Alphabetic Symbols and Similar Condensed Appellations in All Fields, 1984- Ed. by E.T. Crowley. Detroit: Gale Research. irregular. Inter-edition supplements.
(See related title AJ66)

AJ69 Pugh, Eric. THIRD DICTIONARY OF ACRONYMS AND ABBREVIATIONS: More Abbreviations in Management, Technology and Information Science. London: Clive Bingley, 1977.
R421 P978D3

AJ70 Rybicki, Stephen. ABBREVIATIONS: A REVERSE GUIDE TO STANDARD AND GENERALLY ACCEPTED ABBREVIATED FORMS. Ann Arbor, MI: Pierian Press, 1971. 334 p.
R421 R989A

Foreign Words and Phrases (Index, then Dictionaries)

AJ71　LOANWORDS INDEX. Ed. by Laurence Urdang. Detroit: Gale Research, 1983. 500 p.
　　　　　　　　　　　　PE1670 L6
　　Indexes 19 dictionaries for about 14 000 words assimilated into English from 80 languages; no definitions. Also lists words by lang.

AJ72　Bliss, Alan J. A DICTIONARY OF FOREIGN WORDS AND PHRASES IN CURRENT ENGLISH. London: Routledge, 1966. 389 p.
　　R422.4 B649　　　　PE1670 B55

AJ73　Guinagh, Kevin. DICTIONARY OF FOREIGN PHRASES AND ABBREVIATIONS. 3d ed. New York: H.W. Wilson, 1982. 288 p.
　　R418 G964　　　　P361 G8

AJ74　Mawson, C.D.S. DICTIONARY OF FOREIGN TERMS. 2d ed. Rev. by C. Berlitz. New York: Crowell, 1975. 368 p.
　　R422.4 M462D2　　　PEI670 M3

Symbols

AJ75　Arnstein, Joel. THE INTERNATIONAL DICTIONARY OF GRAPHIC SYMBOLS. London: Kogan Page, 1983. 239 p.
　　　　　　　　　　　　AZ108 A75
　　Excludes pottery, silvermarks and trademarks, but includes other symbols frequently encountered in domestic, everyday and technical fields. National and international symbols. Arranged by broad fields.

AJ76　Dreyfuss, Henry. SYMBOL SOURCEBOOK: AN AUTHORITATIVE GUIDE TO INTERNATIONAL GRAPHIC SYMBOLS. New York: McGraw Hill, 1972. 292 p.
　　R001.56 D77S　　　AZ108 D74
　　Tables of symbols arranged by subject. Contents page in 18 languages; subject index.

AJ77　Shepherd, Walter. SHEPHERD'S GLOSSARY OF GRAPHIC SIGNS AND SYMBOLS. London: J.M. Dent, 1971. 597 p.
　　R001.56 S548S　　　AZ108 S53
　　Many signs in a broad range of subject. Subject index.

ATLASES, MAPS AND RELATED MATERIALS

For additional coverage of cartography and geography, see Earth Sciences, DG, and Astronomy, DD. Atlases on biblical lands are under the Bible subsection in Literature, BD; see also the Atlas subsection in History, CJ.

GUIDES

AK1 Farrell, Barbara, and Aileen Desbarats. GUIDE FOR A SMALL MAP COLLECTION. Ottawa: Association of Canadian Map Libraries, 1981. 88 p.
025.176 F245G
Covers collection assessment and planning; reviews materials, sources, technical services and reference work. No index.

AK2 Kister, Kenneth F. KISTER'S ATLAS BUYING GUIDE: A CONSUMER'S GUIDE TO MAJOR ATLASES IN PRINT. 3 vols. Phoenix, AZ: Oryx, forthcoming 1983-(85).
Provides a description, evaluation of item, with reference to other reviews. Vol. 1: WORLD ATLASES (1983) with additional vols on national and regional atlases, thematic atlases.

AK3 Nicholson, N.L., and L.M. Sebert. THE MAPS OF CANADA: A GUIDE TO OFFICIAL CANADIAN MAPS, CHARTS, ATLASES AND GAZETTEERS. Hamden, CT: Archon/ Shoe String Press, 1981. 251 p.
R912.71 N627M   GA473.7 A1N53 MAPL
A comprehensive survey and historical guide to official map and chart series. Arranged by series; with a section on important provincial map series.

BIBLIOGRAPHIES AND LIBRARY CATALOGUES

AK4 INTERNATIONAL MAPS AND ATLASES IN PRINT. 2d ed. New York: R.R. Bowker, 1976. 866 p.
R912 A161612   Z6021 I596 MAPL   Sheehy 1CL47
Guide to over 8000 maps, atlases; arranged geographically. Dated, but addresses of European map dealers still of use.

AK5 BIBLIOGRAPHIA CARTOGRAPHICA: INTERNATIONAL DOCUMENTATION OF CARTOGRAPHICAL LITERATURE, 1974- Munich: K.G. Saur. irreg. annual. (Dist.: Shoe String Press).
Z6021 B5 BMER
(Vol. 9, 1982 {1983}). Title, publisher varies. Earlier vols, 1-30, cover a span from 1936-1972. Covers applications, history, theory of cartography. Based on entries from national organizations; essential for large map libraries (over 100 000 maps) or libraries supporting a cartography courses. Recent periodical article citations. Subject list; items from primarily English, German, French sources.

AK6 CATALOGUE OF PUBLISHED MAPS/ CATALOGUE DES CARTES PUBLIEES. 13th ed. Ottawa: Survey and Mapping Branch, Dept of Energy, Mines and Resources, 1974. 362 p.
R912 AC212   Ryder SS5-91
A listing, with description, of maps available from the Canada Map Office. From May, 1978- an ALPHABETIC and NUMERIC MAP CATALOGUE is issued on microfiche, monthly.

AK7   Library of Congress. A LIST OF GEOGRAPHICAL ATLASES IN THE LIBRARY OF CONGRESS. 8 vols. Washington: Library of Congress, 1909-74.
Z6028.U54 MAPL   Sheehy CL185, 1CL50
   Vol. 1 lists atlases held at LC to 1909; vol. 2 is an author and analytical index; vol. 3 is a supplement, 1909-1914, with indexes; vol. 4, 1914-1920, with indexes. Vol. 5 (1958) describes world atlases received at LC 1920-1955, with author list and index. Vol. 6 (1963) covers atlases of Europe, Asia, Africa, Oceana and the Polar regions, 1920-1960. Vol. 7 (1973) covers North and South America. Vol. 8 is the index. Entries give full information with contents notes.

AK8   Library of Congress. National Union Catalog. CARTOGRAPHIC MATERIALS, 1983- Washington: Library of Congress. quarterly; annual cum. microfiche.
   Arrangement is a register of full records with five indexes (name, title, subject, series, geographic classification codes); the indexes cumulative through the years, i.e. the 1984 index provides access to both the 1983 and 1984 register. Records all single and multi-sheet thematic map sets, atlases and maps treated as serials by LC. Only LC MARC records included; the records of other institutions to be added at a future date.

AK9   Public Archives of Canada. NATIONAL MAP COLLECTION CATALOGUE/ CATALOGUE DE LA COLLECTION NATIONALE DE CARTES ET PLANS. 16 vols. Boston: G.K. Hall, 1976.
Z6028.N384   Ryder SS5-92
   Almost 98 000 catalogue cards reproduced in area, author, subject sections. Represents less than 15% of the collection (in 1976). The Archives have published other subject catalogues of the holdings of Canadian and international maps and atlases, e.g. COUNTY ATLASES OF CANADA (1970) (912.71 AM466).

DIRECTORIES TO COLLECTIONS

AK10   WORLD DIRECTORY OF MAP COLLECTIONS. IFLA Publication, no. 8. Munich: Verlag Dokumentation, 1976. 326 p. (Dist.: UNIPUB)
GA192 W67 MAPL
   Lists over 280 collections in 45 countries. In addition to directory information, it notes subject and chronological range of collection, classification scheme, publications, etc.

AK11   MAP COLLECTIONS IN THE UNITED STATES AND CANADA: A DIRECTORY. 3d ed. New York: Special Libraries Association, 1978. 230 p.
026.912 S74M2   Sheehy CL197

AK12   DIRECTORY OF CANADIAN MAP COLLECTIONS. 4th ed. Compiled by Lorraine Dubreuil. Ottawa: Association of Canadian Map Libraries, 1980. 144 p.
026.912 D598M   Ryder SS5-95

ATLASES

International

AK13   THE CAMBRIDGE PHOTOGRAPHIC ATLAS OF THE PLANETS. (See DD25)

AK14   THE TIMES ATLAS OF THE WORLD. 2d rev. ed. New York: Times Books, 1983.
                         G1021.T55 1980 GENR MAPL Sheehy CL53
     The (London) Times Atlas prepared in its "comprehensive" format by John Bartholomew & Sons of Edinburgh. This edition revises the "6th comprehensive" (1980). With maps on as large a scale as possible, this atlas is in 3 pts, a preliminary section (introductory text, thematic maps, various tables and assorted articles); a map section; an index. The condensed form is THE TIMES CONCISE ATLAS OF THE WORLD (1980).

AK15   THE TIMES ATLAS OF THE OCEANS. Ed. by Alastair Couper. New York: Van Nostrand Reinhold, 1983. 292 p.
                         G2800.T5S MAPL
     Maps and photos with text; 17 chapters and appendixes to cover all aspects of ocean research, resources, environment, uses and policies.

AK16   Goode, John Paul. GOODE'S WORLD ATLAS. 16th ed. Ed. by E.B. Espenshade, and J. Morrison. Chicago: Rand McNally, 1980. 384 p.
          R912 G647W2   G1019.G67 MAPL   Sheehy CL204
     A small, school and general reference atlas noted for accuracy and legibility; with maps of urban areas and a discussion of projections.

AK17   HAMMOND LARGE TYPE WORLD ATLAS. Rev. ed. Maplewood NJ: Hammond, 1981.
                         G1021.H2727 (1979 ed.) MAPL
     Intended for elementary school, but useful for the visually handicapped. Major administrative boundaries, cities, towns, lakes and rivers (but not roads) are indicated in this atlas and gazetteer.

AK18   NATIONAL GEOGRAPHIC ATLAS OF THE WORLD. 5th ed. Washington: National Geographic Society, 1981. 330 p.
          R912 N277 (1966)   G1019.N28 (1975) GENR MAPL   Sheehy 1CL54
     Primarily administrative maps; excellent gazetteer.

AK19   NEW OXFORD ATLAS. 3d rev. ed. London: Oxford Univ. Press, 1978. 202 p.
                         G1019.N493 MAPL   Sheehy CL55
     A metric atlas with topographic, administrative, thematic maps.

AK20   THE NEW INTERNATIONAL ATLAS. Chicago: Rand McNally, 1980.
          R912 R187I (1969 ed.)   G1019.R35S MAPL   Sheehy 2CL37
     Earlier editions called THE INTERNATIONAL ATLAS. A multilingual reference atlas with topographic and thematic maps plus maps of major urban areas.

Atlases with a National Emphasis (U.S. and Canada)

For regional atlases in Canada, consult Ryder SS5-12 to SS5-17. For economic atlases, see CB17 and CB18.

AK21   NATIONAL ATLAS OF THE UNITED STATES OF AMERICA. Washington: Geological Survey, 1970. 417 p.
                         G1200.U57 MAPL, GENR   Sheehy CL230
     "The 765 maps ... constitute a scientific presentation in cartographic format, of the principal characteristics of the country, including its physical features, historical evolution, economic activities, socio-cultural conditions, administrative subdivisions, and place in world affairs."

AK22   THE NATIONAL ATLAS OF CANADA. 4th ed. Ottawa: Published by the Macmillan Company of Canada in association with the Dept of Energy, Mines and Resources and Information Canada, 1974. 254 p.
R912 C211A4   G115.C356 MAPL, GENR   Ryder SS5-11
Title varies. French ed.: L'ATLAS NATIONAL DU CANADA. This edition originally issued as loose sheets in portfolio, by the Surveys and Mapping Branch, Dept of Energy, Mines and Resources. A thematic atlas with maps based on 1971 census and population statistics from 1961 census. (See also AK23).

AK23   CANADA GAZETTEER ATLAS. Toronto: Macmillan of Canada in cooperation with Energy, Mines and Resources and Supply and Services, 1980. 164 p.
GENR
French ed.: CANADA ATLAS TOPONYMIQUE (Guerin, 1980). A companion volume to the NATIONAL ATLAS OF CANADA (AK22). Concise informative introduction; 48 maps, mainly political and demographic. Gazetteer index of 30 000 names in two sections, populated places and physical features. Names in index are as on maps; names authorized in both languages are shown in both, and as authorized by provinces, territories.

AK24   ATLAS LAROUSSE CANADIEN. 2d ed. Quebec: Les Editions française, 1978. 160 p.
G1019.A85 MAPL
An international atlas for school, general reference with expanded section of topographic, thematic maps prinicipally of Eastern Canada. Limited coverage of other parts of the world.

AK25   THE ATLAS OF CANADA AND THE WORLD. Prepared under the direction of H. Fullard, B.M. Willett. Milwaukee, WI: G.P. Raintree, 1979. 184 p.
G1021.A75 MAPL, GENR
French ed.: LE GRAND ATLAS DU CANADA ET DU MONDE (Les Editions françaises, 1979). Similar to ATLAS LAROUSSE CANADIEN (AK24) but with fewer world thematic maps and a more pronounced bias toward Eastern Canada. The cartographic firm is Geo. Philip of the U.K. joined with juvenile book publisher to produce a typical school reference atlas.

GAZETTEERS

AK26   THE COLUMBIA LIPPINCOTT GAZETTEER OF THE WORLD. New York: Columbia Univ. Press, 1952. 2148 p. SUPPLEMENT 1962.
R910.3 C72   G103.L7 MAPL GENR   Sheehy CL56
A standard gazetteer, useful for older names.

AK27   THE TIMES INDEX GAZETTEER OF THE WORLD. London: The Times, 1965. 964 p.
R910.3 T583   G103.T5 MAPL GENR   Sheehy CL57
A guide to 345 000 place names, with coordinates and map key for places included in major atlases from Times.

AK28   WEBSTER'S NEW GEOGRAPHICAL DICTIONARY. Rev. ed. Springfield, MS: Merriam, 1980. 1568 p.
R910.3 W38 (1972 ed.)   G103.W45 (1977 ed.)   Sheehy CL61
Identifies, locates, gives pronunciation for Can., U.S. places.

AK29   GAZETTEER OF CANADA/ REPERTOIRE GEOGRAPHIQUE DU CANADA, 1952-   Ottawa: Permanent Committee on Geographical Names, Surveys and Mapping Branch, Dept of Energy, Mines and Resources. irregular. ADDITIONS AND CORRECTIONS, 195[?]-   annual.
R917.1 C21   Ryder SS5-68
   Published in parts with a separate vol. for each province and territory except Quebec (see AK30). Most volumes are in a second ed. Places are identified, located by description and coordinates.

AK30   REPERTOIRE TOPONYMIQUE DU QUEBEC. (1978) [Prepared by] La Commission de la toponymie. Quebec: Editeur officiel du Québec, 1979. 1200 p. SUPPLEMENT 1977-78 (an addenda); 1978-79.
              F5451.R48 MAPL, GENR   Ryder SS5-82
   Gazetteer for provinces other than Quebec represented in AK29. This gazetteer includes physical features, administrative regions and municipalities with general location, coordinates. Between main vol. and smaller supplements, some 80 000 approved names are listed.

Place Names

For regional, native place names, see Ryder SS5-72 to SS5-83.

AK31   Sealock, R.B.; M.M. Sealock, and M. Powell. BIBLIOGRAPHY OF PLACE-NAME LITERATURE: UNITED STATES AND CANADA. 3d ed. Chicago: American Library Association, 1982. 436 p.
R929.4 AS43B3   Z6824.S4   Sheehy CL120

AK32   Hamilton, William B. THE MACMILLAN BOOK OF CANADIAN PLACE NAMES. Toronto: Macmillan of Canada, 1978. 340 p.
R917.1003 H222M   Ryder SS5-69
   The origin of about 1800 place names arranged alphabetically by province. Largely replaces ORIGIN AND MEANING OF PLACE NAMES IN CANADA by G.H. Armstrong (Macmillan, 1930) (R917.1 A735).

AK33   Harder, Kelsie B. ILLUSTRATED DICTIONARY OF PLACE NAMES: UNITED STATES AND CANADA. New York: Van Nostrand Reinhold, 1976. 631 p.
              E155.H37 MAPL GENR   Sheehy CL38

BIOGRAPHY

GENEALOGY AND HERALDRY (See also Ryder's section, HA-2)

AL1   Filby, P. William. AMERICAN AND BRITISH GENEALOGY AND HERALDRY: A SELECTED LIST OF BOOKS. 3d ed. Boston, MA: New England Historic Genealogical Society, 736 p.
        929.3 AF479 (1st ed., 1970)   Z5305 G7F55
        Much expanded over 2d ed. (ALA, 1976) with more entries for Canadian, international English language titles. About 9700 entries, cut-off date of 1981; general works, local histories.

AL2   Burke, John B. BURKE'S GENEALOGICAL AND HERALDIC HISTORY OF THE PEERAGE, BARONETAGE, AND KNIGHTAGE. 105th ed. London: Burke's Peerage, 1970. 3260 p.
        R929.7 B959 (104th ed.)   CS420.B85   Sheehy AK49
        Includes lineage of British royalty and nobility, tables of precedence and regulations about the wearing of decorations. One of several biographical publications by Burke's Peerage, e.g. BURKE'S LANDED GENTRY (R9929.72 B959).

AL3   DEBRETT'S PEERAGE AND BARONETAGE 1980: With Her Majesty's Royal Warrant Holders. Ed. by P. Montague-Smith. London: Debrett, 1979. 2336 p.
                    CS420.D32   Sheehy AK55, 1AK17
        Title and publisher vary; an annual until 1976. Contains information on the royal family, the peerage, Privy Counsellors, Scottish Lords of Session, baronets, Scottish chieftains. More concise listings than BURKE'S (AL2). DEBRETT'S annual until 1976. thereafter irregular. DEBRETT'S HANDBOOK is a Who's Who of England, Wales, Scotland, Northern Ireland.

AL4   Baxter, Angus. IN SEARCH OF YOUR ROOTS: A GUIDE FOR CANADIANS SEEKING THEIR ANCESTORS. Rev. ed. Toronto: Macmillan, 1980. 293 p.
                    CS16.B39   Ryder HA2-2
        A layman's introduction to producing family history, beginning with Canadian sources, but branching primarily to U.K. sources, with some information on U.S., Europe.

AL5   Public Archives of Canada. TRACING YOUR ANCESTORS IN CANADA. 7th ed. Ottawa: Supply and Services, 1983. 38 p.
        R929.10971 T759TA   Ryder HA2-3B
        French ed.: GUIDE DES SOURCES GENEALOGIQUES AU CANADA. A free pamphlet listing and describing, in general terms, the various federal and provincial archives, and other records (census, births, military, immigration) that are a basis for a genealogical search.

BIOGRAPHY - BIBLIOGRAPHIES

AL6   BIOGRAPHICAL BOOKS, 1876-1949. New York: R.R. Bowker, 1983. 1768 p.
        R920 AB582B
        Reproducing cataloguing information from ABPR (AD62), this work lists "virtually every biography published or distributed in the U.S." for the years stated. Autobiographies, letters, diaries, journals, collective biographies, etc. are alphabetically arranged in a name/ subject index containing some 16 500 names and 3500 LC subjects. Nearly comprehensive for U.S. trade publications.

AL7   BIOGRAPHICAL BOOKS, 1950-1980. New York: R.R. Bowker, 1982.
           Completes the coverage of AL6

AL8   Slocum, Robert B. BIOGRAPHICAL DICTIONARIES AND RELATED WORKS: AN INTERNATIONAL BIBLIOGRAPHY ... Detroit: Gale Research, 1967. 1056 p. FIRST SUPPLEMENT 1972; SECOND SUPPLEMENT 1978.
           R920 AS634   Sheehy AJ1, 1AJ1
           Lengthy subtitle explains that bibliography is compiled from collective biographies, bio-bibliographies, epitaphs, genealogical sources, dictionaries of anonyms and pseudonyms, government directories, indexes, portrait catalogs and other bibliographies. Entries are arranged into universal, national or area, vocational groups with author, title, subject indexes.

INDEXES

AL9   BIOGRAPHY INDEX: A CUMULATIVE INDEX TO BIOGRAPHICAL MATERIAL IN BOOKS AND MAGAZINES, 1946- New York: H.W. Wilson. quarterly; annual, triennial cumulations.
           (IND)   Sheehy AJ2
           An index to biographical material in current popular and scholarly books and journals mostly in the English language. Includes an index by profession and other groups.

AL10   BIOGRAPHY AND GENEALOGY MASTER INDEX. 2d ed. Ed. by Miranda C. Herbert, and Barbara McNeil. 8 vols. Detroit: Gale Research, 1980. SUPPLEMENT 1981-82 (1982); 1983 (2 vols, 1983).
           920.073 B615B (1st ed.) Z5305.U5B56   Sheehy 1AJ2
           First edition called BIOGRAPHICAL DICTIONARIES MASTER INDEX (1975-76) with SUPPLEMENT (1980). BDGI claims over 3 million citations gathered from more than 350 contemporary who's whos and other works of collective biography, including those listed in this note. The Gale Biographical Index Series, includes HISTORICAL BDI (1980); AUTHOR BDI (1978) with SUPPLEMENT (1980); JOURNALIST BDI (1979); PERFORMING ARTS BDI (2d ed., 1982); CHILDREN'S AUTHORS AND ILLUSTRATORS (3d ed., 1981); WRITERS FOR YOUNG ADULTS (1979).
           BIO-BASE (2d ed., 1981) (microfiche, with printed bibliog. of sources) is an index to nearly 4 million entries in biographical dictionaries. SUPPLEMENT forthcoming.

AL11   Hyamson, Albert M. A DICTIONARY OF UNIVERSAL BIOGRAPHY OF ALL AGES AND ALL PEOPLES. 2d ed. London: Routledge, 1962. 679 p.
           R920.3 H992   Sheehy AJ8
           Provides brief identification, as well as an index, to persons listed in 24 standard (retrospective) biographical works.

AL12   BIOGRAPHY ALMANAC. 2d ed. Ed. by Susan L. Stetler. 2 vols. Detroit: Gale Research, 1983. SUPPLEMENT (forthcoming).
           Covers over 23 000 "newsmakers" from Biblical times to the present. Vol. 1 alphabetically arranges brief biographies under popular name, with citations to sources. Vol. 2 arranges the biogs in various chronologies and in geographic regions. The suppl., covering over 2500 persons, revises entries and adds new entries for changes

resulting from prominence or death. Some overlap with volumes indexed in BGMI (AL10).

AL13   Riches, Phyllis M. AN ANALYTICAL BIBLIOGRAPHY OF UNIVERSAL COLLECTED BIOGRAPHY: Comprising Books Published in the English Tongue in Great Britain, Ireland, American and the British Domains. London: Library Association, 1934. 709 p. Reprint/ Gale Research, 1980.
R920 AR52   Sheehy AJ15
Of antiquarian interest; an alphabetical subject index to over 56 000 biographies in 3000 collective biographical works with chronological and subject or occupation indexes. Biographees are from B.C. to the 20th century before 1933.

AL14   Royal Commonwealth Society. BIOGRAPHY CATALOGUE OF THE LIBRARY OF THE ROYAL COMMONWEALTH SOCIETY. London: RCS, 1961. 511 p. (Dist. Gale).
R920.3 AR888   Sheehy AJ182
Indexes periodical articles and books in the library for information about persons living in the Commonwealth and those connected with British imperial affairs living elsewhere.

Obituaries -- Indexes and Annuals

AL15   THE NEW YORK TIMES OBITUARIES INDEX, 1858-1968. New York: New York Times, 1969. 1136 p.
R920.3 N532   Sheehy AJ25

AL16   OBITUARIES ON FILE. Comp. by Felice Levy. 2 vols. New York: Facts on File, 1979.
CT120 L43
Short notices culled from FACTS ON FILE (AH21) 1940 through 1978, arranged in one alphabetical sequence with chronological and subject (incl. vocational and geographical reference) indexes.

AL17   THE ANNUAL OBITUARY, 1980- Chicago: St James Press, 1983- annual; cum. index.
CT120 A55
Essays (from 500 to 3000 words), with photograph and bibliog. references, on prominent persons who died during the year. Entry is chronological within months. Alphabetical and profession indexes.

INTERNATIONAL BIOGRAPHICAL DICTIONARIES

AL18   BIOGRAPHIE UNIVERSELLE, ANCIENNE ET MODERNE. 2d ed. 45 vols. Paris: Desplaces, 1843-65. Reprint/ 10 vols. Graz: Akademische Druck-u Verlagsanstalt, 1966.
CT143.M5   Sheehy AJ17
Of historic interest, as a source of biographical information from all countries to original publication date.

AL19   CHAMBERS BIOGRAPHICAL DICTIONARY. Rev. ed. Edinburgh: Chambers, 1974. 1432 p.
R920.3 C976   CT103.C4
Provides bibliogs; a paperbound edition revised in 2 vols. (1976).

AL20   CURRENT BIOGRAPHY, 1940-   New York: H.W. Wilson. monthly; annual cum.; cum. index. INDEX 1940-1970 (1973).
R920.3 C976.
     Although international, coverage is primarily concerned with Americans. Includes information about appr. 400 people in public life, with portraits and bibliogs. Articles are verified by biographees before inclusion in annual vol. Has obituaries, which are generally short (cf AL17) and cites an earlier reference.

AL21   THE INTERNATIONAL DICTIONARY OF WOMEN'S BIOGRAPHY. Comp./ edited by Jennifer S. Uglow. New York: Continuum Pub., 1983. 534 p.
     Short biographies of about 1500 women throughout history.

AL22   THE INTERNATIONAL WHO'S WHO, 1935-   London: Europa. annual.
R920.3 I61   CT120.I5
     Brief information on prominent people in all fields. Europa also publishes, in irregular editions, regional titles, (WHO'S WHO IN LEBANON 1982/83 {1983}) or occupational titles, in 'The International Red Series' (see also AL25) (WHO'S WHO IN MEDICINE, 5th ed., 2 vols, 1981; ... IN TECHNOLOGY, 2d ed., 2 vols, 1983; ... IN THE ARTS AND LITERATURE, 3d ed., 4 vols, 1982; ... IN FASHION, 3 vols. 1982).

AL23   THE NEW YORK TIMES BIOGRAPHICAL SERVICE, 1970-   Ann Arbor, MI: University Microfilms International, 1984-   monthly.
CT120.N45
     Published by NY Times/ Arno Press until 1981, by Microfilming Corporation of America to 1983, then by UMI which also supplies back years. Name varies on binders as BIOGRAPHICAL EDITION; looseleaf compilation of newsworthy figures in the NY TIMES. Cum. name index.

AL24   WEBSTER'S BIOGRAPHICAL DICTIONARY. Springfield, MA: Merriam Webster, 1972. 1679 p.
R920.3 W38   CT103.W4
     Brief information on figures throughout history to early 20th century. Universal but intended for English speakers. Scant revision since first printing in 1943. Has useful lists of rulers, etc.

AL25   WHO'S WHO. The International Red Series. Wörthsee, West Germany: Who's Who Verlag. varying frequencies.
     Some titles in the series available under the Europa imprint (see AL22). The series, 18 titles to end of 1983, is published in English and has entries, in alphabetical order by name, for life and career history of prominent persons. Most editions have a subject index. The "National Editions" (WHO'S WHO IN GERMANY {2 vols, 8th ed., 1983}; WHO'S WHO IN ITALY {3d ed., 1980} etc.) are biennial; the "Special Editions" (see AL22n) are triennial.

AL26   WHO'S WHO IN EUROPEAN INSTITUTIONS AND ORGANIZATIONS, 1982- Wörthsee, West Germany: Who's Who Verlag. biennial.
     An "International Red Book Who's Who" (see AL25); appr. 3500 personalities in organizations, associations, European parliament etc.

AL27   WHO'S WHO IN THE WORLD, 1971/72-   Chicago: Marquis. biennial.
R920.3 W628W   CT120.W47
     (7th ed., 1984/85 {1984}). Represents all fields of endeavour, listing more than 24 000 biographees in brief sketches covering education, career, politics and special achievement.

AL28   WHO WAS WHO IN THE GREEK WORLD, 776 B.C.- 30 B.C. Ed. by Diana Bawder. Ithaca, NY: Cornell Univ. Press, 1982. 227 p.
   Companion to AL29; brief description, with bibliog., of over 750 persons, with 6 family trees, brief history, maps, glossary.

AL29   WHO WAS WHO IN THE ROMAN WORLD, 753 B.C. - A.D. 476. Ed. by Diana Bawder. Ithaca, NY: Cornell Univ. Press, 1980. 256 p.
   Companion to AL28; brief description, with bibliog., of over 900 prominent persons including non-Romans (e.g. rulers like Cleopatra) and early Christians (e.g. Paul). Has maps, photos, some family trees.

NATIONAL BIOGRAPHICAL DICTIONARIES

Great Britain

AL30   DICTIONARY OF NATIONAL BIOGRAPHY FROM EARLIEST TIMES TO 1900. 63 vols. London: Smith, Elder, 1885-1901. Reissued/ 22 vols. Oxford, 1963-64. SUPPLEMENT 1901-11; 1912-21; 1922-30; 1931-40; 1941-50; 1951-1960; 1961-70 (1981).
   R920.3 D55B2   Sheehy AJ165,AJ167
   The major British work, including important people in Great Britain, Ireland and the Commonwealth. Excludes living persons. Extensive bibliographies. Supplements have cumulative indexes. CORRECTIONS AND ADDITIONS 1923-1963 (G.K. Hall, 1966); THE COMPACT EDITION OF DNB TO 1960 (2 vols, 1975, miniprint).

AL31   THE CONCISE DICTIONARY OF NATIONAL BIOGRAPHY. 2 vols. London: Oxford Univ. Press, 1961.
   R920.3 D55C2
   Vol. 1 epitomizes the main work and first supplement; vol. 2 covers 1912 to 1950.

AL32   WHO'S WHO, 1849-   London: Black. annual
   R920.3 W62   DA28.W6   Sheehy AJ187
   Concise authoritative biographies of distinguished living Britons and international figures.

AL33   WHO WAS WHO. London: Black, 1961-   irregular decennial. Vol. 1, 1897-1915; Vol. 2, 1916-28; Vol. 3, 4th ed., 1929-40; Vol. 4, 3d ed., 1941-50; Vol. 6, 1961-70.
   R920.3 W62AW   DA28.W65
   These companion volumes to WHO'S WHO (AL22) include entries for deceased people, as they appeared in the original volumes with death dates and sometimes added or corrected information.

United States

AL34   NATIONAL CYCLOPEDIA OF AMERICAN BIOGRAPHY. Clifton, NJ: James T. White, 1892-   irregular.
   R920.3 AN27I5 (Index vols. 1-51) E176.N2814   Sheehy AJ43, AJ44
   A comprehensive dictionary from earliest days of American history but with emphasis after 1850. Includes over 60 000 biographees in two series, the "Permanent Series" on deceased people and the "Current Series" on the living. Revised INDEX VOLUME 1979 (R920.3 AN27I5) has a

subject, topical, name index to both series (71 vols in all) to 1979. A companion publication is NOTABLE NAMES IN AMERICAN HISTORY (1973) acting as a cross reference for individuals and institutions.

AL35   DICTIONARY OF AMERICAN BIOGRAPHY. 20 vols. New York: Scribner, 1928-77. 7 supplements cum. index. COMPLETE INDEX GUIDE TO VOLS I-X AND SUPPLEMENTS 1-7, 1981.
R920.3 D553   Sheehy AJ41
   The 7th supplement (1981) covers 1961-1965. Eligible for inclusion were deceased people who made a significant contribution to American life. The index volume includes a list of contributors with citations to their articles and an occupation index.

AL36   CONCISE DICTIONARY OF AMERICAN BIOGRAPHY. 3d ed. New York: Scribner's, 1980. 1333 p.
R920.3 D553C   E176.D564
   Includes 17 000 entries from original DAB through 1980 suppl.

AL37   WHO'S WHO IN AMERICA. A Biographical Dictionary of Notable Living Men and Women, 1899-   2 vols. Chicago: Marquis. biennial.
R920.3 W62AM   E663.W56
   Includes a wide range of Americans and some international figures. Four regional volumes (...IN THE EAST; ...WEST; ...MIDWEST; ...SOUTH AND SOUTHWEST) are also indexed in the main set. Volumes by profession (...IN GOVERNMENT, ...IN FINANCE AND INDUSTRY) or by designation (... OF AMERICAN WOMEN) also published. AN INDEX TO ALL BOOKS 1984 (2 vols, 1983) is an alphabetic, geographic aid to ten current Marquis biographies.

AL38   WHO WAS WHO IN AMERICA. Chicago: Marquis, 1942-   irregular. HISTORICAL Vol. 1607-1896; Vol. 1, 1897-1942; Vol. 2, 1943-50; Vol. 3, 1951-60; Vol. 4, 1961-68, subtitled WITH WORLD NOTABLES; Vol. 5, 1969-73; Vol. 6, 1974-76; Vol. 7, 1977-81. annual; cum. index. INDEX 1607-1981 (1981).
R920.3 W62AH   E663.W54

Canada (see also Ryder HA1)

AL39   DICTIONARY OF CANADIAN BIOGRAPHY. Ed. by Francess Halpenny. Toronto: Univ. of Toronto Press, 1965-   In progress. Vol. 1, 1000-1700; vol. 2, 1701-40; vol. 3, 1741-70; vol. 4, 1771-1800; vol. 5, 1801-1820; vol. 9, 1861-70; vol. 10, 1871-80; vol. 11, 1881-90. INDEX TO VOLS 1-4: 1000-1800 (1981).
R920.3 D554   Ryder HA1-11
   (Vol. 8, 1851-60, forthcoming Fall 1985). French ed.: DICTIONNAIRE BIOGRAPHIQUE DU CANADA (Presses de l'Univ. Laval) (R920.3 D554A) ed. by Jean Hamelin. Patterned on DNB, but departing from alphabetical arrangement, this major work of Canadian scholarship has volumes to organized to demonstrate social as well as biographical history from the year 1000 to its planned cut-off for biographees who died in/before 1900. Volumes cover a time span with entries alphabetically arranged within volume. Each vol. with index; separate INDEX is a cumulative name, with geographical, professional or other designation.

AL40   Morgan, Henry J. THE CANADIAN MEN AND WOMEN OF THE TIME: A Handbook of Canadian Biography of Living Characters. 2d ed. Toronto: William Briggs, 1912. 1218 p.
R920.3 M84C2   Ryder HA1-19
   This and first edition (1898) are important for coverage, often with portraits, for noteworthy persons of the late 1800's. Morgan's SKETCHES OF CELEBRATED CANADIANS (Hunter Rose, 1862) contains some 460 biographies of pre-Confederation Canadians in Upper Canada (Ontario) and Lower Canada (Quebec).

AL41   STANDARD DICTIONARY OF CANADIAN BIOGRAPHY. Ed. by Charles G.D. Roberts, and Arthur L. Tunnell. 2 vols. Toronto: Trans-Canada Press, 1934-38.
R920.3 S785   Ryder HA1-27
   Biographies, with bibliographies, of Canadians who died 1875-1937.

AL42   THE MACMILLAN DICTIONARY OF CANADIAN BIOGRAPHY. 4th ed. Ed. by W.A. McKay. Toronto: Macmillan, 1978. 914 p.
R920.3 M167   Ryder HA1-16
   Contains sketches (30 to 600 words) about more than 5000 noteworthy Canadians deceased before 1976. First edition (1926) and subsequent editions edited by W. Stewart Wallace. Fourth edition adds dimension of business, science, arts to the emphasis on authors, politicians, government people in the 3rd edition. In 4th ed., politics and government still account for about a third of the entries; with corrections to earlier entries and updated bibliographical references.

AL43   CREATIVE CANADA: A BIOGRAPHICAL DICTIONARY OF TWENTIETH CENTURY CREATIVE AND PERFORMING ARTISTS. 2 vols. Toronto: Univ. of Toronto Press, 1971-72.
R920.3 C912   Ryder HU1-10
   Compiled at the Univ. of Victoria Library, vols include about 1000 biographees, both then living or deceased, whether native-born or not, who have contributed to Canadian culture.

AL44   BIOGRAPHIES CANADIENNES FRANÇAISES, 1920-   Montreal: Editions BCF. irregular.
R920.3 B615B   F5452.B58   Ryder HA1-85
   Title varies. Last 26th edition, 1979-80. Portraits and short factual entries; parallel publication to AL46.

AL45   THE CANADIAN WHO'S WHO: With Which is Incorporated Canadian Men and Women of the Time: A Biographical Dictionary of Notable Living Men and Women, 1910-   Ed. by Kieran Simpson. Toronto: Univ. of Toronto Press, 1978-   annual.
R920.3 C21   F5009.C3   Ryder HA1-7
   Title, publisher and frequency varies. Within recent decade, it was issued triennially with 5 supplements (THE CANADIAN BIOGRAPHICAL SERVICE), and a pamphlet "Who's What in CANADIAN WHO'S WHO" (1981). Acquisition (1978) by the Univ. of Toronto Press ended the supplementary material, and established the freq. as annual with the 14th (1979) edition. Descriptions, with addresses, about the life, honours, profession, leisure interests of notable living Canadians. More than 7000 biographies in alphabetical order; entrants selected on the basis of merit or by virtue of their position.

AL46   WHO'S WHO IN CANADA, 1910-   Toronto: Global Press Division, Gage Pub., 1984-   biennial. illus.
R920.3 W62C   F5009.W62   Ryder HA1-30
   Title, subtitle and publisher varies. Portraits usually accompany the one page or so entries assigned to some 2000 biographees. Previously a random arrangement with name index, the 75th anniversary edition, 1984/85 uses an alphabetical listing and adds a corporate index listing the company with its principal officers and their titles.

AL47   WHO'S WHO OF CANADIAN WOMEN, 1984-   Ed. by Evelyn Davidson. Toronto: Trans-Canada Press, 1983-   annual. SUPPLEMENT (to 1st ed.) 1984
   Women in Canadian business, finance, law, media, government, the arts. Trans-Canada also publishes a WHO'S WHO IN CANADIAN BUSINESS, ... IN CANADIAN FINANCE, ... IN CANADIAN LAW.

AUTHORS (Additional information in Literature, BD)

AL48   Allibone, Samuel A. A CRITICAL DICTIONARY OF ENGLISH LITERATURE AND BRITISH AND AMERICAN AUTHORS: Living and Deceased from the Earliest Accounts to the Latter Half of the Nineteenth Century. 3 vols. Philadelphia: G.W. Childs, 1863-71. SUPPLEMENT 2 vols, 1891. Reprint/ 5 vols. Gale Research, 1965.
R820.9 A43A   Sheehy BD374,BD427
   Of historical interest. Biographical sketches list works with dates and excerpts from criticism. Includes many minor authors.

AL49   AUTHOR BIOGRAPHIES MASTER INDEX: A Consolidated Guide to Biographical Information Concerning Authors Living and Dead as It Appears in a Selection of Principal Biographical Dictionaries Devoted to Authors, Poets, Journalists and Other Literary Figures. Ed. by Dennis La Beau. 2 vols. Detroit: Gale Research, 1978. 1177 p. SUPPLEMENT 1980.
Z5304.A8A88
   Part of the 'Gale Biographical Index Series' (AL10) where information also appears in BGMI. ABMI plus suppl. indexes nearly 200 literary reference works to provide access to over 200 000 authors.

AL50   DICTIONARY OF LITERARY BIOGRAPHY. Detroit: Gale Research, 1978-   In progress
   Twenty-one volumes in this set available to Spring 1984, with an additional 3 in preparation. Each vol. or set (of 2 parts) in this multi-volume series covers a specific literary movement (Vol. 1, THE AMERICAN RENAISSANCE IN NEW ENGLAND, 1978), genre (Vol. 8, set of 2, TWENTIETH-CENTURY AMERICAN SCIENCE FICTION WRITERS, 1981) or period (Vol. 14, set of 2, BRITISH NOVELISTS SINCE 1960, 1983) follows a similar format. Alphabetically arranged essays have description of life and work, career chronology and references. DLB YEARBOOK (1980-) revises entries on included writers and adds newly prominent writers. A DLB: DOCUMENTARY SERIES (3 vols) reproduces samples of texts, literary documents pertaining to the author and reviews.

AL51   CONTEMPORARY AUTHORS: A Bio-bibliographical Guide to Current Writers in Fiction, General Nonfiction, Poetry, Journalism, Drama, Motion

Pictures, Television and Other Fields, 1962-   Detroit: Gale Research. Vol. 101, 1984-   annual; cum. index alternate years.
R920.3 C761C2   Z1224.C62
    Vols 1 - 100, with periodic cum. indexes, are issued in sets of 4, to cover the vol. year. Concise information on new and established authors, media personalities, mostly American. Has personal facts, career, full bibliography of works and comment on any work in progress. A "Permanent Series" issued for biographies of deceased or "no longer active" authors. A supplementary "New Revision Series" extracts information from main set on very active authors or ones for whom information is frequently needed.

AL52   CONTEMPORARY LITERARY CRITICS. 2d ed. Ed. by Elmer Borklund. Detroit: Gale Research, 1982. 600 p.
                    PN99 G72G5
    Bio-biographical information on 155 influential English language critics of the 20th century.

AL53   Magill, Frank N. CYCLOPEDIA OF WORLD AUTHORS. New York: Harper, 1958. 1198 p.
R803 M194W   PN41.M26
    Discusses the life and work of 750 authors represented in Magill's MASTERPIECES OF WORLD LITERATURE IN DIGEST FORM (R808.8 M194).

AL54   Grant, Michael. GREEK AND LATIN AUTHORS 800 B.C.-A.D.1000. New York: H.W. Wilson, 1980. 500 p.
    Earliest time span of the standard 'Wilson Author Series' (AL54 to AL61) with portraits, biographical and critical information, bibliog. on familiar Classical writers and their works. AN INDEX TO THE WILSON AUTHOR SERIES (1976) locates authors in the chronological series of titles available in the mid-70s.

AL55   Kunitz, Stanley H., and Vineta Colby. EUROPEAN AUTHORS, 1000-1900. 1967. 1016 p.
R920.3 K96E   Sheehy BD88

AL56   _____., and Howard Haycraft. AMERICAN AUTHORS, 1600-1900. 1938. 584 p.
R920.3 K96AM   Sheehy BD229

AL57   _____. BRITISH AUTHORS BEFORE 1800. 1952. 584 p.
R920.3 K96B   Sheehy BD429

AL58   _____. BRITISH AUTHORS OF THE NINETEENTH CENTURY. 1936. 677 p.
R920.3 K96B2   Sheehy BD430

AL59   _____. TWENTIETH CENTURY AUTHORS. 1942. 1577 p. SUPPLEMENT 1955
R920.3 K96T   Sheehy BD89, BD89a

AL60   Wakeman, John. WORLD AUTHORS, 1950-1970. 1975. 1593 p.
R920.3 K96TA   Sheehy BD89an

AL61   _____. WORLD AUTHORS, 1970-1975. 1979. 893 p.

Children's Authors

AL62 Kunitz, Stanley J., and Howard Haycraft. THE JUNIOR BOOK OF AUTHORS. 2d ed. New York: H.W. Wilson, 1951. 309 p.
   R920.3 K96J2   Sheehy BD300
       In the pattern of the 'Wilson Author Series' (see AL54 etc.) the series of children's authors is represented by AL62 to AL66.

AL63 Fuller, Muriel. MORE JUNIOR AUTHORS. 1963. 235 p.
   R920.3 F967   Sheehy BD301

AL64 de Montreville, Doris, and Donna Hill. THIRD BOOK OF JUNIOR AUTHORS. 1972. 320 p.
   R920.3 K96J3

AL65 _____, and Elizabeth Crawford. FOURTH BOOK OF JUNIOR AUTHORS AND ILLUSTRATORS. 1978. 370 p.
   R920.3 K96J4
       Has cum. index for earlier titles in series. Articles written in a simple style for younger readers.

AL66 Holtze, Sally Holmes. FIFTH BOOK OF JUNIOR AUTHORS. New York: W.W. Wilson, 1983.

AL67 YESTERDAY'S AUTHORS OF BOOKS FOR CHILDREN. 2 vols. Ed. by Anne Commire. Detroit: Gale Research, 1977-78.
   R920.3Y47
       About 80 authors or illustrators from early times to 1960 described in well-illustrated essays.

AL68 TWENTIETH CENTURY CHILDREN'S WRITERS. 2d ed. Ed. by Daniel Kirkpatrick. London: St Martin's Press, 1983. 1024 p.
       Bio-bibliographical short essay, comment from the author and brief signed criticism; appendix for notable 19th century authors.

AL69 SOMETHING ABOUT THE AUTHOR: Facts and Pictures about Authors and Illustrators of Books for Young People, 1971- Detroit: Gale Research. annual; cum. index.
   R920.3 C734S
       Taken from CONTEMPORARY AUTHORS (AL51) Portraits, photographs, book illustrations. Author/ illustrator index.

AL70 PROFILES 2: Authors and Illustrators, Children's Literature in Canada. Ed. by Irma McDonough. Ottawa: Canadian Library Assoc., 1982. 170 p.
       Sketches of 45 personalities taken from IN REVIEW (AC25); a new edition of PROFILES (1971) which has 20 (illustrated) of the sketches.

Canadian Authors (See also section BD, and Ryder, HU6)

AL71 Hamel, Reginald; John Hare and Paul Wyczynski. DICTIONNAIRE PRATIQUE DES AUTEURS QUEBECOIS. Montreal: Fides, 1976. 725 p.
             PS9081.H34   Ryder HU6-23
       Alphabetical arrangement biobibliographies of French language authors in Quebec (and other provinces) with photographs.

AL72   Sylvestre, Guy; Brandon Conron and Carl Klinck. CANADIAN WRITERS/ ECRIVAINS CANADIENS. 2d ed. Montreal: Editions HMH, 1966. 186 p.
       R920.3 S985C   Ryder HU6-28
          Has information about 300 authors from 1608 to 1966, with chronological table of important works and index of titles. Biographies (50 to 1000 words) are in English or French according to the language of the biographee.

AL73   Thomas, Clara. CANADIAN NOVELISTS, 1920-1945. Toronto: Longmans, 1946. 129 p.
       R920.3 T45S   Ryder HU6-89.

AL74   WHO'S WHO IN CANADIAN LITERATURE, 1983/84- Ed. by Gordon Ripley, and Anne Mercer. Toronto: The Reference Press, 1983-
       R819 W628W
          Authors, playwrights, critics, translators active in the broad field. Over 600 brief biographies, dates, address, publications, in English or French according to the entrant's preference.

GOVERNMENT INFORMATION

GUIDE

AM1   Cherns, J.J. OFFICIAL PUBLISHING: AN OVERVIEW; AN INTERNATIONAL SURVEY AND REVIEW OF THE ROLE, ORGANISATION AND PRINCIPLES OF OFFICIAL PUBLISHING. Oxford: Pergamon, 1979. 527 p.
070.595 C521C
Expensive coverage for content; survey based on study of twenty countries with publishing recorded in considerable detail.

GREAT BRITAIN

Directory and Guides

AM2   Richard, Stephen. comp. DIRECTORY OF BRITISH OFFICIAL PUBLICATIONS: A DIRECTORY OF SOURCES. N.Y.: Mansell, 1981. 352 p.
Z2009 R535 GOVT
Lists over 1000 publishers with the services they offer, type of publication and addresses.

AM3   Butcher, David. OFFICIAL PUBLICATIONS IN BRITAIN. London: Clive Bingley, 1983. 161 p.
015.41 B983P
A concise introduction which explains recent changes.

AM4   Johansson, Eve. CURRENT BRITISH GOVERNMENT PUBLISHING. London: Assoc. of Assistant Librarians, 1978. 64 p.
025.1734 J65C
Problems and needs in a nutshell.

AM5   Ollé, James G.H. AN INTRODUCTION TO BRITISH GOVERNMENT PUBLICATIONS. 2d ed. London: Assoc. of Assistant Librarians, 1973. 175 p.
025.173 O49I2
A standard text.

AM6   Pemberton, John E. BRITISH OFFICIAL PUBLICATIONS. 2d rev. ed. Oxford: Pergamon Press, 1973. 328 p.
015.42 P394B2
Useful for information not covered in the briefer guides.

AM7   Rodgers, Frank. A GUIDE TO BRITISH GOVERNMENT PUBLICATIONS. New York: H.W. Wilson, 1980. 750 p.
015.41R691G
Extensive coverage of both parliamentary and executive publications with background information on the issuing body.

Major Bibliographies

AM8   Great Britain. GOVERNMENT PUBLICATIONS, 1922-   London: HMSO, 1923- annual; quinquennial consolidated index.
(PER)
With INDEX 1922-1973 (Carrollton Press, 1976). Not all departments or publications. Supplemented by the DAILY LIST and MONTHLY CATALOGUE.

AM9   _____. MONTHLY SELECTION OF BOOKS PUBLISHED. London: HMSO.
       (PER)

AM10   _____. SECTIONAL LISTS. London: HMSO. irregular.
       (PER)   GOVT
           Useful subject bibliographies.

AM11   CATALOGUE OF BRITISH OFFICIAL PUBLICATIONS NOT PUBLISHED BY HMSO, 1980- Cambridge: Chadwyck Healey, 1981- bimonthly; annual cumulation.
           Includes the publications of over 300 government departments, nationalized industries, research institutes, quasi-autonomous non-governmental organizations and other official bodies. Includes monographs, serials, newspapers, some publicity items, atlases, some maps but excludes items editors judge too ephemeral, too specialized or groups of items well catalogued elsewhere (e.g. maps). Available online; microfiche document delivery service.

UNITED STATES

Guides

AM12   Andriot, John L. GUIDE TO U.S. GOVERNMENT PUBLICATIONS, 1962- McLean, VA: Documents Index. irregular. (Microfiche publication, 1981-).
       R015.73 A673   Z1223 Z7G82 GOVT   Sheehy AG18, 1AG6
           A comprehensive listing of publications by Superintendent of Documents classification scheme. Includes both serial and monographic publications.

AM13   GOVERNMENT REFERENCE BOOKS, 1968/69- Littleton, CO: Libraries Unlimited. biennial.
       R015.73 G721   Sheehy AG16
           Lists, describes over 1400 documents; bibliographies, catalogues, compendia, directories etc.

AM14   Morehead, Joe. INTRODUCTION TO UNITED STATES PUBLIC DOCUMENTS. 3d ed. Littleton, CO: Libraries Unlimited, 1983. 377 p.
       015.73 M8I3   Z1223 Z7M67 GOVT   Sheehy 1AG5
           An account of the basic sources and bibliographic structure of federal government publications; emphasis is on current sources. Edition has been "extensively revised and updated to include changes in the production and distribution ... proliferation of online databases and microform collections." Describes administrative machinery, activities of agencies like NTIS, ERIC.

AM15   Nakata, Yuri. FROM PRESS TO PEOPLE: COLLECTING AND USING U.S. GOVERNMENT PUBLICATIONS. Chicago: American Library Association, 1979. 212 p.
       025.173 N163F   Z688 G6N34   Sheehy 2AG4
           "Designed as a handbook for the beginning document-librarian and for others interested in promoting the use of government documents." Emphasizes reference service and document delivery to patron.

AM16   Newsome, Walter L. NEW GUIDE TO POPULAR GOVERNMENT PUBLICATIONS: FOR LIBRARY AND HOME REFERENCE. Littleton, CO: Libraries Unlimited, 1978.
       R015.73 P748G2   Sheehy 2AG5

AM17   Schmeckebier, Laurence F., and Roy B. Eastin. GOVERNMENT PUBLICATIONS AND THEIR USE. 2d rev. ed. Washington: Brookings Institution, 1969. 502 p.
R025.173 S34G3   Z1223 Z7S3   Sheehy AG13
    Reliable standard aid to date of publication. Has detailed description of official guides, catalogues and indexes, an assessment of their value and advice on their use.

Major Bibliographies

AM18   Poore, Benjamin Perley. A DESCRIPTIVE CATALOGUE OF THE GOVERNMENT PUBLICATIONS OF THE UNITED STATES, SEPTEMBER 5, 1774 - March 4, 1881. 2 vols. Washington: GPO, 1885. Reprint/ New York: Johnson, 1962.
R015.73 P823   US1GP-Y5021 GOVT   Sheehy AG20
    Incomplete but still useful for this period. Arranged chronologically with brief annotations; indexed by subject, personal author and government agency.

AM19   CHECKLIST OF UNITED STATES PUBLIC DOCUMENTS, 1789-1909. 3d ed. rev. and enl. Washington: GPO, 1911. 1707 p. Reprint/ New York: Kraus, 1962.
R015.73 U58C   US1GP-11C37 GOVT   Sheehy AG23
    Reproduced shelf list of the Public Documents Department Library. Originally planned as 2 vol. set. The second (index) vol. never published.

AM20   CIS U.S. SERIAL SET INDEX 1789-1969. Washington: Congressional Information Service, 1975-1979.
                                             Sheehy 1AG7
    Updated by CIS INDEX (AM27). Thoroughly indexes the most important historical collection of U.S. government publications. Microfiche document delivery service available from CIS.

AM21   CHECKLIST OF UNITED STATES PUBLIC DOCUMENTS, 1789-1976. Checklist 76. Arlington, VA: U.S. Historical Documents Institute, 1976.
    Microfilm edition of shelf list of Public Documents Library on 118 reels. Includes and updates AM19 above. Indexed in 5 hardcover vols.

AM22   CUMULATIVE TITLE INDEX TO U.S. PUBLIC DOCUMENTS, 1789-1976. 16 vols. Arlington, VA: U.S. Historical Documents Institute, 1977.
    Indexes CHECKLIST 76 (AM21).

AM23   Ames, John G. COMPREHENSIVE INDEX TO THE PUBLICATIONS OF THE UNITED STATES GOVERNMENT, 1881-1893. 2 vols. Washington: GPO, 1905. Reprint/ Johnson, 1962.
R015.73 U58   US1GP-Z4C58 GOVT   Sheehy AG21
    Each page in three columns. The middle column provides the main arrangement, alphabetical by keyword, usually a catchword from an inverted title. The first column cites issuing agency; the third column has the classification number. With personal name index.

AM24   CATALOG OF THE PUBLIC DOCUMENTS OF CONGRESS AND OF ALL DEPARTMENTS OF THE GOVERNMENT OF THE UNITED STATES, 1893-1940. 25 vols. Washington: GPO, 1896-45. Reprint/ Hein.
                       US1GP-C16 GOVT   Sheehy AG24
    A comprehensive record for the period.

AM25   MONTHLY CATALOG OF UNITED STATES GOVERNMENT PUBLICATIONS, 1895- Washington: GPO. monthly.
(PER)   US1GPMS1 GOVT   Sheehy AG25, 2AG9
Title varies, from 1951, title as above. Lists documents, by issuing office, within a month after publication. Before 1976, catalog arranged alphabetically by issued agency, except for publications of Congress which were subdivided by form and issuing entity. There is no annual cumulation; to 1975, the Dec. issue contains an annual index. There are decennial indexes, 1941-1950; 1951-1960; quinquennial indexes, 1961-1965; 1966-1970; and a cumulation for 1971 to June 1976.
From July 1976, entries are in full catalogue format with LC subject headings. Entries are arranged alphanumerically by Superintendent of Documents classification notation. From Dec. 1976, there are semi-annual and separate annual cum. index vols; author, title, subject, series/ reports, stock numbers, title keyword indexes.
Commercially published adjuncts to the MONTHLY CATALOG include CUMULATIVE SUBJECT INDEX TO THE MONTHLY CATALOG OF U.S. GOVERNMENT PUBLICATIONS, 1895-1899 (2 vols); CUMULATIVE SUBJECT INDEX ..., 1900-1971 (15 vols); CUMULATIVE PERSONAL AUTHOR INDEXES ..., 1941-1975 (5 vols).

AM26   MONTHLY CHECKLIST OF STATE PUBLICATIONS, 1910-   Prepared by the Library of Congress. Washington: GPO.
(PER)   Z1223.5 A1U5 GOVT   Sheehy AG47

AM27   CIS INDEX, 1970-   Washington: Congressional Information Service. monthly, annual.
                     Z1223 Z9C8 GOVT   Sheehy CJ83, 2CJ48
An index to the contents of all Congressional publications. Available online. Microfiche document delivery service from CIS.

AM27   AMERICAN STATISTICS INDEX, 1973-   Washington: Congressional Information Service. monthly; quarterly cumulated indexes; annual.
                     Z7554 U5A54 GOVT   Sheehy CG76
Comprehensive guide and index to U.S. government publications containing statistics. Available online. Microfiche document delivery service from CIS.

AM28   United States. SUBJECT BIBLIOGRAPHIES, 1975-   Washington: Superintendent of Documents. irregular.
                                                Sheehy AG28
A series of about 300 topical bibliographies. Replaces PRICE LISTS OF GOVERNMENT PUBLICATIONS.

AM29   _____. NEW BOOKS, 1982-   Washington: GPO. bimonthly.
(PER)
Unannotated list of all new titles placed on sale during preceding two weeks. Free.

AM30   U.S. GOVERNMENT BOOKS, 1982-   Washington: GPO. quarterly.
(PER)
Annotated entries of popular monograph and serial publications available for sale. Includes 1000 best sellers, 10% of list replaced each quarter. First issue free.

CANADA

Structure, Organization and Procedures of the Government

Federal

AM31   Canada. Dept of Justice. A CONSOLIDATION OF THE CONSTITUTION ACTS, 1867 TO 1982. Ottawa: Supply and Services, 1983.
R342.02 C212C

AM32   Canada. House of Commons. PERMANENT AND PROVISIONAL STANDING ORDERS OF THE HOUSE OF COMMONS, DECEMBER 22, 1982. Ottawa: Queen's Printer, 1982. INDEX (1983).
328.71 C212S
    Official guide to procedure in the House.

AM33   Canada. Treasury Board. "Chapter 335: Publishing." ADMINISTRATIVE POLICY MANUAL. Ottawa, 1978. 42 p. (xerographic copy).
R070.595 C212A
    Federal government's rules for publishing; the depository system.

AM34   CANADA YEAR BOOK. (See AH12)
R317.1 C212
    See chaps: "The Constitution and the Legal System"; "Government."

AM35   CANADIAN PARLIAMENTARY HANDBOOK/ REPERTOIRE PARLEMENTAIRE CANADIAN, 1982- Comp. by John Bejermi. Ottawa: Borealis Press. 532 p. irreg.

AM36   (1983/84 ed., rev. Sept 1983) Begins with a note on the parliamentary process, introduces the Senate and senators, House of Commons and members, some information on the Library of Parliament. Duplicates material found in other sources like CANADIAN PARLIAMENTARY GUIDE, almanacs and current biographies.

AM36   Forsey, Eugene. HOW CANADIANS GOVERN THEMSELVES. Ottawa: Supply and Services, 1979. 40 p. (free pamphlet).
354.71 F732H
    An elementary guide to Canadian government.

AM37   GOVERNMENT OF CANADA TELEPHONE DIRECTORY: NATIONAL CAPITAL REGION. Ottawa: Dept of Communications, Government Telecommunications Agency. semi-annual.
R354.71 C212   Ryder SS6-23

AM38   INDEX TO FEDERAL PROGRAMS AND SERVICES. 5th ed. Ottawa: Task Force on Service to the Public, 1984. 550 p.
R354.71 I38I
    French ed.: PROGRAMMES ET SERVICES DU GOUVERNEMENT FEDERAL. Lists programs, services available from 131 federal departments, agencies and Crown corporations. Directory information; subject index.

AM39   ORGANIZATION OF THE GOVERNMENT OF CANADA. 13th ed. Ottawa: Treasury Board Secretariat and Macmillan, 1980. 635 p.
354.71 C212RG   Ryder SS6-27

AM40   Stewart, John B. THE CANADIAN HOUSE OF COMMONS: PROCEDURE AND REFORM.
             Montreal: McGill/ Queen's Univ. Press, 1976. 337 p.
          328.71072 S849C
                An informative guide to the work of the House, by an insider.

AM41   Van Loon, Richard, and M.S. Whittington. THE CANADIAN POLITICAL SYSTEM.
             3d ed. Toronto: McGraw, 1981. 839 p.
          320.971 V261C2 (1976 ed.)   JL61 V3
                A standard textbook.

Ontario

For similar publications of and about government in the other provinces and the
territories, see Ryder SS6-35 to SS6-68. See also the bibliographies, AM58 TO
AM98 below.

AM42   GOVERNMENT OF ONTARIO TELEPHONE DIRECTORY. Toronto: Ministry of
             Government Services. semi-annual.
          R354.713 G712G   Ryder SS6-52

AM43   Macdonald, Donald C. ed. GOVERNMENT AND POLITICS IN ONTARIO. 2d ed.
             Toronto: Van Nostrand, 1980. 454 p.
          320.9713 G721G (1975 ed.)   F5526 G69

AM44   Ontario. Legislative Assembly. STANDING ORDERS OF THE LEGISLATIVE
             ASSEMBLY, AUGUST 1981. Toronto, 1981.

AM45   Ontario. Ministry of Government Services. Citizens' Inquiry Bureau. KWIC
             INDEX TO YOUR ONTARIO GOVERNMENT SERVICES, 19?- Toronto: annual.
          R354.713 O59N
                Frequency varied; now annual in publication. (7th ed., 1982/83).

Government Publications in Canadian Libraries

AM46   Bishop, Olga B. CANADIAN OFFICIAL PUBLICATIONS. Oxford: Pergamon Press,
             1981.
          015.71 B622C
                A useful overview with emphasis on historical documents.

AM47   Canadian Library Association. "A Submission to the Standing Joint
             Committee on Regulations and Other Statutory Instruments." Ottawa:
             Canadian Library Association, 1978. (Appendix RS1-23 to the MINUTES OF
             PROCEEDINGS AND EVIDENCE, No. 34, June 27, 1978, pp. 59-65.)

AM48   CASLIS Workshop on Federal Documents. ACCESS TO FEDERAL GOVERNMENT
             DOCUMENTS. Papers presented at CLA Annual Conference, June 1979.
             Ottawa: Canadian Library Association, 1980. 70 p.
          025.2834 C111A

AM49   Farr, Robin M. A REVIEW OF THE ONTARIO GOVERNMENT PUBLICATIONS SERVICE.
             Toronto: Ministry of Government Services, 1979. (pamphlet).
          070.59509713 F239R

AM50   Fox, Paul W. ed. POLITICS: CANADA; PROBLEMS IN CANADIAN GOVERNMENT. 5th ed. Toronto: McGraw-Hill Ryerson, 1982.
342.71 F793P4 (4th ed.)
   Contains "A Description and Guide to the Use of Canadian Government Publications," pp. 18-36, by R.B. Land.

AM51   Friedland, M.L., in collaboration with P.E.J. Jewett, and L.J. Jewett. ACCESS TO THE LAW: A STUDY CONDUCTED FOR THE LAW REFORM COMMISSION OF CANADA. Toronto: Carswell/Methuen, 1975. 198 p.
342.71 F899A
   Some suggested reforms implemented, but much remains to be done.

AM52   Jarvi, Edith. ACCESS TO CANADIAN GOVERNMENT PUBLICATIONS IN CANADIAN ACADEMIC AND PUBLIC LIBRARIES. Ottawa: Canadian Library Association, 1976. 116 p.
070.595 J38AA   Ryder GR3-3
   Describes bibliographical control of federal and provincial government publications, including distribution to libraries.

AM53   Pemberton, John. ed. BIBLIOGRAPHICAL CONTROL OF OFFICIAL PUBLICATIONS. Oxford: Pergamon Press, 1982. 172 p.
025.3434 B582B
   Discusses current national schemes as a step toward a definitive system of bibliographic control of official publications. Canada is represented in articles on the Library of Parliament, the Legislative Library of B.C. and the CODOC system, Guelph University, Ontario.

AM54   Pross, A.P., and C.A. Pross. GOVERNMENT PUBLISHING IN THE CANADIAN PROVINCES: A PRESCRIPTIVE STUDY. Toronto: Univ. of Toronto Press, 1972. 178 p.
070.595 P966
   A major study which led to improvements.

AM55   Task Force on Government Information. TO KNOW AND BE KNOWN: REPORT. 2 vols. Ottawa: Queen's Printer, 1969.
001.50971 C212
   An important statement on federal government publishing, even though some aspects are out of date.

Major Bibliographies of Canadian Government Publications

Federal and Provincial Coverage

AM56   CANADIANA. (See AD77)
(1950-)
   From 1950-51, federal documents were with monographs; 1952-1980 in separate section; from 1981, with monographs in Pt 1. Provincial documents included from 1953 in a separate section, and from 1981, with monographs in Pt 1.

AM57   MICROLOG INDEX, 1979-   Toronto: Micromedia, 1979-   monthly; annual cumulation.
R015.71 M626M   Ryder GR3-4
   Supersedes PUBLICAT INDEX, 1977-78 (R015.71 P976I) and PROFILE INDEX, 1973-78 (R015.71 P964P).

Bibliographies of Federal Government Publications

AM58   Higgins, Marion V. CANADIAN GOVERNMENT PUBLICATIONS: A MANUAL FOR LIBRARIANS. Chicago: American Library Association, 1935. 582 p.
R025.173 H63 (1841-1933)   Ryder GR3-2
A large proportion of federal publications from 1867 to 1931 are recorded; the period from 1841 to 1867 is covered less adequately. For each issuing office there is an outline of organization, history, function, with a list of documents. Sets such as sessional papers are not analyzed.

AM59   GOVERNMENT OF CANADA PUBLICATIONS CATALOGUE, 1979- Ottawa: CGPC, Supply and Services, 1953- weekly, quarterly, with annual index.
R015.71 C21G (1953-)   Ryder GR3-6
Supersedes CANADIAN GOVERNMENT PUBLICATIONS CATALOGUE with change from frequency of daily, monthly and annual.

AM60   SPECIAL LIST OF CANADIAN GOVERNMENT PUBLICATIONS, 1953- Ottawa: CGPC, Supply and Services. irregular. (Green list).
R015.71 C21G   Ryder GR3-7

AM61   PUBLISHING NEWS, 1977- Ottawa: CGPC, Supply and Services. irregular.
R015.71053 C212P
An annotated listing of new publications designed for bookstores.

AM62   SUBJECT LIST, 1977- Ottawa: CGPC, Supply and Services. irregular.
R015.71 C21G
French ed.: VEDETTE MATIERE. Each list covers one topic such as "Energy and Environment," "Parliamentary Reports and Legislation," "History and Archaeology," "Sports and Leisure."

AM63   INVENTORY LIST: GOVERNMENT OF CANADA PUBLICATIONS, 1979- Ottawa: CGPC, Supply and Services. bimonthly.
Priced publications of the Provincial and Territorial governments.

Bibliographies of the Provincial and Territorial Governments
(From East to West and North)
Bibliographies, AD81 to AD98, listed in the section on National Bibliography may also contain government publications within their scope.

AM64   Pross, Catherine A. A GUIDE TO IDENTIFICATION AND ACQUISITION OF CANADIAN GOVERNMENT PUBLICATIONS: PROVINCES AND TERRITORIES. 2d ed. Occasional Paper, No. 16. Halifax: Dalhousie Univ. Libraries and Dalhousie Univ. School of Library Service, 1983. 103 p.
R025.173 P966G2   Ryder GR4-4

AM65   LIST OF PUBLICATIONS OF THE GOVERNMENT OF NEWFOUNDLAND AND LABRADOR, 1974-1979. St John's: Information Services. irregular; ceased publication.
R015.718 N547L (1974-1979)

AM66   Bishop, Olga B. PUBLICATIONS OF THE GOVERNMENTS OF NOVA SCOTIA, PRINCE EDWARD ISLAND, NEW BRUNSWICK, 1758-1952. Ottawa: National Library of Canada, 1957. 237 p.
R015.716 B622 (1758-1952)   Ryder GR4-7
Includes useful historical notes.

AM67   PUBLICATIONS OF THE PROVINCE OF NOVA SCOTIA, 1967-   Prepared by the Legislative Library. Halifax: Queen's Printer, 1968-   annual. Supplemented by the QUARTERLY CHECKLIST, June 1980- .
R015.716 N935 (1967-)
Also available is a PUBLICATIONS CATALOGUE: NOVA SCOTIA GOVERNMENT BOOKSTORE, irregular, quarterly supplements.

AM68   P.E.I. PROVINCIAL GOVERNMENT PUBLICATIONS CHECKLIST, 1976-   Charlottetown: Island Information Service. monthly.
R015.717 P954P (1976-)

AM69   Guilbeault, Claude. GUIDE TO OFFICIAL PUBLICATIONS OF NEW BRUNSWICK 1952 - 1970. Ottawa: Univ. of Ottawa Library School, 1974. 382 p. M.L.S. thesis.
MFILM 1039 (1952-1970)

AM70   NEW BRUNSWICK GOVERNMENT DOCUMENTS, 1956-   Prepared by the Legislative Library. Fredericton: Queen's Printer. annual, limited distribution of irregular supplements.
R015.715 N53 (1955-)

AM71   BIBLIOGRAPHIE DU QUEBEC, 1821-1967. (In progress. See AD87)
R015.714 B582B (1821-1967)

AM72   Beaulieu, André; Jean-Charles Bonenfant, and Jean Hamelin. REPERTOIRE DES PUBLICATIONS GOUVERNEMENTALES DU QUEBEC DE 1867 A 1964. Quebec: Imprimeur de la Reine, 1968. SUPPLEMENT 1965-1968. By A. Beaulieu, J. Hamelin, and G. Bernier. (Editeur officiel de Québec, 1970).
R015.714 B377 (1867-1968)   Ryder GR-25

AM73   BIBLIOGRAPHIE DU QUEBEC. (See AD88)
R015.714 AB582B (1968-)
Pt 2 lists government publications.

AM74   CATALOGUE DE L'EDITEUR OFFICIEL, 1974-   Quebec: Ministère des communications [par le Bureau de l'Editeur officiel]. irregular.
R015.714 Q3QA (1974-)   Ryder GR4-27
Supersedes PUBLICATIONS ... 1967-74.

AM75   CHOIX DE PUBLICATIONS GOUVERNEMENTALES, 1975-   Quebec: Ministère des communications [par le Bureau de l'Editeur officiel]. irregular.
R015.714 C546C (1975-)
Selected, annotated list arranged by subject; author, title index.

AM76   REPERTOIRE DES PUBLICATIONS GOUVERNEMENTALES GRATUITES, 1976-   Quebec: Communications-Québec, Direction géerérale des communications gouvernmentales, Ministère des communications. irregular
R015.714 Q3G (1976-)
(3d ed., 1980). A list of free publications.

AM77   LISTE MENSUELLE DES PUBLICATIONS DU GOUVERNMENT DU QUEBEC, 1981-   Quebec: Service de diffusion des publications, Ministère des Communications.
R015.714053 Q3L (1981-)

AM78   Bishop, Olga B. PUBLICATIONS OF THE GOVERNMENT OF THE PROVINCE OF UPPER CANADA AND OF GREAT BRITAIN RELATING TO UPPER CANADA, 1791-1840. Toronto: Ministry of Citizenship and Culture, 1984.
(1791-1840)
With the publication of this title, Ontario's record becomes the most comprehensive for any of the provinces or the federal government.

AM79   _____. PUBLICATIONS OF THE GOVERNMENT OF THE PROVINCE OF CANADA, 1841-1867. Ottawa: National Library of Canada, 1963. 351 p.
R015.71 B622 (1841-1867)   Ryder GR3-5
The Province of Canada consisted of Canada West (Ontario) and Canada East (Quebec). Over 1400 titles arranged by department with list of printers and a chronology of parliamentary sessions.

AM80   _____. PUBLICATIONS OF THE GOVERNMENT OF ONTARIO, 1867-1900. Toronto: Ministry of Government Services, 1976. 409 p.
R015.713 B622P (1867-1900)   Ryder GR4-20
A chronological list, under the divisions of government with a short history of each branch of government. Author, title, subject index and a library location.

AM81   MacTaggart, Hazel I. PUBLICATIONS OF THE GOVERNMENT OF ONTARIO, 1901-1955. A Checklist Compiled for the Ontario Library Association. Toronto: Univ. of Toronto Press for the Queen's Printer, 1964. 303 p.
R015.713 M175 (1901-1955)   Ryder GR4-21
Arranged by issuing department with author, title, suject index and library locations.

AM82   _____, assisted by Kenneth E. Sunquist. PUBLICATIONS OF THE GOVERNMENT OF ONTARIO, 1956-1971: A Checklist. Toronto: Ministry of Government Services, 1975. 410 p.
R015.713 M175A (1956-1971)   Ryder GR4-22
Continues AM81, and the coverage is continued by the MONTHLY CHECKLIST (AM83).

AM83   ONTARIO GOVERNMENT PUBLICATIONS: MONTHLY CHECKLIST, 1972- Prepared by the Research and Information Services, Legislative Library, 1979- Toronto: Ministry of Government Services. ANNUAL CATALOGUE, 1979- .
R015.713 059 (1979-)   Ryder GR4-23
Publisher varies, from 1972-79, published by the Ministry of Government Services, with annual cumulation. From Jan. 1984, incorporates CATALOGUE DES PUBLICATIONS EN FRANCAISE DU GOUVERNEMENT DE L'ONTARIO, published twice a year from 1979-1983.

AM84   ONTARIO GOVERNMENT PUBLICATIONS REPORT, 1981- Toronto: Ministry of Government Services. irregular.
R015.713 059GB (1981-)
An in-print price list.

AM85   Morley, Marjorie. A BIBLIOGRAPHY OF MANITOBA FROM HOLDINGS IN THE LEGISLATIVE LIBRARY OF MANITOBA. Winnipeg: Legislative Library of Manitoba, 1970. 267 p.
R015.712 AM864B (1830-1970)   Ryder GR1-82
Over 2000 items arranged alphabetically by author; includes listing of some 300 newspapers and periodicals as well as books.

AM86   MANITOBA GOVERNMENT PUBLICATIONS, 1970-   Winnipeg: Cultural Affairs and
          Historical Resources, 1975-   monthly; annual.
          R015.712 M278A (1970-)   Ryder GR4-18
             Published by the Legislative Library, 1970-74.

AM87   LOOKING FOR MANITOBA GOVERNMENT PUBLICATIONS: AN ANNOTATED BIBLIOGRAPHY
          OF BOOKS AND PAMPHLETS. Ed. by John Tooth. Winnipeg: Public Library
          Services Branch, Dept of Tourism, Recreation and Cultural Affairs,
          1978. 265 p.
          R016.7127 AL863L (-1978)   Ryder GR4-19

AM88   MacDonald, Christine. PUBLICATIONS OF THE GOVERNMENT OF THE NORTH-WEST
          TERRITORIES, 1867-1905, AND OF THE PROVINCE OF SASKATCHEWAN,
          1905-1952... Regina: Legislative Library, 1952. 110 p.
          R015.712 M13 (1867-1905)   Ryder GR4-15, GR4-29
             Alberta was included in the Territories. Arranged by issuing body
          with author/ subject index.

AM89   CHECKLIST OF SASKATCHEWAN GOVERNMENT PUBLICATIONS, 1976-   Regina:
          Legislative Library, 1977-   annual.
          R015.7124 S252C (1976-)   Ryder GR4-30
             Supplemented by SASKATCHEWAN GOVERNMENT PUBLICATIONS, 1979-
          bimonthly.

AM90   Forsyth, Joseph. GOVERNMENT PUBLICATIONS RELATING TO ALBERTA: A
          Bibliography of Publications of the Government of Alberta from
          1905-1968, and of the Government of Canada Relating to the Province of
          Alberta from 1867 to 1968. 8 vols. Tylers Green, High Wycombe, Bucks,
          Eng.: University Microfilms, 1972. (Thesis submitted for Fellowship of
          the Library Association, 1971).
                          Z1392 A4F67 GOVT   Ryder GR4-14

AM91   PUBLICATIONS CATALOGUE, 1974-   Edmonton: Public Affairs Bureau.
          quarterly; annual.
          R015.7123 A333P (1973-)   Ryder GR4-13

AM92   British Columbia Provincial Archives. DICTIONARY CATALOGUE OF THE
          PROVINCIAL ARCHIVES OF BRITISH COLUMBIA. 8 vols. Boston: G.K. Hall,
          1971.
          R015.711 B862D (1774-1970)   Ryder GR1-24
             The Archives has divisions for manuscripts, visual records, maps
          and includes material relating to Canada west of the Great Lakes, the
          Pacific Northwest and the Territories.

AM93   Lowther, Barbara. A BIBLIOGRAPHY OF BRITISH COLUMBIA: LAYING THE
          FOUNDATIONS, 1849-1899. Victoria: Univ. of Victoria, 1968. 328 p.
          R015.711 B582 (1858-1871)   Ryder GR1-62
             (See related titles, AD96) Includes government publications of the
          two colonies of Vancouver Island and British Columbia, and after their
          union in 1866, of the united colony of B.C. to 1871, the year the
          province entered Confederation.

AM94   Holmes, Marjorie C. PUBLICATIONS OF THE GOVERNMENT OF BRITISH COLUMBIA,
          1871-1947. Victoria: Provincial Library, 1950. 254 p.
          R015.711 H75 (1871-1947)   Ryder GR4-17
             Publications arranged by issuing departments with extensive notes
          on departments.

AM95   BRITISH COLUMBIA GOVERNMENT PUBLICATIONS MONTHLY CHECKLIST, 1970-
Victoria: Legislative Library.
R015.711 B862BA (1970-   )   Ryder GR4-16

AM96   QUEEN'S PRINTER PUBLICATIONS PRICE LIST, 1981- Victoria: Provincial
Secretary and Government Services. annual, periodic revisions.
R015.711 B862Q (1981-   )

AM97   Northwest Territories. GOVERNMENT PUBLICATIONS CATALOGUE, 1977-
Yellowknife: Dept of Information, Publications and Production
Division, 1978- annual. Supplement twice a year, (May, Nov.).
R015.7192 M879P (1977-   )   Ryder GR4-32
Title varies.

AM98   YUKON BIBLIOGRAPHY. (See AD97)
(1897-   )   Z1392.Y8L6   Ryder GR1-120, -121
Includes some government publications.

Parliamentary Publications

FLIS has samples only; see files at GOVT, Robarts Library.

AM99   Canada. House of Commons. DEBATES, 1867-1874. Ottawa: Queen's Printer, 1967- In progress.
Debates for these years, not officially recorded, are being collated from available sources and published under the auspices of the Library of Parliament.

AM100   _____. _____. DEBATES: OFFICIAL REPORT, 1875- [Hansard]. Ottawa: Queen's Printer. daily, sessional.

AM101   _____. _____. JOURNALS, 1867- Ottawa: Queen's Printer. sessional.
Compiled from the daily VOTES AND PROCEEDINGS.

AM102   Canada. Senate. JOURNALS, 1967- Ottawa: Queen's Printer. sessional.
Compiled from the daily MINUTES OF THE PROCEEDINGS.

AM103   Canada. SESSIONAL PAPERS OF THE DOMINION OF CANADA, 1867-1925. Ottawa: Queen's Printer, 1867-1925.
CA1 YS S27 GOVT

AM104   Canada. ANNUAL DEPARTMENTAL REPORTS OF THE DOMINION OF CANADA, 1925-1930. Ottawa: King's Printer, 1926-1930.
CA1 YX 21 S71 GOVT

AM105   STATUTES OF CANADA, 1867- Ottawa: Queen's Printer. sessional.

AM106   REVISED STATUTES OF CANADA, 1970. 11 vols. Ottawa: Queen's Printer, 1970.
R348.71 C212
Includes APPENDICES, 1 vol.; SUPPLEMENT, 2 vols; INDEX, 1 vol.
Available online.

AM107   CONSOLIDATED REGULATIONS OF CANADA, 1978. 19 vols. Ottawa: Queen's Printer [for the Statute Revision Commission], 1978.
R348.71025 C212C

AM108   THE CANADA GAZETTE, 1867-   Ottawa: Queen's Printer. in 3 pts.
CA1 YX 99 G191 GOVT
From December 13, 1974, in three parts. Pt 1, published every Saturday, contains notices of a general character, proclamations, certain Orders-in-Council and various other classes of statutory notices. Pt 2, published on the second and fourth Wednesday of the month, contains all regulations and statutory instruments required to be published. Pt 3, published irregularly, contains the Public Acts of Canada and certain other ancillary publications, proclamations and updated Tables of Public Statutes.

Legislative Assembly of Ontario: Statutes

Ontario is an example of the organization typical of each province.

AM109   STATUTES OF THE PROVINCE OF ONTARIO, 1867-   Toronto: Queen's Printer. sessional.
R348.713 O59S

AM110   REVISED STATUTES OF ONTARIO, 1980. Being a Revision and Consolidation of the Public General Acts of the Legislature of Ontario, Published under the Authority of the Statutes Revision Act, 1979. 11 vols. Toronto: Queen's Printer, 1980.
R348.713 O59

AM111   REVISED REGULATIONS OF ONTARIO, 1980. A Revision and Consolidation of Regulations Published under the Authority of the Regulations Revision Act, 1979. 8 vols. Toronto: Queen's Printer, 1980. SUPPLEMENT 1982. 2 vols.
R348.713 O59R

PUBLICATIONS FROM INTERNATIONAL ORGANIZATIONS

DOCUMENTS AND PUBLICATIONS

General Guides

AN1   DIRECTORY OF INTERNATIONAL STATISTICS. Statistical Papers, Series M, No. 56, Rev. 1. Vol. 1. New York: United Nations, Statistical Office, 1982. 274 p. (Vol. 2, in preparation).
                     UN2 S13 75M561 rev GOVT
     A guide to statistical series issued by international organizations within and outside the UN system. Includes an inventory of machine-readable databases; covers economic and social statistics. Vol. 2 will describe statistical services of international orgs.

AN2   Dimitrov, Theodore D. WORLD BIBLIOGRAPHY OF INTERNATIONAL DOCUMENTATION. 2 vols. Pleasantville, NY: UNIFO, 1981.
                     Z6464 I6D56 1981 GOVT
     Covers monographs, journal articles, etc. by or about international orgs within and outside the UN system. Also covers material on international relations in general.

Bibliographies and Indexes

AN3   DOCUMENTS OF INTERNATIONAL ORGANIZATIONS: A SELECTED BIBLIOGRAPHY. Vol. 1-3, No. 4; Nov. 1947 - Sept. 1950. Boston: World Peace Foundation.
                     Z6464 I6D6 GOVT
     Covers documents of orgs within and outside the UN system. Intended to fill the gap until the orgs themselves began issuing regular indexes and bibliographies. Cumulative table of contents.

AN4   INDEX TO INTERNATIONAL STATISTICS, 1983- Washington: Congressional Information Service. monthly; quarterly, annual cumulation.
                     HA154I64 GOVT
     An index to, and abstract of, statistical publications and documents of orgs within and outside the UN system. Also covers other international material with substantial statistical content. In two main parts: abstracts, indexes (subject/ name/ geographic, categories, issuing sources, titles, and publication numbers).

AN5   INTERNATIONAL BIBLIOGRAPHY: PUBLICATIONS OF INTERGOVERNMENTAL ORGS, Vol. 11- ;1983- New York: UNIPUB. quarterly
   (PER)   Z6481 I6 GOVT   Sheehy CK201
     Supersedes INTERNATIONAL BIBLIOGRAPHY, INFORMATION, DOCUMENTATION, Vols 1-10; 1973-82. A current awareness bibliography of international orgs within and outside the UN system.

UNITED NATIONS AND THE UN SYSTEM

Guides

AN6   Clews, John. DOCUMENTATION OF THE UN SYSTEM: A Survey of Bibliographic Control and a Suggested Methodolocy for an Integrated UN Bibliography. IFLA/UBC Occasional Papers, No. 8. London: IFLA International Office for UBC, 1981. 20 p.
341.23C625D   JX1977.8 D6C64 GOVT
     Outlines the pattern of documentation of the UN system, the state of bibliographical control, and gives recommendations for an integrated bibliographic system covering all UN orgs.

AN7   DIRECTORY OF UNITED NATIONS INFORMATION SYSTEMS. 2d ed. 2 vols. Geneva: Inter-Organization Board for Information Systems, 1980.
UN9 IOB D37 GOVT
     A guide to information in the UN system. Vol. 1 describes orgs and their systems. Vol. 2 lists information sources, addresses by country.

AN8   Fetzer, Mary K. UNITED NATIONS DOCUMENTS AND PUBLICATIONS: A RESEARCH GUIDE. Occasional Papers No. 76-5. New Brunswick, NJ: Rutgers Univ. Graduate School of LIbrary Service, 1978. 61 p.
341.23 F421U   JX1977.8 D6F47 GOVT

AN9   Hajnal, Peter I. GUIDE TO UNITED NATIONS ORGANIZATION, DOCUMENTATION AND PUBLISHING FOR STUDENTS, RESEARCHERS, LIBRARIANS. Dobbs Ferry, NY: Oceana, 1978. 450 p.
341.23H154G   JX1977 H22 GOVT
     Overview of the structure, functions, evolution of the UN; detailed description of the pattern of UN publications and documentation. An annotated bibliog. of works by and about the UN, a selection of texts, and a survey of other orgs in the UN system.

AN10   Marulli, Luciana. DOCUMENTATION OF THE UNITED NATIONS SYSTEM: CO-ORDINATION IN ITS BIBLIOGRAPHIC CONTROL. Metuchen, NJ: Scarecrow Press, 1979. 225 p.
MFILM 01754   JX1977.8 D6M37 GOVT
     Surveys bibliographic policies, practices of seventeen orgs of the UN system; explores the status of bibliographic control and co-ordination in that system. Has recommendations and bibliography.

AN11   UNITED NATIONS DOCUMENTATION: A BRIEF GUIDE. New York: United Nations, Dag Hammarskjöld Library, 1981. 51 p.
UN2 LI 74U55A
     A practical guide to UN documents, their categories, numbering, distribution and availability, bibliographic control etc. Includes information about documents in microform and suggestions for organizing and maintaining UN document collections.

Bibliographies and Indexes

AN12   Birchfield, Mary E., and Jacqueline Coolman, comps. THE COMPLETE REFERENCE GUIDE TO UNITED NATIONS SALES PUBLICATIONS, 1946-1978. 2 vols. Pleasantville, NY: UNIFO, 1982.
        Z6485 Z9U52 GOVT
    Vol. 1 is the catalogue, listing documents alphanumerically by series symbol, with full bibliog. information including sales no. Vol. 2 contains the indexes (keyword in context, title, sales no.). Updated by lists of new sales publications in UNDOC and by sales catalogue.

AN13   CHECK LIST OF UNITED NATIONS DOCUMENTS, 1946-1953. New York: United Nations, Library.
        Z6481 A5 GOVT   Sheehy CK241
    Partly fills the gap from 1946 to the publishing of UNITED NATIONS DOCUMENTS INDEX (UNDI). In separate parts, each covering a different UN organ, e.g. Security Council, Economic and Social Council, regional commissions, etc. Does not cover General Assembly and Secretariat documents.

AN14   REGISTER OF UNITED NATIONS SERIAL PUBLICATIONS. Geneva: Inter Organization Board for Information Systems, 1982. 261 p.
        UN9 IOB 82R27 GOVT
    An extensive general serials bibliography for most orgs of the UN systems. Includes periodicals, newsletters, reports, proceedings and monographic series.

AN15   UNITED NATIONS DOCUMENTS INDEX, 1950-1973. 24 vols. New York: United Nations, Dag Hammarskjöld Library. monthly; annual cumulation.
        Z6482 U5 GOVT   Sheehy CK242
    UNDI lists and indexes documents, except restricted material and internal papers. For 1950-1962, also includes a selective index to documents of other orgs in the UN system. CUMULATED INDEX to vols 1-13, 1950-1962 (4 vols; Kraus Thomson, 1974). Overlaps with and is continued by AN16.

AN16   UNDEX: UNITED NATIONS DOCUMENTS INDEX, 1970- Jan. 1979. New York: United Nations, Dag Hammarskjöld Library. 10 issues a year; annual cumulation.
        Z6482 U52 GOVT   Sheehy CK245
    Covers non-restricted documents and publications, although less inclusively than UNDI. In three series: A, SUBJECT INDEX (Vols 1-9; 1970-1978); B, COUNTRY INDEX (Vols 1-9; 1970-1978); and C, LIST OF DOCUMENTS ISSUED (Vols 1-6, No. 1: 1974- Jan. 1979). A and B, produced by computer-aided and now defunct UNDIS system, is much less complete than the manually produced C. Series "C" CUMULATIVE EDITION 1974-1977 (3 vols); 1978 [-1979] (1 vol.) (UNIFO, 1979-1980). UNDEX continued by AN17.

AN17   UNDOC: CURRENT INDEX; UNITED NATIONS DOCUMENTS INDEX, 1979- New York: United Nations, Dag Hammarskjöld Library. 10 issues a year; annual cumulation.
        UN2 LI U51 GOVT   Sheehy 2CK69
    Covers non-restricted documents and publications much more inclusively than its predecessor (AN16). Consists of checklist (full

bibliographic record) and author, title, and subject indexes. Also includes lists of maps, sales publications and new document series symbols.

AN18   UNITED NATIONS DOCUMENT SERIES SYMBOLS, 1946-1977. Cumulative List with Indexes. New York: United Nations, Dag Hammarskjöld Library, 1978. 312 p.
026.34113 U58   UN2 LI11 U55 GOVT

An index to the principal numbering scheme for UN documents, i.e. the document series symbols. Gives the names of issuing organs, indicates periods during which each symbol was in use and shows 'restricted' status when applicable. Subject/ title index; updated by listings in UNDEX (AN16) and UNDOC (AN17).

The UN System: UNESCO

In addition to the UN itself, most other orgs in the UN system issue bibliographies, indexes and/or sales catalogues. Some commercially published reference sources are also available. The following entries for the United Nations Educational, Scientific and Cultural Organization (UNESCO) are illustrative.

Guide

AN19   Hajnal, Peter I. GUIDE TO UNESCO. London: Oceana, 1983. 578 p.
341.767 H154G   AS4 U83 H33 GOVT

An overview of UNESCO's evolution, structure and work, with detailed analyses of programming activities, conferences and information (has chap. on documentation and publishing; discussion of the "new world information and communication order"). Includes an annotated bibliography of works by and about UNESCO, with various lists, tables, texts of ducuments.

Bibliographies and Indexes

AN20   BIBLIOGRAPHY OF PUBLICATIONS ISSUED BY UNESCO OR UNDER ITS AUSPICES; THE FIRST TWENTY-FIVE YEARS: 1946-1971. Paris: Unesco, 1973. 385 p.
R342.767 AU582B   UN9 ES 73B36 GOVT

Lists monographic and serial pubs, but excludes documents. Arranged by Universal Decimal Classification; author, title indexes.

AN21   LIST OF UNESCO DOCUMENTS AND PUBLICATIONS, 1949-1973. Paris: Unesco.
UN9 ES L37 GOVT

Covers pubs and general distribution documents. Annual indexes for 1960-1973. Overlaps with, continued by AN22.

AN22   UNESCO LIST OF DOCUMENTS AND PUBLICATIONS, 1972- Paris: Unesco. quarterly; cum. index, annual, multi-annual cumulations.
UN9 ES730 U54 GOVT

Includes most categories of documents and pubs. Produced by Unesco's Computerized Documentation System; with a 'masterfile' sequence no. assigned by computer (full bibliog. record) and subject, title/ series, personal name, meeting and corporate name indexes.

INTERNATIONAL ORGANIZATIONS OUTSIDE THE UN SYSTEM -- EXAMPLES

EUROPEAN COMMUNITIES

Guide

AN23   Jeffries, John. A GUIDE TO THE OFFICIAL PUBLICATIONS OF THE EUROPEAN COMMUNITIES. 2d ed. London: Mansell, 1981. 318 p.
015.4 AJ47G   Z2000 J4 GOVT
A survey of official publishing and publications of the European communities, grouped by issuing organ. Has chap. on bibliog. aids; appendices containing bibliography and other lists.

Bibliography

AN24   PUBLICATIONS OF THE EUROPEAN COMMUNITIES, 1974- Luxembourg: Office for Official Publications of the European Communities. monthly; annual cumulation.
ZZ EM380 P72 GOVT
Subject list of free and priced publications (excluding certain types) of the Communities. Annual cumulations include alphabetical index, list of periodicals. Issues appear both as a regular feature in the BULLETIN OF THE EUROPEAN COMMUNITIES and as a separate offprint; continuing similar lists in the BULLETIN OF THE EUROPEAN ECONOMIC COMMUNITY.

ORGANISATION FOR ECONOMIC CO-OPERATION AND DEVELOPMENT (OECD)

Publications

AN25   Organisation for Economic Co-operation and Development. CATALOGUE OF PUBLICATIONS, 1964- Paris: OECD. biennial; supplements.
ZZ ED C16 GOVT
This sales catalogue groups publications by subject, with author/title index. The only publicly available bibliographic source for OECD as a whole; INDEX OF OECD DOCUMENTS AND PUBLICATIONS, 1977- is not generally available outside the OECD.

Section B
Humanities

HUMANITIES

GUIDE

BA1   Rogers, A. Robert. THE HUMANITIES: A SELECTIVE GUIDE TO INFORMATION SOURCES. 2d ed. Littleton, CO: Libraries Unlimited, 1979. 355 p.
001.3 AA724H2

BIBLIOGRAPHIES AND INDEXES

BA2   ARTS & HUMANITIES CITATION INDEX, 1977- Philadelphia: Institute for Scientific Information, 1978- monthly; triennial cum. 1977-83, annual cum. 1984-
AI3 A6
Covers over 800 major journals in literature, history, languages, religion, philosophy, drama and theatre, art and architecture, music, classics, dance, folklore and the media. In addition to the usual citation indexing, AHCI includes works of art (poems, paintings, films etc.) as indexing terms when those works are the subject of the article. Indexes: citation, permuterm subject, source/ author.

BA3   BRITISH HUMANITIES INDEX, 1962- (See AF11)

BA4   CURRENT CONTENTS: ARTS & HUMANITIES, 1979- Philadelphia: Insitute for Scientific Information. weekly.
Contents pages for ca 950 journals and 125 new books. Covers the same fields as BA2.

BA5   HUMANITIES INDEX, 1974- (See AF12)

PHILOSOPHY

GUIDES

BB1   De George, Richard T. THE PHILOSOPHER'S GUIDE: To Sources, Research Tools, Professional Life, and Related Fields. Lawrence, KS: Regents Press of Kansas, 1980. 261 p.
         Z7125 D445
     Classified guide to materials in philosophy supplemented by sections on research tools in related fields, and general reference sources. Some titles with brief annotations.

BB2   Tice, Terence N., and Slavens, Thomas P. RESEARCH GUIDE TO PHILOSOPHY. Chicago: American Library Association, 1983. 608 p.
     R107 T555R
     Bibliographic essays on the history of philosophy, individual philosophers, and areas of philosophical inquiry, followed by an annotated list of reference works. Author/ title, subject indexes.

BIBLIOGRAPHIES, INDEXES AND ABSTRACTS

BB3   BIBLIOGRAPHIE DE LA PHILOSOPHIE, 1954-   Paris: Vrin. quarterly.
         Z7127 B5
     Abstracts of important new monographs in a classified order. Original language for English, French, German, Italian, and Spanish books; in English or French for others.

BB4   Guerry, Herbert. A BIBLIOGRAPHY OF PHILOSOPHICAL BIBLIOGRAPHIES. Westport, CT: Greenwood Press, 1977. 332 p.
         Z7125 A1G83
     In two parts: bibliographies of individual philosophers; subject bibliographies.

BB5   THE PHILOSOPHER'S INDEX: An International Index to Philosophical Periodicals and Books, 1967- Bowling Green, OH: Philosophy Documentation Center, Bowling Green State Univ. quarterly, annual cum.
         Z7127 P472
     An index, with abstracts of books in English, major journals in English, French, German, Spanish, and Italian; selected journals in other languages. Available online.
     The abstracting service, BULLETIN SIGNALETIQUE: PHILOSOPHIE, 1947- (Paris: Centre Nationale de la Recherche Scientifique) (Z7127 F72) aims to provide exhaustive coverage of current international serial publication in philosophy and allied disciplines.

BB6   _____: A Retrospective Index to Non-U.S. English Language Publications from 1940. 3 vols. Bowling Green, OH: Philosophy Documentation Center, Bowling Green State Univ., 1980.
         Z7127 P45
     Provides coverage of the philosophical literature from 1940 to the beginnings of indexing in the quarterly (BB5); articles published, 1940-66; books published, 1940-78. Available online.

BB7 _____: A Retrospective Index to U.S. Publications from 1940. 3 vols. Bowling Green, OH: Philosophy Documentation Center, Bowling Green State Univ., 1978.
Z7127 P478
Provides coverage for articles published, 1940-66; books published, 1940-76. Available online.

BB8 Rand, Benjamin. BIBLIOGRAPHY OF PHILOSOPHY, PSYCHOLOGY AND COGNATE SUBJECTS. 2 vols. New York: Macmillan, 1905.
Z7125 R3   Sheehy BA18
Classified bibliography of books, articles published to 1902. No author index.

BB9 REPERTOIRE BIBLIOGRAPHIQUE DE LA PHILOSOPHIE, 1949- Louvain: Editions de l'Institut superieur de philosophie. quarterly.
Z7127 R42   Sheehy BA26
Comprehensive classified list of current philosophical literature in English, Latin, seven European languages. Covers books, articles, review articles. Indexes: book reviews, names in Nov. issue.

BB10 Varet, Gilbert. MANUEL DE BIBLIOGRAPHIE PHILOSOPHIQUE. 2 vols. Paris: Presses universitaires de France, 1956.
Z7125 V3
A selective bibliography of books, articles in many languages. Vol. 1 covers basic works in philosophy; vol. 2 philosophy of other disciplines. Emphasis on the period 1914-1934. Extended by G.A. de Brie's BIBLIOGRAPHIA PHILOSOPHIA, 1934-1945 (Bruxelles: Spectrum, 1950-54) (Z7125 B7), a comprehensive bibliog. in twelve languages.

ENCYCLOPEDIAS AND DICTIONARIES

BB11 DICTIONARY OF THE HISTORY OF IDEAS: STUDIES OF SELECTED PIVOTAL IDEAS. 4 vols. Ed. by Philip P. Wiener. New York: Scribner, 1968-73. illus. separate index.
B823.3 D5
An interdisciplinary approach to intellectual history. Significant concepts explored by scholarly contributors in long essays with bibliographies. Index provides name and subject access.

BB12 THE ENCYCLOPEDIA OF PHILOSOPHY. 8 vols. New York: Macmillan, 1967. Reissue/ 4 vols. 1973.
R103 E56   B41 E5
A comprehensive, authoritative encyclopedia with articles by noted scholars. Broad scope, readable style, good bibliographies, excellent index. Largely supersedes James M. Baldwin's DICTIONARY OF PHILSOPHY AND PSYCHOLOGY (1901-05).

BB13 Flew, Anthony. A DICTIONARY OF PHILOSOPHY. New York: St Martin's Press, 1979. 351 p.
B41 D52
Concise definitions of terms and brief articles on major concepts, movements, philosophers. More extensive coverage of Eastern topics is found in DICTIONARY OF PHILOSOPHY AND RELIGION: EASTERN AND WESTERN THOUGHT by William L. Reese (Humanities Press, 1980) (B41 R43).

BB14   Lacey, Alan. A DICTIONARY OF PHILOSOPHY. London: Routledge, 1976. 239 p.
             B41 L3
             "A pocket encyclopedia of philosophy ... with a bias toward explaining terminology." Many entries include bibliographies.

BB15   Urmson, James O. THE CONCISE ENCYCLOPEDIA OF WESTERN PHILOSOPHY AND PHILOSOPHERS. 2d ed. London: Hutchinson, 1975. 319 p. illus.
         R103 U77   B41 U7
             An encyclopedia for the non-specialist reader. Brief articles deal with the most important individuals and theories.

HISTORIES OF PHILOSOPHY

BB16   Brehier, Emile. THE HISTORY OF PHILOSOPHY. 7 vols. Chicago: Univ. of Chicago Press, 1963-69.
                    B77 B72
             Originally published in French (1926-32). A standard history of the development of philosophic thought from the Hellenic period to the early twentieth century.

BB17   Copleston, Frederick. A HISTORY OF PHILOSOPHY. 8 vols. London: Burns and Oates, 1947-66.
                    B72 C6
             Written by a noted Jesuit scholar. The approach is chronological; each vol. with bibliography and index.

DIRECTORIES OF PHILOSOPHERS

BB18   DIRECTORY OF AMERICAN PHILOSOPHERS, 1962/63-   Bowling Green, OH: Philosophy Documentation Center, Bowling Green State Univ. biennial.
                    B935 D5
             Provides up-to-date information on philosophical activities in the U.S. and Canada.

BB19   INTERNATIONAL DIRECTORY OF PHILOSOPHY AND PHILOSOPHERS, 1966-   Bowling Green, OH: Philosophy Documentation Center, Bowling Green State Univ. irregular.
                    B35 I55
             Companion to BB18 for Europe, Central and South America, Asia, Africa, and Australia.

RELIGION

GUIDES

BC1 Adams, Charles J. A READER'S GUIDE TO THE GREAT RELIGIONS. 2d ed. New York: Free Press, 1977. 521 p.
R200 AA211
Critical bibliographic essays by specialists, covering primitive religion, Hinduism, Judaism, Christianity, Islam, religions of Central and South America, China and Japan, Sikhs, Jainas and the ancient world.

BC2 Wilson, John F., and Thomas P. Slavens. RESEARCH GUIDE TO RELIGIOUS STUDIES. Chicago: American Library Association, 1982. 192 p.
BL41 W56
Bibliographic essays and an annotated guide to reference works.

BIBLIOGRAPHIES, ABSTRACTS AND INDEXES

BC3 BULLETIN SIGNALETIQUE: HISTOIRE ET SCIENCES DES RELIGIONS, 1947- Paris: Centre Nationale de la Recherche Scientifique. quarterly.
Z7127 F72
International coverage of religious periodicals with annotations in French. The annual INTERNATIONAL BIBLIOGRAPHY OF THE HISTORY OF RELIGIONS, 1954- (Brill) (Z7833 I53) provides access to the scientific study of religions in books and periodicals.

BC4 Dell, David J., and others. GUIDE TO HINDU RELIGION. Boston: G.K. Hall, 1981. 461 p.
Z7835 B8G84
Annotated bibliography, broad in scope and comprehensive in coverage. Other vols in this ongoing series are GUIDE TO BUDDHIST RELIGION (1981) (Z7860 R48) by Frank Reynolds, and others; GUIDE TO ISLAM (1983) (Z7835 M6G84) by David Ede.

BC5 Mitros, Joseph F. RELIGIONS: A SELECT, CLASSIFIED BIBLIOGRAPHY. Louvain: Editions Nauwelaerts, 1973. 435 p.
Z7751 M57
A bibliography, partially annotated, of materials about major religions, denominations. Intended as a research guide for students. L.M. Karpinsk's THE RELIGIOUS LIFE OF MAN (Scarecrow, 1978) (Z7751 K36), a classified, annotated bibliography, is similar in purpose.

BC6 RELIGION INDEX ONE: PERIODICALS, July/Dec. 1977- Chicago: American Theological Library Association, 1978- semi-annual; biennial cumulation; annual 1985-
Z7753 A52
Continues INDEX TO RELIGIOUS PERIODICAL LITERATURE: An Author Subject Index to Periodical Literature, 1949/52-1977. BC6 covers more than 300 titles in English and other languages in three parts: subject index; author index with abstracts; book review index. Includes periodicals from many denominations. THE CATHOLIC PERIODICAL AND LITERATURE INDEX, 1968- (Catholic Library Association) includes Catholic periodicals and books by or of interest to Catholics.

BC7   RELIGION INDEX TWO: MULTI-AUTHOR WORKS, 1976-   Chicago: American Theological Library Association, 1978-   annual.
                    Z7751 R43
          Index to scholarly works on religious and theological topics. Subject, author indexes.

BC8   RELIGIOUS AND THEOLOGICAL ABSTRACTS, 1958-   Myerstown, PA: Religious and Theological Abstracts. quarterly.
                    BR1 R286
          Abstracts in English for articles from more than 200 journals in various languages. Non-sectarian approach. Classified arrangement with annual author, subject, scripture index.

BC9   RELIGIOUS BOOKS, 1876-1982. 4 vols. New York: R.R. Bowker, 1983.
                    Z7751 R436
          Based on the publishing records of Bowker augmented by entries from NATIONAL UNION CATALOG. Vols 1-3 list appr. 130 000 titles by subject. Vol. 4 is author and title indexes.

ENCYCLOPEDIAS AND DICTIONARIES

BC10   A DICTIONARY OF COMPARATIVE RELIGION. Ed. by S.G.F. Brandon. London: Weidenfeld & Nicolson, 1970. 704 p.
                    BL31 D54
          Concise articles, many with bibliographies, written by specialists. Synoptic and general index. Equally useful and somewhat similar in scope is ABINGDON DICTIONARY OF LIVING RELIGIONS (Abingdon, 1981) (BL31 A24).

BC11   ENCYCLOPEDIA JUDAICA. 16 vols. New York: Macmillan, 1972. illus. YEARBOOK, 1973-
                    DS102 8E55   Sheehy BB387, 1BB75
          Presents a scholarly, comprehensive picture of Jewish life and knowledge. Most of the 25 000 articles are signed; bibliographies emphasize English language material. DECENNIAL BOOK, 1973-1982: EVENTS OF 1972-1981 includes material from the yearbooks with additional information (Jerusalem: Encyclopedia Judaica, 1983) (DS37 E55133).

BC12   THE ENCYCLOPEDIA OF ISLAM. New ed. Leiden: E.J. Brill, 1960-
                    DS37 E5   Sheehy BB346, IBB64
          (Vols 1-4, A-KHA complete; with paper parts to M) Replaces the first ed. 1911-38. Authoritative and scholarly work treating Islamic life, lands, and people.

BC13   ENCYCLOPEDIA OF RELIGION AND ETHICS. 13 vols. Ed. by James Hastings, and others. Edinburgh: T. & T. Clark, 1908-27.
                    BL31 E5   Sheehy BB20
          Many articles now too dated for current work, but still consulted and cited.
          THE ENCYCLOPEDIA OF BIOETHICS, (4 vols, Free Press, 1978) (QH332 E52, BMER, SIGR) is an interdisciplinary approach to ethical and legal problems (abortion, organ transplants, test tube fertilization) current in philosophy, science, and religion. Coverage of concepts, traditions, historical perspective, scientific summary is a balanced

attempt to give a range of views in matters pertaining to the life sciences.

BC14 Humphreys, Christmas. A POPULAR DICTIONARY OF BUDDHISM. London: ARCO, 1962. 223 p.
        BL1403 H8
 Glossary of people, places, terms, concepts for English speaking students of Buddhism.

BC15 NEW CATHOLIC ENCYCLOPEDIA: An International Work of Reference on the Teachings, History, Organization and Activities of the Catholic Church, and on All Institutions, Religions, Philosophies, and Scientific and Cultural Developments Affecting the Catholic Church from Its Beginning to the Present. 15 vols. New York: McGraw Hill, 1967. illus. maps. SUPPLEMENT(s), vol. 16- 1974-
R282.03 N532   BX841 N44   Sheehy BB261
 Not a revision of the CATHOLIC ENCYCLOPEDIA (1907-14), but a new comprehensive work, ecumenical in outlook. Some 17 000 signed articles by specialists, good bibliographies, many illustrations, material on the arts, sciences. Supplements add new material, update articles in the main set. Some editorial staff of NCE continued their work to publish the ENCYCLOPEDIC DICTIONARY OF RELIGION (3 vols, Corpus, 1979) (BL31 E53).

BC16 THE OXFORD DICTIONARY OF THE CHRISTIAN CHURCH. 2d ed. Ed. by F.L.Cross, and E.A. Livingstone. London: Oxford Univ. Press, 1979. 1518 p.
R203 O98
 Broad in scope and intended audience, it contains more than 6000 authoritative articles, many with bibliographies. Emphasis is on the historical development of the Christian church. Also a CONCISE OXFORD DICTIONARY OF THE CHRISTIAN CHURCH (1977). THE NEW INTERNATIONAL DICTIONARY OF THE CHRISTIAN CHURCH (Zondervan, 1978) (BR95 D68), ed. by J.D. Douglas, is similar in scope with particular strength in evangelical topics.

BC17 Piepkorn, Arthur C. PROFILES IN BELIEF: The Religious Bodies of the United States and Canada. 7 vols. New York: Harper and Row, 1977- In progress.
        BR510 P53
 "A formal guide to belief systems" of a large number of religious, particularly Christian, groups.

BC18 THE NEW SCHAFF-HERZOG ENCYCLOPEDIA OF RELIGIOUS KNOWLEDGE: Embracing Biblical, Historical, Doctrinal and Practical Theology and Biblical, Theological and Ecclesiastical Biography from the Earliest Times to the Present Day. 12 vols. New York: Funk & Wagnalls, 1908-12. separate index. Reprint/ 13 vols. Grand Rapids, MI: Baker Book House, 1949-50.
        BR95 S435
 A basic Protestant encyclopedia, based on the 3d ed. of the REALENCYCLOPADIE, founded by J.J. Herzog and edited by A. Hauck. Supplemented by the TWENTIETH CENTURY ENCYCLOPEDIA OF RELIGIOUS KNOWLEDGE: An Extension of the New Schaff-Herzog Encyclopedia of Religious Knowledge (2 vols, Baker Book House, 1955) (BR95 S435).

BC19 YEARBOOK OF AMERICAN AND CANADIAN CHURCHES, 1916- Nashville, TN: Abingdon Press. annual.
BR513 Y4   Ryder HU8-5
Statistical and directory information on Christian churches and organizations. Michel Thériault's LES INSTITUTS DE VIE CONSCREE AU CANADA/ THE INSTITUTES OF CONSECRATED LIFE IN CANADA (National Library of Canada, 1980) (BX2527 T48) identifies 448 religious institutes of Canadian interest.

THE BIBLE

Bibliographies

BC20 British Library [Museum]. Dept of Printed Books. GENERAL CATALOGUE OF PRINTED BOOKS ... vols 17-19. (See AD4)
These three vols provide an excellent bibliography of the Bible. Editions in all languages are listed in vols 17,18; works about the Bible in vol. 19.

BC21 THE READER'S ADVISER. Vol. 3, 1977. pp. 86-127. (See AC18)

Encyclopedias and Dictionaries

BC22 Gehman, Henry S. THE NEW WESTMINSTER DICTIONARY OF THE BIBLE. Philadelphia: Westminster, 1970. 1027 p. illus. maps.
BS440 G4
Guide to the Bible with scriptural references, prononunciation, maps. Protestant viewpoint.

BC23 Hastings, James. DICTIONARY OF THE BIBLE: Dealing with Its Language, Literature and Contents, Including the Biblical Theology. 5 vols. Edinburgh: T. & T. Clark, 1898-1904. illus. maps.
BS440 H52
An older scholarly work based on the Authorized Version and the Revised Version, including the Old Testament Apocrypha. A revised Hastings' DICTIONARY OF THE BIBLE (Scribner, 1963, 1059 p.) (R220.3 H357) ed. by F.C. Grant and H.H. Rowley is based on the Revised Standard Version with cross references from the Revised and Authorized Versions.

BC24 THE INTERNATIONAL STANDARD BIBLE ENCYCLOPEDIA. 4 vols. Rev. ed. Ed. by G.W. Bromiley. Grands Rapids, MI: Eerdmans, 1979- In progress.
BS440 I46
Scholarly articles, many with bibliographies; coloured maps and plates. Conservative approach.

BC25 THE INTERPRETER'S DICTIONARY OF THE BIBLE: An Illustrated Encyclopedia Identifying and Explaining All Proper names and Significant Terms and Subjects in the Holy Scriptures, Including the Apocrypha, with Attention to Archaeological Discoveries and Researches into the Life

and Faith of Ancient Times. 4 vols. New York: Abingdon, 1962. illus. maps. SUPPLEMENT 1976.
R220.3 I61   BS440 I5
A comprehensive and authoritative work for modern Bible study; extensively illustrated.

BC26   McKenzie, John L. DICTIONARY OF THE BIBLE. Milwaukee, WI: Bruce Publishing, 1965. 954 p. illus. maps.
R220.3 MI56   BS440 M36
Scholarly, readable articles with a Roman Catholic viewpoint.

BC27   Miller, M.S., and J. L. Miller. HARPER'S BIBLE DICTIONARY. 8th ed. rev. New York: Harper and Row, 1973. 853 p. illus. maps.
R220.3 M649H   BS440 M52
A popular encyclopedia updated in the light of modern study, with new illustrations and revised maps to show changed place names and reflect recent archaeological findings.

BC28   _____. HARPER'S ENCYCLOPEDIA OF BIBLE LIFE. 3d rev. ed. New York: Harper, 1978. 423 p. illus. maps.
R220.3 M649   BS440 M5
Covers many areas of life including agriculture, apparel, arts, crafts, defense, flora and fauna, professions, trades and worship.

BC29   NEW INTERNATIONAL DICTIONARY OF BIBLICAL ARCHAEOLOGY. Ed. by E.M. Blaiklock, and R. Harrison. Grand Rapids, MI: Zondervan, 1983. 486 p.
BS622 N48
All articles except definitions are signed; many bibliographies and illustrations. ENCYCLOPEDIA OF ARCHAEOLOGICAL EXCAVATIONS IN THE HOLY LAND (4 vols, Prentice Hall, 1975-78) (DS111 A2E5) is a detailed work translated from the Hebrew.

Atlases

BC30   ATLAS OF THE BIBLE. (Ed. by L.H. Grollenberg) Trans. and ed. by J.M.H. Reid, and H.H. Rowley. London: Nelson, 1956. 165 p. illus. maps.
R220.93 G875
Translation of the 2d Dutch ed. ATLAS VAN DE BIJBEL (1954) with scholarly text and many fine illustrations.

BC31   THE MACMILLAN BIBLE ATLAS. Rev. ed. Ed. by Y. Aharoni, and M. Avi-Yonah. New York: Macmillan, 1977. 184 p. illus. maps.
R220.91 A285
Events in Biblical lands from 3000 B.C. to A.D. 200 shown in 264 maps; text by two Hebrew Univ. scholars.

BC32   THE OXFORD BIBLE ATLAS. 2d ed. Ed. by Herbert G. May. London: Oxford, 1974. 144 p. illus. maps.
BS630 M35
Includes historical introduction, article on Bible archaeology, as well as excellent maps and a gazetteer.

BC33   THE WESTMINSTER HISTORICAL ATLAS TO THE BIBLE. Rev. ed. Ed. by G.E. Wright, and F. Filson. Philadelphia: Westminster Press, 1956. 130 p. illus. maps.
R220.91 W949
Authoritative work with good maps, extensive text.

Concordances and Quotations

BC34   AN ANALYTICAL CONCORDANCE TO THE REVISED STANDARD VERSION OF THE NEW TESTAMENT. Comp. by C. Morrison. Philadelphia: Westminster Press, 1979. 770 p.
BS2305 M67
Relates the English translation to the original Greek text. Index/lexicon lists Greek words with all English translations in the RSV.

BC35   COMPLETE CONCORDANCE TO THE BIBLE (DOUAY VERSION). 4th ed. rev. and enl. Ed. by N.W. Thompson, and R. Stock. St Louis, MO: B. Herder, 1945. 1914 p.
R220.1 T474
First pub. in 1942 as CONCORDANCE TO THE BIBLE, Douay Version.

BC36   NELSON'S COMPLETE CONCORDANCE OF THE NEW AMERICAN BIBLE. General Ed. S.J. Hartdegen. Nashville, TN: Nelson, 1977. 1274 p.
BS425 H27
Computer-produced, verbal concordance.

BC37   NELSON'S COMPLETE CONCORDANCE OF THE REVISED STANDARD VERSION BIBLE. Ed. by J.W. Ellison. New York: Nelson, 1957. 2157 p.
R220.2 E47
An exhaustive, computer-produced concordance.

BC38   Stevenson, Burton E. THE HOME BOOK OF BIBLE QUOTATIONS. New York: Harper, 1949. 645 p.
R220.2 S847
Arranged by subject; a collection of familar Bible quotations, based on the Authorized Version.

BC39   Strong, James. THE EXHAUSTIVE CONCORDANCE OF THE BIBLE: Showing Every Word of the Text of the Common English Version of the Canonical Books, and Every Occurrence of Each Word in Regular Order: Together with a Comparative Concordance of the Authorized and Revised Versions, Including the American Variations; Also Brief Dictionaries of the Hebrew and Greek Words of the Original, with References to the English Words. 4 vols in 1. New York: Abingdon, 1890.
R220.2 S847   BS425 S8
A standard work, frequently reprinted.

Lives of the Saints

BC40   Butler, Alban. BUTLER'S LIVES OF THE SAINTS. 4 vols. 2d ed. Ed., rev., supplemented by H. Thurston, and D. Attwater. Montreal: Palm Publishers, 1956.
R920.3 B985   BX4655 B8
The homilies and lives of more obscure saints are omitted. John Delaney's DICTIONARY OF SAINTS (Kaye and Ward, 1982) (BX4655.8 D44)

is a more popular treatment without sources or index. OXFORD DICTIONARY OF SAINTS (Oxford, 1978) (BR1710 F3) by D.H. Farmer lists English saints and saints venerated in England.

OTHER SCRIPTURES

BC41   THE SACRED BOOKS OF THE EAST. 50 vols. Trans. by various Oriental scholars; ed. by F. Max Muller. Oxford: Clarendon Press, 1879-1910.
ROBA
Translations of the most important books of the non-Christian religions that have influenced the life and thought of Asia. Vol. 50 is an analytical index.

HYMNS

BC42   Diehl, Katharine S. HYMNS AND TUNES: AN INDEX. New York: Scarecrow, 1966. 1185 p.
781.1 D MCL MUS
Index to hymns from 78 20th century hymnals, chiefly Protestant, but includes a few Catholic and Jewish hymns. Access to hymns by first line and author; to tunes by composer, melody, name.

BC43   Julian, John. A DICTIONARY OF HYMNOLOGY: Setting Forth the Origin and History of Christian Hymns of All Ages and Nations. 2d rev. ed. with new supplement. London: J. Murray, 1907. 1768 p. Reprint/ 2 vols. New York: Dover, 1957.
R245.03 J94   BV305.J8
Stresses hymns of English-speaking countries.

MYTHOLOGY AND FOLKLORE

BC44   CROWELL'S HANDBOOK OF CLASSICAL MYTHOLOGY. Comp. by Edward Tripp. New York: Thomas Y. Crowell, 1970. 631 p.
Myths of Greece and Rome with reference to literary sources and a pronouncing index. WHO'S WHO IN CLASSICAL MYTHOLOGY (Weidenfeld & Nicholson, 1973) (BL715 G68) by M. Grant, and J. Hazel is similar in coverage, but includes genealogical trees and many illustrations.

BC45   DICTIONNAIRE DES MYTHOLOGIES ET DES RELIGIONS DES SOCIETES TRADITIONELLES ET DU MONDE ANTIQUE. 2 vols. Ed. by Yves Bonnefoy. Paris: Flammarion, 1981.
BL715 D54
Scholarly approach; signed articles, bibliographies, illustrations

BC46   EVERYMAN'S DICTIONARY OF NON-CLASSICAL MYTHOLOGY. 3d ed. Ed. by Egerton Sykes. London: Dent, 1962. 280 p. illus.
BL303 S9
Concise entries for persons, places and concepts in myths and legends of the world.

BC47 Frazer, Sir James G. THE GOLDEN BOUGH: A Study in Magic and Religion. 12 vols. 3d ed. London: Macmillan, 1911-15. Supplement: AFTERMATH. 1936.
BL310 F7
Extensive information on primitive religions and on the growth of beliefs and customs.

BC48 FUNK & WAGNALLS STANDARD DICTIONARY OF FOLKLORE, MYTHOLOGY AND LEGEND. Ed. by Maria Leach. New York: Funk & Wagnalls, 1972. 1236 p.
R398.03 F982   GR35 F8
A one vol. reissue of a standard work, with revisions and minor deletions. Long signed articles on folktales, gods, festivals, rituals, and food customs.

BC49 Fowke, E., and C.H. Carpenter. A BIBLIOGRAPHY OF CANADIAN FOLKLORE IN ENGLISH. Toronto: Univ. of Toronto Press, 1981. 272 p.
398 AF784B   Z5984 C2F69   Ryder SS2-1
Extensive bibliography, without annotations, under headings such as folktales, superstitions, popular beliefs, folk art and material culture. Includes films and recordings.

BC50 Haywood, Charles. A BIBLIOGRAPHY OF NORTH AMERICAN FOLKLORE AND FOLKSONG. 2 vols. 2d ed. New York: Dover, 1961. illus.
Z5984 U5H32
A comprehensive list of material in books and periodicals; includes Canadian references.

BC51 MYTHOLOGY: AN ILLUSTRATED ENCYCLOPEDIA. Ed. by Richard Cavendish. New York: Rizzoli, 1980. 303 p.
BL311 M4S
Geographical arrangement with glossary, bibliography, index; lavishly illustrated in col. and b&w. A GUIDE TO THE GODS (Morrow, 1982) (BL473 C37) by Richard Carlyon is also arranged geographically.

BC52 THE MYTHOLOGY OF ALL RACES. 13 vols. Ed. by Louis H. Gray. Boston: Marshall Jones, 1916-32. illus.
BL25 M8
A comprehensive collection of myths presented and interpreted by specialists. Vol. 13 is the index.

BC53 NEW LAROUSSE ENCYCLOPEDIA OF MYTHOLOGY. New ed. New York: Putnam, 1968. 500 p. illus.
BL310 L453
First published in French in 1935. Essays cover the mythologies of many cultures from prehistoric times to the 20th century.

LITERATURE

WORLD LITERATURE AND COMPREHENSIVE WORKS

GUIDES

BD1   A GUIDE TO EASTERN LITERATURES. Ed. by D.M. Lang. London: Weidenfeld and Nicolson, 1971. 500 p.
Z7046 L35
Essays, chiefly by Oriental scholars, at the Univ. of London, on the history, trends, important writers in a variety of literatures (Arabic, Jewish, Turkish, Indian, Pakistani, Tibetan, Chinese, Japanese, Korean, Burmese). Bibliographies in each section.

BD2   THE READER'S ADVISER. Vols 1 & 2. (See AC18)

BD3   YEAR'S WORK IN MODERN LANGUAGE STUDIES, 1929/30-   London: Modern Humanities Research Association, 1931-   annual.
R011 R286   PB1 Y45
Survey of publications on Latin, Romance, Celtic, Germanic and Slavonic languages and literatures.

BIBLIOGRAPHIES

BD4   Anderson, G.L. ASIAN LITERATURE IN ENGLISH: A GUIDE TO INFORMATION SOURCES. Detroit: Gale Research, 1981. 336 p.
An annotated bibliography of literary works, critical studies and reference sources. Other guides in this extensive 'American Literature, English Literature and World Literatures in English' series are INDIAN LITERATURE IN ENGLISH, 1827-1979 (1981) (Z3208 L5S56); AUSTRALIAN LITERATURE TO 1900 (1980) (Z4021 A54); MODERN AUSTRALIAN PROSE, 1901-1975 (1980) (Z4011 D38).

BD5   THE LITERATURES OF THE WORLD IN ENGLISH TRANSLATION: A BIBLIOGRAPHY. New York: Ungar, 1967-   In progress.
R880 AP252G   ROBA (various nos)
Vol. 1: THE GREEK AND LATIN LITERATURES (Z7018 T7E857); vol. 2: THE SLAVIC LITERATURES (Z7041 L59); vol. 3: THE ROMANCE LITERATURES (Z7033 T7E857). Other vols to include the Celtic, Germanic, other European, Asian, and African literatures.

BD6   MLA INTERNATIONAL BIBLIOGRAPHY OF BOOKS AND ARTICLES ON THE MODERN LANGUAGES AND LITERATURES, 1921-   New York: New York Univ. Press, published for the Modern Language Association of America, 1922-   annual. Reprint/ 1921-1962. New York: Kraus Reprint, 1964.
Z7006 M639 (Index Table 2)
Classified list of articles and books; author, subject indexes. Scope includes linguistics and folklore. Available online. Since 1970, the MLA has also issued an annual ABSTRACTS OF ARTICLES IN SCHOLARLY JOURNALS; published the MLA DIRECTORY OF PERIODICALS: A GUIDE TO JOURNALS AND SERIES IN LANGUAGE AND LITERATURE (1979).

BD7   Patterson, Margaret C. LITERARY RESEARCH GUIDE: An Evaluative, Annotated Bibliography of Important Reference Books and Periodicals on English, Irish, Scottish, Welsh, Commonwealth, American, Afro-American, American Indian, Continental, Classical, and World Literatures, and

Sixty Literature - Related Subject Areas. New York: Modern Language Association, 1983. 559 p.
Z6511 P37 (1976)
Related subject areas include little magazines, textual criticism, women's studies. "Directed toward those students ... who want to be self-educating individuals" with examples, glossary, index. Coverage of literatures other than British, American is not extensive.

BD8   Thompson, George A. KEY SOURCES IN COMPARATIVE AND WORLD LITERATURE: An Annotated Guide to Reference Materials. New York: Ungar, 1982. 383 p.
Z6511 T47
A basic handbook for Classical, European and Oriental literatures.

ENCYCLOPEDIAS, DICTIONARIES AND CRITICISM

BD9   Benet, William R. THE READER'S ENCYCLOPEDIA. 2d ed. New York: Crowell, 1965. 1118 p.
R803 B46R2   PN41 B4   Sheehy BD32
A reference source on world literature and the arts: literary terms, allusions, place names, authors, and painters.

BD10   CARIBBEAN WRITERS: A BIO-BIBLIOGRAPHICAL CRITICAL ENCYCLOPEDIA. Ed. by D.E. Herdeck. Washington: Three Continents Press, 1979. 943 p. illus.
PN849 C3C3
Anglophone, Francophone and Spanish language authors of the literatures of the Caribbean, including the Netherland Antilles and Surinam. Bibliographies of anthologies and critical works follow the biographical sections.

BD11   CASSELL'S ENCYCLOPEDIA OF WORLD LITERATURE. 3 vols. Rev. and enl. Ed. by J. Buchanan-Brown. London: Cassell, 1973.
R803 C343   PN41 C3
Vol. 1 contains histories of individual literatures and schools, definitions, descriptions of genres. Vols 2 and 3 are biographical.

BD12   COLUMBIA DICTIONARY OF MODERN EUROPEAN LITERATURE. 2d ed. Ed. by J-A Bédé, and W.B. Edgerton. New York: Columbia Univ. Press, 1980. 895 p
R803 C72   PN41 C6
Mainly biographical, with signed articles about more than 1800 authors. Some entries for national literatures.

BD13   CONTEMPORARY LITERARY CRITICISM, 1973-   Detroit: Gale Research. irreg.
PN94 C6
(Vol. 25, 1983) Excerpts from books and periodicals concerned with the criticism of major authors and playwrights living (or deceased since 1960). Retrospective coverage is provided by TWENTIETH CENTURY LITERARY CRITICISM, 1978- (vol. 10, 1983) (PN771 T9) for authors 1900-1960, with portraits included from vol. 4. Also by NINETEENTH CENTURY LITERATURE CRITICISM, 1981- (vol. 4, 1983) (PN761 N5) for authors who lived 1800-1900.

BD14   DICTIONARY OF ORIENTAL LITERATURES. 3 vols. Ed. by J. Prusek. New York: Basic Books, 1974.
PN41 P75
Vol. I: EAST ASIA; II: SOUTH AND SOUTH-EAST ASIA; III: WEST ASIA AND NORTH AFRICA. Signed articles, many with bibliographies, about authors, literary forms and genres, schools of writing and movements. International list of contributors; many are Czechoslovakian.

BD15   DIZIONARIO LETTERARIO BOMPIANI DELLE OPERE E DEI PERSONAGGI DI TUTTI I TEMPI E DI TUTTE LE LETTERATURE. 11 vols. Milan: Bompiani, 1947-79.
PN41 D528
An illustrated standard European dictionary of literary and artistic works with biographies of writers, artists, musicians.

BD16   ENCYCLOPEDIA OF WORLD LITERATURE IN THE 20TH CENTURY. 4 vols. Rev. ed. Ed. by L.S. Klein. New York: Ungar, 1981-   In progress.
PN771 E5
Articles on authors, literary movements, genres, national literatures, movements in ideas, literature and related arts.

BD17   A HANDBOOK TO LITERATURE. 4th ed. Ed. by H. C. Holman. Indianapolis, IN: Bobbs Merrill, 1980. 537 p.
PN41 H6
Based on a handbook by Thrall and Hibbard. Explains, for the student of literature, the "words and phrases peculiar to the study of English and American literature." H. Shaw's DICTIONARY OF LITERARY TERMS (McGraw, 1972) (PN44.5 S46) and J.A. Cuddon's A DICTIONARY OF LITERARY TERMS (Deutsch, 1979) (PN41 C83) are also useful.

BD18   Magill, Frank N. MASTERPIECES OF WORLD LITERATURE IN DIGEST FORM. 4 vols New York: Harper, 1952-69.
R808.8 M194   PN44 M32
Includes summaries, very brief comment on essays, poetry, drama, fiction; arranged alphabetically by the title of the work. MAGILL'S LITERARY ANNUAL (2 vols, Salem Press) provides critical evaluations, summaries of the previous year's 200 most significant books, both fiction and non-fiction. Magill's MASTERPLOTS, published in a rev. ed as MASTERPLOTS: 2010 PLOT STORIES AND ESSAY REVIEWS (1976).

BD19   _____. CYCLOPEDIA OF LITERARY CHARACTERS. New York: Harper, 1963. 1280 p.
R803 M194   PN44 M3
Major characters from 1300 world classics are assessed critically. Arrangement is alphabetical by title of work; author, character index

BD20   A NEW READER'S GUIDE TO AFRICAN LITERATURE. 2d ed. Ed. by H.M. Zell; C. Bundy, and V. Coulon. New York: Africana, 1983. 553 p.
PR9798 Z4
Black African authors south of the Sahara writing in English, French and Portuguese. Annotated entries for reference materials, anthologies, criticism, collections, folklore, children's books, periodicals and belles lettres. Illustrated biographies of the most prominent authors; sources for African literature with publishers, booksellers, libraries listed.

BD21 THE OXFORD COMPANION TO CLASSICAL LITERATURE. Ed. by Sir Paul Harvey. Oxford: Clarendon Press, 1974. 468 p.
R913.38 H346C1   DE5 H3
(1st ed., 1937; frequently reprinted) Concise information on classical authors and their works, the literary forms, allusions. Other "companions" are THE OXFORD COMPANION TO FRENCH LITERATURE (1959) (PQ41 H3) by P. Harvey and J. Heseltine; ... TO GERMAN LITERATURE (1976) (PT41 G3) by H. Garland and M. Garland; ... TO SPANISH LITERATURE (1978) (PQ6006 O93) by P. Ward.

BD22 THE PENGUIN COMPANION TO LITERATURE. 4 vols. London: Penguin, 1969-71.
PN41 P45
Concise signed articles, most with bibliographies covering, vol. 1, Britain and the Commonwealth; 2, Europe; 3, U.S., Latin America; 4, Classical, Byzantine, Oriental, African literatures.

ENGLISH LITERATURE

GUIDES, BIBLIOGRAPHIES AND ABSTRACTS

BD23 ABSTRACTS OF ENGLISH STUDIES, 1958- Calgary: English Dept, Univ. of Calgary. monthly.
PR1 A25
Abstracts of articles on British and world literature in English and other languages. Covers language and bibliography as well as themes, types and periods of literature.

BD24 Altick, Richard D., and Andrew H. Wright. SELECTIVE BIBLIOGRAPHY FOR THE STUDY OF ENGLISH AND AMERICAN LITERATURE. 6th ed. New York: Macmillan, 1979. 180 p.
R820 AA468S3   Z2011 A4
Useful authority on materials essential for modern research.

BD25 ANNUAL BIBLIOGRAPHY OF ENGLISH LANGUAGE AND LITERATURE, 1920- London: Modern Humanities Research Association.
Z2011 M69 (Index Table 2)
Excellent bibliography for books, pamphlets, articles, bk reviews. Scope includes media, bibliography, folklore, computer applications.

BD26 Bateson, Frederick W., and Harrison T. Meserole. A GUIDE TO ENGLISH AND AMERICAN LITERATURE. 3d ed. London: Longman, 1976. 334 p.
R820 AB329G2
Annotated bibliographies accompanied by lively essays introducing and reinterpreting each period of English literature. One chapter on American literature.

BD27 Bell, Inglis F., and Jennifer Gallup. A REFERENCE GUIDE TO ENGLISH, AMERICAN AND CANADIAN LITERATURE: An Annotated Checklist of Bibliographic and Other Reference Materials. Vancouver: Univ. of British Columbia, 1971. 139 p.
025.5 AB433R   Z2011 B45
Intended for graduate level research.

BD28   THE CAMBRIDGE GUIDE TO ENGLISH LITERATURE. Ed. by Michael Stapleton. Cambridge: Univ. Press, 1983. 992 p.
PR85 C28
A guide to the literature of the English speaking world, with entries for authors, characters and works.

BD29   'Contemporary Writers of the English Language'. Series ed. James Vinson. London: Macmillan
Series includes DRAMATISTS (3d ed., 1982) (PR106 V5); NOVELISTS (3d ed., 1982) (PR881 C65); POETS (3d ed., 1980) (PR610 C6). Entries feature a brief biography, bibliography and critical essay.

BD30   GREAT WRITERS OF THE ENGLISH LANGUAGE. 3 vols. Ed. by James Vinson. London: Macmillan, 1979.
PR106 G64
Vol. 1: POETS; 2: NOVELISTS AND PROSE WRITERS; 3: DRAMATISTS. Biography, short title list of publications, brief signed essay.

BD31   New, William H. CRITICAL WRITINGS ON COMMONWEALTH LITERATURES: A Selective Bibliography to 1970, with a List of Theses and Dissertations. University Park, PA: Pennsylvania State Univ. Press, 1975. 333 p.
Z2000.9 N48
Lists books and articles on general works, individual authors.

BD32   YEAR'S WORK IN ENGLISH STUDIES, 1919-   London: J. Murray, published for the English Association. annual.
PE58 E6
Brief critical survey of books and articles on English and American literature issued anywhere during the year. Each period discussed in a separate chapter by a specialist.

CRITICAL EXCERPTS

BD33   THE CRITICAL TEMPER: A Survey of Modern Criticism on English and American Literature from the Beginnings to the Twentieth Century. 3 vols. Ed. by Martin Tucker. New York: Ungar, 1969. SUPPLEMENT 1979.
R820.9 C934   ROBA
Presents excerpts from studies of important authors in books and periodicals. Forms part of the 'Library of Literary Criticism' series (Ungar) with vols on modern American, British, Commonwealth, French, German, Latin American, Black, Slavic, Greek and Lation literatures and plans coverage of Near Eastern authors. (Complements BD34).

BD34   THE LIBRARY OF LITERARY CRITICISM OF ENGLISH AND AMERICAN AUTHORS THROUGH THE BEGINNING OF THE TWENTIETH CENTURY. 8 vols. Ed. by Charles W. Moulton. Buffalo: Moulton, 1901-05. /Abridged ed. 4 vols. Rev. and enl. by Martin Tucker. New York: Ungar, 1966.
R809 M927   PR83 M73
Excerpts from criticism of the works of authors from 680-1904.

LITERARY BIOGRAPHY AND ANONYMOUS AUTHORS

See Biography, AL, and its subsection on Authors AL48 to AL74; plus BD listings for general works of reference on literature.

BD35   DICTIONARY OF LITERARY PSEUDONYMS. 3d ed. Ed. by F. Atkinson. London: Clive Bingley, 1982. 305 p.
         Z1041 A84
         Useful for 20th century writers in English.

BD36   Halkett, Samuel, and John Laing. A DICTIONARY OF ANONYMOUS AND PSEUDONYMOUS ENGLISH LITERATURE. 3d ed. Ed. by John Horden. New York: Longman, 1980-   In progress.
         R014 AH17   Z1065 H17   Sheehy AA98
         The most comprehensive index for identifying anonymous, pseudonymous works in the English language. Third ed. in chronological vols. Vol. 1 covers 1475-1640.

BD37   PSEUDONYMS AND NICKNAMES DICTIONARY. (See AJ64)
         Includes literary figures.

NATIONAL LITERATURES Great Britain

BD38   Baugh, Albert C. A LITERARY HISTORY OF ENGLAND. 2d ed. New York: Appleton, 1967. 1605 p.
         R820.9 B346
         A comprehensive history of English literature, including some Scottish and Irish writers, from earliest times to 1939.

BD39   THE CAMBRIDGE HISTORY OF ENGLISH LITERATURE. 15 vols. Cambridge: Univ. Press, 1907-27.
         R820.9 C178   PR83 C2
         This important history is arranged by period with each chapter by a specialist. A reprint concise edition omitted the bibliographies; 3d ed. of the concise version (1970) ed. by George Sampson.

BD40   INDEX TO BRITISH LITERARY BIBLIOGRAPHY. 6 vols. Ed. by T.H. Howard-Hill. Oxford: Clarendon Press, 1969-   In progress.
         Z2011 A1H68
         Vol. 1 covers British literary bibliographies; 2, Shakespearian bibliography; 4-6, bibliography and textual criticism with index in vol. 6. Lists books, substantial parts of books and articles in English, pub. since 1890. Covers authors, periods, regions, genres.

BD41   THE OXFORD COMPANION TO ENGLISH LITERATURE. Ed. by Sir Paul Harvey. 4th ed. rev. by Dorothy Eagle. Oxford: Clarendon Press, 1967. 961 p.
         R820.3 H34C4   PR19 H3
         Includes brief biographies, plot summaries, literary allusions. THE CONCISE OXFORD DICTIONARY OF ENGLISH LITERATURE is based on this work.

BD42   THE NEW CAMBRIDGE BIBLIOGRAPHY OF ENGLISH LITERATURE. 5 vols. Ed. by G. Watson, and I. Willison. Cambridge: Univ. Press, 1969-77.
         R820 AC178CA   Z2011 N45   Sheehy BD376, 1BD83
         Vols 1-4 are chronological: 600-1660; 1660-1800; 1800-1900; 1900-1950 with index in vol. 5. Completely revises the CAMBRIDGE

BIBLIOGRAPHY OF ENGLISH LITERATURE (5 vols, Univ. Press, 1940-57). Entries arranged by period and form, then by authors. Differs from its predecessor by excluding Commonwealth literature and by limiting non-literary sections. Also THE SHORTER NEW CAMBRIDGE BIBLIOGRAPHY OF ENGLISH LITERATURE (1981, 1622 p.) (Z2011 N45).

BD43   OXFORD HISTORY OF ENGLISH LITERATURE. 12 vols. Oxford: Clarendon Press, 1945-   In progress.
R820.9 098   ROBA
By period; scholarly with extensive bibliographies.

United States

BD44   Blanck, Jacob N. BIBLIOGRAPHY OF AMERICAN LITERATURE. New Haven, CT: Yale Univ. Press, 1955-   In progress.
R810.3 B641   Z1225 B55
(Vol. 7, 1983, names beginning with "S") Descriptive bibliography of 1st eds and variants of "the native literature read in book form" from the American Revolution to 1930. Includes illustrations, title pages, locations of copies.

BD45   Gohdes, Clarence L.F. BIBLIOGRAPHICAL GUIDE TO THE STUDY OF THE LITERATURE OF THE U.S.A. 4th ed. rev. and enl. Durham, NC: Duke Univ. Press, 1976. 173 p.
Z1225 G6
Basic guide to techniques of research into the literature.

BD46   Koster, Donald N. AMERICAN LITERATURE AND LANGUAGE: A GUIDE TO INFORMATION SOURCES. Detroit: Gale Research, 1982. 396 p.
Z1225 K68
This annotated guide to secondary sources is vol. 13, 'American Studies Information Guide' series. Other titles include AFRO-AMERICAN LITERATURE AND CULTURE SINCE WORLD WAR II (1979) (Z1229 N39P4) by C.D. Peavy; JEWISH WRITERS OF NORTH AMERICA (1981) (Z1229 J4N32) by I.B. Nadel.

BD47   LITERARY HISTORY OF THE UNITED STATES. 2 vols. 4th ed. rev. Ed. by R.E. Spiller, and others. New York: Macmillan, 1974.
R810 AN712   PS88 L52
Survey from Colonial times to present. Vol. 2 is bibliography. THE CAMBRIDGE HISTORY OF AMERICAN LITERATURE (4 vols, 1917-21 /reprint 1933; 1967) (R810.9 C178) is still a standard.

BD48   Nilon, Charles H. BIBLIOGRAPHY OF BIBLIOGRAPHIES IN AMERICAN LITERATURE. New York: R.R. Bowker, 1970. 483 p.
R810 AN712   Z1225 A1N5
Over 6000 items; books and periodical articles.

BD49   THE OXFORD COMPANION TO AMERICAN LITERATURE. 5th ed. Ed. by James D. Hart. New York: Oxford Univ. Press, 1983. 896 p.
R810.3 H3204 (1965)   PS21 H3
Concise entries on authors, societies, terms, allusions, movements, awards, periodicals etc.

BD50   THE READER'S ENCYCLOPEDIA OF AMERICAN LITERATURE. New York: Crowell, 1962. 1280 p.
R810.3 R285   PS21 R43
   Entries on American, Canadian literatures. Biographies, criticism, fictional characters, genres, glossary of terms. Many portraits.

Canada

BD51   THE ANNOTATED BIBLIOGRAPHY OF CANADA'S MAJOR AUTHORS. 10 vols. Ed. by R. Lecker, and J. David. Downsview, Ont.: ECW Press, 1979- In progress.
Z1375 L43   Ryder HU6-6
   Extensive bibliographies of works by and about Atwood, Laurence, MacLennan, Richler, Roy, Cohen, Lampman, Pratt, Purdy, Buckler, Ross, Davies, Knister, Mitchell, Birney, Livesay, Scott, Smith, Callaghan, Gallant, Hood, Munro, Wilson.

BD52   Barbeau, V., and A. Fortier. DICTIONNAIRE BIBLIOGRAPHIQUE DU CANADA FRANCAIS. Montreal: Académie canadienne française, 1974. 246 p.
Z1365 B3   Ryder GR1-7
   Includes brief biographical notes.

BD53   THE BROCK BIBLIOGRAPHY OF PUBLISHED CANADIAN PLAYS IN ENGLISH, 1766-1978 (BD74)

BD54   CANADIAN WRITERS AND THEIR WORKS. 20 vols. Ed. by R. Lecker; J. David, and E. Quigley. Toronto: ECW Press, 1983-   In progress.
PS8141 C37
   Essays outlining the development of fiction and poetry, each in 10 vols. Biographical essay and critical assessment with bibliography of primary, secondary sources. Fiction, vol. 1 covers Brooke, Moodie, Richardson, Traill and several Victorian writers. Poetry, vol.. 2, covers Campbell, Carman, Lampman, Roberts, Scott.

BD55   DICTIONNAIRE DES OEUVRES LITTERAIRES DU QUEBEC. 3 vols. Sous la direction de Maurice Lemire. Montreal: Fides, 1980.
PS9015 D5
   Vols are chronological, I: des Origines à 1900; II: 1900-1939; III: 1940-1959. An illustrated directory of major works; signed articles with bibliographies; index.

BD56   CANADA'S PLAYWRIGHTS: A BIOGRAPHICAL GUIDE. (BD83)

BD57   Fee, M. CANADIAN FICTION: AN ANNOTATED BIBLIOGRAPHY. (BD92).

BD58   Gnarowski, Michael. A CONCISE BIBLIOGRAPHY OF ENGLISH CANADIAN LITERATURE. Rev. ed. Toronto: McClelland and Stewart, 1978. 145 p.
Z1375 G525
   Includes material to 1975; lists major works by date and type; plus criticism and studies of authors and their works.

BD59   Grandpré, Pierre de. HISTOIRE DE LA LITTERATURE FRANCAISE DU QUEBEC. 4 vols. Montreal: Librairie Beauchemin, 1967-69.
819 G754   PS9063 G733   Ryder HU6-43
   Biographical and bibliographic approach to major literary figures, selected journalists and historians.

BD60   LITERARY HISTORY OF CANADA: Canadian Literature in English. 3 vols. 2d ed. Ed. by Carl F. Klinck. Toronto: Univ. of Toronto Press, 1976.
R819 K65L2   PS8063 K55   Ryder HU6-44
   Expert essays on authors and literature; surveys of work in other disciplines, e.g. history, philosophy, religion, and the physical, biological and social sciences.

BD61   Moyles, R.G. ENGLISH CANADIAN LITERATURE TO 1900: A Guide to Information Sources. Detroit: Gale Research, 1976. 346 p.
810.08 AM938E   Z1375 M693   Ryder HU6-39
   Critical annotations of reference works, travel literature, journals; critical comment in books and periodicals supplied for 12 major, 36 minor authors. One of 3 vols on Canadian literature in the series 'American Literature ...'; others are P. Steven's MODERN ENGLISH CANADIAN POETRY (1978) (Z1377 P7S79) and H. Hoy's MODERN ENGLISH CANADIAN PROSE (1983) (Z1377 F4HG9).

BD62   THE OXFORD COMPANION TO CANADIAN HISTORY AND LITERATURE. Ed. by N. Story. Toronto: Oxford Univ. Press, 1967. 935 p. SUPPLEMENT. Ed. by W. Toye. 1973.
R971.03 S887   PS8015 S7   Ryder HU6-41
   About a third of the articles are on literature. Most are biographical; others survey poetry, fiction, drama, journals, folklore and Indian legends.

BD63   THE OXFORD COMPANION TO CANADIAN LITERATURE. Ed. by W. Toye. Toronto: Oxford Univ. Press, 1983. 843 p.
R819 O98P   PS8015 O93
   Signed entries for authors, notable works, genres, themes, regional literatures, etc. Emphasis on modern writing in both English and French Canada. Cross refs; no index.

BD64   Tremblay, Jean-Pierre. BIBLIOGRAPHIE QUEBECOISE; ROMAN, THEATRE, POESIE, CHANSON: Inventaire des écrits de Canada français. Quebec: Educo Média, 1973. 252 p.
                    Z1377 F8T74
   By genre; cites books, articles. Less selective is BIBLIOGRAPHIE DE LA CRITIQUE DE LITTERATURE QUEBECOISE DANS LES REVUES DE XIXe ET XXe SIECLES (5 vols, Univ. d'Ottawa, 1979) (Z1377 F8C28).

BD65   Union des ecrivans québécois. DICTIONNAIRE DES ECRIVANS QUEBECOIS CONTEMPORAINS. Monteal: Québec/ Amérique, 1983. 399 p.
                    PS8081 D53
   Bio-bibliographies; illustrated.

BD66   Watters, Reginald E. A CHECKLIST OF CANADIAN LITERATURE AND BACKGROUND MATERIALS, 1628-1960. 2d ed. Toronto: Univ. of Toronto Press, 1972. 1085 p.
R015.71 W346C2   Z1375 W3   Ryder HU6-20
   In two parts; 1, records all known titles of poetry, fiction, drama by Anglophone Canadians to 1960; 2, selectively lists items by Canadians of value to the student of Canadian literature or culture.

LITERARY GENRES Poetry

BD67 INDEX TO POETRY FOR CHILDREN AND YOUNG PEOPLE, 1964-1969. Comp. by J.E. Brewton; G.M. Blackburn, and L.A. Blackburn. New York: H.W. Wilson, 1972. SUPPLEMENT 1970-1975 (1978).
R808.81 AB848
Continues INDEX TO CHILDREN'S POETRY (1952, 1954, 1965). Title, subject and first line index to poetry in collections.

BD68 Deutsch, Babette. POETRY HANDBOOK: A DICTIONARY OF TERMS. 4th ed. New York: Funk & Wagnalls, 1974. 203 p.
R808.1014 D486P4   PN44.5 D4
Terms, with examples, used in the criticism, practice of poetry.

BD69 GRANGER'S INDEX TO POETRY 7th ed. Ed. by W.J. Smith, and W.F. Bernhardt New York: Columbia Univ. Press, 1982. 1239 p.
R808.81 AG7515 (1982)   PN1021 G7
This ed. marks a change in editorial policy. Previous GRANGER'S carried over anthologies from earlier eds; 7th ed. goes back only to 1970. Includes 248 vols of poetry collections. Arranged by title and first line; author, subject indexes.

BD70 Kuntz, J.M., and N.C. Martinez. POETRY EXPLICATION: A Checklist of Interpretation Since 1925 of British and American Poems Past and Present. Boston: G.K. Hall, 1980. 570 p.
Z2014 P7K8
Arranged by author, then title of poem.

BD71 PRINCETON ENCYCLOPEDIA OF POETRY AND POETICS. Enl. ed. Ed. by Alex Preminger. Princeton, NJ: Princeton Univ. Press, 1975. 992 p.
R809.1 E56   PN1021 E5
A scholarly work on "the history, theory, technique and criticism of poetry from the earliest times to the present."

Drama Bibliographies

BD72 Breed, P., and F. Sniderman. DRAMATIC CRITICISM INDEX: A Bibliography of Commentaries on Playwrights from Ibsen to the Avant-Garde. Detroit: Gale Research, 1972. 1022 p.
R809.2 D763   Z5781 B8
A selective index to appr. 630 books and over 200 periodicals. Some reviews are included, especially for foreign playwrights.

BD73 THE PLAYER'S LIBRARY: The Catalogue of the Library of the British Drama League. London: Faber, 1950. 1115 p. SUPPLEMENT(s) 1951, 1954, 1956.
Z2014 D7B8   Sheehy BG8
More than 70 000 plays and books on the theatre. Plays, some in European languages, listed alphabetically by author with short notes; books on theatre arranged by subject.

BD74 THE BROCK BIBLIOGRAPHY OF PUBLISHED CANADIAN PLAYS IN ENGLISH, 1766-1978. Ed. by Anton Wagner. Toronto: Playwrights Canada, 1980. 375 p.
R808.82 AB864B   Z1377 D7B72   Ryder HU6-73
An annotated bibliography of some 2000 entries. A BIBLIOGRAPHY OF ENGLISH LANGUAGE THEATRE AND DRAMA IN CANADA, 1800-1914 (Univ. of Alberta, 1976) (Z1377 D7S44) by D. Sedgwick and CANADIAN PLAYS: A

SUPPLEMENTARY CHECKLIST TO 1945 (Dalhousie Univ. Lib. and School of Library Service, 1978) (Z1377 D7054) by P. O'Neill are also useful.

BD75   New York Public Library. Research Libraries. CATALOG OF THE THEATRE AND DRAMA COLLECTIONS. Boston: G.K. Hall, 1967. SUPPLEMENT 1973; 1974.
Z5785 N4; N42; N43
In 3 parts: I: drama collection with author, cultural origin lists; theatre; 2: theatre collection; 3: non-book collection. The BIBLIOGRAPHIC GUIDE TO THEATRE ARTS, 1975- (G.K. Hall) is the supplement.

BD76   Rinfret, Edouard G. LE THEATRE CANADIEN D'EXPRESSION FRANCAISE: Répertoire analytique des origines à nos jours. 4 vols. Ottawa: Leméac, 1975-78.
Z1377 D7R5   Ryder HU6-78
Arranged alphabetically by author; information on performance, cast, plot. Vols 1-3, theatre, radio plays; vol. 4 television plays.

Play Indexes

BD77   CUMULATED DRAMATIC INDEX, 1909-1949: A Cumulation of the F.W. Faxon Company's Dramatic Index. 2 vols. Boston: G.K. Hall, 1965.
R808.82 AC971   AI3 C85
Indexes articles in English and American periodicals.

BD78   Ireland, Norma. INDEX TO FULL LENGTH PLAYS, 1944 TO 1964. Boston: F.W. Faxon, 1965. 296 p.
R808.82 AT48   Z5781 T52
Author/ title/ subject alphabetical index with author, adapter, number of acts and characters under the title entry. Continues R.G. Thomson's 1895-1944 indexes (F.W. Faxon, 1946, 1956) (Z5781 T5).

BD79   Keller, Dean H. INDEX TO PLAYS IN PERIODICALS. Rev. and expanded. Metuchen, NJ: Scarecrow, 1979. 824 p.
Z5781 K43
Author and title access to plays, published to 1976, in over 200 periodicals, chiefly American and British.

BD80   Logasa, Hannah, and Ver Nooy, Winifred. AN INDEX TO ONE ACT PLAYS, 1900-1964. 6 vols. Boston: F.W. Faxon, 1924-66.
R808.82 AL83   Z5781 L83
Vol. 1, 1900-23, other vols as supplements, 1924-31; 1932-40; 1941-48; 1948-57; 1956-64. Third suppl. adds radio plays; 4th adds TV plays. Index stresses plays for children, young people.

BD81   OTTEMILLER'S INDEX TO PLAYS IN COLLECTIONS: An Author and Title Index to Plays Appearing in Collections Published between 1900 and early 1975. 6th ed. rev. and enl. Ed. by John M. Connor, and Billie M. Connor. Metuchen, NJ: Scarecrow Press, 1976. 523 p.
R808.82 AO8914   Z5781.O8

BD82   PLAY INDEX, 1949- New York: H.W. Wilson, 1953- irreg.
R808.82 AP722   Z5781 F45
(Vol. 6, 1978-82 {1983}). Indexes single plays, collections, radio, TV plays, and plays for children. Cast analysis in author/ title/

subject index. The 6 vols (to 1983) provide access to more 23 000 plays. PLAYS: A CLASSIFIED GUIDE TO PLAY SELECTION (Stacey Directories, annual) (PR1272 P6) lists new plays.

Encyclopedias, Directories and Handbooks

BD83   CANADA'S PLAYWRIGHTS: A BIOGRAPHICAL GUIDE. Toronto: Canadian Theatre Review, 1980. 191 p.
PS8081 C36
Entry includes list of works with photo for more than 60 authors.

BD84   Gassner, John, and Edward Quinn. THE READER'S ENCYCLOPEDIA OF WORLD DRAMA. New York: Crowell, 1969. 1030 p. illus.
R809.2 G253R   PN1625 G3
Treats drama as literature; surveys, biographies, summaries.

BD85   Marlow, Myron. MODERN WORLD DRAMA: AN ENCYCLOPEDIA. New York: E.P. Dutton, 1972. 960 p. illus.
PN1851 M36
Synopses and comment on all major 19th century playwrights who lived into the 20th century and contemporary dramatists.

BD86   McGRAW HILL ENCYCLOPEDIA OF WORLD DRAMA. 5 vols. 2d ed. New York: McGraw Hill, 1984. illus.
PN1625 M3
A guide to major dramatists, with surveys on national, regional drama, non-Western dramatic traditions, influential directors, theatres and companies. Play title list, glossary, index.

Fiction

BD87   Aubin, Allen J. CRIME FICTION 1749-1980: A COMPREHENSIVE BIBLIOGRAPHY. New York: Garland, 1984. 712 p.
Z2014 F4H82
Author list of 60 000 works; indexes by title, setting (primarily geographic), series, series character. David and Ann Skene-Melvin's CRIME, DETECTIVE, ESPIONAGE, MYSTERY, & THRILLER FICTION AND FILM: A Comprehensive Bibliography of Critical Writing through 1979 (Greenwood, 1979) (Z5197 D5S55) indexes books and articles.

BD88   Barron, Neil. ed. ANATOMY OF WONDER: A CRITICAL GUIDE TO SCIENCE FICTION. 2d ed. New York: R.R. Bowker, 1981. 724 p.
Z5917 S36A52
Classified, annotated bibliography, with research aids. Author, title indexes.

BD89   Bleiler, Everett F. THE GUIDE TO SUPERNATURAL FICTION. Kent, OH: Kent State Univ. Press, 1983. 723 p.
PN56 S8B57
Lists some 1800 books, 1750-1960, including Gothic, occult, fantasy and supernatural fiction. Author, title, motif indexes.

BD90   CUMULATED FICTION INDEX, 1945-1960. London: Association of Assistant
        Librarians, 1960. 552p. SUPPLEMENT 1960-1969 (1970); 1970-1974 (1975)
        R808.83 AC72   Z5916 C8
           Short story collections, anthologies, omnibus and condensed books.

BD91   THE ENCYCLOPEDIA OF SCIENCE FICTION AND FANTASY THROUGH 1968. 3 vols.
        Ed. by Donald H. Tuck. Chicago: Advent, 1974-82.
                              Z5917 S36T83
           Bibliographic survey of science fiction, fantasy, weird fiction;
        includes authors, editors, artists, magazines and series. Vols 1, 2
        are biographical entries; 3: lists magazines, pseudonyms, miscellany.

BD92   Fee, Margery, and Ruth Cawker CANADIAN FICTION: AN ANNOTATED BIBLIOGRAPHY
        Toronto: Peter Martin, 1976. 170 p.
        R813 AF295C   Z1377 F4F44   Ryder HU6-86
           Arranged by author; title index, subject guide. Includes selected
        non-fiction, children's stories, French novels in translation, short
        story anthologies with contents note.

BD93   FICTION CATALOG (See AC14)
           Tenth ed. annotated list of 5056 novels; "best fiction in English".

BD94   FICTION 1876-1983: A BIBLIOGRAPHY OF UNITED STATES EDITIONS. 2 vols. New
        York: R.R. Bowker, 1983.
                              Z5916 F49
           Derived from Bowker's database; access by author and title.

BD95   Freeman, William. EVERYMAN'S DICTIONARY OF FICTIONAL CHARACTERS. 3d ed.
        Rev. by Fred Urquhart. London: Dent, 1973. 579 p.
                              PN43 F7
           Identifies over 20 000 fictional characters. Author, title index.

BD96   Gardner, Frank M. SEQUELS. 6th ed. London: Association of Assistant
        Librarians, 1974.
        R823 AG226S5   Z5916 G3
           An author list of some 20 000 titles. Janet Husband's SEQUELS: An
        Annotated Guide to Novels in Series (ALA, 1982) (R808.83 AH9685)
        covers more than 600 authors in concise notes; title index.

BD97   McGarry, Daniel D., and Sarah H. White. WORLD HISTORICAL FICTION GUIDE:
        An Annotated Chronological, Geographical and Topical List of Selected
        Historical Novels. 2d ed. Metuchen, NJ: Scarecrow, 1972. 629 p.
                              Z5917 H6M3
           Very brief annotations.

BD98   Moss, John. A READER'S GUIDE TO THE CANADIAN NOVEL. Toronto: McClelland
        and Stewart, 1981. 399 p.
                              PS8187 M67
           Comment on selected works of some 150 Canadian authors from the
        18th century to 1980. Classifications, awards list and index.

BD99   SCIENCE FICTION BOOK REVIEW INDEX, 1923-1973. Ed. by H.W. Hall. Detroit:
        Gale Research, 1975. 438 p. SUPPLEMENT 1974-1979 (1981)
                              Z5917 S36H35, H36
           Index to reviews published in science fiction magazines, 1923-73,
        and also in general or library journals and fanzines from 1970-1973.

Author entries; title index. Supplement, in same format, adds reviews for appr. 6200 novels, collections.

BD100 SHORT STORY INDEX, 1950- New York: H.W. Wilson, 1955- every four years (1950-54; 1955-58; 1959-63; 1974-78); irreg. annual, 1979-
R808.83 AC77   Z5917 S5C6
Began as SHORT STORY INDEX: An Index to 60 000 Stories from 4320 Collections (to 1949) (H.W. Wilson, 1953) cont. with supplements. From 1974, has stories in periodicals as well as in collections. M.P. Fletcher's SCIENCE FICTION SHORT STORY INDEX, 1950-1979 (ALA, 1981) (R823.0876) is author, title access to stories in 950 anthologies.

BD101 TWENTIETH CENTURY ROMANCE AND GOTHIC WRITERS. Ed. by James Vinson. London: Macmillan, 1982. 898 p.
PR888 L69T86
Part of a series of one vol. biographical works on 20th century writers surveyed by genre. e.g ... WESTERN WRITERS, ... CHILDREN'S WRITERS. Series typically includes list of works and a brief, signed essay for each author. BD101 has title index and references between names, pseudonyms etc.

BD102 Tymn, Marshall, ed. HORROR LITERATURE: A CORE COLLECTION AND REFERENCE GUIDE. New York: R.R. Bowker, 1981. 559 p.
Z2014 H67H67
Bibliographic essays on genres, periods; annotated bibliogs. List of sources; author, title index. FANTASY LITERATURE (1979) (R823.0876 T986F) is a companion vol.

BD103 Walker, W.S. TWENTIETH CENTURY SHORT STORY EXPLICATION: Interpretations 1900-1975, of Short Fiction since 1800. 3d ed. London: C. Bingley, 1977. 880 p. SUPPLEMENT. Hamden, CT: Shoe String Press, 1980. 257 p.
Studies of stories by more than 850 authors. Supplement adds appr. 200 authors, indexing materials to 1978.

CHILDREN'S LITERATURE (See also AL62-AL70)

BD104 Meacham, Mary. INFORMATION SOURCES IN CHILDREN'S LITERATURE: A Practical Reference Guide for Children's Librarians, Elementary School Teachers, and Students of Children's Literature. Westport, CT: Greenwood Press, 1978. 256 p.
Introduces books for the study of the literature as well as the books, indexes etc. for buidling of basic collections. Virginia Haviland's CHILDREN'S LITERATURE: A GUIDE TO REFERENCE SOURCES (Library of Congress, 1966 with supplements to 1969) (028.5 AH388) is the unsurpassed standard older source.

BD105 THE OXFORD COMPANION TO CHILDREN'S LITERATURE. Edited by H. Carpenter and M. Prichard. New York: Oxford Univ. Press, 1984. 587 p.

FINE AND APPLIED ARTS

GUIDES

BE1　Kleinbauer, W.E., and Slavens, T.P. RESEARCH GUIDE TO THE HISTORY OF WESTERN ART. Chicago: American Library Association, 1982. 220 p.
R709 K64R
　　Survey followed by an annotated list of major sources; coverage of methodology good. L.S. Jones' ART RESEARCH MATERIALS AND RESOURCES (Kendall/ Hunt, 1978) (R700 AJ77A) is a practical guide. Sacca and Singer's VISUAL ARTS REFERENCE AND RESEARCH GUIDE (Perspecto, 1983) (700 AS119V) is rather diffuse, but includes computer retrieval.

BE2　Muehsam, Gerd. GUIDE TO BASIC INFORMATION ON SOURCES IN THE VISUAL ARTS. Santa Barbara, CA: Jeffrey Norton/ ABC-Clio, 1978. 266 p.
N742S M88
　　Bibliographic essays on periods in Western art, forms, techniques, national schools of art, primitive art; separate lists of titles.

BIBLIOGRAPHIES, ABSTRACTS AND INDEXES

BE3　Arntzen, E., and R. Rainwater. GUIDE TO THE LITERATURE OF ART HISTORY. Chicago: American Library Association, 1980. 616 p.
Z5931 A67
　　Evaluative annotations for more than 3000 titles; scope includes photography, excludes works on individual artists. Author/ title index.

BE4　ART INDEX, 1929-　New York: H.W. Wilson. quarterly; annual cumulations
(PER)　Z5937 A78 (Index Table 3)
　　A basic index to articles, book reviews; also indexes exhibitions, illustrations. Covers U.S. and other periodcals and museum bulletins.

BE5　ARTBIBLIOGRAPHIES MODERN, vol. 4- , 1973-　Santa Barbara, CA: American Bibliographic Center. semi-annual.
Z5937 A75
　　Supersedes LOMA: LITERATURE ON MODERN ART, vols 1-3, 1970-　An international index, abstracting service for books, articles, exhibition catalogues treating art and design since 1800. The companion ARTBIBLIOGRAPHIES: CURRENT TITLES, bimonthly, reproduces contents pages of over 300 journals. Available online.

BE6　Art Institute of Chicago Ryerson Library. INDEX TO ART PERIODICALS. 11 vols. Boston: G.K. Hall, 1962. SUPPLEMENT. 1975.
Z5937 C55
　　Indexing began in 1907, and after publication of the ART INDEX (BE4) coverage changed to foreign periodicals, museum bulletins to avoid duplication.

BE7　Bradley, I., and P. Bradley. A BIBLIOGRAPHY OF CANADIAN NATIVE ARTS: INDIAN AND ESKIMO ARTS, CRAFTS, DANCE AND MUSIC. Agincourt, Ont.: GLC Publishers, 1977. 107 p.
Z1209.2 C287
　　Some 1500 entries under format, topical headings. Subject index by art form.

BE8   CATALOGUE OF THE LIBRARY OF THE NATIONAL GALLERY OF CANADA/ CATALOGUE DE LA BIBLIOTHEQUE DE LA GALERIE NATIONALE DU CANADA. 8 vols. Boston: G.K. Hall, 1973. FIRST SUPPLEMENT 6 vols, 1981.
Z5939 O88, O883
A dictionary catalogue with entries for books, documents, periodicals, monographs, art catalogues and auction records.

BE9   Chamberlin, Mary W. GUIDE TO ART REFERENCE BOOKS. Chicago: American Library Association, 1959. 418 p.
R700 AC443   Z5931 C45
Annotated, classified guide to over 2500 titles on architecture, painting, sculpture, prints, engravings, drawings and applied arts.

BE10   Ehresmann, Donald L. FINE ARTS: A BIBLIOGRAPHIC GUIDE TO BASIC REFERENCE WORKS, HISTORIES AND HANDBOOKS. 2d ed. Littleton, CO: Libraries Unlimited, 1979. 349 p.
R700 AE33F2   Z5931 E47
Classified annotated list of over 1600 titles, 1830-1978. includes all titles from BE9 which fall within the scope.

BE11   Lucas, E. Louise. ART BOOKS: A BASIC BIBLIOGRAPHY ON THE FINE ARTS. Greenwich, CT: New York Graphic Society, 1968. 245 p.
R700 AL933   Z5931 L93
Includes works on individual artists.

BE12   Metropolitan Museum of Art Library. (New York). LIBRARY CATALOG. 48 vols. 2d ed. Boston: G.K. Hall, 1980. SUPPLEMENT 1982.
Z5939 N44
A dictionary catalogue of books, serials, articles, with 3 vols of sales catalogues. Catalogues of other important collections published by Hall include Harvard Univ. Fine Arts Library (Z5939 H352); the Victoria and Albert (Z5939 V63, V633); Museum of Modern Art (Z5939 N46). THE DICTIONARY CATALOG OF THE ART AND ARCHITECTURE DIVISION OF THE NEW YORK PUBLIC LIBRARY (G.K. Hall, 1975) is updated annually by the excellent BIBLIOGRAPHIC GUIDE TO ART AND ARCHITECTURE, 1975- (Z5939 N48, N482, N483).

BE13   PRINT REFERENCE SOURCES: A Selected Bibliography, 18th - 20th Centuries. 2d ed. Comp. by Lauris Mason, and Joan Ludman. Milwood, NY: KTO Press, 1979. 363 p.
Z5947 A3M37
Printmakers are arranged alphabetically with books, catalogues, articles about each in chronological order. Historical, technical and topical works indexed by the same compilers in FINE PRINT REFERENCES: A Selected Bibliography of Print Related Literature (Kraus, 1982) (Z5947 A3L82).

BE14   RILA: INTERNATIONAL REPERTORY OF THE LITERATURE OF ART/ REPERTOIRE INTERNATIONAL DE LA LITTERATURE DE L'ART, 1975- Williamstown, MA: J. Paul Getty Trust. semi-annual.
N1 A1R15
Indexing and abstracting books, festschriften, more than 400 serials, congress reports, museum publications, and dissertations in art history from antiquity to the present. Classified with author, subject index. Available online.

BE15   REPERTOIRE D'ART ET D'ARCHEOLOGIE (de l'époque paléochretienne à 1939), 1910-   Paris: Centre national de la Recherche Scientifique. 4 issues a year; separate index.
Z5937 R4
Covers a large number of art periodicals from many countries.

ENCYCLOPEDIAS AND DICTIONARIES

BE16   ENCYCLOPEDIA OF WORLD ART. 15 vols. New York: McGraw Hill, 1959-68.
R703 E56
N31 B533
Italian ed.: ENCICLOPEDIA UNIVERSALE DELL'ARTE. Signed articles by international authorities, on architecture, painting, scuplture and the decorative arts. Detailed bibliographies. Appr. half of each vol. consists of b&w and col. plates. Analytical index.

BE17   Hall, James. DICTIONARY OF SUBJECTS AND SYMBOLS IN ART. Rev. ed. London: John Murray, 1979. 349 p.
N33 H28
Introductory guide identifying persons, personal types, objects, activities, concepts depicted in art, mainly Christian or classical. Brief bibliog. lists some major scholarly works in iconography.

BE18   McGRAW HILL DICTIONARY OF ART. 5 vols. Ed. by Bernard S. Myers. New York: McGraw Hill, 1969. illus.
N33 M23
Short entries for definitions, biographies etc. with signed longer articles. Many full col. plates.

BE19   Mayer, Ralph. A DICTIONARY OF ART TERMS AND TECHNIQUES. New York: Crowell, 1969. 447 p.
N33 M36
Explains terms encountered in the study and practice of the visual arts and in their literatures. Mayer's THE ARTIST'S HANDBOOK OF MATERIALS AND TECHNIQUES (4th ed., Viking, 1981) (751 M138 MCL FA) is intended to give the artist an account of materials and methods.

BE20   Munsterberg, Hugo. DICTIONARY OF CHINESE AND JAPANESE ART. New York: Hacker, 1981. 354 p.
N7340 M318
More than 5000 definitions for persons, symbols, concepts, terms, materials, techniques, styles, places. Supplements the often meagre coverage in other sources.

BE21   Murray, Peter, and Linda Murray. DICTIONARY OF ART AND ARTISTS. 4th ed. London: Thames and Hudson, 1976. 493 p.
N31 M8
Biographies of artists; defines technical terms, processes, movements chiefly in Western art since 1300.

BE22   THE OXFORD COMPANION TO ART. Ed. by Harold Osborne. London: Oxford Univ. Press. 1970. 1277 p.
N31 O73
"A non-specialist introduction to the fine arts." Brief articles on national, regional schools of art, styles, techniques, design, iconography; short biographies. Extensive bibliography.

BE23 THE OXFORD COMPANION TO TWENTIETH CENTURY ART. Ed. by Harold Osborne. London: Oxford Univ. Press, 1981. 656 p.
N6490 O94
Articles on artists, styles, groups, technical terms, countries. Substantial selective bibliographies divided by subject; list of illustrations.

BE24 PRAEGER ENCYCLOPEDIA OF ART. 5 vols. New York: Praeger, 1971. illus.
N99 P68
Especially useful for 19th, 20th centuries. A revised, enlarged translation of DICTIONNAIRE UNIVERSEL DE L'ART ET DES ARTISTES. Also published in a condensed, slighty updated, single vol. as PHAIDON ENCYCLOPEDIA OF ART AND ARTISTS (1978).

DIRECTORIES AND AUCTION RECORDS

BE25 AMERICAN ART DIRECTORY, 1898- New York: R.R. Bowker, 1899- biennial.
R708.1 A512   N50 A54
Lists American, Canadian museums, libraries, art organizations and schools, art magazines and newspapers.

BE26 CANADIAN ART SALES INDEX, 1977- Vancouver: Westbridge.
709.71075 C125 MCL FA
Priced list of paintings, watercolours, drawings sold at auction across Canada in the current year. CANADIAN ART AT AUCTION (709.71 S59.2 MCL,FA) records Sotheby's Toronto sales, 1968-80. The international market is covered by guides such as INTERNATIONAL AUCTION RECORD (705 I559 MCL,FA); ANNUAL ART SALES INDEX (745.1075 C58 MCL,FA).

BE27 DIRECTORY OF CANADIAN MUSEUMS AND RELATED INSTITUTIONS/ REPERTOIRE DES MUSEES CANADIENS ET INSTITUTIONS CONNEXES. Ottawa: Canadian Museums Association, 1981. 256 p.
AM21 A2D5
Geographical; institution, category, personnel indexes.

BE28 THE DIRECTORY OF MUSEUMS. 2d ed. Ed. by K. Hudson, and A. Nicholls. London: Macmillan, 1981. 681 p.
AM1 D57
Arranged by country, city. THE OFFICIAL MUSEUM DIRECTORY, 1975- (Amer. Assoc. of Museums) (AM10 O438) lists ca 6000 U.S. institutions

BE29 INTERNATIONAL DIRECTORY OF ARTS, 1958- 2 vols. Frankfurt: Müller.
N50 I6
Includes museums, universities, societies, artists, collectors, dealers, galleries, publishers, restorers, periodicals, booksellers.

BE30 Janson, H.W., and D.J. Janson. HISTORY OF ART: A Survey of the Major Visual Arts from the Dawn of History to the Present Day. 2d ed. Englewood Cliffs, NJ: Prentice Hall, 1977. 767 p. illus.
N5300 J3
Rev. expanded survey, principally of Western art. Other standards are H. Gardner's ART THROUGH THE AGES (6th ed., Harcourt, 1975) (R709 G227); E.H.J. Gombrich's THE STORY OF ART (13th ed., Phaidon, 1978) (R709 G632).

BE31   PELICAN HISTORY OF ART. 50 vols. Ed. by N. Pevsner. Harmondsworth, Eng.: Penguin, 1953-   In progress. illus.
        ROBA
    Covers world painting, scupture, architecture of all periods; each vol. written by an authority. Extensive bibliographies, many plates. A comparable series, THE ARTS OF MANKIND (Thames & Hudson) is in a more popular format with col. illus. and plates throughout the text.

WORKS ON ARTISTS

BE32   Bénézit, Emmanuel. DICTIONNAIRE CRITIQUE ET DOCUMENTAIRE DES PEINTRES, SCULPTEURS, DESSINATEURS ET GRAVEURS DE TOUS LES TEMPS ET DE TOUS LES PAYS: par un groupe d'écrivains specialistes franàais et étrangers. 10 vols. New ed., reset, rev., corr. Paris: Grund, 1976.
        N40 B47   Sheehy BE66, 1BE37
    (1st ed. 1911-23) Comprehensive, with brief biographies of artists both Eastern and Western, from 5th century B.C. to the present. Entries usually list artist's important works, some auction prices, galleries where displayed and bibliography.

BE33   Bryan, Michael. BRYAN'S DICTIONARY OF PAINTERS AND ENGRAVERS. 5 vols. New ed. rev. and enl. under the supervision of George C. Williamson. London: G. Bell, 1903-05. Reprint/ Port Washington, NY: Kennikat Press, 1971.
    (1st ed. 1816) Standard work which lists works, often with location. Illus. by half tone plates. Vol. 5 has artists' monograms.

BE34   CONTEMPORARY ARTISTS. 2d ed. London: Macmillan, 1983. 1041 p.
        701.22 C58   MCL,FA
    Entries include a biographical note, list of exhibitions, bibliography and signed evaluative comment. First ed. (1982) (N6490 C68) did not include a Canadian advisor.

BE35   Havlice, Patricia P. INDEX TO ARTISTIC BIOGRAPHY. 2 vols. Metuchen, NJ: Scarecrow, 1973. SUPPLEMENT. 1981.
        N40 H38, H383
    Index to biographies in 611 works in 10 languages. Suppl. adds 70 titles listing works on women artists as well as European, Japanese, Mexican and Canadian references.

BE36   LAROUSSE DICTIONARY OF PAINTERS. New York: Larousse, 1981. 467 p.
        ND35 L3713
    International scope; signed articles each with at least one illustration. Bibliography and index.

BE37   Mallet, Daniel T. MALLET'S INDEX OF ARTISTS, INTERNATIONAL BIOGRAPHICAL: Including Painters, Sculptors, Illustrators, Engravers and Etchers of the Past and the Present. New York: R.R. Bowker, 1935. 493 p. SUPPLEMENT. 1940. Reprint/ 2 vols. New York: P. Smith, 1948.
        N40 M3
    Still useful as finding list for other sources; covers all artists "exhibited in leading galleries or inquired about by modern students"

BE38   Thieme, Ulrich, and Felix Becker. ALLGEMEINES LEXIKON DER BILDENDEN KÜNSTLER VON DER ANTIKE BIS ZUR GEGENWART, UNTER MITWIRKUNG VON ETWA

400 FACHGELEHRTEN DES IN- UND AUSLANDES. 37 vols. Leipzig: Seeman, 1907-50.

         N40 T4   Sheehy BE103

Authoritative dictionary for artists of all periods: engravers, sculptors, etchers, architects. Bibliographies.

BE39 Vollmer, Hans. ALLGEMEINES LEXIKON DER BILDENDEN KÜNSTLER DES XX JAHRHUNDRETS, UNTER MITWIRKUNG VON FACHGELEHRTEN DES IN- UND AUSLANDES 6 vols. Leipzig: Seemann, 1953-62.

         N40 V6

Complements BE38 for 20th century artists.

BE40 WHO'S WHO IN AMERICAN ART, 1935- New York: R.R. Bowker. biennial.

         N6536 W5

Information on American, Canadian, Mexican painters, sculptors, designers, engravers, craftspeople, cartoonists, photographers, critics, historians, museum personnel.

BE41 WHO'S WHO IN ART: Biographies of Leading Men and Women in the World of Art Today. London: Art Trade Press, 1927- biennial.

         N40 W6

Emphasis on Britain; covers artists, critics, designers, teachers, curators etc. with an appendix of signatures. The DICTIONARY OF CONTEMPORARY ARTISTS (Clio, 1981) (N40 D5) and INTERNATIONAL DIRECTORY OF EXHIBITING ARTISTS (2 vols, Clio, 1982) (N40 I55) are additional sources.

Canada

Titled listed in this section are national in scope, with the exception of one regional title, BE46. Other examples of regional (and national) biographies of artists are in Ryder, HU4-2 to HU4-17.

BE42 ARTISTS IN CANADA/ ARTISTES AU CANADA: A UNION LIST OF FILES/ UNE LISTE COLLECTIVE DES DOSSIERS. Ottawa: Library, National Gallery of Canada, 1982. 358 p.

         N6548 A77

Documents Canadian artists in 20 libraries and galleries across Canada. THE ONTARIO INDEX OF CANADIAN ARTISTS published 1974.

BE43 Harper, J. Russell. EARLY PAINTERS AND ENGRAVERS IN CANADA. Toronto: Univ. of Toronto Press, 1970. 376 p.

         ND248 H37   Ryder HU4-7

More than 4000 artists born before 1867 or working in Canada before 1900. Extensive bibliography.

BE44 MacDonald, Colin S. A DICTIONARY OF CANADIAN ARTISTS. Ottawa: Canadian Paperbacks, 1967- In progress.

  R920.3 M135   N6548 M234

(Vol. 6, names beginning with "R", 1982) brief sketch of artist's life and work citing from newspapers, magazines, catalogues.

BE45 McMann, Evelyn de R. ROYAL CANADIAN ACADEMY OF THE ARTS/ ACADEMIE ROYALE DES ARTS DU CANADA: EXHIBITIONS AND MEMBERS 1880-1979. Toronto: Univ. of Toronto Press, 1981. 448 p.
N17 R618M45   Ryder HU4-55
More than 3000 artists with catalogue entries for some 25 500 exhibited works includes title, sometimes size, price and lender.

BE46 THE INDEX OF ONTARIO ARTISTS. Ed. by H. Wolff. Toronto: Visual Arts Ontario/ Ontario Association of Art Galleries, 1978. 337 p.
R709.713 I38I   N6546 O5154   Ryder HU4-18
Alphabetically lists contemporary Ontario artists with information on life, work. Includes index by medium.

REPRODUCTIONS AND ILLUSTRATIONS

BE47 Andrew, M., and V. Lunn. COLOURED REPRODUCTIONS OF CANADIAN PAINTINGS AVAILABLE FOR PURCHASE. Ottawa: Canadian Library Association, 1975. 29 p.
R759.11 A563C   N4035 A54   Ryder HU9-64
Access by artist's name and title of work. Bilingual.

BE48 Havlice, Patricia P. WORLD PAINTING INDEX. 2 vols. Metuchen, NJ: Scarecrow, 1977. SUPPLEMENT, 1973-1980. 2 vols. 1982.
ND45 H38
Artist and title access to reproductions in 1167 books and catalogues published 1940-1975. The supplement adds 617 titles. Y. Korwin's INDEX TO TWO DIMENSIONAL ART WORKS (2 vols, Scarecrow, 1981) (N7525 K67) includes entries from 250 books published 1960-77 while P.J. Parry's CONTEMPORARY ARTISTS: AN INDEX TO REPRODUCTIONS (Greenwood, 1978) (N6490 P277) covers 60 titles.

BE49 Monro, Isabel S., and Kate M. Monro. INDEX TO REPRODUCTIONS OF AMERICAN PAINTINGS: A Guide to Pictures Occurring in More than Eight Hundred Books. New York: H.W. Wilson, 1948. 731 p. SUPPLEMENT 1964.
R759.13 AM752   ND205 M57
Entries arranged by artist, title of painting and, in some cases, under subject or person represented. Often locates original. Suppl. adds 400 books, catalogues, published 1948-61. Smith and Moure's INDEX TO REPRODUCTIONS OF AMERICAN PAINTINGS (Scarecrow, 1977) (ND205 S575) is intended as an update, but has no title access.

BE50 _____. INDEX TO REPRODUCTIONS OF EUROPEAN PAINTINGS: A Guide to Pictures in More than Three Hundred Books. New York: H.W. Wilson, 1956. 668 p.
R758.9 AM752   ND45 M6

BE51 UNESCO. CATALOGUE OF REPRODUCTIONS OF PAINTINGS, 1860 TO 1979. 11th ed. Paris: UNESCO, 1981. 275 p. illus.
R759 U5B2C10 (1974)   NE1860 A2U52
Lists, illus. with small b&w prints, 1597 paintings since 1860 for which reproductions are available. Text in French, Spanish, English.

BE52 _____. CATALOGUE OF REPRODUCTIONS OF PAINTINGS PRIOR TO 1860. 10th ed. rev. and enl. Paris: UNESCO, 1979. 346 p. illus.
NE1860 A2U5
Complements BE51. Useful as source to identify, verify, locate originals and to purchase reproductions of 1475 works.

ARCHITECTURE

BE53 THE ARCHITECTURAL PERIODICALS INDEX, 1972/73- London: Royal Institute of British Architects, 1974- quarterly.
016.7 R598.2 MCL FA
Supersedes RIBA LIBRARY BULLETIN; RIBA ANNUAL REVIEW OF PERIODICAL ARTICLES. BE53 is international; indexes over 400 journals in design, architecture, construction techniques, environment studies, planning and research.

BE54 'Architecture Series: Bibliography No. 1,'- , 1978- Monticello, IL: Vance. irreg.
Z5941 A74
Separately issued bibliographies on a wide range of topics. More than 1100 published to date with cum. author, title, subject indexes covering Nos 1-154; 155-636.

BE55 Columbia University. AVERY INDEX TO ARCHITECTURAL PERIODICALS. 15 vols. 2d ed. Boston: G.K. Hall, 1973. SUPPLEMENT 1975; 1977; 1979.
Z5941 C6
Architecture broadly defined to include decorative arts, interior design, archaeology, city planning and housing. Indexing from 1934. Available online.

BE56 CONTEMPORARY ARCHITECTS. Ed. by Muriel Emanual. London: Macmillan, 1980. 333 p.
NA680 C646
Entries for some 600 srchitects include biographical note, chronological list of works, bibliography, statement by the biographee, and signed evaluative note. Illus. for each entry.

BE57 A DICTIONARY OF ARCHITECTURE. rev. and enl. Comp. by N. Pevsner; J. Fleming, and H. Honour. London: Penguin, 1975. 556 p. illus.
NA31 P49
Defines terms, describes national schools, styles, movements in world architecture. Includes biographies. Most articles with bibliog.

BE58 Ehresmann, Donald L. ARCHITECTURE: A Bibliographic Guide to Basic Reference Works, Histories, and Handbooks. Littleton, CO: Libraries Unlimited, 1984. 354 p.
ROBA
Classified annotated bibliography of over 1300 titles, 1875-1980.

BE59 Fletcher, B.F. A HISTORY OF ARCHITECTURE ON THE COMPARATIVE METHOD. 18th ed. Rev. by J.C. Palmes. London: Athlone Press, 1975. 1390 p. illus.
R720.9 F612   NA200 F63   Sheehy BE176, 1BE68
(1st ed., 1896). A standard with many drawings, cross sections, maps etc. Part 1, "Ancient Architecture and the Western Sucession." Part 2, "Architecture in the East."

BE60   Harvard University Graduate School of Design. LIBRARY CATALOGUE. 44 vols. Boston: G.K. Hall, 1968. SUPPLEMENT 1970; 1974; 1979.
Z5945 H374, H375
A dictionary catalogue of books, pamphlets, analytics for serials in architecture, landscape, city and regional planning. Another useful catalogue is that of the Avery Memorial Architectural Library, Columbia Univ. (2d ed., G.K. Hall, 1968, with 5 suppls. 1972-82) (Z5945 C652, C653).

BE61   MACMILLAN ENCYCLOPEDIA OF ARCHITECTS. Ed. by A.K.Placzek. 4 vols. New York: Free Press, 1982.
NA40 M25
Biographies of 2400 architects from Imhotep to contemporaries born prior to 1930 or deceased. Signed entries include a list of works and bibliography. Illus., chronologies, name index, index of works and glossary. A briefer work is WHO'S WHO IN ARCHITECTURE FROM 1400 TO THE PRESENT DAY (Weidenfeld and Nicolson, 1977) (NA40 W48).

BE62   Markowitz, Arnold L. HISTORIC PRESERVATION: A GUIDE TO INFORMATION SOURCES. Detroit: Gale Research, 1980. 279 p.
Z1251 A2M37
Broad scope, concise annotations. Indexed by author, organization, title and subject.

BE63   Wodehouse, Lawrence. INDIGENOUS ARCHITECTURE WORLDWIDE. Detroit: Gale Research, 1980. 392 p.
Z5943 V47W62
Vol. 12 in the 'Art and Architecture Information Guide Series' which includes studies of American and British architecture.

PAINTING

BE64   ENCYCLOPEDIA OF PAINTING: Painters and Painting of the World from Prehistoric Times to the Present Day. 4th ed. Ed. by Bernard S. Myers New York: Crown, 1979. 511 p. illus.
ND30 E5
Surveys outstanding painters, movements, styles, techniques, and definitions. Covers China, India, Japan and Persia in single entries. No bibliographies, no index.

Canada

BE65   ART GALLERY OF ONTARIO: THE CANADIAN COLLECTION. Toronto: McGraw Hill, 1970. 603 p. illus.
N6540 A78 ROBA   Ryder HU4-21
The "complete collection of Canadian paintings, drawings, prints, and sculpture ... to the end of June, 1967." Brief biographies with the descriptive notes on an artist's works. Illustrations for about a third of the works.

BE66   CANADIAN WATERCOLOURS AND DRAWINGS IN THE ROYAL ONTARIO MUSEUM. 2 vols. Comp. by Mary Allodi. Toronto: Royal Ontario Museum, 1974. illus.
ND1727 C2T65 ROBA   Ryder HU4-20
Over 2000 items, nearly one quarter illustrated, with biographies for appr. 200 artists. Another work by the same author is PRINTMAKING

IN CANADA: THE EARLEST VIEWS AND PORTRAITS (1980). The collection of the Public Archives of Canada is described in Michael Bell's PAINTERS IN A NEW LAND (McClelland and Stewart, 1973).

BE67 Harper, J. Russell. PAINTING IN CANADA: A HISTORY. 2d ed. Toronto: Univ. of Toronto Press, 1977. 463 p.
R759.11 H294
 A comprehensive, scholarly survey of Canadian painting tracing its development, in text and pictures, from its beginning to the present. Another definitive study by the same author is A PEOPLE'S ART: PRIMITIVE, PROVINCIAL, AND FOLK PAINTING IN CANADA (Univ. of Toronto Press, 1974). Blake McKendry's FOLK ART: PRIMITIVE AND NAIVE ART IN CANADA (Methuen, 1983) includes painting along with other arts and provides a bibliography and checklist of artists.

BE68 A HERITAGE OF CANADIAN ART: THE McMICHAEL COLLECTION. Toronto: Clarke Irwin, 1979. 208 p. illus.
MCL FA   Ryder HU4-31
 A catalogue of the McMichael Canadian Coolection, Kleinburg, Ont. illustrating and documenting nearly 1200 items, with biogrphies of major artists by Paul Duval.

BE69 National Gallery of Canada. CATALOGUE OF PAINTINGS AND SCULPTURE. 4 vols. Ed. by R.H. Hubbard. Toronto: Published for the Trustees by the Univ. of Toronto Press, 1957-65. illus.
R708.11 C212C v.3 N910 07A55   Ryder HU4-23A
 Vol.1: OLDER SCHOOLS; 2: MODERN EUROPEAN SCHOOL; 3: CANADIAN SCHOOL; 4: EUROPEAN DRAWINGS. The 3d vol. is a scholarly, annotated catalogue of the most represetive and largest collection of Canadian sculpture in Canada. Illustrated with photographs, many in colour. Genre, subject, artist indexes.

BE70 Reid, Dennis. A CONCISE HISTORY OF CANADIAN PAINTING. Toronto: Oxford Univ. Press, 1973. 319 p. illus.
ND240 R45 ROBA
 Emphasizes individual artists from 1665-1965.

SCULPTURE

BE71 Bazin, Germain. THE HISTORY OF WORLD SCULPTURE. New York: New York Graphic Society, 1968. 459 p. illus.
MCL FA
 Lavishly illus. with over 1000 col. plates, all well identified. Survey articles; no bibliographies.

BE72 Clapp, Jane. SCULPTURE INDEX. 2 vols. Metuchen, NJ: Scarecrow Press, 1970.
NB36 C55
 Vol. 1: SCULPTURE OF EUROPE AND THE CONTEMPORARY MIDDLE EAST; 2: AMERICAS, ORIENT, PACIFIC AREA AND CLASSICAL WORLD. Identifies pictures of sculpture (in many media, applied and fine arts) in about 950 publications, locates original.

DECORATIVE ARTS

BE73   THE DICTIONARY OF ANTIQUES AND THE DECORATIVE ARTS: A Book of Reference for Glass, Furniture, Ceramics, Silver, Periods, Styles, Technical Terms, etc. Enl. ed. by L.A. Boger, and H.B. Boger. New York: C. Scribner, 1967. 662 p. illus.
R703 B674   703 B57 MCL FA

BE74   Bradley, I., and P. Bradley. A BIBLIOGRAPHY OF CANADIAN NATIVE ARTS. Victoria: GLC, 1977. 107 p.
MCL FA
Over 1500 items, primarily arts and crafts; classified table of entries by specific craft with brief coverage of dance and music. No annotations or index. N. Patterson's CANADIAN NATIVE ARTS (Collier Macmillan, 1973) (709.701 P13 MCL FA) includes a bibliography.

BE75   Ehresmann, Donald L. APPLIED AND DECORATIVE ARTS: A BIBLIOGRAPHIC GUIDE TO BASIC REFERENCE WORKS, HISTORIES, AND HANDBOOKS. Littleton, CO: Libraries Unlimited, 1977. 232 p.
R745 AE33A   Z5956 A68 E47
Classified, annotated bibliography of books published since 1875. Covers folk art, furniture, ceramics, glass, costume and textiles.

BE76   THE PENGUIN DICTIONARY OF DECORATIVE ARTS. Ed. by J. Fleming, and H. Honour. London: A. Lane, 1977. 896 p. illus.
NK30 F54
Concerned with furniture and furnishings, in Europe from the Middle Ages and in America from Colonial times to the present.

BE77   Franklin, Linda C. ANTIQUES AND COLLECTIBLES: A Bibliography of Works in English 16th Century to 1976. Metuchen, NJ: Scarecrow, 1978. 1091 p.
Z5956 A68F7
Comprehensive for books, pamphlets, catalogues, theses, serials in broad subject areas. No annotations, brief bibliography, subject and author indexes.

BE78   Lessard, M., and H. Marquis. ENCYCLOPEDIE DES ANTIQUITES DU QUEBEC: Trois sièles de production artisanale. Montreal: Les Editions de l'Homme, 1971. 526 p. illus.
NK843 Q3L4 ROBA
Translated as COMPLETE GUIDE TO FRENCH CANADIAN ANTIQUES (Gage, 1974). A well illustrated guide to furniture, glass, ceramics, metalwork and other antiques. Bibliography, glossary, index.

BE79   THE OXFORD COMPANION TO THE DECORATIVE ARTS. Ed. by Harold Osborne. Oxford: Clarendon Press, 1975. 865 p. illus.
NK30 O93
Entries for styles, persons, manufacturers, materials, terms, techniques. Bibliographies with individual articles.

BE80   Palardy, Jean. THE EARLY FURNITURE OF FRENCH CANADA. Trans. from the French by Eric McLean. 2d ed. Toronto: Macmillan, 1965. 413 p. illus.
NK2441 P353
A standard work. For Ontario styles, a basic text is H. Pain's THE HERITAGE OF UPPER CANADIAN FURNITURE (Van Nostrand Reinhold, 1978).

BE81   Webster, Donald B. THE BOOK OF CANADIAN ANTIQUES. Toronto: McGraw Hill
       Ryerson, 1974. 352 p. illus.
                    NK841 W42
          Essays by leading authorities on Canadiana. Covers furniture,
       toys, tools, glass, ceramics, textiles and photography, etc.

COINS AND STAMPS

BE82   THE CHARLTON STANDARD CATALOGUE OF CANADIAN COINS, 1952-   Toronto:
       Charlton Press. annual.
       R737.4971 C481C   CJ1861 S8
          A companion pricing guide is THE CHARLTON STANDARD CATALOGUE OF
       CANADIAN GOVERNMENT PAPER MONEY.

BE83   Holmes, Laurence S. HOLME'S SPECIALIZED PHILATELIC CATALOGUE OF CANADA
       AND BRITISH NORTH AMERICA. 11th ed. rev., price revision by J.N.
       Sissons. Toronto: Ryerson Press, 1968. 434 p. illus.
       R383 22971 H751   HE6185 C2H58

BE84   THE MACMILLAN ENCYCLOPEDIC DICTIONARY OF NUMISMATICS. New York:
       Macmillan, 1982. 355 p. illus.
                    CJ69 D67
          Defines currencies, devices, terms, materials, etc; bibliography.

BE85   Morin, Cimon N. CANADIAN PHILATELY: BIBLIOGRAPHY AND INDEX, 1864-1973/
       PHILATELIE CANADIENNE: BIBLIOGRAPHIE ET INDEX, 1864-1973. Ottawa:
       National Library of Canada, 1979. 281 p. SUPPLEMENT. 1983. 246 p.
       R383.23 AM858C   Ryder HU2-80
          Supplement extends coverage to 1980. Includes books, catalogues,
       articles (English or French) on Canadian postal history and philately

BE86   SCOTT'S STANDARD POSTAGE STAMP CATALOGUE, 18?-   New York: Scott
       Publications. annual.
                    HE6226 S48
          (4 vols. 1984 ed.) LYMAN'S STANDARD CATALOGUE OF CANADA -- BNA
       POSTAGE STAMPS (34th ed., Charlton Press, 1983) (HE6185 C22L82)
       claims "up to date retail prices for all Canadian postage stamps."
       Gibbon's STAMPS OF THE WORLD (769.56 MCL FA) is a British guide.

COSTUME

BE87   Arnold, Janet. A HANDBOOK OF COSTUME. London: Macmillan, 1973. 336 p.
       illus.
                    GT510 A75PR
          Guide to primary sources for costume study; many bibliographies.

BE88   Boucher, François. A HISTORY OF COSTUME IN THE WEST. London: Thames &
       Hudson, 1967. 441 p. illus.
       R391 B753
          A study of costume from prehistoric times to the present, with
       over 1000 illustrations, many in colour.

BE89　　THE DICTIONARY OF COSTUME. Comp. by R. Turner Wilson. New York: C. Scribner, 1969. 406 p. illus.
391.003 W38　MCL FA
Descriptions of dress of all times, all parts of the world by the author of THE MODE IN COSTUME, THE MODE IN FURS, and others.

BE90　　THE FASHION DICTIONARY: Fabric, Sewing, and Apparel as Expressed in the Language of Fashion. Rev. and enl. Ed. by Mary B. Picken. New York: Funk & Wagnalls, 1973. 434 p. illus.
TT503 P5
More than 10 000 terms in historical and contemporary dress. FAIRCHILD'S DICTIONARY OF FASHION (Fairchild, 1975) (391.003 C12 MCL,FA) defines fashion terminology; section on designers. FAIRCHILD'S DICTIONARY OF TEXTILES (6th ed. Fairchild, 1979) (677.003 F11 MCL,FA) is also useful.

BE91　　Hiler, H., and M. Hiler. BIBLIOGRAPHY OF COSTUME: A Dictionary Catalog of about Eight Thousand Books and Periodicals. New York: H.W. Wilson, 1939. 911 p.
Z5691 H5
The standard international bibliography. A more recent list is P. Anthony and J. Arnold's COSTUME: A GENERAL BIBLIOGRAPHY (1974).

BE92　　Kesler, Jackson. THEATRICAL COSTUME: A GUIDE TO REFERENCE SOURCES. Detroit: Gale Research, 1979. 308 p.
Z5691 K47
Annotated, classified bibliography updating BE93. Includes design, patterns, psychology of fashion etc. Author, title index.

BE93　　Monro, Isabel S., and Dorothy E. Cook. COSTUME INDEX: A Subject Index to Plates and to Illustrated Text. New York: H.W. Wilson, 1937. 338 p. SUPPLEMENT. 1957.
R391 M752　　　　　Z5691 M75
The set indexes 962 vols, and is an invaluable finding aid to historical costume of most countries and periods. Includes dress of specific classes of persons, such as kings.

BE94　　Payne, Blanche. HISTORY OF COSTUME: From the Ancient Egyptians to the Twentieth Century. New York: Harper, 1965. 607 p. illus.
R391 P346　　　　　GT510 P35
Each chapter has a very brief history followed by descriptions of costumes, illus. by photos or line drawings. WHAT PEOPLE WORE (Viking 1952) (R391 G674) by D. Gorsline is a largely pictorial treatment.

PHOTOGRAPHY

BE95　　Boni, Albert. PHOTOGRAPHIC LITERATURE: An International Bibliographic Guide to General and Specialized Literature on Photographic Processes Techniques; Theory; Chemistry; Physics; Apparatus; Materials & Applications; Industry; History; Biography; Aesthetics. New York: Morgan & Morgan, 1962. 353 p. SUPPLEMENT, 1960-1970 (1972).
R770 AB715
Main vol. includes materials to 1960.

BE96   CONTEMPORARY PHOTOGRAPHERS. New York: St Martin's, 1982. 837 p. illus.
            770.922 C58 MCL FA
        Entries, on 650 photographers, include biographical note, exhibition list, bibliography, personal statement and signed critique.

BE97   THE FOCAL ENCYCLOPEDIA OF PHOTOGRAPHY. 2 vols. Rev. ed. London: Focal Press, 1965. illus.
        R770.3 F652
        Covers the general aspects of photography, such as history, terms, techniques, applications, etc. plus allied fields of cinematography and photomechanical processes. British emphasis with U.S. variants.

BE98   Greenhill, Ralph, and Andrew Birrell. CANADIAN PHOTOGRAPHY, 1839-1920. Toronto: Coach House Press, 1979. 184 p.
        An illustrated history with bibliography and index.

BE99   INTERNATIONAL PHOTOGRAPHY INDEX, 1979-   Boston: G.K. Hall, 1983-
            016.77 I54 MCL FA
        More than 5000 references from periodicals representing 15 countries.

BE100   MACMILLAN BIOGRAPHICAL ENCYCLOPEDIA OF PHOTOGRAPHIC ARTISTS & INNOVATORS New York: Macmillan, 1983. 722 p.
            TR139 B767
        Alphabetical entries include biography, bibliography, collections and reference, if applicable, to section of 144 plates. No index.

BE101   Moss, Martha. PHOTOGRAPHY BOOKS INDEX: A Subject Guide to Photo Anthologies. Metuchen, NJ: Scarecrow, 1980. 286 p.
            779.016 M59 MCL FA
        Provides access by photographer and subject to illustrations in 22 books and catalogues.

MUSIC

GUIDES

BF1 Booth, Mark W. AMERICAN POPULAR MUSIC: A REFERENCE GUIDE. Westport, CT: Greenwood Press, 1983. 212 p.
016.78042 B58   MCL MUS

BF2 Kennington, D., and D.L. Read. THE LITERATURE OF JAZZ: A CRITICAL GUIDE. 2d ed. Chicago: American Library Association, 1980. 236 p.
R781.57 AK36L2
Bibliographic essays on the music, musicians, reference sources, periodicals, jazz education and jazz in the arts. Name, title index.

BIBLIOGRAPHIES AND CATALOGUES

BF3 Bradley, Ian. A SELECTED BIBLIOGRAPHY OF MUSICAL CANADIANA. Rev. ed. Victoria: Univ. of Victoria, 1976. 177 p.
R780.971 AB811S   Ryder HU3-16
A classified list of more than 1300 items. A BASIC BIBLIOGRAPHY OF MUSICAL CANADIANA (Toronto, 1970) is a list by broad category of literature on music in Canada.

BF4 THE BRITISH CATALOGUE OF MUSIC, 1957-   London: Council of the British National Bibliography. quarterly, annual cumulation.
016.780942 B67   MCL FA   Sheehy BH25
"A record of music and books about music recently published in Great Britain based upon the material deposited at the Copyright Receipt Office of the British Library." In three sections: composer and title index; subject index; classified section. Excludes modern dance music and some other kinds of popular music.

BF5 CANADIAN MUSIC: A SELECTED CHECKLIST, 1950-1973. Ed. by Lynne Jarman. Toronto: Univ. of Toronto Press, 1976. 170 p.
R780.971 AM987M   ML120 C3J4   Ryder HU3-21
Based on CANADIANA (AD77) entries; books about music and musicians in classified order with title and author or composer index.

BF6 Canadian Music Centre. CATALOGUE OF CANADIAN CHORAL MUSIC. 3d ed. Toronto: Canadian Music Centre. 1 vol. unpaged.
016.7841 C12   MCL MUS   Ryder Hu3-18B
One of several CMC catalogues on various forms of music.

BF7 Duckles, Vincent comp. MUSIC REFERENCE AND RESEARCH MATERIALS: AN ANNOTATED BIBLIOGRAPHY. 3d ed. New York: Free Press, 1974. 526 p.
R780 AD835M3   ML113 D83
The outstanding guide in the field. More than 1900 works listed with descriptive and evaluative annotations.

BF8 Heyer, Anna H. HISTORICAL SETS, COLLECTED EDITIONS, AND MONUMENTS OF MUSIC: A GUIDE TO THEIR CONTENTS. 2 vols. 3d ed. Chicago: American Library Association, 1980.
ML113 H52
Indexes, by composer and title, the contents of complete editions of composers, published collections and anthologies of compositions.

BF9 Marco, Guy A. INFORMATION ON MUSIC: A Handbook of Reference Sources in European Languages. 7 vols. Littleton, CO: Libraries Unlimited, 1975- In progress.
R780 AM321I
   A classified, annotated bibliography beginning with vol. 1: BASIC AND UNIVERSAL SOURCES; through vol. 2: THE AMERICAS; to other topics, regions, musicians and musical editions to complete the set.

BF10 MUSIC IN PRINT: ANNUAL SUPPLEMENT, 1979-   Philadelphia: Musicdata.
016.78 M785   MCL MUS
   For various types of music, supplements base vols, e.g. CLASSICAL VOCAL MUSIC IN PRINT, ORGAN MUSIC IN PRINT, ORCHESTRAL MUSIC IN PRINT International in scope, from information supplied by publishers.

BF11 Music Library Association. A BASIC MUSIC LIBRARY: ESSENTIAL SCORES AND BOOKS. Chicago: American Library Association, 1978. 173 p.
780 AM9878
   A guide for small and medium sized libraries.

BF12 New York Public Library. Reference Dept. DICTIONARY CATALOG OF THE MUSIC COLLECTION. 33 vols. Boston: G.K. Hall, 1964. SUPPLEMENT, 1964-1971. 10 vols. (1973).
016.78 N266   MCL FA
   Includes books, scores, libretti. Updated by the BIBLIOGRAPHIC GUIDE TO MUSIC, 1975- . Another collection, noted for scores, is that of the Boston Public Library, with published DICTIONARY CATALOG OF THE MUSIC COLLECTION (20 vols, G.K. Hall, 1972; its supplement, 4 vols, 1977) (016.78 B592   MCL FA).

BF13 Proctor, George A. SOURCES IN CANADIAN MUSIC: A BIBLIOGRAPHY OF BIBLIOGRAPHIES. 2d ed. Sackville, N.B.: Mt Allison Univ., 1979. 38 p.
016.780971 P68   MCL MUS   Ryder Hu3-23
   A classified list, partly annotated, of books and articles. His CANADIAN MUSIC OF THE TWENTIETH CENTURY (Univ. of Toronto Press, 1980) (780.971 P68) lists scores and recordings.

BF14 RISM: REPERTOIRE INTERNATIONAL DES SOURCES MUSICALES. Munich: Henle, 1960- In progress.
016.78 R25   MCL MUS
   A major bibliography from the International Musicological Society and the International Association of Music Libraries. The aim is a "catalogue of all available bibliographical musical works, writings about music and textbooks on music from all countries ... to 1800."

BF15 Library of Congress. MUSIC, BOOKS ON MUSIC AND SOUND RECORDINGS, 1953- (See AG22)

INDEXES AND ABSTRACTS

BF16 THE MUSIC INDEX: The Key to Current Music Periodical Literature, 1949- Detroit: Information Coordinators. monthly, annual.
MCL MUS
   Subject and author index. International coverage of ca 400 music periodicals and newsletters. Lists reviews of records, performances, music and books. Slow publication schedule, but worth the wait.

BF17   RILM: ABSTRACTS OF MUSIC LITERATURE, 1967-   New York: International RILM Center, City Univ. of New York. quarterly.
MCL MUS
(1979 issues {1984}) Abstracts of books, articles, essays, reviews, catalogues, and iconographies etc. Organized by subject, author index; final issue each year is an index. Available online.

SONG AND THEMATIC INDEXES

BF18   Barlow, Harold, and Sam Morgenstern. A DICTIONARY OF MUSICAL THEMES. Rev. ed. New York: Crown, 1975. 642 p.
Notation and title indexes identifying 10 000 themes of recorded instrumental pieces grouped by composer with title and first line. The companion, A DICTIONARY OF OPERA AND SONG THEMES (Crown, 1976) (016.784 B13   MCL MUS) indexes over 8000 works by first line and notation to composer list with titles, words, music of first lines.

BF19   Canadian Music Library Association. MUSICAL CANADIANA: A SUBJECT INDEX. Ottawa: Canadian Library Association, 1967. 62 p.
R780.971 AC212   Ryder HU3-19
A preliminary list, by subject, of some 800 vocal and instrumental pieces published in or related to Canada to 1921.

BF20   De Charms, Desirée, and Paul F. Breed. SONGS IN COLLECTIONS: AN INDEX. Detroit: Information Service, 1966. 588 p.
R784 AD293
Indexes 9493 songs in 411 collections, most published 1940-57. Emphasis on solos with piano accompaniment. Arranged by song with indexes to authors, titles, first lines.

BF21   Fuld, James J. THE BOOK OF WORLD FAMOUS MUSIC: CLASSICAL, POPULAR AND FOLK. Rev. ed. New York: Crown, 1971. 688 p.
780.2F MCL MUS
Notes on the composition, publication, performance of 1100 songs. Words and music of first lines; composers, author, title indexes.

BF22   FOLK SONG INDEX: A Comprehensive Guide to the Florence E. Brunnings Collection. New York: Garland, 1981. 357 p.
016.7844 B694   MCL MUS
An alphabetical list of more than 49 000 songs with reference to books, journals and recordings.

BF23   Havlice, Patricia. POPULAR SONG INDEX. Metuchen, NJ: Scarecrow Press, 1975. 933 p. SUPPLEMENT 1978.
016.784 H135
Indexes folk, popular, children's songs, hymns, chanteys and blues from 301 song books, 1940 to 1972, plus 72 books in the supplement.

BF24   Leigh, Robert, comp. INDEX TO SONG BOOKS: A Title Index to over 11 000 Copies of Almost 6800 Songs in 111 Song Books Published between 1933 and 1962. Stockton, CA: The Author, 1964. 237 p.
R784 AL529
Includes only U.S. books, with words and music. No author or composer entries.

BF25   Mercer, Paul NEWFOUNDLAND SONGS AND BALLADS IN PRINT, 1842-1974: A Title and First Line Index. St John's: Memorial Univ., 1979. 343 p.
016.78 M26   Ryder HU3-52.
Includes an annotated list of sources.

BF26   Sears, Minnie E. SONG INDEX: An Index to More than 12 000 Songs in 177 Song Collections, Comprising 262 Volumes. New York: H.W. Wilson, 1926 SUPPLEMENT 1934. Reprint/ 2 vols in 1. Shoe String, 1966.
R784 AS439
Entries for title, composer, author in one alphabet. Limited inclusion of collections without instrumental setting and none with words only. Complemented by H.G. Cushing's CHILDREN'S SONG INDEX (1936) with subject, author, title, composer access, and by the INDEX TO CHILDREN'S SONGS (1979) which indexes 298 books by title, first line and subject.

ENCYCLOPEDIAS, DICTIONARIES AND DIRECTORIES

BF27   ALLGEMEINE ENZYKLOPADIE DER MUSIK. 16 vols. Kassel: Berenreiter Verlag, 1949-79. illus.
780.3 M79   MCL MUS
Comprehensive for music and musicians; long signed articles by specialists and extensive bibliographies.

BF28   DICTIONARY OF CONTEMPORARY MUSIC. Ed. by John Vinton. New York: Dutton, 1974. 834 p. illus.
ML100455
Composers, terms, national styles and other topics important in 20th century concert music in the Western tradition. Longer articles signed and many with bibliographies.

BF29   DIRECTORY OF MUSICAL CANADA, 1981-   Agincourt, Ont.: GLC. triennial.
780.971 G3819981 MCL MUS   Ryder HU3-33
Covers administration, education, libraries, festivals, grants, awards, competitions, music industry; bibliography, discography.

BF30   ENCYCLOPEDIA OF CONCERT MUSIC. Ed. by David Ewen. New York: Hill & Wang, 1959. 566 p.
R780.3 R94
A popular, quick reference source. Emphasizes instrumental works, including opera selections, ballet music in the orchestral repertory. (See related title BF49).

BF31   ENCYCLOPEDIA OF MUSIC IN CANADA. Ed. by Helmut Kallman; Gilles Potvin, and Kenneth Winters. Toronto: Univ. of Toronto Press, 1981. 1076 p.
R780.3 E56E   ML106 C3E6
A major encyclopedia covering "the nation's musical culture in all its breadth and depth." Over 3000 signed entries with bibliographies, discographies, illustrations. Index limited to persons, organizations not covered by individual entries. A French ed. available.

BF32   EVERYMAN'S DICTIONARY OF MUSIC. (Orig. ed. Eric Blom). 5th ed. Rev. by Sir Jack Westrup. London: Dent, 1971. 793 p.
R780 B653   ML100 B47
Extensive revision of a standard quick reference for definitions covering Western music from the 15th century to the present.

BF 33   HARVARD DICTIONARY OF MUSIC. 2d ed. rev. and enl. Ed. by Willi Apel.
           Cambridge MA: Belknap Press, 1969. 935 p.
           R780.3 A641   ML100 A64
              A standard, scholarly work with definitions, surveys and shorter
           entries, excluding biographical entries; many bibliographies.

BF 34   THE NEW GROVE DICTIONARY OF MUSIC AND MUSICIANS. 20 vols. London:
           Macmillan, 1980. illus.
           R780.3 G884 (1954, 1961)   ML100 G8863
              Complete revision of a standard reference through five editions
           (1878-1961). International scope, authoritative scholarship. Includes
           lists of works, discographies. No index except to terms used in the
           articles on non-Western and folk music.

BF 35   THE NEW OXFORD COMPANION TO MUSIC. 2 vols. Ed. by Denis Arnold. Oxford:
           Oxford Univ. Press, 1983. illus.
                         780.321 N266   MCL MUS
              A complete revision of THE OXFORD COMPANION (10th ed., 1970) by
           Percy Scholes. Entries for composers, works, instruments, acoustics,
           musical theory and geographical areas.

BF 36   THE INTERNATIONAL CYCLOPEDIA OF MUSIC AND MUSICIANS. (Orig. ed.: Oscar
           Thompson). 10th ed. Ed. by Bruce Bohle. New York: Dodd, 1975. 2511 p.
                         ML100 T47
              Most entries are brief, but with long signed articles by
           specialists for important persons and subjects. Articles on composers
           followed by a catalogue of works, and in some cases, a chronology.

BIOGRAPHY AND HISTORY

General and International

BF 37   ASCAP BIOGRAPHICAL DICTIONARY. 4th ed. Ed. by Jaques Cattrell Press. New
           York: R.R. Bowker, 1980.
                         780.922 A514   MCL MUS
              Brief sketches of over 8000 members of THE AMERICAN SOCIETY OF
           COMPOSERS, AUTHORS AND PUBLISHERS, with list of member publishers.

BF 38   Baker, Theodore. BAKER'S BIOGRAPHICAL DICTIONARY OF MUSICIANS. 6th ed.
           Rev. by Nicholas Slonimsky. New York: Schirmer, 1978. 1955 p.
           R920.3 B168   ML105 B16
              (1st ed., 1900) The most comprehensive dictionary in English
           covering musicians of all times and countries. Pronunciation for some
           names. Lists composers' major works with date of initial performance.

BF 39   Bull, Storm. INDEX TO BIOGRAPHIES OF CONTEMPORARY COMPOSERS. 2 vols. New
           York: Scarecrow Press, 1964-74.
           R780 B935   ML105 B8
              Analyses 177 biographical works with information about living
           composers, those born in the 20th century, and those deceased since
           1949. Stresses Europe and America.

BF 40   Eisler, Paul E. WORLD CHRONOLOGY OF MUSIC HISTORY. Dobbs Ferry, NY:
           Oceana Publications, 1972-   In progress.
                         780.9 E39   MCL MUS
              (Vol. VI, 1771-1796 {1981}).

BF41   Grout, Donald J. A HISTORY OF WESTERN MUSIC. 3d ed. New York: Norton, 1980.
            780.9 G68   MCL MUS
          A basic history of classical music from ancient Greece to the present. Includes bibliography, chronology and index.

BF42   INTERNATIONAL WHO'S WHO IN MUSIC, 1935-   Cambridge: Melrose. irreg.
            780.922 I59   MCL MUS
          (9th ed., 1980) Lists some 10 000 composers, teachers, critics or other persons associated with music. Appendices for orchestras, libraries, conservatories, awards.

BF43   Marcuse, Sibyl. MUSICAL INSTRUMENTS: A COMPREHENSIVE DICTIONARY. Corrected ed. New York: Norton, 1975. 608 p.
            ML102 I5M37
          A standard dictionary giving brief definitions and references to sources. Curt Sach's THE HISTORY OF MUSICAL INSTRUMENTS (1940) covers the subject chronologically and by cultural area. K. Gieringer's INSTRUMENTS IN THE HISTORY OF WESTERN MUSIC (3d ed., 1978) places instruments in the context of musical periods.

BF44   THE NEW OXFORD HISTORY OF MUSIC. 11 vols. London: Oxford Univ. Press, 1954-   In progress.
          R780.9 O98   780 9N260   MCL MUS
          Intended to replace the OXFORD HISTORY OF MUSIC and to be a survey of music from earliest times to the present, Eastern and primitive as well as Western music. Vol. 11 proposed as chronological tables and index. Each vol. individually titled with bibliographies, index.

Canada

BF45   CREATIVE CANADA: A Biographical Dictionary of Twentieth Century Creative and Performing Artists. (See AL43)

BF46   Kallmann, Helmut. A HISTORY OF MUSIC IN CANADA, 1534-1914. Toronto: Univ. of Toronto Press, 1960. 311 p.
          780.971 K14   ML205 K3
          Stresses the European heritage with emphasis on the social rather than the artistic aspects of pioneer music in Canada. No coverage of Indian or Eskimo music. Bibliography of books and articles.

BF47   Macmillan, Keith, and John Beckwith. CONTEMPORARY CANADIAN COMPOSERS. Toronto: Oxford Univ. Press, 1975. 248 p. illus.
                    ML390 C74S   Ryder HU3-29
          Biographies of 144 the "most active and prominent" professionals with lists of compositions, bibliographies. Also useful is Ronald Napier's A GUIDE TO CANADIAN COMPOSERS (Avondale, 1983) (ML106 C3N3).

BF48   Toomey, K., and S. Willis. MUSICIANS IN CANADA: A BIO-BIBLIOGRAPHICAL FINDING LIST/ MUSICIENS AU CANADA: INDEX BIO-BIBLIOGRAPIQUE. Ottawa: Canadian Association of Music Libraries, 1981. 185 p.
                    ML106 C3C35
          Musicians active in Canada from the 18th century.

OPERA

BF49   THE NEW ENCYLOPEDIA OF THE OPERA. Ed. by David Ewen. New York: Hill and Wang, 1971. 759 p.
R782.103 E94   ML102 O6E9
A popular work about opera and its performance for both frequently performed and less well-known works. (See related title, BF30).

BF50   NEW KOBBE'S COMPLETE OPERA BOOK. Orig. ed. Gustave Kobbe. Ed. and rev. by the Earl of Harewood. London: Putnam, 1976. 1694 p. illus.
R782 108 K75   MT95 K52
The most comprehensive single vol. guide.

BF51   Loewenberg, Alfred. ANNUALS OF OPERA, 1597-1940. 3d ed. Rev. and corr. Totowa, NJ: Rowman and Littlefield, 1978. 1 vol. unpaged.
ML102 O6L6 (1955)
A chronology of nearly 4000 operas, by year of first performance.

BF52   Moore, Frank L. CROWELL'S HANDBOOK OF WORLD OPERA. New York: Crowell, 1961. 683 p.
781M MCL MUS

BF53   PHAIDON BOOK OF THE OPERA. Oxford: Phaidon, 1979. 512 p. illus.
ML102.06 O6I3
Chronological list of 780 operas with synopses and notes. Index of composers, librettists and literary sources.

POPULAR MUSIC

BF54   THE ENCYCLOPEDIA OF JAZZ IN THE SEVENTIES. Comp. by Leonard Feather. New York: Horizon Press, 1976. 393 p.
R785.42 F288
Supplements the ENCYCLOPEDIA OF JAZZ (1962) and THE ENCYCLOPEDIA OF JAZZ IN THE SIXTIES (1966). Includes biographies, photographies, polls, record companies, recordings and bibliography. H. Panassie and M. Gautier's GUIDE TO JAZZ (1973) is a useful source for information about performers, terms, instruments and terms.

BF55   ENCYCLOPEDIA OF FOLK, COUNTRY & WESTERN MUSIC. 2d ed. Comp. by Irwin Stambler, and Grelun Landon. New York: St Martin's Press, 1983. 902 p
781.77303 S74   MCL MUS
Entries for performers and groups, awards, bibliography.

BF56   Harris, S. BLUES WHO'S WHO. New Rochelle, NY: Arlington, 1979. 775 p.
784.0922 H13 MCL MUS
Biographies of performers with bibliographies, film, song indexes. THE BEST OF THE MUSIC MAKERS, (Doubleday, 1979) (780.922 S376 MCL MUS) includes close to 300 popular individuals and groups. Two good biographical references for rock performers are M. Bane's WHO'S WHO IN ROCK (Facts on File, 1981) (784.54009 MCL MUS) and and W. York's WHO'S WHO IN ROCK MUSIC (Scribner's, 1982) (784.54009 MCL MUS).

BF57   THE ROLLING STONE ILLUSTRATED HISTORY OF ROCK & ROLL. Rev. ed. New York: Random House, 1980. 474 p.
780.4209 R58
Essays on groups, individuals, trends in a loose chronology. Discographies and index. LILLIAN ROXON'S ROCK ENCYCLOPEDIA (Rev. ed., Grosset & Dunlap, 1978) (780.3 R598 MCL MUS) is useful for songs and performers.

RECORDED MUSIC

BF58   BIBLIOGRAPHY OF DISCOGRAPHIES. New York: R.R. Bowker, 1977- In progress.
MCL MUS
Already published: CLASSICAL MUSIC (1977) by M. Gray and G. Gibson JAZZ (1981) by D. Allen and POPULAR MUSIC (1983) BY M. Gray. A major comprehensive discography of popular music is THE AMERICAN DANCE BAND DISCOGRAPHY (2 vols, Arlington, 1975) (016.78991 R79 MCL MUS).

BF59   Litchfield, Jack. CANADIAN JAZZ DISCOGRAPHY, 1916-1980. Toronto: Univ. of Toronto Press, 1982.
016.78991 L39   MCL MUS

BF60   SCHWANN-1 RECORD & TAPE GUIDE, 1949-   (See AG23)

PERFORMING ARTS

GENERAL REFERENCE AIDS

BG1   Association of Canadian Television and Radio Artists. FACE TO FACE WITH TALENT. 5th ed. Toronto: ACTRA, 1978. 1 vol. unpaged.
R791.45 A849F2   PN1573 C3A88
A directory of members of ACTRA and Equity, with portraits.

BG2   ENCICLOPEDIA DELLO SPETTACOLO. 9 vols. Rome: Maschere, 1954-62. illus. AGGIORNAMENTO, 1955-65. Rome: Union Editorale, 1966. INDICE REPERTORIO. 1968.
PN1625 E7
A definitive work on staged entertainment including drama, opera, operetta, musicals, dance, variety, pantomine, puppetry, circus, and the media. Signed articles, many illustrations and bibliographies.

BG3   A GUIDE TO CRITICAL REVIEWS. 4 parts. Ed. by James Salem. Metuchen, NJ: Scarecrow Press, 1966-71. SUPPLEMENT 1982.
Z1035 A1S3 (Index Table 1)
An index to articles from popular periodicals. Three of the 4 parts in a 2d ed.; I: AMERICAN DRAMA (1973); II: THE MUSICAL (1976); III: BRITISH AND CONTINENTAL DRAMA (1968). Part IV, THE SCREENPLAY (2 vols, 1st ed., 1971).

BG4   THE LIVELY ARTS INFORMATION DIRECTORY: A Guide to the Fields of Music, Dance, Theatre, Film, Radio and Television for the United States and Canada. Ed. by S. R. Wasserman. Detroit: Gale Research, 1982. 846 p.
PN2289 L55
Organizations, agencies, schools, libraries, festivals, awards etc

BG5   PERFORMING ARTS BIOGRAPHY MASTER INDEX. 2d ed. Ed. by Barbara McNeil, and Miranda Herbert. Detroit: Gale Research, 1981. 701 p.
PN1583 M37
A guide to some 270 000 citations in over 100 reference sources. Very concise; variant forms of names are not consolidated.

BG6   PERFORMING ARTS BOOKS, 1876-1981: Including an International Index of Current Serial Publications. New York: R.R. Bowker, 1981. 1656 p.
Z6935 P43
Entries catalogued by LC since 1876. Main entry under more than 12 000 subjects with access through topical outline of subjects, author and title index. Serials by subject with title index.

BG7   PERFORMING ARTS RESOURCES, 1974-   New York: Theatre Library Association 1975-   annual.
Z675 T36P4
Articles deal with notable collections in libraries and archives, collection management and topics of interest to theatre research.

BG8   Sharp, Harold S., and Majorie Z. Sharp. INDEX TO CHARACTERS IN THE PERFORMING ARTS. 6 vols. Metuchen, NJ: Scarecrow Press, 1966-73.
PN1579 S45
A dictionary of major, minor characters in play, operas, musicals, ballet and in radio and television.

BG9   TOURING ARTISTS' DIRECTORY OF THE PERFORMING ARTS IN CANADA, 1982/83.
             6th ed. Ottawa: Canada Council, 1983. 520 p.
                              790.20971 T59   MCL MUS   Ryder HU3-1
             A guide to professional performers and companies in dance, music,
             opera and theatre across Canada. Portraits and index.

BG10   Wilmoth, Don B. AMERICAN AND ENGLISH POPULAR ENTERTAINMENT: A GUIDE TO
             INFORMATION SOURCES. Detroit: Gale Research, 1980. 465 p.
                              Z7511 W53
                Includes the circus, fairs, magic shows, etc. Brief annotations;
             author, title, subject indexes. Wilmeth's VARIETY ENTERTAINMENT AND
             OUTDOOR AMUSEMENTS (Greenwood, 1982) is limited mostly to U.S.

DANCE

BG11   Balanchine, George. BALANCHINE'S COMPLETE STORIES OF THE GREAT BALLETS.
             Rev. and enl. Garden City, NY: Doubleday, 1977. 838 p.
             R792.8 B171C2
                The stories of over 200 ballets, most in the current repertory.
             With glossary, chronology, annotated recordings list, reading guide.

BG12   Beaumont, Cyril W. COMPLETE BOOK OF BALLETS: A Guide to the Principal
             Ballets of the Nineteenth and Twentieth Centuries. London: Putnam,
             1037. 1100 p. SUPPLEMENT 1945; 1954; 1955.
                              792.84 B24   MCL TH
                Synopses for ballets with choreographer, author, composer,
             designer, date and cast of first performance, excerpts from reviews.

BG13   THE DANCE ENCYCLOPEDIA. Rev. and enl. Ed. by A. Chujoy, and P.W.
             Manchester. New York: Simon and Schuster, 1967. 992 p.
             R793.303 C559   GV1585 C5
                Treats all aspects of dance, emphasizing ballet, including
             history, biography, stage design, criticism, choreography. Most
             entries are brief; some long signed articles by specialists.

BG14   Cohen-Stratyner, Barbara N. BIOGRAPHICAL DICTIONARY OF DANCE. New York:
             Schirmer, 1982. 970 p.
                              GV1705 AIC58
                More than 2900 dance personalities from "the last four centuries
             of dance history in Europe and the Americas, embracing a wide range
             of dance and theatrical genres." No index, glossary or bibliography.

BG15   Collier, Clifford, and Pierre Guilmette. DANCE RESOURCES IN CANADIAN
             LIBRARIES. Resources in Canadian Libraries, No. 8. Ottawa: National
             Library of Canada, 1982. 136 p.
             R026 R432 v.8.
                Includes a bibliography on dance and a list of serials with
             locations. (See AA54 for series)

BG16   THE CONCISE OXFORD DICTIONARY OF BALLET. 2d ed. Ed. by Horst Koegler.
             London: Oxford Univ. Press, 1982. 459 p.
                              GV1585 K62 (1977)
                Entries on all aspects of ballet: dancers, ballets, companies,
             terms, some bibliographical notes. Broader coverage than G. Wilson's
             DICTIONARY OF BALLET (A&C Black, 1974) (GV1585 W5)

BG17   Magriel, Paul D. A BIBLIOGRAPHY OF DANCING: A List of Books and Articles on the Dance and Related Subjects. New York: H.W. Wilson, 1936. SUPPLEMENT. 1966. 229 p.
Z7514 D2M2 ROBA
Covers ballet, mime, folk and national dances. Classified list, partly annotated with indexing for authors, subjects, analytics.

BG18   McDonough, Don. THE COMPLETE GUIDE TO MODERN DANCE. New York: Doubleday, 1976. 534 p. illus.
GV1783 M26
Emphasizes choreographers; includes bibliography.

BG19   New York Public Library. Research Libraries. Performing Arts Research Center. DICTIONARY CATALOG OF THE DANCE COLLECTION. 10 vols. Boston: G.K. Hall, 1973.
Z7514 D2N48; D2B5
Catalogue of a collection often described as the world's most comprehensive resource of print, non-print material on dance. THE BIBLIOGRAPHIC GUIDE TO DANCE, 1975- (annual, 1976-) is a supplement to the collection. The annual, in dictionary catalogue format, lists items catalogued durng the year including books, articles, periodicals, mss, photographs, prints, tapes, scores etc.

THEATRE

BG20   Baker, Blanch M. THEATRE AND ALLIED ARTS: A Guide to Books Dealing with the History, Criticism, and Technic of the Drama and Theatre and Related Arts and Crafts. New York: B. Blom, 1952. 536 p.
R792 AB167   Z5681 B18
About 6000 titles, annotated and arranged in three sections on drama, theatre and actors; stagecraft and allied art; miscellany. Some sections updated in bibliographies such as Richard Stoddard's STAGE, SCENERY, MACHINERY AND LIGHTING (Gale, 1977) (Z5784 S8S79) and his THEATRE AND CINEMA ARCHITECTURE (Gale, 1978) (Z5784 S8S82).

BG21   Ball, John, and Richard Plant. A BIBLIOGRAPHY OF CANADIAN THEATRE HISTORY, 1583-1975. Toronto: Playwrights Co-op, 1976. 160 p. SUPPLEMENT, 1975-1976 (1979).
Z1377 D7B35   Ryder HU3-60
Appr. 2000 entries for books, articles, essays on theatre history in French and English Canada, little theatre, festivals, technical details and biographies. Indexed by author and subject.

BG22   CANADA ON STAGE: CANADIAN THEATRE REVIEW YEARBOOK, 1975- Toronto: Canadian Theatre Review, 1976-
PN2304 C26
Well illustrated review of the year's theatrical activity including festivals, summer and youth theatre, awards. Index.

BG23   Leonard, William T. THEATRE: STAGE TO SCREEN TO TELEVISION. 2 vols. Metuchen, NJ: Scarecrow Press, 1981.
PN2189 L44
Arranged by play's title with synopsis, comment and details of stage performances, operas, ballets, screen and television versions. Indexed by composer, lyricist, librettist, author and playwright. Excludes Greek classics, Shakespeare, Gilbert and Sullivan.

BG24   NEW YORK TIMES THEATER REVIEWS, 1870-   New York: New York Times, 1971-   CUMULATED INDEX, 1870-1919; 1920-1970.
PN1581 N4, N38, N42
Reviews reprinted chronologically, plus appendices of awards and detailed indexes of titles, companies, personal names.

BG25   THE OXFORD COMPANION TO THE THEATRE. 4th ed. Ed. by Phyllis Hartnoll. London: Oxford Univ. Press, 1983. 934 p. illus.
R792.03 H333T3 (1967)   PN2035 H3
Concise, authoritative literate articles on all aspects of the theatre, stressing the stage and performer rather than drama as a literary form. Coverage is international.

BG26   WHO'S WHO IN THE THEATRE: A Biographical Record of the Contemporary Stage, 1912-   2 vols. Detroit: Gale Research. irreg. with suppl.
PN2012 W5
(17th ed., 1981; supplements 1982, 1983) Publisher varies. Vol. 1, biographies of actors, dramatists, directors, designers, composers; a list of living persons covered in previous eds; obituary notes. Vol. 2, lists playbills, 1976-1979 for New York, London, Stratford on Avon and Stratford, Ont. For retrospective biography, WHO WAS WHO IN THE THEATRE, 1912-1976 (4 vols, 1978) presents 4100 biographies, in one sequence, culled from the first 15 editions. For more current information, the annual THEATRE WORLD (Crown) (PN2277 N5D32) covers the season in the U.S. and at Stratford, Ontario.

CINEMA AND FILM

Guides, Bibliographies and Indexes

BG27   THE AMERICAN FILM INSTITUTE CATALOG OF MOTION PICTURES PRODUCED IN THE UNITED STATES. 19 vols. New York: R.R. Bowker, 1971-   In progress.
PN1998 A57
FEATURE FILMS, 1921-30, 2 vols and FEATURE FILMS, 1961-70, 2 vols are available in this set intended to cover features, shorts and newsreels. Title entries with exhaustive index of credits, subjects.

BG28   Armour, Robert A. FILM: A REFERENCE GUIDE. Westport, CT: Greenwood, 1980. 251 p.
PN1993.45 A75
Bibliographic essays on sources for history, production, genres, actors, films. Subject and author indexes. F. Manchel's FILM STUDY: A RESOURCE GUIDE (Fairleigh Dickinson Univ. Press, 1973) (Z5784 M9M34) is a classified, annotated bibliography.

BG29   Bowles, S.E. INDEX TO CRITICAL FILM REVIEWS IN BRITISH AND AMERICAN FILM PERIODICALS TOGETHER WITH: INDEX TO CRITICAL REVIEWS OF BOOKS ABOUT FILM. 2 vols. New York: B. Franklin, 1974-75.
PN1995 B68
Covers 1930-1972. Arranged by film or book title with indexes for directors, authors and reviewers.

BG30   THE BRITISH NATIONAL FILM CATALOGUE, 1963-   (See AG16)

BG31   Dyment, Alan R. THE LITERATURE OF THE FILM: A Bibliographical Guide to the Film as Art and Entertainment, 1936-1970. London: White Lion, 1975. 398 p.
Z5784 M9D88
Classified, annotated bibliog. of ca 1300 English language items.

BG32   Enser, A.G.S. FILMED BOOKS AND PLAYS: A List of Books & Plays from which Films Have Been Made, 1928-1974. London: A. Deutsch, 1975. 549 p.
Z5784 M9E55
Access by title of film, original title and author.

BG33   FILM CANADIANA, 1980/82-   (See AG17)

BG34   FILM LITERATURE INDEX, 1973-   Albany, NY: Filmdex. quarterly
Z5784 M9F45
Subheaded, "A Quarterly Author Subject Periodical Index to the International Literature of Film with Expanded Coverage of Television Periodical Literature." Indexes over 300 periodicals.

BG35   Library of Congress. NUC AUDIOVISUAL MATERIALS, 1983-   (See AG6)

BG36   McCann, R.D., and E.S. Perry. THE NEW FILM INDEX: A Bibliography of Magazine Articles in English 1930-1970. New York: Dutton, 1975. 522 p
Z5784 M9M29
Brief notes; classified arrangement with author index.

BG37   Morris, Peter. CANADIAN FEATURE FILMS, 1913-1969. 3 vols. Ottawa: Canadian Film Institute, 1970-75. illus.
PN1998 M67   Ryder HU3-9A
An annotated review of the films with plot summaries and production notes. Chronologically listed in two sections, Canadian or Canada as location. The CFI library, largest film library in Canada, has "over 10 000 educational, scientific, cultural films ... from the most outstanding productions around the world" accessed by a master title index. CFI's CARD INDEX TO FILMS (1973, 17 microfilm reels) provides basic details on over 100 000 films of all types.

BG38   THE NFB FILM CATALOGUE, 1971/72-   (See AG18)

BG39   Rehrauer, G. THE MACMILLAN FILM BIBLIOGRAPHY: A Critical Guide to the Literature of the Motion Picture. 2 vols. New York: Macmillan, 1982.
Z5784 M9R423
Vol. 1 is brief reviews of over 6700 books arranged alphabetically by title. Vol. 2 is an index for access by subject, author, script. His earlier work: CINEMA BOOKLIST (Scarecrow, 1972-77) (Z5789 M9R42).

BG40   Schuster, Mel. MOTION PICTURE PERFORMERS: A Bibliography of Magazine and Periodical Articles, 1900-1969. Metuchen, NJ: Scarecrow Press, 1971. 702 p. SUPPLEMENT, 1970-74 (1976).
Z5784 M9S35, S352
Articles from popular English language magazines. His MOTION PICTURE DIRECTORS: A Bibliography of Magazine and Periodical Articles 1900-1972 (Scarecrow, 1973) (Z5784 M9S39) follows the same format.

ENCYCLOPEDIAS, DICTIONARIES, ANNUALS AND REVIEWS

BG41   Beattie, Eleanor. A HANDBOOK OF CANADIAN FILM. 2d ed. Toronto: Peter Martin, 1976. 320 p. Illus.
791.43 B369H   PN1993.5 C3B4   Ryder HU3-6
Information about festivals, associations, competitions, collections and performers, film-makers. Added information about Quebec films is in DICTIONNAIRE DU CINEMA QUEBECOIS (Fides, 1978) (PN1993.45 H67) by M. Houle and A. Julien.

BG42   Boussinot, Roger. L'ENCYCLOPEDIE DU CINEMA. 2 vols. Paris: Bordas, 1980.
PN1993.45 B6
An international guide to films, performers, technical terms.

BG43   THE CANADIAN FILM DIGEST YEARBOOK, 1971/72- Toronto: Canadian Film Digest, 1972- annual.
PN1993.5 C3C2   Ryder HU3-8
Information about production, distribution and exhibition of films in Canada. Includes associations, statistics, film study courses, awards, and the year's feature film production.

BG44   CINEMA: A Critical Dictionary: The Major Film-Makers. 2 vols. Ed. by Richard Roud. London: Secker & Warburg, 1980.
PN1993.45 C5
Signed essays on directors, genres, national schools. Indexes for names and film titles.

BG45   Dimmitt, Richard B. A TITLE GUIDE TO THE TALKIES: A Comprehensive Listing of 16 000 Feature Length Films from October, 1922, until December, 1963. 2 vols. New York: Scarecrow Press, 1965. Supplement: A TITLE GUIDE TO THE TALKIES, 1964 THROUGH 1974 (1977).
PN1998 A6695
Information on the literary sources of feature films.

BG46   Halliwell, Leslie. THE FILMGOER'S COMPANION. 7th ed. London: Granada, 1980. 745 p.
PN1993.45 H3
A quick reference aid, emphasizing British and American films with particular emphasis on the 30's and 40's. Also useful, his FILM GUIDE (4th ed., Granada, 1983) (PN1993.45 H27).

BG47   Lentz, Harris M. comp. SCIENCE FICTION, HORROR & FANTASY FILM AND TELEVISION CREDITS. 2 vols. Jefferson, NC: McFarland, 1983.
PN1995.9 S26L46
Subheaded: "Over 10,000 Actors, Actresses, Directors, Producers, Screenwriters, Cinematographers, Art Directors, and Make-Up, Specials Effects, Costume and Other People; Plus Full Cross References from All Films and TV Shows." Vol.1, the people; 2: the films and shows.

BG48   Magill, Frank. ed. MAGILL'S SURVEY OF CINEMA. Englewood Cliffs, NJ: Salem Press, 1980- In progress.
PN1993.45 M3; PN1995.75 M33
Includes ENGLISH LANGUAGE FILMS: FIRST SERIES. (4 vols, 1980) and SILENT FILMS (3 vols, 1982). Films listed alphabetically with brief details of production and players followed by signed critical essay. Indexes provide access to directors, screenwriters, performers, etc.

BG49   THE NEW YORK TIMES FILM REVIEWS, 1913-   New York: New York Times and Arno Press, 1970-   CUMULATED INDEX 1913-1968 (6 vols. 1970).
PN1995 N48, N4834
Reviews arranged chronologically in order of publication.

BG50   THE OXFORD COMPANION TO FILM. Ed. by Liz-Anne Bawden. London: Oxford Univ. Press, 1976. 767 p. illus.
PN1993.45 O9
Covers persons, films, themes, genres, and technical processes.

BG51   WHO WAS WHO ON THE SCREEN. 3d ed. New York: R.R. Bowker, 1983. 788 p.
PN1998.A2
Brief biographies and filmographies for more than 13 000 screen personalities, mostly American, British, German, French. D. Thomson's A BIOGRAPHICAL DICTIONARY OF THE CINEMA (Secker & Warburg, 1975) (PN1998 A2T73) is a lively example of concise biographical writing.

RADIO AND TELEVISION

BG52   Dunning, John. TUNE IN YESTERDAY: THE ULTIMATE ENCYCLOPEDIA OF OLD-TIME RADIO, 1925-1976. 703 p.
PN1991.3 U6D8
Includes articles on the radio shows; index of names.

BG53   NEW YORK TIMES ENCYCLOPEDIA OF TELEVISION. Ed. by Les Brown. New York: Times Books, 1977. 492 p.
PN1992.18 B7
Entries on the history, technology, programs, stars, executives, legal landmarks, rating system, etc. of the medium.

BG54   Halliwell, Leslie. HALLIWELL'S TELEVISION COMPANION. 2d ed. London: Granada, 1982. 713 p.
PN1992.3 G7H36
More than 10 000 entries, for Britain, U.S., on series, TV movies, performers, networks and technical terms. Excludes news and sports.

Section C
Social Sciences

SOCIAL SCIENCES

GUIDES

CA1 Hoselitz, B.F. A READER'S GUIDE TO THE SOCIAL SCIENCES. Rev. ed. New York: Free Press, 1970. 425 p.
R300 AH825R1

CA2 Li, Tze-chung. SOCIAL SCIENCE REFERENCE SOURCES: A PRACTICAL GUIDE. Westport, CT: Greenwood Press, 1980. 315 p.
300 AL693S   Z7161 A1L5
A recent publication in the area, but very general; with chaps on types of materials, on major subdisciplines. Name and titles indexes.

CA3 Roberts, N. USE OF SOCIAL SCIENCES LITERATURE. London: Butterworths, 1977. 326 p.
300 U84U
Guide to the general literature, official publications; several subdisciplines covered.

CA4 White, C.M., and others. SOURCES OF INFORMATION IN THE SOCIAL SCIENCES: A GUIDE TO THE LITERATURE. 2d ed. rev. Chicago: American Library Association, 1973. 702 p.
R300 AW583SA2
The standard guide to the literature.

BIBLIOGRAPHIES; PERIODICAL DIRECTORIES, INDEXES AND UNION LISTS

CA5 A LONDON BIBLIOGRAPHY OF THE SOCIAL SCIENCES: Being the Subject Catalogue of the British Library of Political and Economic Science at the School of Economics ... 4 vols. London: Mansell, 1931-32. SUPPLEMENT(s) 1929-73; irreg. annual 1974-
Z7161 L84
(16th SUPPLEMENT, vol. 39, 1982). Catalogues the holdings of the BL of Political and Economic Science and the Edward Fry Library of International Law. Subject only index; no author access.

CA6 The American Behavioral Scientist. THE ABS GUIDE TO RECENT PUBLICATIONS IN THE SOCIAL AND BEHAVIORAL SCIENCES. Beverly Hills, CA: Sage Publications, 1966-75.
R300 AA512
Now serves as a retrospective bibliog. for the period; includes annotated citations to books, articles, government reports and a few pamphlets. Arranged by author; title, subject indexes.

CA7 BOOK REVIEW INDEX TO SOCIAL SCIENCE PERIODICALS. 4 vols. Ann Arbor, MI: Pierian Press, 1978-1982.
Z7161 A15B65
Covers the period 1964-74 when reviews began to appear in SOCIAL SCIENCES INDEX (AF9).

CA8	CURRENT CONTENTS: SOCIAL AND BEHAVIORAL SCIENCES, 1969- Philadelphia: Institute for Scientific Information. weekly; triannual cum. index. (PER)
	A current awareness service of contents pages from over 1330 journals. Issues include tables of contents of new multi-authored books. Title word index, author index and addresses.

CA9	Directory of Published Proceedings. SERIES SSH: SOCIAL SCIENCES/ HUMANITIES, 1968- Harrison, NY: Inter-Dok. quarterly; annual cum. index, four year cum. index.
	Z7166 D56
	"A bibliographic directory of preprints and published proceedings." Arranged chronologically by date of conference, by location and by name. Indexes by editor, location, keyword/ sponsor.

CA10	Harzfield, Lois A. PERIODICAL INDEXES IN THE SOCIAL SCIENCES AND HUMANITIES: A SUBJECT GUIDE. Metuchen, NJ: Scarecrow, 1978. 174 p.
	300 H343P AI3 H37
	Entries listed by subject.

CA11	INDEX TO SOCIAL SCIENCES AND HUMANITIES PROCEEDINGS, 1979- Philadelphia: Institute for Scientific Information. quarterly, annual cumulation.
	Z7161 I524
	Indexes ca 100 published proceedings each year. In seven indexes: contents of proceedings; category; author/ editor; sponsor; meeting location; subject; corporate.

CA12	PUBLIC AFFAIRS INFORMATION SERVICE BULLETIN. (See AF10)

CA13	SOCIAL SCIENCES INDEX. (See AF9)

CA14	SOCIAL SCIENCES CITATION INDEX, 1966- Philadelphia: Institute for Scientific Information, 1973- monthly, triannual; annual, quinquennial cumulations.
	Z7161 S65
	Citation, source, corporate (geographical, organization), subject indexes to over 1000 journals in all fields of social science. Available online.

CA15	WORLD LIST OF SOCIAL SCIENCE PERIODICALS/ LISTE MONDIALE DES PERIODIQUES SPECIALISES DANS LES SCIENCES SOCIALES. 6th ed. Paris: UNESCO, 1982.
	Z7163 U522
	Over 3500 entries under country of origin. Title, subject index.

ENCYCLOPEDIAS AND DICTIONARIES

CA16	ENCYCLOPAEDIA OF THE SOCIAL SCIENCES. 15 vols. Ed. by E.R.A. Seligman. New York: Macmillan, 1930-34.
	R303 E56
	Scholarly essays on the history of the social sciences precede the main articles. Out of date, but useful as documenting the state of the art for social sciences in the 1930's.

CA17   INTERNATIONAL ENCYCLOPEDIA OF THE SOCIAL SCIENCES. 17 Vols. Ed. by D.L. Sills. New York: Macmillan and The Free Press, 1968. illus/ Reissue. 8 vols (1977).
R303 I61
Emphasizes analysis, research methodology, bibliogrphies in the central social sciences: anthropology, economics, political science, psychology and sociology. BIOGRAPHICAL SUPPLEMENT, vol. 18 (1979).

CA18   Gould, J., and W.L. Kolb. A DICTIONARY OF THE SOCIAL SCIENCES. New York: Free Press, 1964. 761 p.
R303 G697   H41 G6
Authoritative standard for ca 1000 basic concepts; o.p. but not superseded.

CA19   Miller, P.M., and M.J. Wilson. A DICTIONARY OF SOCIAL SCIENCE METHODS. New York: J. Wiley, 1983. 124 p.
H41 M54
"Current methods of inquiry which the empirical social sciences share in common ... to try to explain, illustrate and to set in context the majority of the terms."

CA20   Reading, Hugo F. A DICTIONARY OF THE SOCIAL SCIENCES. London: Routledge & Kegan Paul, 1977. 231 p.
H41 R42
Basic definitions of over 7500 terms for all social sciences except economics and linguistics.

DIRECTORIES

CA21   AMERICAN MEN AND WOMEN OF SCIENCE: SOCIAL AND BEHAVIORAL SCIENCES. 2 vols. 13th ed. New York: R.R. Bowker, 1978.
Q141 A48
Biographies of over 24 000 persons. Discipline, geographic indexes

CA22   CANADIAN REGISTER OF RESEARCH AND RESEARCHERS IN THE SOCIAL SCIENCES. London: Univ. of Western Ontario, Social Science Computing Facility.
Online register (CANREG on CAN/OLE, AB26) of ca 5 000 Canadian social scientists in universities, govt and private sectors. Includes specialization, current research, publications. No print version.

CA23   CANADIAN SOCIAL SCIENCE DATA ARCHIVE. Downsview, Ont.: Institute for Behavioural Research, York Univ., 1981. 127 p.
Z7161 C35 SIGS
Guide to the holdings of the largest social science data archive in Canada. Outlines means of access, descriptions of databases held.

CA24   DIRECTORY OF SOCIAL SCIENCE RESEARCH CENTRES AND INSTITUTES AT CANADIAN UNIVERSITIES. Ottawa:Social Science Federation of Canada, 1981. 141 p.
H62.5 C3D5
Information on 134 centres and institutes and their publications.

CA25   Library of Congress. The National Referral Center. A DIRECTORY OF INFORMATION RESOURCES IN THE UNITED STATES: SOCIAL SCIENCES. Rev. ed. Washington: Library of Congress, 1973. 700 p.
R300 U58D2   AS25 A46

CA26   WORLD DIRECTORY OF SOCIAL SCIENCE INSTITUTIONS/ REPERTOIRE MONDIAL DES INSTITUTIONS DE SCIENCES SOCIALES. 3d rev. ed. Paris: UNESCO, 1982. 535 p.
R300.72 R425R (1977)
A list of international bodies is followed with list by country of institutions and associations.

STATISTICAL INFORMATION

Guides and Encyclopedias

CA27   INDEX TO INTERNATIONAL STATISTICS, 1983-   Washington: Congressional Information Service.
HA154 I64 GOVT
A guide to the statistical publications of about 75 international, intergovernmental organizations. Includes indexes by subjects, names, geographic areas, categories, titles, issuing sources and report nos. Microfiche document delivery service.

CA28   INTERNATIONAL ENCYCLOPEDIA OF STATISTICS, 2 vols. New York: Free Press, 1978.
HA17 I63
Additional material and revised articles on statistical topics that appeared originally in the INTERNATIONAL ENCYCLOPEDIA OF THE SOCIAL SCIENCES (CA17). The ENCYCLOPEDIA OF STATISTICAL SCIENCES (Wiley, in progress) is a comprehensive, broad compendium

CA29   Kalbach, W.E., and McVey, W.W. THE DEMOGRAPHIC BASES OF CANADIAN SOCIETY. 2d ed. Toronto: McGraw Hill Ryerson, 1979. 402 p.
HB3529 K25
Basic information on the structure, characteristics and changing nature of Canada's population; intended for students, lay readers.

CA30   Kendall, M.G., and W.R.A. Buckland. A DICTIONARY OF STATISTICAL TERMS. 4th ed. rev. and enl. London: Longman, for the International Statistical Institute, 1982. 213 p.
HA17 K4
Defines appr. 3000 terms in current use.

CA31   STATISTICS EUROPE: SOURCES FOR SOCIAL, ECONOMIC AND MARKET RESEARCH. 4th ed. Comp. by Joan M. Harvey. Beckenham, Eng.: CBD Research/ Detroit: Gale Research, 1981. 508 p.
Z7554 E83H3
Over 2500 current print sources, arranged by country. Includes information on central statistical offices and other sources of statistical publications. Companion vols are STATISTICS ASIA AND AUSTRALASIA, STATISTICS AFRICA and STATISTICS AMERICA.

CA32   STATISTICS SOURCES. 2 vols. 8th ed. Ed. by P. Wasserman, and J. O'Brien. Detroit: Gale Research, 1983.
Z7551 S84
Subject guide to data (industrial, business, social, educational, financial) and other topics for the U.S. and internationally. Finding

aid to primary sources, especially U.S. publications. AMERICAN STATISTICS INDEX, 1974- (AM27) is a "comprehensive guide and index to the statistical publications of the U.S. government."

Statistical Compilations (See also section on Annuals, AH1 to AH24)

Great Britain

CA33   Central Statistical Office. ANNUAL ABSTRACT OF STATISTICS, 1840-
London: HMSO, 1854-
R314.2 G786A   GOVT
The most often requested time series for vital statistics, social and economic topics; supplemented by MONTHLY DIGEST OF STATISTICS.

United States

CA34   STATISTICAL ABSTRACT OF THE UNITED STATES, 1878-   Washington: Bureau of the Census, 1879-   annual.
R317.3 U58S   GOVT
"The standard summary of statistics on the social, political and economic organizations"; supplemented by POCKET DATA BOOK USA; COUNTY AND CITY DATA BOOK; STATE AND METROPOLITAN DATA BOOK; HISTORICAL STATISTICS OF THE UNITED STATES (1976).

Canada

CA35   CANADA YEAR BOOK. (See AH12)

CA36   CANADIAN STATISTICAL REVIEW, 1926-   Ottawa: Statistics Canada. monthly. with supplementary bulletins
(PER)   Ryder SS10-7
Each monthly issue has a content table highlighting articles from previous years. Articles or overviews which first appear in CSR are sometimes separately published, e.g., HIGHLIGHTS 1981 CENSUS OF CANADA (1983, 52 p.). Information in CSR is partly derived from CANSIM (Canadian Socio-Economic Information Management System), the computerized database of Statistics Canada and is made available as printouts, cards, tape through batch or interactive mode (see AB28). CANSIM has two modules, "Time Series" with current and historical information from a broad range of related socio-economic fields and "Cross Classified" which meets a demand for multi-dimensional data originating from or requested by researchers in demography, health, education, justice etc. The CANSIM SUMMARY REFERENCE INDEX (1980) (R650 C212CC) summarizes contents in the main base by subject and source. The CANSIM MAIN BASE SERIES DIRECTORY (1984) (R050 C212CB) is a detailed guide.

CA37   CENSUS OF CANADA, 1850/51-   Ottawa: Statistics Canada, 1852-
decennial; quinquennial (partial).
R317.1 C212P   GOVT   Ryder SS10-15
Census data for 1981 currently being issued. Three series of tabulations: National series; Provincial series; Profile series (similar to Census Tract Series of earlier censuses). Available in print, microfiche, and computer tapes. Specialized tabulations are produced on a fee basis.

CA38   Leacy, F.H. HISTORICAL STATISTICS OF CANADA. 2d ed. Ottawa: Statistics Canada and Social Science Federation of Canada, 1983. 1 vol. unpaged.
R317.1 H673H2   HA746 U7
Political, social and economic statistics from 1867-1975 (some tables to 1976, 1977).

CA39   Statistics Canada. User Services Division. Reference Products Section. BIBLIOGRAPHY OF FEDERAL DATA SOURCES EXCLUDING STATISTICS CANADA, 1981. Ottawa: Supply and Services, 1982. 189 p.
R015.71 B582B
Sources to social and economic data produced on a regular basis by other federal departments and agencies.

CA40   _____. _____. HISTORICAL CATALOGUE OF STATISTICS CANADA PUBLICATIONS, 1918-1980. Ottawa: Supply and Services, 1982. 337 p.
R015.71 C21GT
Replaces all earlier catalogues. All publications, whether in print or o.p., of the Dominion Bureau of Statistics and its successor Statistics Canada to Dec. 31, 1980. Much early publication available on microfiche from Micromedia.

CA41   STATISTICS CANADA CATALOGUE, 1980-   Ottawa: Statistics Canada, 1981-   annual.
R015.71 C21

Europe; The United Nations

CA42   EUROPEAN HISTORICAL STATISTICS, 1750-1975. 2d rev. ed. Ed. by Brian R. Redman. New York: Facts on File, 1980. 868 p.
HA1107 M5
Gathers major statistical sources for the countries of Europe. Organized by broad subject; extensively documented.

CA43   United Nations. Statistical Office. DEMOGRAPHIC YEARBOOK/ ANNUAIRE DEMOGRAPHIC. New York: United Nations, 1949-   annual
GOVT
"A comprehensive collection of international demographic statistics" for about 220 countries or areas. Special ed. DEMOGRAPHIC YEARBOOK: HISTORICAL SUPPLEMENT (1979) shows a time series, 1948-78.

CA44   United Nations. Statistical Office. STATISTICAL YEARBOOK/ ANNUAIRE STATISTIQUE, 1948-   New York: United Nations, 1949-
R311.3 U58   GOVT
"A comprehensive compendium of the most important internationally comparable data." Supplement: MONTHLY BULLETIN OF STATISTICS. More detailed information on specific aspects is published by the specialized agencies (e.g. UNESCO, see CA45 and AN19-AN22).

CA45   UNESCO STATISTICAL YEARBOOK/ ANNUAIRE STATISTIQUE, 1962-   New York: UNESCO, 1963-
R311.3 U58S   GOVT
Statistics of population, education, science and technology, publishing, culture and communication, films and broadcasting.

URBAN MATERIALS AND INFORMATION

CA46 Armstrong, F.H.; A.F.J. Artibise, and M. Baker. BIBLIOGRAPHY OF CANADIAN URBAN HISTORY. Public Administration Series, Bibliography P538-P543. Monticello, IL: Vance Bibliographies, 1980.
Z5942 A75
In six parts; 1: general topics; pts 2-6: geographic areas.

CA47 Artibise, A.F.J., and G.A. Stelter. CANADA'S URBAN PAST: A Bibliography to 1980 and Guide to Canadian Urban Studies. Vancouver: Univ. of British Columbia Press, 1981. 396 p.
Z7164 U7A77
Includes over 7000 articles, books, reports. General material by topic and specific materials by geographic areas. The "guide" section deals with reseach approaches and resources of all types.

CA48 Council of Planning Librarians. CPL BIBLIOGRAPHIES, 1979- Chicago: CPL Bibliographies. irreg.
Z5942 C68
Continues EXCHANGE BIBLIOGRAPHIES, 1959-79, with COMPREHENSIVE INDEX (1979). A series of bibliographies on many aspects of regional, urban planning and problems. Topics are international in scope.

CA49 DIRECTORY OF CANADIAN URBAN INFORMATION SOURCES. Ottawa: Ministry of State for Urban Affairs, 1977. 251 p.
R301.3607 D598D   Ryder SS3-121
A handbook to urban literature; articles, reference sources. Lists libraries, organizations, universities with relevant courses.

CA50 ENCYCLOPEDIA OF URBAN PLANNING. Ed. in chief, A. Whittick. New York: McGraw Hill, 1974. 1218 p. illus.
HT166 E5
Signed articles (many with bibliogs) on countries, individuals, concepts, national trends.

CA51 INDEX TO CURRENT URBAN DOCUMENTS, 1972- Westport, CT: Greenwood Press. quarterly, annual cum.
Z7164 L815 GOVT
Includes "local government documents issued annually by largest cities, counties in the U.S. and Canada." (Canadian items very limited.) Geographic, subject indexes. Microfiche document delivery.

CA52 INDEX TO MUNICIPAL DATA, 1982. Ottawa: Statistics Canada, 1983. 553 p.
GOVT
Lists Statistics Canada sources of published data for every Canadian municipality, plus a guide to unpublished data and a bibliography of related reference sources.

CA53 MICROLOG INDEX, 1979- (See AM57)
Includes urban materials covered by URBAN CANADA, 1977-78 and by PROFILE INDEX, 1973-76.

CA54   MUNICIPAL GOVERNMENT REFERENCE SOURCES: PUBLICATIONS AND COLLECTIONS. New York: R.R. Bowker, 1978. 341 p.
015.73 AM966M   Z1223.6 A1M85
A guide to over 2000 publications from 167 cities with 100 000+ population; arranged by state and city. Prepared under the auspices of the ALA Government Documents Round Table.

CA55   SAGE URBAN STUDIES ABSTRACTS, 1973-   Beverly Hills, CA: Sage. quarterly.
HT51 S24
Informative abstracts of books, articles, pamphlets, government documents, speeches, reports on all areas of urban studies. Author, subject indexes. Sage also publishes the URBAN AFFAIRS ANNUAL REVIEW.

CA56   URBAN AND REGIONAL REFERENCES, 1945-1969. 7th ed. Ottawa: Canadian Council on Urban and Regional Research, 1970. 796 p. SUPPLEMENT(s), 1970-75.   Ryder SS3-120
R301.364 AC212U7
Covers general sources; physical, population, and social characteristics; urban regional settlement and development; economics, transportation and communication; government and administration. Subject arrangement; author, geographic indexes.

CA57   'Urban Studies Information Guide', 1978-   Detroit: Gale Research. series, occasional.
Titles in this series are separate bibliographic guides on various aspects of urban studies, e.g. URBAN HOUSING (1978); URBAN POLITICS, (1978); URBAN POLICY (1979); URBAN INDICATORS (1980).

ECONOMICS

GUIDES

CB1   Dick, Trevor J. ECONOMIC HISTORY OF CANADA: A GUIDE TO INFORMATION SOURCES. Economics Information Guide Series, vol. 9. Detroit: Gale Research, 1978. 174 p.
        Z7165 C2D48   Ryder SS3-2
    Lists books, articles, dissertations and government publications that contribute significantly to the literature. Comparative evaluation before each group of entries.

CB2   Fletcher, John. INFORMATION SOURCES IN ECONOMICS. 2d ed. Stoneham, MA: Butterworths, 1984. 328 p.
    330 AU84F (1971)
    Provides an overview of the literature, including literature searching; reference tools; unpublished materials; databases and databanks; British, American and international official publications; statistics and a wide range of economics topics.

CB3   Helppie, Charles E., and others. RESEARCH GUIDE IN ECONOMICS. Morristown, NJ: General Learning Press, 1974. 166 p.
    H62 H46
    An introduction for the student; with overview of major resources.

CB4   Kumar, Pradeep. CANADIAN INDUSTRIAL RELATIONS INFORMATION: SOURCES, TECHNICAL NOTES AND GLOSSARY. Kingston, Ont.: Queen's Univ. Industrial Relations Centre, 1979. 166 p.
    331.0971 K96C   HD8106 K84   Ryder SS3-79
    In three parts: "technical notes on concepts, sources and methods of major information series relating to the economy, manpower and labour markets, labour legislation and public policy ..."; bibliog. of sources; glossary of common industrial relations terms.

BIBLIOGRAPHIES, ABSTRACTS AND INDEXES

CB5   ECONOMICS SELECTIONS: AN INTERNATIONAL ANNOTATED BIBLIOGRAPHY, 1954- Series 1: New Books in Economics. New York: Gordon and Breach. quar.
    Z7164 E2E3242
    Title varies. Entries are arranged under subject with author index. Citations, without annotations, published as CUMULATIVE BIBLIOGRAPHY, 1954-1962 and CUMULATIVE BIBLIOGRAPHY, 1963-1970.

CB6   ECONOMIC BOOKS CURRENT SELECTIONS, 1974-   Pittsburgh, PA: Dept of Economics, Univ. of Pittsburgh. quarterly.
    Z7164 E2E3
    An annotated list of all English language economics books, arranged by subject. Author index.

CB7   ECONOMICS WORKING PAPERS: BIBLIOGRAPHY, 1973-   Ed. by J. Fletcher. Dobbs Ferry, NY: Trans-Media Pub. Co. irregular.
                           Z7164 E2E33 BUSI
          Frequency varies. From 1976, subject coverage includes economics, management and business, demography, urban studies, politics. Working papers (drafts unpublished but available), mostly from universities or other institutions, are those received at Univ. of Warwick Library. Subject, author indexes. Microforms normally available.

CB8   INDEX OF ECONOMIC ARTICLES IN JOURNALS AND COLLECTIVE VOLUMES 1886/1924- Homewood, IL: Irwin, 1961-   annual, 1966- .
                           Z7164 E2I45
          Early vols are retrospective from 1886 to 1965. Lists "By subject category and by author, articles in major economic journals (over 230 journals) and in collective volumes" all articles in English or with English summary. Author index. Sponsored by the American Economic Association. Available online.

CB9   INTERNATIONAL BIBLIOGRAPHY OF ECONOMICS/ BIBLIOGRAPHIE INTERNATIONALE DE SCIENCE ECONOMIQUE, 1952-   London: Tavistock Publications, 1955- annual.
                           Z7164 E2I58
          Classified bibliography of books, articles, research reports. Author index; separate English and French subject indexes. A section in UNESCO'S INTERNATIONAL BIBLIOGRAPHY OF THE SOCIAL SCIENCES.

CB10   THE JOURNAL OF ECONOMIC LITERATURE, 1963-   Nashville, TN: American Economic Association. quarterly.
                           HB1 J676
          A review and current awareness journal. Book reviews; annotated list of new books; contents of current journals with subject index to articles, and selected abstracts with author index to subject list. Available online.

CB11   KEY TO ECONOMIC SCIENCE AND MANAGERIAL SCIENCES, 1953-   The Hague: Nijhoff. semi-monthly.
                           HB1 A1E2
          Supersedes ECONOMICS ABSTRACTS. Abstracts (English, French, German or Dutch) are in a classified arrangement and created from some 400 journals and selected books, reports in trade, industry, finance, economics, foreign aid, management, marketing, labour. Annual author, subject index. Available online.

DICTIONARIES AND HANDBOOKS

CB12   Crane, David. A DICTIONARY OF CANADIAN ECONOMICS. Edmonton: Hurtig, 1980. 372 p.
                           HC112 C7   Ryder SS3-8
          Intended as "a convenient source of information about our economic institutions, about traditional economic and business terms and about the ideas of major economists and schools of economic thought."

CB13   Gilpin, Alan. DICTIONARY OF ECONOMIC TERMS. 4th ed. London: Butterworths, 1977. 249 p.
                           HB61 G47
          Primarily for students and economists. A British slant.

CB14   THE MCGRAW HILL DICTIONARY OF MODERN ECONOMICS: A Handbook of Terms and Organizations. 3d ed. New York: McGraw Hill, 1983. 632 p.
R330.3 M147 (1965)   HB61 M3
   Provides definitions of about 1425 frequently used terms, and descriptions of 235 organizations and agencies.

CB15   Moffat, Donald W. ECONOMICS DICTIONARY. New York: Elsevier, 1976. 301 p.
HB61 M54
   "A companion for all who read or listen to the news, ... read trade journals, ... study economics or related business subjects."

DIRECTORY

CB16   DIRECTORY OF ECONOMIC LIBRARIES IN CANADA, 1981. Ed. by Irene Lackner and Gerald Prodrick. London: School of Library and Information Science, Univ. of Western Ontario, 1980.
R026.33 D598D   Ryder SS8-12
   Directory information for 287 collections. Geographic, personal name, subject, and type of library indexes.

ECONOMIC ATLASES

CB17   UNITED STATES AND CANADA. 2d ed. Prep. by the Cartographic Dept of Oxford Univ. Press. An Oxford Regional Economic Atlas. London: Oxford Univ. Press, 1975. 164 p.
R912 O98   G1201 G109 MAPL

CB18   ECONOMIC ATLAS OF ONTARIO. Toronto: Published for the Government of Ontario by the Univ. of Toronto Press, 1969. 113 numbered sections.
R912 E19A   Ryder SS3-11
   Maps on the "aggregate economy, population, manufacturing, resource industries, wholesale and consumer trade, agriculture, recreation, transportation, commerce, and administration." Economic atlases also available for other provinces (e.g. Manitoba, Quebec).

BUSINESS

GUIDES

CC1   Archer, Maurice. AN INTRODUCTION TO CANADIAN BUSINESS. 4th ed. Toronto: McGraw Hill, 1982. 669 p.
658.400971 A672I3 (1978)

CC2   Brownstone, D.M., and G. Carruth. WHERE TO FIND BUSINESS INFORMATION: A Worldwide Guide for Everyone Who Needs the Answers to Business Questions. 2d ed. New York: Wiley Interscience, 1982. 632 p.
R650 AB885W   HF5323 B765
  In three parts: source finder (index); publishers' index; sources of information (publications).

CC3   Frank, N.D., and J. Ganly. DATA SOURCES FOR BUSINESS AND MARKET ANALYSIS. 3d ed. Metuchen, NJ: Scarecrow, 1983. 470 p.
HF5415 F686
  A variety of sources, listed by type of source or publication. Name/ subject index.

CC4   Land, Brian. SOURCES OF INFORMATION FOR CANADIAN BUSINESS. 3d ed. Montreal: Canadian Chamber of Commerce, 1978. 76 p.
650 L253BA3   Ryder SS3-33

CC5   Vernon, K.D.C. USE OF MANAGEMENT AND BUSINESS LITERATURE. London: Butterworths, 1975. 327 p.
650 AV541U
  In three parts: the characteristics of the literature, its bibliographical and reference sources; research materials, statistical publications, company information; surveys of major subject areas of the field.

BIBLIOGRAPHIES

CC6   Baker Library. [Harvard University. Graduate School of Business Administration]. CORE COLLECTION: AN AUTHOR AND SUBJECT GUIDE, 1969-   Boston: Baker Library. annual.
  Updated by RECENT ADDITIONS TO BAKER LIBRARY (10 a year) which also serves as a selection aid. Baker Library is the major research library for material in business, economics, business administration etc. Its AUTHOR TITLE SUBJECT CATALOG (G.K. Hall) (Z7164 C81 H248) and supplements make available the library's holdings from its beginning, before 1850, to 1974. Baker Library also published BUSINESS REFERENCE SOURCES: AN ANNOTATED GUIDE FOR HARVARD BUSINESS STUDENTS (Rev. ed. 1979) (650 AH339).

CC7   Brown, Barbara E. CANADIAN BUSINESS AND ECONOMICS: A GUIDE TO SOURCES OF INFORMATION/ ECONOMIQUE ET COMMERCE AU CANADA: SOURCES D'INFORMATION. Ottawa: Canadian Library Association, 1984. 504 p.
R330 AB877C2   Ryder SS3-30
  Includes over 7000 government, non-government books, periodicals and services arranged by subject. Some entries are annotated. Indexed by author, title, publisher, series.

CC8 BUSINESS DEPARTMENT ACQUISITIONS, 1980- Toronto: Business Dept, Metropolitan Toronto Library, 1970- monthly.
Continues the Dept's ACQUISITIONS LIST, 1970-79; a selection aid.

CC9 BUSINESS & ECONOMICS BOOKS, 1876-1983. 4 vols. New York: R.R. Bowker, 1983.
Z7164 C81B927
Comprehensive listing of over 140 000 publications from the Bowker database. Full bibliographic information; author, subject indexes.

CC10 BUSINESS AND ECONOMICS BOOKS AND SERIALS IN PRINT. New York: R.R. Bowker, 1981. 1836 p.
R650 AB979B
Entries are listed by author, title, subject.

CC11 BUSINESS LITERATURE, 1928- Newark, NJ: Public Library. 10 nos a year. (PER)
Each issue is a short annotated bibliography of books and articles on a particular topic. A selection aid.

CC12 Daniels, Lorna M. BUSINESS INFORMATION SOURCES. Berkeley, CA: Univ. of California Press, 1976. 439 p.
R650 AD185B
Annotated list of business books, reference sources with emphasis on material in the English language.

CC13 DIRECTORY OF INDUSTRY DATA SOURCES: THE UNITED STATES OF AMERICA AND CANADA. 3 vols. 2d ed. Cambridge, MA: Harfax Ballinger Publishing, 1983.
Z7165 U5D5
Basically a bibliography. "To identify and describe sources of marketing and financial information for key industries." Pt 1: general reference sources. Pt 2: industry data sources; 3: data publishers, producers (alphabetic and type of document listings). Subject, title indexes.

CC14 ENCYCLOPEDIA OF BUSINESS INFORMATION SOURCES: A Detailed Listing of Primary Subjects of Interest to Managerial Personnel, with a Record of Sourcebooks, Periodicals, Organizations, Directories, Handbooks, Bibliographies, On-Line Data Bases, and Other Sources of Information on Each Topic. 5th ed. Ed. by Paul Wasserman, and others. Detroit: Gale Research, 1983. 728 p.
R650 AE96A4   HF5353 E52
Basically a bibliography. Sources of current information, arranged by topic.

CC15 ENCYCLOPEDIA OF GEOGRAPHIC INFORMATION SOURCES. 3d ed. Detroit: Gale Research, 1979.
HF5353 E54
"A detailed listing of publications and agencies of interest to managerial personnel, with a record of sourcebooks, periodicals, guides to doing business, government and trade offices, directories, handbooks, bibliographies and other sources of information on each location." Geographic arrangement; companion to CC14 above.

CC16 Uhlan, Miriam. GUIDE TO SPECIAL ISSUES AND INDEXES OF PERIODICALS. 3d ed. New York: Special Libraries Association, 1983. 289 p.
 A similar source is SPECIAL ISSUES INDEX: SPECIALIZED CONTENTS OF BUSINESS, INDUSTRIAL AND CONSUMER JOURNALS, ed. by R. Sicignano, and D. Pritchard (Greenwood, 1982).

INDEXES

CC17 BUSINESS PERIODICALS INDEX, 1958-   New York: H.W. Wilson. monthly, annual cumulation.
 (IND)
                    Z7164 C81B983
 Subject index to about 300 business periodicals, mostly American. Book reviews listed separately at end of issues. Expected online availability, 1985. MANAGEMENT CONTENTS, is a biweekly service, available online, and as BUSINESS PUBLICATIONS INDEX AND ABSTRACTS, 1983- (Gale). THE BUSINESS INDEX [microfiche] indexes some 325 periodicals, newspapers, books and reports. ABI/ INFORM is an online service abstracting ca 400 periodicals.

CC18 CANADIAN BUSINESS INDEX, 1975-   Toronto: Micromedia. monthly, annual cumulation.
 (IND)   Z7164 C81C242
 Formerly CANADIAN BUSINESS PERIODICALS INDEX. Indexes over 170 Canadian serials in business, industry, economics, related fields. Also indexes FINANCIAL POST, FINANCIAL TIMES, and business items in the GLOBE AND MAIL. Separate subject, corporate and personal name indexes. Available online as CANADIAN BUSINESS AND CURRENT AFFAIRS.

CC19 F & S INDEX INTERNATIONAL: INDUSTRIES, COUNTRIES, COMPANIES, 1968- Cleveland, OH: Predicasts. monthly; quarterly, annual cumulations.
                    MCL(BU)
 Access by country, subject and company. Useful for Canadian material. Available online.

ENCYCLOPEDIAS, DICTIONARIES AND HANDBOOKS

CC20 ABC: ASSISTANCE TO BUSINESS IN CANADA: The Federal Government's Catalogue of Business Assistance Programs, Services and Incentives. 2d ed. Ottawa: Min. of State for Economic Development, 1981. 237 p.
 R338.971 A111A2   Ryder SS3-29
 Arranged by problem areas, such as marketing; especially useful for small businesses.

CC21 Ammer, C., and D. Ammer. DICTIONARY OF BUSINESS AND ECONOMICS. Rev. and expanded. New York: Free Press, 1984. 507 p.
              HB61 A53
 Intended for the general reader as well as the student; covers a broad range of terms and concepts.

CC22 THE BLUE BOOK OF CANADIAN BUSINESS. Toronto: Canadian Newspaper Services International, 1976- annual.
 R658.1145B658B   HD2808 B6   Ryder SS3-23
 Profiles over 100 leading Canadian companies, ranks major companies and lists some 2000 companies operating in Canada.

CC23   Statistics Canada. MARKET RESEARCH HANDBOOK/ RECUEIL STATISTIQUE DES ETUDES DE MARCHE, 1975-   Ottawa: Merchandising and Services Division, Statistics Canada, 1976-   annual.
R330.971 C212M   Ryder SS3-89
Previously published in irregular editions. A source of information and reference for analysis of Canadian markets.

CC24   Cheveldayoff, Wayne. THE BUSINESS PAGE: HOW TO READ IT AND UNDERSTAND THE ECONOMY. 2d ed. Ottawa: Deneau, 1980. 320 p.
HC115 C49 BUSI
Guide to basic economics, financial data for general reader.

CC25   ENCYCLOPEDIA OF PROFESSIONAL MANAGEMENT. Ed. in chief. L.R. Bittel. New York: McGraw Hill, 1978. 1304 p.
HD30.15 E5
Intended "to provide managers with clear explanations of fundamental concepts and widely practiced techniques, and specific advice about how to apply them successfully." THE ENCYCLOPEDIA OF MANAGEMENT, by Carl Heyel (3d ed. Van Nostrand Reinhold, 1982) is another useful source.

CC26   THE FINANCIAL POST CANADIAN MARKETS, 1925-   Toronto: Maclean Hunter. annual.
HC111 S82   Ryder SS3-86
Information on 690 urban markets, buying power indices, retail sales, provincial comparisons and special features.

CC27   McGOLDRICK'S HANDBOOK OF THE CANADIAN CUSTOMS TARIFF AND EXCISE DUTIES, 1892-   Montreal; McMullin. annual.
HJ6092 A6M3

CC28   MUNN'S ENCYCLOPEDIA OF BANKING AND FINANCE. 7th ed. rev. and enl. Ed. by F.L. Garcia. Boston: Bankers Publishing, 1973. 953 p.
HG151 M8

CC29   Newman, D.M., and J.P. Newman. CANADIAN BUSINESS HANDBOOK. 3d ed. Toronto: McGraw Hill Ryerson, 1979. 673 p.
R650.0202 N552C3   Ryder SS3-34

CC30   SURVEY OF BUSINESS ATTITUDES AND INVESTMENT SPENDING INTENTIONS, 1977-   Ottawa: Conference Board in Canada. quarterly.
Continues SURVEY OF CONSUMER BUYING INTENTIONS 1975-1977, nos 1-3.

DIRECTORIES

CC31   Bell Canada. CANADIAN TELEPHONE DIRECTORY PRICE LIST: Directories Published in Canada, Effective January 1. Montreal: Bell Canada, 19?-   annual.

CC32   CANADIAN BOOK OF CORPORATE MANAGEMENT, 1977-   Toronto: Dun & Bradstreet Canada. annual.
HG4090 C36   Ryder SS3-83
Marketing directory with specific information on Canada's top 6000 corporations, public and private.

CC33   CANADIAN KEY BUSINESS DIRECTORY, 1974-   Toronto: Dun & Bradstreet Canada. annual.
                         HF5071 C38
   (1983 ed.) Lists 14 000 companies with $500 000 or more net worth, $25 million plus sales, or 250 or more employees. GUIDE TO CANADIAN MANUFACTURERS (1979-) has market information on 10 000 manufacturing locations.

CC34   CANADIAN TRADE INDEX, 1900-   Toronto: Canadian Manufacturers' Association, 1901-   annual.
                   T12.5 C2C25   Ryder SS3-24
   Manufacturers names, addresses and products; companies listed under province and city; classified list of products with their manufacturers.

CC35   CONSULTANTS AND CONSULTING ORGANIZATIONS DIRECTORY: A Reference Guide to Concerns and Individuals Engaged in Consultation for Business and Industry. 5th ed. Ed. by P. Wasserman, and J. McLean. Detroit: Gale Research, 1982. 1385 p. Inter edition supplement: NEW CONSULTANTS.
                         HD69 C6C6

CC36   DIRECTORY OF LABOUR ORGANIZATIONS IN CANADA/ REPERTOIRE DES ORGANISATIONS DE TRAVAILLEURS AU CANADA, 1911-   Ottawa: Ministry of Labour.
                   HD6523 D57   Ryder SS3-67
   Includes information on national, international unions, local organizations and central congresses.

CC37   THE FINANCIAL POST DIRECTORY OF DIRECTORS, 1930-   Toronto: Maclean Hunter, 1931-   annual.
       R658.151 F491   HG4090 Z5D5   Ryder SS3-3
   For Canadian companies, lists directors, executives with their positions, directorships, addresses.

CC38   THE FINANCIAL POST 500: Canada's Largest Industrial, Financial, Merchandising, Property and Resource Companies, 1964-   Toronto: Maclean Hunter. annual.
       Subtitle varies. Issued as a journal (Summer) supplement to THE FINANCIAL POST. The 1984 ed. adds an additional 500, plus new investors on Canada's stock exchanges to the regular features on business trends etc. The TORONTO STOCK EXCHANGE '300' STOCK PRICE INDEXES: ANNUAL UPDATE also has information on stocks, industries.

CC39   THE FINANCIAL POST SURVEY OF INDUSTRIALS, 1927-   Toronto: Maclean Hunter, 1928-   annual.
       R338 F491   HG5151 F53   Ryder SS3-25
   Financial information on all Canadian public industrial corporations. FINANCIAL POST SURVEY OF MINES AND ENERGY RESOURCES is a similar compilation for that area.

CC40   FRASER'S CANADIAN TRADE DIRECTORY, 1913-   3 vols. Toronto: Fraser's Trade Directories. annual.
       R670 F842   HF3223 F7   Ryder SS3-26
   Includes product classifications, trade names index and a brief list of all foreign firms with agents in Canada.

CC41   NATIONAL TRADE AND PROFESSIONAL ASSOCIATIONS OF THE UNITED STATES, 1966-   Washington: Columbia Books. annual.
R061 N277N   HD2425 D5332
   Currently lists ca 6000 associations -- trade, professional, scientific and technical, labour unions. Alphabetical list with subject, geographic indexes.

CC42   SCOTT'S INDUSTRIAL DIRECTORY ONTARIO MANUFACTURERS, 1958-   Oakville, Ont.: Scott's Industrial Directories. biennial.
R670 S431   HC117 O6S2
   Designed for industrial sales. Main arrangement is geographical by community, with company, product indexes. Similar directories are compiled for Quebec, Atlantic and Western provinces.

CC43   STANDARD & POOR'S REGISTER OF CORPORATIONS, DIRECTORS AND EXECUTIVES, 1928-   3 vols. New York: Standard & Poor's. annual; cumulative SUPPLEMENT(s) 3 times a year.
                    HG4057 A43
   Vol. 1: is corporate listings; 2: individual listings; 3: indexes.

CC44   THOMAS REGISTER OF AMERICAN MANUFACTURERS AND THOMAS REGISTER CATALOG FILE, 1905-   18 vols. New York: Thomas. annual.
R670 T463T   T12 T6
   The standard American buyers' guide. Current format: vols 1-10: products and services; vols 11-12: profiles; vols 13-18 catalogs of companies.

CC45   WHO'S WHO IN FINANCE AND INDUSTRY, 1936-   Chicago: Marquis. biennial.
R920.3 W927F   HF3023 A2W5
   Predominantly American biographies. WHO'S WHO IN CANADIAN BUSINESS (4th ed., Trans Canada Press, 1983) and WHO'S WHO IN CANADIAN FINANCE (5th ed., Trans Canada Press, 1983) offer information on the Canadian business community.

BUSINESS SERVICE PUBLICATIONS

Several American firms publish a variety of services that include Canada in their coverage, e.g. Predicasts (Cleveland,OH); Standard and Poor's (New York) providing investment services, special editions for libraries and information databases. Many business information publishers have online services.

CC46   DIRECTORY OF BUSINESS AND FINANCIAL SERVICES. 7th ed. Ed. by M.M. Grant, and N. Cote. New York: Special Libraries Association, 1976. 232 p.
R330 D598
   (8th ed., in preparation) Selected list of newsletters, bulletins and other services for business, economics, finance.

CC47   BUSINESS LAW REPORTS, 1977-   Agincourt, Ont.: Carswell. monthly. looseleaf.

CC48   CANADIAN BUSINESS SERVICE, 1941-   Toronto: Canadian Business Service. weekly. looseleaf.
   Includes BLUE BOOK OF CBS STOCK REPORTS. Surveys financial trends.

CC49   CANADIAN TAX REPORTS, 1939-   Don Mills, Ont.: CCH Canadian Limited. weekly.
       CCH publishes other services (e.g. CANADIAN CORPORATION LAW REPORTS) in topical law.

CC50   CANADIAN TAX SERVICE, 1948-   Don Mills, Ont.: Richard de Boo. weekly. looseleaf.

CC51   Dun & Bradstreet of Canada. REFERENCE BOOK, 1859-   Toronto: Dun & Bradstreet. 6 issues a year.
       Credit rating guide to Canadian companies; arranged by province, by city, by company name, "for confidential use of subscribers only."

CC52   FINANCIAL POST CORPORATION SERVICE, 1929-   Toronto: Maclean Hunter.
                           BUSI
       Card service for investment information on Canadian securities.

CC53   INSIDER: CANADIAN COMPANIES, 19?-   Toronto: Micromedia. weekly.
       Microfiche subscription service for reports filed by some 3000 companies. DISCLOSURE: U.S. COMPANIES (Dist.: Micromedia) is a service for reports of the Fortune 500 corporations.

CC54   MOODY'S BANK & FINANCE MANUAL, 1909-   New York: Moody's Investors Services. annual. Supplement: NEWS REPORTS. semi-weekly.
                         HG4961 M65
       One of many services from Moody's. Other manuals are INDUSTRIALS, MUNICIPAL AND GOVERNMENT, PUBLIC UTILITIES, TRANSPORTATION. Entries have a brief history of company, description of plants and products, list of officers, financial information (balance sheets, dividends).

POLITICAL SCIENCE

GUIDES

CD1   Clement, Wallace; and Daniel Drache. A PRACTICAL GUIDE TO CANADIAN POLITICAL ECONOMY. Toronto: James Lorimer, 1978. 183 p.
Z7165 C2C53
A bibliographic essay; followed by a topical bibliography.

CD2   Harmon, Robert B. DEVELOPING THE LIBRARY COLLECTION IN POLITICAL SCIENCE. Metuchen, NJ: Scarecrow Press, 1976. 198 p.
320 AH288D
Useful for small to medium-sized libraries.

CD3   Holler, Frederick L. INFORMATION SOURCES OF POLITICAL SCIENCE. 3d rev. ed. Santa Barbara, CA: ABC-Clio, 1981. 278 p.
Z7161 H64
An annotated bibliography of 1750 entries. In six parts: general reference, social sciences, American government, politics and law, international relations, political theory, and public administration.

BIBLIOGRAPHIES AND ABSTRACTS

CD4   ABC POL SCI: A Bibliography of Contents: Political Science & Government, 1969-   Santa Barbara, CA: ABC-Clio. 6 issues a year.
Z7163 A13
Provides contents pages from about 300 journals. Indexes: permuted subject and author. Ten year CUMULATIVE INDEX, 1969-1978.

CD5   FOREIGN AFFAIRS BIBLIOGRAPHY: A Selected and Annotated List of Books on International Relations, 1919-   New York: R.R. Bowker for Council on Foreign Relations, 1933-   .
R327 AF714   Z6463 F73
(Latest is Vol. 5, 1962-1972 {1976}). FOREIGN AFFAIRS 50 YEAR BIBLIOGRAPHY (1972) is an annotated list of about 2000 books.

CD6   Grasham, W.E., and G. Julian. CANADIAN PUBLIC ADMINISTRATION: BIBLIOGRAPHY/ ADMINISTRATION PUBLIQUE CANADIENNE: BIBLIOGRAPHIE. Toronto: Institute of Public Administration of Canada, 1972. 261 p. SUPPLEMENT, 1971-72 (1974); 1973-75 (1977); 1976-78 (1980); 1979-82 (1984).
Z7165 C2G7   Ryder SS6-103
Covers the broad field including books, articles, theses, government publications in a topical arrangement.

CD7   Heggie, Grace F. CANADIAN POLITICAL PARTIES, 1867-1968: A HISTORICAL BIBLIOGRAPHY. Toronto: Macmillan, 1977. 603 p.
Z7165 C2H4   Ryder SS6-97
Includes 8850 annotated references, published before 1970, for popular and scholarly works on the development of federal politics. Peter Weinrich's SOCIAL PROTEST FROM THE LEFT IN CANADA, 1870-1970 (Univ. of Toronto Press, 1982) attempts to cover all publications of the CCF, NDP, Communist, Socialist, and Labour parties, trade unions and various movements.

CD8   INTERNATIONAL BIBLIOGRAPHY OF POLITICAL SCIENCE/ BIBLIOGRAPHIE INTERNATIONALE DE SCIENCE POLITIQUE, 1953-   London: Tavistock Publications, 1954-   annual.
Z7163 I64
A classified bibliography of books and articles. Author index; separate English and French subject indexes. A section of UNESCO's INTERNATIONAL BIBLIOGRAPHY OF THE SOCIAL SCIENCES.

CD9   INTERNATIONAL POLITICAL SCIENCE ABSTRACTS/ DOCUMENTATION POLITIQUE INTERNATIONALE, 1951-   Paris: International Political Science Association, 1952-   bimonthly.
JA36 I5
Non-evaluative abstracts of periodical articles, in broad subject areas with subject index. Annual author, cum. subject indexes.

CD10   Page, D.M. A BIBLIOGRAPHY OF WORKS ON CANADIAN FOREIGN RELATIONS, 1945-1970. Toronto: Canadian Institute of International Affairs, 1973. 442 p. SUPPLEMENT(s) 1971-75 (1977); 1976-80 (1982).
Z6465 C2P3   Ryder SS6-79
The 1976-80 suppl. comp. by Jane Barrett, and Jane Beaumont. Organized by broad subject area, with name and subject indexes. No annotations.

CD11   PEACE RESEARCH ABSTRACTS JOURNAL, 1964-   Dundas, Ont.: Peace Research Institute. monthly.
JX1901 P43
"An official publication of the International Peace Research Association." Abstracts on many subjects relating to disarmament, peace, war, and international relations. Classified arrangement; author index in each issue. Annual author and subject indexes.

CD12   POLITICAL SCIENCE ABSTRACTS, 1980-   New York: IFI/Plenum, 1981- annual.
Z6461 U6632
Supersedes URS: POLITICAL SCIENCE ... (CD15). Each issue covers about 10 000 books, articles, briefly abstracted. Subject, author indexes.

CD13   THESES IN CANADIAN POLITICAL STUDIES/ THESES CANADIENNES EN SCIENCE POLITIQUE. Kingston: Canadian Political Science Assoc., 1970. 71 p. SUPPLEMENT, 1971/72-
Z7161 T44   Ryder SS6-72
Supplements bring coverage to 1981. Includes theses completed and in progress at Canadian and foreign universities.

CD14   UNITED STATES POLITICAL SCIENCE DOCUMENTS, 1975-   Pittsburgh, PA: NASA Industrial Applications Center, Univ. of Pittsburgh, 1976-
Z7163 U58
Comprehensive database in political policy and social sciences. Abstracts about 135 major American journals. Indexes by subject (using POLITICAL SCIENCE THESAURUS), author, journal name, geographic area, proper name. Available online.

CD15 UNIVERSAL REFERENCE SYSTEM: POLITICAL SCIENCE, GOVERNMENT AND PUBLIC POLICY SERIES. 10 vols. Princeton, NJ: Princeton Research Pub., 1965-69. Annual SUPPLEMENT(s) 1967-1979 (IFI/Plenum, 1972-79).
Z6461 U663
A comprehensive index to books, articles, pamphlets in the social sciences. Each of the ten basic URS vols covers a different subject. The annual vols. supplement the whole set. (Continued by CD12).

DICTIONARIES

CD16 Dunner, Joseph. DICTIONARY OF POLITICAL SCIENCE. Totowa, NJ: Littlefield, Adams, 1970. 585 p.
R320.3 D923   JA61 D8

CD17 Laqueur, Walter. A DICTIONARY OF POLITICS. Rev. ed. New York: Free Press, 1974. 565 p.
D419 L3

CD18 McMenemy, John. THE LANGUAGE OF CANADIAN POLITICS: A GUIDE TO IMPORTANT TERMS AND CONCEPTS. Toronto: J. Wiley, 1980. 294 p.
JA61 M36   Ryder SS6-71
Intended to provide "a comprehensive summary of terms and concepts in Canadian government and politics, with reference to some of the current or standard academic works on these subjects."

CD19 Plano, Jack C., and Roy Olton. THE INTERNATIONAL RELATIONS DICTIONARY. 3d ed. Santa Barbara, CA: ABC-Clio, 1982. 488 p.
JX1226 P55
A dictionary of concepts, theories, specific facts, events and institutions. Organized under broad topics, with index.

CD20 Safire, William. SAFIRE'S POLITICAL DICTIONARY. 3d ed. New York: Random House, 1978. 845 p.
JK9 S2
Especially useful for American politics.

ANNUALS AND HANDBOOKS (World and Area; Canada)

CD21 EUROPA YEAR BOOK. (See AH2)

CD22 EVERYONE'S UNITED NATIONS. 9th ed. New York: United Nations, 1979.
R341.13 U58E9   JX1977 A37E9; GOVT
EVERYMAN'S UNITED NATIONS (a companion vol., 8th ed.) covers the organization from 1945-1965. CA22 emphasizes the UN since 1965. The two vols. form a basic history of the organization.

CD23 Herman, Valentine, and Françoise Mendel. PARLIAMENTS OF THE WORLD: A REFERENCE COMPENDIUM. London: Macmillan, 1976. 985 p.
JF501 H47
Based on a comprehensive comparative survey of parliaments conducted by the Inter-Parliamentary Union.

CD24 THE MUNICIPAL YEAR BOOK, 1934- Washington: International City Management Association. annual.
R352.073 M966M   JS301 M8
"The authoritative source book of urban data and developments." Profiles individual cities, counties in the U.S.; intergovernmental relations; salaries of officials; directory and information sources; statistical tables. Some Canadian coverage, but principally American. Vols. include five year cumulative indexes.

CD25 POLITICAL HANDBOOK OF THE WORLD, 1928- New York: McGraw Hill [for the Council on Foreign Relations and Center for Social Analyis]. annual.
JF37 P6
Articles on countries give basic statistics, information on news media, government and politics. Articles on intergovernmental orgs provide information on officers, membership, origin and development.

CD26 THE STATESMAN'S YEAR-BOOK. (See AH3)

CD27 WORLDMARK ENCYCLOPEDIA OF THE NATIONS: A Practical Guide to the Geographic, Historical, Political, Social and Economic Status of All Nations, Their International Relationships, and the United Nations System. 5 vols. 5th ed. New York: Worldmark Press, 1976. illus.
R910.3 W927W3 (1967)   G103 W65
A standard guide.

CD28 YEARBOOK OF THE UNITED NATIONS, 1946/47- New York: United Nations, Office of Public Information, 1947-
R341.13 U58Y   GOVT
Annual review, with documentary references, of the activities of the UN and its agencies.

CD29 THE YEARBOOK OF WORLD AFFAIRS, 1947- London: Stevens.
JX21 Y4
Includes annual literature survey, "Trends and Events" and essays on topics of current interest. Published under the auspices of the London Institute of World Affairs.

Canada See also "Structure, Organization, Procedures of the Government" AM31-AM45

CD30 Bourinot, John G. BOURINOT'S RULES OF ORDER. (See AH50)
Parliamentary procedure; "a manual on the practices and usages of the House of Commons."

CD31 Campbell, Colin. CANADIAN POLITICAL FACTS, 1945-1976. Toronto: Methuen, 1977. 151 p.
JL78 1977 C34   Ryder SS6-69
A useful compilation despite some inaccuracies.

CD32 THE CANADIAN DIRECTORY OF PARLIAMENT, 1867-1967. Ed. by J.K. Johnson. Ottawa: Public Archives of Canada, 1968. 731 p.
R920.3 C212C   JL131 A55   Ryder SS6-13
The standard biographical reference work on past members of Parliament. Brief, factual information.

CD33   GUIDE TO CANADIAN MINISTRIES SINCE CONFEDERATION, JULY 1, 1867 - FEBRUARY 1, 1982. Ottawa: Privy Council and Public Archives, 1982. 326 p.
R354.7104 G946G   Ryder SS6-16
   A chronological list of ministries with an alphabetical list of departments; incumbents' names and dates of service.

CD34   THE CANADIAN PARLIAMENTARY GUIDE, 1862-   Ed. by Pierre G. Normandin. Ottawa: Normandin.
R328.71 C21   Ryder SS6-20
   Title and publisher vary. Includes biographies of current members of parliament and the provincial legislatures, a record of election results, and other information on Canada's government.

LAW AND LEGAL MATERIALS

GUIDES

CE1   Banks, Margaret A. USING A LAW LIBRARY: A GUIDE FOR STUDENTS AND LAWYERS IN COMMON LAW PROVINCES OF CANADA. 3d ed. Toronto: Carswell, 1980. 212 p.
340.0971 B218U2
    Student's guide to the organization of law libraries and the sources and materials of legal research.

CE2   Cohen, Morris L. HOW TO FIND THE LAW. 8th ed. St Paul, MN: West Publishing, 1983. 600 p.
340.072073 C678 H7
    A standard student's guide.

CE3   Gall, Gerald L. THE CANADIAN LEGAL SYSTEM. 2d ed. Toronto: Carswell, 1983. 348 p.
KF385 ZA2G3 LAW
    A comprehensive overview of the legal system for lay persons, students and lawyers.

CE4   Jacobstein, J. Myron, and Roy M. Mersky. FUNDAMENTALS OF LEGAL RESEARCH. 2d ed. Mineola, NY: Foundation Press, 1981. 614 p.
340.072 J17F2
    Formerly POLLACK'S FUNDAMENTALS OF LEGAL RESEARCH. The chapter on Canadian legal research, by D.T. MacEllvan, has concise explanations, and sample pages from Canadian legal research aids; his CANADIAN LEGAL RESEARCH HANDBOOK (Butterworths, 1983) is an extensive guide.

CE5   Murphy, Paul T. CANADIAN LEGAL RESEARCH GUIDE: ONTARIO AND CANADIAN FEDERAL MATERIAL. Rev. ed. Windsor, Ont.: Faculty of Law, Univ. of Windsor, 1981. 42 p.
R340.072 M978CA
    Intended particularly for beginning law students.

BIBLIOGRAPHIES

CE6   Boult, Reynald. BIBLIOGRAPHIE DU DROIT CANADIEN/ A BIBLIOGRAPHY OF CANADIAN LAW. New ed. Ottawa: Canadian Law Information Council, 1977. 661 p. SUPPLEMENT 1982.
R340.0971 AB764B2   Z6458 C2B6
    Provides access to over 14 000 articles, treatises and texts, by broad subject areas. Author, subject indexes are cumulated in suppl.

CE7   CLIC'S LEGAL MATERIALS LETTER/ BULLETIN D'INFORMATION JURIDIQUE, 1977- Ottawa: Canadian Law Information Council. bimonthly.
(PER)
    Information on recent legal materials, for the librarian, student, layman, practitioner.

CE8 Dykstra, Gail S. A BIBLIOGRAPHY OF CANADIAN LEGAL MATERIALS/ UNE BIBLIOGRAPHIE DE DOCUMENTATION JURIDIQUE CANADIENNE. Toronto: Butterworths, 1977. 113 p.
R342.71 AD996BA   Z6458 C2D85
Comprehensive, bilingual, annotated bibliography of Canadian legal materials published from 1973-76. Arranged by subject. Includes a directory of law book publishers.

CE9 Ferguson, Margaret, and San San Sy. LEGAL MATERIALS FOR HIGH SCHOOL LIBRARIES IN ALBERTA. Edmonton: Legal Resource Centre, Faculty of Extension Studies, Univ. of Alberta, 1983. 50 p.
Annotated bibliography; useful beyond the province.

CE10 INDEX TO CURRENT LEGAL RESEARCH IN CANADA/ REPERTOIRE DES RECHERCHES MEMEES ACTUELLEMENT AU CANADA DANS LE DOMAINE JURIDIQUE. Ottawa: Dept of Justice, 1972-
GOVT
Information on research in progress at Canadian universities and government agencies, departments. Provides lists of available Law Reform Commission publications for all provinces.

CE11 Jenner, Catherine. BIBLIOGRAPHY OF LEGAL MATERIALS FOR NON-LAW LIBRARIANS. Toronto: Ministry of Citizenship and Culture, 1984.
"A selected, annotated list of lay legal materials for Ontario public libraries." In two parts: primary materials and reference works; secondary materials by broad subjects.

CE12 LAW INFORMATION: CURRENT BOOKS, PAMPHLETS, SERIALS. 2 vols. New York: R.R. Bowker.
Publications of specialized legal publishers, bar associations, government agencies, professional groups as well as trade publishers. Access by author, subject, title. LAW BOOKS, 1876-1981 (R.R. Bowker, 1981) is a comprehensive list of over 130 000 entries.

CE13 LEGAL BIBLIOGRAPHY FOR LAWYERS OF B.C. Vancouver: The Law Library Foundation, 1982. 1 vol. looseleaf.
KF1 L398 LAW
Arranged by subject; subject, title, index; publisher information.

CE14 Wilson, Margaret. A LEGAL COLLECTION FOR NON-LEGAL LIBRARIES IN BRITISH COLUMBIA. Rev. ed. Vancouver: Legal Services Society, 1981. 94 p.
An annotated bibliography; particularly useful for public libraries. Arranged by broad subject with author, title, indexes; publisher list. Useful beyond the province.

INDEXES AND UNION LISTS

CE15 Canadian Association of Law Libraries. PERIODICALS IN CANADIAN LAW LIBRARIES, A UNION LIST. 2d ed. Downsview, Ont.: York University Law Library, 1973. 190 p. SUPPLEMENT 1977.
Z6459 C35
Supplement brings information to 1976.

CE16   INDEX TO CANADIAN LEGAL PERIODICAL LITERATURE, 1963-   Montreal: Index to Canadian Legal Periodical Literature. quarterly, cumulates.
(PER)
Publisher varies, begun by the Canadian Assoc. of Law Libraries. Separate author, subject indexes to articles in Canadian legal journals and legal articles in other journals; table of cases.

CE17   INDEX TO LEGAL PERIODICALS, 1908-   New York: H.W. Wilson, 1909- monthly and cumulates.
(PER)
Subject and author index to ca 400 periodicals from the U.S., U.K., Canada, Australia and New Zealand. LEGAL RESOURCE INDEX (Information Access Corp.) indexes over 600 legal periodicals, newspapers and other materials, available online and in cumulative microfiche issues monthly; CURRENT LAW INDEX (Information Access Corp) is a print version for the periodical literature indexed. Such systems as LEXIS (Mead Central Data) and QL Systems (AB31) in Ottawa provide online access to legal information, case and statute law.

CE18   CHECKLISTS OF LAW REPORTS AND STATUTES IN CANADIAN LAW LIBRARIES/ LISTES DE CONTROLE DES RECUEILS DE JURISPRUDENCE ET DES STATUTS DANS LES BIBLIOTHEQUES DE DROIT DU CANADA. 4 vols. Ottawa: Resources Survey Division, National Library of Canada, 1977-   occasional.
R348 AC213C
Vols cover Canadian law reports; U.K. and Irish Republic law reports; U.S. law reports; Canadian statutes and regulations. Comprises a union list of holdings.

DICTIONARIES

CE19   THE ENCYCLOPEDIA OF WORDS AND PHRASES, LEGAL MAXIMS: 1825-1978. 4 vols. 3d ed. Ed. by Gerald D. Sanagan. Toronto: Richard deBoo, 1979.
KE183 E56
Standard Canadian authority; defines legal terms as determined by court practice and as outlined by judicial opinion.

CE20   Flynn, William J. A HANDBOOK OF CANADIAN LEGAL TERMINOLOGY. Rev. ed. Don Mills, Ont.: General Publishing, 1981. 117 p.
R340.0971 F648H   KE183 F63
"Simplified interpretations of the most common legal terms." William Stevens' BASIC LEGAL TERMINOLOGY is intended for students in legal courses at a community college level.

CE21   JOWITT'S DICTIONARY OF ENGLISH LAW. 2 vols. 2d ed. London: Sweet and Maxwell, 1977.
KJ8757 D5
A standard lawyer's reference work, written for lawyers or those with prior knowledge of the law and the English legal system.

CE22   Yogis, John A. CANADIAN LAW DICTIONARY. Woodbury, NY: Barron's Educational Series, 1983. 243 p.
KF156 Y63 LAW
A basic dictionary for the student and lay person.

DIRECTORIES

CE23   CANADIAN DIRECTORY OF PUBLIC LEGAL INFORMATION. 13 vols. Ottawa: Canadian Law Information Council, 1979.
R340.0971 C212C
  Set includes ten provincial directories, an index volume and two federal vols (one Eng., one Fr.). For each provincial directory there is a list of all public, private, governmental agencies which provide information or advice on the law. Subject, name, geographic index.

CE24   CANADIAN LEGAL DIRECTORY, 1911-   Toronto: J.H. Wharton, annual.
R347.02 C212   K C2126
  The major sections are the geographic and alphabetic lists of lawyers and law firms.

CE25   CANADIAN LAW LIST, 1883-   Toronto: Canadian Law Book. annual.
R347.02 C212L   K C21275
  Main listing of law firms and lawyers is by geographic area; with name listing.

ANTHROPOLOGY AND ETHNOLOGY

BIBLIOGRAPHIES; ABSTRACTS, INDEXES AND ANNUALS

CF1   Abler, Thomas, and Sally M. Weaver. A CANADIAN INDIAN BIBLIOGRAPHY, 1960-1970. Toronto: Univ. of Toronto Press, 1974. 732 p.
                 Z1209.2 C2A64   Ryder SS1-18
      An annotated bibliography, listing books, monographs, journal articles, unpublished papers, reports, federal and provincial government documents. Includes a case law digest as "an attempt to bring together all case law relating to Indian legal questions decided since 1 July, 1867."

CF2   ABSTRACTS IN ANTHROPOLOGY, 1970-   Farmingdale, NY: Baywood Publishing. quarterly.
                 GN1 A17
      Includes archaeology; cultural, physical anthropology; linguistics. International in scope but English language material predominates. Author and subject indexes.

CF3   ANNUAL REVIEW OF ANTHROPOLOGY, 1972-   Palo Alto, CA: Annual Reviews.
                 GN1 A56
      Scholarly articles, with extensive bibliographies, on current problems in all branches of anthropology. Subject index.

CF4   ANTHROPOLOGICAL INDEX TO CURRENT PERIODICALS IN THE MUSEUM OF MANKIND LIBRARY, 1963-   London: Royal Anthropological Institute. 4 a year.
                 Z5112 A52
      Covers archaeology, ethnomusicology, physical anthropology, human biology, cultural anthropology, ethnography, linguistics. Subarranged by topic under geographical areas.

CF5   ANTHROPOLOGICAL LITERATURE: AN INDEX TO PERIODICAL ARTICLES AND ESSAYS, 1979-   New York: Redgrave Publishing. quarterly.
                 Z5112 A56
      Compiled by the Tozzer Library, Peabody Museum, Harvard Univ. In four sections: cultural/ social; archaeology; biological/physical; linguistics. Indexes: joint author; archaeological site/ culture; ethnic and linguistic group; geographic. Annual cum. indexes.

CF6   Corley, Nora T. RESOURCES FOR NATIVE PEOPLES STUDIES. Research Collections in Canadian Libraries: Special Studies, No. 9. Ottawa: Resources Survey Division, National Library of Canada, 1984. 342 p.
     R026 R342
      In English, French language reverse; a directory of Canadian libraries with native studies holdings, a union list of periodicals and bibliography of reference and other relevant material.

CF7   Frantz, Charles. THE STUDENT ANTHROPOLOGIST'S HANDBOOK: A GUIDE TO RESEARCH, TRAINING AND CAREER. Cambridge, MA: Schenkman, 1972. 228 p.
                 GN42 F7
      General guide to the profession; emphasis on resources.

CF8 HRAF SOURCE BIBLIOGRAPHY. Rev. ed. New Haven, CT: Human Relations Area Files, 1976. looseleaf for updating.
R300 AH918H   Z7164 S667H82
   Bibliography on world cultures arranged geographically, with alphabetical cultural unit, and author indexes. R.O. Lagace's NATURE AND USE OF HRAF FILES (1974) (300 L172N) is a guide to assist in locating information in the files. George P. Murdock's OUTLINE OF CULTURAL MATERIALS (5th ed., HRAF, 1982) and his OUTLINE OF WORLD CULTURES (6th ed., HRAF, 1983) are related publications.

CF9 Hirschfelder, Arlene, and others. GUIDE TO RESEARCH ON NORTH AMERICAN INDIANS. Chicago: American Library Association, 1983. 330 p.
Z1209.2 N67H57
   Selected, annotated guide to about 1100 English language books, articles, government documents and other written materials in 27 fields. The "goal is to present a selection of scholarly materials in the various disciplines." Includes material on some Canadian, Central and South American native peoples, but emphasis is on U.S. peoples.

CF10 INTERNATIONAL BIBLIOGRAPHY OF SOCIAL AND CULTURAL ANTHROPOLOGY/ BIBLIOGRAPHIE INTERNATIONALE D'ANTHROPOLOGIE SOCIALE ET CULTURELLE, 1955- London: Tavistock Publications. annual.
Z7161 I593
   Classified bibliography of books and articles. Author index, separate English and French subject indexes. A section of UNESCO's INTERNATIONAL BIBLIOGRAPHY OF THE SOCIAL SCIENCES.

CF11 Meiklejohn, C. ANNOTATED BIBLIOGRAPHY OF THE PHYSICAL ANTHROPOLOGY AND HUMAN BIOLOGY OF CANADIAN ESKIMOS AND INDIANS. Toronto: Dept of Anthropology, Univ. of Toronto, 1971. 169 p.
Z1210 E7M38
   An annotated list, arranged by main entry. Subject index.

CF12 Murdock, George Peter, and Timothy J. O'Leary. ETHNOGRAPHIC BIBLIOGRAPHY OF NORTH AMERICA. 5 vols. 4th ed. New Haven, CT: Human Relations Area Files Press, 1975.
301.451 AM974 (1960)   Z1209 M8   Ryder SS1-22
   Almost 40 000 entries to provide "basic coverage of the published literature on the Native Peoples of North America" to 1972. Includes books, articles, reports, parts of books, conference proceedings, dissertations. Main arrangement by region.

CF13 Newberry Library. Edward E. Ayer Collection. DICTIONARY CATALOG OF THE EDWARD E. AYER COLLECTION OF AMERICANA AND AMERICAN INDIANS IN THE NEWBERRY LIBRARY. 16 vols. Boston: G.K. Hall, 1961. SUPPLEMENT(s). 3 vols, 1970; 4 vols, 1980.
Z1209 N48
   Extensive collection contains research material on early history of the Americas, Hawaii and the Philippines.

CF14 Newberry Library Center for the History of the American Indian. Bibliographical Series. Bloomington, IN: Indiana Univ. Press.
   A multi-volume series covering a wide variety of topics in a standard format. Recent titles include: Robert Surtees, CANADIAN INDIAN POLICY: A CRITICAL BIBLIOGRAPHY (1982); Neal Salisbury, THE INDIANS OF NEW ENGLAND: A CRITICAL BIBLIOGRAPHY (1982).

CF15 Peabody Museum of Archaeology and Ethnology Library. [Harvard Univ.] AUTHOR AND SUBJECT CATALOGUES OF THE LIBRARY OF THE PEABODY MUSEUM ... (AUTHORS, 26 vols.; SUBJECT 27 vols) Boston: G.K. Hall, 1963. SUPPLEMENT(s) 1-4 (1970-79)
Z5134 H37
Records the holdings of this outstanding anthropology collection, founded in the 1860's. Includes analytic entries from periodicals, conference proceedings, festschriften as well as monographs. The main set of the catalogue includes material to 1962; suppls add material from 1962 to 1977.

CF16 REVIEWS IN ANTHROPOLOGY, 1974-   Pleasantville, NY: Redgrave Pub. Co. quarterly.
GN1 R43
Publishes review articles and lengthy reviews of new books.

CF17 Whiteside, Don. ABORIGINAL PEOPLE: A SELECTED BIBLIOGRAPHY CONCERNING CANADA'S FIRST PEOPLE. Ottawa: National Indian Brotherhood, 1973. 345 p.
Z1209.2 C2W45   Ryder SS1-25
Emphasizes unpublished speeches, reports, work of aboriginals.

ENCYCLOPEDIAS, DICTIONARIES AND HANDBOOKS

CF18 ENCYCLOPEDIA OF ANTHROPOLOGY. Ed. by D.E. Hunter, and P. Whitten. New York: Harper & Row, 1976. 411 p.
GN11 E52
Almost 1400 articles dealing with concepts, language, theories and leading figures in anthropology; entries on topics in related fields.

CF19 HANDBOOK OF NORTH AMERICAN INDIANS. 20 vols. Washington: Smithsonian Institute, 1978-   In progress.
E77 H25
"An encyclopedic summary of what is known about the prehistory, history, and cultures of the aborginal peoples of North America." Regions are treated separately (e.g.: vol. 8, Indians of California).

CF20 Jenness, Diamond. THE INDIANS OF CANADA. 7th ed. National Museum Bulletin, No. 65. Ottawa: National Museum, 1979. 432 p.
R970.1 J54   E78 C2J4
This ed. includes a new foreword and omits appendices.

CF21 Winick, Charles. DICTIONARY OF ANTHROPOLOGY. Totawa, NJ: Littlefield/ Adams, 1966. 578 p.
R572.03 W772   GN11 W5

DIRECTORIES

CF22 FIFTH INTERNATIONAL DIRECTORY OF ANTHROPOLOGISTS. Chicago: Univ. of Chicago Press, 1975. 496 p.
GN20 I5
Dated; one alphabetical list of 4752 entries giving affiliation, research, publication. Geographic, subject/ methodology, institution/ residence indexes.

CF23 GUIDE TO DEPARTMENTS OF ANTHROPOLOGY, 1969/70-   Washington: American
      Anthropological Association. annual.
                           GN43 A2G82
      Covers the U.S. and Canada, including academic depts; museum and
research depts (all with list of faculty, staff). Lists the year's
PhD. theses. The GUIDE TO DEPARTMENTS OF SOCIOLOGY, ANTHROPOLOGY AND
ARCHAEOLOGY IN UNIVERSITIES AND MUSEUMS IN CANADA (National Museum of
Man, 1978) is another useful directory.

SOCIOLOGY AND RELATED TOPICS

GUIDES

CG1 Bart, Pauline, and Linda Frankel. THE STUDENT SOCIOLOGIST'S HANDBOOK. 3d ed. New York: Random, 1980. 249 p.
HM68 B37
Provides an overview of essential journals, bibliographies, abstracting services and other sources.

CG2 McMillan, Patricia, and James R. Kennedy. LIBRARY RESEARCH GUIDE TO SOCIOLOGY: ILLUSTRATED SEARCH STRATEGY AND SOURCES. Library Research Guides, no. 5. Ann Arbor, MI: Pierian Press, 1981. 70 p.
HM15 M38

BIBLIOGRAPHIES AND ANNUALS

CG3 ANNUAL REVIEW OF SOCIOLOGY, 1975- Palo Alto, CA: Annual Reviews.
HM1 A766
Substantial scholarly articles on current problems in a variety of areas. Extensive bibliographies. Subject index; cum. author index.

CG4 Conrad, J.H. REFERENCE SOURCES IN SOCIAL WORK: ANNOTATED BIBLIOGRAPHY. Metuchen, NJ: Scarecrow Press, 1982. 201 p.
HV40 C66
Mainly 1970-80 imprints in social work and related fields. Subject organization under broad fields. Author, title and subject indexes.

CG5 CONTEMPORARY SOCIOLOGY: A JOURNAL OF REVIEWS, 1972- Washington: American Sociological Association. bimonthly.
HM1 C65
Includes review essays, surveys, and book reviews under broad subject headings. Annual index.

CG6 INTERNATIONAL BIBLIOGRAPHY OF SOCIOLOGY/ BIBLIOGRAPHIE INTERNATIONALE DE SOCIOLOGIE, 1951- London: Tavistock, 1952- annual.
Z7161 I594
A classified bibliography of books and articles, with author index and separate English, French subject indexes. A section of UNESCO's INTERNATIONAL BIBLIOGRAPHY OF THE SOCIAL SCIENCES.

CG7 Moscovitch, A.; T. Jennisen, and P. Findlay. THE WELFARE STATE IN CANADA, A SELECTED BIBLIOGRAPHY, 1840 TO 1978. Waterloo, Ont.: Wilfrid Laurier Univ. Press, 1983. 246 p.
Z7164 C4M6
The first part generally treats of the origin and administration of the welfare state in Canada, including statistical sources. The second part covers areas of policy, such as unemployment, prisons, child and family welfare, and health care.

CG8 Wepsiec, Jan. SOCIOLOGY: AN INTERNATIONAL BIBLIOGRAPHY OF SERIAL PUBLICATIONS, 1880-1980. London: Mansell, 1983. 183 p.
Z7164 S68W47
An alphabetical list of 2311 sociology and other journals in the social sciences covering sociological aspects. Subject index.

BIBLIOGRAPHIES: SELECTED SPECIAL TOPICS

Aging

CG9   Edwards, W.M., and F. Flynn. GERONTOLOGY: A CORE LIST OF SIGNIFICANT WORKS. Ann Arbor, MI: Institute of Gerontology, 1976. 160 p.
Z7164 O4E3 SIGR
Emphasis is on social gerontology. Subject bibliography; author, title indexes.

CG10   Place, L.F.; L. Parker, and F.J. Berghorn. AGING AND THE AGED: An Annotated Bibliography and Library Research Guide. Boulder, CO: Westview Press, 1980. 128 p.
Z7164 O4P52
Includes sections for physiological, psychological, social and environmental aspects. Author and title indexes.

CG11   THE SEVENTH AGE: A Bibliography of Canadian Sources in Gerontology and Geriatics, 1964-1972. [Ottawa]: Prepared for the Central Mortgage and Housing Corp. by Environics Research, 1972. 290 p.
Z7164 O4E5
In two parts: a gerontology section further divided into general reference, living arrangments, working and retirement, attitudes and behaviour; author/ subject index.

Child Abuse

CG12   Kalisch, Beatrice J. CHILD ABUSE AND NEGLECT: AN ANNOTATED BIBLIOGRAPHY. Contemporary Problems of Childhood, no. 2. Westport, CT: Greenwood Press, 1978. 535 p.
Z7164 C5K34
Includes over 2000 books, articles, government publications, etc. published 1960-77. Subject arrangement with author, keyword indexes.

CG13   Schlesinger, Benjamin. SEXUAL ABUSE OF CHILDREN: A SELECTED ANNOTATED BIBLIOGRAPHY, 1937-1980. [Toronto: Author], 1981. 74 p.
Z7164 C5S37
About 200 items, organized by subject.

CG14   Wells, Dorothy P., and Charles R. Carroll. CHILD ABUSE: AN ANNOTATED BIBLIOGRAPHY. Metuchen, NJ: Scarecrow, 1980. 450 p.
Z7164 C5S37
Concentrates "on physical and psychological abuse and intentional neglect." Includes books, articles, audio-visual materials, mostly published 1962-76. Organized by subject, with author index.

Death

CG15   Miller, Albert J., and Michael J. Acre. DEATH: A BIBLIOGRAPHICAL GUIDE. Metuchen, NJ: Scarecrow Press, 1977. 420 p.
Z5725 M54
Almost 4000 entries under broad disciplines, plus a list of audio visual resources. Author, subject indexes.

CG16   Lester, D.; B.H. Sell, and K.D. Sell. SUICIDE: A GUIDE TO INFORMATION SOURCES. Social Issues and Social Problems Information Guide, no. 3. Detroit: Gale Research, 1980. 294 p.
RC569 L47
Arranged by type of material, topics. Name, title, subject indexes

Drugs and Alcoholism

CG17   'Addiction Research Foundation Bibliographic Series'. Toronto: Addiction Research Foundation, 1968-   occasional.
Bibliographies cover a variety of topics on drug and alcohol abuse e.g. WOMEN AND PSYCHOACTIVE DRUG USE (1976), ALCOHOL USE AND WORLD CULTURES (1980).

CG18   Andrews, Theodora. A BIBLIOGRAPHY OF DRUG ABUSE, INCLUDING ALCOHOL AND TOBACCO. Littleton, CO: Libraries Unlimited, 1977. 306 p. SUPPLEMENT 1981. 312 p.
Z7164 N17A65
Annotated bibliography in two parts: general reference material, and source material by subject area. Suppl. brings coverage to 1980. Author/ title, subject indexes.

Marriage and the Family

CG19   INTERNATIONAL BIBLIOGRAPHY OF RESEARCH IN MARRIAGE AND THE FAMILY. 2 vols. Minneapolis, MN: Univ. of Minnesota Press, 1967-74.
Z7164 M2I58
Vol. 1: 1900-1964 (1967, 508 p.); vol. 2: 1965-72 (1974, 1530 p.). A comprehensive collection prepared for the Minnesota Family Center. Materials are listed by subject index, KWIC index, bibliographical and author lists.

CG20   INVENTORY OF MARRIAGE AND FAMILY LITERATURE, 1973/74-   Beverly Hills, CA: Sage Publications, 1975-   annual.
Z7164 M2I59
A continuing supplement to CG19 above. Prepared at the Family Social Science Dept, Univ. of Minnesota as "all revelant articles published in professional journals." Subject, author, keyword indexes.

CG21   Nowosielski, Maryna. MARRIAGE AND THE FAMILY: PRELIMINARY CHECK LIST OF NATIONAL LIBRARY HOLDINGS/ MARIAGE ET FAMILLE: INVENTAIRE PRELIMINAIRE DES FONDS DE LA BIBLIOTHEQUE NATIONALE. Ottawa: National Library of Canada, 1980. 130 p.
Z7164 M2N3   Ryder SS9-15
In collaboration with the Vanier Institute of the Family. Includes reference materials, serials and monographs. The Vanier Institute's VARIETIES OF FAMILY LIFESTYLES is a selected, annotated bibliography on family patterns.

CG22   Schlesinger, Benjamin. THE ONE-PARENT FAMILY: PERSPECTIVES AND ANNOTATED BIBLIOGRAPHY. 4th ed. Toronto: Univ. of Toronto Press, 1978. 224 p.
Z5118 F2S36
Includes essays on topics of special interest. Bibliography in chronological, topical arrangement with author index.

CG23   Sell, Kenneth D., and Betty H. Sell. DIVORCE IN THE UNITED STATES, CANADA, AND GREAT BRITAIN: A GUIDE TO INFORMATION SOUJRCES. Social Issues and Social Problems Information Guide, no. 1. Detroit: Gale Research, 1978. 298 p.
Z7164 M2S4
A guide to bibliographies, reference books, statistics and other sources of information. Name, title, and subject indexes. K.D. Sell's DIVORCE IN THE 70s: A SUBJECT BIBLIOGRAPHY (Oryx, 1981) lists over 4700 items in topical order.

Sex and Sex Roles

CG24   Astin, Helen S., and others. SEX ROLES: A RESEARCH BIBLIOGRAPHY. Rockville, MD: National Institute of Mental Health, 1975. 362 p.
MCL
Arranged by topics; includes articles, books, reports, all with lengthy annotations. Author, subject indexes.

CG25   Bullough, V., and others. AN ANNOTATED BIBLIOGRAPHY OF HOMOSEXUALITY. 2 vols. New York: Garland Publishing, 1976.
Z7164 S42A54
Over 12 000 entries, organized by broad topic. Author index. Despite title, most entries lack notes. W. Parker's HOMOSEXUALITY BIBLIOGRAPHY and its supplement (Scarecrow, 1971-77) also cover the literature to 1975.

CG26   Institute for Sex Research. SEX RESEARCH: Bibliographies from the Institute for Sex Research. Comp. by J.S. Scherer, and R.W. Wright. Phoeniz, AZ: Oryx Press, 1979. 212 p.
Z7164 S42I57
Topical organization; includes 4267 entries for books, articles, research reports. Author and subject indexes.

CG27   Institute for Sex Research Library. CATALOG OF THE SOCIAL AND BEHAVIORAL SCIENCES MONOGRAPH SECTION OF THE LIBRARY OF THE INSTITUTE FOR SEX RESEARCH, INDIANA UNIVERSITY. 4 vols. Boston: G.K. Hall, 1975.
Z7164 S42I5
Dictionary catalogue of holdings. Its CATALOG OF PERIODICAL LITERATURE (G.K. Hall, 1976) contains entries for periodical literature indexed to 1975.

ABSTRACTS

CG28   SAGE FAMILY STUDIES ABSTRACTS, 1979-   Beverly Hills, CA: Sage Publications, quarterly.
HQ536 S23
Each issue has about 250 abstracts of important recent books, articles, etc. on marriage, the family, sex roles, counselling. Broad subject arrangement with author, subject indexes.

CG29   HUMAN RESOURCES ABSTRACTS, 1966-   Beverly Hills, CA: Sage Publications. quarterly.
Z7165 U5P222
Formerly POVERTY AND HUMAN RESOURCES ABSTRACTS. A comprehensive source of information: "covers human, social, and manpower problems and solutions ranging from slum rehabilitation and job development training to compensatory education, minority group problems and rural proverty." Includes books and articles in a topical organization with author and subject indexes.

CG30   SOCIAL WORK RESEARCH & ABSTRACTS, 1977-   Albany, NY: National Association of Social Workers. quarterly; annual cum. index.
HV1 A27
Supersedes ABSTRACTS FOR SOCIAL WORKERS, 1965-1977. Arranged by broad topics for areas of service, social policy and action, methods, the profession, history and related fields. Author, subject indexes.

CG31   SOCIOLOGICAL ABSTRACTS, 1952-   New York: Sociological Abstracts. 5 issues a year. annual cum. index.
HM1 S67
Sponsored in part by the International Sociological Association. Non-evaluative abstracts in a classified arrangement by broad subjects with subdivisions; author, subject indexes. Each issue has the "International Reviews of Publications in Sociology" a bibliog. of book reviews from the journals abstracted. Available online.

ENCYCLOPEDIAS, DICTIONARIES AND HANDBOOKS

CG32   DICTIONARY OF SOCIAL WELFARE. By Noel Timms, and Rita Timms. London: Routledge & Kegan Paul, 1982. 217 p.
HV12 T54
Defines current terminology in social welfare and social policy. Most entries include reference to further information.

CG33   ENCYCLOPEDIA OF SOCIAL WORK. 2 vols. 17th ed. Ed. in chief, John Turner. Washington: National Association of Social Workers, 1977. SUPPLEMENT 1980; 1983/84.
HV35 S6A
Articles on many problems and activities in social welfare, biographies of outstanding social workers, statistical tables and a agency directory. A regular series of suppls to the 17th ed (to 1987) update statistics, add topical articles. Beginning in 1987, the NASW plans publication of AG33 at ten year intervals.

CG34   ENCYCLOPEDIA OF SOCIOLOGY. New & updated. Guilford, CT: DPG Reference Publishing, 1981. 317 p.
HM17 E5
Over 1000 articles, "subject maps" and guides, cross references.

CG35   HANDBOOK OF CONTEMPORARY DEVELOPMENTS IN WORLD SOCIOLOGY. Ed. by R.P. Mohan, and D. Martindale, Westport, CT: Greenwood Press, 1975. 493 p.
HM19 H23
Each country is discussed in a separate chapter.

CG36   INTERNATIONAL ENCYCLOPEDIA OF POPULATION. 2 vols. Ed. in chief, John A. Ross. New York: Free Press, 1982.
HB849.2 I55
Companion to INTERNATIONAL ENCYCLOPEDIA OF THE SOCIAL SCIENCES (CA17) and INTERNATIONAL ENCYCLOPEDIA OF STATISTICS (CA28). Covers demography, fertility, marriage, mortality, morbidity and migration. Geographic coverage in separate articles for the 11 largest countries and Canada. Articles are an overview of available knowledge.

CG37   A MODERN DICTIONARY OF SOCIOLOGY. By George A. Theodorson, and Achilles G. Theodorson. New York: Crowell, 1969. 469 p.
HM17 T5
Comprehensive list of terms; for both students and professionals.

CG38   A NEW DICTIONARY OF SOCIOLOGY. By G. Duncan Mitchell. London: Routledge & Kegan Paul, 1979. 244 p.
HM17 M56
Intended for students; most entries refer to additional sources.

DIRECTORIES

CG39   DIRECTORY OF CANADIAN HUMAN SERVICES/ REPERTOIRE DES SERVICES SOCIAUX AU CANADA. Ottawa: The Canadian Council on Social Development, 1943- biennial.
HV104 C3813   Ryder SS9-21
Lists organizations in, or related to, social development field. Geographical arrangement.

CG40   DIRECTORY OF COMMUNITY SERVICES IN METROPOLITAN TORONTO. Toronto: Community Information Centre of Metropolitan Toronto, 1972-   irreg.
R360 D598D   HV110 T6C6
Frequency varies. Includes services provided by major social sevice and government agencies. Organizations listed alphabetically. Subject index and separate section on emergency services.

WOMEN'S STUDIES

Bibliographies

CG41   Ballou, Patricia K. WOMEN: A BIBLIOGRAPHY OF BIBLIOGRAPHIES. Boston: G.K. Hall, 1980. 155 p.
Z7961 A1B34
Includes 557 bibliographies, published 1970-79, most entries annotated. Organized by specific subjects, some geographical. Name index. M.Ritchie's WOMEN'S STUDIES: A CHECKLIST OF BIBLIOGRAPHIES (Mansell, 1980) includes material published to 1978.

CG42   Canadian Research Institute for the Advancement of Women. WOMEN AND WORK: AN INVENTORY OF RESEARCH/ LA FEMME ET LE TRAVAIL: UN INVENTAIRE DE RECHERCHES. Ottawa: CRIAW, 1978. 85 p.
Z7963 E7C35   Ryder SS9-25
Books, articles, reports, arranged by subject. Name/ subject index

CG43   Frey, L.; M. Frey, and J. Schneder. WOMEN IN WESTERN EUROPEAN HISTORY: A Select Chronological, Geographical and Topical Bibliography. Westport, CT: Greenwood Press, 1982-   In progress.
Z7961 F74
Arranged by topics under broad chronological periods. "Planned to make available to the scholar and non-specialist recent and past research on women." Subject, name and author indexes.

CG44   Harrison, Cynthia E. WOMEN IN AMERICAN HISTORY: A BIBLIOGRAPHY. Santa Barbara, CA: ABC-Clio, 1979. 374 p.
Z7962 H37
Abstracts of articles from periodicals and collections published 1963-76. Topical and geographical arrangement. Includes some Canadian material. Detailed subject; author index.

CG45   Hauck, Philomena. SOURCEBOOK ON CANADIAN WOMEN. Ottawa: Canadian Library Association, 1979. 111 p.
Z7964 C3H48   Ryder SS9-26
"An annotated guide to books, periodicals, pamphlets, audiovisual materials and general information sources." English language only; items arranged by broad subject.

CG46   Light, Beth, and Veronica Strong-Boag. TRUE DAUGHTERS OF THE NORTH: Canadian Women's History, An Annotated Bibliography. Toronto: Ontario Institute for Studies in Education, 1980. 210 p.
Z7964 C3L54   Ryder HA4-77
The sources "both primary and secondary by which Canadians may ... improve their understanding of women's experience and role in the creation of the modern community." Organized by topic under broad chronological headings; author index.

CG47   Mazur, C. and S. Pepper. WOMEN IN CANADA 1965 TO 1975: A BIBLIOGRAPHY. Hamilton, Ont.: McMaster Univ. Library Press, 1976. 174 p.
Z7964 C3H37   Ryder SS9-32
Books, articles, reports, arranged by subject. Author index.

CG48   Stephenson, Marylee. WOMEN IN CANADA. Rev. ed. Don Mills, Ont.: General Publishing, 1977. 368 p.
HQ1453 S74   Ryder SS9-33n
Articles, with bibliographies, on various issues; a bibliography of 1100 items: "social science materials on Canadian women" 1950-75.

CG49   Stineman, Esther. WOMEN'S STUDIES: A RECOMMENDED CORE BIBLIOGRAPHY. Littleton, CO: Libraries Unlimited, 1979. 670 p.
Z7961 S75
Over 1700 annotated entries for books and periodicals, including a large section of fiction and other creative work. Arranged by broad topics; author, title, subject indexes.

CG50   Williamson, Jane. NEW FEMINIST SCHOLARSHIP: A GUIDE TO BIBLIOGRAPHIES. Old Westbury, NY: Clearinghouse of Women's Studies, 1979. 139 p.
Z7961 A1W54
Includes 391 English language bibliographies, resource lists and literature reviews. Subject arrangement with author, title indexes.

CG51 THE WOMEN'S ANNUAL: THE YEAR IN REVIEW, 1980-   Boston: G.K. Hall, 1981-
              HQ1105 W6
   Articles on the trends and literature include extensive bibliographies. Author/ title, subject indexes.

CG52 WOMEN'S HISTORY SOURCES: A Guide to Archive and Manuscript Collections in the United States. 2 vols. Ed. by Andrea Hinding. New York: R.R. Bowker, 1979.
              Z7964 U49H56
   Guide to over 10 000 collections in 1000 repositories. Each entry gives a description of the collection, its dates, scope and related publications. Detailed name/ subject index.

CG53 WOMEN'S RESOURCE CATALOGUE. Ottawa: Secretary of State, Women's Program, 1982. 73, 64 p.
              Z7964 C3W65
   Lists "print and audio-visual materials by, for and about Canadian women ... (limited to) inexpensive, readily available Canadian resources published no earlier than 1975." Organized by 'issues' with lists of sources; English and French language items.

Abstracts

CG54 RESOURCES FOR FEMINIST RESEARCH/DOCUMENTATION SUR LA RECHERCHE FEMINISTE 1972-   Toronto: Dept of Sociology, Ontario Institute for Studies in Education. quarterly, cum. index.
              HQ1101 C32   Ryder SS9-28
   "An interdisciplinary, international periodical of research on women and sex roles ... (also) book reviews, bibliographies." Two issues each year ar on specific themes, another focuses on book reviews. Author, subject indexes.

CG55 WOMEN'S STUDIES ABSTRACTS, 1972-   Rush, NY: Rush Publishing. quarterly.
              HQ1101 W4
   Abstracts of articles in both specialized and general periodicals. Arranged by topic; subject and author indexes.

PSYCHOLOGY

GUIDE

CH1   McInnis, Raymond G. RESEARCH GUIDE FOR PSYCHOLOGY. Reference Sources for the Social Sciences and Humanities, no. 1. Westport, CT: Greenwood Press, 1982. 604 p.
Z7201 M35
Intended as "a research guide that contains the principal information sources in a logically integrated and critically analytical format." A bibliographical guide in 16 topical sections; with chapter on general works by type. Author, title, subject index.

BIBLIOGRAPHIES AND ANNUALS

CH2   ANNUAL REVIEW OF PSYCHOLOGY, 1950-   Palo Alto, CA: Annual Reviews.
BF30 A56
Each review covers a variety of topics in essay format, with extensive bibliographies. Author and subject indexes.

CH3   BIBLIOGRAPHIC GUIDE TO PSYCHOLOGY, 1975-   Boston: G.K. Hall, 1976- annual.
Lists all material catalogued during the year by LC and by the New York Public Library's Research Libraries.

CH4   THE HARVARD LIST OF BOOKS IN PSYCHOLOGY. 4th ed. Cambridge, MA: Harvard Univ. Press, 1971. 108 p.
Z7201 H28
A basic list.

ABSTRACTS

CH5   CHILD DEVELOPMENT ABSTRACTS AND BIBLIOGRAPHY, 1927-   Chicago: Univ. of Chicago Press for the Society for Research in Child Development. 3 a year.
HQ750 A1C47
Abstracts of periodical articles arranged by broad subject; book reviews arranged by author. Author and subject indexes; cumulated indexes in last issue of volume.

CH6   PSYCHOLOGICAL ABSTRACTS: Non-evaluative Summaries of the World's Literature in Psychology and Related Disciplines, 1927-   Arlington, VA: American Psychological Association. monthly.
BF1 P65
Each issue is organized by broad subject areas with narrower subdivisions. Author and brief subject indexes. Expanded, integrated indexes published semi-annually. Cumulated indexes, currently three year periods. Records since 1967 available online as PsycINFO.

ENCYCLOPEDIAS AND DICTIONARIES

CH7 ENCYCLOPEDIA OF PSYCHOLOGY. 4 vols. Ed. by R.J. Corsini. New York: J. Wiley, 1974.
BF31 E554
Covers some 1200 major topics in brief articles; has biogs, description of tests and summary of psychology worldwide. THE ENCYCLOPEDIA OF PSYCHOLOGY (3 vols, 1972/ re-issue 1 vol., Seabury Press, 1979), with short definitions and longer articles, is an authoritative general treatment for the layman and specialist.

CH8 THE ENCYCLOPEDIC DICTIONARY OF PSYCHOLOGY. Ed. by Rom Harré, and Roger Lamb. London: Blackwell Reference, 1983. 718 p.
BF31 E555
Covers the broad range of psychological topics. Alphabetical organization with cross references and index for improved access. Many articles include bibliographies.

CH9 Harriman, Philip L. DICTIONARY OF PSYCHOLOGY. London: Peter Owen, 1972. 364 p.
BF31 H34

CH10 INTERNATIONAL ENCYCLOPEDIA OF PSYCHIATRY, PSYCHOLOGY, PSYCHOANALYSIS & NEUROLOGY. 12 vols. Ed. in chief, Benjamin B. Wolman. New York: Van Nostrand, 1977. Progress vols, 1983- (Aesculapius Publishers).
RC334 I57

CH11 LONGMAN DICTIONARY OF PSYCHOLOGY AND PSYCHIATRY. Ed. in chief, Robert M. Goldenson. New York: Longman, 1984. 815 p.
BF31 L66
Over 21 000 brief entries, with emphasis on current terms. Broad coverage of both fields.

CH12 Wolman, Benjamin B. DICTIONARY OF BEHAVIORAL SCIENCE. New York: Van Nostrand Reinhold, 1973. 478 p.
BF31 N64
For university students and professionals.

HANDBOOKS ON TESTS

CH13 Buros, Oscar K. ed. THE EIGHTH MENTAL MEASUREMENTS YEARBOOK. 2 vols. Highland Park, NJ: Gryphon Press, 1978.
R153.9 B967Y7   Z58144 P8B932
"Designed to assist test users in education, psychology and industry to make more intelligent use of standardized tests of every description." Tests are arranged by type. Indexes of test titles and names; classified index of tests.

CH14 TESTS IN PRINT III: An Index to Tests, Test Reviews, and the Literature on Specific Tests. Ed. by James V. Mitchell. Lincoln, NE: Buros Inst. of Mental Measurements, Univ. of Nebraska-Lincoln, 1983. 714 p.
Z5814 E9T47
"Descriptive listings and references, without reviews, of commercially published tests that are in print and available for purchase and use ... [and] a comprehensive index to the contents of Mental Measurements Yearbooks" (see CH13). Includes 2672 tests.

DIRECTORIES AND BIOGRAPHIES

CH15   Canadian Psychological Association. DIRECTORY, 1960-   Montreal: C.P.A.
BF30 C35   Ryder SC13-1
Lists current members, present, past officers of the C.P.A.

CH16   DIRECTORY OF THE AMERICAN PSYCHOLOGICAL ASSOCIATION. Washington: American Psychological Association. triennial.
BF11 A67
A comprehensive current listing of some 54 000 members of the APA; providing education, specialty, employment information.

CH17   Zusne, Leonard. NAMES IN THE HISTORY OF PSYCHOLOGY: A BIOGRAPHICAL SOURCEBOOK. Washington: Hemisphere Publishing, 1975. 489 p.
BF109 A1Z85
Includes brief notes on the life and significance to psychology of 526 individuals. No living persons included.

EDUCATION

GUIDES AND BIBLIOGRAPHIES

CI1   Auster, Ethel. REFERENCE SOURCES ON CANADIAN EDUCATION: AN ANNOTATED BIBLIOGRAPHY. OISE Bibliography Series, No. 3. Toronto: Ontario Institute for Studies in Education, 1978. 114 p.
370.971 AA934R   Z5815 C2A9   Ryder SS4-1
With subject and author/title indexes.

CI2   Camp, William L., and Bryan L. Schwark. GUIDE TO PERIODICALS IN EDUCATION AND ITS ACADEMIC DISCIPLINES. 2d ed. Metuchen, NJ.: Scarecrow Press, 1975. 552 p.
370.5 AC186   Z5813 C2P   Sheehy 1CB27
Arranged topically with detailed information; submission of manuscripts. EDUCATION AND EDUCATION - RELATED SERIALS: A DIRECTORY (Libraries Unlimited, 1977) is a similar list.

CI3   'Education Information Guide Series'. Detroit: Gale Research. In progress.
Each vol. in the series is a guide to information sources in a sub-field of education. Representative titles include: MUSIC EDUCATION; THE PHILOSOPHY OF EDUCATION; U.S. HIGHER EDUCATION.

CI4   FREE! (See AC34)
A Canadian newsletter describing free materials (pamphlets, posters, magazines) primarily for educators.

CI5   FREE AND INEXPENSIVE LEARNING MATERIALS, 1941- Nashville, TN: George Peabody College for Teachers, Office of Educational Services. biennial.
371.3 AG348
Title and order information for instructional aids; organized topically.

CI6   Harris, Robin S., and others. A BIBLIOGRAPHY OF HIGHER EDUCATION IN CANADA/ BIBLIOGRAPHIE DE L'ENSEIGNEMENT SUPERIEUR AU CANADA. Studies in Higher Education in Canada. Toronto: Univ. of Toronto Press, 1960. 158 p. SUPPLEMENT 1965; 1971; 1981.
R378.71 AH315   Z5815 C2H32   Ryder SS4-27
Series title varies. Entries are arranged under broad headings with subdivisions. Includes books, periodical articles, theses and reports. SELECT BIBLIOGRAPHY ON HIGHER EDUCATION (1961- Association of Universities and Colleges of Canada) has similar current coverage.

CI7   Kennedy, James R. LIBRARY RESEARCH GUIDE TO EDUCATION: Illustrated Search Strategy and Sources. Library Research Guides, no. 3. Ann Arbor, MI: Pierian Press, 1979. 80 p.
LB1028 K46
Includes a bibliography of basic reference sources.

CI8   Woodbury, Marda. A GUIDE TO SOURCES OF EDUCATIONAL INFORMATION. 2d ed. Arlington, VA: Information Resources Press, 1982. 430 p.
370 AW885G (1976)   Z5811 W65
"The coverage is largely current and American." A guide to the research process, printed research tools, special subjects, instructional materials, and non-print sources.

ABSTRACTS AND INDEXES

CI9 BRITISH EDUCATION INDEX, 1954- London: Bibliographic Services Division, British Library. quarterly; annual cum.
(PER)   Z5813 B7
"Aims to list and analyse the subject content of all articles of permanent educational interest ... in a wide range of English language periodicals." Indexes over 300 periodicals, mostly British. Proceedings of selected conferences are included. In two parts: subject list of articles; author list.

CI10 CANADIAN EDUCATION INDEX/ REPERTOIRE CANADIEN SUR L'EDUCATION, 1965- Toronto: Canadian Education Association. 3 issues a year, including annual cumulation.
(IND)   Z5813 C3
A cooperative work of Canadian education libraries. Author, subject index to a selected list of over 200 Canadian education periodicals, books, pamphlets, reports.

CI11 EDUCATION INDEX: A Cumulative Author Subject Index to a Selected List of Educational Periodical and Yearbooks, 1929- New York: H.W. Wilson, 1932- monthly; quarterly, annual cumulation.
(IND)   Z5813 E23   Sheehy CB83, 1CB29
Indexes by subject and author about 330 titles, including some also indexed by CIJE (CI12). Important yearbooks, proceedings, selected U.S. govt publications. Separate list of book reviews.

CI12 ERIC. CURRENT INDEX TO JOURNALS IN EDUCATION, 1969- (see AA12)
(IND)
CIJE indexes over 700 journals, including some indexed in EDUCATION INDEX (CI11). CIJE has main entry section arranged by broad subjects; subject, author, journal contents index. Available online.

CI13 ERIC. RESOURCES IN EDUCATION, 1966- (see AA13)
(IND)   LB1028 A1E382
Formerly titled RESEARCH IN EDUCATION. Includes abstracts of research and other types of material collected by ERIC clearinghouses. Available online.

STATISTICS

CI14 Statistics Canada. EDUCATION STATISTICS. 81 Series. Ottawa: Statistics Canada, Education Division.
GOVT
The statistical series for education publications, including serials and monographs, e.g . EDUCATION STATISTICS; FINANCIAL STATISTICS OF EDUCATION, ENROLMENT IN COMMUNITY COLLEGES, EDUCATION IN CANADA.

ENCYCLOPEDIAS AND DICTIONARIES

CI15 ENCYCLOPEDIA OF EDUCATION. 10 vols. Ed. by L.C. Deighton. New York: Macmillan, 1970.
R370.3 E56D   LB15 E46
Provides a single reference source describing the entire range of educational interests and practices.

CI16   ENCYCLOPEDIA OF EDUCATIONAL RESEARCH. 4 vols. 5th ed. Ed. in chief, Harold E. Mitzel. New York: Free Press, 1982.
LB15 E49
Sponsored by the American Educational Research Assoc. Substantial articles on a wide variety of topics, most with extensive bibliog. Name and topical index.

CI17   Good, Carter V. DICTIONARY OF EDUCATION. 3d ed. New York: McGraw Hill, 1973. 681 p.
R370.3 G646   LB15 G6
Defines technical, professional terms and concepts in education, as well as terms in related fields.

CI18   THE INTERNATIONAL ENCYCLOPEDIA OF HIGHER EDUCATION. 10 vols. San Francisco: Jossey Bass, 1977.
LB15 I57
"A first attempt to bring together all major aspects of international higher education." Substantial articles on subjects and geographic areas. Name and subject indexes.

CI19   Page, G.T.; J.B. Thomas, and A.R. Marshall. INTERNATIONAL DICTIONARY OF EDUCATION. London: Kogan Page, 1977. 381 p.
LB15 P34
Over 10 000 brief entries for all aspects and levels of education. International terminology; with wide coverage of national, international organizations and associations.

DIRECTORIES AND HANDBOOKS

CI20   THE CEA HANDBOOK, 1970- Toronto: Canadian Education Assoc. annual.
L905 C44   Ryder SS4-24B
Bilingual, "Le Ki-es-Ki" lists officials of provincial education depts, school boards, federal government depts, senior staff of teacher education institutions.

CI21   COMMONWEALTH UNIVERSITIES YEARBOOK: A Directory to the Universities of the Commonwealth and the Handbook of Their Association, 1914- 4 vols. London: Assoc. of Commonwealth Universities. maps. annual.
R378.058 C734   LB2310 Y5   Sheehy CB16B
Under each country, lists principal officers, teaching staff, and general information on each institution granting degrees. For larger countries, there is an article on the university system. Indexes: institutions and topics; subjects of study; names.

CI22   DIRECTORY OF CANADIAN UNIVERSITIES/ REPERTOIRE DES UNIVERSITES CANADIENNES, 1948- Ottawa: Assoc. of Universities and Colleges of Canada. biennial.
R378.71 C212   Ryder SS4-36
Continues UNIVERSITIES AND COLLEGES OF CANADA. Describes studies, admission requirements, fees, costs, academic year, grading system, research facilities, programs for degree, diploma and certificate. Companion: ACADEMIC AND ADMINISTRATIVE OFFICERS AT CANADIAN UNIVERSITIES (1979- annual).

CI23   DIRECTORY OF EDUCATION STUDIES IN CANADA, 1968/69-   Toronto: Canadian Education Assoc. annual.
LB1028 A1D58

List of studies, theses completed in the field. Subject arrangement with author index. INVENTORY OF RESEARCH INTO HIGHER EDUCATION IN CANADA (Assoc. of Universities and Colleges of Canada) informs on research in progress.

CI24   INTERNATIONAL HANDBOOK OF UNIVERSITIES AND OTHER INSTITUTIONS OF HIGHER EDUCATION, 1959-   Paris: International Assoc. of Universities. triennial.
R378.058 I61   L900 I58

Complements COMMONWEALTH UNIVERSITIES YEARBOOK (CI21) and AMERICAN UNIVERSITIES AND COLLEGES. Covers institutions of higher education in all other parts of the world.

CI25   THE NATIONAL FACULTY DIRECTORY, 1970-   4 vols. Detroit: Gale Research. annual.
R378.12 N277N   L901 N24

Subtitle indicates scope as "An Alphabetical List, with Addresses, of about 597,000 Members of Teaching Faculties at Junior Colleges, Colleges and Universities in the United States and at Selected Canadian Institutions." From 1984, an annual supplement of changes and new entries published.

CI26   PATTERSON'S AMERICAN EDUCATION, 1904-   Mount Prospect, IL: Educational Directories. annual.
L901 P3

Comprehensive list of schools, colleges, universities. School systems listed by state and town, other institutions by speciality.

CI27   WORLD LIST OF UNIVERSITIES/ LISTE MONDIALE DES UNIVERSITES, 1965-   Paris: International Association of Universities. triennial.
L900 I5732

Title varies. Directory of univesities and other institutions of higher education, national academic and student bodies, international and regional organizations concerned with higher education.

CI28   WORLD OF LEARNING, 1947-   London: Europa. annual.
R060 W89

Organized by country; with brief information on learned societies, libraries, museums, galleries, universities and colleges. Section on international bodies. Institution index.

HISTORY

BIBLIOGRAPHIES; ABSTRACTS AND INDEXES

CJ1   American Historical Association. GUIDE TO HISTORICAL LITERATURE. New York: Macmillan, 1961. 962 p.
R900 AA51   Z6201 A55
   Dated, but of some use as an annotated guide to important literature in all historical fields.

CJ2   Boyce, Gray C. LITERATURE OF MEDIEVAL HISTORY, 1930-1975. 5 vols. New York: Kraus, 1981.
Z6203 B6
   Sponsored by the Medieval Academy of America. A comprehensive guide to the literature, especially for Western Europe, excluding works specifically on English history. Organized in three parts: 1, general works, reference, auxillary; 2, general histories, chronologically; 3, medieval culture. The INTERNATIONAL MEDIEVAL BIBLIOGRAPHY, 1967-   (Univ. of Leeds) (Z6203 I6) indexes over 800 journals in its semi-annual issues. (See also CJ7)

CJ3   HISTORICAL PERIODICALS DIRECTORY. Ed. by Eric H. Boehm, and others. 5 vols. Santa Barbara, CA: ABC-Clio, 1981-   In progress.
Z6205 H654
   Vol. 1: U.S.A. AND CANADA; 2: EUROPE: WEST, NORTH, CENTRAL AND SOUTH; 3: EUROPE: EAST AND SOUTHEAST, USSR; 4: AFRICA, ASIA AND PACIFIC AREA, LATIN AMERICA AND WEST INDIES; 5: INTERNATIONAL ORGANIZATIONS, ADDENDA, INDEXES. An international guide updating Boehm's HISTORICAL PERIODICALS: AN ANNOTATED WORLD LIST (Clio Press, 1961) (R905 AB671). CJ3 includes scholarly and popular periodicals published or discontinued since 1960 with titles alphabetically listed under country of publication. Dale R. Steiner's HISTORICAL JOURNALS: A HANDBOOK FOR WRITERS AND REVIEWERS (ABC-Clio, 1981) has detailed information on over 350 major North American journals.

CJ4   THE COMBINED RETROSPECTIVE INDEX SET TO JOURNALS IN HISTORY, 1838-1974. Washington: Carollton Press, 1977-78.
MCL
   Covers 150 000 articles in 234 English language periodicals. Many never before consistently indexed.

CJ5   HISTORICAL ABSTRACTS, 1955-   Santa Barbara, CA: ABC-Clio. quarterly; cum. annual index; quinquennial index.
D299 H5
   Abstracts ca 2000 historical serials worldwide covering all areas except North America. Published in two parts. Part A: MODERN HISTORY ABSTRACTS, 1450 - 1914. Part B: TWENTIETH CENTURY ABSTRACTS, 1914 TO THE PRESENT. Subject, biographic, geographic permuted index. From 1980, includes citations for books, theses, selected journals. Available online.

CJ6   INTERNATIONAL BIBLIOGRAPHY OF HISTORICAL SCIENCES, 1926- International Committee of Historical Sciences; ed. with the contribution of the National Committees. New York, Munich: K.G. Saur. annual.
          Z6205 I62
     Broad geographic and topical coverage of articles and monographs. Topical organization; name and geographic indexes.

CJ7   Kuehl, Warren F. DISSERTATIONS IN HISTORY: AN INDEX TO DISSERTATIONS COMPLETED IN HISTORY DEPARTMENTS OF THE UNITED STATES AND CANADIAN UNIVERSITIES. Lexington, KY: Univ. of Kentucky Press, 1972-1973/ Santa Barbara, CA: ABC-Clio, 1983.
          Z6201 K8
     Vol. 1 covers 1873-1960; 2: 1961-1970; 3: 1970- June, 1980. Supplemented by DOCTORAL DISSERTATIONS IN HISTORY, 1973- (American Historical Association).

CJ8   Paetow, Louis J. A GUIDE TO THE STUDY OF MEDIEVAL HISTORY. Prep. under the auspices of the Mediaeval Academy of America. Rev. and corrected ed. by Gray C. Boyce and addendum by Lynn Thorndike. Millwood, NY: Kraus Reprint, 1980. 643 p.
          Z6203 P19
     This ed. includes material published to 1931. (See also CJ2)

CJ9   Poulton, H.J., and M.S. Howland. THE HISTORIAN'S HANDBOOK: A DESCRIPTIVE GUIDE TO REFERENCE WORKS. Norman, OK: Univ. of Oklahoma Press, 1972. 304 p.
     R900 AP876H   Z6201 P68
     To aid both students and scholars in the social sciences by a survey or reference works in history, important titles in allied fields. Organized by type of material. Elizabeth Frick's LIBRARY RESEARCH GUIDE TO HISTORY: ILLUSTRATED SEARCH STRATEGY AND SOURCES (Pierian Press, 1980) is a less detailed guide. MATERIALS & METHODS FOR HISTORY RESEARCH by Carla Stoffle and Simon Karter (Neal Schuman, 1979) takes a workbook approach using question sets and answers.

CJ10   Powell, James M. MEDIEVAL STUDIES: AN INTRODUCTION. Syracuse, NY: Syracuse Univ. Press, 1976. 389 p.
          D116 M4
     A guide to the literature, supplementing CJ7 with imprints to 1974; (see also CJ2). GUIDE TO THE SOURCES OF MEDIEVAL HISTORY, by R.C. Van Caenegem (North Holland, 1978) is another useful guide.

CJ11   THE READER'S ADVISER. Vol. 3. (See AC18)

CJ12   RECENTLY PUBLISHED ARTICLES, 1976- Washington: American Historical Association. 3 issues a year.
          Z6205 R4
     Formerly included in the AMERICAN HISTORICAL REVIEW. International coverage with citations in general and geographic sections. No index.

CJ13   Waserman, Manfred. BIBLIOGRAPHY ON ORAL HISTORY. Rev. ed. New York: Oral History Association, 1975. 53 p.
          Z6201 W37
     Annotated bibliography of 306 items.

ENCYCLOPEDIAS, DICTIONARIES AND HANDBOOKS

CJ14   DICTIONARY OF THE MIDDLE AGES. Ed. in chief, John R. Strayer. New York: Scribners, 1982-   In progress. illus.
        D114 D5
        When complete will have ca 5000 entries, ranging from brief definitions to major articles; bibliographies primarily English language. Intended for high school, university, specialist levels.

CJ15   THE ENCYCLOPEDIA OF HISTORIC PLACES. 2 vols. Ed. by Courtlandt Canby. New York: Facts on File, 1984. illus.
        D9 C29
        Detailed coverage on all geographic locations of historical significance; ancient times to present.

CJ16   Langer, William L. THE NEW ILLUSTRATED ENCYCLOPEDIA OF WORLD HISTORY: Ancient, Medieval, and Modern History Chronologically Arranged. 2 vols. New York: Abrams, 1975.
        R902 L27E4 (1968)   D21 L28
        A quick reference guide; arranged by period, then by area. An illus. ed. of his ENCYCLOPEDIA OF WORLD HISTORY.

CJ17   MACMILLAN CONCISE DICTIONARY OF WORLD HISTORY. Comp. by Bruce Wetterau. New York: Macmillan, 1983. 867 p.
        D9 W47
        About 10 000 entries for people, places, events, etc. including chronologies for major events, countries, wars. THE OXFORD CLASSICAL DICTIONARY (2d ed., Clarendon Press, 1970) (R913.38 O98) is an example of a concise reference source for a specific period.

CHRONOLOGIES AND TABLES (See also "Holidays and Events" AH39-AH44)

CJ18   Freeman-Grenville, G.S.P. CHRONOLOGY OF WORLD HISTORY: A CALENDAR OF PRINCIPAL EVENTS FROM 3000 BC to AD 1976. 2d ed. London: R. Collings/ Totowa, NJ: Rowman and Littlefield, 1978. 746 p.
        D11 F75
        Considered the best general geographical approach to political and military history.

CJ19   Grun, Bernard. THE TIMETABLES OF HISTORY: A Horizontal Linkage of People and Events. New York: Simon and Schuster, 1975. 661 p.
        D11 G78
        Covers 5000 B.C. to 1974, in columns for history and politics, literature and theatre, religion, philosophy and learning, visual arts, music, science, technology and growth, and daily life.

CJ20   HARBOTTLE'S DICTIONARY OF BATTLES. 3d ed. Rev. by George Bruce. New York: Van Nostrand, 1981. 303 p.
        R903H255   D25 A2H2
        Concise information on some 2400 battles from antiquity to 1979. Arranged alphabetically by name of battle with index for proper or personal names/ ships/ countries but not repeating names of battles.

CJ21 Steinberg, S.H. HISTORICAL TABLES 58 B.C. - A.D. 1978. 10th ed. Ed. by C. Steinberg, and J. Paxton. London: Macmillan, 1979. 269 p.
D11S83
Acknowledges some bias for British Commonwealth and U.S. Very little Canadian content. Information is in six columns read vertically for comparison of momentous events. Column headings, e.g. cultural life, constitutional history, countries overseas, change slightly to suit the times surveyed.

ATLASES

CJ22 ATLAS OF CLASSICAL ARCHAEOLOGY. Ed. by M.I. Finley. London: Chatto & Windus, 1977. 256 p. illus. maps.
G1046 E15A8 MAPL
Over 100 archaeological sites, city plans in 13 geographical areas relating to Greek and Roman times. Directed also to the traveller.

CJ23 Shepherd, William R. HISTORICAL ATLAS. 9th ed. New York: Barnes & Noble, 1964. 341 p. (two sections paged, maps).
R911 S54H8   G1030 S4
Covers world history to 1964, with emphasis on Europe and North America, in chronological arrangement.

CJ24 THE TIMES ATLAS OF WORLD HISTORY. Ed. by Geoffrey Barraclough. London: Times Books, 1978. 360 p. illus. maps. (Dist.: Hammond).
G1030 T54 MAPL
Presents historical geography worldwide, with glossary and index of historical place names. Includes 600 maps. Divides world history into seven chronological stages dealing with all regions of the world within the stages from "early man" to "global civilisation." THE TIMES CONCISE ATLAS OF WORLD HISTORY (Dist.: Hammond, 1982) is a "shorter less elaborate atlas on a reduced scale" condensed from the 1978 atlas and providing good coverage of all major world events from prehistoric times to 1980; while emphasizing European history, it does cover British and Hispanic colonialism, U.S. after 1783, Latin America after 1808 and recent history of Afica and China.

CJ25 Kerr, D.G.G. HISTORICAL ATLAS OF CANADA. 3d rev. ed. Don Mills, Ont.: Nelson, 1975. 100 p. maps.
R911 K41H2 (1966)   Ryder HA4-37A, -37B
Chronological arrangement, from pre-historic times to the present.

CJ26 Trudel, Marcel. ATLAS DE LA NOUVELLE FRANCE/ AN ATLAS OF NEW FRANCE. 2d ed. Quebec: Presses de l'Univ. Laval, 1973. 219 p. maps.
R911 T866 (1961)   Ryder HA4-39
Reproductions of maps relating to the history of French Canada. A revision of ATLAS HISTORIQUE DU CANADA FRANÇAIS DES ORIGINES A 1867.

CJ27 Gentilcore, R. Louis, and C. Grant Head. ONTARIO'S HISTORY IN MAPS. Toronto: Univ. of Toronto Press, 1984. 300 maps, 304 p.
With a cartobibliography by Joan Winearls. Text and maps show the development of the province as recorded in earliest European mss and printed maps, through the watercolour maps of Simcoe era to 19th and 20th century skills, concerns, values as reflected in the maps.

GENERAL HISTORIES

CJ28 THE CAMBRIDGE ANCIENT HISTORY. 3d ed. Cambridge: Univ. Press, 1970- In progress.
  R930 C178   D57 C25
   The standard, comprehensive general ancient history.

CJ29 THE CAMBRIDGE MEDIEVAL HISTORY. 8 vols/ 6 vols. Cambridge: Univ. Press, 1911-36. maps.
  940.1 C178   D117 C3
   A 2 vol. abridgement (1952) and a 2d ed., in 2 pts, of Vol. 4 (1966-67).

CJ30 THE CAMBRIDGE MODERN HISTORY. 13 vols. Cambridge: Univ. Press, 1902-12.
      D208 C16

CJ31 THE NEW CAMBRIDGE MODERN HISTORY. 14 vols Cambridge: Univ.Press, 1957-70
  R940.2 C178
   Covers history from the Renaissance to the present. New ed. has no bibliographies and few footnotes. Supplemented by a BIBLIOGRAPHY OF MODERN HISTORY (1968) by John Roach.

CJ32 THE CAMBRIDGE HISTORY OF THE BRITISH EMPIRE. 8 vols in 9. Cambridge: Univ. Press, 1929-59.
      DA30 C3
   Vol. 8, on Africa is in a second ed.

Great Britain

CJ33 ANNUAL BIBLIOGRAPHY OF BRITISH AND IRISH HISTORY, 1901/33- London: Institute of Historical Research, Univ. of London, 1934-
      Z2016 A6

CJ34 BIBLIOGRAPHY OF BRITISH HISTORY. Oxford: Clarendon Press. In progress.
   A series of major bibliographies with extensive coverage by periods of British history: English history to 1485; Tudor period, 1485-1603; Stuart period, 1603-1714; then 1714-1789; 1789-1851; 1851-1914.

CJ35 Conference on British Studies. BIBLIOGRAPHICAL HANDBOOKS. Cambridge: Univ. Press.
   Bibliographical coverage by period. Less extensive, less detailed than the Oxford series.

CJ36 ENGLISH HISTORICAL DOCUMENTS. 13 vols. London: Eyre, 1953- In progress: 2d ed., 1979- In progress.
  R942 E58 v. 2   DA26 E56
   An extensive collection of original documents for British history, A.D. 500 to 1914. Notes, references, introductory essay in each vol.

CJ37 OXFORD HISTORY OF ENGLAND. 15 vols. Oxford: Clarendon Press, 1936-
  Some vols in 2d or 3d ed.
      ROBA

CJ38 Steinberg, S.H., and I.H. Evans. eds. STEINBERG'S DICTIONARY OF BRITISH HISTORY. 2d ed. London: E. Arnold, 1970. 421 p.
  R942 S819   DA34 S7

United States

CJ39   A GUIDE TO THE STUDY OF THE UNITED STATES OF AMERICA: Representative Books Reflecting the Development of American Life and Thought. Washington: Library of Congress, 1960. 1193 p. SUPPLEMENT, 1956-1965 (1976).
R016.9173 U58   Z1215 U53
    Full bibliographic information for each entry with descriptive, evaluative annotations. A second suppl. 1966-1975 is in progress.

CJ40   AMERICA, HISTORY AND LIFE, 1964-   Santa Barbara, CA: ABC-Clio. annual and quinquennial indexes.
E171 A54
    Abstracts of literature on U.S. and Canadian history. From 1974, published in four parts: A: article citations, abstracts (3 a year); B: index to book reviews (2 a year); C: American history bibliography (annual); D: indexes to parts A-C (annual), subject permuted, author, book title and reviewer. Available online. The CLIO BIBLIOGRAPHY SERIES has topical selections from the main database, e.g.: URBAN AMERICA (1983), THE AMERICAN AND CANADIAN WEST (1979).

CJ41   Beers, Henry P. BIBLIOGRAPHIES IN AMERICAN HISTORY, 1942-1978: GUIDE TO MATERIALS FOR RESEARCH. 2 vols. Woodbridge CT: Research Publications, 1982.
Z1236 A1B4
    Broad coverage. Vol. 1, organized by topic; vol. 2, by geography. Name/ subject index.

CJ42   BIBLIOGRAPHIC GUIDE TO NORTH AMERICAN HISTORY, 1978-   (See CJ70n)

CJ43   HARVARD GUIDE TO AMERICAN HISTORY. Ed. by F. Freidel, assisted by R.K. Showman. 2 vols. 2d ed. Cambridge, MA: Belknap Press, 1974.
R973 AH339 (1963)
    A detailed bibliography organized by broad subject with materials to 1970. Intended for student, scholar and lay reader.

CJ44   WRITINGS ON AMERICAN HISTORY: A SUBJECT BIBLIOGRAPHY OF ARTICLES, 1974-   Washington: American Historical Association. annual.
Z1236 W77
    The U.S. sections of RECENTLY PUBLISHED ARTICLES (CJ12) are a core with additions. In sections: chronological, geographical, subjects with subdivisions. Author index.

CJ45   INDEX TO BOOK REVIEWS IN HISTORICAL PERIODICALS, 1972-   Metuchen, NJ: Scarecrow Press, 1975-   annual.
Z6208 B6I6
    Indexes about 100 journals, many not indexed in other book review indexes. U.S. history is emphasized.

CJ46   DICTIONARY OF AMERICAN HISTORY. Rev. ed. 8 vols. New York: Scribners, 1976-78.
E174 A43
    A first choice for quick reference. Considerably rev. and enlarged with analytical index. CONCISE DICTIONARY OF AMERICAN HISTORY (latest ed., Scribner, 1983) is based on this work. Companion vol.: ATLAS OF AMERICAN HISTORY (rev., 1978).

CJ47   Commager, Henry S. DOCUMENTS OF AMERICAN HISTORY. 2 vols. 9th ed. New York: Appleton, 1973.
       R973 C734 (1963)
       A selection of important U.S. documents, arranged chronologically with notes and bibliographic references.

CJ48   ENCYCLOPEDIA OF AMERICAN HISTORY. 6th ed. Ed. by R.B. Morris and assoc. ed. J.B. Morris. New York: Harper and Row, 1982. 1285 p. maps.
       E174.5 E52
       In four sections: basic chronology; topical chronology; 500 notable Americans; structure of federal government.

Canada

Bibliographies (See also "Library Catalogues" AD64-AD66; "Bibliographies" AD67-AD80, and "Regional Bibliographies" AD81-AD98)

CJ49   Aubin, Paul, and Paul-André Linteau. BIBLIOGRAPHIE DE L'HISTOIRE DU QUEBEC ET DU CANADA, 1966-1975. 2 vols. Quebec: Institut Québécois de recherche sur la culture, 1981.
       Z1382 A8
       Includes about 22 000 articles, books, theses, in three main divisions: systematic and analytic and author classifications. Available online as the HISCABEQ database.

CJ50   Beaulieu, A.; J. Hamelin, and B. Benoit. GUIDE D'HISTOIRE DU CANADA. Les Cahiers de l'institut d'histoire, No. 13. Quebec: Presses de l'Univ. Laval, 1969. 540 p.
       Z1382 B4
       An extensive guide; many annotated entires in sections on sources, historiography, aids, studies, auxiliary fields and periodicals.

CJ51   Bishop, O.B.; B. Irwin, and C.G. Miller. BIBLIOGRAPHY OF ONTARIO HISTORY 1867-1976. (See AD90).

CJ52   REGISTER OF POST-GRADUATE DISSERTATIONS IN PROGRESS IN HISTORY AND RELATED SUBJECTS/ REPERTOIRE DES THESES EN COURS PORTANT SUR DES SUJETS D'HISTOIRE ET AUTRES SUJETS CONNEXES, 1966-   Ottawa: Canadian Historical Association. annual.
       Z6201 C3
       A guide to work in progress, mainly in Canada. Broad chronological and geographical arrangement. Name index.

CJ53   Cotnam, Jacques. CONTEMPORARY QUEBEC: AN ANALYTICAL BIBLIOGRAPHY. Toronto: McClelland and Stewart, 1973. 112 p.
       Z1392 Q3C65
       A bibliography planned for students. Claudette Cardinal's THE HISTORY OF QUEBEC: A BIBLIOGRAPHY OF WORKS IN ENGLISH (Centre for the Study of Anglophone Quebec, 1981) has entries for ca 3500 books, articles, theses, on the history of Quebec to 1976.

CJ54   A READER'S GUIDE TO CANADIAN HISTORY. 2 vols. Toronto: Univ. of Toronto Press, 1982.
                          Z1382 R4
        A guide to and critical assessment of articles, papers, books. Vol. 1: BEGINNINGS TO CONFEDERATION, ed. by D.A. Muise, is a largely regional approach. Vol. 2: CONFEDERATION TO THE PRESENT, ed. by J.L. Granatstein and P. Stevens has both topical and regional chapters.

CJ55   REVIEW OF HISTORICAL PUBLICATIONS RELATING TO CANADA. 22 vols. Toronto: Univ. of Toronto Press, 1897-1919.
        An annual survey of reviews of books and papers on Canadian history in the broad sense. Continued in CANADIAN HISTORICAL REVIEW.

CJ56   Smith, Dwight L. THE HISTORY OF CANADA: AN ANNOTATED BIBLIOGRAPHY. Clio Bibliography, no. 10. Santa Barbara, CA: ABC-Clio Information Services, 1983. 327 p.
                        Z1382 H57
        Based on the AMERICA: HISTORY AND LIFE (CJ40); 3362 articles "related to Canadian history in any way" which appeared 1973-78. Chronological approach, subdivided by topics with regional section. Detailed subject, author indexes.

CJ57   Thibault, Claude. BIBLIOGRAPHIA CANADIANA. Don Mills, Ont.: Longman, 1973. 795 p.
R971 AT425B   Ryder HA4-13
        A chronological and topical bibliography of over 25 000 entries for printed items on Canadian history. In four parts: sources for research; French colonial regime; British North America; Dominion of Canada. Not annotated.

Series and General Histories (For "Local History" in Canada, see CJ72-CJ74)

CJ58   'The Canadian Centenary Series.' A HISTORY OF CANADA ... Toronto: McClelland and Stewart, 1963-   In progress.
        A comprehensive history intended for the general reader as well as the scholar. Each vol. by a noted historian.

CJ59   'Champlain Society' Publications. Toronto: Champlain Society, 1907-   First series, 1907- . Second series (Hudson Bay Co. Papers), 1938-1949. Third series (Ontario), 1957-   occasional.
                        F5004 C45
        Each vol. contains texts of important documents; scholarly introd.

CJ60   Shortt, Adam, and Arthur G. Doughty. CANADA AND ITS PROVINCES: A HISTORY OF THE CANADIAN PEOPLE AND THEIR INSTITUTIONS. 23 vols. Toronto: Publisher's Association of Canada, 1913-1917. illus.
                        F5011 S57
        A comprehensive work covering history, political, economic and cultural development of Canada. Vol. 23: index, bibliog.

Documents and Handbooks

CJ61 Bliss, J.M. CANADIAN HISTORY IN DOCUMENTS, 1763-1966. Toronto: Ryerson, 1966. 397 p.
R971 B649

CJ62 Brunet, M.; G. Frégault, and M. Trudel. HISTOIRE DU CANADA PAR LES TEXTES. 2 vols. Rev. and enl. ed. Montreal: Fides, 1963.
971 B895

CJ63 Reid, J.H.S.; K, McNaught, and H.S. Crowe. A SOURCE-BOOK OF CANADIAN HISTORY: SELECTED DOCUMENTS AND PERSONAL PAPERS. Rev. ed. with index. Toronto: Longman, 1964, 485 p.
R971 R356

CJ64 Story, Norah. THE OXFORD COMPANION TO CANADIAN HISTORY AND LITERATURE. Toronto: Oxford Univ. Press, 1967. 935 p. maps. SUPPLEMENT, ed. by William Toye (1973).
R971.03 S887.

Archives

CJ65 DIRECTORY OF CANADIAN RECORDS AND MANUSCRIPT REPOSITORIES. (See AA50)

CJ66 Public Archives of Canada. CATALOGUE OF THE PUBLIC ARCHIVES LIBRARY. (See AD116)

CJ67 _____. GENERAL INVENTORY: MANUSCRIPTS. (See AD117)

CJ68 A UNION LIST OF MANUSCRIPTS IN CANADIAN REPOSITORIES/ CATALOGUE COLLECTIF DES MANUSCRIPTS DES CONSERVES DANS LES DEPOTS D'ARCHIVES CANADIEN. (See AD117n)
In 3 parts: description of entries (arranged by name); catalogue by repository; index.

CJ69 ONTARIO'S HERITAGE: A GUIDE TO ARCHIVAL RESOURCES. 15 vols. Cheltenham, Ont.: Boston Mills Press, 1978- In progress.
CD3645 0605
A project of the Toronto Area Archivists to survey systematically local records in Ontario and to publish regional guides to resources.

LOCAL HISTORIES

CJ70 Hobbs, John L. LOCAL HISTORY AND THE LIBRARY. 2d rev. ed. by George A. Carter. London: Deutsch, 1973. 344 p.
026.9 H68L

CJ71 UNITED STATES LOCAL HISTORIES IN THE LIBRARY OF CONGRESS: A BIBLIOGRAPHY 4 vols. Baltimore, MD: Magna Carta Book Co., 1975. SUPPLEMENT AND INDEX, 1976.
Z1250.U59
Catalogue for a major collection of local histories. Another major collection is presented in the DICTIONARY CATALOG OF THE LOCAL HISTORY AND GENEALOGY DIVISION OF THE NEW YORK PUBLIC LIBRARY

RESEARCH LIBRARIES (G.K. Hall, 1974) which includes listings for over 100 000 vols and is supplemented by the annual BIBLIOGRAPHIC GUIDE TO NORTH AMERICAN HISTORY, 1978- (G.K. Hall). This annual lists material catalogued in the year by LC and NYPL on all aspects of U.S. and Canadian history.

CJ72   DIRECTORY OF HISTORICAL SOCIETIES AND AGENCIES IN THE UNITED STATES AND CANADA, 1956/57- Nashville, TN: American Association for State and Local History, 1956- biennial.
R906 D598   E172 D57
   Active societies, arranged by state and town with name index.

CJ73   CANADIAN LOCAL HISTORIES TO 1950: A BIBLIOGRAPHY. Toronto: Univ. of Toronto Press, 1967- In progress.
971 AM864
   Vol. 1: THE ATLANTIC PROVINCES: NEWFOUNDLAND, NOVA SCOTIA, NEW BRUNSWICK, PRINCE EDWARD ISLAND (1967) by William F.E. Morley. Vol. 2: LA PROVINCE DE QUEBEC (1971) by W.F.E. Morley and A. Beaulieu. Vol. 3: ONTARIO AND THE CANADIAN NORTH (1978) by W.F.E. Morley.

CJ74   Aitken, Barbara B. LOCAL HISTORIES OF ONTARIO MUNICIPALITIES, 1951-1977: A BIBLIOGRAPHY. Toronto: Ontario Library Association, 1978. 120 p.
971.3 AA311L3
   Includes 1700 local histories.

CJ75   Spencer, Loraine, and Susan Holland. NORTHERN ONTARIO: A BIBLIOGRAPHY. Toronto: Univ. of Toronto Press, 1968. 121 p.
917.13 AS745

Section D
Science and Technology

SCIENCE AND TECHNOLOGY

GUIDES

DA1   Chen, C-C. 1977. SCIENTIFIC AND TECHNICAL INFORMATION SOURCES. Cambridge, MA: MIT Press. 519 p.
500 C518S   Z7401 C48 ENGR; PASR
   Primarily a brief guide for science and engineering librarians and library school students. R. Aluri and J. Robinson's A GUIDE TO U.S. GOVERNMENT SCIENTIFIC AND TECHNICAL RESOURCES (1983, Libraries Unlimited) describes flow of information with a number of resources.

DA2   Herner, S.; G.P. Allen, and N.D. Wright. 1980. A BRIEF GUIDE TO SOURCES OF SCIENTIFIC AND TECHNICAL INFORMATION. 2d ed. Arlington, VA: Information Resources Press. 160 p.
R500 AH558 B2   Q223 H42 ENGR

DA3   Malinowsky, H.R., and J.M. Richardson. 1980. SCIENCE AND ENGINEERING LITERATURE: A GUIDE TO REFERENCE SOURCES. 3d ed. Littleton, CO: Libraries Unlimited. 342 p.
R500 AM251S3   Z7401 M28 (1976) ENGR
   Major bibliographic sources for primary and secondary literature.

DA4   Parker, C.C., and R.V. Turley. 1975. INFORMATION SOURCES IN SCIENCE AND TECHNOLOGY. London: Butterworths. 223 p.
R507 P238I   Q224 P37 PASR
   British, intended for practising scientists, engineers, students. D. Grogan's SCIENCE AND TECHNOLOGY: AN INTRODUCTION TO THE LITERATURE (1976, 3d rev., C. Bingley) (507.G874 S3; Q223 G76 PASR) introduces readers, students without formal scientific training to the various forms of literature in scientific fields, exclusive of medicine.

DA5   Subramanyam, K. 1981. SCIENTIFIC AND TECHNICAL INFORMATION RESOURCES. New York: M. Dekker. 416 p.
507 S941S   T10.7 S93 ENGR
   Brief comment as introduction to titles in different fields.

BIBLIOGRAPHIES AND SELECTION AIDS

DA6   Canada Institute for Scientific and Technical Information. RECENT ADDITIONS TO THE LIBRARY, No. 1, 1962-   Ottawa: CISTI. semi-monthly.

DA7   HANDBOOKS AND TABLES IN SCIENCE AND TECHNOLOGY. 1983. 2d ed. Ed. by R.H. Powell. Phoenix, AZ: Oryx Press. 384 p.
                        Z7405 T3H35 PASR
   Comprehensive annotated list of ca 2000 sci-tech handbooks (tabulated data, physical constants, properties of materials etc.). Indexed by subject and author.

DA8   NEW TECHNICAL BOOKS, 1915-   New York: New York Public Library. monthly (except Aug. and Sept.)
                        Z1035 A1N45 PASR
   A classified, selected list from introductory college to research level. Entries usually describe and evaluate contents. Covers pure and applied sciences but generally excludes medical, natural sciences.

DA9   PUBLICATIONS OF THE NATIONAL RESEARCH COUNCIL OF CANADA, 1916-   Ottawa: CISTI. annual.
Z5055 C2N3 PASR
A cumulative listing of papers on experimental work carried out in NRC's laboratories.

DA10   SCIENCE BOOKS AND FILMS, 1965-   Washington: American Association for the Advancement of Science. 5 issues a year. Annual cum. index.
Supersedes SCIENCE BOOKS. Evaluatives trade, text, reference books. Books are also substantively reviewed in the AAAS members' journal SCIENCE. A monograph, AAAS SCIENCE BOOK LIST ... for secondary school, college students and non-specialists (1970) and SUPPLEMENT (1978) (500 AD285A3; Z7401 W64 PASR) helped public, school libraries.

DA11   SCIENTIFIC AND TECHNICAL BOOKS AND SERIALS IN PRINT, 1972-   New York: R.R. Bowker. annual.
Z7401 S38 PASR
Published annually in Dec., includes international sci-tech works by subject and title. More than 100 000 books published or dist. in the U.S.; a spinoff with some enrichment from BIP.

DA12   TECHNICAL BOOK REVIEW INDEX. (See AD62)

PERIODICALS (Union Lists; for Abstracts and Indexes, see DA15-DA22)

DA13   UNION LIST OF SCIENTIFIC SERIALS IN CANADIAN LIBRARIES. (See AE18)

DA14   WORLD LIST OF SCIENTIFIC PERIODICALS PUBLISHED IN THE YEARS 1900-1960. 1963-65. 3 vols. 4th ed. London: Butterworths.
500 AW927   Z7403 W92 PASR
A comprehensive union list for over 60 000 sci-tech periodicals held in British libraries. Supplemented from 1964 by WORLD LIST OF SCIENTIFIC PERIODICALS, a part of BUCOP (see AE14)

ABSTRACTS, INDEXES TO PERIODICALS AND OTHER MATERIALS

DA15   APPLIED SCIENCE AND TECHNOLOGY INDEX. (See DL6)

DA16   CURRENT CONTENTS ... 1961-   Philadelphia: Institute for Scientific Information. weekly.
various libs: BMED; PASR; ENGR; FLIS
A 'current awareness' alerting service separately published in 7 sections. Each weekly issue (section) reproduces tables of contents from most recent issues of journals and outstanding books in the relevant fields. Five of the 7 sections are in the sciences (life sciences; clinical practice; agriculture; biology and environmental sciences; engineering, technology and applied sciences). Each issue contains a subject index, author index and directory.

DA17   CURRENT TECHNOLOGY INDEX. (See DL9)

DA18   ENGINEERING INDEX. (See DL11)

DA19   GENERAL SCIENCE INDEX, 1978-   (See AF7)

DA20   REFERATIVNYJ ZHURNAL, 1953-   Moscow: VINITI. monthly.
various libs: PASR

A comprehensive abstracting service; published in subject sections (e.g. INFORMATICS ABSTRACTS, see AA17). International in scope; science sections (the primary interest) have the abstract in Russian.

DA21   SCIENCE ABSTRACTS, 1898-   4 series. Hitchin, Herts, Eng.: Institution of Electrical Engineers/ Piscataway, NJ: Institute of Electrical and Electronic Engineers. monthly.

A major international service for a broad range of physical, mathematical, engineering sciences abstracting periodicals, papers etc. The separately titled series (parts) are:
   A: PHYSICS ABSTRACTS, 1898-
   B: ELECTRICAL AND ELECTRONIC ABSTRACTS, 1966-
   C: COMPUTER AND CONTROL ABSTRACTS, 1966-
   D: IT FOCUS, 1983-   [Information Technology]
Titles of foreign language articles and abstracts (varying in length with series, 100 - 300 words) are in English and often signed. Annual detailed author and subject indexes appear with usually quinquennial cum. Available online as INSPEC; use with INSPEC THESAURUS.

DA22   SCIENCE CITATION INDEX, 1961-   (See AF17)

An international interdisciplinary index to the literature of science, engineering, technology, medicine. Covers books as well as some 3500 journals. Available online as SCISEARCH.

Patents and Trademarks

DA23   Canada. Patent Office. THE PATENT OFFICE RECORD/ LA GAZETTE DU BUREAU DES BREVETS, 1873-   Ottawa: CGPC, Supply and Services. weekly.
BMED; MTCL

Former title: THE CANADIAN PATENT OFFICE RECORD. Numbered entries are arranged in classes according to the Patent Office domestic classification scheme. An outline of the 403 main classes appears in the first January issue each year. Index of inventors and patentees in each issue, with annual cum. index. Separate indexing aids, e.g. SUBJECT MATTER INDEX, CLASS SCHEDULES AND CLASS LISTINGS are useful adjuncts for searches through the POR prior to 1982. For patents issued after Jan. 1982, the POR is the only publicly available access. The POR has gradually diminished the amount of information available, discontinuing drawings and abstracts as part of the entry.

Canada's POR follows the pattern of U.K., U.S. patent gazettes. Great Britain's weekly notice is in the OFFICIAL JOURNAL (PATENTS), 1889- (Patent Office) (MTCL); U.S. notices are in the weekly OFFICIAL GAZETTE OF THE UNITED STATES PATENT OFFICE, 1836- (Superintendent of Documents) (MTCL) THE INPADOC PATENT GAZETTE, 1973- (Vienna: International Patents Documentation Center) collates information from gazettes and journals of 45 countries, and publishes various indexes to aid in bringing related patents together.

For an understanding of the patent process in Canada, the MANUAL OF PATENT OFFICE PRACTICE (Supply and Services, 1980) (T226 K6C3 ENGR) supplies information and instructions.

DA24   Canada. Trade Marks Office. TRADE MARKS JOURNAL/ JOURNAL DES MARQUES DE COMMERCE. 1953-   Ottawa: CGPC, Supply and Services. weekly.
                         MTCL
           Trade mark is shown; arranged by registration no. with statement on wares, service to which mark applies; also amendments, cancellations, extensions.

Proceedings, Conference Papers

DA25   BIBLIOGRAPHIC GUIDE TO CONFERENCE PUBLICATIONS, 1975-   2 vols. Boston: G.K. Hall. annual.
                         Z5051 B5 PASR
           A dictionary catalogue of entries catalogued by the New York Public Library and LC during the year.

DA26   CONFERENCE PAPERS INDEX, vol. 6-   1978-   Louisville, KY: Data Courier. monthly; cum. annual index.
                         Z7409 C6 PASR
           Supersedes CURRENT PROGRAMS, 1973-77. Programs of scientific and technological conferences grouped by subject. Available online.

DA27   DIRECTORY OF PUBLISHED PROCEEDINGS: SEMT: SCIENCE, ENGINEERING, MEDICINE, TECHNOLOGY, 1965-   Harrison, NY: InterDok. monthly (except July, Aug.); annual cumulation.
                         Z7409 D56 PASR
           Lists proceedings chronologically by conference date with indexes for editor, location, subject/ sponsor.

DA28   INDEX TO SCIENTIFIC AND TECHNICAL PROCEEDINGS, 1978-   Philadelphia: Institute for Scientific Information. monthly; semi-annual cumulation.
                         Z7409 I56 PASR
           Multidisciplinary coverage of over 3000 proceedings, 80 000 papers annual. Entries provide complete bibliographic description and contents table for papers; 6 indexes (subject; author/ editor; sponsor; category; location).

Theses, Research and Technical Reports

DA29   DISSERTATIONS ABSTRACTS INTERNATIONAL: B: PHYSICAL SCIENCES AND ENGINEERING, 1967-   monthly.
                         Z5053 D513 PASR
           Arranged by subject categories with keyword and author indexes. (See AF29 for general description; see also AF30 for CANADIAN THESES).

DA30   GOVERNMENT REPORTS ANNOUNCEMENTS AND INDEX, vol. 75, no. 7-   1975- Springfield, VA: National Technical Information Service. biweekly.
          (IND)   Z7916 U5316
           Supersedes GOVERNMENT REPORTS ANNOUNCEMENT and GOVERNMENT REPORTS INDEX. An abstract journal covering U.S. govt sponsored research and development reports including those of the Dept of Commerce, NASA, ERDA. Arranged by subject and indexed by corporate author, personal author, subject, contract no., accession report no. Annual cum. index.

WEEKLY GOVERNMENT ABSTRACTS is a current awareness bulletin. Available online as NTIS.

The National Technical Information Service, 1961- (NTIS), a division of the U.S. Dept of Commerce, is a major supplier of sci-tech information, and the central source for the public sale of U.S. and foreign govt sponsored research (including patented information, development and engineering reports, analyses prepared by national, local govt agencies, their contractors or rantees. NTIS has microfiche document delivery service and publishes directories, bibliographies, technical reports. NTIS alerting services include weekly newletters for specific fields in technology, science.

DA31   RESEARCH IN BRITISH UNIVERSITIES, POLYTECHNICS AND COLLEGES. (See AF28)

Translations

DA32   INDEX TRANSLATIONUM, 1948-   (See AF43)

DA33   TRANSLATIONS REGISTER INDEX, 1967-   Chicago: National Translations Center, John Crerar Library. semi-monthly.
Z7401 T74 PASR

The National Translations Center is a depository for unpublished English translations of literature from the natural, physical, medical and social sciences. The 'register' announces new accessions; the 'index' (semi-annual cum.) ists titles from the register and items listed by NTIS in GOVERNMENT REPORTS ANNOUNCEMENTS AND INDEX (DA30).

DA34   WORLD TRANSINDEX, 1978-   Delft, Netherlands: International Translations Centre. monthly.
Z7403 W94 PASR

Supersedes WORLD INDEX OF SCIENTIFIC TRANSLATIONS ... noting articles, patents, standards, in sci-tech fields translated from East European and Asiatic languages into Western languages.

ENCYCLOPEDIAS AND YEARBOOKS

DA35   THE BOOK OF POPULAR SCIENCE. 10 vols. New York: Grolier. issued annually.
R503 B724   Q162 B68 PASR

(1st ed., 1924). Topics are treated under broad subject headings for an audience at the elementary and secondary school level. Vol. 10 has bibliography and index.

DA36   BRITANNICA YEARBOOK OF SCIENCE AND THE FUTURE, 1969-   (See AI4)

A science suppl. to the ENCYCLOPEDIA BRITANNICA, emphasizing American scientific accomplishments. Has feature articles with bibliographies and reviews the scientific year; also lists annual awards, prizes in science.

DA37   DICTIONARY OF THE HISTORY OF SCIENCE. 1981. Ed. by W.F. Bynum, and others. New York: Princeton Univ. Press. 494 p.

Brief encyclopedic entries placing concepts from 5 centuries of Western natural science in context of their development.

DA38   McGRAW HILL ENCYCLOPEDIA OF SCIENCE AND TECHNOLOGY. 1982. 15 vols. 5th ed. New York: McGraw Hill.
R503 M14   Q121 M3 PASR
A comprehensive work covering all branches of physical, natural and applied science. Arranged alphabetically; articles are usually short with cross references to more specific subjects. The longer articles have bibliographies. Analytical and topical indexes. Supplemented by a YEARBOOK OF SCIENCE AND TECHNOLOGY, 1962- .

DA39   SCIENCE YEAR: THE WORLD BOOK SCIENCE ANNUAL, 1965-   (See AI11)
Feature articles on selected topics, and a review of major scientific developments for the year. Includes biographies, obituaries, lists of awards and prizes. Three year cum. index.

DA40   VAN NOSTRAND'S SCIENTIFIC ENCYCLOPEDIA. 1982. 6th ed. New York: Van Nostrand Reinhold. 3067 p. illus.
Q121 V3 PASR
Earlier ed. VNR SCIENTIFIC ENCYCLOPEDIA (1976); a one vol. standard. Articles tend to be technical; longer articles signed, most articles brief; with cross references (no index), tables, bibliogs. Emphasizes the physical sciences, but newer technologies, information science represented. AA40 has measurement in English and metric units.

DICTIONARIES

DA41   A DICTIONARY OF NAMED EFFECTS AND LAWS IN CHEMISTRY, PHYSICS AND MATHEMATICS. 1980. Ed. by D.W.G. Ballentyne, and D.R. Lovett. 4th ed. London: Chapman and Hall. 350 p.
Q123 B3 PASR
Arrangement is alphabetical by name of the effect or law with explanations, formulae and illustrations.

DA42   ACRONYMS, INITIALISMS AND ABBREVIATIONS DICTIONARY. (See AJ65).

DA43   DICTIONARY OF SCIENCE & TECHNOLOGY: ENG-FRENCH/ FR-ENGLISH. 1979. 2 vols. Ed. by A.F. Dorian. New York: Elsevier Scientific.
Q123 D68
Detailed, comprehensive coverage of some 150 000 terms. A similar title, DICTIONARY OF SCIENCE & TECHNOLOGY: GERMAN - ENGLISH (1982, 2 vols, 2d ed.) is intended for English speakers working with German.

DA44   FRENCH-ENGLISH SCIENCE AND TECHNOLOGY DICTIONARY. 1976. 4th ed. Ed. by L. De Vries, and S. Hochman. New York: McGraw Hill. 736 p.
Q123 Q37 PASR

DA45   GERMAN-ENGLISH SCIENCE AND TECHNOLOGY DICTIONARY. 1978. 4th ed. Ed. by L. De Vries. New York: McGraw Hill. 704 p.
Q123 D4 PASR
The text, with addendum, provides some 65 000 terms. Bilingual Ger. and Eng. is in the COMPACT DICTIONARY OF EXACT SCIENCE AND TECHNOLOGY (1980, 2 vols., Weisbaden: Rucera.

DA46   McGRAW HILL DICTIONARY OF SCIENTIFIC AND TECHNICAL TERMS. 1984. 3d ed. New York: McGraw Hill. 1781 p.
Q123 M15 PASR
An illustrated short entry dictionary with over 100 000 entries, abbreviations and multiple definitions given. Uses SI units.

DIRECTORIES OF SOCIETIES, RESEARCH AND INFORMATION SERVICES

(See also "Directories" AH27-AH31, and "Information Industries" AB17-AB24).

DA47   WORLD GUIDE TO SCIENTIFIC ASSOCIATIONS AND LEARNED SOCIETIES. 1982. 3d ed. Ed. by M. Zils. Handbook of Information Documentation and Information, vol. 13. Munich: K.G. Saur. 619 p. (Dist.: Gale Research)
        Q145 W67 PASR
    Over 18 000 associations and societies, arranged geographically, for some 130 countries. This ed. adds the arts to sci-tech coverage.

DA48   DIRECTORY OF ENGINEERING SOCIETIES AND RELATED ORGANIZATIONS. 1982. New York: American Assoc. of Engineering Societies.
        TA12 D38 ENGR

DA49   DIRECTORY OF CANADIAN SCIENTIFIC AND TECHNICAL DATABASES/ REPERTOIRE DES BASES DE DONNEES SCIENTIFIQUES ET TECHNIQUES AU CANADA. (See AB21)

DA50   DIRECTORY OF FEDERALLY SUPPORTED RESEARCH IN UNIVERSITIES, 1972/73-   2 vols. Ottawa: Information Exchange Centre, CISTI.
        Q180 C2D5 PASR
    (11ed., 1982-83 {1983}). Lists over 12 500 projects reported by federal govt funding agencies. Five colour coded parts: in Vol. 1: (1) projects listed by grant agency with investigator's name, affiliation, project title, amount; (2) investigators; (3) fiscal breakdown by agency; (4) fiscal breakdown by province; Vol. 2: KWOC subject index arranged alphabetically by Eng. and Fr. terms in the titles. DA50 is available online (IEC database on CISTI's CAN/OLE); fiscal totals not available in the online version.

DA51   SCIENTIFIC AND TECHNICAL SOCIETIES OF CANADA. 1982. 6th ed. Ottawa: CISTI. 130 p.
  R506 S416 ST6   Q21 S37 ENGR; Q21 N34 PASR
    Information is given in the language (Eng., Fr.) of the society.

DIRECTORIES OF MEETINGS

DA52   FORTHCOMING INTERNATIONAL SCIENTIFIC AND TECHNICAL CONFERENCES, 1966- London: Aslib. quarterly.
        Q10 F67 PASR
    Chronological arrangement with 3 indexes for subject, location, organization. Main issue (Feb.) with cum. supplements other quarters.

DA53   WORLD MEETINGS OUTSIDE UNITED STATES AND CANADA, 1968- New York: Macmillan Information. quarterly.
        Q101 W6 PASR

DA54   WORLD MEETINGS UNITED STATES AND CANADA, 1963- New York: Macmillan Information. quarterly.
        Q10 T44 PASR
    A 2 year registry of future medical, scientific, technical meetings. Indexed by date, keyword, deadline, location, sponsor.

BIOGRAPHICAL DICTIONARIES AND DIRECTORIES

DA55   Asimov, I. ASIMOV'S BIOGRAPHICAL ENCYCLOPEDIA OF SCIENCE AND TECHNOLOGY: The Lives and Achievements of 1510 Great Scientists from Ancient Times to the Present, Chronologically Arranged. 1982. 2d rev. ed. New York, Doubleday. 941 p. illus.
    Articles primarily concerned with achievements; index. Compare CONCISE DSB (DA56n) which covers more scientists but with less depth.

DA56   DICTIONARY OF SCIENTIFIC BIOGRAPHY. 1970-80. 15 vol. New York: Scribner. SUPPLEMENT.
    Q141 D53 PASR
    Published under the auspices of the American Council of Learned Societies and intended as a contribution for science parallel to the DAB (AL35) and DNB (AL30). The DSB includes persons of all periods, places who have contributed to the advancement of natural sciences and mathematics. No living persons included. There is a CONCISE DSB (1981) for quick reference, and J. Carvill's FAMOUS NAMES IN ENGINEERING (1981, Butterworths) (Q141 C37 ENGR) is useful for identification.

DA57   McGRAW HILL MODERN SCIENTISTS AND ENGINEERS. 1982. 3 vols. illus.
    Autobiographical entries (for the most part) from over 1100 of the world's achievers in scientific fields. Topical index; bibliogs

DA58   AMERICAN MEN AND WOMEN OF SCIENCE: PHYSICAL AND BIOLOGICAL SCIENCES. 1982. 7 vols. Ed. by Jaques Cattrell Press. New York: R.R. Bowker.
    R509.2 A512A482   Q141 A482
    Includes Canadian scientists in the physical, mathemetical, biological and engineering sciences; giving personal, educational, professional data. Discipline and geographice indexes. A retrospective companion vol. is the BIOGRAPHICAL DICTIONARY OF AMERICAN SCIENCE; 17TH THROUGH 19TH CENTURIES (1979, Greenwood) (Q141 E37 PASR).

DA59   WHO'S WHO IN TECHNOLOGY TODAY, 1979-   4 vols. Woodbridge, CT: Research Publications. irreg. annual
    T39 W5 ENGR
    (4th ed., 1984) Over 26 000 American engineers and scientists and their contribution in some 1400 areas of sci-tech. Vol. 4 is a name and subject index to other vols on Electronic & Physics; Mechanical, Civil & Earth Sciences; Chemical & Bioscience Technologies. WHO'S WHO IN ENGINEERING (1982, 5th ed., Amer. Assoc. of Eng. Societies) (TA139 E373 ENGR) is a similar publication covering U.S. engineers; includes a section on American and Canadian engineering societies.

DA60   DIRECTORY OF PROFESSIONAL ENGINEERS OF ONTARIO. 1980. Toronto: Assoc. of Professional Engineers of Ontario. 918 p.
    TA12 D4 ENGR

MATHEMATICS

GUIDES

DB1　BIBLIOGRAPHY AND RESEARCH MANUAL IN THE HISTORY OF MATHEMATICS. 1973. By K.O. May. Toronto: Univ. of Toronto Press. 818 p.
　　　　　　　Z66451 M35 PASC　　　　Ryder SC9-12
　　Annotated bibliography, 31 000 items, from secondary literature.

DB2　Dorling, A.R. 1977. USE OF MATHEMATICAL LITERATURE. Boston: Butterworths. 260 p.
　　510 U84U　　　　QA41.7 U83 PASR
　　A graduate level guide which covers literature and topical areas for mathematics; organizations, reference works, education, history.

DB3　Schaefer, B.K. 1979. USING THE MATHEMATICAL LITERATURE: A PRACTICAL GUIDE. New York: Marcel Dekker. 141 p.
　　510.72 S294U　　　　QA41.7 S3 PASR
　　Mostly American sources for research, applications, expositions.

BIBLIOGRAPHIES AND ABSTRACTS

DB4　INDEX OF MATHEMATICAL PAPERS, 1970-　Providence, RI: American Mathematical Society. semi-annual
　　　　　　　Z6653 I55 PASR
　　International and acts as index, 1973- to MATHEMATICAL REVIEWS.

DB5　MATHEMATICAL REVIEWS, 1940-　Providence, RI: American Mathematical Society. monthly.
　　　　　　　QA1 M424 PASR
　　Abstracts (English, French, German) of books, periodical articles in the international literature of mathematical research. Arranged by subject with author index. AMS also publishes a biweekly list of new publications, CURRENT MATHEMATICAL PUBLICATIONS.

DB6　STATISTICAL THEORY AND METHOD ABSTRACTS, 1959-　London: Longman for the International Statistical Institute. quarterly.
　　　　　　　QA276 S83 PASR
　　Merged in 1964 with the INTERNATIONAL JOURNAL OF ABSTRACTS: STATISTICAL THEORY AND METHOD. Detailed, evaluative abstracts in classified order. Author index.

HANDBOOKS AND TABLES

DB7　Burlington, R.S. 1973. HANDBOOK OF MATHEMATICAL TABLES AND FORMULAS. 5th ed. New York: McGraw Hill. 500 p.
　　　　　　　QA47 B8 PASR
　　Intended for the student and specialist. In two parts: 1: formulas, definitions, theorems from elementary mathematics; 2: logarithmic and trigonometric tables.

DB8　CRC HANDBOOK OF MATHEMATICAL SCIENCE. 1978. 5th ed. Ed. by William H. Beyer. Palm Beach, FL: CRC Press. 982 p.
　　　　　　　QA47 H322 (1978) PASR; ENGR
　　Supersedes the HANDBOOK OF TABLES FOR MATHEMATICS.

DB9   Korn, G.A., and T.A. Korn. 1968. MATHEMATICAL HANDBOOK FOR SCIENTISTS AND ENGINEERS: Definitions, Theorems and Formulas for Reference and Review. New York: McGraw Hill. 1130 p.
          QA37 K74 PASR
          A comprehensive collection of data. Subject index.

DB10   National Research Council. 1926-33. INTERNATIONAL CRITICAL TABLES. 7 vols. New York: McGraw Hill.
          Q199 N32 PASR

DICTIONARIES AND ENCYCLOPEDIAS

DB11   ENCYCLOPEDIC DICTIONARY OF MATHEMATICS. 1977. 2 vols. Comp. by the Mathematical Society of Japan. Cambridge, MA: M.I.T. Press.
          QA5 N5 PASR
          Trans. from the Japanese; 436 articles. Basic and comprehensive.

DB12   INTERNATIONAL DICTIONARY OF APPLIED MATHEMATICS. 1960. Comp. by W.F. Freiberger. Princeton, NJ: Van Nostrand. 1173 p.
          QA5 I5 PASR; ENGR
          Encyclopedic dictionary; lengthy explanations for applications of mathematics in engineering, physical sciences. French, German, Russian, Spanish indexes.

DB13   MATHEMATICS DICTIONARY. 1976. 4th ed. Ed. by G. James, and R.C. James. Princeton, NJ: Van Nostrand Reinhold. 509 p.
          QA5 J3 PASR
          All branches: arithmetic, calculus, probability, statistics, etc.

DB14   McGRAW HILL DICTIONARY OF PHYSICS AND MATHEMATICS. 1978. Ed. by D.N. Lapedes. New York: McGraw-Hill. 1074 p.
          QC5 M23 PASR
          Some 20 000 definitions of terms in physics, math, related fields.

DB15   THE VNR CONCISE ENCYCLOPEDIA OF MATHEMATICS. 1977. New York: Van Nostrand Reinhold. 816 p.
          QA40 V18 PASR
          Includes both theoretical and practical aspects of mathematics with numerous examples and illustrations.

DIRECTORIES

DB16   WORLD DIRECTORY OF MATHEMATICIANS. 1979. 6th ed. Ed. by the International Mathematical Union. Kyoto: Kyoto Univ. Dept of Mathematics.
          QA30 W67 PASR
          Alphabetical name and address list of 20 000 mathematicians. Geographical index.

COMPUTER SCIENCE

GUIDES, BIBLIOGRAPHIES AND REVIEWS

DC1   COMPUTER REVIEWS, 1960-   New York: Association for Computing Machinery. monthly.
QA76 C68 PASR
Short signed reviews of computer literature in classified arrangement. Author index for each vol. Cumulative bibliography and subject index to CR is called ACM GUIDE TO COMPUTING LITERATURE.

DC2   COMPUTER SCIENCE RESEARCH: A GUIDE TO PROFESSIONAL LITERATURE. 1981. Ed. by D. Myers. White Plains, NY: Knowledge Industry Publications for the American Society for Information Science. 346 p.
R001.64 AM996C
Comprehensive compilation of several thousand essential reference works. Covers all aspects of data processing. Serves practitioners, librarians, students, consultants and systems analysts.

DC3   INTERNATIONAL COMPUTER BIBLIOGRAPHY, 1960-70. 2 vols. New York: Science Associates International.
R651.8 AI61   Z6654 C17I5 02 PASR
Prepared at the Centre for Studies in Information Processing, Amsterdam. Vol. 1 covers 1960-68; vol. 2, 1969-70. Includes 10 000 abstracts of books, technical reports from 40 countries. Emphasis on applications in coverage of use, applications, effect of computers in scientific, commercial, industrial, social environments.

ABSTRACTS

DC4   COMPUTER ABSTRACTS, 1957-   British Channel Islands: Technical Information Co. monthly.
QA76 C54 PASR
Abstracts books, articles in ca 100 periodicals, conference proceedings, U.S. govt reports, patents. International coverage.

DC5   COMPUTER AND CONTROL ABSTRACTS, 1966-   monthly. (See DA21)
TJ212 C56 ENGR
Scans over 3000 journals, over 1000 conference proceedings, books, reports, dissertations in brief abstracts (100-150 words) covering international literature; 24 000+ items carried yearly in this service which is Series C of SCIENCE ABSTRACTS. Available online as INSPEC.

DC6   IT FOCUS, [Information Technology], 1983-   monthly. (See DA21)
Purpose "to assist managers to keep up to date with the latest significant developments in Information Technology by presenting information selected and summarized from the wide and growing range of publications." Short abstracts (100-150 words) in this service which is series D of SCIENCE ABSTRACTS. Available online as INSPEC.

HANDBOOKS

DC7   AUTOMATIC DATA PROCESSING HANDBOOK. 1977. New York: McGraw Hill.
QA76 A888 (1977) PASC
Covers data and information processing; management developments.

DC8 McGRAW HILL'S COMPILATION OF DATA COMMUNICATION STANDARDS. 1978. New York: McGraw Hill. 1133 p.
TK5105 M3 ENGR (1978)
Both international and American data communication standards.

ENCYCLOPEDIAS AND DICTIONARIES

DC9 ABBREVIATIONS: The Comprehensive Dictionary of Abbreviations and Letter Symbols for the Computer Era. 1983. 2 vols. Ann Arbor, MI: Pierian Press.
Some 70 000, showing up to as many as 14 variant, acceptable abbreviations for areas for computer data entry, transmission, output. Vol.1 is abbreviation to word; vol. 2, word to abbreviation.

DC10 ENCYCLOPEDIA OF COMPUTER SCIENCE AND TECHNOLOGY, 1975- 20 vols. Ed. by J. Belxer, and others. New York: Marcel Dekker. In progress.
QA76 15 E5 PASR

DC11 COMPUTER DICTIONARY. 1980. 3d ed. Ed. by C.J. Sippl, and R.J. Sippl. Indianapolis, IN: H.W. Sams. 624 p.
R651 803 S61S (1966)   QA76 S512 (1980)
A "browsing" dictionary, with encyclopedic definitions, intended for computer users rather than specialists.

DC12 DICTIONARY OF DATA PROCESSING: Including Applications in Industry, Administration and Business. 1977. 3d rev. ed. New York: Elsevier/ North Holland. 347 p.
651.2603 T846 (1964)   QA76 15 W57 (1977)1

DC13 ENCYCLOPEDIA OF COMPUTER SCIENCE AND ENGINEERING. 1983. 2d ed. by A. Ralston, and E.D. Reilly. New York: Van Nostrand Reinhold. . 1664 p.
QA76.15 E48 PASR; ENGR
Clear concise information for the non-specialist. Greatly expanded edition of the ENCYCLOPEDIA OF COMPUTER SCIENCE. Almost 600 articles classified under 9 categorical headings such as Hardware, Mathematics of Computing, Applications etc. Useful cross references, detailed index, multilingual glossary.

DIRECTORIES

For directories to databases and online search manuals, see AB17-AB32.

DC14 BOWKER/ BANTAM 1984 COMPLETE SOURCEBOOK OF PERSONAL COMPUTING. 1983. New York: R.R. Bowker/ Bantam. 646 p. illus.
A product directory for hardware, software; lists books, clubs, associations, distributors, producers etc. in a one stop compendium.

DC15 DATA COMMUNICATIONS: BUYER'S GUIDE, 1979-   New York: McGraw Hill, 1980- annual.
HD9696 T43 ENGR
Covers equipment with vendor index.

DC16 DIRECTORY OF ONLINE INFORMATION RESOURCES. 1980. 6th ed. Rockville, MD: CSG Press.
R025.4025 D598D B6
Covers some 225 bibliographic and non-bibliographic databases.

ASTRONOMY

GUIDES AND BIBLIOGRAPHIES

DD1   BIBLIOGRAPHY OF ASTRONOMY, 1970-1979. 1982. By R. Sealand, and S. Martin. Littleton, CO: Libraries Unlimited. 407 p.
Z5151 S38 PASR
Updates D.A. Kemp's ASTRONOMY AND ASTROPHYSICS: A BIBLIOGRAPHICAL GUIDE (1970, Macdonald Technical and Scientific) (Z5151 K45 PASR). DD1 is an international classified, annotated bibliog. of selected items.

DD2   BIBLIOGRAPHY OF NON-COMMERCIAL PUBLICATIONS OF OBSERVATORIES AND ASTRONOMICAL SOCIETIES. 1973. Rev. ed. Utrecht, Netherlands: Sonnenborgh Observatory.
QB81 B52 DUNO
Prepared under the auspices of IFLA/FIAB, Section of Astronomical Libraries. INDEX TO OBSERVATORY PUBLICATIONS includes discontinued and current series, addresses.

DD3   HISTORY OF MODERN ASTRONOMY AND ASTROPHYSICS. 1982. New York: Garland. 432 p.
Z5154 H58 D48 PASC
Comprehensive coverage of major sources and important journal articles from the invention of the telescope to the present.

DD4   Seal, R.A. 1977. A GUIDE TO THE LITERATURE OF ASTRONOMY. Littleton, CO: Libraries Unlimited. 306 p.
R520 AS438G   Z5252 S4
Introductory, annotated list of books, periodicals in astronomy and closely related fields.

ABSTRACTS

DD5   ASTRONOMY AND ASTROPHYSICAL ABSTRACTS, 1969-   Berlin: Springer Verlag. semi-annual.
QB1 A8875 PASR
Supersedes ASTROMISCHER JAHRESBERICHT, 1899-1969. International in scope with abstracts primarily in English (some in French or German). Arranged by broad subject categories with author, subject indexes.

DD6   ASTRONOMY AND ASTROPHYSICS MONTHLY INDEX, 1976-   Sierra Madre, CA: Olivetree Associates. monthly.
Z5153 A7 PASS
Covers some 30 professional journals. Author, title indexes.

ANNUALS AND REVIEWS

DD7   ADVANCES IN ASTRONOMY AND ASTROPHYSICS, 1962-   New York: Academic Press. annual.
QB1 A1717 DUNO
Selected authoritative surveys of recent research. Subject index and index to authors cited.

DD8 ANNUAL REVIEW OF ASTRONOMY AND ASTROPHYSICS, 1963- Palo Alto, CA: Annual Reviews.
       QB1 A2884
  Broad technical survey for the professional astronomer.

DD9 VISTAS IN ASTRONOMY, 1955- Oxford: Pergamon Press. annual.
       QB3 V56
  Each vol. generally covers a specific field.

ENCYCLOPEDIAS AND DICTIONARIES

DD10 THE CAMBRIDGE ENCYCLOPEDIA OF ASTRONOMY. 1977. Ed. by S. Mitton. New York: Crown. 481 p.
       QB43.2 C35 PASR
  Definitive sourcebook. A treatise for lay people on modern astronomy and astrophysics. Long chapters in classified arrangement.

DD11 CATALOGUE OF THE UNIVERSE. 1979. Comp. by P. Murdin, and D. Allen. New York: Crown/ London: Cambridge Univ. Press. 256 p.
       QB44 2 M869 PASC
  "Photographs and descriptive articles about a comprehensive selection of objects in our universe."

DD12 CONCISE ENCYCLOPEDIA OF ASTRONOMY. 1976. 2d ed. Ed. by A. Weigert, and H. Zimmerman. London: Adam Hilger. 532 p.
       QB14 W413 PASR
  Some 1500 authoritative entries on all aspects of astronomy for laypersons. Illus., photographs, tables.

DD13 DICTIONARY OF ASTRONAUTICS: ENG-FRENCH/ FR-ENGLISH. 1964. 2d ed. Ed. by A. Martin. Montreal: Editions Martin. 237 p.
       TL788 M37 (1964) ENGI Ryder SC3-1
  Covers astronomy, astronautics, physics, electronics, missiles, radio, radar etc.

DD14 THE FACTS ON FILE DICTIONARY OF ASTRONOMY. 1979. Ed. by V. Illingworth. New York: Facts on File. 378 p.
       QB14 I42 ROMU
  Wide coverage; precise definitions; illus., diagrams, tables. Technical language and inclusion of mathematical, physical formulae inhibit use by lay people.

DD15 GLOSSARY OF ASTRONOMY AND ASTROPHYSICS. 1980. 2d ed. Ed. by J. Hopkins. Chicago: Univ. of Chicago Press.
       QB14 H66 PASR
  General dictionary for astronomy, astrophysics, related physical, chemical terms. Defines 2300 terms; not recommended for the novice.

HANDBOOKS

DD16 THE AMATEUR ASTRONOMER'S HANDBOOK. 1980. 4th ed. By J. Muirden. New York: Crowell. 404 p.
       QB44 S558 DUNO
  "Everything the amateur astronomer needs to know" for observations in the northern hemisphere. Glossary, bibliog.; list of societies.

DD17   ASTRONOMICAL ALMANAC, 1981-   Washington: GPO/ London: HMSO. annual.
                    QB81 U6 A77 SIGS
        Supersedes AMERICAN EPHEMERIS AND NAUTICAL ALMANAC (1852-1980, GPO) (QB8 U6 PASS) and ASTRONOMICAL EPHEMERIS (HMSO). Has data for space sciences, astronomy, geodesy, surveying, navigation, other areas.

DD18   ASTRONOMY DATA BOOK. 1979. 2d ed. Ed. by J.H. Robinson, and J. Muirden. New York: John Wiley. 272 p.
                    QB64 R58 PASR
        Reference for the student and amateur astronomer. Glossary; tables; short articles.

DD19   ASTROPHYSICAL FORMULAE: A Compendium for the Physicist & Astrophysicist. 1980. 2d ed. Berlin/ New York: Springer Verlag. 783 p.
                    QB461 L36 (1980) PASR
        Complements DD20. Gives formulae, derivations, applications rather than lists of data.

DD20   ASTROPHYSICAL QUANTITIES. 1973. 3d ed. Comp. by C.W. Allen. London: Athlone, 310 p.
                    QB461 A564
        Includes experimental, theoretical values, constants, conversion factors. Intended for advanced students and professional astronomers.

DD21   BURNHAM'S CELESTIAL HANDBOOK: An Observer's Guide to the Universe Beyond the Solar System. 1978. 3 vols. 2d ed. By R. Burnham. New York: Dover.
                    QB64 B85 PASR
        The comprehensive English language guide to celestial objects.

DD22   THE LAROUSSE GUIDE TO ASTRONOMY. 1978. Ed. by D. Baker. New York: Larousse. 288 p.
                    QB442 B36 (1978) PASR
        General coverage, written primarily for a British audience.

DD23   PICTORIAL GUIDE TO THE PLANETS. 1981. 3d ed. Ed. by J. Jackson, and J. Baumert. New York: Harper and Row. 246 p.
                    QB601 J3 PASC
        Stresses exploration, discoveries of solar system, space science.

DD24   OBSERVER'S HANDBOOK, 1907-   Toronto: Royal Astronomical Society of Canada. annual.
                    QB64 R6 PASR   Ryder SC3-2
        Tables of data for the year for Canadian observers.

DD25   WHITNEY'S STAR FINDER: A Field Guide to the Heavens. 1981. New York: Knopf. 102 p.

ATLASES

DD26   THE CAMBRIDGE PHOTOGRAPHIC ATLAS OF THE PLANETS. 1983. Ed. by G. Briggs, and F.W. Taylor. New York: Cambridge Univ. Press. 224 p. 215 photos.
        A survey of the evolution of the solar system; a record of recent discoveries about the planets.

DD27   MASTER LIST OF NONSTELLAR OPTICAL ASTRONOMICAL OBJECTS. Comp. by R. Dixon, and G. Sonneborn. 1980. Columbus, OH: Ohio State Univ. Press. 835 p.
QB65 O56
Consolidates 85 000 listings from 270 catalogues of nonstellar objects for (prof. and amateur) astronomers, engineers, physicists.

DD28   THE RAND MCNALLY NEW CONCISE ATLAS OF THE UNIVERSE. 1978. Rev. ed. Ed. by P. Moore. Chicago: Rand McNally. 190 p.
Rev. ed. of the ATLAS OF THE UNIVERSE (1970) (QB44 2 M66 BMER). As much an encyclopedia as an atlas. Most changes in the rev. ed. are in the solar system.

DD29   Smithsonian Institution. Astrophysical Observatory. STAR ATLAS OF REFERENCE STARS AND NONSTELLAR OBJECTS. 1969. Cambridge, MA: M.I.T. Press. 13 p. 152 charts.
QB65 SI55 PASC
Appr. 250 000 stars recorded on the charts. Indexes.

DD30   THE TIMES ATLAS OF THE MOON. 1969. Ed. by H.A.G. Lewis. London: Times Newspapers. 110 p.
QB595 T5 PASR
Over 100 pages of maps, all same scale, with text and illus. on lunar mapping, lunar landscape and flight.

PHYSICS

GUIDES AND BIBLIOGRAPHIES

DE1   Heilbron, J.L. and B.R. Wheaton. 1981. LITERATURE ON THE HISTORY OF PHYSICS IN THE 20TH CENTURY. Berkeley, CA: Office of the History of Science and Technology, Univ. of California. 485 p.
Z7141 H45 PASC
Comprehesive bibliography on all types of physics literature, in suject arrangement.

DE2   Melton, L.R. 1978. AN INTRODUCTORY GUIDE TO INFORMATION SOURCES IN PHYSICS. Philadelphia: Heyden and Son.
Z7141 M528 (1978) PHYS

ABSTRACTS AND INDEXES

DE3   CURRENT CONTENTS: PHYSICAL, CHEMICAL AND EARTH SCIENCES, 1961-   weekly. (See DA16)
001 PASR

DE4   CURRENT PAPERS IN PHYSICS, 1966-   London: Institute of Electrical Engineers. semi-monthly.
QC1 P4813 PASR
Selective coverage, bibliographic citation only. Available online through INSPEC (DE7).

DE5   CURRENT PHYSICS INDEX, 1975-   New York: American Institute of Physics. quarterly; annual cum. index.
QC1 C86 PASR
Supersedes CURRENT PHYSICS ADVANCE ABSTRACTS; CURRENT PHYSICS TITLES. DE5 is an index, with abstracts, to journals published by AIP and member societies. Classified arrangement; author, subject index. Available online as SPIN (DE11).

DE6   INIS ATOMINDEX: An International Abstracting Service, 1970-   Vienna: International Atomic Energy Agency. semi-monthly; semi-annual cum. ind
Z6160 I18 PASR
Partially supersedes NUCLEAR SCIENCE ABSTRACTS and IAEA's LIST OF REFERENCES ON ATOMIC ENERGY. A cooperative effort of over 60 countries and international organizations contributing to the International Nuclear Information System. Main section classed by subject. Many INIS reports on microfiche document delivery.

DE7   INSPEC [International Information Services for the Physics and Engineering Communities], 1967-   monthly. (See DA21)
A fully integrated computer-based operation of IEE/IEEE information services; the print equivalent is SCIENCE ABSTRACTS (DA21). With four available files: A: PHYSICS ABSTRACTS; B: ELECTRICAL AND ELECTRONIC ABSTRACTS; C: COMPUTER AND CONTROL ABSTRACTS; D: INFORMATION TECHNOLOGY ABSTRACTS. INSPEC is available through commercial online systems, and through CAN/OLE (AB26) or CAN/SDI (AB27) at CISTI. Use with INSPEC THESAURUS 1983 (1982).

DE8   NUCLEAR SCIENCE ABSTRACTS, 1947-1976. 33 vols. Oak Ridge, TN: U.S. Atomic Energy Commission, Division of Technical Information.
              QC770 N877 PASR
           Ceased publication with vol. 33, no. 12, June 1976. Coverage in ENERGY INFORMATION ABSTRACTS (DK9) and INIS ATOMINDEX (DE6).

DE9   PHYSICS ABSTRACTS, 1898-65/ vol. 69-   1966-   semi-monthly; cum. index monthly, semi-annual. (See DA21).
              QC1 P4843 PASR
           Covers all areas of modern physics in a classified arrangement, and is "Section A" of SCIENCE ABSTRACTS. Available online as INSPEC.

DE10   PHYSICS BRIEFS/ PHSYIKALISCHE BERICHTE, 1979-   New York: American Institute of Physics. semi-monthly
              QC1 P83 PASR
           Supersedes PHYSIKALISCHE BERICHTE, 1920-1978. An international abstract journal for all fields of physics; all types of literature.

DE11   SPIN [Searchable Physics Information Notices] 1971-   New York: American Institute of Physics.
           A computerized database covering all major areas of physics, astronomy from any English language journal, plus Russian articles, and conference proceedings from AIP and its member societies. Physics articles from other American journals are also included. CURRENT PHYSICS INDEX (DE5), with wider coverage, is the print equivalent.

REVIEWS AND ANNUALS

DE12   ANNUAL REVIEW OF NUCLEAR SCIENCE, 1952-   Palo Alto, CA: Annual Reviews.
              QC770 A5 PHYS
           Reviews of recent significant developments, with extensive bibliographies. Author and subject indexes.

DE13   REPORTS ON PROGRESS IN PHYSICS, 1934-   London: Institute of Physics and Physical Society. annual.
              QC1 R37 PHYS
           Extensive reviews articles by specialists.

DE14   REVIEWS OF MODERN PHYSICS, 1929-   New York: American Institute of Physics. quarterly.
              QC1 R4 PHYS
           Reviews, at advanced level, articles in current research.

ENCYCLOPEDIAS AND DICTIONARIES

DE15   THE ENCYCLOPEDIA OF PHYSICS. 1974. 2d ed. Ed. by R.M. Besancon. New York: Van Nostrand Reinhold. 1067 p.
           R530.03 B554 (1966)   QC5 B47 PASR
           Articles written to be of "primary value to the type of reader most apt to look for the particular topic." Some advanced material as well as articles at a lower technical level.

DE16   ENCYCLOPEDIA OF PHYSICS. 1980. Ed. by R.G. Lerner, and G.L. Trigg. Reading, MA: Addison Wesley. 1157 p.
QC5 E545 ENGR
Authoritative coverage of physics, astrophysics and related topcis for graduate students and professionals. Some articles assume advanced levels of mathematics and physics.

DE17   ENCYCLOPEDIC DICTIONARY OF PHYSICS. 1961-64. 9 vols. Ed. by J. Thewlis. Oxford: Pergamon Press. SUPPLEMENT 5 vols (1966-75).
QC5 E5 PASR
Covers "general, nuclear, solid state, molecular, chemical, metal and vacuum physics, astronomy, geophysics, biophysics, related subjects." Bibliogs with most articles. Vol. 9: multilingual glossary (Eng/ Fr/ Ger/ Sp/ Rus/ Jap) listing ca 13 000 terms taken from the titles of articles; the CONCISE DICTIONARY OF PHYSICS AND RELATED SUBJECTS (1979) is a condensed version of this glossary.

DE18   McGRAW HILL DICTIONARY OF PHYSICS AND MATHEMATICS. 1978. Ed. by D.N. Lapedes. New York: McGraw Hill. 1074 p.
QC21 M23 PASR

HANDBOOKS

DE19   AMERICAN INSTITUTE OF PHYSICS HANDBOOK. 1972. 3d ed. New York: McGraw Hill, 2200 p.
QC61 A5 PASR
Prepared for those employing physical methods in research. Arranged by broad subject areas. Subject index.

DE20   FUNDAMENTAL MEASURES AND CONSTANTS FOR SCIENCE AND TECHNOLOGY. 1974. Comp. by F.D. Rossini. Cleveland, OH: CRC Press.
QC39 R66

DE21   HANDBOOK OF CHEMISTRY AND PHYSICS: A Ready Reference Book of Chemical and Physical Data, 1913-   (See DF'26)
R540 H236 (1972/73)   QD65 H3 PASR
A concise summary of major definitions, formulas, tables and examples of elementary and intermediate technical physics. Extensive subject index.

DE22   HANDBOOK OF PHYSICAL CALCULATIONS. 1976. Ed. by J.J. Tuma. New York: McGraw Hill. 370 p.
QC61 T85 PASR

DE23   TABLES OF PHYSICAL AND CHEMICAL CONSTANTS AND SOME MATHEMATICAL FUNCTIONS. 1973. 14th ed. Ed. by G.W.C. Kay, and T.H. Laby. London: Longman.
QC61 K3 PASR
Includes tables in general physics, chemistry, atomic and nuclear physics. SI units used.

CHEMISTRY

GUIDES AND BIBLIOGRAPHIES

DF1 Anthony, A. 1979. GUIDE TO BASIC INFORMATION SOURCES IN CHEMISTRY. New York: Jeffrey Norton. 219 p.
QD8.5 A57 PASR
A useful introduction for student or librarian.

DF2 Maizell, R.E. 1979. HOW TO FIND CHEMICAL INFORMATION: A Guide for Practicing Chemists, Teachers and Students. New York: J. Wiley. 261 p.
QD8.5 M34 PASR
Comprehensive on all aspects, organization of chemical literature.

DF3 USE OF CHEMICAL LITERATURE. 1979. 3d ed. Ed. by R.T. Bottle. London: Butterworths, 306 p.
540 AB751 U3
International coverage, with British emphasis, for all types of chemical literature; some chapters, by individual authors, are encyclopedic in nature.

ABSTRACTS AND INDEXES

DF4 ANALYTICAL ABSTRACTS, 1954-   London: Chemical Society. monthly. annual index.
QD71 A49 PASR
Decennial INDEX 1954-1983; quinquennial INDEX 1964-1968. Covers all areas of analytical chemistry in a broad subject arrangement. No index in monthly issues; annual author, subject indexes.

DF5 CHEMICAL ABSTRACTS, 1907-   Columbus, OH: Chemical Abstracts Service. weekly. annual cum. index. Decennial indexes, 1907-1956; quinquennial 1957-
QD1 C45 PASR
The comprehensive abstracting service for world chemical and chemical engineering literature. Issues are arranged in 80 sections under broad fields: applied, organic, macro molecular, physical and analytic chemistry, and chemical engineering. Each issue has author, keyword subject, numerical patent indexes and a patent concordance. Annual cum. includes author, generic subject, chemical substance, ring systems, patent formula, patent concordance indexes. Available online as CASEARCH, through commercial services and CISTI services (AB26, AB27). CA CONDENSATES are weekly tapes of CA without abstracts. Other services include CASIA (CA Subject Index Alert) and CA INDEX GUIDE for general subject vocabulary.

DF6 CHEMICAL ABSTRACTS SERVICE SOURCE INDEX, 1907-1979. 1980. [CASSI]. Columbus, OH: Chemical Abstracts Service.
Z5523 C5 PASR
Supersedes ACCESS: Key to the Source Literature of the Chemical Sciences. CASSI has bibliographical descriptions for source literature of chemical sciences with key to library holdings. Kept current by CHEMICAL ABSTRACTS SERVICE SOURCE INDEX, 1970-   quarterly suppl.

DF7   CHEMICAL TITLES, 1960-   Columbus, OH: Chemical Abstracts Service. biweekly.
      QD1 C45 PASR

DF8   CURRENT ABSTRACTS OF CHEMISTRY AND INDEX CHEMICUS, 1960-   Philadelphia: Institute for Scientific Information. weekly, quarterly, annual; index
      QD1 PASR
      Title varies: vols 1-35, INDEX CHEMICUS; from vol. 36- INDEX CHEMICUS forms the second section of the vol. Indexes: molecular formula, author, keyword, biological activity, corporate, new reactions, labelled compounds. Abstract section covers articles on the synthesis, isolation and identification of new compounds, and reporting new chemical reactions or syntheses.

DF9   CURRENT CHEMICAL REACTIONS, 1979-   Philadelphia: Institute for Scientific Information. monthly.
      QD501 C84 CHEM
      Literature on new synthetic methods or modifications improving known methods. Included with subscription to CURRENT ABSTRACTS OF CHEMISTRY AND INDEX CHEMICUS (CF8).

DF10 CURRENT CONTENTS: PHYSICAL, CHEMICAL AND EARTH SCIENCES, 1961-   weekly. (See DA16)
      QD1 PASR

ANNUALS AND REVIEWS

DF11 ADVANCES IN CHEMICAL ENGINEERING, 1956-   New York: Academic Press. irregular.
      TP145 A4 ENGS

DF12 RUSSIAN CHEMICAL REVIEWS, 1968-   London: Chemical Society. monthly.
      QD1 U713 CHEM
      English translation of Russian review journal, USPEKHI KHIMII.

DF13 CHEMICAL REVIEWS, 1924-   Washington: American Chemical Society. monthly.
      QD1 C58 CHEM
      Review articles with extensive bibliographies.

ENCYCLOPEDIAS AND DICTIONARIES

DF14 CHEMICAL SYNONYMS AND TRADE NAMES: A Dictionary and Commercial Handbook. 1978. 8th ed. Oxford: Technical Press.
      TP9 G28 (1979) ENGR
      Comprehensive listing with over 35 000 definitions; trade names keyed to manufacturers (when known).

DF15 COMPREHENSIVE ORGANIC CHEMISTRY. 1979. 6 vols. Ed. by D. Barton, and W.D. Ollis. Elmsford, NY: Pergamon.
      QD245 C65 PASR
      Vol. 6 contains indexes for formula, subject, author, reaction, reagent; with additional bibliographic references.

DF16 CONDENSED CHEMICAL DICTIONARY. 1981. 10th ed. Ed. by G.G. Hawley. New York: Van Nostrand Reinhold. 1135 p.
    QD5 C5 (1981) PASR
  Recent developments in all aspects of applied chemistry in this quick reference source. This ed. revises coverage of pollution, waste control, chemical manufacturing equipment and energy sources. Hampel and Hawley's GLOSSARY OF CHEMICAL TERMS (1976) is a short dictionary for non-specialists.

DF17 A DICTIONARY OF NAMED EFFECTS AND LAWS IN CHEMISTRY, PHYSICS AND MATHEMATICS. (See DA41)
    QD5 B32 (1980) ENGR

DF18 DICTIONARY OF ORGANIC COMPOUNDS. 1965. 5 vols. 4th ed. New York: Oxford Univ. Press. annual SUPPLEMENT(s).
    QD251 D492 CHEM
  "The Constitution and Physical, Chemical and other properties of the principal carbon compounds and their derivatives, together with the relative literature referenced."

DF19 THE ENCYCLOPEDIA OF CHEMISTRY. 1973. 3d ed. Ed. by C.A. Hampel, and G.G. Hawley. New York: Van Nostrand Reinhold. 1198 p.
    QD5 E58 PASR
  Intended for students, lay persons, or experts outside their specialization. Third ed. increased emphasis on environmental chemistry, chemistry of life processes.

DF20 FACTS ON FILE DICTIONARY OF CHEMISTRY. 1981. Ed. by J. Daintith. New York: Facts on File.
    QD5 D26 DENT
  Some 2000 entries for important and commonly used chemical terms.

DF21 THE INTERNATIONAL ENCYCLOPEDIA OF PHYSICAL CHEMISTRY AND CHEMICAL PHYSICS, 1960- 100 vols. London: Pergamon Press. In progress.
    QD453 I5
  A comprehensive account of all aspects of the domain of science between chemistry and physics, primarily for the graduate and research worker. Theoretical, rather than practical aspects are emphasized. In 20 general topic groups, each with several vols.

DF22 KIRK OTHMER ENCYCLOPEDIA OF CHEMICAL TECHNOLOGY, 1978-1983. 25 vols. 3d ed. New York: John Wiley. SUPPLEMENT 1984.
    TP9 E685 PASR
  Authoritative coverage of chemical engineering. Each vol. is self contained. All articles, with bibliogs, written by specialists. Complements the ENCYCLOPEDIA OF CHEMICAL PROCESSING AND DESIGN (DL24).

DF23 McGRAW HILL ENCYCLOPEDIA OF CHEMISTRY. 1983. Ed. by S. Parker. New York: McGraw Hill. 1200 p.
    QD5 M36 (1983) PASR
  Up-to-date, comprehensive one vol. encyclopedia containing 790 articles from the McGRAW HILL ENCYCLOPEDIA OF SCI. AND TECH. (DA38).

HANDBOOKS

DF 24   THE CHEMICAL FORMULARY: Collection of Commercial Formulas for Making Thousands of Products in Many Fields. 1933-77. 20 vols. New York: Chemical Publishing.
                        TP151 C53 PASR
     Contains formulas, obtained from reputable sources, for products from every type of chemical industry. Useful supplementary information includes list of incompatible chemicals, lists of suppliers and first aid for chemical injuries.

DF 25   DANGEROUS PROPERTIES OF INDUSTRIAL METHODS. 1979. 5th ed. Ed. by N. Sax. New York: Van Nostrand. 1118 p.
                        T55 S37 (1979) ENGI
     Lists ca 15 000 common industrial and laboratory materials with incompatibilities and toxicological data for humans, animals.

DF 26   HANDBOOK OF CHEMISTRY AND PHYSICS: A Ready Reference Book of Chemical and Physical Data, 1913-   Cleveland, OH: CRC Press. 1 vol. various paging. irreg.
R540 H236 (1972/73)   QD65 H3 PASR
     Authoritative all purpose handbook including mathematical tables, organic and inorganic compounds, general chemical, general physical constants and miscellaneous data. Subject index.

DF 27   HANDBOOK OF REACTIVE CHEMICAL HAZARDS. 1979. 2d ed. By L. Bretherick. London: Butterworths. 1281 p.
                        T55.3 H3 B73 (1979) ENGR
     Important safety guide; includes many hazardous materials not ordinarily described.

DF 28   LANGE'S HANDBOOK OF CHEMISTRY. 1979. 12th ed. Ed. by J.A. Dean. New York: McGraw Hill. 1462 p.
R540 L274H (1973)   TP151 L3 PASR
     (1st ed. 1934) Ready access to chemical and physical data required in laboratory and in manufacturing.

DIRECTORIES

DF 29   CANADIAN CHEMICAL REGISTER. 1978. Ottawa: Chemicals Branch, Dept of Industry, Trade and Commerce. 244 p. irregular.
                    TP12 C24 PASS   Ryder SC5-1
     Section 1 is an index of chemicals made in Canada, name of producing company, plant locations. Section 2 is an index of companies listing head office, plant locations, products.

EARTH SCIENCES

See also the AK section on Atlases, Maps and Related Materials.

GUIDES

DG1   Brewer, J.G. 1978. THE LITERATURE OF GEOGRAPHY: A Guide to its Organization and Use. 2d ed. London: Clive Bingley. 264 p.
         910 AB847I2
         "Planned as an introductory guide, identifying the most useful, most significant and most authoritative sources within each branch of geography." Reference books and bibliographic sources emphasized.

DG2   Lock, C.B. Muriel. GEOGRAPHY AND CARTOGRAPHY. 1976. 3d ed. rev. and enl. London: Clive Bingley. 762 p.
         900 L813G3
         Combined revision of author's older titles GEOGRAPHY: A REFERENCE HANDBOOK and MODERN MAPS AND ATLASES. Has title list with index.

DG3   Mackay, J. 1973. SOURCES OF INFORMATION FOR THE LITERATURE OF GEOLOGY: AN INTRODUCTORY GUIDE. London: Geological Society. 61 p.
         QE33 M34 PASR
         Introduction to the literature, brief guide to sources.

DG4   Ward, D.C., and M.W. Wheeler. 1981. GEOLOGIC REFERENCE SOURCES: A Subject and Regional Bibliography of Publications and Maps in the Geological Sciences. 3d ed. Metuchen, NJ: Scarecrow Press, 500 p.
         550 AW257 (1967)   Z6031 W3 PASR
         Introduction to the literature of the geosciences; materials at both introductory and advanced levels.

DG5   Wood, D.N. 1973. USE OF EARTH SCIENCES LITERATURE. Hamden, CT: Archon Books, 459 p.
         050.7 AW874U   Z6031 W67 PASR
         Guide to reference works, abstracting and indexing services, periodicals, for the field generally and its subdisciplines.

BIBLIOGRAPHIES

DG6   ARCTIC BIBLIOGRAPHY. (See AD97)
         Z6005 P7 A75 BMER

DG7   BIBLIOGRAPHY OF NORTH AMERICAN GEOLOGY, 1923-71. Washington: U.S. Geological Survey. annual.
         Z6034 A5U48 PASR
         Coverage continued by DG13. DG7 covers the North American continent, adjacent islands and American possessions. Arranged by author with subject index.

DG8   Bryan, M.L. 1979. REMOTE SENSING OF EARTH RESOURCES: A GUIDE TO INFORMATION SOURCES. Detroit: Gale Research. 188 p.
         Z6004 R3B79 ROBA
         Draws together literature from a wide range of disciplines. Includes technical reports, conference proceedings, published course notes as well as books and articles. Includes chap. on workshops and training courses.

DG9   CATALOGUE OF THE LIBRARY OF THE ARCTIC INSTITUTE OF NORTH AMERICA. (Montreal). 1968. 4 vols. Boston: G.K. Hall. SUPPLEMENT 1971, 1 vol.; 1974, 2 vols; 1980, 3 vols.
Z6005 P7 A7 ENGR; GEOL   Ryder GR1-115
   The Arctic Institute, fded 1945, and originally located in Montreal, became in 1979, a research institute at the Univ. of Calgary. This catalogue represents one of the largest collections devoted to polar regions, with particular strength in the Arctic, sub-Arctic regions. Main set describes the 9000 books, 20 000 pamphlets and reprints with 1200 periodical titles, and many analytic entries for periodical contents. Related titles are the ARCTIC BIBLIOGRAPHY (DG6; AD97) and ASTIS, 1979- (Arctic Science and Technology Information System, Univ. of Calgary) a bibliography available on microfiche annually.

DG10   GEOTITLES WEEKLY: GEOSCIENCE BIBLIOGRAPHY, 1969-   London: Geosystems, weekly.
Z6032 G37 PASR
   A comprehensive weekly classified international subject bibliog. for all forms of geological literature. Indexes: serial source, author, locational, geographical, stratigraphical. Cum index available on microfiche as GEOTITLES REPERTORIUM, 1969- . DG10 available online as GeoArchive.

DG11   INDEX TO THE PUBLICATIONS OF THE GEOLOGICAL SURVEY OF CANADA, 1970- Ottawa: CGPC, Supply and Services [for the Geological Survey]. annual. CUMULATION 1959-1974 (1975); 1975-1979 (1980).
R015.71 C21GD   Z6034 C19A4, A4112   Ryder SC6-11A,B,C
   Lists publications by type (memoirs, bulletins, papers, maps, etc) and then chronologically. Includes a finding list by area (Canada, provinces, territories, NTS quadrants) and author index. There is a retrospective vol. INDEX TO THE PUBLICATIONS OF THE GEOLOGICAL SURVEY OF CANADA, 1845-1958 (1961, Queen's Printer, 378 p.).

ABSTRACTS AND INDEXES

DG12   ABSTRACTS OF NORTH AMERICAN GEOLOGY, 1966-71. Washington: GPO [for the U.S. Geological Survey]
QE71 U6 PASR
   Continued by DG13. Abstracts from covers books, technical papers on the geology of North America, Greenland, the West Indies and U.S. island possessions.

DG13   BIBLIOGRAPHY AND INDEX OF GEOLOGY, vol. 32- , 1968-   Boulder, CO: Geological Society of America. monthly.
Z60333 G4 PASR
   Supersedes BIBLIOGRAPHY AND INDEX OF GEOLOGY EXCLUSIVE OF NORTH AMERICA, vol. 1-31, 1933-67. Abstracts earth science literature of the world in books, serials, reports, maps and North American theses. Arranged by subject fields; subject and author indexes. From 1977, only the indexes cumulate. Available online via GEOREF.

DG14   CURRENT CONTENTS: PHYSICAL, CHEMICAL AND EARTH SCIENCES, 1961-   weekly. (See DA16)

DG15　　　GEOPHYSICAL ABSTRACTS, 1929-71. Washington: GPO.
　　　　　　　　　　　　QE500 U5 PASR
　　　International literature pertaining to the physics of the solid earth and to geophysical exploration.

DG16　　　GEOPHYSICAL ABSTRACTS, 1977-　Norwich, Eng.: GEO Abstracts, Univ. of East Anglia. 7 parts, 6 issues a year.
　　　　　　　　　　　　QE500 G35　PASR; G1 G3252
　　　Supersedes GEOMORPHOLOGICAL ABSTRACTS, 1960-76. The separately available parts in GA are: A: LANDFORMS AND THE QUATERNARY; B: CLIMATOLOGY AND HYDROLOGY; C: ECONOMIC GEOGRAPHY; D: SOCIAL AND HISTORICAL GEOGRAPHY; E: SEDIMENTOLOGY; F: REGIONAL AND COMMUNITY PLANNING; G; REMOTE SENSING, PHOTOGRAMMETRY & CARTOGRAPHY. Fills the gap left by cessation of DG15, and widens the coverage. Annual indexes, and cumulative indexes to bring all parts, plus related ECOLOGICAL ABSTRACTS, to 1980 in preparation.

DG17　　　MINERALOGICAL ABSTRACTS, 1920-　London: Mineralogical Society of Great Britain and Mineralogical Society of America. quarterly.
　　　　　　　　　　　　QE351 M54 PASR
　　　Covers mineralogy, geochemistry, meteorites, petrology etc, in a subject arrangement with author index.

DG18　　　OCEANIC ABSTRACTS, 1964-　Lousiville, KY: Data Courier. bimonthly.
　　　　　　　　　　　　Z6004 P6025
　　　Includes geology, pollution, fisheries, shipping etc. Covers all types of literature on all aspects of the ocean. Available online.

DG19　　　WATER RESOURCES ABSTRACTS, 1968-　Urbana, IL: American Water Resources Association. monthly. looseleaf.
　　　　　　　　　　　　HD1691 W18 PASR
　　　Indicative abstracts covering all aspects of water resources.

REVIEWS AND ANNUALS

DG20　　　ADVANCES IN GEOLOGY, 1965-　New York: Academic Press, irreg.
　　　　　　　　　　　　QC801 A283 GEOL
　　　Lengthy surveys, with bibliographies, by experts in the field.

DG21　　　CANADIAN MINERALS YEARBOOK, 1901-　Ottawa: Dept of Energy, Mines and Resources, 1962-　annual.
　　　　　　　　　　　　TN26 A342 ENGI　　　　　　Ryder SC6-24
　　　Title, publisher varies. Statistics, developments in the industry.

DG22　　　EARTH SCIENCE REVIEWS,1966-　Amsterdam: Elsevier. quarterly.
　　　　　　　　　　　　QE1 E14 GEOL
　　　International in scope, this serial includes reviews of new books, forthcoming events and recent journal contents of interest.

DG23　　　INTERNATIONAL GEOLOGY REVIEW, 1959-　Washington: American Geological Institute. annual.
　　　　　　　　　　　　QE1 I577 GEOL
　　　English translations of important articles, especially Russian, Chinese and Japanese, which are not readily available.

DG24   United States. Bureau of Mines. MINERALS YEARBOOK, 1932/33- Washington: GPO. annual.
                                TN23 U612 PASR
"A record of the performance of the world's mineral industry" for metals, minerals, fuels by type, mineral industries of the U.S. and other countries. A major statistical source.

ENCYCLOPEDIAS AND DICTIONARIES

DG25   A DICTIONARY OF EARTH SCIENCES. 1977. Comp. by S.E. Stiegler. London: Macmillan. 301 p.
                                QE5 D54 PASR
Concise definitions of terms for the non-specialist.

DG26   A DICTIONARY OF GEOLOGY. 1978. 5th ed. Comp. by J. Challinor. Cardiff: Univ. of Wales Press. 350 p.
      R550.3 C437D3 (1967)   QE5 C45 PASR
Contains some 1500 names and terms with many quotations.

DG27   A DICTIONARY OF MINING, MINERAL AND RELATED TERMS. 1968. Comp. and ed. by P.W. Thrush, and the Staff of the Bureau of Mines. Washington: GPO. 1269 p.
                                TN9 T5 PASR
Includes about 55 000 terms applying to metal and coal mining, quarrying, geology, metallurgy, ceramics, clays, glassmaking, mineralogy and general terminology.

DG28   'Encyclopedia of Earth Sciences' 1966- New York: Van Nostrand Reinhold. Series, occasional.
                              PASR (various nos)
Each vol., separately titled, covers a specialized aspect of earth sciences. Vol. 1: ENCYCLOPEDIA OF OCEANOGRAPHY (1966); 2: ... OF ATMOSPHERIC SCIENCES AND ASTROGEOLOGY (1967); 3: ... OF GEOMORPHOLOGY (1968); 4A: ... OF GEOCHEMISTRY AND ENVIRONMENTAL SCIENCES (1972); 6: ... OF SEDIMENTOLOGY (1978); 7: ... OF PALEONTOLOGY (1979); 8, Pt 1: ... OF WORLD REGIONAL GEOLOGY: WESTERN HEMISPHERE (1976); 12: ... OF SOIL SCIENCES (1979); 15: ... OF BEACHES AND COASTAL ENVIRONMENTS (1982); 48: ... OF MINERALOGY (1981) and so on.

DG29   McGRAW HILL ENCYCLOPEDIA OF THE GEOLOGICAL SCIENCES. 1978. Ed. by D.N. Lapedes. New York: McGraw Hill. 915 p.
                            QE5 M29 (1978) PASR
Articles, reprinted with additional material and updating, from the McGRAW HILL ENCYCLOPEDIA OF SCIENCE AND TECHNOLOGY (DA38). Covers geology, geophysics, geochemistry, oceanography and meteorology.

DG30   McGRAW HILL ENCYCLOPEDIA OF OCEAN AND ATMOSPHERIC SCIENCES. 1980. Ed. by S.P. Parker. New York: McGraw Hill. 580 p.
                              GC9 M32 (1979)
Articles, reprinted with additional material and updating, from the McGRAW HILL ENCYCLOPEDIA OF SCIENCE AND TECHNOLOGY (DA38). Covers geology, geophysics, geochemistry and related fields.

DG31   OCEAN AND MARINE DICTIONARY. 1979. Comp. by D.F. Tver. Ithaca, NY: Cornell Maritime Press. 388 p.
                              GC9 T86 GENR

DG32   THE OCEAN WORLD ENCYCLOPEDIA. 1980. Ed. by D.G. Groves, and L.M. Hunt. New York: McGraw Hill. 448 p.
GC9 G76 GENR
Nearly 500 articles; well illus. with drawings, halftones, maps.

DG33   STANDARD DICTIONARY OF METEORLOGICAL SCIENCES: ENGLISH/ FRENCH, FRENCH/ ENGLISH. 1971. Comp. By G.J. Proulx. Montreal: McGill/ Queen's Univ. Press. 307 p.
QC854 P7 PASR

DG34   VNR COLOR DICTIONARY OF MINERALS AND GEMSTONES. 1982. New York, Van Nostrand Reinhold. 159 p.
Intended for the collector who wishes to identify specimens; 1000+ minerals included with superb colour photos and clean concise text. Access to minerals is by name or by description.

HANDBOOKS

DG35   AUDUBON SOCIETY FIELD GUIDE TO NORTH AMERICAN ROCKS AND MINERALS. 1978. New York: Knopf. 850 p.
QE443 C45 PASR
Provides all revelant data necessary to identify each rock and mineral, including chemistry, descriptions, etc.; with col. plates.

DG36   CATALOGUE OF CANADIAN MINERALS. 1970. Comp. by R.J. Traill. Ottawa: Dept of Energy, Mines and Resources. 649 p. SUPPLEMENT 1974.
List of Canadian mineral resources in alphabetical order.

DG37   GEOLOGY AND ECONOMIC MINERALS OF CANADA. 1970. 2 vols. 5th ed. Ottawa: Geological Survey of Canada.
QE145 A43   Ryder SC6-8
Vol.1 contains concisely summarized factual data arranged by the major geologic regions of Canada; vol. 2 is a folio of complementary maps and charts including geological, tectonic, mineral deposits, glacial and other maps.

DG38   MANUAL OF MINERALOGY. 1977. 19th ed. Ed. by C.S. Hurlburt. New York: Wiley. 532 p.
QE372 D2
A textbook useful as a reference book. Subject, mineral indexes.

DIRECTORIES

DG39   Canadian Geoscience Council. CURRENT RESEARCH, 1978-   Ottawa: Geological Survey of Canada. annual.
QE185 A223 MAPL
Supersedes CURRENT RESEARCH IN THE GEOLOGICAL SCIENCES IN CANADA, 1950-77.

BIOLOGICAL SCIENCES

GUIDES AND BIBLIOGRAPHIES

DH1   ANIMAL IDENTIFICATION: A REFERENCE GUIDE. 1980. 3 vols. London: Natural History Section, British Museum. 1980.
QL351 A53 ROMU
    Lists primary sources leading to identification of any animal from any part of the world.

DH2   Bottle, R.T., and H.V. Wyatt. 1972. THE USE OF BIOLOGICAL LITERATURE. 2d ed. London: Butterworths. 379 p.
574 AB751   QH315 B67 BMER
    Deals with the primary and secondary source literature in general as well as the uses in specific disciplines; stresses practical use.

DH3   Davis, E. 1981. USING THE BIOLOGICAL LITERATURE: A PRACTICAL GUIDE. New York: M. Dekker. 276 p.
QH303 D39 BMER
    Based on a large university biology collection, this work intended for undergraduate biology students is useful to anyone searching biological literature. Covers broad subject fields in pure, not applied, biology.

DH4   Froton, J.S. 1982. A BIO-BIBLIOGRAPHY FOR THE HISTORY OF BIOCHEMICAL SCIENCES SINCE 1800. Philadelphia: American Philosophical Society. 885 p.
Z5524 B54 F68 BMER

DH5   Kerker, A.E., and H.T. Murphy. 1968. BIOLOGICAL AND BIOMEDICAL RESOURCE LITERATURE. Lafayette, IN: Purdue Univ. Press. 226 p.
R574 AK39B   Z5320 K4   BMER
    Emphasis on the major treatises and taxonomic tools. Elementary textbooks, popular and clinical medical works are excluded. In two main parts: materials of general interest; materials of special interest, by subject.

DH6   Smith, R.C., and W.M. Reid. 1980. GUIDE TO THE LITERATURE OF THE LIFE SCIENCES. 9th ed. Minneapolis, MN: Burgess. 223 p.
574 AS658 G8 (1972)   Z7991 S5 BMER
    A library guide covering the broad range of biological sciences dealing with the literature, including computer-based retrieval, and literature problems in the field.

ABSTRACTS AND INDEXES

DH7   AQUATIC SCIENCE AND FISHERIES ABSTRACTS, 1976-   London: Information Retrieval. monthly.
QH90 A64 ZOOL
    Reviews 3000+ journals on all aspects relating to fish.

DH8   BIOLOGICAL ABSTRACTS, 1926-   Philadelphia: Biosciences Information Service. semi-monthly; semi-annual cum index.
QH301 B37 BMER
Abstracts journals in the life sciences, by broad subjects with many sub-headings. Indexes in each issue for author, biosystem, generic, concept, permuted subject. Available online. (See also DH8)

DH9   BIOLOGICAL ABSTRACTS/RRM, 1980-   Philadelphia: Biosciences Information. Service. monthly
Z5321 B5 BMER
Supersedes BIORESEARCH INDEX. Acts as an index to research reports, reviews, meetings, not covered in DH8.

DH10   BIOLOGICAL AND AGRICULTURAL INDEX, 1916-   (See DJ10)

DH11   CURRENT CONTENTS: LIFE SCIENCES, 1958-   weekly. (See DA16)

DH12   INTERNATIONAL ABSTRACTS OF BIOLOGICAL SCIENCES, 1954-   Oxford: Pergamon Press. monthly.
QH301 I63 BMER
"Attempts to cover the more important papers in experimental biology." Abstracts arranged under broad subjects, with subdivisions. Monthly issues with author index; vols with subject, author index.

DH13   MICROBIOLOGY ABSTRACTS, 1965-   London: Information Retrieval. monthly.
QR1 I52 BMER
Issued in three sections: A: INDUSTRIAL AND APPLIED MICROBIOLOGY; B: BACTERIOLOGY; C: ALGOLOGY, MYCOLOGY AND PROTOZOOLOGY. About 20 000 abstracts annually.

DH14   ZOOLOGICAL RECORD, 1864-   London: Zoological Society of London. annual.
Z7991 Z8 BMER
Title varies. Cites the important literature in three parts, 20 sections. Eacg section covers one genus with contents list, author, subject and systematic index.

REVIEWS AND ANNUALS

DH15   ANNUAL REVIEW OF BIOCHEMISTRY, 1932-   Palo Alto, CA: Annual Reviews.
QP501 A7 BMES
Authoritative articles with lengthy bibliographies. Index of authors, subject cited.

DH16   BIOLOGICAL REVIEWS, 1923-   Cambridge: Cambridge Univ. Press. quarterly
QH1 B55 BMER
Comprehensive review of particular topics; extensive references.

DH17   THE BOTANICAL REVIEW, 1935-   New York: Botanical Gardens. quarterly.
QK1 B56 BOTA
Interprets botanical progress in long review articles.

DH18   INTERNATIONAL ZOO YEARBOOK, 1959-   London: Zoological Society.
QL76 I55 BMER
Reviews recent developments; directory of zoos and aquaria.

ENCYCLOPEDIAS AND DICTIONARIES

DH19   DICTIONARY OF BIOLOGY: ENGLISH/ GERMAN/ FRENCH/ SPANISH. 1976. Comp. by G. Haensch, and G. Haberkamp de Anton. New York: Elsevier. 483 p.
        QH302.5 H33 BMER
    Arranged by English term, then equivalents in other languages.

DH20   DICTIONARY OF ZOOLOGY. 3d ed. Ed. by A.W.A. Lefwich. London: Constable & Co. 478 p.
        QL9 L4 BMER

DH21   THE ENCYCLOPEDIA OF BIOLOGICAL SCIENCES. 1970. 2d ed. Ed. by P. Gray. New York: Van Nostrand Reinhold. 1027 p.
    R574.03 G781E2   QH13 G7 BMER
    Signed articles on many aspects of the biological sciences, biophysics and biochemistry. Articles vary in length depending on the topic, and most include short bibliographies. Subject index.

DH22   Grzimek, Bernhard. GRZIMEK'S ANIMAL LIFE ENCYCLOPEDIA. 1972-76. 13 vols. New York: Van Nostrand Reinhold.
        QL45 G813 BMER
    Arranged by animal groups. Covers evolution, physical descriptions, range, diet etc. in concise style. Animal name glossary appended in English, German, French and Russian.

DH23   HENDERSON'S DICTIONARY OF BIOLOGICAL TERMS. 1979. 9th ed. Ed. by I.F. Henderson, and D.W. Henderson. New York: Van Nostrand Reinhold. 510 p
        QH13 H4 BMER
    Identifies 22 000 terms. Useful appendices including table of classification of plant and animal kingdom.

DH24   ILLUSTRATED NATURAL HISTORY OF CANADA. 1971-74. Toronto: Natural Science of Canada. illus.
    R500.971 I29   Ryder SC10-6
    A treatment for lay people. Each separately titled vol. covers a different area of Canada or topic (e.g. THE GREAT LAKES, THE NATURE OF FISH) giving a scientific list of rocks, plants etc.; bibliogs.

HANDBOOKS

DH25   Altman, P.L. and D.S. Dittmer. 1972-74. BIOLOGICAL DATA BOOK. 2 vols. 2d ed. Washington: Federation of American Societies for Experimental Biology.
        QH310 A38 BMER
    A basic reference in biology, containing quantitative and descriptive tables, charts, diagrams. The Federation also publishes other specialized handbooks.

DH26   Banfield, W.F. 1977. THE MAMMALS OF CANADA. Toronto: Univ. of Toronto Press for the National Museum of Natural Sciences. 438 p.
        QL721 B34 BMER   Ryder SC10-1
    Covers 196 species of animals, excluding fossils, known to have occurred since historical times in Canada or its coastal waters.

DH27   CODE INTERNATIONAL DE NOMENCLATURE ZOOLOGIQUE/ INTERNATIONAL CODE OF ZOOLOGICAL NOMENCLATURE. 1961. London: International Trust for Zoology. 176 p.
QL353 I5 BMED
As ratified at the 15th International Congress of Zoology, London.

DH28   THE FLORA OF CANADA. 1978-79. 4 vols. By H.J. Scroggan. Ottawa: National Museums of Canada.
QK201 S39 GEOL; BMED; BOTA   Ryder SC4-8
Identifies 4153 species of ferns, flowering plants found in Canada

DH29   HANDBOOK OF BIOCHEMISTRY AND MOLECULAR BIOLOGY. 1976. 9 vols. 3d ed. Cleveland, OH: CRC Press.
QP514.2 H34 BMER
For the graduate student and research worker. The 3d ed. is an extensive revision. One of several handbooks published by CRC Press.

DH30   HANDBOOK OF FRESHWATER FISHERY BIOLOGY. 1969. 2 vols. Comp. and ed. by K.D. Carlander. Amers, IA: Iowa State Univ. Press.
QL625 C373

DH31   INTERNATIONAL CODE OF BOTANICAL NOMENCLATURE. 1972. Utrecht: Oosthoek. 426 p.
QK9 I67 BOTA
The standard regulations for the establishment of botanical names as ratified at the 11th International Botanical Congress, Seattle. Text in English, French and German.

DH32   STATISTICAL TABLES FOR BIOLOGICAL, AGRICULTURAL AND MEDICAL RESEARCH. 1974. Comp. By R.A. Fisher, and F. Yates. 6th ed. rev. and enl. New York: Hafner. 146 p.
HA33 F53 (1963) ZOOL
Comprehensive collection of tables, with usefulness of each table explained. Bibliography on statistical methods appended. A standard statistical reference of wide applicability in scientific research.

DH33   UFAW HANDBOOK ON THE CARE AND MAINTENANCE OF LABORATORY ANIMALS. 1976. 5th ed. Comp. by the Universities Federations for Animal Welfare. London: Churchill Investigations. 635 p.
QL55 U65 BMED
Describes procedures for humane treatment of laboratory animals.

DH34   SYNOPSIS AND CLASSIFICATION OF LIVING ORGANISMS. 1982. 2 vols. Ed. by S.P. Parker. New York: McGraw Hill.
QH83 S78 BMED; ROMU
Compendium showing systematic positions of all living organisms, down to the family level. Includes 8300 brief articles arranged in taxonomic order with reference to the literature; 170 contributors from 12 countries writing in semi-technical language.

DIRECTORIES

DH35   Botvin, B. SURVEY OF CANADIAN HERBARIA. 1980. Quebec: Laval Univ. 187 p.
QK76 C2 B65 BMED
Brief description of 410 public and private herbaria; of which 160 are no longer in existence.

DH36　　INDEX HERBORIORUM: Guide to the Location and Contents of the World's Public Herbaria. 1964. 5th ed. Ed. by J. Lanjouw. Utrecht: International Association for Plant Taxonomy.
　　　　　　　　　　QK75 L32 (1964) BMER
　　　　Dated but still useful for its 7000 herbaria, 20 000 collectors.

DH37　　NATURALISTS DIRECTORY INTERNATIONAL, 1878-　　South Orange, NJ: PCL Publications. annual.
　　　　　　　　　　QH35 N3 BMES
　　　　Professional, amateur naturalists listed geographically with name, address, subject of interest. Also lists museums, societies, serials.

HEALTH SCIENCES

GUIDES AND BIBLIOGRAPHIES

DI1 Basler, D.K., and T.G. Basler. 1977. HEALTH SCIENCE LIBRARIANSHIP: A GUIDE TO INFORMATION SOURCES. Detroit: Gale Research. 186 p.
026.61 AB15H   Z675 M4B33 BMER

DI2 Blake, J.B., and C. Roos. 1967. MEDICAL REFERENCE WORKS, 1679-1966: A SELECTED BIBLIOGRAPHY. Chicago: Medical Library Association. 343 p. SUPPLEMENT(s), 1970-
610.AM48B63   Z6658 B63 BMER
Bibliography, based on the holdings of the U.S. National Library of Medicine, is arranged subject, then by type of work. Indexes: author, subject, title. Suppl. is corrections, additions to main vol.

DI3 Chen, C-C. 1977. THE SOURCEBOOK ON HEALTH SCIENCES LIBRARIANSHIP. Metuchen, NJ: Scarecrow Press. 307 p.
R610 AC518S   Z675 M4C47 BMER

DI4 HANDBOOK OF MEDICAL LIBRARY PRACTICE. 1982. 4th ed. Chicago: Medical Library Association.
026.61 M48H3   Z675 M4H33 (1982) BMER

DI5 MEDICAL BOOKS AND SERIALS IN PRINT, 1978- 2 vols. New York: R.R. Bowker. annual.
                       Z6658 M42 BMER
Author, title, subject indexes to i.p. titles. Lists appr. 9000 serials, 50 000 books, texts, etc. Covers all fields of medicine, health care, nutrition etc. including veterinary medicine.

DI6 Morton, L.T. 1983. A MEDICAL BIBLIOGRAPHY: An Annotated Check-list of Texts Illustrating the History of Medicine. 4th ed. Aldershot, Eng.: Gower. 1000 p.
R610 AG242M3   Z6658 G243 (1983) BMER
(1st ed., 1943). Earlier editions, GARRISON AND MORTON'S MEDICAL BIBLIOGRAPHY ... Important contributions to medical literature, (e.g., biography, bibliography, lexicography). Personal name, subject index.

DI7 _____. 1977. USE OF MEDICAL LITERATURE. 2d ed. London: Butterworths. 462 p.
610 M889 U2   R118 M67 BMER
"Attempts to provide a comprehensive guide" to general medical information plus specialized topics.

DI8 National Library of Medicine. [United States]. CURRENT CATALOG, 1966- Bethesda, MD: National Library of Medicine. quarterly; annual, quinquennial cumulation.
                       Z6676 U486 BMER
Supersedes NLM CATALOG. All items (except audio-visual) received at the NLM. Subject and name sections. Weekly proof sheets of NLM cataloguing issued by the Medical Library Association.

DI9 Roper, F. 1980. AN INTRODUCTION TO REFERENCE SOURCES IN THE HEALTH SCIENCES. Chicago: Medical Library Association, 252 p.
R026.61 F784I   Z6658 R66 BMER

ABSTRACTS AND INDEXES

DI10   CONFERENCE PROCEEDINGS IN THE HEALTH SCIENCES, 1969-   Ottawa: Canada Institute for Scientific and Technical Information.
        Z6658 C6 BMER

DI11   CUMULATIVE INDEX TO NURSING & ALLIED HEALTH LITERATURE (CINAHL), 1983- Glendale, CA: CINAHL. bimonthly, annual cumulation.
        With newsletter; uses NLM's subject headings for journals in nursing, some allied fields (e.g. administration) and selected items from INDEX MEDICUS (DI14) and from the popular media on health issues.

DI12   CURRENT CONTENTS: CLINICAL PRACTICE, 1973-   weekly. (See DA16)
        BMER

DI13   EXCERPTA MEDICA, 1947-   Amsterdam: Excerpta Medica Foundation. monthly; monthly, annual cum. index.
        R100 E895 BMER
        International abstracting service for medical, related literature. Issued by subject in separately published sections. Author, subject indexes. Available online.

DI14   INDEX MEDICUS: Including Bibliography of Medical Reviews, 1960- Bethesda, MD: monthly, annual; annual cum. index.
        Z6660 I42 BMER
        Index to some 2250 biomedical journals and selected monographs. Each issue has "Bibliography of Medical Reviews" (subject, author section); "Index Medicus" (subject, author section); both separately available in the annual cumulations. Other NLM publications include ABRIDGED INDEX MEDICUS, covering some 100 English language journals, and recurring subject bibliographies derived from the IM database. Available online as MEDLINE, part of the MEDLARS system.
        For assistance in locating journal holdings, the union list CANADIAN LOCATIONS OF JOURNALS INDEXED FOR MEDLINE/ DEPOTS CANADIENS DES REVUES INDEXEES POUR MEDLINE, (1979, 9th ed., CISTI) (Z6660 C52 BMER) should be consulted.

REVIEWS AND ANNUALS

DI15   National Library of Medicine. [United States]. BIBLIOGRAPHY OF MEDICAL REVIEWS, 1955-   Bethesda, MD: National Library of Medicine.
        Z6658 U52 BMER

DI16   'Annual Review' Series, 1950-   Palo Alto, CA: Annual Reviews.
        BMES
        In depth reviews, with extensive bibliographies, in over 20 subject areas.

DI17   'Yearbook' Series, 1901-   Chicago: Year Book Medical Publishers. annual.
        BMES
        Issued in over 20 separate series for various medical fields. Informative abstracts of important medical works reported in the literature. Subject, author indexes.

ENCYCLOPEDIAS AND DICTIONARIES

DI18 THE A TO Z OF WOMEN'S HEALTH: A CONCISE ENCYCLOPEDIA. 1983. Ed. by C. Ammer. New York: Facts on File. 481 p.
Cross references and subject index aid in using this encyclopedia, of some 900 short entries, covering principal diseases, health maintenance, sexual behaviour, other subjects related to women.

DI19 BLAKISTON'S GOULD MEDICAL DICTIONARY. 1979. 4th ed. New York: McGraw Hill. 1632 p.
R121 B62 (1979) BMER
Comprehensive standard dictionary.

DI20 BUTTERWORTHS' MEDICAL DICTIONARY. 1978. 2d ed. London: Butterworths. 1942 p.
R121 B87 (1978) BMER

(1st ed}, 1961, BRITISH MEDICAL DICTIONARY) A standard dictionary.

DI21 DORLAND'S ILLUSTRATED MEDICAL DICTIONARY. 1981. 26th ed. Philadelphia: W.B. Saunders. various paging.
R121 D73 (1981) BMER
Standard; the 25th ed. was extensively revised. Used by NLM for preparation of INDEX MEDICUS (DI14).

DI22 MELLONI'S ILLUSTRATED MEDICAL DICTIONARY. 1979. I. Dox, ed. Baltimore: Williams & Wilkins. 530 p.
R121 D76 (1979) BMER

DI23 ELSEVIER'S MEDICAL DICTIONARY IN FIVE LANGUAGES: ENGLISH, FRENCH, ITALIAN, SPANISH AND GERMAN. 1975. 2d rev. ed. Amsterdam: Elsevier. 1452 p.
R121 E45 (1975) BMER

DI24 DICTIONNAIRE ANGLAIS FRANCAIS DES SCIENCES MEDICALES/ ENGLISH FRENCH DICTIONARY OF MEDICAL AND PARAMEDICAL SCIENCES. 1978. Comp. by W.J. Gladstone. St Hyacinthe, Que.: Edisem. 1153 p.
R121 G52 BMER

DI25 Magalini, S., and E. Scrascia. 1981. DICTIONARY OF MEDICAL SYNDROMES. 2d ed. Philadelphia: Lippincott. 944 p.
RC69 M35 (1981) BMER

DI26 Miller, B.F., and C.B. Keane. 1978. ENCYCLOPEDIA AND DICTIONARY OF MEDICINE, NURSING AND ALLIED HEALTH. 2d ed. Philadelphia: Saunders. 1148 p.
R121 M65 (1978) BMER

DI27 STEDMAN'S MEDICAL DICTIONARY. 1982. 24th ed. Baltimore, MD: Williams & Wilkins. 1678 p.
R121 S8 (1982) BMER
A standard reference.

DI28 White, W.F. 1977. LANGUAGE OF THE HEALTH SCIENCES: A Lexical Guide to Word Parts, Word Roots and Their Meanings. New York: Wiley, 193 p.
R123 W43 BMER

HANDBOOKS

DI29   AMERICAN DRUG INDEX. 1980. Philadelphia: Lippincott. 730 p.
RS356 A53 (1980) BMER
A standard, list of drugs, including generic brand, U.S.P., N.F. and chemical names.

DI30   CANADIAN DRUG IDENTIFICATION CODE/ CODE CANADIEN D'IDENTIFICATION DES DROGUES, 1974-   Ottawa: Health and Welfare. irreg.
RS 6 C35 BMER

DI31   CANADIAN ENCYCLOPEDIA OF DRUG THERAPY. 1981. Pointe Claire, Que.: STA Communications. 800 p.
RS356 C35 BMER

DI32   COMPENDIUM OF PHARMACEUTICALS AND SPECIALITIES (CPS), 1960-   Toronto: Canadian Pharmaceutical Association.
RS141.23 C62 BMER
(CPS, 17th ed. 1982, 800 p.) Information on appr. 3000 drug products; medications with indications, contra indications, precautions, adverse effects, overdose symptoms, treatments, dosage and suppliers. With product recognition charts in col.

DI33   HANDBOOK OF NON PRESCRIPTION DRUGS. 1982. 7th ed. Washington: American Pharmaceutical Association. 682 p.
RM671 A1H35 (1982) BMER

DI34   MERCK INDEX: AN ENCYCLOPEDIA OF CHEMICALS AND DRUGS. 1976. 9th ed. Rahway, NJ: Merck & Co. 1952 p.
RS356 M524 (1956) BMER
Includes some 10 000 descriptions of individual substances, 8000 structural displays, over 50 000 synonyms of chemicals, drugs. Mostly includes only single substances; cross index of names; formula index.

DI35   PHYSICIANS DESK REFERENCE. 1979. 33d ed. Oradell, NJ: Medical Economics 2047 p.
RS75 P5 (1979) BMER
A similar title, but one with information suitable for lay persons, is THE PHYSICIAN'S DRUG MANUAL: PRESCRIPTION AND NONPRESCRIPTION DRUGS (1981, Doubleday). THE ESSENTIAL GUIDE TO NONPRESCRIPTION DRUGS (1983, Harper) reviews the active ingredients and the therapeutic claims of preparations in a manner also suitable for lay interest. These titles complement handbooks intended for professional or technical users.

DIRECTORIES

DI36   MEDICAL AND HEALTH INFORMATION DIRECTORY. 1980. 2d ed. Ed. by A. Kruzas. Detroit: Gale Research. 835 p.
R118.4 U6M4 (1980) BMER
Subtitled: "A Guide to State, National and International Organizations, Government Agencies, Educational Institutions, Hospitals, Grant-awarded Sources, Health Care Delivery Agencies, Journals, Newsletters, Review Serials, Abstracting Services, Publishers, Research Centers, Computerized Data Banks, Audio-visual Services, and Libraries and Information Centers."

DI37   AMERICAN MEDICAL DIRECTORY, 1906-   Chicago: American Medical Association. biennial.
        R712 A1A6 BMER
    Lists physicians alphabetically; and with hospitals geographically

DI38   CANADIAN HOSPITAL DIRECTORY, 1953-   Toronto: Canadian Hospital Association. annual.
        RA977 C33 BMER
    Information on hospitals, nursing homes, associations, educational programs, etc. Buyers' guide for supplies and equipment.

DI39   CANADIAN MEDICAL DIRECTORY, 1955-   Toronto: Seccombe House. annual.
        R713.01 C3 BMER
    Lists physicians alphabetically, geographically; information on medical, nursing schools, associations and societies.

DI40   ENCYCLOPEDIA OF MEDICAL ORGANIZATIONS AND AGENCIES. 1983. Comp. and ed. by A.T. Kruzas. Detroit: Gale Research. 780 p.
    Heavily American in orientation. Concentrates on international, national, state associations, agencies, schools; foundations, funding agencies and information, database services. Updates, duplicates related directory DI36.

AGRICULTURAL SCIENCES

GUIDES AND BIBLIOGRAPHIES

DJ1 BIBLIOGRAPHY OF AGRICULTURE, 1942- Phoenix, AZ: Oryx Press. monthly.
Z5071 U52 BMER
CUMULATION 1970-78, on microfiche. Indexes the pertinent items in the U.S. National Agricultural Library. Entries are by title under broad subjects, with separate lists of new govt publications (federal, state, FAO) and translations. Each issue has geographic, personal/corporate author, subject indexes. Available online as AGRICOLA.

DJ2 Bush, E.A.R. 1974. AGRICULTURE: A BIBLIOGRAPHIC GUIDE. 2 vols. London: Macdonald.
Z5071 B87 BMER
Annotated guide to 9400 general and specialized bibliographies; most imprints are between 1958 and 1971.

DJ3 GUIDE TO SOURCES FOR AGRICULTURAL AND BIOLOGICAL RESEARCH. 1981. Ed. by J.R. Blanchard, and L. Farrel. Berkeley, CA: Univ. of California Press. 735 p.
Z5071 G83 BMER
Literature from 1958-1979 on food production, wildlife management, agricultural implications of pollution control, maintenance of the environment. Updates LITERATURE OF AGRICULTURAL RESEARCH (1958).

DJ4 FOOD SCIENCE AND TECHNOLOGY: A BIBLIOGRAPHY OF RECOMMENDED MATERIALS. 1978. Beltsville, MD: National Agriculture Library. 231 p.
R664 AF686F
Prep. by the National Agriculture Library and SLA's Food and Nutrition Division. Lists item useful in building basic collections in 14 areas of food science.

DJ5 INFORMATION SOURCES IN AGRICULTURE AND FOOD SCIENCE. 1981. Ed. by G.P. Lilley. London: Butterworths. 618 p.
Mostly British resources, in 2 pts. General sources, databases, maps as sources, statistics, libraries and their uses. Specialized areas like agri-engineering, herbicides, husbandry, agrarian history.

DJ6 National Agricultural Library. [United States]. CATALOG, 1966- Totawa, NJ: Rowman & Littlefield. monthly; semi-annual, annual cum. index.
Z5076 U5 BMER
Supplements the DICTIONARY CATALOG OF THE NATIONAL AGRICULTURAL LIBRARY (DJ17). Entries arranged by broad subjects; indexes for specific subjects, personal and corporate authors, titles.

DJ7 _____. DICTIONARY CATALOG OF THE NATIONAL AGRICULTURAL LIBRARY, 1862-1965. 1967-70. 73 vols. New York: Rowman & Littlefield.
Z881 U4D5
About a million entries; author/ title/ subjects for monographs, serials, analytics in this major collection.

DJ8 PUBLICATIONS OF THE CANADIAN DEPT OF AGRICULTURE, 1867-1974. 1975. 2d rev. ed. Ottawa: Dept of Agriculture. 341, 136 p.
R015.71 C212P2   Z5075 C2C32 BMER
English and French publications listed, indexed separately.

ABSTRACTS AND INDEXES

DJ9   AGRINDEX, 1975-   Rome: Food and Agriculture Organization, United Nations. monthly. (Dist.: UNIPUB).
Z5073 A456 BMER
Produced from AGRIS, the international information system for the agricultural sciences and technology, with references to current international research and development literature relevant to food, agriculture and allied fields. Classified subject order; indexes for personal and corporate authors, commodities, report and patent nos. Available online to participating governments, organizations.

DJ10   BIOLOGICAL & AGRICULTURAL INDEX, 1916-   New York: H.W. Wilson. monthly (except Aug.); cumulates.
Z5073 A452 BMER
Subject index to ca 150 general American, Canadian, Commonwealth journals biology, agriculture and related sciences. No author index.

DJ11   CAB ABSTRACTS. Farnham, Eng.: Commonwealth Agricultural Bureaux.
BMER (various call nos)
CAB publishes 25 abstract journals (e.g.: REVIEW OF PATHOLOGY, VETERINARY BULLETIN, DAIRY SCIENCE ABSTRACTS, NUTRITION ABSTRACTS, AGRICULTURE ENGINEERING ABSTRACTS, SOILS AND FERTILIZERS) covering international literature. Appr. 125 000 items from some 8500 journals abstracted annually. Available online as CAB ABSTRACTS.

DJ12   CURRENT CONTENTS: AGRICULTURE, BIOLOGY AND ENVIRONMENTAL SCIENCES, 1961- weekly. (See DA16).
BMER

DJ13   FARM AND GARDEN INDEX, 1978-   Mankato, MN: Minnesota Scholarly Press. quarterly
Thorough coverage of appr. 120 periodicals in relevant area.

DIRECTORIES

DJ14   NORTH AMERICAN HORTICULTURE: A REFERENCE GUIDE. 1982. New York: Scribner's [with coop. American Horticultural Society]. 362 p.
Directory of horticulture organizations, societies, clubs, provincial and state associations. Also covers nomenclature, registration authorities, educational programs, herbaria, arboreta, major flower shows, and world records for vegetables, fruits, flowers.

ANNUALS AND REVIEWS

DJ15   ADVANCES IN AGRONOMY, 1949-   New York: Academic Press. annual
Z405 A24 BOTA
Prepared under the auspices of the American Society of Agronomy.

DJ16   ADVANCES IN FOOD RESEARCH, 1948-   New York: Academic Press. irreg.
TX537 A25 HYGI
Critical review with bibliographies, at the professional level.

ENCYCLOPEDIAS AND DICTIONARIES

DJ17   BLACK'S VETERINARY DICTIONARY. 1975. Comp. by G.P. West. 11th ed. London: A. & C. Black. 853 p.
        SF609 M5 BMER
    A standard dictionary for all areas of veterinary practice.

DJ18   DICTIONARY OF AGRICULTURE: German/ English/ French/ Spanish/ Russian/ 1975. Ed. by G. Haensch, and G.H. Kamp de Anton. 4th ed. New York: Elsevier Scientific. 999 p.
        S411 H34 BMER

DJ19   THE DICTIONARY OF HOUSE PLANTS. 1974. Comp. by R. Hay, and others. New York: McGraw Hill in coop. with the Royal Horticultural Society.
        SB419 D53 BMER
    Lists plants, by scientific name with reference from popular name. Description, growing information. Col. plates for 506 plants.

DJ20   THE ENCYCLOPEDIA OF MARINE RESOURCES. 1969. Comp. by F.E. Firth. New York: Van Nostrand Reinhold. 740 p.
        SH201 F56 BMER
    Covers the "most significant aspects of the ocean's resources with summaries of a few closely related topics."

DJ21   WORLD FOOD BOOK. 1981. Comp. by D. Crabbe, and S. Lawson. New York: Nichols. 240 p.
        HD9000.5 W567 (1981) ROBA
    Encyclopedic coverage of subjects concerned with production, processing, distribution, consumption of food.

HANDBOOKS AND DICTIONARIES

DJ22   CRC HANDBOOKS OF FOOD ADDITIVES. 1979. 2 vols. 2d ed. Cleveland, OH: Chemical Rubber Co.
        TX553 A3C2
    Information on properties, uses of direct food additives. In 2 pts: 1: introd. to additives in broad areas; 2: U.S. regulatory status of additives with summaries about the use of frequently employed ones.

DJ23   Clayton, J.S. 1977. SOILS OF CANADA. 2 vols. Ottawa: Research Branch, Dept of Agriculture.
        S599 1 A1S6 BMED   Ryder SC2-1C
    A report with glossary and maps.

DJ24   A GEOGRAPHIC ATLAS OF WORLD WEEDS. 1979. New York: Wiley Interscience. 391 p.
        SB611 G38 BMED
    Not an atlas; but a checklist of 7000 weed species.

DJ25   HORTUS THIRD: A CONCISE DICTIONARY OF PLANTS CULTIVATED IN THE UNITED STATES AND CANADA. 1976. New York: Macmillan. 1290 p.
        SB45 B22 (1976) BOTA
    Describes propagation, care, use of all species and varieties.

DJ26   PESTICIDE INDEX. 1976. 5th ed. College Park, MD: Entomological Society of America. 328 p.
SB951 P487 BMES
Alphabetic list providing available information on pesticides.

DJ27   THE YEARBOOK OF AGRICULTURE, 1894- Washington: U.S. Dept of Agriculture.
S21 A35 BMES
Title varies. Not a review of the year. Each issue, with distinctive title, is devoted to a single topic.

DJ28   WESTCOTT'S PLANT DISEASE HANDBOOK. 1979. 4th ed. New York: Van Nostrand.
SB731 W47 (1979) SIGS
Covers diseases, garden chemical, classification of pathogens.

ATLASES

DJ29   ATLAS OF CANADIAN AGRICULTURE. 1979. Comp. By M.J. Troughton. London, Ont.: Dept of Geography, Univ. of Western Ontario. 104 p.
Ryder SC2-1
A portfolio of maps based on the 1971 Census of Agriculture.

ENVIRONMENTAL SCIENCES AND ENERGY RESOURCES

GUIDES AND BIBLIOGRAPHIES

DK1   Armstrong, J.M. 1980. CANADIAN ENERGY BIBLIOGRAPHY. Toronto: Ontario Library Association. 140 p.
         Z5853 P83 A75 ENGR   Ryder SC6-5
     Some 600 annotated entries.

DK2   Balachandran, S. 1980. ENERGY STATISTICS: A GUIDE TO INFORMATION SOURCES. Detroit: Gale Research. 272 p.
         Z5853 P83 B25 ENGR
     Detailed analyses of recurring statistical data in 40 serials, with other sources noted.

DK3   Clark, B.D.; R. Bisset, and P. Walthern. 1980. ENVIRONMENTAL IMPACT ASSESSMENTS: A BIBLIOGRAPHY WITH ABSTRACTS. New York: Mansell/ R.R. Bowker. 524 p.
         Z5863 I57 C47 BMER; ENGR
     For private developers, public agencies, and professionals.

DK4   SOURCEBOOK ON THE ENVIRONMENT: A GUIDE TO THE LITERATURE. 1978. Comp. by K. Hammond and others. Chicago: Univ. of Chicago. 613 p.
         Z5861 S66 BMER
     Goal is to provide, through 24 bibliographic essays with bibliographies, a broad guide to selected aspects of the literature.

ABSTRACTS AND INDEXES

DK5   ABSTRACTS ON HEALTH EFFECTS OF ENVIRONMENTAL POLLUTANTS, 1972- Philadelphia: Biosciences Information Service of Biological Abstracts. monthly.
         RA565 A126 BMER
     Material of interest to health related environmental pollution research. Indexes: concept, author, biosystematic, generic, subject.

DK6   AIR POLLUTION ABSTRACTS, 1970- Research Triangle Park, NC: Air Pollution Technical Information Center. monthly.
         Z6673 A35 PASR

DK7   CURRENT CONTENTS: AGRICULTURE, BIOLOGY AND ENVIRONMENTAL SCIENCES, 1961- weekly. (See DA16)
         BMER

DK8   ENERGY ABSTRACTS, 1974- New York: Engineering Index. monthly.
         TJ163.2 E54 ENGR
     Multidisciplinary service which includes records from ENGINEERING INDEX and other databases.

DK9   ENERGY INFORMATION ABSTRACTS, 1976- New York: Environment Information Center. monthly; annual cum index: THE ENERGY INDEX, 1973-
         HD9502 A1E6 ENGR
     Covers reports, conference papers, government documents, 10000 journals. Available online as ENERGLINE.

DK10   ENVIRONMENT ABSTRACTS, 1971-   New York: Environment Information Center. monthly; annual cum. index, ENVIRONMENT INDEX.
Z5862 E59 PASR
Covers reports, conference papers, government documents, journals, legislation, research by broad subjects. Indexes: subject, author, industry. Available online as ENVIROLINE.

DK11   POLLUTION ABSTRACTS, 1970-   Louisville, KY: Data Courier. bimonthly.
TD180 P75 PASR
Surveys worldwide technical literature on the environment. Entries arranged by subject with keyword, author indexes. Available online.

DK12   SOLAR ENERGY INDEX, 1980-   Comp. by the Arizona State Univ. Library. Elmsford, NY: Pergamon Press.
Z5853 S63 A74 ENGR

DK13   WATDOC, 1972-   Ottawa: Environment Canada. online; no print version.
Journals, reports, conference proceedings, and international items selected by Environment Canada staff.

ENCYCLOPEDIAS

DK14   ENCYCLOPEDIA OF ENVIRONMENTAL SCIENCES AND ENGINEERING. 1976. 2 vols. Ed. by J.R. Pfafflin, and E.N. Ziegler. New York: Gordon and Breech.
TD9 E5 ENGR
Overview of environmental areas and related engineering practice.

DK15   McGRAW HILL ENCYCLOPEDIA OF ENERGY. 1981. 2d ed. New York: McGraw Hill. 838 p. illus.
R020.257 L697L (1976 ed.) TJ163.2 M3 (1981) ENGR
Over 300 signed articles with brief bibliographies. Material taken from the McGRAW HILL ENCYCLOPEDIA OF SCIENCE AND TECHNOLOGY (DA38) with additions.

DK16   McGRAW HILL ENCYCLOPEDIA OF ENVIRONMENTAL SCIENCE. 1980. 2d ed. New York: McGraw Hill. 858 p. illus.
QH540.4 M24 PASR
Updated, expanded by specialists; the 250 articles reflect trends, technology at the level of non-specialist.

DK17   THE WORLD ENERGY BOOK: AN A-Z ATLAS AND STATISTICAL SOURCE BOOK. 1978. Ed. by D. Crabbe, and R. McBride. New York: Nichols. 258 p.
HD9502 A2W669 ENGR
An encyclopedic coverage of global energy sources.

DICTIONARIES

DK18   A DICTIONARY OF THE ENVIRONMENT. 1977. Comp. by M. Allaby. New York: Van Nostrand Reinhold. 532 p.
QH540.4 A44 BMED
Explains 6000 words, phrases from all environmental disciplines.

DK19   ENERGY DICTIONARY. 1979. Comp. by D.V. Hunt. New York: Van Nostrand Reinhold. 518 p.
                    TJ163.2 H85 ENGR
      Authoritative, concise entries for terms in broad field of energy.

DK20   SOLAR ENERGY DICTIONARY. 1982. Comp. By D.V. Hunt. New York: Industrial Press, 1982. 411 p.
                    TJ810 H86 ENGR
      Broad scope covers biomass, ocean energy, hydro-electric power in addition to solar energy.

HANDBOOKS

DK21   HANDBOOK OF ENVIRONMENTAL CONTROL. 1973-78. 6 vols. Cleveland, OH: CRC Press.
                    TD145 C2 ENGR
      Covers air pollution, solid waste, water supply, waste treatment, hospital and health care in separate vols.

DK22   CANADA WATER YEAR BOOK, 1975-   Ottawa: Dept of the Environment. irreg.
                    GN707 C354 BMER
      A series on the fresh water resources in Canada.

DK23   ENERGY HANDBOOK. 1978. Comp. by R.L. Loftness. New York: Van Nostrand Reinhold. 741 p.
                    TJ163.2 L63 ENGR
      Concise coverage of energy alternatives. Illus. with bibliogs.

DK24   INSTRUMENTATION FOR ENVIRONMENTAL MONITORING, 1972-   4 vols. Berkeley, CA: Lawrence Berkeley Laboratory, Univ. of California. looseleaf.
                    TD177 C3 PASR
      Vols arranged by type of control; include descriptions, evaluations of instruments and techniques.

DK25   TOXIC SUBSTANCES SOURCEBOOK. 1978. New York: Environment Information Center. 550 p.
                    T55.3 H3T6 BMER

DIRECTORIES

DK26   CANADIAN CONSERVATION DIRECTORY. 1978/79. 3d ed. Ottawa: Canadian Nature Federation. 86 p.
                S920 C3 PASR   Ryder SC7-1
      International, national, and provincial list of ca 400 agencies, groups in conservation, natural history, environment; 250 consultants.

DK27   CANADIAN ENERGY DIRECTORY. 1980. Comp. by W. Powell. Toronto: Ontario Library Association. 520 p.
                    HD9502 C32 C34 ENGR

DK28   CONSERVATION DIRECTORY, 1956- Washington: National Wildlife Federation. annual.
S430 C78 BMER
Lists organizations, agencies, officials concerned with natural resources. U.S. federal and state organizations; Canadian federal and provincial organizations and citizens' groups for both countries.

DK29   DIRECTORY OF CANADIAN ENVIRONMENTAL EXPERTS. 1980. Ottawa: Canada Institute for Scientific and Technical Information. 482 p.
TD178.7 C2N32 BMER

DK30   ENERGY: SOURCES OF PRINT AND NON-PRINT MATERIALS. 1980. By M. Crowley. New York: Neal Schuman Pub. 341 p.
HD9500 A2 C76 ROBA

DK31   ENVIRONMENT SOURCE BOOK: A Guide to Environmental Information in Canada. 1978. Ottawa: Supply and Services. 115 p.
R301.31 C212E   TD171.5 C2C22 BMER
A directory of organizations, agencies concerned with environment.

DK32   WORLD ENERGY DIRECTORY. 1981. London: Hodgson. 567 p.
TJ163.2 W675 ENGR
Companion to DK33. Guide to organizations, research in non-atomic energy. Some 200+ organizations in 80 countries listed, with projects.

DK33   WORLD NUCLEAR DIRECTORY. 1981. 6th ed. London: Hodgson.
QC770 W65 PASS
Companion to DK32. Guide to organizations, research in atomic energy. Some 2500 organizations in 90 countries listed.

ENGINEERING AND TECHNOLOGY

GUIDES

DL1   Mildren, K.W. 1976. USE OF ENGINEERING LITERATURE. London: Butterworths. 621 p.
       620 AM641U   Z5851 U73
       A guide to structure, organization of literature and to sources of information in the discipline as a whole and in its sub-divisions.

DL2   Mount, E. 1976. GUIDE TO BASIC INFORMATION SOURCES IN ENGINEERING. New York: John Wiley. 196 p.
       607 M928G   T10.7 M68 ENGI
       Brief annotations primarily for engineering students, researchers.

BIBLIOGRAPHIES

DL3   BIBLIOGRAPHIC GUIDE TO TECHNOLOGY, 1975-   Boston: G.K. Hall. annual.
                               Z7913 B5 ENGR
       Includes acquisitions of the Research Libraries of the New York Public Library, Library of Congress and Engineering Societies Library.

DL4   Engineering Societies. 1963. CLASSED SUBJECT CATALOG, ENGINEERING SOCIETIES LIBRARY. [New York]. 12 vols. Boston: G.K. Hall. Ten SUPPLEMENT(s) 1964-1973 (10 vols, 1965-1974).
       R017.1 E57   Z5854 N47 ENGR
       Additional supplements, 1974- , appear as BIBLIOGRAPHIC GUIDE TO TECHNOLOGY (DL3). The Engineering Societies Library is the largest engineering library in the U.S. It is an historic archive for engineering material as well as current resource. The catalogues monographs, pamphlets, serials, reports, films, govt publications, etc. The main set of this catalogue lists about 185 000 items. The index vol. is available separately.

DL5   _____. 1982. CLASSED SUBJECT CATALOG, ENGINEERING SOCIETIES LIBRARY. 2d ed. Rev. and updated. Boston. G.K. Hall. 22 microfilm reels.
       A cumulative ed., in one alphabet, of DL4 with revisions to reflect current terminology, new areas of engineering (e.g., energy, bioengineering, lasers, computer technology).

ABSTRACTS AND INDEXES

DL6   APPLIED SCIENCE & TECHNOLOGY INDEX, 1913-   New York: H.W. Wilson. monthly; cumulates.
       (PER)   Z7913 I7 ENGR
       Subject only index to over 200 periodicals from all fields.

DL7   COMPUTER AND CONTROL ABSTRACTS, 1966-   monthly; semi-annual cum. index
       (See DA21)
                               TJ212 C56 ENGR
       Covers some 30 000 items each year in a classified arrangement, with author, subject index. DL7 is "Series C" of SCIENCE ABSTRACTS, available online as INSPEC.

DL8   CURRENT CONTENTS: ENGINEERING, TECHNOLOGY AND APPLIED SCIENCES, 1961- weekly. (See DA16)
                         ENGR

DL9   CURRENT TECHNOLOGY INDEX, 1981-   London: Library Association, 1962- monthly; annual cumulation.
                         Z7913 B7 ENGR

     Supersedes BRITISH TECHNOLOGY INDEX, 1962-1980. A subject index to articles in over 350 technical journals in general technology, applied engineering, chemical technology, manufacturing. Author, catchword, trade name indexes.

DL10   ELECTRICAL AND ELECTRONICS ABSTRACTS, vol. 69- , 1966-   monthly, semi-annual cum. index. (See DA21)
                         TK1 E35 ENGR

     "Forms the world's major English language abstracting service (for) electrotechnology." Covers all aspects of the area; entries in a classified order with author, subject index. DL10 is "Series B" of SCIENCE ABSTRACTS; available online as INSPEC.

DL11   ENGINEERING INDEX, 1884-   New York: Engineering Index. monthly; annual cumulation.
                         Z5851 E62 ENGR

     EI is a "compilation of abstracts and items covering the world's significant technological literature and conferences encompassing all engineering disciplines." Subject arranged with subdivisions; author index. Available online as COMPENDEX.

DL12   SCIENTIFIC AND TECHNICAL AEROSPACE REPORTS, 1963-   Washington: NASA, Scientific and Technical Information Office. semi-monthly; cum index.
                         TL501 S3 PASR

     STAR covers the literature of space and aeronautics contained in technical reports commissioned by the U.S. and other national govts. Subject arrangement. Indexes: subjects, corporate and personal authors, contract and report nos. Companion publication, INTERNATIONAL AEROSPACE ABSTRACTS, 1961- , covers other forms of literature.

ANNUALS AND REVIEWS

DL13   ADVANCES IN APPLIED MECHANICS, 1948-   New York: Academic Press, irreg.

DL14   ADVANCES IN CHEMICAL ENGINEERING, 1956-   New York: Academic Press. irreg.
                         TP145 A4 ENGS

DL15   ADVANCES IN NUCLEAR SCIENCE AND TECHNOLOGY, 1962-   New York: Academic Press. biennial.
                         TK9001 A3 ENGS

     Reviews current topics in selected fields; of interest primarily to nuclear engineers.

DL16   PROGRESS IN AEROSPACE SCIENCES, 1961-   Oxford: Pergamon Press. annual.
                         TL500 P7 ENGS

     Title varies. Long, critical reviews of work in areas of recent substantial advance. Subject index; index of authors cited.

DL17   PROGRESS IN MATERIALS SCIENCE, 1949-   Oxford: Pergamon Press. annual.
      TN1 P7 ENGS

ENCYCLOPEDIAS AND DICTIONARIES

DL18   AVIATION AND SPACE DICTIONARY. 1980. 6th ed. Fallbrook, CA: Aero Publisher. 272 p.
      TL600 A85 (1980) ENGR
  For the non-specialist.

DL19   DICTIONARY OF PUBLIC TRANSPORT. 1982. Washington: Lea Transportation Reseach Corp.
      HE141 D5 ROBA
  Tri-lingual (English, French, German) dictionary of 2000 terms. Part 1 of a forthcoming INTERNATIONAL TRANSIT HANDBOOK AND COMPENDIUM sponsored by federal agencies in U.S., Canada and West Germany.

DL20   DICTIONARY OF SOIL MECHANICS AND FOUNDATION ENGINEERING. 1981. Ed. by J. Barker. London: Construction Press. 210 p.
      TP710 B37 ENGR

DL21   DICTIONARY OF TELECOMMUNICATIONS. 1981. Ed. by S.J. Aries. London: Butterworths. 329 p.
      TK5102 A74 ENGR
  For the non-specialist; short definitions, some brief essays.

DL22   DICTIONARY OF WASTE AND WATER TREATMENT. 1981. Ed. by J.S. Scott, and P. Smith. Woburn, MA: Butterworths. 359 p.
      TD791 S35 ENGR
  Some 6000 brief definitions of U.K., U.S. terminology.

DL23   ELSEVIER'S DICTIONARY OF CHEMICAL ENGINEERING IN SIX LANGUAGES. 1968. Amsterdam: Elsevier.
      TP9 E37 ENGR
  Arranged on an English language base, American spelling, with references from French, Spanish, Italian, Dutch, German.

DL24   ENCYCLOPEDIA OF CHEMICAL PROCESSING AND DESIGN, 1976-   New York: Marcel Dekker. In progress.
      TP9 E66 ENGR
  Comprehensive encyclopedia; complements the more theoretical KIRK OHMER (DF22). Emphasizes design of equipment, systems, controls used in chemical processing.

DL25   GLOSSARY OF MARINE TECHNOLOGY TERMS. 1980. London: Heinemann. 177 p.
      V23 G56 ENGR
  Some 1400 terms defined.

DL26   INTERNATIONAL DICTIONARY OF HEATING, VENTILATING AND AIR CONDITIONING. 1980. Documentation Committee, European Heating and Ventilating Associations. London: E. & FN Spon. 482 p.
      TH7007 I6 ENGR
  Specialized multilingual dictionary in 9 languages.

DL27   Jay, F. 1977. IEEE STANDARD DICTIONARY OF ELECTRICAL AND ELECTRONICS TERMS. 2d ed. New York: Institute of Electrical and Electronics Engineers. 882 p. (Dist.: Wiley Interscience).
TK9 1478 ENGR
Alphabetic list of words, phrases; reference to source of standardization.

HANDBOOKS AND STANDARDS

DL28   American Society for Testing and Materials. ANNUAL BOOK OF ASTM STANDARDS, 1939- Philadelphia: ASTM.
TA401 A653 ENGR
Voluntary standards for materials, products, systems, services. Each type or group is in a separate vol. Comprehensive indexes.

DL29   ASHRAE HANDBOOK AND PRODUCT DIRECTORY, 1972- 4 vols. New York: American Society of Heating, Refrigerating and Air Conditioning Engineers. annual.
TH7011 A4 ENGR
Four vols (APPLICATIONS; EQUIPMENT; SYSTEMS; FUNDAMENTALS) revised individually on a 4 year cycle. Each vol. has a handbook section and a product section which is updated annually.

DL30   ASM METALS REFERENCE BOOK: A Handbook of Data About Metals and Metal Working. 1983. Metals Park, OH: American Society for Metals.
TA459 A78 (1983) ENGR
Compendium of numerical and graphical data.

DL31   CRC COMPOSITE INDEX FOR CRC HANDBOOKS. 1977. 2d ed. Cleveland, OH: CRC Press. 1111 p.
QD65 C74 (1977) ENGR

DL32   CRC HANDBOOK OF MATERIALS SCIENCE. 1974-1980. 4 vols. Ed. by C.T. Lynch. Cleveland, OH: CRC Press.
TA403.4 L94 ENGR

DL33   ENCYCLOPEDIA OF INTEGRATED CIRCUITS: A PRACTICAL HANDBOOK OF ESSENTIAL REFERENCE DATA. 1981. Comp. by W, Buchsbaum. Englewood Cliffs, NJ: Prentice Hall. 420 p.
TK7874 B77

DL34   ENGINEERING FORMULAS. 1979. 3d ed. Ed. by K. Gieck. New York: McGraw Hill.
TA151 G4713 (1979) ENGR

DL35   HANDBOOK OF ENGINEERING FUNDAMENTALS. 1975. Ed. by O. Eshbach, and M. Souders. New York: J. Wiley. 1562 p.
TA151 E8 (1975) ENGI

DL36   HANDBOOK OF STEEL CONSTRUCTION. 1980. Willowdale, Ont.: Canadian Institute of Steel Construction.
TA684 C25 (1980) ENGR
Concise source of design properties for structural shapes produced in Canada, in SI units.

DL37   KEMPE'S ENGINEERS YEAR-BOOK, 1894-   London: Morgan-Grampton Books Pub.
       TA151 A1K4 ENGR
  Standard handbook covering all major aspects of engineering.

DL38   MATERIALS HANDBOOK. 1977. 11th ed. Ed. by G.S. Brady, and H.R. Clauser. New York: McGraw Hill. 1011 p.
       TA403 B75 (1977) ENGI
  Data on 14 000 different materials, grouped in classes, with information on their characteristics.

DL39   Marcus, J. 1980. MODERN ELECTRONIC CIRCUITS REFERENCE MANUAL. New York: McGraw Hill.
       TK78 G7 M345 ENGR

DL40   MARKS' STANDARD HANDBOOK FOR MECHANICAL ENGINEERS. 1978. 8th ed. New York: McGraw Hill.
       TJ151 M37 (1978) ENGR
  This ed. incorporates both SI and U.S. Customary System of Units.

DL41   METALS HANDBOOK, 1980-   9th ed. 11 vols. Metals Park, OH: American Society for Metals. In progress.
       TA459 A53 ENGR
  All aspects of metals covered in this comprehensive set.

DL42   NATIONAL BUILDING CODE OF CANADA, 1941-   Ottawa: National Research Council.
       TH226 N28 (1980) ENGR

DL43   Sax, N.I. 1979. DANGEROUS PROPERTIES OF INDUSTRIAL MATERIALS. 5th ed. New York: Van Nostrand Reinhold. 1118 p.
       T55 S37 (1979) ENGI
  Provides "concise, hazard analysis information about nearly 15 000 common industrial and laboratory materials." Has countermeasures.

DL44   STANDARD HANDBOOK FOR CIVIL ENGINEERS. 1983. 2d ed. Ed. by F.S. Merritt. New York: McGraw Hill. 1 vol. unpaged.
       TA151 S8 (1983) ENGI

DL45   STANDARD HANDBOOK FOR ELECTRICAL ENGINEERS. 1978. 11th ed. Ed. by D.G. Fink. New York: McGraw Hill. 1 vol. unpaged.
       TK151 S83 (1978) ENGI

DL46   STANDARD HANDBOOK FOR PLANT ENGINEERING. 1983. Ed. by T.C. Rossler. New York: McGraw Hill. 1 vol. unpaged.
       TS184 S7 ENGI
  Detailed, handbook for a field affected by rapid technology change. Data on how equipment works and its maintenance.

DL47   Standards Council of Canada. 1982. DIRECTORY AND INDEX OF STANDARDS/ REPERTOIRE DES NORMES. Ottawa: Standards Council of Canada. 705 p.
  R389.60971 578D (1977)   Z914 A22N28 ENGR
  Contains numerical, keyword listings of all standards published by the accredited standards writing organizations in the National Standards System of Canada.

DL48   STRUCTURAL ENGINEERING HANDBOOK. 1979. 2d ed. Ed. by E.H. Gaylord, and C.N. Gaylord. 2d ed. New York: McGraw Hill. 1219 p.
       TA635 G3 (1979) ENGI

DL49   Tuma, J.J. 1979. ENGINEERING MATHEMATICS HANDBOOK: Definitions, Theories, Formulas, Tables. 2d ed. New York: McGraw Hill. 394 p.
       TA332 T85 (1979) ENGI
       (1st ed. 1975, TECHNOLOGY MATHEMATICS HANDBOOK)

DL50   WORLD METRIC STANDARDS FOR ENGINEERING. 1978. New York: Industrial Press.
       TA368 K93 ENGR

TITLE INDEX

Entries for titles cited in the annotations and a few author entries for titles in Section A. An 'n' after the item no. indicates that the entry is in the note.

A TO Z OF WOMEN'S HEALTH: ... ENCYCLOPEDIA, DI18
ABBREVIATIONS: A REVERSE GUIDE, AJ70
ABBREVIATIONS, ACRONYMS, CIPHERS AND SIGNS, AJ65
ABBREVIATIONS: ... COMPUTER ERA, DC9
ABC: ASSISTANCE TO BUSINESS IN CANADA, CC20
ABC POL SCI: A BIBLIOGRAPHY, CD4
ABHB: ANNUAL BIBLIOGRAPHY OF THE HISTORY OF THE PRINTED BOOK AND LIBRARIES, AA3
ABINGDON DICTIONARY OF LIVING RELIGIONS, BC10n
ABORIGINAL PEOPLE: A SELECTED BIBLIOGRAPHY, CF17
ABRIDGED INDEX MEDICUS, DI14n
ABRIDGED READERS' GUIDE (ARGPL), AF6n
ABS GUIDE TO RECENT PUBLICATIONS IN THE SOCIAL AND BEHAVIORAL SCIENCES, CA6
ABSTRACTING AND INDEXING SERVICES DIRECTORY, AF1
ABSTRACTS IN ANTHROPOLOGY, CF2
ABSTRACTS OF ARTICLES IN SCHOLARLY JOURNALS, BD6n
ABSTRACTS OF ENGLISH STUDIES, BD23
ABSTRACTS OF NORTH AMERICAN GEOLOGY, DG12
ABSTRACTS ON HEALTH EFFECTS OF ENVIRONMENTAL POLLUTANTS, DK5
ACADEMIC AMERICAN ENCYCLOPEDIA, AI7
ACADEMIC AND ADMINISTRATIVE OFFICERS AT CANADIAN UNIVERSITIES, CI22n
ACCESS TO CANADIAN GOVT PUBS IN ... LIBS, AM52
ACCESS TO FEDERAL GOVERNMENT DOCUMENTS, AM48
ACCESS TO THE LAW, AM51
ACRONYMS AND ABBREV. IN LIB. AND INFO. WORK, AA37
ACRONYMS, INITIALISMS AND ABBREVIATIONS, AJ66
Addiction Research Foundation Bibliographies, CG17
ADVANCES IN AGRONOMY, DJ15
ADVANCES IN APPLIED MECHANICS, DL13
ADVANCES IN ASTRONOMY AND ASTROPHYSICS, DD7
ADVANCES IN CHEMICAL ENGINEERING, DF11, DL14
ADVANCES IN FOOD RESEARCH, DJ16
ADVANCES IN GEOLOGY, DG20
ADVANCES IN LIBRARIANSHIP, AA22
ADVANCES IN NUCLEAR SCIENCE AND TECHNOLOGY, DL15
AGING AND THE AGED: ... BIBLIOGRAPHY, CG10
AGRICULTURE: A BIBLIOGRAPHIC GUIDE, DJ2
AGRINDEX, DJ9
AIR POLLUTION ABSTRACTS, DK6
ALA GLOSSARY OF LIB. AND INFORMATION SCIENCE, AA33
ALA HANDBOOK OF ORGANIZATION ..., AA56
ALA WORLD ENCYCL. OF LIB. & INFO. SERVICES, AA27
ALA YEARBOOK, AA23
ALBERTA BIBLIOGRAPHY, AD95
ALCOHOL USE AND WORLD CULTURES, CG17n
ALLGEMEINE ENZYKLOPADIE DER MUSIK, BF27

ALLGEMEINES LEXIKON DER BILDENDEN KÜNSTLER, BE38-BE39
AMATEUR ASTRONOMER'S HANDBOOK, DD16
AMERICA HISTORY AND LIFE, CJ40
AMERICAN AND BRITISH GENEALOGY AND HERALDRY, AL1
AMERICAN AND CANADIAN WEST, CJ40n
AMERICAN ART DIRECTORY, BE25
AMERICAN AUTHORS, 1600-1900, AL56
AMERICAN BIBLIOGRAPHY, AD42, AD43
AMERICAN BIBLIOGRAPHY ... 1801-1819, AD44
AMERICAN BOOK PRICES CURRENT, AD107
AMERICAN BOOK PUBLISHING RECORD, AD62
AMERICAN BOOK TRADE DIRECTORY, AB10
AMERICAN CATALOGUE OF BOOKS, 1876-1910, AD46
AMERICAN DOCTORAL DISSERTATIONS, AF26
AMERICAN DRUG INDEX, DI29
AMERICAN FILM INSTITUTE CATALOG, BG27
AMERICAN HERITAGE DICTIONARY, AJ10
AMERICAN INSTITUTE OF PHYSICS HANDBOOK, DE19
AMERICAN LIBRARY DIRECTORY, AA42
AMERICAN LIBRARY RESOURCES, AA51
AMERICAN LITERATURE AND LANGUAGE ..., BD46
AMERICAN MEDICAL DIRECTORY, DI37
AMERICAN MEN AND WOMEN OF SCIENCE, DA58
AMERICAN MEN AND WOMEN OF SCIENCE: SOCIAL AND BEHAVIORAL SCIENCES, CA21
AMERICAN POPULAR MUSIC: A REFERENCE GUIDE, BF1
AMERICAN REFERENCE BOOKS ANNUAL, AC1
AMERICAN SOCIETY OF COMPOSERS, AUTHORS AND PUBLISHERS, BF37n
AMERICAN STATISTICS INDEX, AM27
American Studies Information Guide series, BD46n
AMERICAN THESAURUS OF SLANG, AJ58
AMERICAN UNIVERSITIES AND COLLEGES, CI24n
AMERICANISMOS DICCIONARIO ILUSTRADO SOPENA, AJ34
AMY VANDERBILT COMPLETE BOOK OF ETIQUETTE, AH48
ANALYTICAL ABSTRACTS (Chemistry), DF4
ANALYTICAL BIBLIOGRAPHY OF UNIVERSAL COLLECTED BIOGRAPHY, AL13
ANALYTICAL CONCORDANCE TO THE REVISED STANDARD VERSION (NT), BC34
ANATOMY OF WONDER, BD88
ANIMAL IDENTIFICATION: A REFERENCE GUIDE, DH1
ANNIVERSARIES AND HOLIDAYS, AH41
ANNOTATED BIBLIOG. OF CANADA'S MAJOR AUTHORS, BD51
ANNOTATED BIBLIOGRAPHY OF HOMOSEXUALITY, CG25
ANNOTATED BIBLIOGRAPHY OF THE PHYSICAL ANTHROPOLOGY ... ESKIMOS AND INDIANS, CF11
ANNUAIRE DU QUEBEC, AH19

ANNUAL ABSTRACT OF STATISTICS, CA33
ANNUAL ART SALES INDEX, BE26n
ANNUAL BIBLIOG. OF BRITISH AND IRISH HISTORY, CJ33
ANNUAL BIBLIOG. OF ENG. LANGUAGE AND LIT., BD25
ANNUAL BOOK OF ASTM STANDARDS, DL28
ANNUAL DEPARTMENTAL REPORTS OF THE DOMINION OF CANADA, AM104
ANNUAL OBITUARY, AL17
ANNUAL REGISTER, AH1
ANNUAL REVIEW OF ANTHROPOLOGY, CF3
ANNUAL REVIEW OF ASTRONOMY AND ASTROPHYSICS, DD8
ANNUAL REVIEW OF BIOCHEMISTRY, DH15
ANNUAL REVIEW OF INFO. SCI. AND TECHNOLOGY, AA24
ANNUAL REVIEW OF NUCLEAR SCIENCE, DE12
ANNUAL REVIEW OF PSYCHOLOGY, CH2
ANNUAL REVIEW OF SOCIOLOGY, CG3
Annual Review series, medical sciences, DI16
ANNUALS OF OPERA, BF51
ANTHROPOLOGICAL INDEX TO CURRENT PERIODICALS ... MUSEUM OF MANKIND LIBRARY, CF4
ANTHROPOLOGICAL LITERATURE INDEX, CF5
ANTIQUES AND COLLECTIBLES: A BIBLIOGRAPHY, BE77
APPLIED AND DECORATIVE ARTS: (bibliog.), BE75
APPLIED SCIENCE & TECHNOLOGY INDEX, DL6
APPRAISAL, AC46
AQUATIC SCIENCE AND FISHERIES ABSTRACTS, DH7
ARCHITECTURAL PERIODICALS INDEX, BE53
ARCHITECTURE, BE58
Architecture Series: Bibliography, BE54
ARCTIC BIBLIOGRAPHY, AD97
Arctic Institute of North America CATALOGUE, DG9
ARMS, FLAGS AND EMBLEMS OF CANADA, AH45
Art and Architecture Information Guides, BE63n
ART BOOKS: A BASIC BIBLIOGRAPHY, BE11
ART GALLERY OF ONTARIO: CANADIAN COLLECTION, BE65
ART INDEX, BE4
ART RESEARCH MATERIALS AND RESOURCES, BE1n
ARTBIBLIOGRAPHIES MODERN, BE5
ARTIST'S HANDBOOK OF MATERIALS AND TECHNIQUES, BE19n
ARTISTS IN CANADA, BE42
ARTS & HUMANITIES CITATION INDEX, BA2, AF19
ASCAP BIOGRAPHICAL DICTIONARY, BF37
ASHRAE HANDBOOK AND PRODUCT DIRECTORY, DL29
ASIAN LITERATURE IN ENGLISH, BD4
ASIMOV'S BIOGRAPHICAL ENCYC. OF SCI-TECH., DA55
ASLIB DIRECTORY, AA43
ASM METALS REFERENCE BOOK, DL30
ASSOCIATIONS' PUBLICATIONS IN PRINT, AD55
ASTRONOMICAL ALMANAC, DD17
ASTRONOMY AND ASTROPHYSICAL ABSTRACTS, DD5
ASTRONOMY AND ASTROPHYSICS MONTHLY INDEX, DD6
ASTRONOMY DATA BOOK, DD18
ASTROPHYSICAL FORMULAE, DD19
ASTROPHYSICAL QUANTITIES, DD20

ATLANTIC BOOK CHOICE: ... ELEMENTARY SCHOOL COLLECTIONS, AC24n
ATLANTIC PROVINCES CHECKLIST, AD81
ATLAS DE LA NOUVELLE FRANCE/ AN ATLAS OF NEW FRANCE, CJ26
ATLAS LAROUSSE CANADIEN, AK24
ATLAS OF CANADA AND THE WORLD, AK25
ATLAS OF CANADIAN AGRICULTURE, DJ29
ATLAS OF CLASSICAL ARCHAEOLOGY, CJ22
ATLAS OF THE BIBLE, BC30
AUDIOVISUAL MARKET PLACE, AG1
AUDUBON SOCIETY FIELD GUIDE TO NORTH AMERICAN ROCKS AND MINERALS, DG35
AUSTRALIAN AND NEW ZEALAND LIB. RESOURCES, AA52n
AUTHOR BIOGRAPHIES MASTER INDEX, AL49
AUTOMATIC DATA PROCESSING HANDBOOK, DA7
AVERY INDEX TO ARCHITECTURAL PERIODICALS, BE55
AVIATION AND SPACE DICTIONARY, DL18
AWARDS, HONORS AND PRIZES, AH32
Ayer Collection, Anthropology, CF13
AYER DIRECTORY OF PUBLICATIONS, AE5
BAKER'S BIOGRAPHICAL DICTIONARY OF MUSICIANS, BF38
BALANCHINE'S COMPLETE STORIES (ballet), BG11
BARNHART DICTIONARY OF NEW ENGLISH, AJ14n
Bartlett's quotations, AF34
BASIC BIBLIOGRAPHY OF MUSICAL CANADIANA, BF3n
BASIC LEGAL TERMINOLOGY, CE20n
BASIC MUSIC LIBRARY: ... SCORES AND BOOKS, BF11
BBC PRONOUNCING DICTIONARY OF BRITISH NAMES, AJ46
BEST BUYS IN PRINT, AD108
BEST OF THE MUSIC MAKERS, BF56n
BEST REFERENCE BOOKS SELECTED FROM ARBA, AC1n
Besterman, AD20
BIBLIOGRAPHER'S MANUAL ..., AD30
BIBLIOGRAPHIA CANADIANA, CJ57
BIBLIOGRAPHIA CARTOGRAPHICA, AK5
BIBLIOGRAPHIC GUIDE TO CONFERENCE PUBNS, DA25
BIBLIOGRAPHIC GUIDE TO DANCE, BG19n
BIBLIOGRAPHIC GUIDE TO MUSIC, BF12n
BIBLIOGRAPHIC GUIDE TO NORTH AMER HIST CJ42 CJ70n
BIBLIOGRAPHIC GUIDE TO PSYCHOLOGY, CH3
BIBLIOGRAPHIC GUIDE TO TECHNOLOGY, DL3
BIBLIOGRAPHIC GUIDE TO THEATRE ARTS, BD75n
BIBLIOGRAPHIC INDEX, AD21
BIBLIOGRAPHICAL CONTROL OF OFFICIAL PUBNS, AM53
BIBLIOGRAPHICAL GUIDE TO THE STUDY OF THE LITERATURE (U.S.), BD45
BIBLIOGRAPHICAL HANDBOOKS (history), CJ35
BIBLIOGRAPHICAL SERVICES THROUGHOUT THE WORLD, AD22
BIBLIOGRAPHIE/ BIBLIOGRAPHY OF CANADIAN LAW, CE6
BIBLIOGRAPHIE DE BIBLIOGRAPHIES QUEBECOISES, AD84
BIBLIOGRAPHIE DE LA CRITIQUE DE LITTERATURE QUEBECOISE ..., BD64n

BIBLIOGRAPHIE DE LA FRANCE-BIBLIO, AD100
BIBLIOGRAPHIE DE LA PHILOSOPHIE, BB3
BIBLIOGRAPHIE DE L'HISTOIRE DU QUEBEC ET DU
    CANADA, CJ49
BIBLIOGRAPHIE DU QUEBEC, AD88
BIBLIOGRAPHIE DU QUEBEC, 1821-1967, AD87
BIBLIOGRAPHIE QUEBECOISE, BD64
BIBLIOGRAPHIES IN AMERICAN HISTORY, CJ41
BIBLIOGRAPHY AND INDEX OF GEOLOGY, DG13
BIBLIOGRAPHY AND RESEARCH MANUAL IN THE HISTORY OF
    MATHEMATICS, DB1
BIBLIOGRAPHY OF AGRICULTURE, DJ1
BIBLIOGRAPHY OF AMERICAN LITERATURE, BD44
BIBLIOGRAPHY OF ASTRONOMY, DD1
BIBLIOGRAPHY OF BIBLIOGRAPHIES IN AMERICAN
    LITERATURE, BD48
BIBLIOGRAPHY OF BRITISH COLUMBIA, AD96
BIBLIOGRAPHY OF BRITISH HISTORY, CJ34
BIBLIOGRAPHY OF CANADIAN BIBLIOGRAPHIES, AD23
BIBLIOGRAPHY OF CANADIAN CHILDREN'S BOOKS, AD70
BIBLIOGRAPHY OF CANADIAN FOLKLORE IN ENGLISH, BC49
BIBLIOGRAPHY OF CANADIAN LEGAL MATERIALS, CE8
BIBLIOGRAPHY OF CANADIAN NATIVE ARTS, BE7, BE74
BIBLIOGRAPHY OF CANADIAN THEATRE HISTORY, BG21
BIBLIOGRAPHY OF CANADIAN URBAN HISTORY, CA46
BIBLIOGRAPHY OF CANADIANA, AD66
BIBLIOGRAPHY OF COSTUME, BE91
BIBLIOGRAPHY OF DANCING, BG17
BIBLIOGRAPHY OF DISCOGRAPHIES, BF58
BIBLIOGRAPHY OF DRUG ABUSE, ... ALCOHOL AND
    TOBACCO, CG18
BIBLIOGRAPHY OF ENGLISH LANGUAGE THEATRE AND DRAMA
    IN CANADA, BD72n
BIBLIOGRAPHY OF FEDERAL DATA SOURCES EXCLUDING
    STATISTICS CANADA, CA39
BIBLIOGRAPHY OF HIGHER EDUCATION IN CANADA, CI6
BIBLIOGRAPHY OF LEGAL MATERIALS FOR NON-LAW
    LIBRARIANS, CE11
BIBLIOGRAPHY OF LIBRARY ECONOMY, AA4
BIBLIOGRAPHY OF MANITOBA, AM85
BIBLIOGRAPHY OF MEDICAL REVIEWS, DI15
BIBLIOGRAPHY OF MODERN HISTORY, CJ31n
BIBLIOGRAPHY OF NEWFOUNDLAND, AD82
BIBLIOGRAPHY OF NON-COMMERCIAL PUBLICATIONS OF
    OBSERVATORIES AND ASTRONOMICAL SOCIETIES, DD2
BIBLIOGRAPHY OF NORTH AMERICAN FOLKLORE AND
    FOLKSONG, BC50
BIBLIOGRAPHY OF NORTH AMERICAN GEOLOGY, DG7
BIBLIOGRAPHY OF ONTARIO HISTORY, AD90
BIBLIOGRAPHY OF PHILOSOPHICAL BIBLIOGRAPHIES, BB4
BIBLIOGRAPHY OF PHILOSOPHY, PSYCHOLOGY ..., BB8
BIBLIOGRAPHY OF PLACE-NAME LITERATURE: U.S. AND
    CANADA, AK31
BIBLIOGRAPHY OF PUBLICATIONS (UNESCO), AN20
BIBLIOGRAPHY OF THE PRAIRIE PROVINCES, AD93
BIBLIOGRAPHY OF UPPER CANADIAN IMPRINTS,
    1801-1841, AD91
BIBLIOGRAPHY OF WORKS ON CANADIAN FOREIGN
    RELATIONS, CD10
BIBLIOGRAPHY ON ORAL HISTORY, CJ13
BIBLIOTHECA BRITANNICA, AD31
BIBLIOTHECA CANADENSIS, AD71
BIG BOOK OF HALLS OF FAME, AH60
BIO-BIBLIOGRAPHY FOR THE HISTORY OF BIOCHEMICAL
    SCIENCES, DH4
BIOGRAPHICAL BOOKS, AL6-AL7
BIOGRAPHICAL DICTIONARIES, AL8
BIOGRAPHICAL DICTIONARIES MASTER INDEX, AL10n
BIOGRAPHICAL DICTIONARY OF AMERICAN SCIENCE, DA58n
BIOGRAPHICAL DICTIONARY OF DANCE, BG14
BIOGRAPHICAL DICTIONARY OF THE CINEMA, BG51n
BIOGRAPHIE UNIVERSELLE, AL18
BIOGRAPHIES CANADIENNES FRANCAISES, AL44
BIOGRAPHY ALMANAC, AL12
BIOGRAPHY AND GENEALOGY MASTER INDEX, AL10
BIOGRAPHY CATALOGUE OF THE LIBRARY OF THE ROYAL
    COMMONWEALTH SOCIETY, AL14
BIOGRAPHY INDEX, AL9
BIOLOGICAL ABSTRACTS, DH8
BIOLOGICAL ABSTRACTS/RRM, DH9
BIOLOGICAL & AGRICULTURAL INDEX, DJ10
BIOLOGICAL AND BIOMEDICAL RESOURCE LITERATURE, DH5
BIOLOGICAL DATA BOOK, DH25
BIOLOGICAL REVIEWS, DH16
BLACK'S VETERINARY DICTIONARY, DJ17
BLAKISTON'S GOULD MEDICAL DICTIONARY, DI19
BLUE BOOK OF CANADIAN BUSINESS, CC22
BLUE BOOK OF CBS STOCK REPORTS, CC48n
BLUES WHO'S WHO, BF56
BOL'SHAIA SOVETSKAIA ENTSIKLOPEDIIA, AI21n
BOLSHOI ANGLO- RUSSKII SLOVAR/ NEW ENG- RUSSIAN
    DICTIONARY, AJ37
BOOK OF CANADIAN ANTIQUES, BE81
BOOK OF NEWFOUNDLAND, AI24n
BOOK OF POPULAR SCIENCE, DA35
BOOK OF WORLD FAMOUS MUSIC, BF21
BOOK PUBLISHING ANNUAL, AB2
BOOK REVIEW DIGEST, AC58
BOOK REVIEW INDEX, AC59
BOOK REVIEW INDEX: A MASTER CUMULATION, AC59n
BOOK REVIEW INDEX TO SOCIAL SCI. PERIODICALS, CA7
BOOK TRADE IN CANADA, AB1
BOOKLIST, AC30
BOOKMAN'S GLOSSARY, AB7
BOOKS FOR COLLEGE LIBRARIES, AC21
BOOKS FOR PUBLIC LIBRARIES, AC9
BOOKS IN CANADA, AC54
BOOKS IN ENGLISH, AD38
BOOKS IN OTHER LANGUAGES, AC8
BOOKS IN PRINT, AD51-AD54

BOOKS IN SERIES, AD59-AD60
BOOKS 1976-82 NOW OP, AD36
BOOKS ON DEMAND, AD109
BOOKS OUT OF PRINT, AD56
BOTANICAL REVIEW, DH17
BOURINOT'S RULES OF ORDER, AH50, CD30
BOWKER ANNUAL OF LIBRARIES AND THE BOOK TRADE, AB3
BOWKER ANNUAL OF LIB. & BOOK TRADE INFO., AA25
BOWKER/ BANTAM 1984 COMPLETE SOURCEBOOK OF
    PERSONAL COMPUTING, DC14
BRIEF GUIDE TO SOURCES OF SCI. & TECH. INFO., DA2
BRITAIN: AN OFFICIAL HANDBOOK, AH7
BRITANNICA ATLAS, AI4n
BRITANNICA DISCOVERY, AI13n
BRITANNICA JUNIOR, AI13
BRITANNICA YEARBOOK OF SCIENCE ..., DA36, AI4
BRITISH AND IRISH LIBRARY RESOURCES, AA52
BRITISH AUTHORS BEFORE 1800, AL57
BRITISH AUTHORS OF THE NINETEENTH CENTURY, AL58
BRITISH BOOK NEWS, AC31
BRITISH BOOKS IN PRINT, AD34
BRITISH CATALOGUE OF AUDIOVISUAL MATERIALS, AG5
BRITISH CATALOGUE OF MUSIC, BF4
BRITISH COLUMBIA GOVT PUBNS MTHLY CHECKLIST, AM95
BRITISH EDUCATION INDEX, CI9
BRITISH HUMANITIES INDEX, AF11, BA3
BRITISH LIBRARY GENERAL CATALOGUE, AD3-AD5, AD6
British Museum Catalogues, AD3-AD5, AD6
BRITISH NATIONAL BIBLIOGRAPHY, AD37
BRITISH NATIONAL FILM CATALOGUE, AG16
BRITISH OFFICIAL PUBLICATIONS, AM6
BRITISH PAPERBACKS IN PRINT, AD35
BRITISH TECHNOLOGY INDEX, DL9n
BRITISH UNION CATALOGUE OF PERIODICALS, AE13-AE14
BROCHURES QUEBECOISES, AD85
BROCK BIBLIOGRAPHY (Can. plays), BD53, BD72
BROCKHAUS ENZYKLOPADIE, AI18n
BRS MANUAL, AB25
BRYAN'S DICTIONARY OF PAINTERS AND ENGRAVERS, BE33
BULLETIN OF THE CENTER FOR CHILDREN'S BOOKS, AC48
BULLETIN SIGNALETIQUE: HISTOIRE ET SCIENCES DES
    RELIGIONS, BC3
BURKE'S GENEALOGICAL AND HERALDIC HISTORY ..., AL2
BURNHAM'S CELESTIAL HANDBOOK, DD21
BUSINESS & ECONOMICS BOOKS, CC9
BUSINESS & ECONOMICS BOOKS, SERIALS IN PRINT, CC10
BUSINESS DEPARTMENT ACQUISITIONS (MTL), CC8
BUSINESS INFORMATION SOURCES, CC12
BUSINESS LAW REPORTS, CC47
BUSINESS LITERATURE, CC11
BUSINESS PAGE: HOW TO READ IT, CC24
BUSINESS PERIODICALS INDEX, CC17
BUSINESS PUBLICATIONS INDEX AND ABSTRACTS, CC17n
BUTLER'S LIVES OF THE SAINTS, BC40
BUTTERWORTHS' MEDICAL DICTIONARY, DI20

CA CONDENSATES, DF5n
CAB ABSTRACTS, DJ11
CAMBRIDGE ANCIENT HISTORY, CJ28
CAMBRIDGE BIBLIOGRAPHY OF ENGLISH LIT., BD42n
CAMBRIDGE ENCYCLOPEDIA OF AFRICA, AI27n
CAMBRIDGE ENCYCLOPEDIA OF ASTRONOMY, DD10
CAMBRIDGE ENCYCLOPEDIA OF CHINA, AI27
CAMBRIDGE ENCYCLOPEDIA OF RUSSIA, AI27n
CAMBRIDGE GUIDE TO ENGLISH LITERATURE, BD28
CAMBRIDGE HISTORY OF AMERICAN LITERATURE, BD47n
CAMBRIDGE HISTORY OF ENGLISH LITERATURE, BD39
CAMBRIDGE HISTORY OF THE BRITISH EMPIRE, CJ32
CAMBRIDGE ITALIAN DICTIONARY, AJ35
CAMBRIDGE MEDIEVAL HISTORY, CJ29
CAMBRIDGE MODERN HISTORY, CJ30
CAMBRIDGE PHOTOGRAPHIC ATLAS OF THE PLANETS, DD26
CAN/OLE MANUAL, AB26
CAN/SDI PROFILE DESIGN MANUAL, AB27
CANADA AND ITS PROVINCES: A HISTORY, CJ60
CANADA GAZETTE, AM108
CANADA GAZETTEER ATLAS, AK23
CANADA HANDBOOK, AH13
CANADA ON STAGE, BG22
CANADA: SYMBOLS OF SOVEREIGNTY, AH46
CANADA WATER YEAR BOOK, DK22
CANADA YEAR BOOK, AH12
CANADA'S PLAYWRIGHTS, BD83
CANADA'S SPORTING HEROES, AH60n
CANADA'S URBAN PAST: A BIBLIOGRAPHY, CA47
CANADIAN ADVERTISING, AE6
CANADIAN ALMANAC & DIRECTORY, AH16
CANADIAN ANNUAL REVIEW ..., AH15
CANADIAN ANNUAL REVIEW OF PUBLIC AFFAIRS, AH14
CANADIAN ANTIQUARIAN BOOK SELLERS DIRECTORY, AB11
CANADIAN ART AT AUCTION, BE26n
CANADIAN ART SALES INDEX, BE26
CANADIAN BOOK OF CORPORATE MANAGEMENT, CC32
CANADIAN BOOK REVIEW ANNUAL, AC10
CANADIAN BOOKS FOR CHILDREN, AC22n.
CANADIAN BOOKS FOR YOUNG PEOPLE, AC22
CANADIAN BOOKS IN PRINT, AD78-AD79
CANADIAN BUSINESS AND ECONOMICS: A GUIDE, CC7
CANADIAN BUSINESS HANDBOOK, CC29
CANADIAN BUSINESS INDEX, CC18
CANADIAN BUSINESS SERVICE, CC48
CANADIAN CATALOGUE OF BOOKS, AD76
CANADIAN CATALOGUE OF BOOKS, 1791-1895, AD72
Canadian Centenary series (history), CJ58
CANADIAN CHEMICAL REGISTER, DF29
CANADIAN CHILDREN'S LITERATURE, AC49
CANADIAN CONSERVATION DIRECTORY, DK26
CANADIAN CONSUMER, AH35
CANADIAN DICTIONARY FOR CHILDREN, AJ19
CANADIAN DIRECTORY OF PARLIAMENT, 1867-1967, CD32
CANADIAN DIRECTORY OF PUBLIC LEGAL INFO., CE23

CANADIAN DRUG IDENTIFICATION CODE, DI30
Canadian Education Assoc. HANDBOOK, CI20
CANADIAN EDUCATION INDEX, CI10
CANADIAN ENCYCLOPEDIA, AI23
CANADIAN ENCYCLOPEDIA OF DRUG THERAPY, DI31
CANADIAN ENERGY BIBLIOGRAPHY, DK1
CANADIAN ENERGY DIRECTORY, DK27
CANADIAN ESSAY AND LITERATURE INDEX, AF31
CANADIAN FEATURE FILMS, AG16, BG37
CANADIAN FICTION ... BIBLIOGRAPHY, BD92
CANADIAN FILM DIGEST YEARBOOK, BG43
CANADIAN GOVERNMENT PUBLICATIONS, AM58
CANADIAN HISTORY IN DOCUMENTS, CJ61
CANADIAN HOSPITAL DIRECTORY, DI38
CANADIAN HOUSE OF COMMONS, AM40
CANADIAN INDIAN BIBLIOGRAPHY, CF1
CANADIAN INDIAN POLICY: ... BIBLIOGRAPHY, CF14n
CANADIAN INDUSTRIAL RELATIONS INFORMATION, CB4
CANADIAN JAZZ DISCOGRAPHY, BF59
CANADIAN KEY BUSINESS DIRECTORY, CC33
CANADIAN LAW DICTIONARY, CE22
CANADIAN LAW LIST, CE25
CANADIAN LEGAL DIRECTORY, CE24
CANADIAN LEGAL RESEARCH GUIDE, CE5
CANADIAN LEGAL RESEARCH HANDBOOK, CE4n
CANADIAN LEGAL SYSTEM, CE3
CANADIAN LIBRARY DIRECTORY, AA44
CANADIAN LIBRARY HANDBOOK, AA28
CANADIAN LITERATURE, AC32
CANADIAN LOCAL HISTORIES TO 1950 (bibliog), CJ73
CANADIAN LOCATIONS OF JOURNALS INDEXED FOR MEDLINE, DI14n
CANADIAN MEDICAL DIRECTORY, DI39
CANADIAN MEN AND WOMEN OF THE TIME, AL40
CANADIAN MINERALS YEARBOOK, DG21
CANADIAN MUSIC: A SELECTED CHECKLIST, BF5
CANADIAN MUSIC OF THE TWENTIETH CENTURY, BF13n
CANADIAN NEWS FACTS, AH23
CANADIAN NEWS INDEX, AF20
CANADIAN NEWSPAPERS ON MICROFILM, AE24
CANADIAN NOVELISTS, AL73
CANADIAN OFFICIAL PUBLICATIONS, AM46
CANADIAN PARLIAMENTARY GUIDE, CD34
CANADIAN PARLIAMENTARY HANDBOOK, AM35
CANADIAN PERIODICAL INDEX, AC60, AF12
CANADIAN PHILATELY, BE85
CANADIAN PHOTOGRAPHY, 1839-1920, BE98
CANADIAN POLITICAL FACTS, 1945-1976, CD31
CANADIAN POLITICAL PARTIES, CD7
CANADIAN POLITICAL SYSTEM, AM41
CANADIAN PRESS NEWSFILES, AF21-
CANADIAN PUBLIC ADMINISTRATION: BIBLIOGRAPHY, CD6
CANADIAN PUBLISHING DIRECTORY, AB6n
CANADIAN REFERENCE SOURCES, AC4
CANADIAN REGISTER OF RESEARCH AND RESEARCHERS IN THE SOCIAL SCIENCES, CA22
CANADIAN SELECTION, AC11
CANADIAN SELECTION: FILMSTRIPS, AG29
CANADIAN SERIALS DIRECTORY, AE7
CANADIAN SOCIAL SCIENCE DATA ARCHIVE, CA23
CANADIAN STATISTICAL REVIEW, CA35
CANADIAN TAX REPORTS, CC49
CANADIAN TAX SERVICE, CC50
CANADIAN TELEPHONE DIRECTORY PRICE LIST, CC31
CANADIAN THESES, AF30
CANADIAN TRADE INDEX, CC34
CANADIAN WATERCOLOURS AND DRAWINGS (Royal Ont. Museum), BE66
CANADIAN WHO'S WHO, AL45
CANADIAN WRITERS, AL72
CANADIAN WRITERS AND THEIR WORKS, BD54
CANADIANA, AD77, AG20
CANADIANA 1867-1900, AD73
CANSIM, CA35n
CANSIM USER'S MANUAL ..., AB28
CARIBBEAN WRITERS, BD10
CASIA (CA Subject Index Alert), DF5n
CASSELL'S ENCYCLOPEDIA OF WORLD LITERATURE, BD11
CASSI, DF6
CATALOG, Library of the Institute for Sex Research, Indiana Univ., CG26
CATALOG OF MUSEUM PUBLICATIONS AND MEDIA, AC12
Catalog, Engineering Societies Library, DL4-DL5
CATALOG OF LOCAL HISTORY AND GENEALOGY (New York Public Lib.), CJ71n
CATALOG OF PUBLIC DOCUMENTS OF CONGRESS ..., AM24
CATALOG OF THE THEATRE AND DRAMA COLLECTIONS, BD75
Catalogs of art libraries, BE12n
Catalogs of music collections, BF12, BF15
CATALOGUE DE L'EDITEUR OFFICIEL (Que), AM74
CATALOGUE GENERAL ... BIBLIOTHEQUE NATIONALE (France), AD1-AD2
CATALOGUE OF BRITISH OFFICIAL PUBNS, AM11
CATALOGUE OF CANADIAN CHORAL MUSIC, BF6
CATALOGUE OF CANADIAN MINERALS, DG36
CATALOGUE OF PAINTINGS AND SCULPTURE (Nat. Gallery of Can.), BE69
CATALOGUE OF PROV. ARCHIVES (B.C.), AM92
CATALOGUE OF PUBLICATIONS (OECD), AN25
CATALOGUE OF PUBLISHED MAPS, AK6
CATALOGUE OF THE LIBRARY OF THE ARCTIC INSTITUTE OF NORTH AMERICA, DG9
CATALOGUE OF THE LIBRARY OF THE NATIONAL GALLERY OF CANADA, BE8
CATALOGUE OF THE UNIVERSE, DD11
CATALOGUES, LIBRARY OF THE PEABODY MUSEUM, CF15
CATHOLIC PERIODICAL AND LITERATURE INDEX, BC6n
CEA HANDBOOK, CI20
CENSUS OF CANADA, CA36

CHAMBERS BIOGRAPHICAL DICTIONARY, AL19
Champlain Society publications, CJ59
CHARLTON STANDARD CATALOGUE OF CAN. COINS, BE82
CHARLTON STANDARD CATALOGUE OF CAN. GOVERNMENT PAPER MONEY, BE82n
CHECK LIST OF CANADIAN IMPRINTS, 1900-1925, AD75
CHECK LIST OF UNITED NATIONS DOCUMENTS, AN13
CHECKLIST OF AMERICAN IMPRINTS, AD45
CHECKLIST OF CANADIAN DIRECTORIES, AH26
CHECKLIST OF CANADIAN ETHNIC SERIALS, AE17n
CHECKLIST OF CANADIAN LITERATURE, BD66
CHECKLIST OF SASKATCHEWAN GOVERNMENT PUBNS, AM89
CHECKLIST OF U.S PUBLIC DOCUMENTS, AM19, AM21
CHECKLISTS OF LAW REPORTS AND STATUTES IN CANADIAN LAW LIBRARIES, CE18
CHEMICAL ABSTRACTS, DF5
CHEMICAL ABSTRACTS SERVICE SOURCE INDEX, DF6
CHEMICAL FORMULARY, DF24
CHEMICAL REVIEWS, DF13
CHEMICAL SYNONYMS AND TRADE NAMES, DF14
CHEMICAL TITLES, DF7
CHILD ABUSE: AN ANNOTATED BIBLIOGRAPHY, CG14
CHILD ABUSE AND NEGLECT: (bibliog), CG12
CHILD DEVELOPMENT ABSTRACTS AND BIBLIOGRAPHY, CH5
CHILDREN'S BOOK REVIEW INDEX, AC59n
CHILDREN'S CATALOG, AC23
CHILDREN'S LITERATURE: A GUIDE, BD104n
Children's Literature Service, NLC, AC26n
CHOICE, AC33
CHOIX DE PUBLICATIONS GOUVERNEMENTALES (Que), AM75
CHRONOLOGY OF WORLD HISTORY, CJ18
CIJE, AA12
CINAHL, DI11
CINEMA: A CRITICAL DICTIONARY, BG44
CIRCULAR 15; 14: TEXTBOOKS, AC24n
CIS INDEX, AM26
CIS U.S. SERIAL SET INDEX, AM20
CISTI databases, DA49
CISTI RECENT ADDITIONS TO THE LIBRARY, DA6
CLA DIRECTORY & MEMBERS' HANDBOOK, AA57
CLASSED SUBJECT CATALOG, ENGINEERING SOCIETIES LIBRARY, DL4-DL5
CLIC'S LEGAL MATERIALS LETTER, CE7
CM: CANADIAN MATERIALS FOR SCHOOLS AND LIB., AC50
CODE INTERNATIONAL DE NOMENCLATURE ZOOLOGIQUE/ INTERNATIONAL CODE, DH27
COIN: A DIRECTORY OF COMPUTERIZED INFORMATION IN CANADA, AB20
COLLEGE & RESEARCH LIBRARIES, AC41
COLLIER'S ENCYCLOPEDIA, AI2
COLOURED REPRODUCTIONS OF CANADIAN PAINTINGS AVAILABLE FOR PURCHASE, BE47
COLUMBIA DICTIONARY OF MODERN EUROPEAN LIT., BD12
COLUMBIA LIPPINCOTT GAZETTEER, AK26

Columbia Univ. Library Service Library. DICTIONARY CATALOG, AA5
COLUMBO'S CANADIAN QUOTATIONS, AF40
COLOMBO'S CANADIAN REFERENCES, AF41
COMBINED RETROSPECTIVE INDEX SET TO JOURNALS IN HISTORY, CJ4
COMBINED RETROSPECTIVE INDEX TO BOOK REVIEWS IN SCHOLARLY JOURNALS, AC61
COMMONWEALTH UNIVERSITIES YEARBOOK, CI21
COMPACT DICTIONARY OF CANADIAN ENGLISH, AJ18n
COMPENDEX, DL11n
COMPENDIUM OF PHARMACEUTICALS AND SPECIALITIES, DI32
COMPLETE BOOK OF BALLETS, BG12
COMPLETE CONCORDANCE TO THE BIBLE (DOUAY), BC35
COMPLETE GUIDE TO FRENCH CANADIAN ANTIQUES, BE78n
COMPLETE GUIDE TO MODERN DANCE, BG18
COMPLETE HEBREW ENGLISH DICTIONARY, AJ40
COMPLETE REFERENCE GUIDE TO UNITED NATIONS SALES PUBLICATIONS, AN12
COMPREHENSIVE ETYMOLOGICAL DICTIONARY, AJ44
COMPREHENSIVE INDEX TO THE PUBNS U.S. GOVT, AM23
COMPREHENSIVE ORGANIC CHEMISTRY, DF15
COMPTON'S ENCYCLOPEDIA AND FACT-INDEX, AI8
COMPTON'S PRECYCLOPEDIA, AI14
COMPUTER ABSTRACTS, DC4
COMPUTER AND CONTROL ABSTRACTS, DC5, DA21, DL7
COMPUTER DICTIONARY, DC11
COMPUTER READABLE DATA BASES, AB19
COMPUTER REVIEWS, DC1
COMPUTER SCIENCE RESEARCH: A GUIDE, DC2
CONCISE AMERICAN HERITAGE DICTIONARY, AJ10n
CONCISE BIBLIOG. OF ENGLISH CANADIAN LIT., BD58
CONCISE DICTIONARY OF AMERICAN BIOGRAPHY, AL36
CONCISE DICTIONARY OF CANADIANISMS, AJ55n
CONCISE DICTIONARY OF NATIONAL BIOGRAPHY, AL31
CONCISE ENCYCLOPEDIA OF ASTRONOMY, DD12
CONCISE ENCYCLOPEDIA OF WESTERN PHILOSOPHY, BB15
CONCISE HISTORY OF CANADIAN PAINTING, BE70
CONCISE OXFORD DICTIONARY, AJ6
CONCISE OXFORD DICTIONARY OF BALLET, BG16
CONDENSED CHEMICAL DICTIONARY, DF16
CONFERENCE PAPERS INDEX, DA26
CONFERENCE PROCEEDINGS ... HEALTH SCIENCES, DI10
CONSER, AE12
CONSERVATION DIRECTORY, DK28
CONSOLIDATED REGULATIONS OF CANADA, AM107
CONSOLIDATION OF THE CONSTITUTION ACTS, AM31
CONSULTANTS AND CONSULTING ORGS DIRECTORY, CC35
CONSUMER REPORTS, AH36
CONSUMER SOURCEBOOK, AH37
CONSUMERS INDEX TO PRODUCT EVALUATIONS AND INFORMATION SOURCES, AH38
CONTEMPORARY ARCHITECTS, BE56
CONTEMPORARY ARTISTS, BE34

CONTEMPORARY ARTISTS: ... TO REPRODUCTIONS, BE48n
CONTEMPORARY AUTHORS, AL51
CONTEMPORARY CANADIAN COMPOSERS, BF47
CONTEMPORARY LITERARY CRITICISM, BD13
CONTEMPORARY LITERARY CRITICS, AL52
CONTEMPORARY PHOTOGRAPHERS, BE96
CONTEMPORARY QUEBEC: ... BIBLIOGRAPHY, CJ53
CONTEMPORARY SOCIOLOGY: A JOURNAL OF REVIEWS, CG5
Contemporary Writers series, BD29
CONTRIBUTIONS TO ... CATALOGUE OF CANADIANA, AD68
CORPUS ALMANAC OF CANADA, AH17
COSTUME INDEX, BE93
COUNTY ATLASES OF CANADA, AK9n
CPL BIBLIOGRAPHIES, CA48
CRC COMPOSITE INDEX FOR CRC HANDBOOKS, DL31
CRC HANDBOOK OF MATERIALS SCIENCE, DL32
CRC HANDBOOK OF MATHEMATICAL SCIENCE, DB8
CRC HANDBOOKS OF FOOD ADDITIVES, DJ22
CREATIVE CANADA, AL43
CRIME ... FICTION AND FILM, BD87n
CRIME FICTION 1749-1980, BD87
CRITICAL DICTIONARY OF ... AUTHORS, AL48
CRITICAL TEMPER, BD33
CRITICAL WRITINGS ON COMMONWEALTH LITS, BD31
CROWELL'S HANDBOOK OF CLASSICAL MYTHOLOGY, BC44
CROWELL'S HANDBOOK OF WORLD OPERA, BF52
CUMULATED DRAMATIC INDEX, BD77
CUMULATED FICTION INDEX, BD90
CUMULATED MAGAZINE SUBJECT INDEX, 1907-1949, AF5
CUMULATIVE BOOK INDEX, AD48
CUMULATIVE BOOK LIST, AD33
CUMULATIVE INDEX TO NURSING & ALLIED HEALTH
   LITERATURE, DI11
CUMULATIVE TITLE INDEX TO U.S. PUBLIC DOCTS, AM22
CURRENT ABSTRACTS OF CHEM. AND INDEX CHEMICUS, DF8
CURRENT BIOGRAPHY, AL20
CURRENT BOOK REVIEW CITATIONS, AC13
CURRENT BRITISH GOVERNMENT PUBLISHING, AM4
CURRENT CHEMICAL REACTIONS, DF9
CURRENT CONTENTS, DA16
   _____: AGRICULTURE, BIOLOGY AND ENVIRONMENTAL
   SCIENCES, DJ12, DA16, DK7
   _____: ARTS & HUMANITIES, BA4
   _____: CLINICAL PRACTICE, DI12, DA16
   _____: ENGINEERING, TECHNOLOGY AND APPLIED
   SCIENCES, DL8, DA16
   _____: LIFE SCIENCES, DH11, DA16
   _____: PHYSICAL, CHEMICAL AND EARTH SCIENCES,
   DG14, DA16, DF10, DE3
   _____: SOCIAL AND BEHAVIORAL SCIENCES, CA8
CURRENT INDEX TO JOURNALS IN EDUCATION, AA12, CI12
CURRENT LAW INDEX, CE17n
CURRENT PAPERS IN PHYSICS, DE4
CURRENT PHYSICS INDEX, DE5
CURRENT RESEARCH (Geological Sciences), DG39
CURRENT RESEARCH IN LIB. AND INFO. SCIENCE, AA11
CURRENT TECHNOLOGY INDEX, DL9
CUSS LIST, AE20
CYCLOPEDIA OF LITERARY CHARACTERS, BD19
CYCLOPEDIA OF WORLD AUTHORS, AL53
DANCE ENCYCLOPEDIA, BG13
DANCE RESOURCES IN CANADIAN LIBRARIES, BG15
DANGEROUS PROPERTIES OF INDUSTRIAL MATERIALS, DL43
DANGEROUS PROPERTIES OF INDUSTRIAL METHODS, DF25
DATA COMMUNICATIONS: BUYER'S GUIDE, DC15
DATA SOURCES FOR BUSINESS AND MARKET ANALYSIS, CC3
DAUGHTERS OF THE NORTH, CG46
DAYS TO REMEMBER, AH39
DEADLINE DATA ON WORLD AFFAIRS, AH20
DEATH: A BIBLIOGRAPHICAL GUIDE, CG15
DEBATES (Can. govt), AM99-AM100
DEBRETT'S ETIQUETTE AND MODERN MANNERS, AH47
DEBRETT'S PEERAGE, AL3
DEMOGRAPHIC BASES OF CANADIAN SOCIETY, CA29
DEMOGRAPHIC YEARBOOK, CA43
Dept of Agriculture publications, DJ8
DESCRIPTIVE CATALOGUE ... GOVT PUBS (U.S), AM18
DEUTSCHE BIBLIOGRAPHIE, AD104
DEUTSCHE NATIONALBIBLIOGRAPHIE, AD105
DEUTSCHES WÖRTERBUCH, AJ28
DEVELOPING THE LIB. COLLECTION IN POLI. SCI., CD2
DICCIONARIO DE LA LENGUA ESPANOLA, AJ33n
DICTIONARIES, ENCYCLOPEDIAS AND OTHER WORD-RELATED
   BOOKS, AJ2
DICTIONARY BUYING GUIDE, AJ3
DICTIONARY CATALOG OF THE EDWARD E. AYER
   COLLECTION OF AMERICANA AND AMERICAN INDIANS IN
   THE NEWBERRY LIBRARY, CF13
DICTIONARY CATALOGUE OF THE PROVINCIAL ARCHIVES OF
   BRITISH COLUMBIA, AM92
DICTIONARY OF ACRONYMS (lib. sci), AA39
DICTIONARY OF AGRICULTURE (five lang), DJ18
DICTIONARY OF AMERICAN BIOGRAPHY, AL35
DICTIONARY OF AMERICAN ENGLISH, AJ53
DICTIONARY OF AMERICAN HISTORY, CJ46
DICTIONARY OF AMERICAN LIBRARY BIOGRAPHY, AA58
DICTIONARY OF AMERICAN SLANG, AJ59
DICTIONARY OF AMERICANISMS, AJ54
DICTIONARY OF ANONYMOUS AND PSEUDONYMOUS ENGLISH
   LITERATURE, BD37
DICTIONARY OF ANTHROPOLOGY, CF21
DICTIONARY OF ANTIQUES ... DECORATIVE ARTS, BE73
DICTIONARY OF ARCHITECTURE, BE57
DICTIONARY OF ART AND ARTISTS, BE21
DICTIONARY OF ART TERMS AND TECHNIQUES, BE19
DICTIONARY OF ASTRONAUTICS: ENG/FR, DD13
DICTIONARY OF BALLET, BG16n
DICTIONARY OF BEHAVIORAL SCIENCE, CH12
DICTIONARY OF BIOLOGY: ENG/ GER/ FR/ SPANISH, DH19
DICTIONARY OF BOOKS RELATING TO AMERICA, AD39 AD41

DICTIONARY OF BUSINESS AND ECONOMICS, CC21
DICTIONARY OF CANADIAN ARTISTS, BE44
DICTIONARY OF CANADIAN BIOGRAPHY, AL39
DICTIONARY OF CANADIAN ECONOMICS, CB12
DICTIONARY OF CANADIAN ENGLISH, AJ16n
DICTIONARY OF CANADIAN QUOTATIONS, AF42
DICTIONARY OF CANADIANISMS, AJ55
DICTIONARY OF CATCH PHRASES, AJ60n
DICTIONARY OF CHINESE AND JAPANESE ART, BE20
DICTIONARY OF CLICHES, AJ60n
DICTIONARY OF COMPARATIVE RELIGION, BC10
DICTIONARY OF CONTEMPORARY ARTISTS, BE41n
DICTIONARY OF CONTEMPORARY MUSIC, BF28
DICTIONARY OF COSTUME, BE89
DICTIONARY OF DATA PROCESSING, DC12
DICTIONARY OF EARTH SCIENCES, DG25
DICTIONARY OF ECONOMIC TERMS, CB13
DICTIONARY OF EDUCATION, CI17
DICTIONARY OF FOREIGN PHRASES AND ABBREV., AJ73
DICTIONARY OF FOREIGN TERMS, AJ74
DICTIONARY OF FOREIGN WORDS AND PHRASES, AJ72
DICTIONARY OF GEOLOGY, DG26
DICTIONARY OF HOUSE PLANTS, DJ19
DICTIONARY OF HYMNOLOGY, BC43
DICTIONARY OF INFORMATION TECHNOLOGY, AA35
DICTIONARY OF LIBRARY AND EDUC. TECHNOLOGY, AG3
DICTIONARY OF LITERARY BIOGRAPHY, AL50
DICTIONARY OF LITERARY PSEUDONYMS, BD35
DICTIONARY OF LITERARY TERMS, BD17n
DICTIONARY OF MEDICAL SYNDROMES, DI25
DICTIONARY OF MINING, MINERAL ... TERMS, DG27
DICTIONARY OF MODERN ENGLISH USAGE, AJ48
DICTIONARY OF MODERN WRITTEN ARABIC, AJ41
DICTIONARY OF MUSICAL THEMES, BF18
DICTIONARY OF NAMED EFFECTS AND LAWS IN CHEMISTRY, PHYSICS AND MATHEMATICS, DA41, DF17
DICTIONARY OF ORGANIC COMPOUNDS, DF18
DICTIONARY OF NATIONAL BIOGRAPHY, AL30
DICTIONARY OF NEWFOUNDLAND ENGLISH, AJ56
DICTIONARY OF OPERA AND SONG THEMES, BF18n
DICTIONARY OF ORIENTAL LITERATURES, BD14
DICTIONARY OF PHILOSOPHY, BB13, BB14
DICTIONARY OF POLITICAL SCIENCE, CD16
DICTIONARY OF POLITICS, CD17
DICTIONARY OF PRONUNCIATION, AJ47
DICTIONARY OF PSYCHOLOGY, CH9
DICTIONARY OF PUBLIC TRANSPORT, DL19
DICTIONARY OF SAINTS, BC40n
DICTIONARY OF SCIENCE & TECHNOLOGY: ENG/FR, DA43
DICTIONARY OF SCIENCE & TECHNOLOGY: GER/ENG, DA43n
DICTIONARY OF SCIENTIFIC BIOGRAPHY, DA56
DICTIONARY OF SLANG AND UNCONVENTIONAL ENG., AJ60
DICTIONARY OF SOCIAL SCIENCE METHODS, CA19
DICTIONARY OF SOCIAL WELFARE, CG32

DICTIONARY OF SOIL MECHANICS AND FOUNDATION ENGINEERING, DL20
DICTIONARY OF STATISTICAL TERMS, CA30
DICTIONARY OF SUBJECTS AND SYMBOLS IN ART, BE17
DICTIONARY OF TELECOMMUNICATIONS, DL21
DICTIONARY OF THE BIBLE, BC23, BC26
DICTIONARY OF THE ENVIRONMENT, DK18
DICTIONARY OF THE HISTORY OF IDEAS, BB11
DICTIONARY OF THE HISTORY OF SCIENCE, DA37
DICTIONARY OF THE MIDDLE AGES, CJ14
DICTIONARY OF THE SOCIAL SCIENCES, CA18, CA20
DICTIONARY OF THE UNDERWORLD, AJ60n
DICTIONARY OF UNIVERSAL BIOGRAPHY, AL11
DICTIONARY OF WASTE AND WATER TREATMENT, DL22
DICTIONARY OF ZOOLOGY, DH20
DICTIONNAIRE ALPHABETIQUE, AJ25
DICTIONNAIRE ANG-FR/ ENG-FRENCH DICT. OF MEDICAL AND PARAMEDICAL SCIENCES, DI24
DICTIONNAIRE BIBLIOG. DU CANADA FRANCAIS, BD52
DICTIONNAIRE CANADIEN, AJ22
DICTIONNAIRE CRITIQUE ... DES PEINTRES, BE32
DICTIONNAIRE DE LA LANGUE QUEBECOISE, AJ21
DICTIONNAIRE DES ECRIVANS QUEBECOIS CONTEMPORAINS, BD65
DICTIONNAIRE DES MYTHOLOGIES ..., BC45
DICTIONNAIRE DES OEUVRES LITTERAIRES (Que), BD55
DICTIONNAIRE DU CINEMA QUEBECOIS, BG41n
DICTIONNAIRE NORD-AMERICAN, AJ20
DICTIONNAIRE PRATIQUE DES AUTEURS QUEBECOIS, AL71
DIRECTORIES OF CANADIAN LIBRARIES, AA41
DIRECTORY AND INDEX OF STANDARDS, DL47
DIRECTORY (Canadian Psych. Assoc), CH15
DIRECTORY OF AMERICAN PHILOSOPHERS, BB18
DIRECTORY OF ANTHROPOLOGISTS, CF22
DIRECTORY OF ASSOCIATIONS IN CANADA, AH31
DIRECTORY OF BRITISH OFFICIAL PUBLICATIONS, AM2
DIRECTORY OF BUSINESS AND FINANCIAL SERVICES, CC46
DIRECTORY OF CANADIAN ENVIRONMENTAL EXPERTS, DK29
DIRECTORY OF CANADIAN HUMAN SERVICES, CG39
DIRECTORY OF CANADIAN MUSEUMS, BE27
DIRECTORY OF CANADIAN RECORDS AND MANUSCRIPT REPOSITORIES, AA50, AD115
DIRECTORY OF CANADIAN SCIENTIFIC AND TECHNICAL DATABASES, AB21, DA49
DIRECTORY OF CANADIAN UNIVERSITIES, CI22
DIRECTORY OF CANADIAN URBAN INFO. SOURCES, CA49
DIRECTORY OF COMMUNITY SERVICES IN METROPOLITAN TORONTO, CG40
DIRECTORY OF DIRECTORIES, AH25
DIRECTORY OF ECONOMIC LIBRARIES IN CANADA, CB16
DIRECTORY OF EDUCATION STUDIES IN CANADA, CI23
DIRECTORY OF ENGINEERING SOCIETIES ..., DA48
DIRECTORY OF FEDERALLY SUPPORTED RESEARCH IN UNIVERSITIES, DA50

DIRECTORY OF HISTORICAL SOCIETIES AND AGENCIES
   (U.S., Can.), CJ72
DIRECTORY OF INDUSTRY DATA SOURCES, CC13
DIRECTORY OF INFORMATION RESOURCES IN THE UNITED
   STATES: SOCIAL SCIENCES, CA25
DIRECTORY OF INTERNATIONAL STATISTICS, AN1
DIRECTORY OF LABOUR ORGANIZATIONS IN CANADA, CC36
DIRECTORY OF LIBRARY ASSOCIATIONS IN CANADA, AA59
DIRECTORY OF LIBRARY CONSULTANTS '85, AA60
DIRECTORY OF LIBRARY STAFF ORGANIZATIONS, AA46
DIRECTORY OF MUSEUMS, BE28
DIRECTORY OF MUSICAL CANADA, BF29
DIRECTORY OF ONLINE DATABASES, AB22
DIRECTORY OF ONLINE INFORMATION RESOURCES, DC16
DIRECTORY OF PROFESSIONAL ENGINEERS (Ont), DA60
DIRECTORY OF PUBLISHED PROCEEDINGS: SEMT, DA27
DIRECTORY OF SOCIAL SCIENCE RESEARCH CENTRES ...
   AT CANADIAN UNIV., CA24
DIRECTORY OF SPECIAL LIBS AND INFO. CENTERS, AA45
DIRECTORY OF THE AMER. PSYCHOLOGICAL ASSOC., CH16
DIRECTORY OF UNITED NATIONS INFO. SYSTEMS, AN7
DISCLOSURE: U.S. COMPANIES, CC53n
DISSERTATIONS ABSTRACTS INTERNATIONAL, DA29
DISSERTATIONS ABSTRACTS INTERNATIONAL, AF29
DISSERTATIONS IN HISTORY (U.S., Can.), CJ7
DIVORCE IN THE 70s: A SUBJECT BIBLIOGRAPHY, CG23n
DIVORCE IN THE UNITED STATES, CANADA AND GREAT
   BRITAIN: A GUIDE, CG23
DIZIONARIO LETTERARIO ..., BD15
DOCTORAL DISSERTATIONS IN HISTORY, CJ7n
DOCUMENTATION OF THE UN SYSTEM, AN6
DOCUMENTATION OF THE UNITED NATIONS SYSTEM, AN10
DOCUMENTS OF AMERICAN HISTORY, CJ47
DOCUMENTS OF INTERNATIONAL ORGANIZATIONS, AN3
DORLAND'S ILLUSTRATED MEDICAL DICTIONARY, DI21
DRAMATIC CRITICISM INDEX, BD72
DUDEN BILDWÖTERBUCH, AJ32n
DUDEN DAS GROSSE WÖRTERBUCH, AJ29
Dun & Bradstreet REFERENCE BOOK, CC51
EARLY AMERICAN IMPRINTS 1639-1800, AD42n
EARLY CANADIAN CHILDREN'S BOOKS, AD69
EARLY FURNITURE OF FRENCH CANADA, BE80
EARLY PAINTERS AND ENGRAVERS IN CANADA, BE43
EARTH SCIENCE REVIEWS, DG22
ECONOMIC ATLAS OF ONTARIO, CB18
ECONOMIC BOOKS CURRENT SELECTIONS, CB6
ECONOMIC HISTORY OF CANADA: A GUIDE, CB1
ECONOMICS DICTIONARY, CB15
ECONOMICS SELECTIONS, CB5
ECONOMICS WORKING PAPERS: BIBLIOGRAPHY, CB7
EDUCATION INDEX, CI11
Education Information Guide series, CI13
EDUCATION STATISTICS, Canada, CI14
EDUCATIONAL DOCUMENTS ABSTRACTS, AA14
EDUCATIONAL DOCUMENTS INDEX, AA15.

EDUCATIONAL MEDIA YEARBOOK, AG2
Educational Resources Information Center, AA12n
EFLA EVALUATIONS, AG28
EIGHTEENTH CENTURY SHORT TITLE CATALOGUE, AD28
EIGHTH MENTAL MEASUREMENTS YEARBOOK, CH13
ELECTRICAL AND ELECTRONICS ABSTRACTS, DL10, DA21
ELSEVIER'S DICTIONARY OF CHEM. ENGINEERING, DL23
ELSEVIER'S DICTIONARY OF LIBRARY SCIENCE ..., AA34
ELSEVIER'S MEDICAL DICTIONARY, DI23
ENCICLOPEDIA BARSA, AI19n
ENCICLOPEDIA DELLO SPETTACOLO, BG2
ENCICLOPEDIA ITALIANA, AI20
ENCICLOPEDIA UNIVERSAL ILUSTRADA, AI19
ENCYCLOPAEDIA OF THE SOCIAL SCIENCES, CA16
ENCYCLOPAEDIA UNIVERSALIS, AI15
ENCYCLOPEDIA AMERICANA, AI3
ENCYCLOPEDIA AND DICTIONARY OF MEDICINE, NURSING
   AND ALLIED HEALTH, DI26
ENCYCLOPEDIA BRITANNICA, AI4
ENCYCLOPEDIA BUYING GUIDE, AI1
ENCYCLOPEDIA CANADIANA, AI22
ENCYCLOPEDIA INTERNATIONAL, AI9
ENCYCLOPEDIA JUDAICA, BC11
ENCYCLOPEDIA OF AMERICAN HISTORY, CJ48
ENCYCLOPEDIA OF ANTHROPOLOGY, CF18
ENCYCLOPEDIA OF ARCHAEOLOGICAL EXCAVATIONS IN THE
   HOLY LAND, BC29n
ENCYCLOPEDIA OF ASSOCIATIONS, AH27
ENCYCLOPEDIA OF BIOETHICS, BC13n
ENCYCLOPEDIA OF BIOLOGICAL SCIENCES, DH21
ENCYCLOPEDIA OF BUSINESS INFORMATION SOURCES, CC14
ENCYCLOPEDIA OF CHEMICAL PROCESSING ..., DL24
ENCYCLOPEDIA OF CHEMISTRY, DF19
ENCYCLOPEDIA OF COMPUTER SCI. & ENGINEERING, DC13
ENCYCLOPEDIA OF COMPUTER SCI. & TECHNOLOGY, DC10
ENCYCLOPEDIA OF CONCERT MUSIC, BF30
Encyclopedia of Earth Sciences series, DG28
ENCYCLOPEDIA OF EDUCATION, CI15
ENCYCLOPEDIA OF EDUCATIONAL RESEARCH, CI16
ENCYCLOPEDIA OF ENVIRONMENTAL SCIENCES AND
   ENGINEERING, DK14
ENCYCLOPEDIA OF FOLK, COUNTRY & WESTERN MUSIC,
   BF55
ENCYCLOPEDIA OF GEOGRAPHIC INFO. SOURCES, CC15
ENCYCLOPEDIA OF HISTORIC PLACES, CJ15
ENCYCLOPEDIA OF INFO. SYSTEMS AND SERVICES, AB17
ENCYCLOPEDIA OF INTEGRATED CIRCUITS, DL33
ENCYCLOPEDIA OF ISLAM, BC12
ENCYCLOPEDIA OF JAZZ, BF54
ENCYCLOPEDIA OF LIB. AND INFORMATION SCIENCE, AA29
ENCYCLOPEDIA OF MANAGEMENT, CC25n
ENCYCLOPEDIA OF MARINE RESOURCES, DJ20
ENCYCLOPEDIA OF MEDICAL ORGS AND AGENCIES, DI40
ENCYCLOPEDIA OF MUSIC IN CANADA, BF31
ENCYCLOPEDIA OF NEWFOUNDLAND AND LABRADOR, AI24

ENCYCLOPEDIA OF ONTARIO, AI25
ENCYCLOPEDIA OF PAINTING, BE64
ENCYCLOPEDIA OF PHILOSOPHY, BB12
ENCYCLOPEDIA OF PHYSICS, DE15, DE16
ENCYCLOPEDIA OF PROFESSIONAL MANAGEMENT, CC25
ENCYCLOPEDIA OF PSYCHOLOGY, CH7
ENCYCLOPEDIA OF RELIGION AND ETHICS, BC13
ENCYCLOPEDIA OF SCIENCE FICTION AND FANTASY, BD91
ENCYCLOPEDIA OF SOCIAL WORK, CG33
ENCYCLOPEDIA OF SOCIOLOGY, CG34
ENCYCLOPEDIA OF SPORTS, AH59
ENCYCLOPEDIA OF THE THIRD WORLD, AI30
ENCYCLOPEDIA OF UKRAINE, AI29
ENCYCLOPEDIA OF URBAN PLANNING, CA50
ENCYCLOPEDIA OF WORDS ... LEGAL MAXIMS, CE19
ENCYCLOPEDIA OF WORLD ART, BE16
ENCYCLOPEDIA OF WORLD LITERATURE (20th cent), BD16
ENCYCLOPEDIC DICTIONARY OF MATHEMATICS, DB11
ENCYCLOPEDIC DICTIONARY OF PHYSICS, DE17
ENCYCLOPEDIC DICTIONARY OF PSYCHOLOGY, CH8
ENCYCLOPEDIC DICTIONARY OF RELIGION, BC15n
ENCYCLOPEDIE DES ANTIQUITES DU QUEBEC, BE78
ENCYCLOPEDIE DU BON FRANÇAIS, AJ23
ENCYCLOPEDIE DU CINEMA, BG42
ENCYCLOPEDIE DU QUEBEC, AI26
ENERGY ABSTRACTS, DK8
ENERGY DICTIONARY, DK19
ENERGY HANDBOOK, DK23
ENERGY INFORMATION ABSTRACTS, DK9
ENERGY: SOURCES OF PRINT AND NON-PRINT ..., DK30
ENERGY STATISTICS: A GUIDE, DK2
ENGINEERING FORMULAS, DL34
ENGINEERING INDEX, DL11
ENGINEERING MATHEMATICS HANDBOOK, DL49
Engineering Societies Library CATALOG, DL4-DL5
ENGLISH CANADIAN LITERATURE TO 1900 ..., BD61
ENGLISH HISTORICAL DOCUMENTS, CJ36
ENGLISH ITALIAN, IT/ENGLISH DICTIONARY, AJ36
ENGLISH LANGUAGE FILMS, BG48n
ENGLISH RUSSIAN, RUS/ ENGLISH DICTIONARY, AJ38
ENVIRONMENT ABSTRACTS, DK10
ENVIRONMENT SOURCE BOOK, DK31
ENVIRONMENTAL IMPACT ASSESSMENTS, (bibliog), DK3
EPONYMS DICTIONARIES INDEX, AJ63
ERIC, AA12-AA16, CI12
ESSENTIAL GUIDE TO NONPRESCRIPTION DRUGS, DI35n
ESSAI DE BIBLIOGRAPHIE CANADIENNE, AD64
ESSAY AND GENERAL LITERATURE INDEX, AF32
ESTC, AD28
ETHNOGRAPHIC BIBLIOGRAPHY OF NORTH AMERICA, CF12
EUROPA YEAR BOOK, AH2
Europa yearbooks, AH2n
EUROPEAN AUTHORS, 1000-1900, AL55
EUROPEAN HISTORICAL STATISTICS, CA42
Evans, AD42, AD43

EVERYMAN'S DICTIONARY OF FICT. CHARACTERS, BD95
EVERYMAN'S DICTIONARY OF MUSIC, BF32
EVERYMAN'S DICTIONARY OF NON-CLASSICAL MYTH, BC46
EVERYMAN'S UNITED NATIONS, CD22n
EVERYONE'S UNITED NATIONS, CD22
EXCERPTA MEDICA, DI13
EXHAUSTIVE CONCORDANCE OF THE BIBLE, BC39
F & S INDEX INTERNATIONAL, CC19
FACE TO FACE WITH TALENT, BG1
FACTS ON FILE, AH21
FACTS ON FILE DICTIONARY OF ASTRONOMY, DD14
FACTS ON FILE DICTIONARY OF CHEMISTRY, DF20
FAIRCHILD'S DICTIONARY OF FASHION, BE90n
FAMILIAR QUOTATIONS, AF34
FAMOUS NAMES IN ENGINEERING, DA55n
FANTASY LITERATURE, BD102n
FARM AND GARDEN INDEX, DJ13
FASHION DICTIONARY, BE90
FEATURE FILMS, BG27n
FICTION CATALOG, AC14, BD93
FICTION 1876-1983: A BIBLIOGRAPHY, BD94
FIFTH INTERNAT. DIRECTORY OF ANTHROPOLOGISTS, CF22
FILM: A REFERENCE GUIDE, BG28
FILM CANADIANA, AG17
FILM EVALUATION GUIDE, AG28n
FILM LITERATURE INDEX, BG34
FILM STUDY: A RESOURCE GUIDE, BG28n
FILMED BOOKS AND PLAYS, BG32
FILMGOER'S COMPANION, BG46
FINANCIAL POST CANADIAN MARKETS, CC26
FINANCIAL POST CORPORATION SERVICE, CC52
FINANCIAL POST DIRECTORY OF DIRECTORS, CC37
FINANCIAL POST 500, CC38
FINANCIAL POST SURVEY OF INDUSTRIALS, CC39
FINANCIAL POST SURVEY OF MINES AND ENERGY RESOURCES, CC39n
FINE ARTS: A BIBLIOGRAPHIC GUIDE, BE10
FINE PRINT REFERENCES, BE13n
FLIS "Serials Currently Received," AA8
FLORA OF CANADA, DH28
FOCAL ENCYCLOPEDIA OF PHOTOGRAPHY, BE97
FOLK SONG INDEX, BF22
Follett, AJ49
FOOD SCIENCE AND TECHNOLOGY: A BIBLIOGRAPHY, DJ4
FOREIGN AFFAIRS BIBLIOGRAPHY, CD5
FORTHCOMING BOOKS, AD57-AD58
FORTHCOMING INTERNATIONAL SCIENTIFIC AND TECHNICAL CONFERENCES, DA52
Fowler, AJ48
FRASER'S CANADIAN TRADE DIRECTORY, CC40
FREE, AC34, CI4
FREE AND INEXPENSIVE LEARNING MATERIALS, CI5
FRENCH-ENG SCIENCE AND TECHNOLOGY DICTIONARY, DA44
FRENCH PERIODICAL INDEX, AF15
FROM PRESS TO PEOPLE, AM15

FUNDAMENTAL MEASURES AND CONSTANTS FOR SCIENCE AND TECHNOLOGY, DE20
FUNDAMENTALS OF LEGAL RESEARCH, CE4
FUNK & WAGNALLS ... INTERNATIONAL DICTIONARY, AJ11
FUNK & WAGNALLS NEW ENCYCLOPEDIA, AI5
FUNK & WAGNALLS STANDARD COLLEGE DICTIONARY, AJ17
FUNK & WAGNALLS STANDARD DICT OF FOLKLORE, BC48
GAGE CANADIAN DICTIONARY, AJ16
Gagnon collection, AD64
GENERAL SCIENCE INDEX, AF7
GEODATA: THE WORLD ALMANAC GAZETTEER, AH6n
GEOGRAPHIC ATLAS OF WORLD WEEDS, DJ24
GEOGRAPHY AND CARTOGRAPHY, DG2
GEOLOGIC REFERENCE SOURCES, DG4
Geological Survey of Canada publications, DG11
GEOLOGY AND ECONOMIC MINERALS OF CANADA, DG37
GEOPHYSICAL ABSTRACTS, DG16
GEOPHYSICAL ABSTRACTS 1929-71 (U.S.), DG15
GEOTITLES WEEKLY: GEOSCIENCE BIBLIOGRAPHY, DG10
GERMAN BOOKS IN PRINT (VLB), AD106
GERMAN ENG SCIENCE AND TECHNOLOGY DICTIONARY, DA45
GERONTOLOGY: A CORE LIST, CG9
GESAMTVERZEICHNIS DES DEUTSCHSPRACHIGEN SCHRIFTTUMS, AD102-AD103
GLOSSARY OF ASTRONOMY AND ASTROPHYSICS, DD15
GLOSSARY OF MARINE TECHNOLOGY TERMS, DL25
GOLDEN BOUGH, BC47
GOODE'S WORLD ATLAS, AK16
GOVERNMENT AND POLITICS IN ONTARIO, AM43
GOVERNMENT OF CANADA PUBLICATIONS CATALOGUE, AM59
GOVERNMENT OF CANADA TELEPHONE DIRECTORY, AM37
GOVERNMENT OF ONTARIO TELEPHONE DIRECTORY, AM42
GOVERNMENT PUBLICATIONS, AM8
GOVERNMENT PUBLICATIONS AND THEIR USE, AM17
GOVERNMENT PUBLICATIONS CATALOGUE (NWT), AM97
GOVERNMENT PUBLICATIONS RELATING TO ALBERTA, AM90
GOVERNMENT PUBLISHING ... CANADIAN PROVINCES, AM54
GOVERNMENT REFERENCE BOOKS, AM13
GOVERNMENT REPORTS ANNOUNCEMENTS AND INDEX, DA30
GRAN ENCICLOPEDIA RIALP, AI19n
GRAND DICTIONNAIRE ENCYCL. LAROUSSE, AI17, AJ24
GRANDE ENCYCLOPEDIE, AI16
GRANDE LAROUSSE DE LA LANGUE FRANCAISE, AJ24n
GRANGER'S INDEX TO POETRY, BD69
GREAT SOVIET ENCYCLOPEDIA, AI21
GREAT WRITERS OF THE ENGLISH LANGUAGE, BD30
GREEK AND LATIN AUTHORS, AL54
GREEK ENGLISH LEXICON, AJ42
GROSSE BROCKHAUS, AI18
GRZIMEK'S ANIMAL LIFE ENCYCLOPEDIA, DH22
GUIDE D'HISTOIRE DU CANADA, CJ50
GUIDE FOR A SMALL MAP COLLECTION, AK1
GUIDE TO ART REFERENCE BOOKS, BE9
GUIDE TO BASIC INFORMATION ... VISUAL ARTS, BE2
GUIDE TO BASIC INFORMATION ... CHEMISTRY, DF1
GUIDE TO BASIC INFORMATION ... ENGINEERING, DL2
GUIDE TO BRITISH GOVERNMENT PUBLICATIONS, AM7
GUIDE TO BUDDHIST RELIGION, BC4n
GUIDE TO CANADIAN COMPOSERS, BF47n
GUIDE TO CANADIAN MANUFACTURERS, CC33n
GUIDE TO CANADIAN MINISTRIES SINCE CONFEDERATION, CD33
GUIDE TO CANADIAN PHOTOGRAPHIC ARCHIVES, AG25
GUIDE TO CRITICAL REVIEWS, BG3
GUIDE TO DEPARTMENTS OF ANTHROPOLOGY, CF23
GUIDE TO DEPARTMENTS OF SOCIOLOGY, ANTHROPOLOGY & ARCHAEOLOGY IN UNIV. & MUSEUMS IN CANADA, CF23n
GUIDE TO DIALOG SEARCHING, AB29
GUIDE TO EASTERN LITERATURES, BD1
GUIDE TO ENGLISH AND AMERICAN LITERATURE, BD26
GUIDE TO HINDU RELIGION, BC4
GUIDE TO HISTORICAL LITERATURE, CJ1
GUIDE TO IDENTIFICATION ... CAN. GOVT PUBNS, AM64
GUIDE TO ISLAM, BC4n
GUIDE TO LEGISLATIVE LIBRARIES AND PUBLIC AND SCHOOL LIBRARY AGENCIES IN CANADA, AA41n
GUIDE TO MICROFORMS IN PRINT, AD111
GUIDE TO OFFICIAL PUBLICATIONS OF N.B., AM69
GUIDE TO PERIODICALS ... PUBLIC LIBRARIES OF METROPOLITAN TORONTO, AE21
GUIDE TO PERIODICALS IN EDUCATION, CI2
GUIDE TO PROVINCIAL LIB. AGENCIES IN CANADA, AA41n
GUIDE TO REFERENCE BOOKS, AC5
GUIDE TO REFERENCE BOOKS SCHOOL MEDIA CENTERS, AC7
GUIDE TO REFERENCE MATERIAL, AC6
GUIDE TO REPRINTS, AD110
GUIDE TO RESEARCH ON NORTH AMERICAN INDIANS, CF9
GUIDE TO SOURCES FOR AGRI. AND BIOL. RESEARCH, DJ3
GUIDE TO SOURCES OF EDUCATIONAL INFORMATION, CI8
GUIDE TO SPECIAL ISSUES ... PERIODICALS, CC16 AE11
GUIDE TO SUPERNATURAL FICTION, BD89
GUIDE TO THE GODS, BC51n
GUIDE TO THE LITERATURE OF ART HISTORY, BE3
GUIDE TO THE LITERATURE OF ASTRONOMY, DD4
GUIDE TO THE LITERATURE OF THE LIFE SCIENCES, DH6
GUIDE TO THE OFFICIAL PUBLICATIONS OF EUROPEAN COMMUNITIES, AN23
GUIDE TO THE SOURCES OF MEDIEVAL HISTORY, CJ10n
GUIDE TO THE STUDY OF MEDIEVAL HISTORY, CJ8
GUIDE TO THE STUDY OF THE U.S.A, CJ39
GUIDE TO U.S. GOVERNMENT PUBLICATIONS, AM12
GUIDE TO U.S. GOVERNMENT SCI-TECH RESOURCES, DA1n
GUIDE TO UNESCO, AN19
GUIDE TO UNITED NATIONS ORGANIZATION ..., AN9
GUINNESS BOOK OF RECORDS; SPORTS RECORDS, AH52, AH57
HALLIWELL'S TELEVISION COMPANION, BG54
HAMMOND LARGE TYPE WORLD ATLAS, AK17
HANDBOOK OF BIOCHEM. AND MOLECULAR BIOLOGY, DH29
HANDBOOK OF CANADIAN FILM, BG41

HANDBOOK OF CANADIAN LEGAL TERMINOLOGY, CE20
HANDBOOK OF CHEMISTRY AND PHYSICS, DE21, DF26
HANDBOOK OF CONTEMPORARY DEVELOPMENTS IN WORLD
    SOCIOLOGY, CG35
HANDBOOK OF COSTUME, BE87
HANDBOOK OF ENGINEERING FUNDAMENTALS, DL35
HANDBOOK OF ENVIRONMENTAL CONTROL, DK21
HANDBOOK OF FRESHWATER FISHERY BIOLOGY, DH30
HANDBOOK OF MATHEMATICAL TABLES AND FORMULAS, DB7
HANDBOOK OF MEDICAL LIBRARY PRACTICE, DI4
HANDBOOK OF NON PRESCRIPTION DRUGS, DI33
HANDBOOK OF NORTH AMERICAN INDIANS, CF19
HANDBOOK OF PHYSICAL CALCULATIONS, DE22
HANDBOOK OF REACTIVE CHEMICAL HAZARDS, DF27
HANDBOOK OF STEEL CONSTRUCTION, DL36
HANDBOOK TO LITERATURE, BD17
HANDBOOKS AND TABLES IN SCI. AND TECHNOLOGY, DA7
HARBOTTLE'S DICTIONARY OF BATTLES, CJ20
HARPER'S BIBLE DICTIONARY, BC27
HARPER'S ENCYCLOPEDIA OF BIBLE LIFE, BC28
HARRAP'S ENG/FR DICTIONARY OF SLANG, AJ27n
HARRAP'S NEW STANDARD FR/ENG DICTIONARY, AJ27
HARRAP'S STANDARD GER/ENG DICTIONARY, AJ30
HARRISON TAPE GUIDE, AG21
HARVARD DICTIONARY OF MUSIC, BF33
HARVARD GUIDE TO AMERICAN HISTORY, CJ43
HARVARD LIST OF BOOKS IN PSYCHOLOGY, CH4
Harvard Univ. Business Lib. CORE COLLECTION, CC6
Harvard Univ. Peabody Museum catalogue, CF15
Harvard Univ. Sch. of Design LIB. CATALOGUE, BE60
HEALTH SCIENCE LIBRARIANSHIP: A GUIDE, DI2
HENDERSON'S DICTIONARY OF BIOLOGICAL TERMS, DH23
HERITAGE OF CANADIAN ART: THE McMICHAEL
    COLLECTION, BE68
HERITAGE OF UPPER CANADIAN FURNITURE, BE80n
HIGH DAYS AND HOLIDAYS IN CANADA, AH40
HISTOIRE DE LA LITTERATURE ... DU QUEBEC, BD59
HISTOIRE DU CANADA PAR LES TEXTES, CJ62
HISTORIAN'S HANDBOOK, CJ9
HISTORIC PRESERVATION, BE62
HISTORIC SITES OF ONTARIO, AI25n
HISTORICAL ABSTRACTS, CJ5
HISTORICAL ATLAS, CJ23
HISTORICAL ATLAS OF CANADA, CJ25
HISTORICAL CATALOGUE OF STATISTICS CANADA
    PUBLICATIONS, CA40
HISTORICAL JOURNALS: A HANDBOOK, CJ3n
HISTORICAL PERIODICALS DIRECTORY, CJ3
HISTORICAL SETS, COLLECTED EDITIONS, AND MONUMENTS
    OF MUSIC, BF8
HISTORICAL STATISTICS OF CANADA, CA38
HISTORICAL TABLES 58 B.C. - A.D. 1978, CJ21
HISTORY OF ARCHITECTURE, BE59
HISTORY OF ART, BE30
HISTORY OF CANADA: AN ANNOTATED BIBLIOGRAPHY, CJ56

HISTORY OF COSTUME, BE94
HISTORY OF COSTUME IN THE WEST, BE88
HISTORY OF MODERN ASTRONOMY AND ASTROPHYSICS, DD3
HISTORY OF MUSIC IN CANADA, BF45
HISTORY OF PHILOSOPHY, BB16, BB17
HISTORY OF QUEBEC: A BIBLIOGRAPHY, CJ53n
HISTORY OF WESTERN MUSIC, BF41
HISTORY OF WORLD SCULPTURE, BE71
HOLDINGS OF CANADIAN SERIALS IN NLC, AE17
HOLME'S SPECIALIZED PHILATELIC CATALOGUE, BE83
HOME BOOK OF BIBLE QUOTATIONS, BC38
HOMOSEXUALITY BIBLIOGRAPHY, CG25n
HORN BOOK MAGAZINE, AC51
HORROR LITERATURE, BD102
HORTUS THIRD: ... DICTIONARY OF PLANTS, DJ25
HOW CANADIANS GOVERN THEMSELVES, AM36
HOW TO FIND CHEMICAL INFORMATION, DF2
HOW TO FIND THE LAW, CE2
HOYT'S NEW CYCLOPEDIA OF ... QUOTATIONS, AF37
HRAF SOURCE BIBLIOGRAPHY, CF8
Human Relations Area Files, CF8
HUMAN RESOURCES ABSTRACTS, CG29
HUMANITIES: ... GUIDE TO INFORMATION SOURCES, BA1
HUMANITIES INDEX, AF8
HYMNS AND TUNES: AN INDEX, BC42
IBZ, AF16
IEEE STANDARD DICTIONARY OF ELECTRICAL AND
    ELECTRONICS TERMS, DL27
ILLUS. DICTIONARY OF PLACE NAMES: (U.S, Can), AK33
ILLUSTRATED NATURAL HISTORY OF CANADA, DH24
IMPRIMES DANS LE BAS-CANADA, AD65n, AD87n
IN CANADA: THE EARLEST VIEWS AND PORTRAITS, BE66n
IN REVIEW: CANADIAN BOOKS FOR YOUNG PEOPLE, AC25
IN SEARCH OF CANADIAN MATERIALS, AC24
IN SEARCH OF YOUR ROOTS (Canada), AL4
INDEX CHEMICUS, DF8n
INDEX DE L'ACTUALITE, AF23
INDEX HERBORIORUM, DH36
INDEX MEDICUS, DI14
INDEX OF ECONOMIC ARTICLES, CB8
INDEX OF MANUSCRIPTS IN THE BRITISH LIBRARY, AD113
INDEX OF MATHEMATICAL PAPERS, DB4
INDEX OF ONTARIO ARTISTS, BE46
INDEX TO ART PERIODICALS, BE6
INDEX TO ARTISTIC BIOGRAPHY, BE35
INDEX TO BIOGRAPHIES OF CONTEMP. COMPOSERS, BF39
INDEX TO BOOK REVIEWS IN HIST. PERIODICALS, CJ45
INDEX TO BRITISH LITERARY BIBLIOGRAPHY, BD40
INDEX TO CANADIAN LEGAL PERIODICAL LIT., CE16
INDEX TO CHARACTERS IN THE PERFORMING ARTS, BG8
INDEX TO CHILDREN'S SONGS, BF26n
INDEX TO CRITICAL FILM REVIEWS, BG29
INDEX TO CURRENT LEGAL RESEARCH IN CANADA, CE10
INDEX TO CURRENT URBAN DOCUMENTS, CA51
INDEX TO EDUCATION JOURNALS, AA12n

INDEX TO EDUCATIONAL AUDIO TAPES, AG7
INDEX TO EDUCATIONAL OVERHEAD TRANSPARENCIES, AG8
INDEX TO EDUCATIONAL RECORDS, AG9
INDEX TO EDUCATIONAL SLIDES, AG10
INDEX TO EDUCATIONAL VIDEO TAPES, AG11
INDEX TO 8MM MOTION CARTRIDGES, AG12
INDEX TO FEDERAL PROGRAMS, AM38
INDEX TO FESTSCHRIFTEN IN LIBRARIANSHIP, AA9, AA10
INDEX TO FULL LENGTH PLAYS, BD78
INDEX TO INTERNATIONAL STATISTICS, AN4, CA27
INDEX TO LEGAL PERIODICALS, CE17
INDEX TO MUNICIPAL DATA, CA52
INDEX TO OBSERVATORY PUBLICATIONS, DD2n
INDEX TO ONE ACT PLAYS, BD80
INDEX TO PLAYS IN PERIODICALS, BD79
INDEX TO POETRY FOR CHILDREN, BD67
INDEX TO PRODUCERS AND DISTRIBUTORS, AG15
INDEX TO RELIGIOUS PERIODICAL LITERATURE, BC6n
INDEX TO REPRODUCTIONS OF AMERICAN PAINTINGS, BE49
INDEX TO REPRODUCTIONS OF EUROPEAN PAINTINGS, BE50
INDEX TO SCI. AND TECHNICAL PROCEEDINGS, DA28
INDEX TO 16 MM EDUCATIONAL FILMS, AG13
INDEX TO SOC. SCI. & HUMANITIES PROCEEDINGS, CA11
INDEX TO SONG BOOKS, BF24
INDEX TO THE PUBNS ... GEOL. SURVEY CANADA, DG11
INDEX TO THESES (U.K), AF27
INDEX TO TWO DIMENSIONAL ART WORKS, BE48n
INDEX TRANSLATIONUM, AF43
INDEXES, ABSTRACTS, DIGESTS, AF2
INDIANS OF CANADA, CF20
INDIGENOUS ARCHITECTURE WORLDWIDE, BE63
INFORMATICS ABSTRACTS, AA17
INFORMATION INDUSTRY MARKET PLACE, AB18
INFORMATION ON MUSIC, BF9
INFORMATION PLEASE ALMANAC, AH4
INFORMATION REPORTS AND BIBLIOGRAPHIES, AA6
INFORMATION SCIENCE ABSTRACTS, AA18
INFORMATION SOURCES IN AGRI. AND FOOD SCIENCE, DJ5
INFORMATION SOURCES IN CHILDREN'S LIT., BD104
INFORMATION SOURCES IN ECONOMICS, CB2
INFORMATION SOURCES IN SCIENCE AND TECHNOLOGY, DA4
INFORMATION SOURCES OF POLITICAL SCIENCE, CD3
Information Technology [IT] ABSTRACTS, DA6, DA21
INIS ATOMINDEX, DE6
INSIDER: CANADIAN COMPANIES, CC53
INSPEC, DE7
Institute for Sex Research Library CATALOG, CG26
INSTITUTS DE VIE CONSCREE AU CANADA, BC19n
INSTRUMENTATION FOR ENVIRONMENTAL MONITORING, DK24
INTERNATIONAL ABSTR. OF BIOLOGICAL SCIENCES, DH12
INTERNATIONAL ACRONYMS, INITIALISMS, ABBREV., AJ68
INTERNATIONAL AEROSPACE ABSTRACTS, DL12n
INTERNATIONAL AUCTION RECORD (Art), BE26n
INTERNATIONAL BIBLIOGRAPHY, AN5
INTERNATIONAL BIBLIOGRAPHY OF ECONOMICS, CB9

INTERNATIONAL BIBLIOGRAPHY OF HIST. SCIENCES, CJ6
INTERNATIONAL BIBLIOGRAPHY OF POLI. SCIENCE, CD8
INTERNATIONAL BIBLIOGRAPHY OF RESEARCH IN MARRIAGE
   AND THE FAMILY, CG19
INTERNATIONAL BIBLIOGRAPHY OF SOCIAL AND CULTURAL
   ANTHROPOLOGY, CF10
INTERNATIONAL BIBLIOGRAPHY OF SOCIOLOGY, CG6
INTERNATIONAL BIBLIOGRAPHY OF THE HISTORY OF
   RELIGIONS, BC3n
INTERNATIONAL BOOK TRADE DIRECTORY, AB10n
INTERNATIONAL BOOKS IN PRINT, AD99
INTERNATIONAL CODE BOTANICAL NOMENCLATURE, DH31
INTERNATIONAL CODE ZOOLOGICAL NOMENCLATURE, DH27
INTERNATIONAL COMPUTER BIBLIOGRAPHY, DC3
INTERNATIONAL CRITICAL TABLES, DB10
INTERNATIONAL CYCLOPEDIA OF MUSIC ..., BF36
INTERNATIONAL DICTIONARY OF APPLIED MATH, DB12
INTERNATIONAL DICTIONARY OF EDUCATION, CI19
INTERNATIONAL DICTIONARY OF GRAPHIC SYMBOLS, AJ75
INTERNATIONAL DICTIONARY OF HEATING, VENTILATING
   AND AIR CONDITIONING, DL26
INTERNATIONAL DICTIONARY OF SPORTS AND GAMES, AH58
INTERNATIONAL DICTIONARY OF WOMEN'S BIOG, AL21
INTERNATIONAL DIRECTORY OF ACRONYMS IN LIBRARY,
   INFORMATION, COMPUTER SCIENCES, AA40
INTERNATIONAL DIRECTORY OF ARTS, BE29
INTERNATIONAL DIRECTORY OF ... ARTISTS, BE41n
INTERNATIONAL DIRECTORY OF PHILOSOPHY ..., BB19
INTERNATIONAL ENCYCLOPEDIA OF HIGHER EDUC, CI18
INTERNATIONAL ENCYCLOPEDIA OF PHYSICAL CHEMISTRY
   AND CHEMICAL PHYSICS, DF21
INTERNATIONAL ENCYCLOPEDIA OF POPULATION, CG36
INTERNATIONAL ENCYCLOPEDIA OF PSYCHIATRY ..., CH10
INTERNATIONAL ENCYCLOPEDIA OF STATISTICS, CA28
INTERNATIONAL ENCYCLOPEDIA ... SOC. SCIENCES, CA17
INTERNATIONAL FOUNDATION DIRECTORY, AH28
INTERNATIONAL GEOLOGY REVIEW, DG23
INTERNATIONAL GUIDE TO LIBRARY, ARCHIVAL AND
   INFORMATION SCIENCE ASSOCIATIONS, AA61,
INTERNATIONAL HANDBOOK OF UNIVERSITIES, CI24
INTERNATIONAL INDEX TO MULTI-MEDIA INFO, AG32
International Information Services for the Physics
   and Engineering Communities, DE7
INTERNATIONAL LITERARY MARKET PLACE, AB10n
INTERNATIONAL MAPS AND ATLASES IN PRINT, AK4
INTERNATIONAL MEDIEVAL BIBLIOGRAPHY, CJ2n
INTERNATIONAL PHOTOGRAPHY INDEX, BE99
INTERNATIONAL POLITICAL SCIENCE ABSTRACTS, CD9
International Red Series, biography, AL22n
INTERNATIONAL RELATIONS DICTIONARY, CD19
INTERNATIONAL STANDARD BIBLE ENCYCLOPEDIA, BC24
INTERNATIONAL TRANSIT HANDBOOK ..., DL19n
INTERNATIONAL WHO'S WHO, AL22
INTERNATIONAL WHO'S WHO IN MUSIC, BF42
INTERNATIONAL ZOO YEARBOOK, DH18

INTERNATIONALE BIBLIOGRAPHIE DER
   ZEITSCHRIFTENLITERATUR, AF16
INTERPRETER'S DICTIONARY OF THE BIBLE, BC25
INTRODUCTION TO BRITISH GOVT PUBLICATIONS, AM5
INTRODUCTION TO CANADIAN BUSINESS, CC1
INTRODUCTION TO ... SOURCES HEALTH SCIENCES, DI9
INTRODUCTION TO U.S PUBLIC DOCUMENTS, AM14
INTRODUCTORY GUIDE TO ... SOURCES IN PHYSICS, DE2
INVENTAIRE CHRONOLOGIQUE, AD86
INVENTORY LIST (CGPC), AM63
INVENTORY OF MARRIAGE AND FAMILY LITERATURE, CG20
INVENTORY OF RESEARCH INTO HIGHER EDUC (Can) CI23n
IRREGULAR SERIALS & ANNUALS, AE4
IT FOCUS, DA6, DA21
JOURNAL OF ECONOMIC LITERATURE, CB10
JOURNALS (Can. govt), AM101
JOWITT'S DICTIONARY OF ENGLISH LAW, CE21
JUNIOR BOOK OF AUTHORS (Wilson series), AL62-AL66
JUNIOR HIGH SCHOOL LIBRARY CATALOG, AC27
KEESING'S CONTEMPORARY ARCHIVES, AH22
KEMPE'S ENGINEERS YEAR-BOOK, DL37
KEY SOURCES IN COMPARATIVE AND WORLD LIT., BD8
KEY TO ECONOMIC SCI. AND MANAGERIAL SCIENCES, CB11
KIRK OTHMER ENCYCLOPEDIA OF CHEM. TECHNOLOGY, DF22
KIRKUS REVIEWS, AC35
KISTER'S ATLAS BUYING GUIDE, AK2
KODANSHA ENCYCLOPEDIA OF JAPAN, AI28
KWIC INDEX TO YOUR ONTARIO GOVT SERVICES, AM45
Lande Collection, AD65
LANGENSCHEIDT'S ENCYCL DICTIONARY ENG/GERMAN, AJ31
LANGE'S HANDBOOK OF CHEMISTRY, DF28
LANGUAGE OF CANADIAN POLITICS, CD18
LANGUAGE OF THE FOREIGN BOOK TRADE, AB8
LANGUAGE OF THE HEALTH SCIENCES, DI28
LAROUSSE DICTIONARY OF PAINTERS, BE36
LAROUSSE GUIDE TO ASTRONOMY, DD22
LAURENTIANA PARUS AVANT 1821, AD66
LAW BOOKS, CE12n
LAW INFORMATION: CURRENT BOOKS ... SERIALS, CE12
LAWRENCE LANDE COLLECTION OF CANADIANA ..., AD65
LAYING THE FOUNDATIONS, AD96n
LEGAL BIBLIOGRAPHY FOR LAWYERS OF B.C., CE13
LEGAL COLLECTION FOR NON-LEGAL LIBS (B.C.), CE14
LEGAL MATERIALS FOR HIGH SCHOOL LIBS (Alta), CE9
LEGAL RESOURCE INDEX, CE17n
LETTERS IN CANADA, AC36
LIBRARIANS' GLOSSARY OF TERMS ..., AA36
LIBRARIAN'S HANDBOOK, AA31
LIBRARIAN'S PRACTICAL DICTIONARY IN 22 LANGS, AA38
LIBRARY AND INFORMATION SCIENCE: A GUIDE ..., AA1
LIBRARY AND INFORMATION SCIENCE ABSTRACTS, AA19
LIBRARY AND INFORMATION SCIENCE DICTIONARIES, AA32
LIBRARY ASSOCIATION YEAR BOOK, AA23n
LIBRARY JOURNAL, AC37
LIBRARY LITERATURE, AA20

Library of Congress Catalogues, AD7-AD19
Library of Congress - MONOGRAPHIC SERIES, AD17
Library of Congress - SUBJECTS, AD18
LIBRARY OF LITERARY CRITICISM ..., BD34
LIBRARY RESEARCH GUIDE TO EDUCATION, CI7
LIBRARY RESEARCH GUIDE TO HISTORY, CJ9n
LIBRARY RESEARCH GUIDE TO SOCIOLOGY, CG2
LIBRARY SCIENCE DISSERTATIONS 1925-1972, AA7
LIBRARY TECHNOLOGY REPORTS, AA30
LILLIAN ROXON'S ROCK ENCYCLOPEDIA, BF57n
LIST OF GEOGRAPHICAL ATLASES (LC), AK7
LIST OF PUBNS OF THE GOVT OF NEWF & LABRADOR, AM65
LIST OF UNESCO DOCUMENTS ..., AN21
LISTE DES LIVRES DISPONIBLES (Can), AD80, AD89
LISTE MENSUELLE ... DU GOUVERNMENT DU QUEBEC, AM77
LITERARY AND LIBRARY PRIZES, AH33
LITERARY HISTORY OF CANADA, BD60
LITERARY HISTORY OF ENGLAND, BD37
LITERARY HISTORY OF THE UNITED STATES, BD47
LITERARY MARKET PLACE, AB12
LITERARY RESEARCH GUIDE, BD7
LITERATURE OF GEOGRAPHY, DG1
LITERATURE OF JAZZ, BF2
LITERATURE OF MEDIEVAL HISTORY, CJ2
LITERATURE OF THE FILM, BG31
LITERATURES OF THE WORLD IN ENG. TRANSLATION, BD5
LITERATURE ON THE HISTORY OF PHYSICS, DE1
LIVELY ARTS INFORMATION DIRECTORY, BG4
LIVRES DE L'ANNEE (France), AD100n
LIVRES DISPONIBLES/ FRENCH BOOKS IN PRINT, AD101
LIVRES DU MOIS (France), AD100n
LIVRES ET AUTEURS QUEBECOISES, AC16
LOANWORDS INDEX, AJ71
LOCAL HISTORIES OF ONTARIO MUNICIPALITIES, CJ74
LOCAL HISTORY AND THE LIBRARY, CJ70
LOMA: LITERATURE ON MODERN ART, BE5n
LONDON BIBLIOGRAPHY OF THE SOCIAL SCIENCES, CA5
LONGMAN DICTIONARY OF CONTEMPORARY ENGLISH, AJ7
LONGMAN DICTIONARY OF ENGLISH IDIOMS, AJ7n
LONGMAN DICTIONARY OF PSYCHOLOGY PSYCHIATRY, CH11
LOOKING FOR MANITOBA GOVERNMENT PUBLICATIONS, AM87
LURELU, AC29n
LYMAN'S STANDARD CATALOGUE OF CANADA, BE86n
MACMILLAN BIBLE ATLAS, BC31
MACMILLAN BIOG ENCYCL PHOTOGRAPHIC ARTISTS, BE100
MACMILLAN BOOK OF CANADIAN PLACE NAMES, AK32
MACMILLAN BOOK OF PROVERBS ..., AF38
MACMILLAN CONCISE DICT. OF WORLD HISTORY, CJ17
MACMILLAN DICTIONARY FOR CHILDREN, AJ19n
MACMILLAN DICTIONARY OF CANADIAN BIOGRAPHY, AL42
MACMILLAN ENCYCLOPEDIA OF ARCHITECTS, BE61
MACMILLAN ENCYCLOPEDIC DICT. OF NUMISMATICS, BE84
MACMILLAN FILM BIBLIOGRAPHY, BG39
MAGAZINE INDUSTRY MARKETPLACE, AB12n
MAGAZINES FOR LIBRARIES, AC15

MAGILL'S LITERARY ANNUAL, BD18n
MAGILL'S SURVEY OF CINEMA, BG48
MALLET'S INDEX OF ARTISTS, BE37
MAMMALS OF CANADA, DH26
MANAGEMENT CONTENTS, CC17n
MANITOBA GOVERNMENT PUBLICATIONS, AM86
MANUAL OF MINERALOGY, DG38
MANUAL OF PATENT OFFICE PRACTICE, DA23n
MANUEL DE BIBLIOGRAPHIE, AC3
MANUEL DE BIBLIOGRAPHIE PHILOSOPHIQUE, BB10
MAP COLLECTIONS IN THE U.S AND CAN., AK11
MAPS OF CANADA, AK3
MARKET RESEARCH HANDBOOK, CC23
MARKS' STANDARD HANDBOOK FOR MECHANICAL ENG., DL40
MARRIAGE AND THE FAMILY: ... CHECKLIST (NLC), CG21
MASTER LIST OF NONSTELLAR OPTICAL ASTRONOMICAL
   OBJECTS, DD27
MASTERPIECES OF WORLD LIT. IN DIGEST, BD18, AL53n
MASTERPLOTS, BD18n
MATERIALS & METHODS FOR HISTORY RESEARCH, CJ9n
MATERIALS HANDBOOK (engineering), DL38
MATHEMATICAL HANDBOOK FOR SCIENTISTS AND
   ENGINEERS, DB9
MATHEMATICAL REVIEWS, DB5
MATHEMATICS DICTIONARY, DB13
McGOLDRICK'S HANDBOOK OF THE CANADIAN CUSTOMS
   TARIFF AND EXCISE, CC27
McGRAW HILL DICTIONARY OF ART, BE18
McGRAW HILL DICTIONARY OF MODERN ECONOMICS, CB14
McGRAW HILL DICTIONARY OF PHYSICS AND MATHEMATICS,
   DB14, DE18
McGRAW HILL DICTIONARY OF SCI. & TECH. TERMS, DA46
McGRAW HILL ENCYCLOPEDIA OF CHEMISTRY, DF23
McGRAW HILL ENCYCLOPEDIA OF ENERGY, DK15
McGRAW HILL ENCYCLOPEDIA OF ENVIR. SCIENCE, DK16
McGRAW HILL ENCYCLOPEDIA OF OCEAN AND ATMOSPHERIC
   SCIENCES, DG30
McGRAW HILL ENCYCLOPEDIA OF SCI. AND TECH., DA38
McGRAW HILL ENCYCLOPEDIA OF GEOL. SCIENCES, DG29
McGRAW HILL ENCYCLOPEDIA OF WORLD DRAMA, BD86
McGRAW HILL MODERN SCIENTISTS AND ENGINEERS, DA57
McGRAW HILL'S COMPILATION OF DATA COMMUNICATION
   STANDARDS, DC8
MEDIA REVIEW DIGEST, AG31
MEDIA SELECTION HANDBOOK, AG4
MEDICAL AND HEALTH ANNUAL, AI4n
MEDICAL AND HEALTH INFORMATION DIRECTORY, DI36
MEDICAL BIBLIOGRAPHY, DI6
MEDICAL BOOKS AND SERIALS IN PRINT, DI5
MEDICAL REFERENCE WORKS, 1679-1966, DI2n
MEDIEVAL STUDIES: AN INTRODUCTION, CJ10
MEDLARS, DI14n
MEDLINE, DI14n
MELLONI'S ILLUSTRATED MEDICAL DICTIONARY, DI22
MERCK INDEX, DI34

MERIT STUDENTS ENCYCLOPEDIA, AI10
METALS HANDBOOK, DL41
Metropolitan Museum of Art Library. CATALOG, BE12
MICROBIOLOGY ABSTRACTS, DH13
MICROFORM MARKET PLACE, AB13
MICROFORM REVIEW, AC42
MICROLOG INDEX, AM57, CA53
MINERALOGICAL ABSTRACTS, DG17
MINERALS YEARBOOK, DG24
MLA DIRECTORY OF PERIODICALS, BD6n
MLA INTERNATIONAL BIBLIOGRAPHY ..., BD6
MODERN AMERICAN USAGE, AJ49
MODERN DICTIONARY OF SOCIOLOGY, CG37
MODERN ELECTRONIC CIRCUITS REFERENCE MANUAL, DL39
MODERN ENGLISH CANADIAN POETRY, BD61n
MODERN ENGLISH CANADIAN PROSE, BD61n
MODERN WORLD DRAMA: AN ENCYCLOPEDIA, BD85
MONTHLY CATALOG OF UNITED STATES GOVT PUBS, AM25
MONTHLY CHECKLIST OF STATE PUBLICATIONS, AM26
MONTHLY SELECTION OF BOOKS PUBLISHED (HMSO), AM9
MOODY'S BANK & FINANCE MANUAL, CC54
Moody's publications, CC54
MOTION PICTURE DIRECTORS, BG40n
MOTION PICTURE PERFORMERS, BG40
MUNICIPAL GOVERNMENT REFERENCE SOURCES, CA54
MUNICIPAL YEAR BOOK, CD24
MUNN'S ENCYCLOPEDIA OF BANKING AND FINANCE, CC28
MURET SANDERS GERMAN DICTIONARY, AJ31n
MUSIC, BOOKS ON MUSIC AND SOUND RECORDINGS, AG22
MUSIC EDUCATION, CI3n
MUSIC IN PRINT, BF10
MUSIC INDEX, BF16
MUSIC REFERENCE AND RESEARCH MATERIALS, BF7
MUSICAL CANADIANA: A SUBJECT INDEX, BF19
MUSICAL INSTRUMENTS ... DICTIONARY, BF43
MUSICIANS IN CANADA, BF48
MYTHOLOGY: AN ILLUSTRATED ENCYCLOPEDIA, BC51
MYTHOLOGY OF ALL RACES, BC52
NAMES IN THE HISTORY OF PSYCHOLOGY ..., CH17
National Agricultural Lib (U.S.) CATALOG, DJ6-DJ7
NATIONAL ATLAS OF CANADA, AK22
NATIONAL ATLAS OF THE UNITED STATES, AK21
NATIONAL BUILDING CODE OF CANADA, DL42
NATIONAL CYCLOPEDIA OF AMERICAN BIOGRAPHY, AL34
NATIONAL DIRECTORY OF NEWSLETTERS ..., AE8
NATIONAL FACULTY DIRECTORY, CI25
National Film Board catalogues, AG17-18
NATIONAL GEOGRAPHIC ATLAS, AK18
NATIONAL INDEX OF AMERICAN IMPRINTS (to 1800) D43
National Info. Center for Educ. Materials, AG7n
National Lib.of Medicine (U.S), CATALOG, DI8
NATIONAL MAP COLLECTION CATALOGUE (PAC), AK9
NATIONAL NEWSPAPER INDEX, AF22
NATIONAL REGISTER OF MICROFORM MASTERS, AD112
National Research Council publications, DA9

National Technical Information Service, DA30n
NATIONAL TRADE AND PROFESSIONAL ASSOCS (U.S), CC41
NATIONAL UNION CATALOG OF MS COLLECTIONS, AD114
NATIONAL UNION CATALOG(s), AD10-AD16, AD114
NATURALISTS DIRECTORY INTERNATIONAL, DH37
NAVIGATIONS, TRAFFIQUES & DISCOVERIES, AD96n
NELSON'S COMPLETE CONCORDANCE (Bible), BC36-BC37
NEW ASSOCIATIONS AND PROJECTS, AH27n
NEW BOOK OF KNOWLEDGE, AI12
NEW BOOKS, (U.S. GPO), AM29
NEW BRUNSWICK GOVERNMENT DOCTS, AM70
NEW CAMBRIDGE BIBLIOG. OF ENG. LITERATURE, BD42
NEW CAMBRIDGE MODERN HISTORY, CJ31
NEW CATHOLIC ENCYCLOPEDIA, BC15
NEW CENTURY DICTIONARY AND CYCLOPEDIA, AJ8
NEW DICTIONARY OF SOCIOLOGY, CG38
NEW EMILY POST'S ETIQUETTE, AH49
NEW ENCYLOPEDIA OF THE OPERA, BF49
NEW FEMINIST SCHOLARSHIP: ... (bibliog), CG50
NEW FILM INDEX, BG36
NEW GROVE DICTIONARY OF MUSIC AND MUSICIANS, BF34
NEW GUIDE TO POPULAR GOVERNMENT PUBLICATIONS, AM16
NEW ILLUS. ENCYCLOPEDIA OF WORLD HISTORY, CJ16
NEW INFORMATION SYSTEMS AND SERVICES, AB17n
NEW INTERNATIONAL ABBREVIATIONS DICTIONARY, AJ67
NEW INTERNATIONAL ATLAS, AK20
NEW INTERNATIONAL DICT. BIBLICAL ARCHAEOLOGY, BC29
NEW KOBBE'S COMPLETE OPERA BOOK, BF50
NEW LAROUSSE ENCYCLOPEDIA OF MYTHOLOGY, BC53
NEW OXFORD ATLAS, AK19
NEW OXFORD COMPANION TO MUSIC, BF35
NEW OXFORD HISTORY OF MUSIC, BF44
NEW PERIODICAL TITLE ABBREVIATIONS, AE1n
NEW READER'S GUIDE TO AFRICAN LITERATURE, BD20
NEW RESEARCH CENTERS, AH29
NEW SABIN, AD40
NEW SCHAFF-HERZOG ENCYCLOPEDIA OF RELIGIOUS KNOWLEDGE, BC18
NEW SERIAL TITLES, AE16
NEW SERIAL TITLES, 1950-1970: SUBJECT GUIDE, AE16n
NEW SPECIAL LIBRARIES, AA45n
NEW TECHNICAL BOOKS, DA8
NEW WESTMINSTER DICTIONARY OF THE BIBLE, BC22
New York Public Lib. CATALOG MUSIC COLLECTION BF12
_____. CATALOG DANCE COLLECTION, BG19
_____. CATALOG LOCAL HIST., GENEALOGY, CJ71n
NEW YORK REVIEW OF BOOKS, AC55
NEW YORK TIMES BIOGRAPHICAL SERVICE, AL23
NEW YORK TIMES BOOK REVIEW, AC56
NEW YORK TIMES ENCYCLOPEDIA OF TELEVISION, BG53
NEW YORK TIMES FILM REVIEWS, AG33, BG49
NEW YORK TIMES INDEX, AF24
NEW YORK TIMES OBITUARIES INDEX, AL15
NEW YORK TIMES THEATER REVIEWS, BG24
Newberry Library, CF13

Newberry Library ... American Indian bibliographies, CF14
NEWFOUNDLAND SONGS AND BALLADS IN PRINT, BF25
NEWNES DICTIONARY OF DATES, AH42
NEWSCOM, AH24
NEWSPAPERS IN MICROFORM, AE22-AE23
NFB FILM CATALOGUE, AG18
NICEM Indexes, AG7-AG15
NINETEENTH CENTURY LITERATURE CRITICISM, BD13n
NINETEENTH CENTURY READERS' GUIDE, AF4,
NINETEENTH CENTURY SHORT TITLE CATALOGUE, AD29
NLM CATALOG, DI8n
NOTABLE CANADIAN CHILDREN'S BOOKS, AC26
NORTH AMERICAN HORTICULTURE, DJ14
NORTHERN ONTARIO: A BIBLIOGRAPHY, CJ75
NTIS, DA30n
NUC AUDIOVISUAL MATERIALS, AG6
NUC CARTOGRAPHIC MATERIALS, AK8
NUC REGISTER OF ADDITIONAL LOCATIONS, AD10n
NUCLEAR SCIENCE ABSTRACTS, DE8
OBITUARIES ON FILE 1940-78, AH21n
OBITUARIES ON FILE, AL16
OBSERVER'S HANDBOOK, DD24
OCEAN AND MARINE DICTIONARY, DG31
OCEAN WORLD ENCYCLOPEDIA, DG32
OCEANIC ABSTRACTS, DG18
OFFICIAL GAZETTE, U.S. PATENT OFFICE, DA23n
OFFICIAL JOURNAL (PATENTS), (U.K.), DA23n
OFFICIAL MUSEUM DIRECTORY, BE28n
OFFICIAL PUBLICATIONS IN BRITAIN, AM3
OFFICIAL PUBLISHING, AM1
-OLOGIES AND -ISMS, AJ62
ONE-PARENT FAMILY: PERSPECTIVES ... BIBLIOG. CG22
ONLINE BIBLIOGRAPHIC DATABASES, AB23
ONLINE DATABASE SEARCH SERVICES DIRECTORY, AB24
ONT. GOVT PUBLICATIONS: MONTHLY CHECKLIST, AM83
ONT. GOVERNMENT PUBLICATIONS REPORT, AM84
ONTARIO'S HERITAGE: ... ARCHIVAL RESOURCES, CJ69
ONTARIO'S HISTORY IN MAPS, CJ27
OPENING DAY COLLECTION, AC33n
ORBIT USER MANUAL, AB30
ORGANIZATION OF THE GOVERNMENT OF CANADA, AM39
ORIGIN AND MEANING OF PLACE NAMES IN CANADA, AK32n
OTTEMILLER'S INDEX TO PLAYS IN COLLECTIONS, BD81
OUTSTANDING ACADEMIC BOOKS AND NONPRINT ..., AC33n
OUVRAGES DE REFERENCE DU QUEBEC, AC2
OXFORD AMERICAN DICTIONARY, AJ12
OXFORD BIBLE ATLAS, BC32
OXFORD COMPANION, BF35n
OXFORD COMPANION TO AMERICAN LITERATURE, BD49
OXFORD COMPANION TO ART, BE22
OXFORD COMPANION TO CAN. HIST. & LIT., BD62, CJ64
OXFORD COMPANION TO CANADIAN LITERATURE, BD63
OXFORD COMPANION TO CHILDREN'S LITERATURE, BD105
OXFORD COMPANION TO CLASSICAL LITERATURE, BD21

OXFORD COMPANION TO ENGLISH LITERATURE, BD41
OXFORD COMPANION TO FILM, BG50
OXFORD COMPANION TO THE DECORATIVE ARTS, BE79
OXFORD COMPANION TO THE THEATRE, BG25
OXFORD COMPANION TO TWENTIETH CENTURY ART, BE23
Oxford Companions (French, German, Spanish), BD21n
OXFORD DICTIONARY OF ENGLISH ETYMOLOGY, AJ45
OXFORD DICTIONARY OF QUOTATIONS, AF35
OXFORD DICTIONARY OF SAINTS, BC40n
OXFORD DICTIONARY OF THE CHRISTIAN CHURCH, BC16
OXFORD DUDEN PICTORIAL ENGLISH DICTIONARY, AJ32n
OXFORD DUDEN PICTORIAL GER/ENG DICTIONARY, AJ32
OXFORD ENGLISH DICTIONARY, AJ4
OXFORD GUIDE TO ENGLISH USAGE, AJ50
OXFORD HISTORY OF ENGLAND, CJ37
OXFORD HISTORY OF ENGLISH LITERATURE, BD43
OXFORD HISTORY OF MUSIC, BF44n
OXFORD ILLUSTRATED DICTIONARY, AJ6n
OXFORD LATIN DICTIONARY, AJ43
P.E.I. PROVINCIAL GOVERNMENT ... CHECKLIST, AM68
PAINTING IN CANADA, BE67
PAIS BULLETIN, AF10
PAPERBOUND BOOKS IN PRINT, AD63
PARLIAMENTS OF THE WORLD, CD23
PATENT OFFICE RECORD (Canada), DA23
PATTERSON'S AMERICAN EDUCATION, CI26
Peabody Museum of Archaeology and Ethnology Lib. catalogue, CF15
PEACE RESEARCH ABSTRACTS JOURNAL, CD11
PELICAN HISTORY OF ART, BE31
PENGUIN COMPANION TO LITERATURE, BD22
PENGUIN DICTIONARY OF DECORATIVE ARTS, BE76
PEOPLE'S CHRONOLOGY, AH43
PERFORMING ARTS BIOGRAPHY MASTER INDEX, BG5
PERFORMING ARTS BOOKS, BG6
PERFORMING ARTS RESOURCES, BG7
PERIODEX, AF13
PERIODICAL INDEXES ... SOC. SCI. & HUM., CA10
PERIODICAL TITLE ABBREVIATIONS, AE1
PERIODICALS IN CANADIAN LAW LIBS, UNION LIST, CE15
PERMANENT AND PROVISIONAL STANDING ORDERS OF THE HOUSE OF COMMONS, AM32
PESTICIDE INDEX, DJ26
PHAIDON BOOK OF THE OPERA, BF53
PHILOSOPHER'S GUIDE, BB1
PHILOSOPHER'S INDEX, BB5-BB7
PHILOSOPHY OF EDUCATION, CI3n
PHOTOGRAPHIC LITERATURE, BE95
PHOTOGRAPHY BOOKS INDEX, BE101
PHOTOS CANADA, AG24
PHYSICIANS DESK REFERENCE, DI35
PHYSICIAN'S DRUG MANUAL: PRESCRIPTION AND NONPRESCRIPTION DRUGS, DI35n
PHYSICS ABSTRACTS, DE9, DE21
PHYSICS BRIEFS, DE10

PICTORIAL GUIDE TO THE PLANETS, DD23
PICTURESQUE EXPRESSIONS, AJ61
PINYIN CHINESE ENGLISH DICTIONARY, AJ39
PLACES IN ONTARIO, AI25n
PLAY INDEX, BD82
PLAYER'S LIBRARY ..., BD73
PLAYS: A CLASSIFIED GUIDE, BD82n
PLEINS FEUX SUR LA LITTERATURE DE JEUNESSE AU CANADA FRANCAISE, AC29n
POETRY EXPLICATION, BD70
POETRY HANDBOOK: A DICTIONARY OF TERMS, BD68
POLITICAL HANDBOOK OF THE WORLD, CD25
POLITICAL SCIENCE ABSTRACTS, CD12
POLITICS: CANADA, AM50
Pollard and Redgrave, AD24
POLLUTION ABSTRACTS, DK11
POOLE'S INDEX, AF3
POPULAR DICTIONARY OF BUDDHISM, BC14
POPULAR SONG INDEX, BF23
PRACTICAL GUIDE TO CANADIAN POLITICAL ECONOMY, CD1
PRAEGER ENCYCLOPEDIA OF ART, BE24
Prince Edward Island Bibliography, AD83
PRINCETON ENCYCLOPEDIA OF POETRY AND POETICS, BD71
PRINT REFERENCE SOURCES, BE13
PRINTED RECORD, AD74
PROFILES IN BELIEF, BC17
PROFILES 2, AL70
PROGRESS IN AEROSPACE SCIENCES, DL16
PROGRESS IN MATERIALS SCIENCE, DL17
PRUDENTIAL'S BOOK OF CAN. WINNERS AND HEROES, AH53
PSEUDONYMS AND NICKNAMES, AJ64
PSYCHOLOGICAL ABSTRACTS, CH6
PUBLIC AFFAIRS INFORMATION SERVICE BULLETIN, AF10
Public Archives of Canada Catalogues, AD116-AD117
_____, NATIONAL MAP COLLECTION CATALOGUE, AK9
PUBLIC LIBRARY CATALOG, AC17
PUBLICATIONS CATALOGUE (Alta Govt), AM91
PUBLICATIONS OF THE CAN. DEPT OF AGRICULTURE, DJ8
PUBLICATIONS OF THE EUROPEAN COMMUNITIES, AN24
PUBLICATIONS OF THE GOVT OF BRITISH COLUMBIA, AM94
PUBLICATIONS OF THE GOVT OF ONTARIO, AM80-AM82,
PUBLICATIONS OF THE GOVT OF THE NWT, AM88
PUBLICATIONS OF THE GOVT ... PROV. OF CANADA, AM79
PUBLICATIONS OF THE GOVT ... UPPER CANADA, AM78
PUBLICATIONS OF THE GOVTS OF N.S, P.E.I, N.B, AM66
PUBLICATIONS OF THE NATIONAL RESEARCH COUNCIL, DA9
PUBLICATIONS OF THE PROVINCE OF N.S, AM67
PUBLISHERS' CATALOGS ANNUAL, AD50
PUBLISHERS' DIRECTORY, AB14
PUBLISHERS, DISTRIBUTORS & WHOLESALERS (U.S), AB15
PUBLISHERS' INTERNATIONAL DIRECTORY, AB16
PUBLISHER'S PRACTICAL DICTIONARY IN 20 LANGS, AB9
PUBLISHERS' TRADE LIST ANNUAL, AD49
PUBLISHERS WEEKLY, AB5
PUBLISHING NEWS, AM61

QL SYSTEMS MANUAL, AB31
QUEBECOIS DICTIONARY, AJ21n
QUEEN'S PRINTER PUBNS PRICE LIST (B.C.), AM96
QUICK CANADIAN FACTS, AH18
QUILL AND QUIRE, AB6, AC39
QUOTABLE WOMAN, AF36
R&D PROJECTS IN DOCUMENTATION, LIBRARIANSHIP, AA21
RADAR, AF14
RADIALS BULLETIN, AA11n
RAND MCNALLY NEW CONCISE ATLAS, DD28
RANDOM HOUSE COLLEGE DICTIONARY, AJ13
RANDOM HOUSE DICTIONARY, AJ13
RANDOM HOUSE ENCYCLOPEDIA, AI6
READER'S ADVISER, AC18
READERS ADVISORY SERVICE, AC40
READER'S ENCYCLOPEDIA, BD9
READER'S ENCYCLOPEDIA OF AMERICAN LITERATURE, BD50
READER'S ENCYCLOPEDIA OF WORLD DRAMA, BD84
READERS' GUIDE (RGPL), AF6
READER'S GUIDE TO CANADIAN HISTORY, CJ54
READER'S GUIDE TO THE CANADIAN NOVEL, BD98
READER'S GUIDE TO THE GREAT RELIGIONS, BC1
READER'S GUIDE TO THE SOCIAL SCIENCES, CA1
RECENTLY PUBLISHED ARTICLES (history), CJ12
RECOMMENDED BEST BOOKS FOR SMALL AND MEDIUM-SIZED LIBRARIES..., AC1n
REFERATIVNYJ ZHURNAL, DA20, AA17
REFERENCE AND SUBSCRIPTION BOOKS REVIEWS, AC19
REFERENCE BOOKS FOR SMALL AND MEDIUM-SIZED LIBRARIES, AC20
REFERENCE GUIDE TO ENGLISH, AMERICAN AND CANADIAN LITERATURE, BD27
REFERENCE SERVICES REVIEW, AC44
REFERENCE SOURCES IN LIBRARY AND INFORMATION SERVICES: A GUIDE, AA2
REFERENCE SOURCES IN SOCIAL WORK, CG4
REFERENCE SOURCES ON CANADIAN EDUCATION, CI1
REGISTER OF POST-GRADUATE DISSERTATIONS IN PROGRESS IN HISTORY, CJ52
REGISTER OF U.N. SERIAL PUBLICATIONS, AN14
RELIGION INDEX ONE, BC6
RELIGION INDEX TWO, BC7
RELIGIONS: A SELECT, CLASSIFIED BIBLIOGRAPHY, BC5
RELIGIOUS AND THEOLOGICAL ABSTRACTS, BC8
RELIGIOUS BOOKS, BC9
REMOTE SENSING OF EARTH RESOURCES: A GUIDE, DG8
REPERTOIRE BIBLIOGRAPHIQUE DE LA PHILOSOPHIE, BB9
REPERTOIRE D'ART ET D'ARCHEOLOGIE, BE15
REPERTOIRE DES PUBNS GOUVERNEMENTALES (Que), AM72
REPERTOIRE DES PUBNS GOUVERNEMENTALES GRATUITES (Que), AM76
REPERTOIRE INTERNAT. DES SOURCES MUSICALES, BF14
REPORTS ON PROGRESS IN PHYSICS, DE13
REPRINT BULLETIN BOOK REVIEWS, AC45
RESEARCH CENTERS DIRECTORY, AH29
RESEARCH COLLECTIONS IN CANADIAN LIBRARIES, AA54
RESEARCH GUIDE FOR PSYCHOLOGY, CH1
RESEARCH GUIDE IN ECONOMICS, CB3
RESEARCH GUIDE TO PHILOSOPHY, BB2
RESEARCH GUIDE TO RELIGIOUS STUDIES, BC2
RESEARCH GUIDE TO THE HISTORY OF WESTERN ART, BE1
RESEARCH IN BRITISH UNIVERSITIES ..., AF28
RESEARCH LIBS AND COLLECTIONS IN THE U.K., AA55
RESOURCES FOR FEMINIST RESEARCH, CG54
RESOURCES FOR NATIVE PEOPLES STUDIES, CF6
RESOURCES IN EDUCATION, AA13, CI13
REVIEW OF HISTORICAL PUBLNS RELATING TO CAN., CJ55
REVIEW OF THE ONTARIO GOVT PUBNS SERVICE, AM49
REVIEWING LIBRARIAN, AC52
REVIEWS IN ANTHROPOLOGY, CF16
REVIEWS OF MODERN PHYSICS, DE14
REVISED REGULATIONS OF ONTARIO, AM11
REVISED STATUTES OF CANADA, AM106
REVISED STATUTES OF ONTARIO, AM110
RIE, AA12
RILA, BE14
RILM: ABSTRACTS OF MUSIC LITERATURE, BF17
RISM, BF14
Robert's DICTIONNAIRE, AJ25
ROBERT'S RULES OF ORDER, AH51
Roget, AJ51
ROLLING STONE ILLUS. HISTORY OF ROCK & ROLL, BF57
ROYAL CANADIAN ACADEMY OF THE ARTS, BE45
RQ, AC43
RULES OF THE GAME, AH61
RUSSIAN CHEMICAL REVIEWS, DF12
Ryder, AC5
Sabin, AD39, AD41
SACRED BOOKS OF THE EAST, BC41
SAFIRE'S POLITICAL DICTIONARY, CD20
SAGE FAMILY STUDIES ABSTRACTS, CG27
SAGE URBAN STUDIES ABSTRACTS, CA55
SASKATCHEWAN BIBLIOGRAPHY, AD94
SCHOOL LIBRARY JOURNAL, AC53
SCHOOL LIBRARY MEDIA ANNUAL, AA26
SCHWANN guides, BF60
SCIENCE ABSTRACTS, DA21
SCIENCE AND ENGINEERING LITERATURE: A GUIDE, DA3
SCIENCE AND TECHNOLOGY: INTROD. TO THE LIT., DA4n
SCIENCE BOOKS AND FILMS, DA10
SCIENCE CITATION INDEX, DA22, AF17
SCIENCE FICTION BOOK REVIEW INDEX, BD99
SCIENCE FICTION, HORROR & FANTASY FILM AND TELEVISION CREDITS, BG47
SCIENCE FICTION SHORT STORY INDEX, BD100n
SCIENCE YEAR, AI11n, DA39
SCIENTIFIC AND TECHNICAL AEROSPACE REPORTS, DL12
SCIENTIFIC AND TECHNICAL BOOKS AND SERIALS IN PRINT, DA11
SCIENTIFIC AND TECHNICAL INFO. RESOURCES, DA5

SCIENTIFIC AND TECHNICAL INFO. SOURCES, DA1
SCIENTIFIC AND TECHNICAL SOCIETIES OF CANADA, DA51
SCOTT'S INDUSTRIAL DIRECTORY OF ONTARIO
  MANUFACTURERS, CC42
SCOTT'S STANDARD POSTAGE STAMP CATALOGUE, BE86
SCULPTURE INDEX, BE72
Searchable Physics Information Notices, DE11
SECOND BARNHART DICTIONARY OF NEW ENGLISH, AJ14
SECTIONAL LISTS (HMSO), AM10
SELECT BIBLIOGRAPHY ON HIGHER EDUCATION, CI6n
SELECTED BIBLIOGRAPHY OF MUSICAL CANADIANA, BF3
SELECTIVE BIBLIOGRAPHY ENG. AND AMER. LIT., BD24
SENIOR HIGH SCHOOL LIBRARY CATALOG, AC28
SEQUELS, BD96
SERIALS FOR LIBRARIES, AE2
SERIES SSH: SOCIAL SCIENCES/ HUMANITIES, CA9
SESSIONAL PAPERS OF THE DOMINION OF CANADA, AM103
SEVENTH AGE: A BIBLIOG. OF CANADIAN SOURCES, CG11
SEX RESEARCH BIBLIOGS, CG26
SEX ROLES: A RESEARCH BIBLIOGRAPHY, CG24
SEXUAL ABUSE OF CHILDREN: ... BIBLIOGRAPHY, CG13
Sheehy, AC4
SHEPHERD'S GLOSSARY OF GRAPHIC SIGNS SYMBOLS, AJ77
SHORT STORY INDEX, BD100
SHORT-TITLE CATALOGUE ... 1475-1640, AD24-AD25
SHORT-TITLE CATALOGUE ... 1641-1700, AD26-AD27
SHORTER OXFORD DICTIONARY, AJ5
SILENT FILMS, BG48n
16MM FILMS AVAILABLE ... PUBLIC LIBRARIES OF
  METROPOLITAN TORONTO, AG19
SOCIAL PROTEST FROM THE LEFT IN CANADA, CD7n
SOCIAL SCIENCE CITATION INDEX, AF18
SOCIAL SCIENCE REFERENCE SOURCES, CA2
SOCIAL SCIENCES & HUMANITIES INDEX, AF8n-AF9
SOCIAL SCIENCES CITATION INDEX, CA14
SOCIAL SCIENCES INDEX, AF9
SOCIAL WORK RESEARCH & ABSTRACTS, CG30
SOCIOLOGICAL ABSTRACTS, CG31
SOCIOLOGY: AN INTERNAT. BIBLIOG. OF SERIAL(s), CG8
SOILS OF CANADA, DJ23
SOLAR ENERGY DICTIONARY, DK20
SOLAR ENERGY INDEX, DK12
SOMETHING ABOUT THE AUTHOR, AL69
SONG INDEX, BF26
SONGS IN COLLECTIONS, BF20
SOURCE-BOOK OF CAN. HIST.: ... DOCUMENTS, CJ63
SOURCEBOOK OF LIBRARY TECHNOLOGY, AA30n
SOURCEBOOK ON CANADIAN WOMEN, CG45
SOURCEBOOK ON HEALTH SCIENCES LIBRARIANSHIP, DI3
SOURCEBOOK ON THE ENVIRONMENT: A GUIDE, DK4
SOURCES FOR SERIALS, AE3n
SOURCES IN CANADIAN MUSIC: BF13
SOURCES OF FR. CAN. CHILDREN'S ... BOOKS, AC29
SOURCES OF INFORMATION FOR CANADIAN BUSINESS, CC4
SOURCES OF INFORMATION FOR ... GEOLOGY, DG3

SOURCES OF INFORMATION IN THE SOCIAL SCIENCES, CA4
SPECIAL ISSUES INDEX: SPECIALIZED CONTENTS OF
  BUSINESS ... JOURNALS, CC16n
SPECIAL LIST OF CANADIAN GOVT PUBLICATIONS, AM60
SPEECH INDEX, AF39
SPIN, DE11
SPORT BIBLIOGRAPHY, AH55
SPORTS AND RECREATION INDEX, AH56
STAGE, SCENERY, MACHINERY AND LIGHTING, BG20n
STAMPS OF THE WORLD, BE86n
STANDARD & POOR'S REGISTER OF CORPORATIONS,
  DIRECTORS AND EXECUTIVES, CC43
STANDARD DICTIONARY OF CANADIAN BIOGRAPHY, AL41
STANDARD DICTIONARY OF METEORLOGICAL SCIENCES:
  ENG-FR/ FR-ENG., DG33
STANDARD HANDBOOK FOR CIVIL ENGINEERS, DL44
STANDARD HANDBOOK FOR ELECTRICAL ENGINEERS, DL45
STANDARD HANDBOOK FOR PLANT ENGINEERING, DL46
STANDARD PERIODICAL DIRECTORY, AE9
Standards Council of Canada DIRECTORY AND INDEX OF
  STANDARDS, DL47
STANDING ORDERS LEGISLATIVE ASSEMBLY (Ont.), AM44
STAR (sci-tech reports), DL12
STAR ATLAS OF REFERENCE STARS NONSTELLAR OBJ. DD29
STATESMAN'S ... GAZETTEER, AH3n
STATESMAN'S YEAR-BOOK, AH3
STATISTICAL ABSTRACT OF THE UNITED STATES, CA34
STATISTICAL TABLES FOR BIOLOGICAL, AGRICULTURAL
  AND MEDICAL RESEARCH, DH32
STATISTICAL THEORY AND METHOD ABSTRACTS, DB6
STATISTICAL YEARBOOK (U.N.), CA44
STATISTICS AFRICA, CA31n
STATISTICS AMERICA, CA31n
STATISTICS ASIA AND AUSTRALASIA, CA31n
STATISTICS CANADA CATALOGUE, CA41
STATISTICS EUROPE, CA31
STATISTICS SOURCES, CA32
STATUTES OF CANADA, AM105
STATUTES OF THE PROVINCE OF ONTARIO, AM109
STC CATALOGUE(s), AD24-AD27
STEDMAN'S MEDICAL DICTIONARY, DI27
STEINBERG'S DICTIONARY OF BRITISH HISTORY, CJ38
STRUCTURAL ENGINEERING HANDBOOK, DL48
STUDENT ANTHROPOLOGIST'S HANDBOOK, CF7
STUDENT SOCIOLOGIST'S HANDBOOK, CG1
SUBJECT BIBLIOGRAPHIES, (U.S. GPO), AM28
SUBJECT COLLECTIONS, AA49
SUBJECT COLLECTIONS IN EUROPEAN LIBRARIES, AA53
SUBJECT DIRECTORY OF SPECIAL LIBRARIES, AA45n
SUBJECT GUIDE TO BOOKS IN PRINT, AD54
SUBJECT GUIDE TO FORTHCOMING BOOKS, AD58
SUBJECT INDEX OF MODERN BOOKS (Brit. Lib.), AD6
SUBJECT LIST (CGPC), AM62
SUFFIXES AND OTHER WORD FINAL ELEMENTS, AJ62n
SUICIDE: A GUIDE, CG16

SURVEY OF BUSINESS ATTITUDES AND INVESTMENT
   SPENDING INTENTIONS, CC30
SURVEY OF CANADIAN HERBARIA, DH35
SYMBOL SOURCEBOOK, AJ76
SYNOPSIS & CLASSIFICATION LIVING ORGANISMS, DH34
TABLES OF PHYSICAL AND CHEMICAL CONSTANTS AND SOME
   MATHEMATICAL FUNCTIONS, DE23
TECHNICAL BOOK REVIEW INDEX, AC62
TESSIER, AG30
TESTS IN PRINT III, CH14
THEATRE AND ALLIED ARTS, BG20
THEATRE AND CINEMA ARCHITECTURE, BG20n
THEATRE CANADIEN D'EXPRESSION FRANCAISE, BD76
THEATRE: STAGE TO SCREEN TO TELEVISION, BG23
THEATRE WORLD, BG26n
THEATRICAL COSTUME, BE92
THESAURUS OF ENGLISH WORDS AND PHRASES, AJ51
THESAURUS OF ERIC DESCRIPTORS, AA16
THESES IN CANADIAN POLITICAL STUDIES, CD13
THIRD DICTIONARY OF ACRONYMS AND ABBREV., AJ69
THOMAS REGISTER OF AMERICAN MANUFACTURERS, CC44
TIMES ATLAS OF THE MOON, DD30
TIMES ATLAS OF THE OCEANS, AK15
TIMES ATLAS OF THE WORLD, AK14
TIMES ATLAS OF WORLD HISTORY, CJ24
TIMES INDEX, AF25
TIMES INDEX GAZETTEER, AK27
TIMES LITERARY SUPPLEMENT, AC57
TIMETABLES OF HISTORY, CJ19
TITLE GUIDE TO THE TALKIES, BG45
TO KNOW AND BE KNOWN, AM53
Toronto Public Library Collection, AD66
TOURING ARTISTS' DIRECTORY OF THE PERFORMING ARTS
   IN CANADA, BG9
TOXIC SUBSTANCES SOURCEBOOK, DK25
TRACING YOUR ANCESTORS IN CANADA, AL5
TRADE MARKS JOURNAL, DA24
TRANSLATIONS REGISTER INDEX, DA33
TRESOR DE LA LANGUE FRANCAISE, AJ26
TUNE IN YESTERDAY, BG52
TWENTIETH CENTURY AUTHORS, AL59
TWENTIETH CENTURY CHILDREN'S WRITERS, AL68
TWENTIETH CENTURY LITERARY CRITICISM, BD13n
TWENTIETH CENTURY ROMANCE & GOTHIC WRITERS, BD101
TWENTIETH CENTURY SHORT STORY EXPLICATION, BD103
Twentieth Century Writers series, BD101n
U.S. BOOK PUBLISHING YEARBOOK AND DIRECTORY, AB4
U.S. GOVERNMENT BOOKS, AM30
U.S. HIGHER EDUCATION, CI3n
UFAW HANDBOOK ON THE CARE AND MAINTENANCE OF
   LABORATORY ANIMALS, DH33
ULRICH'S INTERNATIONAL PERIODICALS DIRECTORY, AE3
UNESCO CATALOGUE OF REPRODUCTIONS OF PAINTINGS,
   AG26-AG27, BE51-BE52
UNESCO LIST OF DOCUMENTS AND PUBLICATIONS, AN22

UNESCO STATISTICAL YEARBOOK, CA45
UNESCO'S INTERNATIONAL BIBLIOGRAPHY OF THE SOCIAL
   SCIENCES, CB9n, CD8n, CF10n, CG6n
UNION LIST OF CANADIAN NEWSPAPERS, AE25
UNION LIST OF MS, CAN. REPOSITORIES, AD117n, CJ68
UNION LIST OF NON-CANADIAN NEWSPAPERS, AE25n
UNION LIST OF SCI. SERIALS IN CAN. LIBRARIES, AE18
UNION LIST OF SERIALS ... U.S. AND CANADA, AE15
UNION LIST OF SERIALS IN THE SOCIAL SCIENCES AND
   HUMANITIES HELD BY CAN.LIBRARIES, AE19
UNITED NATIONS DOCUMENT SERIES SYMBOLS, AN18
UNITED NATIONS DOCUMENTATION, AN11
UNITED NATIONS DOCUMENTS AND PUBLICATIONS, AN8
UNITED NATIONS DOCUMENTS INDEX, AN15-AN17
UNITED STATES AND CANADA (economic atlas), CB17
UNITED STATES CATALOG, AD47
UNITED STATES LOCAL HISTORIES (in LC), CJ71
UNITED STATES POLITICAL SCIENCE DOCUMENTS, CD14
UNIVERSAL REFERENCE SYSTEM: POLITICAL SCIENCE CD15
URBAN AND REGIONAL REFERENCES, CA56
Urban Studies Information Guide series, CA57
USE OF BIOLOGICAL LITERATURE, DH2
USE OF CHEMICAL LITERATURE, DF3
USE OF EARTH SCIENCES LITERATURE, DG5
USE OF ENGINEERING LITERATURE, DL1
USE OF MANAGEMENT AND BUSINESS LITERATURE, CC5
USE OF MATHEMATICAL LITERATURE, DB2
USE OF MEDICAL LITERATURE, DI7
USE OF SOCIAL SCIENCES LITERATURE, CA3
USING A LAW LIBRARY: A GUIDE, CE1
USING THE BIOLOGICAL LIT.: A PRACTICAL GUIDE, DH3
USING THE MATHEMATICAL LITERATURE, DB3
UTLAS SYSTEMS MANUAL, AB32
VAN NOSTRAND'S SCIENTIFIC ENCYCLOPEDIA, DA40
VARIETIES OF FAMILY LIFESTYLES, CG21n
VARIETY ENTERTAINMENT AND OUTDOOR AMUSEMENTS, BG9n
VERTICAL FILE INDEX, AF33
VERZEICHNIS LIEFERBARER BUCHER/ GERMAN BOOKS IN
   PRINT, AD106
VISTAS IN ASTRONOMY, DD9
VISUAL ARTS REFERENCE AND RESEARCH GUIDE, BE1n
VNR COLOR DICTIONARY OF MINERALS & GEMSTONES, DG34
VNR CONCISE ENCYCLOPEDIA OF MATHEMATICS, DB15
VNR'S SCIENTIFIC ENCYCLOPEDIA, DA40n
Walford, AC6
WALFORD'S CONCISE GUIDE TO REF. MATERIALS, AC6n,
WATDOC, DK13
WATER RESOURCES ABSTRACTS, DG19
WEBSTER'S BIOGRAPHICAL DICTIONARY, AL24
WEBSTER'S NEW COLLEGIATE DICTIONARY, AJ9n
WEBSTER'S NEW DICTIONARY OF SYNONYMS, AJ52
WEBSTER'S NEW GEOGRAPHICAL DICTIONARY, AK28
WEBSTER'S THIRD NEW INTERNATIONAL DICTIONARY, AJ9
WEEKLY GOVERNMENT ABSTRACTS, DA30n
WEEKLY RECORD, AD61

WELFARE STATE IN CANADA, ... BIBLIOGRAPHY, CG7
WESTCOTT'S PLANT DISEASE HANDBOOK, DJ28
WESTERN CANADA SINCE 1870, AD92
WESTMINSTER HISTORICAL ATLAS TO THE BIBLE, BC33
WHERE TO FIND BUSINESS INFORMATION, CC2
Whitaker's ALMANACK, AH5
WHITAKER'S CLASSIFIED MONTHLY BOOK LIST, AD32
WHITAKER'S PUBLISHERS IN THE U.K., AD32n
WHITNEY'S STAR FINDER, DD25
WHO KNOWS WHAT: CANADIAN LIB. EXPERTISE, AA62
WHO WAS WHO, AL33
WHO WAS WHO IN AMERICA, AL38
WHO WAS WHO IN THE GREEK WORLD, AL28
WHO WAS WHO IN THE ROMAN WORLD, AL29
WHO WAS WHO IN THE THEATRE, BG26n
WHO WAS WHO ON THE SCREEN, BG51
WHO'S WHO, AL32
WHO'S WHO IN AMERICA, AL37
WHO'S WHO IN AMERICAN ART, BE40
WHO'S WHO IN ART, BE41
WHO'S WHO IN CANADA, AL46
WHO'S WHO IN CANADIAN BUSINESS, CC45n
WHO'S WHO IN CANADIAN FINANCE, CC45n
WHO'S WHO IN CANADIAN LITERATURE, AL74
WHO'S WHO IN ENGINEERING, DA58n
WHO'S WHO IN EUROPEAN INST. AND ORGS, AL26
WHO'S WHO IN FINANCE AND INDUSTRY, CC45
WHO'S WHO IN LIB. AND INFORMATION SERVICES, AA63
WHO'S WHO IN ROCK, BF56n
WHO'S WHO IN TECHNOLOGY TODAY, DA59
WHO'S WHO IN THE THEATRE, BG26
WHO'S WHO IN THE WORLD, AL27
WHO'S WHO International Red Series, AL25
WHO'S WHO OF CANADIAN WOMEN, AL47
WILLING'S PRESS GUIDE, AE10
WILSON LIBRARY BULLETIN, AC46
Wing, AD26
WINSTON DICTIONARY OF CANADIAN ENGLISH, AJ18
WOMEN: A BIBLIOGRAPHY OF BIBLIOGRAPHIES, CG41
WOMEN AND PSYCHOACTIVE DRUG USE, CG17n
WOMEN AND WORK: AN INVENTORY OF RESEARCH, CG42
WOMEN IN AMERICAN HISTORY: A BIBLIOGRAPHY, CG44
WOMEN IN CANADA, CG48
WOMEN IN CANADA 1965 TO 1975: A BIBLIOGRAPHY, CG47
WOMEN IN WESTERN EUROPEAN HISTORY, CG43
WOMEN'S ANNUAL: THE YEAR IN REVIEW, CG51
WOMEN'S BOOK OF WORLD RECORDS ACHIEVEMENTS, AH54
WOMEN'S HISTORY SOURCES, CG52
WOMEN'S RESOURCE CATALOGUE, CG53
WOMEN'S STUDIES ABSTRACTS, CG55
WOMEN'S STUDIES: A CHECKLIST OF BIBLIOG., CG41n
WOMEN'S STUDIES: A RECOMMENDED CORE, CG49
WORLD ALMANAC, AH6
WORLD ALMANAC DICTIONARY OF DATES, AH44
WORLD AUTHORS, AL60-61

WORLD BIBLIOGRAPHY OF BIBLIOGRAPHIES ..., AD20
WORLD BIBLIOGRAPHY OF INTERNAT. DOCUMENTATION, AN2
WORLD BOOK DICTIONARY, AJ15
WORLD BOOK ENCYCLOPEDIA, AI11
WORLD CHRONOLOGY OF MUSIC HISTORY, BF40
WORLD DICTIONARIES IN PRINT 1983, AJ1
WORLD DICTIONARY OF AWARDS AND PRIZES, AH34
WORLD DIRECTORY OF MAP COLLECTIONS, AK10
WORLD DIRECTORY OF MATHEMATICIANS, DB16
WORLD DIRECTORY OF SOC. SCIENCE INSTITUTIONS, CA26
WORLD ENERGY BOOK: AN A-Z ATLAS AND STATISTICAL SOURCE BOOK, DK17
WORLD ENERGY DIRECTORY, DK32
WORLD FOOD BOOK, DJ21
WORLD GUIDE TO LIBRARIES: INTERNATIONALES BIBLIOTHEKS-HANDBUCH, AA47
WORLD GUIDE TO LIBRARY SCHOOLS AND TRAINING COURSES IN DOCUMENTATION, AA48
WORLD GUIDE TO SCI. ASSOC; LEARNED SOCIETIES, DA47
WORLD HISTORICAL FICTION GUIDE, BD97
WORLD LIST OF SCIENTIFIC PERIODICALS, DA14
WORLD LIST OF SOCIAL SCIENCE PERIODICALS, CA15
WORLD LIST OF UNIVERSITIES, CI27
World Literature in English series, BD4
WORLD MEETINGS (sci-tech), DA53-DA54
WORLD METRIC STANDARDS FOR ENGINEERING, DL50
WORLD NUCLEAR DIRECTORY, DK33
WORLD OF LEARNING, CI28
WORLD PAINTING INDEX, BE48
WORLD TRANSINDEX, DA34
WORLDMARK ENCYCLOPEDIA OF THE NATIONS, CD27
WRITINGS ON AMERICAN HISTORY (bibliog.), CJ44
YEARBOOK OF AGRICULTURE, DJ27
YEARBOOK OF AMERICAN AND CANADIAN CHURCHES, BC19
YEARBOOK OF INTERNATIONAL ORGANIZATIONS, AH30
YEARBOOK OF SCIENCE AND TECHNOLOGY, DA38n
YEARBOOK OF SCIENCE AND THE FUTURE, AI4n
YEARBOOK OF THE UNITED NATIONS, CD28
YEARBOOK OF WORLD AFFAIRS, CD29
Yearbook series, medical sciences, DI17
YEARS OF GROWTH, AD96n
YEAR'S WORK IN ENGLISH STUDIES, BD32
YEAR'S WORK IN MODERN LANGUAGE STUDIES, BD2
YESTERDAY'S AUTHORS OF BOOKS FOR CHILDREN, AL67
YUKON BIBLIOGRAPHY, AD98
ZOOLOGICAL RECORD, DH14

Z 1035.1 .J32 1984

Guide to basic reference
materials for Canadian